PETRARCH

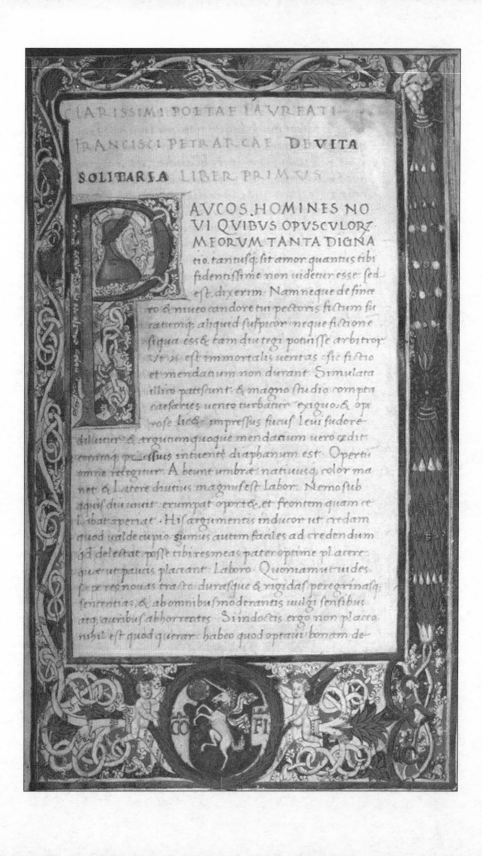

CLARISSIMI POETAE LAVREATI

FRANCISCI PETRARCAE DE VITA

SOLITARIA LIBER PRIMVS

PAVCOS HOMINES NO
VI QVIBVS OPVSCVLORZ
MEORVM TANTA DIGNA
tio, tantusq; sit amor, quantus tibi
fidentissime non uidetur esse: sed
est. dixerim. Nam neque de since
ro & niueo candore tui pectoris fictum sit
ranemq; aliquid suspicor. neque fictione
siqua esset tam diu tegi potuisse arbitror
ut sicut est immortalis ueritas, sic fictio
et mendacium non durant. Simulata
illico patescunt: & magno studio compta
caesaries uento turbatur: exiguo & ope
rose licet impressus fucus leui sudore
diluitur: & argumentumque mendacium uero cedit:
contraq; pressus intuentes diaphanum est. Opertus
omne retegitur: Abeunt umbrae natiuusq; color ma
net & Latere diutius magnus est Labor. Nemo sub
aquis diu uiuit: erumpat oportet, et frontem quam ce
labat aperiat. His argumentis inducor ut credam
quod ualde cupio: sumus autem faciles ad credendum
id delectat: posse tibi res meas pater optime pl acere:
q; ut paucis placeant. Laboro. Quoniam ut uides
sic res nouas tracto durasque & rigidas peregrinasq;
sententias, & ab omnibus moderantis uulgi sensibus
atq; auribus abhorrentes. Si indoctis ergo non placeo,
nihil est quod querar: habeo quod optaui bonam de

PETRARCH

A Critical Guide to the Complete Works

Edited by

Victoria Kirkham and

Armando Maggi

THE UNIVERSITY OF CHICAGO PRESS

Chicago and London

The University of Chicago Press, Chicago 60637
The University of Chicago Press, Ltd., London
© 2009 by The University of Chicago
All rights reserved. Published 2009.
Paperback edition 2012
Printed in the United States of America

21 20 19 18 17 16 15 14 13 12   2 3 4 5 6

ISBN-13: 978-0-226-43741-5 (cloth)
ISBN-13: 978-0-226-43742-2 (paper)
ISBN-10: 0-226-43741-8 (cloth)
ISBN-10: 0-226-43742-6 (paper)

Frontispiece: Francesco Petrarca, *De vita solitaria* (opening page). Courtesy The Newberry Library, Chicago (NL call no. Case Ms f95).

The University of Chicago Press gratefully acknowledges the generous support of the Henry Salvatori Fund at the University of Pennsylvania Center for Italian Studies, and the Division of the Humanities at the University of Chicago, toward the publication of this book.

Library of Congress Cataloging-in-Publication Data

Petrarch : a critical guide to the complete works / edited by Victoria Kirkham and Armando Maggi.
    p.   cm.
  Includes bibliographical references and index.
  ISBN-13: 978-0-226-43741-5 (cloth : alk. paper)
  ISBN-10: 0-226-43741-8 (cloth : alk. paper)
  1. Petrarca, Francesco, 1304–1374—Criticism and interpretation.   I. Kirkham, Victoria.   II. Maggi, Armando.
  PQ4540.P48 2009
  851′.1—dc22

                                                          2008045155

♾ This paper meets the requirements of ANSI/NISO Z39.48–1992 (Permanence of Paper).

CONTENTS

ILLUSTRATIONS

ACKNOWLEDGMENTS

This book has its origins in an international conference, "The Complete Petrarch: A Life's Work," which took place in 2004 as the First Annual Joseph and Elda Coccia Centennial Celebration of Italian Culture at the University of Pennsylvania. Sponsored by the Center for Italian Studies at Penn and supported by a generous gift from the Coccia Foundation, that event still lives in its accompanying library exhibit, "Petrarch at 700," open to visitors at http://www.library.upenn.edu/exhibits/rbm/petrarch/. The volume editors are grateful to the Coccias for their academic philanthropy, to Millicent Marcus, who as Director of the Center for Italian Studies graciously assisted in the conference planning, and to Nicola Gentile, Associate Director of the Center, who provided essential, energetic organizational support.

The volume editors would also like to thank our respective institutions, both for making possible scholarly leave time that has gone into the preparation of this volume and for sharing equally in the financial subvention of its publication. We express our appreciation to Danielle Allen, who during her tenure as Dean of the Humanities at the University of Chicago, contributed to that funding. Penn's part came in the form of a Henry Salvatori Research Grant, kindly authorized by the Faculty Advisory Committee of the Penn Center for Italian Studies under the collegial directorship of Michael Cole.

Victoria Kirkham and Armando Maggi
January 2008

NOTE ON BIBLIOGRAPHICAL FORMS AND ABBREVIATIONS

Faced with the variants of our poet's name in Italian, Latin, and English, we have chosen in the interest of consistency to follow for this English language volume the single designation *Petrarch*. The list below cross-references variant titles and translations of the sources referred to in the text.

Africa (ed. Festa). See also *Petrarch's Africa* (trans. Bergin and Wilson).

Bucolicum carmen (ed. and trans. Bachmann); *Bucolicum carmen* (Eclogues, trans. Bergin). See also *Laura occidens* (ed. Martellotti).

Collatio (Oration). *Collatio laureationis* (ed. Godi). See *Collatio in Capitolio* (trans. Develay); Petrarch's *Coronation Oration* (trans. Wilkins). Cf. *Arenga . . . Novarie, Arenga . . . Mediolani, Arenga . . . Veneciis (Speeches to the Novarese, the Milanese, the Venetians); Collatio brevis coram illustri domino Joanne, Francorum rege* (Brief oration in the presence of John, king of the French), (ed. and Ital. trans. Godi), in *Opere latine* (ed. Bufano).

Contra medicum. Invective contra medicum. See *Invectives.*

De ignorantia. De sui ipsius et multorum ignorantia (ed. Fenzi). See also *Invectives.*

De otio religioso (ed. Rotondi and Martellotti). See also *On Religious Leisure* (ed. and trans. Shearer); *Le Repos religieux* (ed. Marion).

De remediis. De remediis utriusque fortune. Les remèdes aux deux fortunes (ed. and trans. Carraud). See also *Petrarch's Remedies for Fortune Fair and Foul* (trans. Rawski).

De viris illustribus (ed. Martellotti). See also *De gestis Cesaris* (ed. Razzolini); *De viris illustribus* (ed. Schneider); *De vita et rebus gestis C. Julii Caesari* (ed. Schneider); *La vita di Scipione l'Africano* (ed. Martellotti).

De vita solitaria (ed. Noce); *De vita solitaria* (ed. Enenkel). See also *De vita solitaria. La vie solitaire: 1346-1366* (ed. and trans. Carraud); *The Life of Solitude* (trans. Zeitlin).

Disperse. See *Rime disperse.*

Epystole. Metrical Epistles. See *Poesie minori del Petrarca* (ed. Rossetti); also *Petrarch at Vaucluse: Letters in Verse and Prose* (ed. and trans. Wilkins); *Poesie latine* (ed. and trans. Martellotti and Bianchi).

Familiares. Rerum familiarum libri. See *Epistolae de rebus familiaribus* (ed.

Fracassetti); *Epistole* (ed. Dotti); *Le familiari* (ed. Rossi and Bosco); *Le familiari* (ed. Dotti), *Lettere* (trans. Fracassetti), *Letters on Familiar Matters* (trans. Bernardo); *Rerum familiarum* (ed. Dotti).

Fragmenta. See *Rerum vulgarium fragmenta.*

Invectives (ed. and trans. Marsh). See also *Invective contra medicum* (ed. Ricci and Martinelli), *Contro un medico* (ed. Di Leo), *De sui ipsius et multorum ignorantia* (ed. Fenzi).

Itinerarium. Itinerarium ad sepulchrum domini nostri Yhesu Christi. See *Petrarch's Guide to the Holy Land: Itinerary to the Sepulcher of Our Lord Jesus Christ* (ed. and trans. Cachey).

Lettere disperse. Lettere disperse, varie e miscellanee (ed. Pancheri).

Posteritati (Letter to Posterity). See *Lettera ai Posteri* (ed. Villani).

Rerum vulgarium fragmenta (ed. Belloni, et al). See also *Canzoniere* (ed. Contini); *Canzoniere* (ed. Santagata); *Il Canzoniere e i Trionfi* (ed. Moschetti); *Petrarch's Lyric Poems* (ed. and trans. Durling); *Rime* (ed. Carducci); *Rime, Trionfi e poesie latine* (ed. Neri et al.).

Rime disperse. Rime disperse di Francesco Petrarca (ed. Solerti).

Psalmi. Psalmi penitentiales. See *Les Psaumes pénitentiaux* (ed. Cochin); *Salmi penitenziali* (ed. Gigliuzzi); *I sette salmi* (ed. Garghella).

Secretum. De secretu conflictu curarum mearum. See *Opere latine* (ed. Bufano); *Prose* (ed. Martellotti, et al.); *Secretum* (ed. Carrara); *Il mio segreto* (ed. Fenzi), *The Secret* (trans. Quillen).

Seniles. Rerum senilium libri. See *Letters of Old Age* (trans. Bernardo, et al.); *Lettres de la vieillesse. Rerum senilium* (ed. Nota); *Senile V 2* (ed. Berté).

Sine nomine. Liber sine nomine. See *Petrarcas 'Buch ohne Namen'* (ed. Piur); *Sine nomine: Lettere polemiche e politiche* (ed. Dotti), *Petrarch's Book without a Name* (trans. Zacour).

Testamentum. See *Petrarch's Testament* (ed. and trans. Mommsen).

Triumphi (ed. Ariani). See also *Trionfi, Rime estravaganti, Codice degli abbozzi* (ed. Pacca and Paolino); *Die Triumphe* (ed. Appel); *The Triumphs of Petrarch* (trans. Wilkins).

Abbreviations:

For the *Rerum vulgarium fragmenta: RVF; Triumphi: Triumphus Cupidinis* (Triumph of Love) = *TC; Triumphus Pudicitie* (Triumph of Chastity) = *TP; Triumphus Fame* (Triumph of Fame) = *TF; Triumphus Mortis* (Triumph of Death) = *TM; Triumphus Temporis* (Triumph of Time) = *TT; Triumphus Eternitatis* (Triumph of Eternity) = *TE.*

In the Bibliography: *PL = Patrologia latina; CCL = Corpus Christianorum. Series Latina*

CHRONOLOGY OF PETRARCH'S LIFE AND WORKS

Victoria Kirkham

1304 July 20 Born in Arezzo to the notary Pietro di Parenzo (Ser Petracco) and his wife, Eletta Canigiani.

1305–11 Lives at Incisa, Valdarno.

1305 Nov. Papacy moves to France; Clement V installed as pope in Lyons.

1307 His brother Gherardo born.

1311 Family moves to Pisa, where Petrarch may have seen Dante.

1312 Father finds employment at papal court in Avignon; family settles fifteen miles away, in Carpentras.

1312–16 Studies Latin grammar, rhetoric with schoolmaster Convenevole da Prato. Becomes friends with Guido Sette, future archbishop of Genoa.

1314 Clement V dies; John XXII elected new pope.

1316 fall –1320 Studies law at University of Montpellier.

1318 or 1319 His mother dies; soon afterward (or within a few years) Petrarch will compose a Latin elegy for her, *Breve panegyricum defuncte matri*.

1320 fall–1326 Studies civil law at Bologna with Gherardo and Guido Sette. Returns home for intervals in 1321 (after student riots close the university) and 1325. At Bologna he also becomes friends with Giacomo Colonna and his brother Agapito.

1325 Begins receiving small income for service to Stefano Colonna the Elder and his son Giacomo

1325 Feb. First recorded book purchase, Augustine's *De civitate dei*, for 12 florins, in Avignon.

1326 April Ser Petracco dies. Petrarch and Gherardo return to Provence.

1326 May–1337 summer Avignon.

1327 April 6 Sees and falls in love with Laura, church of St. Claire, Avignon.

1328–29 Petrarch works on philological restoration of Livy's *Decades*.

1330 summer Visits Giacomo Colonna, bishop of Lombez, Gascony, in foothills of the Pyrenees. His companions Lello di Pietro Stefano dei Tosetti from Rome ("Laelius") and the Flemish musician Ludwig van Kempen ("Socrates") become his lifelong friends.

1330 fall At Avignon enters service of Giacomo's brother, Cardinal Giovanni Colonna as household chaplain, in which he will remain active until 1337, thereafter serving discontinuously until 1347.

1333 spring and summer Trip to northern Europe. In Liège discovers Cicero's orations, among them *Pro Archia*.

Ca. 1333–34 Probably in Avignon meets the Augustinian monk Dionigi da Borgo San Sepolcro, who gives him the copy of Augustine's *Confessions* he would carry with him always. Makes a list of some fifty of his "favorite books"; writes a comedy, *Philologia Philostrati* (lost). Acquires a house in Vaucluse; forges enduring friendship with Philippe de Cabassoles, bishop of Cavaillon.

1334 Death of Pope John XXII; accession of Benedict XII.

1335 Jan. 25 Canon in cathedral at Lombez in the Pyrenees, appointed by Benedict XII. Petrarch did not take resident possession but received income from it; resigned 1355.

1335 June 1 Copies prayer on guard leaf of his manuscript containing Cassiodorus's *De anima* and Augustine's *De vera religione*.

1335 summer In Avignon meets Azzo da Correggio and Guglielmo da Pastrengo, sent as ambassadors by Mastino della Scala, lord of Verona, who had seized Parma. At their request he successfully makes a case for papal support of Mastino.

1336 The Sienese painter Simone Martini visits Avignon; paints portrait of Laura at Petrarch's request.

1336 April 24–26 Ideal date of ascent of Mount Ventoux (*Familiares* 4.1).

End 1336–early 1337 Visits Giacomo Colonna in Rome, staying first in Capranica with Orso dell'Anguillara, husband of Agnese Colonna (sister of Stefano the Younger, Giacomo, Agapito, and Cardinal Giovanni).

1337 summer–1341 Feb. Vaucluse and Avignon.

1337 In his service to Giovanni Colonna, escorts a protégé of the cardinal's to Mary Magdalene's legendary cavern, near Marseilles; writes Latin poem on that saint. Birth of his natural son, Giovanni.

End of 1337 Begins work on *De viris illustribus*.

1337–39 *Epystole* 1.4, invitation to Dionigi da Borgo San Sepolcro to visit him at Vaucluse.

1338 April Petrarch's father's stolen Virgil manuscript comes back into his possession; he commissions Simone Martini to paint frontispiece.

1338 or 1339, Good Friday Idea for *Africa* comes to him, April 6. Continues *De viris illustribus.*

1340 Azzo da Correggio visits Avignon and receives papal support for taking control of Parma from tyrant Mastino della Scala.

1340 Sept. 1 Receives invitations to be crowned poet laureate from University of Paris and Roman Senate; accepts latter.

1340–41 Petrarch drafts *Collatio laureationis.*

1341–42 Conception of *Triumphi*? (or in 1351–52?).

1341–43 Continues drafting *De viris illustribus.*

1341 Feb. 16 Departs Avignon with Azzo da Correggio for Naples and Rome.

1341 Feb.–March In Naples for coronation examination with King Robert; becomes friends with Barbato da Sulmona and Giovanni Barrili.

1341 April 8 Pronounces *Collatio laureationis;* crowned poet laureate and declared Roman citizen by Orso dell'Anguillara in audience hall of Senatorial Palace on Capitoline in Rome.

1341 May 22/23–1342 Jan. Visits Parma at invitation of new Coreggio rulers. Azzo da Correggio provides him with a country home, his "Italian Helicon," south of their city in the valley of the Enza near a wooded highland called Selvapiana. There he returns to his *Africa* and *De viris illustribus.* His friend Giacomo Colonna dies.

1342 Dionigi da Borgo San Sepolcro dies; Petrarch studies Greek with the Basilian monk Barlaam.

1342 April 25 Benedict XII dies.

1342 May 7 Clement VI succeeds him.

1342 May 22 Obtains canonry at Pisa, resigned sometime before March 1355.

1342 Aug. 21 First form of *Rerum vulgarium fragmenta.*

1342 spring–1343 Sept. Vaucluse and Avignon. Intense work on "Roman plan" of *De viris illustribus.*

1342–43 Ideal date of *Secretum.* Probably begun in 1347.

1342 May 22–1355 Clement VI appoints him canon in cathedral of Pisa; he receives its income through a procurator.

1343 23 lives in *De viris illustribus* complete; daughter Francesca born of unknown mother. Petrarch sends fragment of *Africa* to Barbato da Sulmona.

Early 1343 Cola di Rienzo arrives in Avignon for several months; he and Petrarch become friends. New pope Clement VI in bull of Jan. 27 declares 1350 a year of Jubilee.

1343 Feb. Learns of death of King Robert of Anjou in Naples on Jan. 20.

1343 April Petrarch's brother Gherardo becomes Carthusian monk at Montrieux.

1343 summer Begins *Rerum memorandarum libri*.

1343 Aug. 24 Awarded rectory of S. Angelo in Castiglione Fiorentino by Clement VI.

1343 Sept.–Dec. Frustrating diplomatic mission to Naples in wake of King Robert of Anjou's death on behalf of Pope Clement and Cardinal Colonna (*Familiares* 5.6); Barbato da Sulmona copies the Mago episode from *Africa* and publicizes it against poet's wishes.

1343 Dec.–1345 Feb. Petrarch's second stay in Parma.

1343–45 Continues *Rerum memorandarum libri*, *Africa*.

1344 Buys a house in Parma. Engages Moggio Moggi to tutor his son Giovanni.

1345 23 Feb. Flees Parma (*Familiares* 5.10), under attack by Visconti and Gonzaga enemies of Obizzo d'Este, to whom Azzo da Correggio had ceded city. Via Bologna and Modena retreats to Verona.

1345 spring At Verona his friend Guglielmo da Pastrengo shows him the manuscripts of Cicero's *Ad Atticum,* preserved in cathedral library. Transcribes Cicero's letters. Meets Dante's son Jacopo.

1345 spring–summer Returns to *Rerum memorandarum libri,* then abandons it.

1345 fall Brief return to Parma, then Verona; long journey through Tyrol and Rhone valley.

1345 late–1347 Nov. Vaucluse and Avignon.

1346 spring Composes during Lent *De vita solitaria,* on which work continues to 1366, completed in 1371.

1346 summer Begins *Bucolicum carmen.*

1346 Oct. 29 Assigned canonry at Parma by Clement VI.

Ca. 1347 Cardinal Colonna sends Petrarch a big white dog.

1347 Visits his brother in the Carthusian monastery at Montrieux. He writes an ecclesiastical petition to live nearby with Socrates. Writes *De otio religioso;* probably begins *Secretum.*

1347 summer Petrarch demonstrates support of Cola, who seized power May 20; sends him *Bucolicum carmen* 5, under cover letter (*Disperse* 11). Cf. *Sine nomine* 2, 3. He breaks with Giovanni Colonna (*Bucolicum carmen* 8, "Divortium"), who represents the political faction Cola opposed.

1347 Nov. 20 Departs for Italy as Clement VI's envoy to Mastino della

Scala in Verona to halt King Louis of Hungary's invasion; mission not accomplished. Disillusioned by Cola's failure (*Familiares* 7.7).

End of 1347 Abandons support for Cola di Rienzo, who abdicates Dec. 15.

1347–48 *Psalmi penitentiales* probably composed at this time.

1348 Petrarch in Parma and Verona. Laura (April 6) and Giovanni Colonna (July 3) die from the Black Death, news communicated in letters from Socrates. Period of despairing metrical epistle "Ad se ipsum"; *Bucolicum carmen* 9–11.

1348 March–1351 June Petrarch's third period of (discontinuous) association with Parma.

1348 Aug. 23 Clement VI approves Petrarch's petition for the archdeaconate of Parma, a "fat" benefice that he held, almost always in absentia, for many years.

1349 Probable first revision of *Secretum*.

1349 March Visits Padua at invitation of Jacopo da Carrara.

1349 April 18 Petrarch takes possession of a lucrative canonry in Padua, which he held for at least fifteen years and possibly until his death.

Late 1349–early 1350 Begins to collect *Familiares*.

1350 Conceives collection of metrical epistles and composes dedicatory letter to Barbato da Sulmona (*Epystole* 1.1); Proemial sonnet of *Rerum vulgarium fragmenta*, "Voi ch'ascoltate in rime sparse il suono."

1350 13 Jan. Dedicatory letter of *Familiares* to Socrates.

1350 Oct. Trip to Rome for the Jubilee with stops each way in Florence, where he meets Giovanni Boccaccio, Zanobi da Strada, Francesco Nelli, and Lapo da Castiglionchio, who introduces him to Quintilian.

1351 *Posteritati* drafted.

1351 March Boccaccio visits him in Padua with offer of a chaired professorship at University of Florence.

1351 summer—1353 May Last period in Vaucluse and Avignon. Another version of *De viris illustribus*.

1351 fall Turns down offer of appointment as papal secretary; composes more letters for the *Sine nomine*.

1351–52 Conception of *Triumphi*? First versions of *Triumphus Cupidinis* and *Triumphus Fame*?

1352–53 *Invective contra medicum*, continually revised late into the 1360s.

1352 6 Dec. Clement VI dies.

1352 18 Dec. Innocent VI is chosen as new pope.

1353 May–1361 Petrarch's eight years in Milan.

1353 Nov. 8 Oration to the Venetian Senate as Visconti ambassador.

1353 Nov. Godfather at the baptism of Marco, son of Bernabò Visconti and Beatrice della Scala.

1354 Oct. 7 Oration to the Milanese on death of Archbishop Giovanni Visconti.

1354 Dec. Emperor Charles IV receives Petrarch at Mantua.

1354–60 Composition of *De remediis utriusque fortune.*

1355 *Invectiva contra quendam magni status hominem sed nullius scientie aut virtutis.* Receives as gift from Boccaccio a handsome manuscript of Augustines's commentary (*Enarrationes*) on the Psalms.

1355 March Exchanges canonry at Lombez for rural church of S. Maria de Capellis in diocese of Teano, previously held by Ludwig van Kempen (Socrates).

1356 Year of earliest surviving datings of the *Triumphi.*

1356 May–Aug. Mission to Basel and Prague to meet with Emperor Charles IV, who names Petrarch a Count Palatine.

1356 Oct. 18 Basel struck by earthquake, about which Petrarch speaks in *De remediis* 2.91 and *Seniles* 10.2.

1356–58 Correggio form of *Rerum vulgarium fragmenta.*

1357 Completes *Bucolicum carmen* (which will be further reworked) with a twelfth eclogue; sends first eclogue to Barbato with revised proemial letter, written in 1350. Corrects *Triumphus Cupidinis* (on which he continues work until 1360); revises *De otio religioso.*

1357–59 Composes last three letters of *Sine nomine* to Nelli.

1358 April–May Writes *Sine nomine* 18.

1358 19 June Oration to the city of Novara as Visconti ambassador.

1358–59 winter In Padua.

1358 spring Writes pilgrimage guide (*Itinerarium ad sepulchrum domini nostri Yhesu Christi*) for Giovanni Mandelli. In Padua meets Leontius Pilatus.

1359 Epistle to Jacopo Bussolari on behalf of Bernabò Visconti to send dogs from Pavia to Milan. By this year he had composed a *Vita* of the Roman playwright Terence.

1359 spring Boccaccio visits him in Milan for a month.

1359 spring–1361 spring In Milan.

1359–1362/63 Chigi form of *Rerum vulgarium fragmenta.*

1360 Completes first draft of last major work, *De remediis utriusque fortune.* His son comes to live with him.

1361 Reworks *De vita solitaria.*

1361 Jan. 13 Oration at Paris before King John the Good as Gian Galeazzo Visconti's ambassador.

1361 spring–1362 April Petrarch leaves plague outburst in Milan for Padua.

1361 summer Petrarch's son Giovanni dies in plague epidemic in Milan. Socrates dies.

1362 (or 1364?) Death of Azzo da Correggio.

1362 May Returns to Padua.

1362 Sept.–end of 1367 Resides mainly in Venice, the city to which he promises his library.

1362 Sept. 12 Innocent VI dies.

1362 Sept. 28 Urban V takes the papal tiara.

1363 spring Hosts Boccaccio in Venice.

1363 fall Learns of deaths of Francesco Nelli and Barbato da Sulmona.

1363 Oct.–early 1364 Works on *Triumphus Fame.*

1364 Makes additions to *Bucolicum carmen;* publishes *Epystole.* Hires Giovanni Malpighini as his scribe.

1365 As of this year Petrarch held a canonry at Monselice, near Arquà.

1366 Urges Urban V to restore the papacy to Rome (*Seniles* 7.1).

1366 Jan. or Feb. Petrarch's grandson born to his daughter Francesca and Francesco da Brossano at his home in Arquà.

1366 spring Completes *De vita solitaria* and sends a copy to the dedicatee, Philippe de Cabassoles.

1366 Sept. 1 Petrarch is revising *De remediis;* writes Donato Albanzani that he has nearly finished it (*Sen.* 5.4).

1366 Oct. 4 Completes *De remediis.*

1366 fall Giovanni Malpighini completes transcription of *Familiares;* begins to copy *Rerum vulgarium fragmenta* (Vat. Lat. 3195). Petrarch concludes *Bucolicum carmen.*

1366 Dec. Receives a copy of the translation of Homer by Leontius Pilatus, whom Boccaccio had brought to Florence to carry out that task.

1367–70 Writes *De sui ipsius et multorum ignorantia,* which he will dedicate to Donato Albanzani.

1367 Giovanni Malpighini leaves the service of Petrarch, who continues copying *Rerum vulgarium fragmenta* himself, work that will continue until his death. Death of Guido Sette.

1367 June Urban V returns to Italy.

1367–1370 Living in Padua, under Francesco il Vecchio da Carrara. Writes *De sui ipsius et multorum ignorantia.*

1368 May 19 Petrarch's grandson Francesco dies in Pavia.

1368 summer Returns to work on *De viris illustribus*, at request of Francesco da Carrara; perhaps begins *De gestis Cesaris*.

1369 Begins building his house at Arquà.

1370 March–1374 July Resides at his house in Arquà.

1370 April 4 Writes his *Testamentum* in anticipation of journey to Rome.

1370 late April Falls seriously ill in Ferrara en route to Rome, to celebrate Urban V's return to that city in 1366; weakened health forces Petrarch to return to Padua.

1370 Sept. Urban V returns to Avignon.

1370 19 Dec. Death of Urban V in Avignon.

1370 30 Dec. Gregory XI named pope.

1371 Petrarch in declining health; defies his doctors; writes a supplement to *De vita solitaria* on the life of Saint Romuald.

1371–72 Final revision of *Posteritati*.

1371–74 Last version of *De viris illustribus*.

1372 Aug. His old friend Philippe de Cabassoles dies.

1372 Nov. 15 Petrarch forced by upheavals of war waged by Carrara on Venice to flee Arquà and seek refuge in Padua.

1373 Translates Boccaccio's tale of patient Griselda (*Decameron* 10.10) into Latin as *De insigni obedientia et fide uxoria* and sends it to Boccaccio (*Seniles* 17.3).

1373–74 Last stages of Vatican 3195.

1373 Jan. 4 Sends Malatesta form of *Rerum vulgarium fragmenta* to Pandolfo Malatesta. Queriniana form of *Rerum vulgarium fragmenta* dates from same year.

1373 March *Invectiva contra eum qui maledixit Italie*.

Early summer 1373 Returns to Arquà after war between Padua and Venice. Corrections to *Triumphus Cupidinis*.

1373 Sept. 27 Petrarch travels to Venice to deliver on behalf of Francesco da Carrara the Elder an oration to the Venetians on Oct. 2 and introduce Francesco Novello da Carrara, who will acknowledge Padua's submission to the Adriatic city.

1373 Nov. 28 Letter to Francesco da Carrara the Elder on princely government (*Seniles* 14.1).

1374 Ninth and last reordering of poems in *Rerum vulgarium fragmenta*.

1374 15 Jan.–12 Feb. Drafts *Triumphus Eternitatis*. Final touches follow.

1374 July 18/19 Death of Petrarch.

Fig. 1. Giorgio Vasari, *Portrait of Six Tuscan Poets* (1543–44). Oil on panel. The William Hood Dunwoody Fund, The Minneapolis Institute of Arts.

A LIFE'S WORK

Victoria Kirkham

Keenly oriented to the poetic landscape around him and powerful in his authority, Petrarch predicted his place in literary history. That prophecy occurs in 1364, when he writes from Venice to his soul mate in the life of letters, Giovanni Boccaccio (*Seniles* 5.2).[1] Here he confronts questions that tug perennially at creative minds. They haunted him almost obsessively. How do I rate compared to past writers? Where do I stand among my contemporaries? What will posterity think of me? In response, the poet decrees Italy's classic canon. Claiming for himself not first but second place, he recognizes that Dante Alighieri (1265–1321) precedes him, both in time and stature, while he, Francesco (1304–74), outranks his close Certaldan friend Boccaccio (1313–75). He sees himself as second in a trio that critical tradition would hallow and christen the "Three Crowns of Florence."

This letter joins a lifelong procession of literary works, from biographies of heroic Romans and the epic *Africa*, to his *Collatio laureationis* (*Coronation Oration*), *Secretum*, *Posteritati* (*Letter to Posterity*), *Triumphi* (*Triumphs*), and *Testamentum* (*Testament*), all pervasively concerned with the measurement of human worth. As much an essay as an epistle, the letter begins and ends with outbursts of disdain for the cultural poverty of his day, embodied by those court beggars who merely perform others' poetry, as well as by that multitude of philistines in positions of authority who remain stubbornly contemptuous of antiquity. Within these framing passages Petrarch mounts his central message, a meditation on hierarchies of men and languages. Pointedly unnamed, as Petrarch rates the moderns Dante rises to the top—but in Italian, the second-class tongue, one that the epistler only admits to having toyed with in his youth.[2]

Although he was quite right about his slot in the canon, Petrarch could not imagine what a reversal history would bring to his ladder of the languages. Latin, privileged from his perspective as the Roman tongue, al-

1

ready within a hundred years after his death, was falling out of fashion as Tuscans reaffirmed their native tradition, by then two centuries strong. Petrarch and his contemporary Boccaccio, whose friendship from the mid-trecento had inaugurated a new age of classical humanism, with passing generations were no longer seen as sons of the ancients but as avatars of the vernacular. Their genius came to be concentrated in single genres—for Boccaccio the novella, for Petrarch the lyric. Just one small book, a *Petrarchino*, epitomizes Petrarch's enormous literary success in Giorgio Vasari's 1543–44 *Portrait of Six Tuscan Poets* (fig. 1).[3] As the female medallion profile on its cover declares, Vasari has rendered Madonna Laura's handsome cleric-lover, who modestly, if not disparagingly, referred to his collected lyric poetry as mere "fragments" and "trifles."[4] Centered in the painting are the Three Crowns of Florence, with Dante dominant, Petrarch in second place beside him (but not a hint of his voluminous Latin output, eclipsed in an era of *Petrarchismo*),[5] and Boccaccio as third at the rear between them. By posing them in this way, the painter overlays outlooks inherited from a chain of writers ascending back to the trecento, to an endpoint—or actually, a source—that originates with what Petrarch himself had written.

Restoring nearly forgotten pieces to an equal footing with Petrarch's most famous works, this volume collects twenty-three essays, one each for every work or genre in a prolific corpus that pushes its readers in many directions from a single creative center, the poet at the hub of a literary panopticon. Our contributors' charge was to write about one title in the Petrarchan corpus, answering the simple question, "Quid est"? "What is it?" Our goal was to study Petrarch less through his enormous influence on later centuries, a topic others have richly illuminated,[6] than among his contemporaries and cultural antecedents. How did Petrarch engage with them, establish his distinct authorial persona, and innovate vis-à-vis the tradition?

Part 1, "An Enduring Vernacular Legacy," leads off with his lyric masterwork, *Rerum vulgarium fragmenta*, and proceeds to the *Triumphs*, long paired with it in manuscripts and printed editions. Concluding this section are all the uncollected rhymes condemned to exclusion from those 366 poems that Petrarch chose to "beatify" with a place in his songbook.

Foundational for part 2, "Literary Debut, Latin Humanism, and Orations," are the lives of famous men (*De viris illustribus*) and the epic *Africa*, historical works conceived between 1337–39. Petrarch's first sustained literary projects, they announce the promise that led him for laurels to Rome, where he pronounced his *Coronation Oration* in 1341. Five more public speeches would follow for princely patrons. Last in this early group of writings born of the poet's enthusiasm for the classical world is his encyclopedic "temple" of memorable things, *De rerum memorandarum libri IV*, initiated in 1343.

Part 3, "Contemplative Serenity," embraces works all begun around 1346–47: the *Bucolicum carmen* (*Eclogues*), *De vita solitaria* (*The Life of Solitude*), and *De otio religioso* (*On Religious Leisure*). The latter two form an ideal diptych: one on the layman's quietude in this secular world, the other on monastic retreat, a life that Petrarch's brother Gherardo had chosen when he sealed himself in a Cistercian monastery.

Part 4, "Journeys into the Soul," follows the poet as he turns inward for self-examination, staging this probing as a dialogue in his *Secretum*. He expresses feelings of guilt through his alter ego Augustinus; this sentiment drives somber prayers he wrought during roughly the same period, the seven *Psalmi penitentiales* (ca. 1348). These psalms and his "secret" mental struggle precede by about ten years a spiritual sibling, the pilgrimage guide he wrote for a friend (1358), *Itinerarium ad sepulchrum domini nostri Yhesu Christi* (*Itinerary to the Sepulcher of our Lord Jesus Christ*).

Part 5, "Life's Turbulence," turns to the *De remediis utriusque fortune* (*Remedies for Fortune Fair and Foul*) and displays Petrarch wielding a poison pen in his *Invective contra medicum* (*Invectives against a Physician*) and *De sui ipsius et multorum ignorantia* (*On His Own Ignorance and That of Many Others*). Axiomatic musings on Fortune's two sides mine a vein of pessimistic thought. These dialogues draw, as do the invectives, on philosophical and rhetorical mastery, but the poet's art springs from real-life situations, expressing frustration, anger, and fear.

Part 6, "Petrarch the Epistler," opens with *Epystole* (*Metrical Epistles*), which includes his earliest known work (on the death of his mother) and proceeds to his diatribes on the corrupt papacy in Avignon, *Liber sine nomine* (*The Book without a Name*). Next come *Lettere disperse* (*Scattered Letters*), never edited by him for publishing or judged incompatible with his ideal self-image, a portrait that he projected in the *Familiares* (*Letters on Familiar Matters*) and the *Seniles* (*Letters of Old Age*).

This introduction presents the essays, interweaves biographical background, and integrates information on writings not covered by the contributors (two of the four invectives, several single letters, prayers, ecclesiastical petitions, and miscellaneous Latin poetry). A chronology of Petrarch's life and works precedes. The volume epilogue takes up Petrarch's last will and testament, strongly individual in its creative stamp.

Part 1. An Enduring Vernacular Legacy

For centuries, people read Petrarch's collected lyric "fragments" as a love story in two parts, divided between Lady Laura in life and in death. In the essay that launches our collection, "The Self in the Labyrinth of Time," Teodolinda Barolini argues meaning on more abstract planes. Petrarch takes on the persona of lover, true enough, but as author he is a philosopher meditating on time, "the medium that fragments us, makes us multiple and metamorphic." The *Rerum vulgarium fragmenta*, "which thematizes fragmentation or multiplicity in its very title, conjures the existence of the self in time." Yet chronology is not strict because order in the abstract is Petrarch's concern. Leaving open the question of whether we have his "final" form of the text, Barolini discerns a beginning, middle, and end in the macrostructure, although less assertive than the narrative attempted in the *Triumphi*. Tokens of evanescence and instability, the lyric fragments constantly undercut each other, denying rigid templates.

Writing of the *Triumphi* as "The Poem of Memory," Fabio Finotti too finds that its author undercuts a medieval ideal of ascent to God in the structural progression from Love to Chastity, Death, Fame, Time, and Eternity. Here Petrarch programmatically counters Dante, Finotti finds, transforming a universal, eschatological vision into a subjective, psychological experience. "Moral order yields to memorial order." If the *Divina commedia* in its movement toward God was centripetal, the *Triumphi* is centrifugal, carrying the reader away to the poet's classical literary sources. "Subjective love for a woman, long reflected upon in solitude, and the collective worship of the past stem from the same roots and share an identical capacity to transform time from an agent of destruction to a locus of condensation and radiation of vibrant, perennial images."

With Justin Steinberg's project, "Petrarch's Damned Poetry and the Poetics of Exclusion," we pass from the canonical poet to the forgotten poet. Surprisingly, Steinberg shows, Petrarch lavished as much attention on the poems he omitted from his master collection as he did for those he "saved." What determined their rejection, Steinberg asserts, was their rootedness in history. Contrary to the image he carefully crafted for posterity, the "disperse" (uncollected rhymes) involve him in "exchanges, performances, and contingent and ephemeral functions of poetry that typify the northern courts of fourteenth-century Italy."[7] This is not the Petrarch of the *Rerum vulgarium fragmenta,* which as a system of lyrics pulls away from historical particulars, rising into an ahistorical, abstract sphere—a book that, to say it with Barolini, stages the poet metaphysically.

Part 2. Literary Debut, Latin Humanism, and Orations

Ironically, "the first modern man of letters" entrusted the bulk of his legacy to a language from the past, not the words taken in with his mother's milk.[8] To that maternal Tuscan, boyhood years would have added Provençal after his father Ser Petracco settled the family in 1312 at Carpentras, near Avignon. There, too, Petrarch studied Latin with the schoolmaster Convenevole da Prato and perhaps with his father, a notary at the papal court who had a love of the classics and owned the Virgil manuscript that his son inherited. That codex, for which Petrarch commissioned a beautiful frontispiece by Simone Martini, became a precious repository for personal information—autograph notes on the story of the manuscript's theft and recovery (1338), the date he first saw Laura (1327) and when she died (1348), the deaths of his difficult son Giovanni; his patron Giovanni Colonna, "Socrates," and other friends.[9] Of his son, taken by a plague epidemic in Milan in the summer of 1361, he writes:

> Our Giovanni, born to my toiling and my sorrow, brought me heavy and constant cares while he lived, and bitter grief when he died. He had known few happy days. He died in the year of our Lord 1361, in the 25th year of his age, in the night between Friday and Saturday the 9th and 10th of July. The news of his death reached me in Padua late on the afternoon of the 14th. He died in Milan in the unexampled general devastation wrought by the plague, which hitherto had left that city immune from such evils, but now has found it and has invaded it.[10]

The poet's ideal literary biography begins with a poem to his mother, Eletta Canigiani, in the bookish Latin he was learning from his teachers. These verses, a "brief panegyric" on her death, eventually joined the collection of his metrical letters, the *Epystole.* Wilkins, considering it Petrarch's earliest surviving poem, dates the *Breve panegyricum defuncte matri* to "soon after her death," which befell in 1318 or 1319. More recent scholars put it a few years later, a reasonable assumption given his habit of retrodating (as he did *Familiares* 4.1 to the Augustinian monk Dionigi on his ascent of Mount Ventoux). The text, moreover, is not exclusively about "Eletta

Dei tam nomine quam re" (Elect by God, in name and deed), who has departed, leaving behind young Petrarch and his brother in life's whirlwind at the crossroads of Pythagoras. Petrarch expresses his own sorrow and his hopes for glory. Its length, thirty-eight Latin hexameters, duplicates his mother's age at her passing, a calculated coincidence:

> Versiculos tibi nunc totidem, quot praebuit annos
> vita, damus . . . (vv. 35–36).[11]
> [We give you as many little verses as the years your life
> has reached. . . .]

The poet, who makes his mother a saint in the mold of Augustine's mother Monica from the *Confessions*, interweaves into this highly constructed display piece at least a dozen other literary citations, among them Prudentius, Virgil, Ovid, Statius, Propertius, Catullus, Lucan, Claudian, Seneca, and Cicero.[12]

From his pen as a mature writer, epistles to the dead will continue to flow, imagined as companionable dialogues with some of his most admired ancients—Cicero (who gets two letters), Seneca, Varro, Quintilian, Livy, Horace, Virgil, and Homer [*Familiares* 24.3–12]). Probably in 1333, the year a trip to northern Europe netted his discovery at Liège of Cicero's oration *Pro Archia*, Petrarch composed a list of his favorite books, "Libri mei peculiares." There are about fifty entries, nearly half by Cicero or Seneca. He inscribed it in a thirteenth-century manuscript that contained Cassiodorus's *De anima* (*On the Soul*) and Augustine's *De vera religione* (*On True Religion*).[13]

By the 1330s Petrarch's fascination with philology and antiquity had already come together in detective work on Livy's *Ab urbe condita libri* (*History of Rome*), a classic all but lost during the Middle Ages. He is credited with the first "scholarly edition" of the fragments then known, the First, Third, and Fourth Decades.[14] Apparently related by theme was the comic play he wrote for his patron Cardinal Giovanni Colonna, whom he actively served from 1330 to 1337. A single verse from it survives, recalled in Petrarch's letter to Colonna's uncle (*Familiares* 2.7): "you will remember in my *Philology*, which I wrote only to drive out your cares through entertainment, what my Tranquillinus says, 'The greater part of man dies waiting for something.'"[15] Boccaccio refers to it enthusiastically in his *Vita* of Petrarch (1341–42) as "pulcerrimam comediam" (a most beautiful comedy). From that mention and another by Petrarch himself in a letter to Barbato da Sulmona (*Familiares* 7.16), we know the full title, *Philologia Philostrati* (*Filostrato's Philology*).[16]

Poetry and philology became Petrarch's twin pursuits, enabled early by patronage. As a tonsured cleric he obtained income-bearing ecclesiastical appointments, but he never took holy orders or performed pastoral duties. Wilkins has documented these benefices, the main source of his livelihood, in a chronology that begins formally with a canonry of 1335 at Lombez, where Petrarch had been attached since 1330 to the household of Cardinal Giovanni Colonna. Normally, the candidate himself petitioned for the appointment in a document subsequently formalized by a papal secretary. Some of these petitions preserve traces of the applicant's original wording and can thus be counted among Petrarch's writings.[17] Iconographic tradition from within a decade of his death that has gone unchanged to this day, even allowing for variations as a lover and laureate (as in Vasari's panel, fig. 1), depicts him long-robed in this profession as a cleric, with his face framed by a snugly wrapped hood, or *cappuccio*.[18]

Petrarch's first major literary undertakings, conceived around 1337–39, bespeak his passion for Roman history. *De viris illustribus* (*On Famous Men*), from Ronald Witt's perspective in "The Rebirth of the Romans as Models of Character," wrestles with and rejects medieval antecedents through a complex succession of authorial variants, always clear on moral purpose: "what leads to virtues or to the contraries of virtues."[19] To models like the lives of famous men by his friend Guglielmo da Pastrengo and Boccaccio's *De casibus virorum illustrium* (*The Fates of Illustrious Men*), Petrarch brought significant innovations. Unlike Boccaccio, who gave his laureated colleague a generous speaking part in *De casibus virorum illustrium*, Petrarch sealed off the past, as if with a No Trespassing sign: No contemporaries allowed, not Giovanni of Certaldo, not any of the powerful Colonna clan, not even the wishful Emperor Charles IV (*Familiares* 19.3).[20]

Related to *De viris illustribus* is the little *Collatio inter Scipionem, Alexandrum, Annibalem et Pyrrhum*, a fragment preserved in a single copy at the University of Pennsylvania Library. The word "collatio," which can mean a "speech," "discourse," or "formal oration" (as in *Collatio laureationis, The Coronation Oration*), in this context means rather "comparison." So the title could be translated "Comparison of Scipio, Alexander, Hannibal, and Pyrrhus." Taking suggestions from Livy, Petrarch imagines a conversation among the three foreigners (all of whom have lives in *De viris illustribus* because of their impact on Roman history) to decide who is the most meritorious military hero. The Roman general Scipio, a priori superior to the other three, does not participate. Whereas Livy had given top honors to Alexander the Great, Petrarch overturns his source to declare Hannibal best—after Scipio, of course—and Alexander weakest. Both here and in *De viris illustribus,* he strips the legendary Macedonian of his medieval glitter as a paragon of largesse, reducing him to a wrathful, wine-loving, effeminate creature. Perhaps drafted for eventual importation into a letter,[21] this sketch displays Petrarch's habit of rating subjects—men, their deeds, their words—on a scale of worth. This practice will persist in the *Rerum memorandarum libri* (*Books of Things to Be Remembered*) and well beyond, when in his eclogues and treatises on solitude he will stage debates on the active and contemplative ways of life.

Scipio's great victory over Hannibal in the Second Punic War (3rd cent. BCE) was to pass into heroic verse as the *Africa,* what Simone Marchesi calls "Petrarch's Philological Epic." Close in spirit to *De viris illustribus,* the *Africa* challenges Dante's typology with philology, as Petrarch transcends medieval tradition to restore classical forms. Through the rhetorical devices of analepses and prolepses (flashbacks and flash-forwards), Marchesi finds, he grafts extensive material to the main narrative line, such as his story of Dido, which illustrates Petrarch's theory of "mellification" (*Familiares* 23.19). In much the same way as he collects the scattered fragments of his soul (in the *Secretum*) and of his rhymes (in *Rerum vulgarium fragmenta* 1.1), the philological poet, like a bee who visits many flowers to make honey, "will assemble in one volume (*corpus in unum colliget*) the fragmentary matter of Scipio's deeds."[22] Marchesi continues:

> Petrarch's own inscription in the history of Scipio as a belated singer of Rome and its general, is a move that initially only contributes to authenticate him as a member of the authorial canon of epic poets rapidly sketched in the prologue. Virgil, Statius, and Lucan (1.50–55)—and now also Petrarch—have sung world-historical wars of the past and have thus occupied, for material and stylistic merits, a relatively secure position in the pan-chronic system of cultural history. . . . The closest mytho-poetic equivalent to the cultural dynamics envisioned by Petrarch seems to be Dante's "bella scola" (fair school) of poetry, the quintet of poets by the noble castle who engage in technical conversation that the poem refrains from relating (*Inferno* 4.104–05, *Purgatorio* 22.10–18).

Yet Petrarch feared the great Florentine's ghost, suspects Marchesi, who sees an analogy between the Babel of Hannibal's evil camp and the linguistic multiformity of Dante's *Divina commedia.* "Displaced from Dante to Hannibal and from poetics to politics, the threat of a different poem and of a different poetic lineage haunts Petrarch's poem."[23]

Of Petrarch's six surviving orations, a small corpus unto itself, by far the most famous is his *Collatio laureationis* (*Coronation Oration*), delivered at the Capitoline Hill on Easter Sunday (April 8), 1341, but not published until 1876.[24] The poet himself preserved to history this dazzling occasion in many scattered references, mostly in his epistles, notably a self-apologetic account in his *Posteritati* (*Letter to Posterity*, 1351). Less modest are verses he embedded a decade earlier in the final canto of his epic *Africa*.[25] Scipio has conquered Hannibal, and as the victorious Roman fleet returns home from its African campaign, the poet Ennius holds the hero and his men spellbound on deck, recounting a dream in which blind Homer had appeared to him with a prophetic vision of the Bard's Tuscan successor, that young "Franciscus" who will recall the Muses long exiled to Mount Helicon:

> At last in tardy triumph he will climb
> the Capitol. Nor shall a heedless world
> nor an illiterate herd, inebriate
> with baser passions, turn aside his steps
> when he descends, flanked by the company
> of Senators, and from the rite returns
> with brow girt by the glorious laurel wreath.[26]

Two Roman senators, Orso dell'Anguillara and Giordano Orsini, did in fact bestow the crown. Afterward, it was probably Orso who then read the *Privilegium laureae domini Francisci petrarche*. Closely related to the *Collatio laureationis* and assumed to be Petrarch's composition, this document of about a thousand words lays out the "privilege of the laurel" to which Dominus Franciscus Petrarca is now entitled, a list of eight awards. The *Privilegium* declares him "a great poet and historian," not only for the works he has already written but for those he intends to write in the future; it gives him the right to crown other poets, extends all honors pertaining to professors of the liberal arts, and pronounces him a Roman citizen. Given Petrarch's veneration for Rome, he particularly cherished the last title.[27]

The *Collatio laureationis* survives as the centerpiece of an event that Petrarch himself orchestrated from beginning to end. His *Familiares* (4.4) relate the arrival of invitations on the same day, *mirabile dictu*, from Rome and Paris. He naturally chose the former and journeyed to Naples first so King Robert of Anjou could certify his fitness for the honor. Of Robert, whose patria was Provence and who was himself a writer, Petrarch always speaks most admiringly. The Angevin king, for example, is the only modern deemed worthy of memory in *Rerum memorandarm libri*, where he appears in the treatise on wisdom under the rubric "De studio et doctrina" (On study and learning, 1.10). Petrarch apostrophizes him (1.37): "O voice truly philosophical and most worthy of veneration of all scholarly men, how much you delighted me!"[28]

Following the structural pattern of his other public addresses, he puts new wine in an old bottle and adapts to homiletic form an entirely secular speech, not hung on biblical chapter and verse but lines from Virgil's *Georgics* (3.291–92): "Sed me Parnasi deserta per ardua dulcis / raptat amor" (But a sweet longing urges me upward over the lonely slopes of Parnassus). Dennis Looney's essay, "The Beginnings of Humanistic Oratory: Petrarch's *Coronation Oration*," emphasizes precisely the innovative classical character of the *Collatio*, one quarter of which is made up of Latin citations from fifteen authors in nearly two dozen quotes. It epitomizes the tremendous enthusiasm for Rome and its culture that fired the poet, not yet thirty years old. Before turning twenty, in 1333, he had found in Liège Cicero's oration *Pro Archia*. Cicero there argues that the Greek poet Archias should be permitted to live in Rome as a citizen. Begging the court's indulgence, Cicero departs from legal custom and offers an apologia for literature. That will serve as a crucial model for the 1341 speech at a place on the Capitoline Hill where Petrarch believed (mistakenly) the Roman himself had once orated.[29] As Looney writes, "Petrarch dared to imagine, for his part, the role of poetry and the poet in restoring the ancient polis at the center of a unified Christian republic, at the center of the Holy Roman Empire."

Later Petrarch would deliver other orations, under circumstances very different from the spectacle he staged for himself on Rome's Capitoline Hill to extol the life of letters. Almost forgotten because they don't fit his sleek self-portraits as a freedom-loving intellectual, they are here assembled for scrutiny in Victoria Kirkham's essay, "Petrarch the Courtier: Five Public Speeches (*Arenga facta Veneciis, Arringa facta Mediolani, Arenga facta in civitate Novarie, Collatio brevis coram Iohanne Francorum rege, Orazione per la seconda ambasceria veneziana*)." In fact, the poet served a succession of powerful lords—the Colonna at Avignon, the Correggio at Parma, the Visconti at Milan, and the Carrara at Padua—performing courtly duties that ranged from appearances as a trophy guest at the banquet table to poet-on-call, humanist secretary, orator, and ambassador. Dating from the twenty-year period (1353–73) when his fame was at its height and his display value greatest, these five speeches unabashedly promote the politics of ruling despots. Although they contradict our mythic picture of Petrarch, they reflect a system of courtly patronage that would flourish in the Renaissance.

"Rhetoric was the coin that paid for his keep," permitting him leisure for serious literary projects.

Around summer's end of 1343 in Vaucluse and Avignon, Petrarch began *Rerum memorandarum libri*. This "book of things to be remembered" presses the poet's love of history into a different, experimental mold. Although rooted like *De viris illustribus* and *Africa* in the classical world, it departs from the Suetonian biographical model and heroic poetry. Here Petrarch packages anecdotes ranging in length from 40 to 1,400 words to describe exemplary behavior, ranking the famous for moral merit, just as he had set the Three Crowns of Florence in a hierarchy of poetic talent (*Seniles* 5.2). In a departure from his *De viris illustribus*, Romans of antiquity are here joined by Greeks, "foreigners" (as in Valerius Maximus, an important model), and select moderns—King Robert of Naples, Dante, and fourteenth-century popes. We too, he says with his bridges from past to present, can emulate and equal the ancients. Although interrupted by a frustrating diplomatic mission to Naples in late 1343, the book continued to occupy Petrarch afterward in Parma, where he had taken up residence at the invitation of its new lord, Azzo da Correggio. But when it was only about one-fourth finished, struggles for power among northern Italian princes forced him to flee his haven, under siege from the Visconti of Milan and the Gonzaga of Mantua. After a harrowing escape on February 23, 1345, Petrarch lost interest in these collected morality lessons, "memorable" though he once may have imagined them. The structure he called a "most religious temple" remained incomplete, unknown until its posthumous rediscovery.[30]

In its original ambitious plan, *Rerum memorandarum libri* was to be a treatise in twelve books on the four cardinal or pagan virtues. Preludial thoughts on "solitude, leisure, study, and discipline" lead Petrarch to his temple's threshold, where he pays tribute to Cicero, who had defined the virtues and their facets at the end of *De inventione*. A pre-Christian (d. 43 BCE), the Roman orator knows the classical foundation, which, completed by Saint Paul's triad of faith, hope, and charity, formed the medieval cycle of seven virtues. Cicero's ethical structure rests on prudence, temperance, fortitude, justice—a tetrad that ruled the forty honorable souls in Dante's limbo, among them Marcus Tullius himself alongside Seneca (*Inferno* 4).[31] Prudence, Cicero explains, is the knowledge of things good, bad, and neutral. Its parts are memory (of the past), intelligence (of the present), and foresight (of the future). Petrarch divided his treatment of "Sapientia" (Wisdom) accordingly, but he carried the project barely as far as Temperance, beginning with a chapter on its facet "Modesty."

Enthusiasts after his death, first among them Coluccio Salutati, rescued the incomplete edifice from oblivion. Why, if posterity thought so highly of this project, did Petrarch abandon it? Paolo Cherchi invites us to ponder that puzzle in his essay, "The Unforgettable *Books of Things to Be Remembered.*" Petrarch, we know, was constantly putting aside one project to begin another and then returning to this or that unfinished manuscript—to the point that his entire corpus, like the life it mirrors, was always a "work in progress." In this case, it seems that he did briefly take up the project again not long after leaving Parma, while in Verona, but in the latter city through Guglielmo da Pastrengo he came to know Cicero's *Ad Atticum* (*Letters to Atticus*), which fired him with the idea to collect his own correspondence. Cherchi, however, concurs with others who have suggested that political tumult and exciting manuscript discoveries cannot alone explain the derailment of *Rerum memorandarum libri.* For Petrarch it "was becoming imperative . . . to look for his own character and care less or not at all about the great souls of the past. It was the period in which Petrarch, following the exhortation of Augustine recorded in the *Secretum* . . . begins the conversion into his own interiority."

Part 3. Contemplative Serenity

Petrarch turns to himself and his historical present when at Vaucluse in 1346 he conceives the *Bucolicum carmen,* a single "pastoral song" articulated as twelve eclogues. In a letter to his brother Gherardo (*Familiares* 10.4), Petrarch offers a key to the sequence, which was completed in 1357. Stefano Carrai, in "Pastoral as Personal Mythology in History," traces in these eclogues an allegorically veiled journey through the poet's life and times—his childhood, Gherardo's entry into a Carthusian monastery, the death of Robert of Anjou, Cola di Rienzo's attempted political reform in Rome, his "divorce" from service to Cardinal Giovanni Colonna, the black death of 1348, and the Hundred Years' War. As with the *Rerum vulgarium fragmenta,* he carefully ordered this macrotext. The corrupt, whoring Church is central to an overarching structure interwoven with Petrarch's personal mythology as a poet and, Carrai finds, "firmly rooted in a medieval world view."

Petrarch's own pastoral retreat, Vaucluse, belonged to the diocese of Philippe de Cabassoles, bishop of Cavaillon, fittingly the dedicatee of *De vita solitaria,* drafted during Lent in 1346 but not completed until 1371. The title of Armando Maggi's essay in this volume, "'You will be my solitude': Solitude as Prophecy," announces the poet's paradoxical ideal of "a non-alone solitude" to contemplate, or "prophesy," a future Jerusalem for the soul. If the "Holy Land" of Italy is the center for his meditations, the ultimate utopian nowhere "place" of solitude is the friend—Philippe on one level and on a higher plane, Christ. Assuming "the image of a prototypical humanist-like hermit," Petrarch believes "that a noble spirit will find repose nowhere save in God, in whom is our end, or in himself, and his private thoughts, or in some intellect united by a close sympathy with his own."

Leisure and solitude, conditions for contemplation that launch Petrarch's examples of Wisdom in the *Rerum memorandarum libri*, herald a treatise complementary to *De vita solitaria*.[32] Just one year after drafting that book for Philippe, and again during Lent, he set down *De otio religioso* (*On Religious Leisure*). Destined for his brother's Carthusian community, which received the gift in 1356, it circulated widely in European monasteries. Susanna Barsella, in "A Humanistic Approach to Religious Solitude," sees *De otio* as a creative mix of genres, at once epistle (hence dialogue), treatise, and homily, through which Petrarch imagines the monastery as a defensive citadel where the monks fight secular dangers in a religious solitude redefined as classical otium.

Part 4. Journeys into the Soul

The restless writer without "earth" or "sky" to call his own, the man never a native but everywhere a wanderer, "peregrinus ubique," as he wrote in a metrical epistle to his Neapolitan friend Barbato da Sulmona (*Epystole* 3.19), traveled the cities of Europe while ceaselessly exploring the landscape of his soul. Wilkins catalogs him in eighty-three places during his life span of seventy years (July 20, 1304—July 18/19, 1374), not counting return trips to some that were magnets. The pull most powerful, though, came from the boundless continent inside his mind.[33] That is where he goes the day he climbs Mount Ventoux, an ascent described in what is surely the best-known of his *Familiar Letters* (*Familiares* 4.1). Addressed to his Augustinian father confessor Dionigi da Borgo San Sepolcro, it translates a three-day alpine experience into a moral allegory. Since he has only then reached his thirty-second year (hence the fictional dating to April 26, 1336, of a letter actually composed nearly twenty years later),[34] he falls short of the perfect age that Christ had attained at his death, thirty-three. Petrarch is not yet thirty-two. That chronological discrepancy signifies his defective spiritual state, the realization of which sweeps over him at the windy mount's peak. As he takes in the view, he opens his pocket copy of Augustine's *Confessions*, a gift from Dionigi. It speaks to him as an oracle. From looking outward at the created world, he must turn his thoughts inward and thence travel mentally upward. The route is an itinerary to God: *extra nos, intra nos, supra nos* (outside ourselves, inside ourselves, above ourselves). Petrarch plays out his suspended state, beyond the sensual turbulence of youth but still far from the inner quiet of a safe harbor, against a parallel scene in the *Confessions,* the book through which Augustine constantly kept him company. Augustine had received his oracle from a source nearer the divine, an epistle of Saint Paul. It came to him, moreover, under a fig tree in the garden of his salvation when he had reached thirty-two, a fuller age, at a Christological threshold. In his thirty-third year, Augustine at last rejected the stubbornness that let him keep saying, "Give me chastity, Lord, but not yet." His aversion to God and perversion of the will yielded at last to full Christian conversion.[35]

Petrarch summons Augustine, vested with such authority, as his interlocutor in the *Secretum,* a three-day dialogue that dramatizes turmoil in his soul, a psychomachia. He casts as the two sides of his divided will Augustinus, who speaks with Christian reason, and Franciscus, who wants to postpone his reform much as Augustine had done in the *Confessions* before his oracle in the garden. The debate unfolds with Lady Truth as witness. Franciscus defends himself, referring to Augustine's treatise *De vera religione* (*On True Religion*): "I read it intently. I was like a traveler, far from his homeland and eager to see the world, who, crossing the unfamiliar border of some famous city, is captivated by the sweetness of the sights and stops frequently here and there to study everything he sees." But Augustinus counters reproachfully, sounding much like Petrarch's penitential thoughts at the summit of Mount Ventoux, "What good has all your reading done you? . . . What does it matter if you have learned about the orbits of the planets, if you know the expanse of the oceans and the course of the stars, about the properties of plants and rocks and the secrets of nature? What difference does all of this make if you do not know yourself?"[36]

As David Marsh puts it in "The Burning Question: Crisis and Cosmology in the *Secret,*" "instead of Augustinian confessions, Franciscus seems only to offer Petrarchan concessions about his spiritual shortcomings." Augustinus, like Virgilius in the *Divine Comedy,* takes on as his charge Franciscus, a new "Dante," yet at the Pythagorean crossroads he can't seem to turn away from the left, morally sinister, fork of the road.[37] He is squandering and scattering his assets on the *Africa,* Augustinus accuses, which the poet thought of burning rather than leaving it for someone else to finish. Although in the timeframe of eternity, *sub specie aeternitatis,* Franciscus should abandon his Latin historical works, in the end he still resists. "I will collect the scattered fragments of my soul," he promises—but not yet.[38]

A more intense, soul-searching, true spiritual anguish pervades Petrarch's *Psalmi penitentiali* (*Seven Penitential Psalms*), perhaps close in time
to the despairing metrical epistle *Ad se ipsum* (*To Himself*), written from an
abyss of grief for loved ones lost to the Black Death of 1348. The best copy
of these *Psalms*, widely diffused in the early centuries but still lacking a
critical edition, is in the form of a beautifully decorated scroll at Lucerne
(see fig. 7 below), probably made for presentation to Gian Galeazzo Visconti, infant son of Galeazzo (brother of co-ruler and dog breeder Bernabò) and future groom to the princess Isabelle, daughter of King John II of
France.[39] Petrarch, who claims to have written them in a single day, many
years later sends a copy to Sagremor de Pommiers, formerly a secretary of
Emperor Charles IV and newly a Cistercian monk. Urging "Sagreamor"
to live by his name ("sacred love") and "yearn for the lord of heaven," Petrarch refers to the gift as something "inelegant" and private, "the seven
psalms that I long ago composed for myself in my misery" (*Seniles* 10.1).[40]

What he writes, as Ann Matter announces with her title "Petrarch's
Personal Psalms," are seven original Latin prayers, his own compositions,
"in a type of poetic prose reminiscent of Hebrew."[41] To frame her argument
Matter provides valuable background on the scriptural Psalms and reviews
the sparse reception history of Petrarch's, best characterized as "a work in
progress, the spiritual musings of a sensitive soul who is in conversation, if
not in conflict, with the Christianity he has inherited." Dating from after
his brother Gherardo embraced the strictest of monastic disciplines by becoming a Carthusian in 1343 and probably from the period when Petrarch
was writing the *Secretum* (a date still debated), these personal psalms describe "sincere personal laments" and "regrets for foolishness, falling down
when he felt strong, obstinacy in sin."[42]

Other shorter, scattered prayers give insight into Petrarch's religious
practice, faith, and human fears. Vulnerability to the elements looms in his
petitions for protection from tempests. He prays to the Blessed Agatha that
"winds and vapors of impending storms be mercifully turned away from
our heads." A prayer to Saint Lawrence, martyred by fire on the grate,
hints at the terror lightning could strike as fire from the sky.[43] A "daily
prayer" (*oratio quotidiana*) asks for help on his journey through life:

> Jesus Christ, my salvation, if human misery can bend you to mercy,
> be with me, a miserable man, and benevolently grant my prayers.
> Make my pilgrimage pleasing to you, and direct all my steps to
> the pathway of eternal salvation. Deign to be near me at the end
> of my days and at that final hour of death. Remember not my sins,

but as my spirit leaves this little body, welcome it, placated, and do not enter into judgment of your servant, Lord. Font of mercy, have mercy on me. Favor my efforts and cover up my deformities on the last day, and do not allow this soul, the work of your hands, to come into the proud dominion of your enemy and mine, nor to be prey to unclean spirits and a laughing stock for starving dogs. My God, have mercy on me, through you, O Savior.[44]

When in 1358 he composed for a nobleman at the Visconti court his *Itinerarium ad sepulchrum domini nostri Yhesu Christi* (*Itinerary to the Sepulcher of our Lord Jesus Christ*), Petrarch created a guidebook for two kinds of journeys, one a travel route through Mediterranean lands, and the other a meditation on the path toward spiritual perfection. Thus Theodore J. Cachey Jr. in "The Place of Petrarch's *Itinerarium*" explains the paradox of this manual, written by an author who had never been to Jerusalem and, held back by fear of seasickness, did not accompany his friend on the journey there. For Cachey, who sees a correlation between the restlessness that made Petrarch an eternal "pilgrim" (*peregrinus ubique*) and his habit of jumping back and forth from one unfinished work to another, the geographical content of this guide is less important than "the spatial self-portrait of the poet at a crossroads in his career." An exile begotten in exile, as he says in the dedicatory letter to Ludwig van Kempen in his *Familiares*, writing was his only home. His unsettled state, Cachey writes,

> expressed on the one hand a profound awareness of man's ultimate irremediable homelessness, and on the other a no less compelling biographical need for dwelling, for some form of temporary shelter. . . . this irresolvable tension is at the heart of Petrarch's intellectual history and produces as its effect in writing not only the place of Petrarch's *Itinerary* but the entire corpus and eventually the place or what has recently been termed "the site of Petrarchism."[45]

Part 5. Life's Turbulence

Petrarch's last great work and his most medieval, *De remediis utriusque fortune* (*Remedies for Fortune Fair and Foul*), drafted in 1360, is a medicinal treatise dedicated to Azzo da Correggio of Parma and divided into two books. The first presents cures for the dangers of good luck; the second, help for troubled times. Ratio (Reason), the doctor and stern judge who counters the lower unstable passions from her citadel in the soul, presides in an allegorical debate with four representatives of her antagonist, Fortune. They are the two sets of twin daughters of Prosperity and Adversity, Joy and Hope and Fear and Sorrow, respectively. Dialogue 120 near the end of book 1, "All kinds of hope," gives a sense of the author's riddling, oblique rhetoric, reminiscent of Abelard's *sic et non* and resonant for Petrarch, trained as a lawyer to debate a question from both sides.

> Hope: I hope for long life.
> Reason: A long-lasting prison. . . .
> Hope: A eulogy at my funeral.
> Reason: A nightingale singing to the deaf. . . .
> Hope: Fame after death.
> Reason: Gentle breezes after shipwreck.[46]

Book 1 ends with a typically oppressive dialogue, "De spe vite eterne" (Hope for life eternal). To Hope's wish for salvation in eternity eight times reiterated, Ratio opposes relentless caveats and restrictions. Petrarch launches book 2 with a dictum from Heraclites, "Strife rules the world," illustrated with combative forces from huge animals to the tiniest insects, from human warfare to battles of scribes with parchment, ink, pens, and paper.[47] A culminating series of dialogues brings crashing down the inevitable finale: "Death Before One's Time," "Violent Death," "Shameful Death," "Sudden Death," "Death Away from Home," "Dying in a State of Sin," "Dying Anxious about one's Fame after Death," "Dying without Children," and the crowning dread, "Dying in Fear of Being Cast Away Unburied."[48] Reason dismisses such a petty concern by remembering the unburied dead who litter the whole world—200,000 Persians with King Cyrus, at Cannae more than 85,000 Romans and allies; 56,000 at the Metaurus River. Left exposed, Reason witheringly argues, your body will simply return to the four elements of which it is made. Her final riposte, the very last words of *De remediis utriusque fortune*, is tantamount to a deaf ear:

> Fear: I am being cast away unburied.
> Reason: Attend to your own business. And let the living worry about this.[49]

Timothy Kircher, "On the Two Faces of Fortune," points us to the author's plan for his readers, "an overarching structural arrangement" that puts death as the ultimate subject proper for human meditation. He synthesizes information on Petrarch's sources, including "Seneca," cited in the prefatory letter (actually the sixth-century bishop Martin of Braga), the author of *De remediis fortuitorum* (*Remedies against Happenstances*), which inspired the title.[50] Encyclopedic in the scope of its *exempla*, *De remediis* is syncretistic in its fusion of Christian doctrine with classical dicta. Kircher explains the psychomachia as related to "conscience in the individual soul," comparing Reason to the Freudian "analyst," and the fluctuating passions in her charge to the "analysand." When will Ratio gain mastery over the "emotional netherworld?" For Petrarch's patient the outlook is not good.

Another kind of medicine, healing as actually practiced in Petrarch's day, dominates his *Contra medicum*. Colorfully propelled by the epideictic rhetoric of blame, these outbursts blast their target with scatological language, the weapon of choice for a "great sewer" whose diagnoses depend on peering into chamber pots.[51] Stefano Cracolici's essay, "The Art of Invective," identifies true events that triggered Petrarch's outrage—inept medical responses to an illness of Pope Clement VI, the sense of personal helplessness during plagues that killed Laura, his son, and close friends. Petrarch takes this to a theoretical level as well, within a framework of medieval taxonomies: the seven Liberal Arts as opposed to the seven Mechanical Arts, defined in parallel by Hugh of Saint-Victor.[52] For Petrarch the polemicist, as Cracolici suggests, poetry too is a form of "egrotantis cura" (a patient's care), but only in the proper hands, when it can bring balm to the soul.

Petrarch himself plays the physician, so to speak, not long after publishing his *Invective contra medicum*, practicing again in the same genre with *Invectiva contra quendam magni status hominem sed nullius scientie aut virtutis* (*Invective against a Man of High Rank with No Knowledge or Virtue*, 1355). "I shall diligently offer you what you shun most," he writes acerbically, "as if forcing a bitter potion on an unwilling patient."[53] In need of cure is Jean de Caraman, a grand-nephew of Pope John XXII whom Clement VI had named a cardinal in 1350. Residing at Avignon, the once friendly cleric has stung Petrarch for compromising himself by accepting Visconti patronage. Armed with antithesis and an arsenal of satire from Juvenal to the Acts of the Apostles, the Italian retaliates. Consorting with tyrants, Petrarch insists, does not taint good character, as confirmed by axiomatic truth ("Virtue is not infected by the proximity of vice") no less than by the examples of Socrates, Plato, Callisthenes, Cato, and Seneca.[54] Petrarch lives subject only to Christ and a small circle of friends. He strives to keep on learning even in old age, as did Solon, Socrates, Plato, and Cato. Luck alone, responsible for elevating Caraman, can't grant good character, intelligence, virtue, and eloquence—qualities that (by silent contrast) Petrarch cultivates. "When you quack like a duck rather than sing like a swan," he sneers, "the cause is not eloquence but loquacity."[55] Caraman, as blind as Fortune who has made him her plaything, is a Judas, a venomous snake, and a churchman who fails to practice poverty—on the contrary, he plunders the poor "in the bazaar of Simon Magus as a zealous if tardy merchant."[56] Ridicule reduces the old simonist to a blabbering buffoon who enjoys his fancy red hat and robes merely because of his family's recent rise to power, not because of any personal merit.

De sui ipsius et multorum ignorantia (*On His Own Ignorance and That of Many Others*), the third of Petrarch's invectives, carries a dedicatory letter to the Tuscan grammarian Donato Albanzani dated 1371 (*Seniles* 13.5). It pits the poet, surprisingly, against four friends of his old age in Venice. A soldier, merchant, aristocrat, and physician, his maligners are a small cross-section of society. Their public disparagement of him, which the self-apologist supposes stems from envy of his reputation, prompts a philosophical meditation on knowledge, first of all his own—or lack of it, readily admitted. From these thoughts he elaborates a hierarchy of great thinkers in history: at the top Plato, closest to Christianity, as no faithful reader of Augustine can doubt; next the less appealing Aristotle, a polymath but far from revealed truth; and then Cicero, who died just as Christ's birth was approaching and "speaks more like an Apostle than a philosopher."[57]

William J. Kennedy, in his essay "The Economy of Invective and a Man in the Middle," departs from traditional interpretations that hammer on the poet's anti-Aristotelianism and puts *De ignorantia* into fresh sociological and psychological perspectives. "Petrarch emerges as a 'man in the middle,' neither part of the established social institutions that might proclaim his scholarly and intellectual competence, nor part of an emergent mercantile commercial order that might reward him with material wealth, communal prestige, and strategic influence." To defend his position, Petrarch "reverts to economic figurations" that Kennedy in Marxist style teases out of a metaphorically well-stocked text: "I have become a poor peddler of learning (*mercator inops literarum*), robbed (*spoliatus*) of my knowledge and fame by these four brigands (*predonibus*)." Freudian analysis uncovers the poet's "most censored thought," his "besetting ignorance" of Greek. Ultimately, "Petrarch seeks to defuse his friends' assault by handing over his property to them," that is, his fame.

Petrarch flattens his opponent with a fourth and last sally into this genre, *Invectiva contra eum qui maledixit Italie* (*Invective against a Detractor of Italy*, 1373). Like the cardinal of the second invective, this "lunatic" suffers from the misfortune of being a Frenchman (*gallus*). In this attack, Petrarch pumps a long-standing cultural bias: Paris, stronghold of the Scholastics, he had rejected for his laureation; the country's language he claimed not to speak; its vernacular literature he knew but rated low. A metrical epistle he sent Guido Gonzaga of Mantua (1342/43) to accompany the *Romance of the Rose* warns the gift's recipient of how poorly it compares with the classics:

> Itala quam reliquas superet facundia lingua,
> Vir prestans, Graiam preter, (si fama sequenda est,
> Si Cicero) nullam excipio, brevis iste libellus
> Testis erit
> . . . . . .
> Ut tuus ille olim melius concivis amoris
> Explicuit sermone pathos, si fabula dives
> Inspicitur frigiaque expirans cuspide Dido
> Seu vates, Verona, tuus, seu nidus amorum
> Fertilis ac notus lascivo carmine Sulmo
> Umbria sive ducem ingenio largita peligno.

> [How far the eloquence of other tongues
> Is by our Latin eloquence surpassed
> (Greek I except, on Cicero's report
> And that of Fame), you for yourself, my lord,
> May see from the little book that I am sending
> . . . .
> How much more nobly, in the days of old
> Your fellow citizen (Virgil) set forth the sorrow
> Of passionate love, in his illustrious tale
> Of Dido's death upon her Phrygian sword!
> And thou, Verona, hadst thy bard (Catullus); and thou,
> Sulmona, fruitful home of amorous song,
> Whose poet (Ovid) learned from him of Umbria (Propertius)].[58]

Petrarch, hierarchically thinking, puts Greek at the top over Latin, next Italy's vernacular, and then languages from other regions. Provençal, absorbed into the *Rerum vulgarium fragmenta,* outranks the *langue d'oïl* native to northern France that has evolved into the modern-day national language. Small wonder that the French, a nation "unteachable by nature," became the butt of his merciless satire in the *Invective against a Detractor of Italy.*[59]

The polemicist bashes this particular "feral" Frank and "barbarian" Gaul for having dared oppose Petrarch's letter urging Pope Urban V to return to Italy (*Seniles* 9.1) in a treatise arguing Avignon's superiority to a supposedly corrupt Rome.[60] His adversary, in real life the theologian Jean d'Hesdin, takes a relentless pounding as puns descend to the animal kingdom and turn that cleric into a ridiculous barnyard rooster ("gallus"). From this connection, a virtual zoo materializes to parade through the pages. Decked with a cock's comb, he has a goose's tongue, the brain of an ox, and the ears of an ass. Petrarch especially scorns him because he is a Scholastic. His nation's vices personified, Hesdin dwells unenlightened in gluttony and drunkenness: "hogs love mud, frogs love the swamp, and bats love darkness."[61] Since he is retorting to a lawyer—a bad one, naturally— Petrarch here puts on his legal robes, stepping forward in an identity often overlooked aside from biographical sketches that make passing mention of university training at Montpellier and Bologna. He proudly asserts his citizenship in the city that is the "highest summit of the world, Rome" (*mundi vertex Roma*), glory deserved for its promulgation of the Justinian code. Because laws are sacrosanct, "the city of Rome can be called 'sacred,' since she is the most venerable home of laws, and the mother or nurse of all the jurists who framed our Latin laws!"[62]

6. Petrarch the Epistler

As a "born-again ancient," Petrarch made his greatest manuscript discovery in the Verona cathedral library, the sixteen books of Cicero's *Ad Atticum* along with two minor collections, to the Roman orator's brother Quintus and to Brutus. From these, which the classics detective excitedly transcribed over several weeks in the spring of 1345 (a period when he also came to know Dante's son Pietro Alighieri), Petrarch took the tremendous idea of collecting his own letters.[63] Eventually, he compiled four epistolary anthologies with a total of 563 letters, mostly substantial pieces, rejecting in the process a thousand others he had written and burned because, he claims, there wasn't room for them.[64] In point of fact, he imposed artful criteria for keeping or "damning" letters, much like those that divide the *Rerum vulgarium fragmenta* from the uncollected rhymes. What survives is a corpus embracing a European community of 150 recipients, making him arguably the most prolific epistler ever up to his time. From student days until a month before his death, when he penned his final missive to Giovanni Boccaccio, the "graphomaniac" carried on his correspondence unflaggingly—"nothing," he correctly foresaw, "but the end of my life will bring an end to my letter writing" (*Seniles* 1.1).[65]

By 1350, he was planning both the prose *Rerum familiarum libri* and his

letters in Latin verse, called simply *Epystole*. The former carries a dedicatory letter to the long-time friend he nicknamed Socrates, in history the
Flemish chanter Ludwig van Kempen, first encountered during the "heavenly" summer of 1330 spent with Giacomo Colonna at the latter's episcopal
seat of Lombez, in the Pyrenees.[66] As of May 1356, Petrarch had nearly
finished eight books; by 1359, twenty, and at completion in 1366, the *Familiares* contained 350 letters distributed over twenty-four books, culminating
with those to the ancients.[67] Meanwhile, he announced a new project in the
final, probably fictional, letter to Socrates: "this work has already grown
enough . . . I have decided to insert into another volume any letters excluded and out of order here; and if I do write others, which will take their
title from my age, they will be collected in another volume."[68]

As promised, he continued letter collecting with the *Rerum senilium
libri* (or *Seniles*), 128 pieces distributed over eighteen books dedicated to
Francesco Nelli—"Simonide" in the epistler's classical pseudonym. Nelli,
already the recipient of more letters than any other correspondent in the
Familiares, belonged to Boccaccio's circle of eager disciples in Florence,
where he was prior of the Church of Santissimi Apostoli. Tutor for a time
to Petrarch's trying son Giovanni in Avignon, he died of plague in 1363,
after two years in Naples as a royal secretary.[69] Ideally, the watershed between *Familiares* and *Seniles* was 1361, but Petrarch never followed strict
chronological order—not even in the anniversary poems of *Rerum vulgarium
fragmenta*—so a few epistles postdating that year cross back into the earlier
volume and vice versa. Generally, the later letters illustrate a philosophical
sense of plenitude. As Petrarch pithily conveys it to Boccaccio, his favored
correspondent in the collection, "I discovered old age to be as fruitful as
youth was flowery" (*Seniles* 8.1). If the *Familiares* rise to their rhetorical
climax with ten letters to deceased ancients, his *Seniles* closes in a reverse
symmetry on the single *Posteritati*. "Petrarch, as Aldo Bernardo puts it in
his introduction to the *Seniles*, "hoped to be for posterity what the ancients
had been for him."[70]

Of the letters he slotted neither for the *Familiares* nor the *Seniles*, Petrarch left some simply uncollected (*Lettere disperse*), like rhymes that were
not included in the *Rerum vulgarium fragmenta*. A small group, however, he
bundled into his acerbic *Sine nomine*. Judged too venomous either for the
world of his "familiars" or the mellow years of his maturity, they are sometimes fictitious. What Italians would call the "red thread" that unites them,
their running theme, is the papacy's "Babylonian captivity," its residence in
Avignon (1309–77), abhorrent to a man passionately convinced of Rome's
supremacy. It left that holy city widowed (*Epystole* 4.1) and reduced Avi-

gnon to a sewer for the "scum of the earth" (*Seniles* 10.2). There "all the filth and lewdness of the whole world empty . . . and thicken and jell," he wrote in 1367 to his boyhood friend Guido Sette, now archbishop of Genoa. With Guido he reminisces of joyful childhood days when they lived among the women and children of men who, like Ser Petracco, housed families for their safety in the outlying community of Carpentras.[71] Fall of the same year saw Petrarch's hopes for a Roman papacy briefly come true under Urban V, but that French pontiff succumbed to pressure from his country-men and retreated to Avignon in 1370. In spite of letters Petrarch sent to a succession of popes urging them to take up residency in Rome, he would die four years before Gregory XI again led the court south in 1378, precip-itating a western schism not healed until the election of Martin V in 1416.

Petrarch articulates the *Sine nomine* as a preface plus nineteen letters, a structure planned with the same numerical forethought evident elsewhere in his writings. The eclogues in his *Bucolicum carmen*, for example, total not 10, as had Virgil's pastoral poems, but 12, replicating the pattern of his *Ae-neid*. After reading Homer in the Latin translation by Leontius Pilatus, Pe-trarch extended the books in his *Familiares* to 24, matching the sum of the Greek model.[72] He conceived the *Rerum memorandarum libri* in four parts corresponding to the four cardinal virtues. His *Psalmi penitentiales* are, of course, seven. His first Latin poem has thirty-eight hexameters, one for each year his mother Eletta had lived, as the verse itself discloses. Book 1 of *De remediis* culminates on Hope's wish for life eternal, simply stated eight times in a speech act allusive to the octave of eternity (a step "beyond" the week of Creation into the next world). Whether the 366 lyric poems of the *Rerum vulgarium fragmenta* represent a temporary or terminal ending, he must have liked that total at the time he achieved it. For Petrarch, the num-ber 6 held special importance.[73] It attaches to the first day he saw Laura and her death, both on April 6; on the same day he decided to compose his *Africa* (left incomplete); it rules the metrics of the sestina, a form to which he returns obsessively in his lyrics; the *Triumphi* are six; the *Epystole* fill a template that brings their total to sixty-six. Numerology, far less pervasive in the Petrarchan corpus than in the poetics of his more "medieval" prede-cessor Dante and his contemporary Boccaccio (who moved away from it after becoming friends with Petrarch), puts words in the mouth of Francis-cus at second day's end in the *Secretum*, when Augustine proposes resum-ing for a final session on the morrow:

"Truly, I love the number three with my whole being, not so much because of the three graces as because it is held to be the number that is most akin to the divine. And this is the conviction not only of you and others who profess the true religion and who have absolute faith in the Trinity. So do the pagan philosophers who used this number in the worship of the gods. My beloved Virgil, in fact, seems to have known this when he said, 'God delights in the uneven number.'"[74]

By the code of Pythagorean numerology, to which Petrarch here alludes, 19 is a variant expression of 9. In a traditional Christian meaning, however, 9 signifies shortfall vis-à-vis the perfect 10.[75] Not by accident Petrarch addresses ten letters to the ancients in book 24 of the *Familiares* and names ten rivers in his poem in honor of the birth of Marco Visconti, but he reserves the "defective" 9 in its variant 19 for the *Sine nomine*. Avignon as Babylon is hell, "a dwelling place of shadows and spectres," a "city of confusion" (citing Genesis 11:9), "the labyrinth on the Rhone"; its inhabitants include Semiramis, Minos, Rhadamanthus, Cerberus, Tantalus, the Furies, the "servants of Satan"; "There is no light anywhere, no one to lead you, no sign to guide you along the twisted paths, but only gloom on all sides and confusion everywhere. It is only too true, this is Babylon, that powerful chaos of things."[76] As if to confirm our understanding of his intent, Petrarch signs only one of the letters—the ninth—with a subscription that identifies the place from which he writes: "I, an angry exile from Jerusalem, living by the rivers of Babylon, have written these things to you in great haste."[77]

Petrarch's earliest "letter," the panegyric for his mother (d. 1318/19), found its final niche in his one collection of verse epistles (*Epystole* 1.7). Dedicated to Barbato da Sulmona, these sixty-six pieces in three books came together as the *Epystole* in phases between 1350 and 1364, when Petrarch finally released them as a collection. Much as he did for the *Rerum vulgarium fragmenta*, here he erased all traces of the poetic correspondents whose verse sometimes worked in tandem with Petrarch's to make dialogues in the old medieval tradition of the *tenzone*, a verse exchange or debate between poets.[78] Many epistles, however, display historical dedicatees, among them popes (Benedict XII, Clement VI); rulers (King Robert of Naples, Mastino della Scala, lord of Verona; Guido Gonzaga of Mantua, to whom Petrarch sends a copy of the *Romance of the Rose*); patrons (Luchino Visconti, with a gift of pear trees; Bernabò and his newborn son, Petrarch's godson Marco Visconti); friends (Dionigi da Borgo San Sepolcro, Giacomo Colonna, Cardinal Giovanni Colonna, who had sent him a pet dog; the lawyer Guglielmo da Pastrengo; Giovanni Barrili, with regrets that he could not be present in Rome to crown Petrarch, as had been planned, and a description of the event; Socrates; Pietro Alighieri; Boccaccio); enemies (a bad poet and bad man called Zoilus—actually Brizio Visconti, the natural son of Luchino, who co-ruled Milan with his brother Giovanni); and himself (*Ad se ipsum*).

Such variety obeys principles of unity, as Giuseppe Velli demonstrates in his essay on the *Epystole*, "A Poetic Journal." Like the *Familiares* and *Rerum vulgarium fragmenta*, the *Epystole* is an organic whole, greater than the sum of its parts. Disputing older dismissals of the *Epystole* as a "haphazard heap of preexisting material," Velli discerns a careful arrangement of contents across Petrarch's wide geographic, cultural, and affective panorama. Parallels, contrasts, balance, and symmetry govern clusters of letters that create "thematic units." The three books progress morally "from anguished uncertainty to scornful detachment, and finally to the resolute relinquishment of all worldly things" in a triumph of the poet's will. Simultaneously, they flow along a dynamic horizontal reading axis. The love motif abates; poetry grows as a focus to a "massive presence" in this "original manifesto of humanism."

Ronald L. Martinez compellingly lays out strategies that govern the structure and style of Petrarch's *Liber sine nomine* in "*The Book without a Name:* Petrarch's Open Secret." Properly speaking, these letters are "not missives at all," since they lack names of the addressee, sender, date, and place—except for the subscription "in Babylon," which Martinez sees as marking a center. In hungry, fierce eclecticism, they incorporate invective, satire (Juvenal is "godfather of the collection"), Roman comedy, mock-epic, the novella, Senecan tragedy, history, and biblical Lamentations. These "pseudo-letters" are implicitly an "autobiographical narrative" of the poet's escape from Avignon. At the same time they rise rhetorically to a level of universals with a public who will receive them after his death: "Suppression throughout the collection of all but a few contemporary proper names allows Petrarch to shift his frame of reference at will to the ahistorical plane of apocalyptic, where the names of historical individuals fade in the clamor of cosmic events. The imagined audience of the letters is reoriented . . . toward that posterity of which Petrarch was always thinking."

Through Lynn Westwater's eye in "The Uncollected Poet" on Petrarch's *Lettere disperse (Dispersed Letters)*, privileged glimpses open into the workshop where he shaped and polished his collections. Letters that survived more by accident than design, their addressees all told, from 1338 to 1372, represent forty-one correspondents. Material includes the Aretine's only

surviving note in Italian, a mundane business transaction involving payment for some books. A significant chunk comes from the controversial
eight years he served the Visconti, messages like the dog-lover Bernabò's
missive to Jacopo Bussolari that compromised the image he cultivated as
a humanist unfettered by pragmatic necessity. As Westwater puts it, the
Disperse "might be read as part of Petrarch's messy first draft of his life,
circulated in installments."

For the corrected, flowing, and polished version of his life story,
Giuseppe Mazzotta finds a governing figure in "travel," undertaken by
an author self-cast as Ulysses, and hence discusses the *Familiares* as "An
Epistolary Epic." "Compare my wanderings to those of Ulysses," writes
the poet, who like his father lived in "perpetual exile," as he addresses Socrates in the dedicatory letter.[79] Mazzotta pauses at that threshold to view
the full collection, an "art of living," arranged Homerically into twenty-
four books. Unlike Dante's Ulysses, Petrarch the voyager brings his venture full circle with first and final epistles to Socrates, the latter "a prelude"
to yet more activity, the *Seniles*. Careful stitching of pieces within the epic
frame counters plural registers and rambling tendencies of single letters
to a great variety of correspondents, all united with the poet as allies in
"warfare" against their common enemies—his critics and social decline. Petrarch alone, from "an omniscient, transcendent viewpoint encompassing
all styles," as if he were a Machiavellian prince of letters, heroically carries
the "conviction that the fate of present culture depends on him."[80]

Complementing Mazzotta with his focus on the first letter of the *Familiares*, David Wallace turns to the end of the *Seniles*. His *"Letters of Old
Age:* Love between Men, Griselda, and Farewell to Letters" finds it fitting
for the final tale in the *Decameron* to close *Seniles* book 17 (four letters to
Boccaccio). Within a male domain, the *"hortus inclusus* of humanist Latin,"
Francesco can talk with Giovanni about "the shared pleasures of narration," playing "by turns Walter, Griselda, and sometimes, almost, God, the
all-seeing purveyor of *historia*, the *auctor* behind or before every *auctor*." As
Walter, he can and does remind his wife-like friend that "we are not equal
in merit" (*Seniles* 17.2)—the same stance he had taken in *Seniles* 5.2, with
which this introduction opened. As Griselda, he assumes the weaker, passive position vis-à-vis Gualtieri in parallel, Wallace provocatively suggests,
to "his seduction into Visconti patronage [when] he found his own powers
of volition quite flooded out, surrendered to, the will of the prince." Dated
June 8, 1373, Petrarch's final letter to Boccaccio closes with words that
foresee the poet's own impending death, "Farewell, dear friends. Farewell,
dear letters."

Part 7. Epilogue

Death pervades Petrarch's writings, sometimes an ally calling him to salubrious contemplation, sometimes an enemy who visits physical privation. Augustine, as he reaches his peroration in the *Secretum*, instructs his disciple on the first:

> begin to think about death, which you slowly and unknowingly are approaching. Rip off the veil. Dispel the darkness. Fix your eyes on death alone. Beware lest a single day or night pass by that does not compel you to reflect upon your final hour.[81]

Mourning for lost loved ones and epitaphs he composed manifest the second, from which his own body is not exempt. Sharing a friend's bereavement for the loss of a son, Petrarch writes about his own pain at the death of his grandson Franciscus, for whom he ordered a marble tomb in Pavia (*Seniles* 10.4). On it he had six elegiaic couplets inscribed, no use whatsoever to the little boy who left the world at only two years and four months, but a small consolation to the poet:

> Scarcely did I, newly arrived, touch with my tender foot
> > the hard threshold to the path of the world and this fleeting life.
> Francesco was my father, my mother Francesca;
> > following them I took the same name at the baptismal font;
> a lovely child, sweet solace to my parents,
> > now sorrow; for that alone my lot is less blissful.
> Otherwise I am happy, born so quickly, so easily,
> > to the joy of true and eternal life.
> Twice the sun, four times the moon had traveled the turning earth;
> > death—nay, I am deceived—life was in the way.
> The Venetians' city gave me to the earth; Pavia snatched me away;
> > nor should I complain, to this heaven I was meant to return.[82]

Burial seems to have particularly concerned Petrarch. In France, not surprisingly, they do it badly. The porcine "Gallus" he roasts in his *Invectiva contra eum qui maledixit Italie* has not "heard the stipulation of the civil law that wherever a body is buried—the body not only of a free man, but of a slave, and not merely an entire body, but even part of one—that place is considered 'religious.'" That drunkard's countrymen fail to balance needs of communal worship and proper burial: "I have seen the choirs of famous churches in Paris so crowded with tombs of sinners, both men and—even more revolting—women, that there is scarcely room to kneel or approach the altar."[83] Offensive to Petrarch's legal training and clerical sense of decorum, these breaches may betray a more personal fear, death without the dignity of burial. In the *De remediis*, Fear and Reason's culminating dialogue concerns just this issue, "De moriente qui metuit insepultus abici" (Dying in fear of being cast away unburied).

To insure against such a gruesome fate, Petrarch listed no less than seven possible burial sites for himself when on April 4, 1370, in Padua, he composed his last will and testament. Armando Maggi, closing our volume with his essay "To Write As Another: The *Testamentum*," explains these unusual dispositions by redefining the legal document as a literary artifact. From that innovative perspective, a text traditionally read for its nuggets of biographical information becomes "poetry" in the sense of creative writing. As in the *Secretum*, a "dialogue between two opposite identities . . . informs the entire *Testamentum*." One is the modest person Petrarch sees himself to be, Christocentric in his spirituality and devoted to the Virgin Mary. The other is the rich man his enemy the rabble or "vulgus" thinks him to be, "still fettered to the allurements of the world." Were he that "other," he would have written a different will, hence Maggi's title. Even though it preserves some typical notarial formulas, the *Testamentum* is most striking for deviations from standard practice that make it an "unforgettable self-portrait according to the medieval model of *imitatio Christi*." Comparison both with common practice and two other privileged early Italian wills, those of Saint Francis and Boccaccio, makes clear how idealized this one is, an autobiography uniquely Petrarchan.

The fourteenth-century man who was "father and hero of European humanism"[84] produced an opus as expansive as his life, dedicated to restoring classical culture as the ideal forerunner of Christianity's fulfilling message. Giosuè Carducci, Italy's first Nobel Laureate in Literature (1906), memorably captured the introspective personality of this poet laureate in a thumbnail portrait of the Three Crowns: Dante directed his gaze heavenward, Petrarch inward, and Boccaccio worldward.[85] Yet Petrarch was outgoing, too, in his quest for public laurels and his endless travels. Born in the Tuscan town of Arezzo, restlessly he moved from one place and patron to another, by horse, barge, sailing vessel, and foot, from Prague to

Naples, from the Ardennes to the Pyrenees, from the Rhine to the Tiber.[86] As he passed through many places, so he was many things—philosopher, rhetorician, orator, polemicist, allegorist, melancholic, cleric, church canon, archdeacon, contemplative, courtier, philologist, linguist, playwright, pilgrim, flaneur, gardener, horticulturalist, archeologist, numismatist, poet, historian, counselor of princes, political reformer, liutanist, art collector, employer of servants, library assistants, and copyists ("verily the plague of noble minds"),[87] bibliophile, lover, brother, father, grandfather, godfather, essayist, first modern scholar, ambassador, diplomat, peace negotiator, lawyer, reader, mountain climber, epistler, dandy, friend, translator, glossator, exegete, and encyclopedist.

Readers have long debated whether his opus depicts a modern subject "characterized by a distinct singular interiority" or summons a still medieval concept of personhood through a dense weaving of classical and patristic *auctoritates*.[88] Asking "Quid est?" of each work he wrote, we can perhaps also come closer to knowing "Quis est?" Who is "Petrarch" the author-complex? How shall we understand the man, his writings, and the dynamic interaction between them? Francesco De Sanctis's nineteenth-century notions of a "purist" who inaugurated a new literature of "formal beauty, female beauty, and natural beauty," as Italy "turned its back on the Middle Ages,"[89] have yielded to the tensions of paradox and polarity, the seeming contradictions of a single powerful personality who defies pigeon-holing. He fascinates precisely because he eludes facile typing and rigidly constructed niches. Medieval and Renaissance, Latin and vernacular, classical and Christian, Augustinus and Franciscus, cleric and lover, all mingle in this man, who, as Umberto Bosco asserted, doesn't need any "conversion" theory to explain the oppositions because he never became "other" than what he had been before.[90]

Carducci looks back with double vision upon a towering ancestral specter in the art of poetry. On a cusp between Romanticism's tempestuous melancholy and the searching spirit of twentieth-century philology, he speaks at Petrarch's tomb in Arquà on July 18, 1874, the six-hundredth anniversary of his death. While Carducci sees in his subject "a bit of resemblance" to the romantic hero par excellence, Goethe's young Werther, he prefers to leave that image behind and pull Petrarch forward into a more modern era. For him, Petrarch "was the first to feel what the ancient poets did not . . . that like human society, every individual soul can have a history. . . . Petrarch was the first to denude his conscience esthetically, to question it, to analyze it, and as he did that, he grasped the true and profound meaning of his own elegy, the conflict between the finite man and his infinite aspirations, between the sensible and the ideal, between human and divine, between pagan and Christian."[91]

The image of a wheel, proposed by Manlio Pastore Stocchi, well describes this single man of many diffractions, whose "I" irradiates in so many directions, like spokes from a central hub.[92] This work presents a composite portrait that mirrors the poet as do his own writings. In our anthology of essays, themes running throughout his corpus, from youth to his last years, in Latin as well as Italian, crossing all genre lines, emerge surprisingly and revealingly. What binds these essays and the works they probe is the unifying power of the poet's mind and his recurrent, even obsessive, concerns—ranking people and things; sifting the "saved" from the "damned"—discards left to fend for themselves and survive, if they are lucky, as "dispersed" or uncollected writings; ambition for fame; need for solitude; tireless energies as a scholar; the drive to artistic perfection; the struggle for Christian goodness; his failures as a poet to finish what he started; his relapses as a Christian; the competing objects for his affections—Laura, the queen of heaven, God, Boccaccio, his books, the ancient poets, contemporary friends in an elite circle he drew around himself; disdain for ignorance, acrimony toward enemies; horror of the "populace" (*vulgus*); the wish to be judged fairly by his peers; and hopes for being remembered rightly by posterity.

A sentence from one of the last letters Petrarch ever wrote comes to mind. He has less than three months left to live. Addressing his old friend Boccaccio on April 28, 1373, from his home in Padua, Petrarch quotes one of his beloved ancients, a letter from Seneca to Lucilius: "Much still remains to be done; much will always remain, and even a thousand years hence no one of our descendants need be denied the opportunity of adding his something."[93]

AN ENDURING VERNACULAR LEGACY

CHAPTER ONE

THE SELF IN THE LABYRINTH OF TIME • *Rerum vulgarium fragmenta*

Teodolinda Barolini

Petrarch's enduring collection of lyric poetry, the *Rerum vulgarium fragmenta* (*Fragments of Vernacular Matters;* called variously *Canzoniere, Rime,* and *Rime sparse* but properly and authorially only *Rerum vulgarium fragmenta*),[1] is—like all of Petrarch's work—obsessed with time: the medium that fragments us, makes us multiple and metamorphic, robs us of ontological stillness and wholeness. The *Fragmenta,* which thematizes fragmentation or multiplicity in its very title, conjures the existence of the self in time; we are beings subject to constant incremental change and to radical ontological instability. Aristotle defines time in the *Physics*—"For time is just this, number of motion in respect of 'before' and 'after'" (*Physics* 4.11.219b1)— in a passage cited by Dante in the *Convivio:* "Lo tempo, secondo che dice Aristotele nel quarto de la Fisica, è 'numero di movimento, secondo prima e poi'" (Time, according to Aristotle in the fourth book of the *Physics,* is "number of movement, according to before and after" [*Convivio* 4.2.6]). Asking "does [the 'now'] always remain one and the same or is it always other and other?" (*Physics* 4.10.218a9–10), Aristotle writes, "if the 'now' were not different but one and the same, there would not have been time" (*Physics* 4.11.218b27–28).[2] Time, therefore, comports difference, change, instability, absence of identity, oneness, and being: Petrarch's chosen themes. Hence, although it is not usual to associate Petrarch's lyric sequence, consisting mainly of love poetry, with a philosophical text like Aristotle's *Physics,* it is appropriate: time is a philosophical—indeed, a metaphysical—problem, and to the degree that time is the chief focus and concern of his poetry, Petrarch is a metaphysical poet. Metaphysical concerns, defined as first principles and ultimate grounds, such as being and time, are Petrarch's abiding concerns. The problems that tugged at him ceaselessly—in particular, the nature of time and the existence of the self in time—are metaphysical in nature, and these are the problems that he dramatized in his work.[3]

33

Let us begin by considering what we see when we pick up a copy of Petrarch's poetry book today. We see 366 poems of varied lyrical genres, all interspersed: 317 sonnets, 29 canzoni, 9 sestine, 7 *ballate,* and 4 *madrigali* (for the allocation of these poems throughout the text, see the appendix "Metrical and Thematic Sets in the *Rerum vulgarium fragmenta*" at the end of this essay). In most editions the 366 poems are—correctly—divided into two parts, with part 2 beginning about two-thirds of the way through the text, at poem 264, the canzone *I' vo pensando.* In many editions the two parts incorrectly bear headings that were added early in the editorial tradition: the heading "In vita di madonna Laura" (During the life of Lady Laura) and the heading "In morte di madonna Laura" (After the death of Lady Laura). Later on the beginning of part 2 was moved in order to accommodate the narrative story line told by the invented rubrics. From Pietro Bembo's 1514 edition until Giovanni Mestica's 1896 edition, part 2 begins with sonnet 267, *Oimè il bel viso,* the first poem to register Laura's death, rather than with canzone 264, *I' vo pensando.* While the division of the text into two parts is Petrarch's, the headings and the transposed beginning of part 2 testify to readers' longstanding desire to impose a clear narrative onto the tenuous and opaque love story that the poems do not narrate so much as conjure and suggest.[4]

Of Laura, Petrarch's beloved, we know nothing beyond what he tells us: he first saw her and fell in love with her on April 6, 1327, in the Church of Saint Claire in Avignon. The precise date is declared in sonnet 211, *Voglia mi sprona,* a poem almost excluded from the collection),[5] which concludes: "Mille trecento ventisette, a punto/su l'ora prima, il dì sesto d'aprile,/nel laberinto entrai, né veggio ond'esca" (One thousand three hundred twenty-seven, exactly at the first hour of the sixth day of April, I entered the labyrinth, nor do I see where I may get out of it [*RVF* 211.12–14]). The image of the labyrinth that Petrarch here offers as emblem for his existential experience is particularly telling: he is a writer who specializes in creating texts imbued with aporia, a term for insoluble contradiction or paradox that literally signifies "no passage," impassable, like a labyrinth. But this poet of impasse and dead ends also creates terrible symmetries; thus, Laura died on the same date that he first saw her, April 6, in the plague year of 1348, as specified in sonnet 336, *Tornami a mente:* "Sai che 'n mille trecento quarantotto,/il dì sesto d'aprile, in l'ora prima/del corpo uscìo quell'anima beata" (You know that in one thousand three hundred and forty-eight, on the sixth day of April, at the first hour, that blessed soul left the body [*RVF* 336.12–14]).[6] Laura's identity has eluded numerous attempts to ascertain it. Petrarch's love for her and failed attempts to attain reciprocation from the chaste Laura are the thematic burden of part 1—to the degree that there is a theme to this text beyond the self's metamorphic existence in the labyrinth of time—while, again from the perspective of the "love story," her death and subsequent softening toward her lover dominate part 2.

Both Laura's fierce chastity and later imagined reciprocation are avenues Petrarch uses to dramatize and explore his own psyche, nuancing and psychologizing the narcissism and self-projection that typify the courtly tradition, in which the lady is present as foil to the male lover/poet but not as a subject with her own inner life and moral choices. Petrarch forged his identity against Dante's by going back to the courtly paradigm that Dante inherited, theologized, and then ultimately abandoned; Petrarch's reinstitutionalizing of the courtly paradigm had specific repercussions with respect to the construction of gender in the Italian tradition. Dante constructs women as moral agents in the *Commedia* and even before, already moving away from the courtly paradigm in which women exist only as projections of male desire in moral canzoni like *Doglia mi reca nello core ardire*, whose women possess desires of their own and are full interlocutors who require instruction in moral matters. Petrarch, by contrast, did not write vernacular poems like Dante's *Doglia mi reca*, in which Dante addresses women directly; Petrarch's moral poems, political poems, and poems of friendship address men rather than women. He does not show the commitment to female historicity and selfhood that we find in Dante.[7] Therefore, when we speak of the psychological richness that is dramatized in the *Fragmenta*, we are speaking exclusively about the male lover/poet, as is typical in the courtly tradition.

Petrarch creates opportunities to explore psychological conflict and inner drama, for instance by telling us, for the first time in sonnet 3, *Era il giorno*, that he fell in love on Good Friday: "Era il giorno ch'al sol si scoloraro/per la pietà del suo Factore i rai,/quando i' fui preso" (It was the day when the sun's rays turned pale with grief for his Maker when I was taken [*RVF* 3.1–3]). In this way he builds into his collection a perennial source of tension and contradiction:[8] while he should have been focused on Christ's crucifixion, his eyes heavenward, instead he was falling in love with a mortal creature, his glance earthward. The poet has pinioned himself into a marvelously fertile bind, as we can see for instance in sonnet 62, *Padre del ciel*, a prayer in which he begs God to take pity on his "unworthy pain" by leading his thoughts back from where they are—fixed on Laura—to a "better place," namely, meditation on the crucifixion: "*miserere* del mio non degno affanno;/reduci i pensier' vaghi a miglior luogo;/ramenta lor come oggi fusti in croce" (have mercy on my unworthy pain, lead my wandering thoughts back to a better place, remind them that today you were on the Cross [*RVF* 62.12–14]). Most strikingly, *Padre del ciel* not only tells of the aporia in which Petrarch situates himself, but actually *is* an aporia, incarnate as text, since it is simultaneously a prayer for repentance and a remembrance of the day he first saw Laura: "Or volge, Signor mio, l'undecimo anno/ch'i' fui sommesso al dispietato giogo" (Now turns, my Lord, the eleventh year that I have been subject to the pitiless yoke [*RVF* 62.9–10]).

The issue of whether and when the poet will ever achieve a "conversion" away from Laura to God—there are some poems in which his love for Laura is viewed as a means to reach above the immanent to the transcendent, like Dante's love for Beatrice, but there are others in which such love for a fellow human being, even Laura, is viewed in a negative light as a distraction from loving God—has divided critics. Some read the collection as dramatizing an achieved conversion. Others, including the author of this essay, do not, for instability is at the core of this work: thematically, psychologically, and as we shall see, textually and materially. With respect to the psychology and theology of conversion, instability is signaled by the fact that the collection's famous final poem is a prayer to the Virgin in which Petrarch is, precisely, still praying for help and still commanding his will to be full, while as Augustine notes, "The reason, then, why the command is not obeyed is that it is not given with a full will. *For if the will were full, it would not command itself to be full, since it would be so already.* It is therefore no strange phenomenon partly to will to do something and partly to will not to do it."[9] The logic of conversion is temporal, since conversion is an experience that involves a movement along the arrow of time from a self that is fragmented, changing, and unstable to a self that is whole, unchanging, and still; while the process of achieving conversion may involve much backsliding, as Augustine dramatizes in the *Confessions*, true conversion, once achieved, is by definition a condition from which there is no relapsing. Augustine's meditation in the *Confessions* on the process of achieving fullness of the will is intimately related to his need to tackle the question of time—the medium in which change occurs, and in which fullness cannot occur—within the same text, in book 11.

The *Fragmenta*'s 366 poems are mainly love poems, although there are 11 penitential or anti-love poems in which the lover repents of his love.[10] There are also 7 political poems and a larger group of moral and occasional poems.[11] The political, moral, and occasional poems to friends are interspersed among the love poems, as a way of demonstrating their participation in a universal set of problems. The overlapping of the political and erotic spheres, for instance, is structured into the text not only through sequential ordering but also through lexicon and imagery: one of Laura's variants, the laurel (*lauro*), is connected to glory both political and poetic. Thus, while in this essay it will not be possible to focus on the political poems, I want to state clearly that our interpretation of a political canzone like *Italia mia* (128) must grapple with its position in a series of love poems, and that I do not endorse the interpretive schism best illustrated by the sixteenth-century editor Alessandro Vellutello, who in his 1528 edition of the *Rerum vulgarium fragmenta* placed the political, moral, and occasional poems in a separate third section of his own invention.

The collection's love poems are arranged in a rough chronological order, and this history is highlighted by the existence of a set that critics have dubbed "anniversary poems": poems that commemorate the anniversary of the day and year when Petrarch first fell in love with Laura. The anniversary poems span 24 years, starting with 7 years after 1327, in 1334, and ending 31 years after 1327, in 1358. The fifteen poems mark the following years in the following order: 7 years, 10 years, 11 years, 14 years (twice), 15 years, 16 years, 17 years, 15 years, 20 years (twice), 18 years, 21 years, 24 years (3 years after Laura's death) and 31 years (10 years after her death).[12] These textual markers to April 6, 1327, are—along with the two date poems already cited—the "ciphers" to Petrarch's long obsession: these numbers provide the indispensable platform for any chronological understanding of the events in the *Fragmenta*.

As we can see from the fact that two of the anniversary poems are out of chronological order—a second poem commemorating fifteen years (poem 145) follows the seventeen-year marker, and a poem commemorating eighteen years (poem 266) follows the twenty-year marker—this platform is a shaky one. In truth, chronology and history are often violated by Petrarch, most flagrantly by the two out-of-order anniversary poems, which have caused much consternation in the text's reception. Petrarch's relationship to chronological order is anything but slavish. He views chronology as one more modality to be exploited as he pursues the goal of creating a structure that is itself an aporia: a structure that resists structure. Because it is devoted to dramatizing evanescence, the *Fragmenta* obey no single criterion of order. The collection's overarching theme is the self subjected to multiplicity, caught in the flux of time and change, which Petrarch renders by dramatizing the pressures of time and desire (lack, hence absence of being) through techniques such as Ovidian metamorphoses, through multiple images of multiplicity, such as the many knots of Laura's scattered hair, and through the plays on Laura's name as it morphs into other words (such as *l'aura* [air] and *lauro* [laurel]) and she into other forms. All these devices, to which we shall return, are Petrarch's rhetorical methods for dramatizing radical ontological instability, the instability of being itself.

The name Laura is, as Peter Hainsworth writes, "an exact homophone of 'l'aura' (breeze, breath), something transient, invisible, intangible, and, therefore, insubstantial, and empty, or, alternatively, something cooling, consoling, or even vital when it becomes the breath of life or inspiration."[13] Because Petrarch did not use the diacritical mark we call the apostrophe, Laura's name and the word *l'aura* are written by him in the same fashion. To the degree his collection is a love story, then, it is quite literally a love story about the evanescent and the transient.

If we are to try to capture in our critical nets the deliberately evanescent Petrarchan text, if we hope to say "In rete accolgo l'aura" (In a net I catch the air [*RVF* 239.37]), we need to consider the relevant material documentation. Because of the way Petrarch handled and manipulated the codices in which he wrote, because of the extremely "hands-on" nature of the material constructedness of his texts, he created an opus that requires would-be interpreters to understand the relevant philological and codicological issues.

We are fortunate enough to possess an autograph manuscript of the *Rerum vulgarium fragmenta*, Vaticano Latino 3195. The study of this codex, long dominated by the work of Ernest Hatch Wilkins,[14] has recently been reinvigorated through the production of a facsimile volume with extensive commentary.[15] Although Vaticano Latino 3195 is technically a partial autograph in that Petrarch did not himself copy all the poems in it, it is fully authorial, for the poems not transcribed by Petrarch were transcribed by his secretary Giovanni Malpaghini under his direct supervision.[16] Petrarch was actively working on the *Fragmenta* right up to his death, as we can see from his late renumbering of the last 31 poems. Although Petrarch never had a chance to erase and recopy these poems in their new positions, modern editions of the *Rerum vulgarium fragmenta* print the last 31 poems according to Petrarch's marginal renumbering, assuming that this was his ultimate disposition.[17] Would he have proceeded, had he lived, to erase and recopy these poems according to the beautiful delicate Arabic numerals with which as an old man he renumbered them in his beloved codex? We can never know.[18] As well as unstable in its order, the *Fragmenta* may well be incomplete: the presence in Vaticano Latino 3195 of seven blank pages between the last poem of part 1 and the first poem of part 2 led Wilkins to believe that Petrarch intended to keep adding to part 1 and therefore to conclude that 366 does not represent the final number of poems and that the text is not complete.[19] Whatever our feelings about the suitability of sonnet 263, *Arbor victoriosa triumphale*, a veritable summa of part 1 themes and motifs, for the post of last poem of part 1, we must acknowledge that a sense of incompletion and instability cannot be banished from a text with respect to whose contours we can raise such legitimate doubts.

Alongside the textual instability documented by the material evidence, there is the deliberate thematic and rhetorical instability that Petrarch built into his textual net for gathering the evanescence of human life. In practical terms, the poems are arranged in such a way as to destabilize each other. An example of such disruption operating thematically is provided by the placement of sonnets 60–63: the completedness of sonnet 60, in which the poet curses the laurel/Laura, is compromised by sonnet 61, in which he blesses everything connected with Laura, while sonnet 61 is in its turn destabilized by sonnet 62, a penitential poem, in which the poet's love for Laura is viewed as sinful, while sonnet 62 is then itself undermined by sonnet 63, a love poem. In theoretical terms, the lyric sequence in Petrarch's hands is the form that brings his long meditation on the one and the many to life, for the fragments—the individual poems, the microtexts—exist in two distinct dimensions, simultaneously one and many: in one dimension they are manifestly unstable and incomplete when taken out of the whole, a macrotext whose own shape and teleology confer significance on its parts, but in another they are fully complete, 366 individual entities each endowed with its own beginning, ending, and ability to signify (as witnessed by the anthologization to which many have been subject).[20] The lyrics' simultaneous oneness and 366-ness enact time's simultaneous oneness and manyness, its nature as both continuum and innumerable discrete pieces of the continuum, as Petrarch expresses in this letter: "Thirty years ago—how time does fly! And yet if I cast a glance backward to consider them all together, those thirty years seem as so many days, so many hours, but when I consider them singly, disentangling the mass of my labors, they seem so many centuries."[21]

Time and its passing are the hinges between Petrarch's moral and metaphysical meditations: his exploration of the self's interiority in its multiple fragmented incarnations unable to resolve and to convert into a single stable and full being reflects his understanding of time as a medium that literally cuts the ground out from under us, destabilizing and deracinating us. Time in its metaphysical multiplicity can lead to moral confusion: in the *Secretum* Augustinus cautions Franciscus not to delay his conversion, not to be deceived by the divisibility of time into many units, by the apparent plurality of days (*pluralitas dierum*), for a whole life, even a long one, is really less than the space of one day (*diei unius*).[22] The temporality of Petrarch's message is metaphysical, moral, and finally even reflected in the material and compositional record, giving poignancy and edge to Wilkins's dry description: "The *Canzoniere* contains poems written at various times through the long years of Petrarch's life. It is not a collection made toward the end of his life in a single editorial effort, nor is it a mere gradual accumulation of poems: it is a selective and ordered collection, the fashioning of which, begun in his youth, continued to the day of his death."[23]

Before continuing to characterize the *Fragmenta*, it will be useful to place Petrarch's lyric sequence within the Italian vernacular context. In doing so, we must distinguish between an authorially ordered collection and a scribal collection, between "the *canzoniere* as a literary genre and the *canzoniere* as a codicological genre (the 'anthological collection')."[24] We are currently witnessing, via material culture and the postmodern pastiche, a moment of heightened scholarly interest in the anthological codex, in which a scribe creates an anthology by virtue of collecting material in one codex: the "idea of the anthology," which has set critics looking for the "controlling literary intelligence" of anonymous codices, has gone a long way toward bringing philology back into fashion.[25] The Italian tradition boasts not only a wealth of anonymous codices but also authored anthologies like Chigiano L V 176, in which circa 1363–66 Giovanni Boccaccio transcribed a variety of authors including Petrarch, and thus created the "Chigi form" of the *Fragmenta,,* the only extant version prior to Vaticano Latino 3195.[26]

Vaticano Latino 3195, the codex containing the *Rerum vulgarium fragmenta*, is not an anthology like Chigiano L V 176, not a compilation of disparate texts that someone (someone of genius, in the case of Boccaccio) saw fit to bring together. Rather, it falls into the category of "*canzoniere* as literary genre," the genre of *authorially* collected lyrics, in which the explicitly controlling intelligence of the author has brought lyrics together and determined their order and disposition. "I have transcribed it [that is, the poem] into the order" or "transcribed by me" are common abbreviations from Petrarch's drafts. Given our recent attention to the history of the book, compilation, and anthology, scholars have been exploring the precedents for Petrarch's achievement and in some cases sought to diminish the originality of his contribution. We cannot, however, equate a scribally compiled codex, like the Laurenziana's Rediano 9 that houses Guittone d'Arezzo's verse, and an authorially constructed codex like Vaticano Latino 3195.[27] In considering Petrarch's vernacular precursors, whose poems we read in scribal compilations, we are inevitably driven to look for signs, always thematic, always connected to the persona of the lover and to the events of his love, and from these gleanings we infer unity and authorial purpose. In considering the *Fragmenta*, we are looking instead at a collection whose unity and authorial purpose are a given, and in which abstract order—form—not theme or plot (certainly not the persona of the lover or the events of his love), is the governing paradigm.

Petrarch's method of composition is identical from the time of the early Chigi collection, copied by Boccaccio, if not before.[28] He constructed the *Fragmenta* around a bipartite structure: our current poems 1 and 264 were fixed as the beginnings of parts 1 and 2, and the collection grew by a process of accretion to each part.[29] He copied poems into Vaticano Latino 3195 from his draft notebooks, one of which, known as *il codice degli abbozzi*, is preserved as Vaticano Latino 3196:[30] here we can see Petrarch's haunting personal notations, such as "Responsio mea sera valde" (My response, late indeed), which accompanies a sonnet for Giacomo Colonna written long after his friend's death; we can see the marginalia of a working poet, including the abbreviations for "transcripsi in ordine," by which he indicates that a poem has been copied into the working copy of a final order, cancelling it after transcription by a line drawn through it; we find textual events like the dramatic rehabilitation of the rejected *Voglia mi sprona*, ultimately included in the *Fragmenta* in position 211.[31] From this compositional method the idea of order emerges as primary. Order is a more intangible and abstract concept than history or chronology, not incidentally expressed in numbers (the very numbers that we find ourselves inescapably using to discuss this text), also intangibles. Petrarch kept a sequential count of the collection's sonnets by fifties, starting with poem 130, which as the collection's hundredth sonnet he labeled "C" for *centum*.[32]

Petrarch uses order to dramatize and explore ideas, including the ideas embedded in textuality: the idea of the beginning, the idea of the middle, and the idea of the end. The original beginning, according to Wilkins, is the present sonnet 34, *Apollo, s'anchor vive il bel desio*, an archetypal part 1 poem in which temporal sequence is invoked in the process whereby Apollo loved first what the poet loves now—"difendi or l'onorata et sacra fronde, / ove tu prima, et poi fu' invescato io" (now defend the honored and holy leaves where you first and then I were limed [*RVF* 34.7–8])[33]—only in order to be nullified: in that she is "la donna *nostra*" (*our* lady), both Apollo's Daphne and Petrarch's Laura, whom both together will watch ("sì vedrem poi per meraviglia inseme / seder la donna nostra sopra l'erba," thus we shall then together see a marvel—our lady sitting on the grass [*RVF* 34.12–13]), all identities are conflated and time ceases to exist.[34] By contrast, our present number 1, *Voi ch'ascoltate in rime sparse il suono,* is atypical. Its purpose is to establish temporal sequence: a verse like "quand'era in parte altr'uom da quel ch'i' sono" (when I was in part another man from what I am now [*RVF* 1.4]) suggests narrative movement from the past into the present and seems to promise more such movement leading from the present into the future. In this sense, the poem imposes a beginning in quasi-narrative terms. But, by the same token, it also subverts it, precisely by virtue of its position at the text's beginning. A recantation—"'l pentérsi," repentance (*RVF* 1.13)—at the outset makes no more sense than a sinner's attempt to repent *before* sinning, a logical contradiction treated by Dante in the Guido da Montefeltro episode of the *Inferno* (via the same unusual form of the verb, *pentere,* used in *Voi ch'ascoltate* by Petrarch):[35] "ch'assolver non si può chi non si pente,/né pentere e volere insieme puossi/per la contradizion che nol consente" (For he who does not repent cannot be absolved, nor can one both repent and will at once, because of the contradiction which does not allow it [*Inferno* 27.118–20]). "Forse/tu non pensavi ch'io loïco fossi" (Perhaps you did not think I was a logician! [*Inferno* 27.122–23]), says the devil to Guido as he drags him off to hell. As shown by Augustine in the *Confessions* and by Dante in the *Commedia,* and as Petrarch well knows, the logic of conversion follows the arrow of time: it is not logical to renounce the "breve sogno" *before* engaging in it, *before* succumbing to it, *before* representing it.[36]

Petrarch invokes the category of middle by breaking off part 1 and starting a new part with canzone 264. This canzone, *I' vo pensando,* is a philosophical poem that dramatizes the same moral concerns that we find in Petrarch's *Secretum;* it is clearly indicated in the autograph as the beginning to part 2, separated from sonnet 263 by seven blank pages and further set off as a new beginning by its large ornamental initial, echoing the ornamental initial of sonnet number 1. The two poems that follow canzone 264 refer to Laura alive, and have therefore proven confusing to readers who have wanted Petrarch's text to conform to neat historical and autobiographical categories. As a result, for many centuries editions of the *Fragmenta* began part 2 with sonnet 267, the first sonnet to treat Laura as dead, rather than with canzone 264. By placing sonnets 265 (written in 1350 but as though Laura were still alive) and 266 (an anniversary poem that instructs us to view it as composed in 1345, hence before Laura's death in 1348), right after canzone 264 at the beginning of part 2, Petrarch flouts chronology and indicates—through order—that the significance of part 2 must be grounded in something more abstract and intangible than simple chronology, biography, or history. In my opinion, Petrarch places sonnets 265 and 266 where he does precisely to point us to the deep meaning of part 2, which is not the death of one contingent creature but the nature of contingency and transition itself: the reality that a "2" will always follow a "1," that no human event or mortal being is durable or final. As canzone 264 explains, mortal creatures should not be loved more than their Creator (even when they are inherently good) precisely because they are, in the end, always mortal, contingent, transitory, subject to the passing of time. But this canzone that makes the case for conversion as it formally "converts" to part 2 then denies the lover's own moral conversion in its final verse, "et veggio 'l meglio, et al peggior m'appiglio" (I see the better but I hold onto the worse [*RVF* 264.136]). Thus Petrarch's "middle," well defined by Hainsworth as "the great canzone of aporia in the face of vanity," is a transition that resists transition and is as unstable as his beginning.[37] As for the ending, its instability is both material—in the renumbering of the last 31 poems—and ideological: the order of the poems directly conditions our reading of the ending, as to whether or not the poet has credibly achieved a point from which a conversion is possible. While canzone 366, *Vergine bella*, was by then a fixed point, the textual equivalent of *pace*, the question of how to get to that fixed beacon preoccupied Petrarch up to his death.[38]

The very act of composing a text—of collecting one's lyrics—in and of itself generates a beginning and an ending, but the willed and constructed nature of a beginning or an ending is less evident if a text contains no other formal structure (no chapter divisions or other segmentations). Petrarch's division is a formal structure that, by generating a textual "middle"—in the narratological sense of in medias res rather than in the mathematical sense (poem 264 is closer to two-thirds of the way through the *Fragmenta* than to the halfway point)[39]—also has the effect of throwing into relief the willed and constructed nature of the collection's beginning and ending, and hence of its narrativity.

In a way that I would argue is stunningly new, Petrarch makes time the protagonist of his book of poetry. Time is continually present in the *Fragmenta* through the text's orchestrated narrativity: its deployment of the categories of (unstable) beginning, middle, and end, its dialectically interwoven *contaminatio* of lyric and narrative drives.[40] The poet introduces narrativity through chronology and tenuous thematic linkages, but most of all through various formal measures such as the novel device of dividing his lyric collection into two parts. We can therefore synthesize the principles of construction of the *Fragmenta* as follows. Onto the static organizing principles established by Phelps and Wilkins[41]—general chronological order, variety of form (intermixed sonnets, canzoni, *ballate*, and *madrigali*), and variety of content (love poems for Laura intermixed with moral and

political poems)[42]—we must layer the dynamic principle of dialectically in-
teracting lyric and narrative drives, which offers the poet a way to reflect
the dialectic between fragmentation and unity, between the scattered and
the collected, between particulars and universals, between the contingent
and the transcendent, between the many and the One. The fundamental
characteristic of the Petrarchan lyric sequence, beyond the basic features
set out by Phelps and Wilkins, is its self-conscious, metapoetic, and metaphysically driven exploitation of the principle of order, a textual analogue
of time itself.

Narrativity is thus deliberately injected into the *Fragmenta*, but it is injected opaquely and sparingly. Excess narrativity—actual history or storytelling—is kept at bay. Excess narrativity, or at any rate what the Petrarch
of the *Fragmenta* would consider excess narrativity, will be the future of the
genre: later lyric sequences throughout Europe become ever more overtly
biographical, ever more incapable or unwilling to resist the blandishments
of storytelling. Petrarch is never seduced by narrativity, at least never in
the *Fragmenta* (by contrast, the *Triumphi* could be read as what happens
when Petrarch attempts full-fledged narrativity in the Dantean medium
of terza rima). And what of the past? In canzone 70, *Lasso me*, Petrarch
rehearses the lyric tradition from its Occitan origins to his own time
by citing incipits of Arnaut Daniel,[43] Guido Cavalcanti, Dante, Cino da
Pistoia, and his own canzone 23, thus inscribing himself within the history
of the vernacular lyric. The poets whom he cites wrote lyrics that they never
collected. However, Dante had also proposed, in his *Vita nuova*, a radically
new way of gathering lyrics,[44] taking the steps that are fundamental for
the Petrarchan lyric sequence, namely, that of collecting previously written
lyrics and transcribing them in a new and significant order, and that of de-
ploying lyric/narrative *contaminatio*, embedding his lyrics in a prose frame.
Of Dante's two means for generating narrativity, Petrarch discards the
more explicit, namely, prose, and preserves the more subtle, namely, order.

Another feature of the *Vita nuova* that carries forward into the *Fragmenta*
is the mixing of poetic genres, a major innovation with respect to earlier
lyric collections. I noted that the *Fragmenta*'s 366 poems include 317 sonnets, 29 canzoni, 9 sestine, 7 *ballate*, and 4 *madrigali*, all interspersed. In
Petrarch's system, genre and meter carry significance: for instance, he signals the reader by positioning a number of canzoni in a series, most notably
canzoni 70–73 and canzoni 125–129, and by using meter to highlight—
again, very abstractly—the "story" told by these groupings (thus, canzoni
71–73 have the same meter, which must be factored into our interpretation
of them; canzoni 125 and 126 are almost identical metrically and thus dif-

ferent from the other poems in their canzone series, but my larger point is that each canzone's meter is significant). Meter is connected to narrative deployment again vis-à-vis the sestine, which are carefully positioned throughout the collection. Such sets are not only metrically defined: as we have seen, the anniversary poems are a linked set that are defined by their subject, in that each member of the set commemorates the date of the poet's falling in love on April 6, 1327.

The anniversary poems always remind us of Petrarch's paradoxical relationship with narrativity: on the one hand, he never satisfies his readers with a biographically limpid story line in the manner of Renaissance lyric sequences, but on the other the entire psychodrama he builds with the elements of guilt-inducing Good Fridays and Laura's oft-mentioned chastity is absolutely new (and absolutely not stilnovist) in its personal and psychological dimensions. Beatrice's chastity is simply never a discussion item for Dante. Laura's chastity will be an issue right through the *Fragmenta*, mentioned as late as the final canzone, where he notes that a positive response from Laura would have brought "death to me and dishonor to her" (a me morte et a lei fama rea [*RVF* 366.97]). Petrarch's ability to invoke personal topics but at the same time to remain rigorously abstract is a signature characteristic of his unique poetic voice.

Through the creation of sets of poems (another abstract, indeed mathematical, concept), Petrarch creates opaque "narrative" threads that run through his great web—his "opra d'aragna" (spider's web [*RVF* 173.6])—and that we can isolate and interpret as reflections of the work as a whole. We can distinguish between dispersed sets, both metrical and thematic, that we can cull from the *mare magnum* of the *Fragmenta* in order to read each set as a group, and sequential sets, again both metrical and thematic. Petrarch fashions such formal mechanisms as a means of introducing narrativity into *Fragmenta*, injecting narrativity/temporality into his static and time-resistant lyric collection in the following ways:

- the marking of a beginning, "middle," and end;
- the division of the text into two parts;
- the interspersing of the lyric genres, a technique that effectively constructs metrically marked dispersed sets, encouraging us to cull and to "read" the set of all canzoni as a group, all sestine as a group, all *ballate* as a group, and all *madrigali* as a group;
- the creation of thematically marked dispersed sets, most originally the set of anniversary poems, which commemorate a particular moment in time;
- the creation of other thematically marked dispersed sets, such as the

set of political poems (these sets can include subsets, such as the set of
sonnets on Avignon), the set of penitential poems, the set of poems to
friends like Sennuccio del Bene, the set of poems that mention the place
Vaucluse, etc.;

- the creation of many more thematically dispersed sets, not included in
  appendix 1, such as the set of poems that feature Ovidian mythological
  characters, with its many subsets, for example: poems featuring Daphne
  and Apollo, poems featuring Eurydice and Orpheus, etc.;
- the creation of sequential sets through metrical means: the deployment
  of metrical similarity and even identity to set off series of canzoni from
  other canzoni and to highlight them within the sea of sonnets (e.g.,
  70–73, 125–129);
- the creation of sequential sets through lexical repetition: the use of lexical linkages between poems to create lexically marked sequential sets
  on a spectrum from the very tenuous to the very obvious, for example
  (at the obvious end of the spectrum), the so-called "*l'aura* poems" (*L'aura
  gentil* [194], *L'aura serena* [196], *L'aura celeste* [197], and *L'aura soave*
  [198]). Note that these sets are typically unstable and imperfect, hence
  the interpolation of sonnet 195, *Di dì in dì*, into the *l'aura* sequence;
- the creation of sequential sets through thematic means: for example, the
  series of sonnets we could call the "death sequence" that adumbrates
  Laura's death (roughly 246–254, but again imperfect as a series); and
- the creation of imbricated or overlapping sets, such as friendship poems
  that are also love poems, underscoring the polyvalence of discourse;
  these can become textual analogues for aporia: for example, a penitential
  poem that is also an anniversary poem, such as *Padre del ciel* (62).

A set itself is an abstract concept, and the creation of sets allows the poet
to play with abstract concepts. Thus, the overlapping of two apparently
contradictory sets in one poem allows the poet to materialize the idea of
insoluble contradiction or aporia in textual form, as in *Padre del ciel*, which
is both a penitential poem and an anniversary poem; another example is
Giovene donna sotto un verde lauro (30), which is both a time-resistant sestina
and a time-affirming anniversary poem.[45]

The second appended chart, "Structure of the *Rerum vulgarium fragmenta*," presents a compact reading of the *Fragmenta*, along with a numerological note. There is a structural tension between the bipartite structure
generated by Petrarch's division of the poems into two parts—263 in part 1
and 103 in part 2—and a tripartite structure that I posit using as an endpoint
canzone 129. Petrarch's part 1 arrives at a first climax in the extraordinary

and anomalous series of five canzoni that runs from 125 to 129, a series that dramatizes an ecstatic *oblio*—oblivion and release from time—of both Augustinian and Dantean proportions in canzone 126, *Chiare, fresche et dolci acque,* and then the definitive reconsignment of the self to time and to *storia* in canzoni 127, 128, and 129.[46] If we use the last poem of this series as an endpoint (in support of this endpoint, we remember that Petrarch's sequential count of the collection's sonnets starts immediately after canzone 129 with poem 130, the hundredth sonnet, noted by him with the label "C" for *centum*), there are 129 poems in the first part of part 1 and 134 poems in the second part of part 1.[47] Therefore, the tripartite structure generated by the implicit endpoint of canzone 129 yields the breakdown: 129 // 134 // 103. The interplay between an overt bipartite structure and an implicit tripartite structure creates the fundamental dyadic versus triadic dynamic that is coded into the *Fragmenta* through the number 6: the number of time and Petrarch's number, as Calcaterra has shown.[48] Moreover, the dynamic of dyad versus triad is the structural basis of the sonnet (founded on the tension between the octave, divisible by 2 but not by 3, and the sextet, divisible by 2 and also by 3) and the lyric genre that is arguably Petrarch's favorite, the type of canzone called the sestina, founded on the number six.

The *Fragmenta* begin with a concentrated micro-*canzoniere,* consisting of poems 1 to 23, which includes an introductory sequence, poems 1 to 5 (poems 2 and 3 provide "plot" information regarding the lover's falling in love and poems 4 and 5 provide information about the beloved), and culminates with the first sestina, poem 22, and the first canzone, poem 23. Sonnet 5, *Quando io movo i sospiri a chiamar voi,* is the first poem to invoke Apollo and to thematize the intertwined identities of lover and poet, the latter figured in the laurel (*lauro*) sacred to Apollo and used to wreath the brows of poets. We shall see the poet rise triumphant out of the ashes of the lover's despair in canzone 23, *Nel dolce tempo de la prima etade,* and we noted the benefit of time-resistance brought about by his being linked to Apollo as the lover of "la donna nostra" in *Apollo, s'anchor vive il bel desio* (*RVF* 34), but the first invocation of Apollo—god of music and poetry and would-be lover of Daphne, who fled from the god and was changed into a laurel—occurs in sonnet 5 and offers the poet a bleak scenario.

This sonnet, the first poem to contain the word *il fine*—the end—is a famous play on the beloved's name, parsed as LAU-RE-TA, and it instructs us that narrativity resides in her, in her name, represented here as syllabified by time:

LAUdando s'incomincia udir di fore
il suon de' primi dolci accenti suoi.
Vostro stato REal, che 'ncontro poi,
raddoppia a l'alta impresa il mio valore;
ma: TAci grida il fin, ché farle honore
è d'altri homeri soma che da' tuoi. (5.3–8)

[When I move my sighs to call you and the name that Love wrote
on my heart, the sound of its first sweet accents is heard without
in LAU-ds. Your RE-gal state, which I meet next, redoubles my
strength for the high enterprise; but "TA-lk no more!" cries the
ending, "for to do her honor is a burden for other shoulders than
yours."]

In *Confessions* 13.15, angels are able to look upon God's face and read in it
"sine syllabis temporum"—"without the syllables of time." The syllabification of Laura's name, by contrast, recalls Augustine's syllabification of the
hymn *Deus Creator omnium* as an analogue for time's passing in *Confessions*
11.27. As Augustine sounds out the syllables of the hymn in order to try
to grasp the nature of time, so Petrarch's *sospiri* sound out the nature of
Laura as a being inexorably temporal. Moreover, in a passage that tinges
Petrarch's exit into *oblio* and return to *storia* in canzone 126, Augustine
describes his return from ecstatic simultaneity in the vision at Ostia as a
falling back into sound, language, and therefore time, in the form of beginnings and endings: "et remeavimus ad strepitum oris nostri, ubi verbum
et incipitur et finitur" (we returned to the sound of our own speech, in
which each word has a beginning and an ending [*Confessions* 9.10]). Learning from Augustine, who returns from extratemporal vision at Ostia to the
sound of language, and thus to time, in the form of syllables and words that
possess beginnings and endings, Petrarch understands the textual and the
temporal to be parallel modalities.[49]

Sonnet 5 dramatizes the enmeshedness of time and narrative. Particularly noteworthy are the narrative markers that the poet has linked to the
syllables of the beloved's name: LAU with "s'incomincia," RE with "poi,"
and TA with "il fin." The first syllable corresponds to beginnings, the middle syllable to middles, and the last syllable to endings; thus, to the extent
that the text engages a being defined as existing in time, such as *Laureta*, it
engages the temporal/narrative problems of beginnings, middles, and ends.
The anomalous spelling of her name as *Laureta* evokes *l'aura* and *rete*, the
evanescent caught in the net of time and text, as in "In rete accolgo l'aura"

(*RVF* 239.37). The ominous "TAci, grida il fin," where *il fin*—the end—shouts "Be silent" to the poet, suggests the ultimate ending and the ultimate silence: the silence of death. The subordination of the poet to the violence of *il fin* also foreshadows the poem's final tercet, where we find that Apollo may disdain the mortal poet's presumptuous attempt to write of the god's evergreen boughs: "se non che forse Apollo si disdegna/ch'a parlar de' suoi sempre verdi rami/lingua mortal presumptüosa vegna" (except that perhaps Apollo is incensed that any mortal tongue should come presumptuous to speak of his eternally green boughs [*RVF* 5.12–14]). The poet's mortality, his finitude—his "lingua mortal"—is thus firmly established by sonnet 5's conclusion, as well as the link between the final syllable of the beloved's name and finality, between Laura/*l'aura* and the multitude of finite things that are the opposite of the nonfinite plenitude of God.

Laura indeed *is* multiplicity. Her hair (in Italian, we should not forget, *capelli* is plural), scattered to the wind in "mille dolci nodi" (a thousand sweet knots [*RVF* 90.2]) in *Erano i capei d'oro a l'aura sparsi*, is the chief of many poetic signifiers of her function as carrier of multiplicity. More important even than the hair being "scattered"—"sparsi" like the "rime sparse" in the proemial sonnet—is their existing in the past tense: sonnet 90 begins with the imperfect of the verb *essere* (to be): "Erano." Her hairs of gold *were* scattered by the wind. Unlike Beatrice, who exists in an iconic present tense until she dies, when she is reborn into an even more potent present tense, Laura exists primarily in the past. Laura's poet does not keep her immune from the passage of time; rather, he uses her to mark the passage of time. The imperfect tense is the tense of ongoing incomplete action in the past, the tense of memory, and in it the poet captures and caresses the past as he conjures it and holds it in his memory, thinking of the golden hair and "the lovely light [that] burned without measure in her eyes, which are now so stingy of it" (e 'l vago lume oltra misura ardea/di quei begli occhi ch'or ne son sì scarsi [*RVF* 90.3–4]). Verse 4 brings us to the present tense: it is a present in which Laura's eyes, like Laura herself, have aged.

Petrarch's Laura does what no stilnovist or Dantean lyric love lady had done before her—she ages—and her aging, as in *Erano i capei d'oro a l'aura sparsi*, is a catalyst for the discourse of time, change, and multiplicity. The "I" and his memories and his thought processes are the poem's true subject; the lady—evanescent, transient, mortal—is the vehicle for catching the "I" in the process, catching him in the web. The imperfect tense that defines Laura in this poem—"Non *era* l'andar suo cosa mortale,/ma d'angelica forma" (Her walk *was* not that of a mortal thing but of some angelic form [*RVF* 90.9–10])—is the marker of her mortality, which functions as a catalyst for the poet to meditate on his own mortality. Her step may not seem mortal, but mortal is precisely what it is, and the "angelic form" she possesses is claimed in a spirit of elegiac hyperbole, not in a spirit of genuine mystical affirmation. She is no longer the Lady as Manifestation of the Transcendent, who exists as a source of wonder and awe in a syntactic eternal present in Dante's sonnet *Tanto gentile e tanto onesta pare*, but rather a source of nostalgia and self-reflection: the Lady as Measurer of My Mortality.[50]

Alongside Augustine's *Confessions*, Dante's *Commedia*, and the vernacular lyric tradition extending back to the Occitan troubadours, the major intertextual presence in the *Fragmenta* is Ovid's *Metamorphoses*,[51] a text that dramatizes instability and multiplicity by capturing characters in the moment when multiplicity most overtly afflicts them: in the moment of metamorphosis. Change, which we all experience incrementally and continuously and mostly without noticing it (except for those occasions when we wake up and realize that everything has changed), dominates Ovid's *Metamorphoses*, in which change is not incremental but sudden and catastrophic (so that we cannot fail to notice it), and it similarly dominates Petrarch's canzone 23. Known as the *canzone delle metamorfosi* for the six Ovidian metamorphoses that it recounts, *Nel dolce tempo de la prima etade* held particular importance for Petrarch (it is the poem with which he represents himself in the lyric history recounted by canzone 70), telling the story of how the narrator both fell in love and became a poet. The two occurrences are strictly linked, as the narrator declares in the first strophe: he will sing of his "fierce desire" (*fera voglia* [*RVF* 23.3]) "because, singing, pain becomes less bitter" (*perché cantando il duol si disacerba* [*RVF* 23.4]). Writing poetry is therefore the balm of the lover. But nothing is straightforward in the Petrarchan universe, and the second strophe introduces us to the first metamorphosis of *Nel dolce tempo*, when love and the lady transformed the lover into a laurel: "e i duo mi trasformaro in quel ch'i' sono, / facendomi d'uom vivo un lauro verde, / che per fredda stagion foglia non perde" (those two transformed me into what I am, making me of a living man a green laurel that loses no leaf for all the cold season [*RVF* 23.38–40]). Therefore to love was for Petrarch to be transformed into a laurel, to become a poet, so that the very poetry that lessens the pain of love is also the cause of it. But at the same time the transformation into a laurel is positive: he becomes a "green laurel that loses no leaf for all the cold season," gaining the immortality of a poet. The double role of poetry that will haunt this text is here disclosed, and the ambiguous relations of poet and lover are established.

Nel dolce tempo proceeds to narrate the vicissitudes of the lover/poet through a series of Ovidian transformations: he is changed into a swan, like Phaeton's uncle Cygnus, in the second metamorphosis and, in the third metamorphosis, transformed into a stone, as Battus by disguised Mercury. His resuscitation at this point—the low point of the canzone—comes through poetry; it is precisely here that the poet enters to tell us he must speed up the narrative: "Ma perché 'l tempo è corto, / la penna al buon voler non pò gir presso: / onde più cose ne la mente scritte / vo trapassando" (But because time is short, my pen cannot follow closely my good will; wherefore I pass over many things written in my mind [*RVF* 23.90–93]). As a result of this taking stock of himself through use of the poet's voice, he can use poetry to break violently free: "le vive voci m'erano interditte; / ond'io gridai con carta et con incostro" (Words spoken aloud were forbidden me; so I cried out with paper and ink [*RVF* 23.98–99]). When he cannot speak with "living words"—that is, when he cannot live and love—he can cry out in paper and ink (note the urgency of "gridai"), he can write. What he writes is a disclaimer of self in the language of metamorphosis; he who changes shapes, taking other identities through love, does not possess his self: "Non son mio, no" ("I am not my own, no" [*RVF* 23.100]).[52] And yet the disclaimer of self functions as an affirmation of self: in the act of writing, he is revived. In fact, as he says at the beginning of the next (sixth) stanza, he believed to transform himself thus from "unworthy" to "worthy," and this belief made him "ardito" (bold [*RVF* 23.103])—that is, he is taking charge of his self rather than waiting for her next blow.

In the fourth metamorphosis, the lover becomes a fountain, like Byblis, a woman in love with her brother and the aggressor in her illicit romance. It is worth noting that the gender alignments within the metamorphoses of canzone 23 are not fixed and stable but shift throughout the canzone, as both lover and beloved are aligned eventually with mythical figures of both genders. These shifts in gender alignment, as also in the relative status of victim or aggressor, reflect in microcosm the collection as a whole, where we can trace similar shifts as we move from poem to poem. Thus the mythological and imagistic aspects of *Nel dolce tempo* follow the same unstable, nonlinear, and labyrinthine course that marks the entire collection. From the point of view of gender, therefore, it is difficult to develop a persuasive model on the basis of any one myth or any one trope or any one textual strategy, since every myth, trope, or strategy applied to Laura (including particularizing description) will in turn be applied to the lover/poet himself.[53]

The fifth metamorphosis depicts the lover turned into hard flint and disembodied voice, like Echo, another female aggressor rejected by her beloved (Narcissus, who in other poems will be Petrarch's counterpart:

here he is Echo, elsewhere Narcissus), while in the sixth metamorphosis Petrarch deploys correct gender alignment for one of his favorite myths: here, where for the first time in the canzone the roles are entirely congruent in terms of sex and identity, he is Actaeon transformed into a stag for having gazed upon Diana. This transformation takes us, eerily, into the present tense—he is *still*, like Actaeon, being chased by his hounds through the woods: "ch'i' sentì' trarmi de la propria imago,/et in un cervo solitario et vago/di selva in selva ratto mi trasformo:/et anchor de' miei can' fuggo lo stormo" (for I felt myself drawn from my own image and into a solitary wandering stag from wood to wood quickly I am transformed and still I flee the belling of my hounds [*RVF* 23.157–60]).

But after announcing that he is "still" in the state to which he was transformed in the sixth metamorphosis, Petrarch cancels time and change and multiplicity in the poem's *congedo* or leavetaking, where he tells us that he never left the first state, that of the laurel: "né per nova figura il primo alloro/seppi lassar" (nor for any new shape could I leave the first laurel [*RVF* 23.167–68]). This final declaration follows upon the identification of his poet's self with none other than Jove: in a reference to Jove's rape of Ganymede, he is the eagle that rises through the air "raising her whom in my words I honor" (*alzando lei che ne' miei detti honoro* [*RVF* 23.166]). When, at the end of this poem, he becomes a male god, he does not become Apollo, who loses Daphne, but Jove, who gets what he wants, though like Apollo he acts through poetry. By the time he concludes that he has never left the laurel for any new shape, he has transformed being the laurel so that he is not Daphne the victim, nor Apollo the failed pursuer, but Jove the conqueror, "alzando lei che ne' miei detti honoro."

Nel dolce tempo brilliantly displays the change that is not change—the refusal to change because change brings death and endings—which is at the heart of part 1 of the *Fragmenta*. Change that is not change is associated in the lyric tradition with the sestina, a canzone that has been rigidified (by the use of six rhyme words rather than sounds) and stylized (by the use of *retrogradatio cruciata*, an organization that causes the six rhyme words to appear over the course of six strophes in every possible combination by proceeding backwards [*retrogradatio*] and by alternating or "crossing" [*cruciata*]) to the point where it becomes the textual equivalent of the illusion that time has stopped. Petrarch's precursors in the writing of sestine were Arnaut Daniel and Dante, whose *rime petrose* to a stone-lady include one sestina, *Al poco giorno e al gran cerchio d'ombra*. Petrarch cultivated the sestina form, putting eight sestine in part 1 of the *Fragmenta*, the first immediately preceding canzone 23, and one (a double sestina) in part 2.

Echoing Dante's *rime petrose*, Petrarch frequently refers to his stonelike qualities (again we see his penchant for gender reversals, for in the *rime petrose* the *pietra* is not the male poet but the female figure, characterized by her cold and stony rejection of the lover): in *Nel dolce tempo* he calls himself "un quasi vivo et sbigottito sasso" (an almost living and terrified stone [*RVF* 23.80]) and in *Di pensier in pensier* he is "pietra morta in pietra viva" (a dead stone on the living rock [*RVF* 129.51]). Stoniness may imply a death of the soul's emotions but it also suggests the immortality of the "rock of ages." Canzone 23 perfectly reflects the principle of change that is not change in its linguistic texture: dense, convoluted, an icon to reified—or, as Petrarch would put it, "petrified"—immobility.

Nel dolce tempo is characterized by compact impenetrability, metrical as well as thematic, boasting a heavy stanzaic pattern consisting of a twenty-verse strophe (the longest strophe of any canzone in the collection), packed with mostly hendecasyllables (19 hendecasyllables and only one *settenario*, the shorter verse that Petrarch uses to lighten his canzoni). Its structural counterpart in part 2 of the *Fragmenta* is canzone 323, *Standomi un giorno solo a la fenestra*, which is separated from *Nel dolce tempo* by 300 poems and which presents, by contrast, a limpidly flowing twelve-verse strophe containing two *settenari*. The storylike flow of canzone 323 is a stylistic correlative of the governing principles of part 2: time flows, nothing lasts, death comes. As the poet declares, "ogni cosa al fin vola" (Everything flies to its end [*RVF* 323.55]). For all their divergences, the two canzoni also bear witness at either end of the collection to its abiding concerns. Known as the *canzone delle visioni* for its six mythologically informed narrative visions of Laura's death, canzone 323 depicts tableaux that draw on and invert the metamorphoses of canzone 23. In *Standomi un giorno* he sees her as a beautiful wild creature chased by hounds (whereas he was the one hunted by hounds as Actaeon in *Nel dolce tempo*), as a rich ship sunk by a sudden tempest (he figures himself as a ship throughout the sequence, e.g., *Passa la nave mia colma d'oblio*, poem 189), as a laurel (to which he links himself in poem after poem) that is destroyed by lightning, as a fountain engulfed by a chasm (we saw him become a fountain in canzone 23), as a phoenix that turns its beak on itself, and then, finally, as Eurydice bitten by a snake. But, in the same kind of affirmation through poetry that we saw in *Nel dolce tempo*, if Laura is Eurydice then Petrarch is Orpheus—the singer who charmed wild beasts with the beauty of his song and moved Hades to allow him to bring his beloved back to life.

While in part 1 of the *Fragmenta* Petrarch overtly resists narrativity, in part 2 he apparently accepts it, but these two divergent stylistic and thematic responses are part of a unitary strategy: in part 1 narrative is avoided because the goal is to stop time, resist death; in part 2 narrative is invoked because in order to preserve Laura as she was he must preserve her in time. He thus adopts opposite and apparently contradictory strategies to achieve the same results.[54] When she is alive, he needs to cancel time. When she is dead, he needs to appropriate it, bringing her back to life in his poetry. Petrarch's form of acceptance is thus finally as resistant to time's passing as the overt refusals to acknowledge change of part 1, summed up by sonnet 145's "sarò qual fui, vivrò com'io son visso" (I shall be what I have been, shall live as I have lived [RVF 145.13]). In poetry, as an Orpheus who succeeds in recovering his Eurydice, Petrarch can make Laura live again. And now she can be everything he always wanted her to be, she can be literally as he fantasized in canzone 126, *Chiare, fresche et dolci acque*, the canzone whose incipit invokes the sweet waters of the beautiful place where he loved Laura, and where he imagines that she will return to find him dead and will weep over his grave:

> Tempo verrà anchor forse
> ch'a l'usato soggiorno
> torni la fera bella et mansueta,
> et là 'v'ella mi scorse
> nel benedetto giorno
> volga la vista disiosa et lieta,
> cercandomi: et, o pieta!,
> già terra in fra le pietre
> vedendo, Amor l'inspiri
> in guisa che sospiri
> sì dolcemente che mercé m'impetre,
> et faccia forza al cielo,
> asciugandosi gli occhi col bel velo. (*RVF* 126.27–39)

[There will come a time perhaps when to her accustomed sojourn the lovely, gentle wild one will return and, seeking me, turn her desirous and happy eyes toward where she saw me on that blessed day, and oh the pity! Seeing me already dust among the stones, Love will inspire her to sigh so sweetly that she will win mercy for me and force Heaven, drying her eyes with her lovely veil.]

Here we have a quintessentially part 1 scene, whose complex temporal shifts reflect the tangled strategies required to find solace in imagination when the poet does not have a completely free hand: he imagines a future time (*Tempo verrà*), necessarily hypothetical (*forse*), in which Laura will return to their shared past, their "usato soggiorno." The love that she never showed him in the real past is imagined in a past that is projected into the future within the present of the poem.

In part 2, when Laura is dead, Petrarch the poet can make this scene occur without any such intricate projections of past memory into a hypothetical future. Rather, he can now simply go—in the present—to their "accustomed sojourn" in Vaucluse and look for signs of her: "Così vo ricercando ogni contrada/ov'io la vidi" (Thus I go searching through every region where I saw her [*RVF* 306.9–10; see also 280, 288, 301, 304, 305, 320]). Although this search often results only in traces of Laura (*Lei non trov'io: ma suoi santi vestigi,* her I do not find, but I see her holy footprints [*RVF* 306.12]), it can also lead to more substantive results: thus in sonnet 281 his calling yields visions of Laura, "Or in forma di nimpha o d'altra diva" (Now in the form of a nymph or other goddess [*RVF* 281.9]), which have materialized to the point where he can say that he sees her "calcare i fior' com'una donna viva" (treading the fresh grass like a living woman [*RVF* 281.13]). Indeed, she is sufficiently "donna viva" that he can specify her piteous attitude toward him: "mostrando in vista che di me le 'ncresca" (showing by her face that she is sorry for me [*RVF* 281.14]).

Variants of this event occur in poem after poem in part 2 of the *Fragmenta*, where Laura and her poet develop a closeness never seen in part 1. For instance, there are poems in which she returns to console him. These poems constitute the logical next step after the successful search described in sonnet 281; her concern leads her to return with the express purpose of consoling her lover, as we learn in sonnet 282: "Alma felice che sovente torni/a consolar le mie notti dolenti" (Happy soul who often come back to console my sorrowing nights [*RVF* 282.1–2]). In this poem the process of materialization begun in sonnet 281, where she appears "com'una donna viva," is crystallized in his recognition of her unique presence, manifested "a l'andar, a la voce, al volto, a' panni" (by your walk, by your voice, by your face, by your dress [*RVF* 282.14]). She returns similarly in sonnet 283 (*Ben torna a consolar tanto dolore/madonna, ove Pietà la riconduce,* My lady does indeed come back to console so much sorrow, for pity leads her back [*RVF* 283.9–10]) and in sonnet 343, where her consolation takes the form of listening to and commenting on his life's story, which causes her to weep: "et come intentamente ascolta et nota/la lunga historia de le pene mie!" (and how intently she listens to, and takes note of, the long history of my sufferings! [*RVF* 343.10–11]). In sonnet 285, on the other hand, she is the storyteller recounting the events of their shared life (*contando i casi de la vita nostra* [*RVF* 285.12]). These events (see also sonnets 284 and 286) are summed up by a verse in sonnet 285, "spesso a me torna co l'usato affecto" (she often returns to me with her usual affection [*RVF* 285.7]), which exemplifies the process whereby the affection she shows in death is projected backward onto her life: "*usato* affecto" refers to her "usual" affection, although such affection was by no means a feature of part 1.

There are also in part 2 poems in which Laura is cited speaking to her beloved in direct discourse; in sonnets 342 and 359 she not only comes to him and speaks to him, but also sits on his bed and dries his tears. In general throughout part 2, Petrarch literalizes the turning-back topos: from a trope of memory, in part 1, it becomes a literal description of her various returns to him. Thus, *rimembrare* gives way to *richiamare, rivedere, ricercare, ritrovare,* and the expression "tornami inanzi" (*RVF* 268.46) or "Tornami avanti" (she returns before me [*RVF* 272.9]) becomes a textual emblem for part 2, as for instance in sonnet 336, where the opening "Tornami a mente" (She returns to mind) allows the poet to build up to the vivifying exclamation: "Ell'è ben dessa; anchor è in vita" (That is she, she is still alive! [*RVF* 336.7]). "She is still alive"—"anchor è in vita"—is a perfect emblem for the powerful work of the poet's imagination in part 2 of the *Rerum vulgarium fragmenta,* where Laura's death does not serve—as Beatrice's death does for Dante—to prompt him finally to realize "che quanto piace al mondo è breve sogno" (that whatever pleases in the world is a brief dream [*RVF* 1.14]), but rather liberates him to fashion her as the lover he had always wanted. In part 2 of the *Fragmenta* Petrarch caresses the *breve sogno,* the poet's own particular set of personal non-universals within the flux of fragmentation and multiplicity, with even greater vigor than in part 1.

Petrarch's obsessive focus on the self within the labyrinth of fragmentation, multiplicity, desire, and time and his long meditation on the one and the many, the fragments and the whole, is reflected in his life: in ways that are not equally true of other authors, the multiplicity of Petrarch's many writings refract one set of issues and concerns; they ring changes on the same set of bells. As Petrarch would say: "Solo d'un lauro tal selva verdeggia" (From only one laurel tree such a wood grows green [*RVF* 107.12]). Petrarch is an author who worries, in the *Secretum,* about works left uncompleted (*Labores ... interruptos* [206]), about the *Africa* half-finished ("semiexplicitam" [192]), and who also describes himself as "inexpletum" (74), unfulfilled, incomplete. The way Petrarch worked—the way he put down one *labor* to pick up another, keeping many projects going simultaneously

rather than bringing one to completion before starting another—is fragmented and labyrinthine rather than integral and linear: "nel laberinto entrai" (*RVF* 211.14). From what we know of Petrarch's life as a writer we can
get some sense of an inner life more horizontal than vertical, more committed to making multiple connections among the many morphing *lauri* in
the one *selva* than to moving from one integral *lauro* to an utterly discrete
something else.

At the same time the very fragmentariness of some of the *labores* only
adds to the sense of their all ultimately belonging to one overarching life—
one authored and authorized self—which, once gathered, once *raccolto*, once
etymologically perfected through death and hindsight, is in fact strangely
cohesive and complete.

What I have just described, the many incomplete works or fragments
that yet make a "complete Petrarch," a completed and authored self, could
also serve as an emblem of his most famous work. The fact that we can
find precedents to Petrarch's great lyric sequence should not cause us to
overlook what is distinctively new in his creation: new and perhaps unique.
The enormous influence of Petrarch's collection of vernacular lyrics notwithstanding, it is entirely possible that, defined as we have defined it, this
lyric sequence is a unique exemplar, a category of one. Petrarch would certainly not mind the outcome of singularity for his text (especially since it
was accompanied by imitation): he praises the Virgin in his final canzone
as "unica et sola" ("single and sole" [*RVF* 366.133]). For her there is no second, no "part 2" will ever follow her "part 1," for of her it can be said (and
how like Petrarch it is to say it!) that she is "Vergine sola al mondo, senza
exempio" (Virgin unique in the world, unexampled [*RVF* 366.53]) and that
of her "né prima fu simil, né seconda" (*RVF* 366.55). This last verse, usually translated loosely as "whom none ever surpassed or even approached,"
literally means that with respect to her there was never a first (a superior)
or a second (a similar but lesser exemplar). Because she is literally unique,
literally a category of one, she has no seconds. She is not multiple; she is
not in flux; she is not evanescent. Petrarch diverges in his praise of the Virgin in *Vergine bella* from Dante's prayer to the Virgin in *Paradiso* 33 in this
most significant use of numbers: the all-important "ciphers," the indicators
of multiplicity and flux that he never ceases to use, even when he uses them
to say that in this case they do not apply. For this poet of multiplicity and
time there is no higher value than unicity and singularity, qualities that
exempt their possessor from time, and in the *Rerum vulgarium fragmenta* he
created a unique and singular text.

APPENDIX 1
Metrical and Thematic Sets in the *Rerum vulgarium fragmenta**

Allocation	Part 1.1	Part 1.2	Part 2
Canzone number	23, 28, 29, 37, 50, 53, 70, 71, 72, 73, 105, 119, 125, 126, 127, 128, 129	135, 206, 207	264, 268, 270, 323, 325, 331, 359, 360, 366
No. of *canzoni*	17	3	9
Total no. of *canzoni* per part	20		9
Total no. of *canzoni*	29		
Sestina number	22, 30, 66, 80	142, 214, 237, 239	332
No. of *sestine*	4	4	1
Total no. of *sestine* per part	8		1**
Total no. of *sestine*	9		
Ballata number	11, 14, 55, 59, 63	149	324
No. of *ballate*	5	1	1
Total no. of *ballate* per part	6		1
Total no. of *ballate*	7		

*The *Rerum vulgarium fragmenta* contains 366 poems: 317 sonnets, 29 *canzoni*, 9 *sestine* (of which the last is a *sestina doppia* or double sestina), 7 *ballate*, 4 *madrigali*, all interspersed.
**Sestina doppia*.

Madrigale number	52, 54, 106, 121	None	None
No. of *madrigali*	4	None	None
Total no. of *madrigali* per part	4, all in part 1		None
Anniversary poem number (date-poems in brackets)	30, 50, 62, 79, 101, 107, 118, 122	145, [211], 212, 221	266, 271, 278, [336], 364
No. of anniversary poems	8	3	4
Total no. of anniversary poems per part	11		4
Total no. of anniversary poems	15		
Political poem number	27, 28, 53, 128	136, 137, 138	None
No. of political poems	4	3	None
Total no. of political poems per part	7, all in part 1		None
Occasional/ moral/friendship poem number	7, 8, 9, 10, 24, 25, 26, 38, 39, 40, 58, 68, 92, 98, 103, 104, 108, 112, 113, 119	143, 144, 166, 179, 232, 238, 244	266, 269, 287, 322

(*continued*)

No. of occasional poems	20	7	4
Total no. of occasional/ moral/friend- ship poems per part	27		4
Total no. of occasional/ moral/friend- ship poems	31		
Penitential poem number	1, 62, 80, 81	142, 189	264, 355, 364, 365, 366
No. of penitential poems	4	2	5
Total no. of penitential poems per part	6		5
Total no. of penitential poems	11		

APPENDIX 2
Structure of the *Rerum vulgarium fragmenta**

Part 1. Poems 1–263

1.1. Through the first climax and fall, this section consists of 129 poems (1–129).

- How to begin? A micro-*canzoniere*, 1–23, includes introductory sequence, 1–5, and culminates with 22, the first *sestina*, and 23, the first *canzone* (*canzone delle metamorfosi*).
- *Canzone* 23, emblematic of part 1—change which is stasis—marks the end of the beginning; its counterpart in part 2 is *canzone* 323.
- Establishing the problematic: from 24 to 124, including occasional poems, political poems, penitential poems, Vaucluse poems.
- Release from time/return to time, ecstatic *oblio* versus *storia* in *canzoni* sequences: adumbrated in 70–73, activated in 125–129.

1.2. This section rehearses the problematic established in 1.1 and shows less application of principles of chronology, variety of form, and variety of content. It consists of 134 poems, starting with the poem marked by Petrarch as the 100th sonnet (130–263).

- Stasis and repetition: "sarò qual fui, vivrò com'io son visso" (I shall be what I have been, shall live as I have lived [145.13]), echoing Dante's Capaneo, "Qual io fui vivo, tal son morto" (As I was alive, so am I dead [*Inf.* 14.51]).
- Much formal and thematic linkage, many little subsets or clusters that enhance the feeling of a great interconnected web in this section, which however does not contain the dramatic climaxes created by the great sweeps of *canzoni* found in the earlier section.
- Anticipation of Laura's death, the "death sequence": 246–254.

---

*Note the dynamic of a bipartite structure [263 + 103 = 366] versus a tripartite structure [129 + 134 + 103 = 366]. The dynamic of dyad versus triad is the structural basis of the sonnet and *sestina*. Moreover, 2 and 3 are factors of the number 6, the number of time, Petrarch's number (see Calcaterra 1942), a number that is also present in the following ways: importance of April 6; importance of the *sestina* (poem 66 is a *sestina*); majority of *canzoni* have a *fronte* of 6 verses; 6 *canzoni* begin with *settenari* 366 = 6 × 60 + 6; *canzone* 23 and *canzone* 323 include 300 poems and exclude 66 poems.

Part 2. Poems 264–366

Part 2 begins with canzone 264 and consists of 103 poems (264–366).

- *Trans-ire:* How to change? The question of conversion posed thematically and formally. The beginning of part 2: 264–269.
- Fantasy of *canzone* 126, where he imagined she took pity on him, now made "real": "calcando i fior' com'una donna viva / mostrando in vista che di me le 'ncresca" (treading the grass like a living woman, showing by her face that she is sorry for me [281.13–14]).
- Less variety of content: no political poems.
- Canzone 323 (*canzone delle visioni*) offsets 23, is emblematic of part 2's acceptance of change, marks beginning of the end.
- How to end? Petrarch's renumbering of final 31 poems.

CHAPTER TWO

THE POEM OF MEMORY · *Triumphi*

Fabio Finotti

With his *Triumphi* Petrarch shifts from the lyrical *Rerum vulgarium fragmenta* to an allegorical narrative genre, responding to the *Divina commedia* as does his friend Boccaccio with the *Amorosa visione*.[1] This relation to the Dantean model explains both the choice of meter (terza rima) and the textual architecture, which is not fragmentary but characterized by a force of authorial will more powerful than in the *Rime sparse*. Like the *Divina commedia*, the *Triumphi* are a vision favored by sleep,[2] and a guide accompanies the author-persona. Dantean in taste, too, are the astrological metaphors that set the season in spring and the classical image that places it at dawn, the hour of veracious visions. A vertical progression structures the "capitoli," or chapters, like a ladder that the poet-persona climbs, each rung representing a victory and a progression over the one preceding. From the *Triumphus Cupidinis* (TC; *Triumph of Love*) he turns to the *Triumphus Pudicitie* (TP; *Triumph of Chastity*), the *Triumphus Mortis* (TM; *Triumph of Death*), the *Triumphus Famae* (TF; *Triumph of Fame*) and then the *Triumphus Temporis* (TT; *Triumph of Time*), until he reaches the destination of his climb, the *Triumphus Eternitatis* (TE; *Triumph of Eternity*).[3] At the work's conclusion, the author himself states the title and the number of triumphs, as well as their course from earth to heaven (*TE* 121–23).

In the *Divina commedia* canto articulation does not correspond strictly to the various groups of souls; thus Petrarch feels free to dedicate four full chapters to the *Triumphus Cupidinis*, three to the *Triumphus Famae*, and two to the *Triumphus Mortis*, whereas the other three are built as single chapters. Modern editorial tradition delivers the poem to us organized in six triumphs and twelve chapters, a sequence in which numerology might fasten on the fatal number 6, the date of Petrarch's enamorment and Laura's death.[4]

Yet beginning with the initial verses, Petrarch establishes an essential difference between his poem and Dante's. The latter presents an itinerary that reflects a collective experience, set in a dark forest "Nel mezzo del cammin di *nostra* vita" (Midway in the journey of our life).[5] The year is 1300, a symbolic number for all Christianity since it coincides with the first Jubilee. The day chosen for starting the voyage is Good Friday; the poet's itinerary through hell, purgatory, and paradise evokes a paradigm of death and resurrection of a Christological and universal character.[6] Petrarch, in contrast, seems determined to project the wholly subjective character of his poem. To Dante's universal and objective experience of "our life," he responds with the "tempo che rinova *i mie'* sospiri" (The season when my sighing is renewed) in the first verse of the *Triumphi*. To Good Friday he brings a date of personal significance, the anniversary of his meeting Laura: "la dolce memoria di quel giorno / che fu principio a sì lunghi martiri" (the memory of that day / Whereon my love and suffering began [*TC* 1.2–3]). In the *Rerum vulgarium fragmenta* that date is identified with the date of the Passion of Christ (3) and April 6, 1327 (211), but in the beginning of the *Triumphi* there is no superimposition of religious time over personal time. Petrarch's poem seems intent on underscoring the lyrical character of its own opening. Dante loses the "straight way" in an oblivious journey down the road of sin and error, whereas Petrarch consciously chooses to step off the main road and isolate himself in a "Vale Enclosed" (Valchiusa). Sleep is not the premise for, but a consequence of his solitude, and it does not bear the allegorical meaning of losing one's way, but the wholly lyrical significance of solace and intimate peace (*TC* 1.7–11). Petrarch's vision is not a product of a divine will as in Dante. From the eschatological horizon of the *Divina commedia*, the *Triumphi* turns to a psychological horizon.

This immersion in a visionary state that is subjective and psychological, rather than objective and metaphysical, is given an emblematic form in the protagonist of Petrarch's poem. Dante is a pilgrim heading toward his destination without turning back to his past, except to contemplate and almost measure the course he has covered. There is a fundamental similarity between the narrative and the existential journeys, between the progression of the story and the *evolution* of the persona-poet. In Petrarch, on the other hand, the first descent into memory, as suggested by the initial verses, is followed by another temporal retrogression that is even more remarkable. In dream, the one who moves is not the poet who has already been captivated by Laura in the *Triumphus Cupidinis* 1.1–9, but the poet in his youth, in his "nova età" (*TC* 1.64), just before his enamorment. The narrative progression coincides, then, not with an existential evolution, as in Dante, but with memory's retrogression. What will happen in the *Triumphi* actually coincides with that which has already happened on earth, whereas in the *Divina commedia* time is mystical and prophetic.

It is quite clear why in the *Triumphi* there is little left of Dantean allegory. The herds of people Dante meets are bearers of historical experience destined to be interpreted with the allegory of the theologians. Within human truth, the *Commedia* seeks to indicate, there is always a superior divine truth. The herds Petrarch meets are, in contrast, representative of a truth that is and will remain human. They allow Petrarch to objectify his personal experience, to give it a more general sense, yet without transcending earthly limits. Further, the vision's source is not the mind of God, who seems to create, support, and guide Dante's journey,[7] but the all-human universe of books, libraries, images, and culture. From there comes the theme of the triumph, already developed in *Africa* 9,[8] and the unbreakable tie between learning and poetry (*TC* 3.7–9).

Contrast Dante's beings from the classical world with Petrarch's. In Dante they acquire their Christian truth and become "real" the moment the poet discerns in them a meaning that is higher than their mythical-literary nature. Charon, Minos, and Medusa are not only forms of the ancient imagination but concrete entities, who act in the hereafter according to a divine order. Petrarch, however, removes the guarantee of supernal will from such mythical entities; they express not an absolute but an earthly order. The first mythological figure he meets is Love:

> quattro destrier, vie più che neve bianchi,
> sovr'un carro di foco un garzon crudo
> con arco in man e con saette a' fianchi. (*TC* 1.22–24)

> [Four steeds I saw, whiter than whitest snow,
> And on a fiery car a cruel youth
> With bow in hand and arrows at his side.]

Love conducts the vision's first triumph. As the guide is quick to inform Petrarch, however, that god is an image with no substance, a form not of divine revelation but of wholly mundane frailty:

> Ei nacque d'otio e di lascivia humana,
> nudrito di penser dolci soavi. (*TC* 1.82–84)

> [Idleness gave him birth, and wontonness,
> And he was nursed by sweet and gentle thoughts.]

The *Triumphi* do not play host to figures of a supernatural revelation but instead to emblems of natural experience.

Petrarch, then, does not look for the greater theological meaning in each character but seeks the more memorable meaning.[9] In portraying Love, for example, Petrarch embraces an essential mise-en-scène of classicist iconology. In this complementary strengthening of personal memory and cultural memory, the *Triumphi* finds a raison d'être, originality, and extraordinary fortune throughout the Renaissance.[10] Many passages from the *Triumphi* are catalogs or repertoires that follow a fashion set in Boccaccio's *Amorosa visione*. Well into the seventeenth century, Italian men of letters and artists made use of these classicist inventories, expanding them as the rediscovery of antiquity offered new scholarly materials.

In Petrarch's unified textual mosaic there is a new humanistic sense of an ancient culture recomposed as a whole, acquired as a compact and organic world, no longer fragmentary and incomplete. The *Triumphi* are driven by the same ambition that inspired *De viris illustribus* right from its proem, to collect "the lives of men so illustrious that the flourishing of their glory and their praises have been handed down in the writings of the most learned men."[11]

Although they open a subjective horizon, we are bound to be disappointed if we look for deep psychological analysis in Petrarch's *Triumphi*. His goal is the completeness of the processions, and characterization as succinct as possible, in situations, gestures, and behavior that can become emblematic of destiny. Thus in *TC* Theseus is represented between Ariadne and Phaedra, and the whole story is summed up in a single tercet (*TC* 1.121–23). The iron shackles forged by Vulcan are enough to evoke Mars's passion for Venus in just two verses (*TC* 1.151–52). Juno calls for no more than a single adjective: "Vedi Iunon *gelosa*" (Behold the *jealous* Juno [*TC* 1.154]), to suggest both reproach, caused by Jupiter's betrayals (which actually head the procession), and persistent everlasting love for her husband.

Petrarch launches an intertextual and intercultural game that involves the reader more actively than Dante had.[12] How many times does Dante interrupt Virgil, asking to hear more about the souls of the hereafter? How many times does he interrogate the spirits himself? The *Triumphi*, by contrast, proceed without significant interruptions. Petrarch himself suggests how his work should be read, underlining the relation between the vision and the humanistic culture it evokes (*TF* 2.1–5). This explains the frequent use of circumlocutions in place of proper names, indicating the personae by means of cultural traits rather than by character or physiognomic features.

Precisely because it calls for interpretative cooperation founded on a rich reference library, the *Triumphi* does not stop at stirring the public's memory but tends to select or exclude readers according to their culture, preferring noblemen of letters to noblemen by birth in a way that will inspire humanistic circles and had already animated a famous passage in *Rerum memorandarum libri* (1.37). There King Robert of Anjou asked Petrarch why he has never been to the court of the king of France, and the poet responded that he had little interest in talking to someone who would not understand him due to cultural deficiency.

In *TC* 2, the dialogue with Massinissa opens with a clear example of this *poetics of identification*. The poet stops Massinissa, who is walking hand in hand with Sophonisba, and right away condenses all essential elements of his story, prompting the sovereign's admiration. If Petrarch then queries Massinissa for information about his life, it will be for reasons other than those that drive the Dante persona to interrogate the souls he encounters. It will not be so much a means to expand his knowledge, but rather a wish to let it flow more voluminously in the poem, as Massinissa himself suggests in his reply (*TC* 2.28–30). Once again the event is not projected toward the future but revolves around what the poet already knows. In this case his persona is expanded into a stronger, moving evocation because cultural memory merges with autobiographical memory. Massinissa, Sophonisba, and Scipio belong to a literary, historical, and fictional group that repeatedly appears in other Petrarchan works, from *Africa* 5 to *De viris illustribus* 6 and 21, *Familiares* 9 and 18, and *Seniles* 13.[13] And memory, in turn, creates another memory, making neither a judgment nor moral analysis as it does in the *Divina commedia:*

> Pien di pietate, e *ripensando* 'l breve
> spatio al gran foco di duo tali amanti,
> pareami al sol aver un cor di neve. (*TC* 2.73–75)

> [O'erwhelmed with pity, thinking of the brief
> Time granted to the love of such a pair,
> My heart was like to snow that melts i' the sun.]

The next conversation too is of a literary and cultural nature, performing a function of rhetorical reinforcement and emotional intensification vis-à-vis Massinissa. While the latter is torn between love and friendship, Seleucus incarnates a conflict that is even more agonizing, one between paternal and marital love (*TC* 2.94–132). Massinissa had to renounce his passion for Sophonisba, pressed by his friend Scipio's demands and by "raison d'état," just as Seleucus had to renounce his wife Stratonice to save his son Antiochus, who otherwise would have died of his love for his step-mother. In this case as well, one notes the care with which Petrarch makes clear his familiarity with the story even before meeting its protagonist. It does not come as a surprise, therefore, that when the dialogue with Seleucus ends, Petrarch pauses in order to recall the words he has just heard, as he had done after meeting Massinissa. Once again the poet depicts himself in the act of creating a new memory out of the old.

Beyond the facts taught us by the past, it is their memorial aura that captures Petrarch's imagination. One could say that in the *Triumphi* Petrarch wishes to depict his own enchantment with certain known historical events precisely in order to call to mind that long and slow sedimentation of memory that makes human experience intriguing and gives it sense, beyond any possible imposed allegorical or symbolic sense.

Petrarch's approach to memory is, as we see, a radical reversal of Dante's. In the *Divina commedia* memory is consecrated by revelation, which transcends it and selects and organizes its details. In the *Triumphi*, by contrast, memory itself consecrates content. Just as Laura lives in a dimension in which she can transform herself into a fantasy of memory, culture in its entirety acquires a universal meaning when it is not a form of divine truth but of human nostalgia. The theological perspective of Dante's poem is substituted in Petrarch's poem by a historical and anthropological perspective, which anticipates the Renaissance perspective explored in its highest form by Angelo Poliziano in the *Silvae*.

The principle that guarantees the unity of the *Triumphi* is now clear. The characters who appear in them—Laura, and no less Narcissus, Sophonisba, or Juno—are forms not of divine truth, nor simply of human history. Otherwise we would be hard-pressed to explain the mixing of persons who actually existed with mythological figures considered wholly fictional, like the Love god, like many "fabulosi e vani amori" (vain and fabled loves) of other gods (*TC* 2.169), and like the fictional characters in Breton romances: "quei che le carte empion di sogni: / Lancilotto, Tristano, e gli altri erranti, / ove conven che 'l vulgo errante agogni" (those who fill our books with dreams: / Lancelot, Tristram, and the other knights / Whose wand'rings lead the common folk astray [*TC* 3.79–81]). Nor could we explain the mixing of secular and guilty love with love that is not only virtuous but also sanctioned by biblical tradition, such as the love of Jacob for Rachel, Isaac for Rebecca, and Abraham for Sarah (*TC* 3.34–39). Those personae and love stories may coexist, however, because they share a common existential characteristic. All are forms of human memory. Truly it is in memory that the Petrarch of the *Triumphi* identifies the center of the new culture and discovers the unitary principle of his writing, divided only in appearance between a conversation with antiquity and a lyrical meditation on amorous themes.

Fame and love, the two central themes that inspire the *Triumphi*, are actually two expressions of memory. Subjective love for a woman, long reflected upon in solitude, and the collective worship of the past stem from the same roots and share an identical capacity to transform time from an agent of destruction to a locus of condensation and radiation of vibrant, perennial images. In the *Triumphi* Petrarch identifies with extreme lucidity the memorial nucleus of his whole source of inspiration, revealed both in the construction of the single chapters and in the complete architecture of the poem. Already in *Triumphus Cupidinis* the central theme of love, long cultivated in "sweet memory" (*TC* 1.2), is interwoven with the themes of glory, of consecration of the past through the rite of triumph, the "joy" of more noble ages:

> Vidi un victorïoso e sommo duce,
> pur com'un di color che 'n Campidoglio
> triumphal carro a gran gloria conduce. (*TC* 1.13–15)

> [A leader, conquering and supreme, I saw,
> Such as triumphal chariots used to bear
> To glorious honor on the Capitol.]

And in all the following encounters in that chapter the moral theme is often relegated to the background, behind the emotion stirred by celebrated individuals, whose fame may be emphasized by antonomasia (*TC* 1.121, 1.135); deictic reference (*TC* 1.124–125); or explicit declarations by the persona-poet (*TC* 2.22) or by his guide (*TC* 3.13–14). This celebratory register produces a paradoxical effect. On the one hand the losers in love experience triumph like a defeat that reverses their past glory, beginning with Caesar (*TC* 1.91–93). On the other hand, triumph is a ceremonial rite that seems to glorify the losers no less than the winners, the participants in the procession no less than its leader.

Moral order yields to memorial order. Ulysses does not transcend earthly order, as in the *Divina commedia*, but his myth remains within the limits of classical memory, symbolically marking the limits of Petrarch's poem in the reuse of antiquity: "Quel sì pensoso è Ulixe, affabile ombra, / che la

casta mogliera aspetta e prega, / ma Circe, amando, gliel ritene e 'ngom-
bra" (Ulysses moves in thought, a kindly soul: / His faithful wife entreats
him to return, / But ardent Circe will not let him go [*TC* 3.22–24]). When
Ulysses reappears in *Triumphus Famae* 2.17–18, his restless curiosity seems
to be always restrained within the boundaries of our "world" according to
classical sources; he does not venture toward a "mondo sanza gente" (world
without people) as in *Inferno* 26.117. In other parts of the poem Petrarch
openly exhibits his passion for a faithful historical reconstruction, in opposition to traditional distortions. Just think of the figure of Dido, who
the poet says died because of her love for her husband and not for Aeneas,
challenging both Virgil and Dante. In his portrayal of the Phoenician
queen Petrarch introduces an energetic call for truth and for a philological
commitment, joining scholarship with poetry:

> e veggio ad un lacciuol Giunone e Dido,
> ch'amor pio del suo sposo a morte spinse,
> non quel d'Enea, *com'è 'l publico grido.* (*TP* 10–12)

> [And if in a single snare Juno may fall,
> And Dido, she whom love for her own spouse
> (Not—as they say—for Aeneas) drove to her death.]

In the evocation of such personages vibrates that same cult of memory
to which Petrarch entrusts his complete corpus. Recall his passionate declaration to the reader in concluding the proem of *De viris illustribus*:

> If the labor of my studies has perhaps at least in part quenched
> the thirst of your expectations, then I ask from you no other kind
> of reward than that I be loved by you, even though I am unknown
> to you, even though I am shut up in my grave, even though I have
> turned into dust. In this same way, I have loved after a thousand
> years many who have helped me in my studies, who were not just
> dead but consumed after so much time.[14]

Among the beloved classics recollected, Laura, a darling form of lyrical memory, fits in naturally and harmoniously. Laura is the one who is
entrusted with the triumphs of Love and Fame, the final redemption of
human time, the solid affirmation of memorial poetry both within the *Triumphus Cupidinis* and the architecture of the whole poem. Within *Triumphus
Cupidinis* it is naturally thanks to Laura that Petrarch can transform him-

self from a spectator to a protagonist of the triumph. Having introduced into the vision a younger *alter ego*, the poet may now describe not only the moment when he actually fell in love, but also being captured in the crowd of Love's losers, confirmed in the guide's words, "tutti siam macchiati d'una pece" (all of us are stained with the same pitch [*TC* 3.91–99]).

Coming after a series of famous and memorable examples, his enamorment shines brightly in a glorious aura, ambiguously combined with a sentiment of moral contrition (*TC* 3.112–20). And the theme of fame is interlaced ever more tightly with that of love. Laura is not just a personal ghost. She is also a literary persona, as Petrarch is keen to point out both in the verses just cited ("cotante carte aspergo," the pages that I fill) and in the direct metapoetic references to his own effort to celebrate the lover's merits (*TC* 3.133–144).

The wish to emphasize Laura's literary dimension yields the repeated intertextual recollections that link *Rerum vulgarium fragmenta* to the *Triumphus Cupidinis*. In his love for Laura Petrarch wishes to sublimate not only his private experience but the cultural process through which personal experience is transformed into collective memory. The poetic coronation of 1341 is nothing other than a symbol of this glorification of memory:

> . . . colsi 'l glorïoso ramo
> onde forse anzi tempo ornai le tempie
> *in memoria di quella ch'io tanto amo.* (*TC* 4.79–81)

> [. . . I plucked the glorious laurel branch
> Wherewith—perhaps too soon—I decked my brow,
> Remembering her whom I so deeply love.]

And so love for Laura opens the way to the last chapter of *Triumphus Cupidinis*, where Petrarch calls to his aid other love poets from the past in order to define more clearly the new humanistic ideal of writing, which by immortalizing earthly experience immortalizes itself. Those that Petrarch seeks are not some unknown poets, but living examples full of passion and fame:

> . . . io volgeva gli occhi in ogni parte
> s'i' ne vedesse alcun di chiara fama,
> o per antiche, o per moderne carte. (*TC* 4.10–12)
> [. . . I was looking here and there to see
> If any of them had risen to renown
> For pages they had writ, or old or new.]

Marching past are Orpheus, Alcaeus, Pindar, Anacreon, Virgil, Ovid, Catullus, and other lyrical poets, from antiquity to the Romance vernacular era in a catalogue where it is difficult to judge whose passion is greater, that of these poets for their beloved ladies or that of Petrarch for their beloved texts and for the works "di quei che volentier già 'l mondo lesse" (companions whom the olden world / Had gladly read [*TC* 4.19–21]). Precisely because of this memorial dimension in which the poet lets himself be increasingly absorbed, life can be fully equated with writing and ripple in front of poet's eyes like a dream before vanishing: "Ben è 'l viver mortal, che sì n'agrada, / sogno d'infermi, e fola di romanzi!" (This mortal life, that we do cherish so, / Is an ill dream, a tale of vain romance! [*TC* 4.65–66]).

Throughout *Triumphus Cupidinis* the poetry of memory is true to itself. In the last chapter, Love takes his prisoners to Cyprus, home of Venus. This voyage offers the opportunity for a description that is wholly inspired by poetic remembrances, recovered and sung with an enthusiasm that goes beyond moral scruples. Only at the beginning, the representation of the island seems to reflect a world that has been devastated by passion and is morally depraved (*TC* 4.106–11). But the canto is then immediately caught up by memory of idyllic tradition, marrying ancient Arcadia to the *locus amoenus* of Romance tradition:

> E rimbombava tutta quella valle
> d'acque e d'augelli, ed eran le sue rive
> bianche, verdi, vermiglie, perse e gialle:
>   rivi correnti di fontane vive
> al caldo tempo su per l'erba fresca,
> e l'ombra spessa, e l'aure dolci estive;
>   poi, quand'è 'l verno e l'aër si rinfresca,
> tepidi soli, e giuochi, e cibi, ed otio
> lento, che i semplicetti cori invesca. (*TC* 4.121–29)

> [And the whole valley echoed with the songs
> Of waters and of birds, and all its swards
> Were white and green and red and yellow and perse.
>   Streamlets that spring from living fountains run
> Through the fresh verdure in the summer heat
> When shade is deep and gentle is the breeze:
>   And then, when winter comes and the air is cool,
> Warm sun, games, food, and torpid idleness
> That casts its evil spell on foolish hearts.]

The memory of poetry is no less strong than the memory of love in guiding a poetic voice that is so far from Dante's, to the verge of identifying
art as man's true transcendence. If we were to look for the last image of
himself that the poet leaves us with in the conclusion of the first triumph,
we would not find him delivering his thoughts outside the dark cage in
which Love has locked him. Even in that "così tenebrosa e stretta gabbia"
(*TC* 4.157) Petrarch continues to transform life into a memorable painting.
Even in that "carcer tetro," for him the progression of time is turned into
the retrogression of memory and the tireless transformation of experiencing into reminding:

> e 'ntanto, *pur sognando libertate,*
> l'alma, che 'l gran disio fea pronta e leve,
> *consolai col veder le cose andate.*
> Rimirando er'io fatto al sol di neve
> tanti spirti e sì chiari in carcer tetro,
> *quasi lunga pictura in tempo breve,*
> *che 'l pie' va inanzi, e l'occhio torna a dietro.* (*TC* 4.160–66)

> [And all the while, dreaming of liberty,
> I fed my soul, impatient for escape,
> By thinking of the loves of olden times.
> Like snow that melts away in the sun was I,
> Gazing at the greats spirits here confined—
> Like one beholding lengthy painted scenes,
> Whose eyes look back, despite his hurried feet.]

The entire structure of Petrarch's poem depends on that same poetry
of memory proposed by *Triumphus Cupidinis*. In its entirety, in fact, the
Triumphi seems to be inspired by the dream of saving the two forms of
memory—fame and love—from the objections expressed extensively by Petrarch to himself in the *Secretum*, selecting Augustine as a stand-in. Love
and glory are insubstantial forms, mistakes, confusions of the soul, says
Augustine. There is no other way to set yourself free from their bonds except actually freeing yourself of the slavery of memory.[15]

Upon superficial examination, the architecture of the *Triumphi* could appear a magnificent staging of Augustine's teachings. The triumph of Love is
quashed by first the triumph of Chastity and then by that of Death. The triumph of Fame, in turn, seems to be canceled by the triumph of Time, which
nullifies any human glory. Finally, in the poem's conclusion, the poet-traveler

seems to be severing all ties with the past, all connections to memory, and is left with nothing but to project himself into eternity, to which the last triumph is dedicated and where nothing dies, nothing passes on, nothing is remembered, since here the absolute present of total truth is in force (*Seniles* 3.9.15).[16]

> Quel che l'anima nostra preme e 'ngombra:
> 'dianzi,' 'adesso,' 'ier,' 'deman,' 'matino' e 'sera,'
> tutti in un punto passeran com'ombra.
>   Non avrà loco 'fu,' 'sarà' ned 'era,'
> ma 'è' solo, 'in presente,' ed 'ora,' ed 'oggi,'
> e sola 'eternità' raccolta e 'ntera. (*TE* 64–69)

> [All that encumbers us and weighs us down,
> "Yesterday" and "tomorrow," "morn" and "eve,"
> "Before" and "soon," will pass like fleeting shadows.
>   "Has been," "shall be," and "was" exist no more,
> But "is" and "now," "the present" and "today,"
> "Eternity" alone, one and complete.]

In reality, Petrarch enacts a series of strategies that countermand the progressive character of the poem's structure. Regarding fame, in *Triumphus Cupidinis* an ambiguous choreography tends to transform losers into winners through processions crowded with examples from antiquity that stir the reader's cultural memory more than his moral judgment. The same procedure is applied in defense of fame on the level of the poem's overall structure. As in *Triumphus Cupidinis*, where Caesar's nobility, Aegeria's song, and Atalanta's race grant myth an autonomous value beyond its spiritual significance, in *Triumphus Fame* the mythic seems to have total autonomy from moral order. Nothing reminds us, reading the *Triumphus Fame*, that its characters, illustrious in glory and celebrated with ceremonial eloquence, are destined to suffer defeat by the *Triumph of Time*, which can blow away fame and submit a man to a second death (*TT* 142–43). Instead, the cumulative effect of the examples focuses attention on glory restored and celebrated, fascinating from the initial verses (*TF* 1.16–35).

Are they sinners? Are they defeated, these personae? Or are they not simply presented as sublime examples of human nobility who can beat death—celebrated in the preceding triumph? This celebratory aspect of Petrarchan memory is underscored by the careful choice of examples. Among the Gracchi only one is worthy of joining the procession (*TF* 1.112–14); as is only one of Emperor Vespasian's sons:

> "Poscia Vespasïan col figlio vidi:
> *il buono e bello,* non già il bello e rio." (*TF* 1.121–22)

> [And then I saw Vespasian and the son
> Who was fair and good (not the other, fair and vile).]

In other cases, as with "the other Alexander," memory repairs injustice delivered by destiny, rescuing worthy men from oblivion or redeeming them from unjust judgments by their contemporaries (*TF* 2.13–15). The protagonists of *Triumphus Fame* appear to be like heroes in a memory that does not rerun the past indiscriminately, but selects from it and relives it, establishing and perpetuating the values of human civilization. The decision to present the triumph as a procession of ancient times, with a quasi-ceremonial solemnity, seems consciously to found that cult of history that will live on until the nineteenth century in Ugo Foscolo's *Sepolcri* (*Sepulchers*) and Giacomo Leopardi's *Canti* (*Songs*), and will make Petrarch not only the poet of his love for Laura, but a master, alongside Dante, of modern thought in Italy and the world.[17]

For many centuries, in fact, history will be taught in Western culture according to the way Petrarch proposes in his *Triumphi*, or more specifically in *Triumphus Fame*, which should be considered the founding act of a memory religion, destined to be embraced and nurtured starting from within the fifteenth-century humanistic schools. For centuries after Petrarch, aside from figures of religious history who are mentioned only briefly (*TF* 2.52–84, 118–20); children will learn about Attilius Regulus, "ch'amò altrui più che se stesso" (Regulus, who loved others more than self [*TF* 1.54]); will admire Torquatus "che'l figliuol percusse / e viver orbo per amor sofferse / della militia, perché orba non fusse" (he who smote his son, / Preferring to be reft of him than that / His troops be reft of spirit and of strength [*TF* 1.64–66]); will relive the heroism of Horatius Cocles and of Gaius Mucius Scaevola (*TF* 1.80–84); will study in gymnasiums all the philosophers listed in the *Triumphus Famae;* and will read poets capable of consecrating the past following Homer's footsteps: "primo pintor *de le memorie* antiche" (first to paint men's ancient memories [*TF* 3.15]). The fame celebrated in Petrarch's triumph is one with a new kind of moral significance, laying the foundation for a pedagogy that will identify in history and in man—rather than in theology and in God—the necessary values for building and maintaining modern civil society: altruism, heroism, generosity, unselfishness, magnanimity, and spiritual ennoblement through the cult of art and letters.

The progressive character of the poem's overall structure is therefore marred by the fact that *Triumphus Fame* tends to be presented as a complete whole by itself, connected not so much to the poem's general organism as to the overflowing network of sources from which it draws, with powerful evocation, its characters. The structure of the *Divina commedia* is centripetal: Dante gathers, combines, recreates the materials of his culture. The structure of the *Triumphi*, on the other hand, is centrifugal. Petrarch creates a map that is open to other texts, producing a sort of hypertext that calls for a vertical reading, without which the poem often would not be understood at all. Memory, then, does not only provide the central theme and problem of the work but also determines its form.

In the second place, the poem's progressive character is weakened by its internal circularity. A few *Triumphus Cupidinis* personae return in *Triumphus Fame*. Petrarch himself points this out (*TF* 1.20–21). Glory, defeated in *Triumphus Mortis*, is then resurrected in *Triumphus Fame*. Time, which has been apparently removed from individual life, finds its redemption in a higher dimension, public and historical. What seemed cancelled returns. The mechanism of memory could not have been suggested more effectively on the overall structural level, with a strategy that finds its highest achievement in its treatment of love.

In the third place, the heroes who embody fame are shown only in the act of triumphing, not of being defeated. Dante does not have any compassion for the defeated, whereas Petrarch, in the act of depicting the *Triumphus Temporis* (*Triumph of Time*), which is supposed to break up the magnificent ranks of Fame, limits himself to a generic discussion of moral philosophy. There are none of the kind of grotesque deformation processes that Dante prescribes for those who embody human errors. The Sun accelerates its course. Time breaks up the ranks of memory, not coincidentally led by historians and poets (*TT* 90), but not one among these ranks is recognizable. Certainly the moralistic discourse on the vanity of glory and of fame, which takes up a large part of this chapter, is not enough to equal the power of the preceding triumph.

All these elements tend to lend the *Triumphi* a memorial and circular, rather than linear, structure. But the fact remains that *Triumphus Temporis* represents a dramatic moment of crisis within the work. The absence of recognizable souls allows the poet-persona to talk to himself and to question explicitly the sense of his work. The point he has reached is the same one where *Rerum vulgarium fragmenta* concluded, as demonstrated by his return to its first and recapitulative sonnet, quoted almost verbatim: 'Segui' già *le speranze e 'l van desio;* / or ò dinanzi agli occhi un chiaro specchio, / *ov'io veggio me stesso e 'l fallir mio"* (I followed then my hopes and vain desires, / But now with mine own eyes I see myself / As in a mirror, and my failings [*TT* 55–57]). The central problem of *Triumphus Temporis* is Petrarch's consideration of the possible failure of his poetry and its inspiration, wholly memorial and human.

If the *Triumphi* were interrupted at that point, it would not have indicated a solution that is different from the contrition of *Rerum vulgarium fragmenta*. But *Triumphus Eternitatis* (*Triumph of Eternity*) belongs to the last days of Petrarch's life; it is the triumph in which the circular and memorial structure of the poem is unexpectedly saved and the conclusion of *Triumphus Temporis* is left behind. And since the heroine of this happy ending is Laura, we must move on from fame to another incarnation of memory: love.

The love theme makes even clearer Petrarch's will to fit the *Triumphi* into a circular structure of memory. In the first place, we saw how the beginning of the poem matches not a progression but a retrogression of consciousness. During *Triumphus Cupidinis* the poet relives his enamorment and the long imprisonment that tie him to Laura, tightly binding sentiment and memory. Laura, meanwhile, through a thick network of intertextual references, becomes an emblem not only of Petrarch's passion but also of his poem. The defense of love, more than what happens in the treatment of fame, becomes one with the defense of poetry.

In passing from the first to the second triumph, the progressive structure of the work should have led to a clear defeat of Love and therefore of passion for Laura which dominates the second part of *Triumphus Cupidinis*. Petrarch, however, is very careful to make a distinction between his beloved and the other amorous heroines. She imprisons the poet but keeps in this triumph her separate place. An ally of Love when catching Petrarch, Laura may at the same time be its adversary in protecting her own freedom (*TC* 3.130–132; 3.145–47). Thanks to this paradox the transition from the first to the second triumph amounts not to a progression but to a return of Laura, whose victory over love is revealed in advance in *Triumphus Cupidinis*, in order to emphasize once more the structural circularity of the poem (*TC* 4.86–90).

The *Triumphus Pudicitiae* becomes thus the second triumph of Laura, who continues to keep a tight grip on the center of Petrarch's heart and poetic inspiration. Love, in fact, does not necessarily have to be nullified but may be sublimated. This is suggested by the example of Dido, driven to suicide not by "vano amor" (vain love) but by "amor pio" (pious love), which guarantees the Phoenician queen a place in the procession of Chastity (*TP* 154–59), shortly after being depicted among the prisoners in *Triumphus Cupidinis* (*TP* 1–12).

Not by accident, in the course of *Triumphus Pudicitiae*, the poet is quite careful to emphasize the union between chastity and beauty: modesty seems truly to increase the appeal of a loved woman (*TP* 90, 174) and hence to increase love rather than turn it off. The last image of this triumph is also dominated by the beauty of Laura, more than ever a symbol of poetry as well, when she shows off her laurel wreath:

> Ivi spiegò le glorïose spoglie
> la bella vincitrice; ivi depose
> le sue victorïose e sacre foglie. (*TP* 184–86)

> [There the fair victress spread her glorious spoils
> And there she left the crown that she had won,
> The sacred laurel crown of victory.]

Laura's beauty continues as a theme of *Triumphus Mortis*, which should produce a definite forward movement in the poem's itinerary, freeing the poet from the tyranny of desire and memory. But the triumph is symptomatic of a retrogressive structure, from Laura's present dissolution to her past life (*TM* 1.1–3). In the rest of the triumph the two strategies employed in *Triumphus Cupidinis* and *Triumphus Temporis* are applied in a radical manner, so as to dissolve from within any progression that might produce a clear rupture between past and present. First, as in *Triumphus Cupidinis*, Laura occupies a place separate from other mortals. It is not death that triumphs over Laura, but once again Laura who triumphs over death, overcoming it and forcing it to admire her (*TM* 1.52–69). Second, medieval signs of human frailty and suffering are missing in Petrarch. The triumph of Death does not bring with it skeletons, symbols of decomposition, or slashed bodies like those that Dante comes across in the *Inferno*. The strategy is the same one that drives *Triumphus Temporis*: the poetry is general, moralistic, and it avoids anything concrete except a brief mention of the stripping of earthly honors and clothes (*TM* 1.79–84). Her flesh dissolves, but her memory remains intact. The behavior of Death toward Laura illustrates this strategy. From the beginning of the triumph, there is a continuous succession of references to the beauty of the beloved woman, surrounded and exalted by the beauty of her lady friends (*TM* 1.1, 1.8, 1.13–15, 1.25–26, 1.34–35, 1.62).

Her passing does not disfigure Laura; rather it preserves her. That beauty, mourned and anxiously scrutinized by her friends (*TM* 1.145–46, 1.158), is miraculously saved beyond life. It is not Laura who takes on the face of death, but the reverse, and so in the moment of her passing the canto returns to the theme of *beauty* with a passionate, pounding insistence:

> Pallida no, ma più che neve bianca,
> che senza venti in un *bel* colle fiocchi,
> parea posar come persona stanca.
>   Quasi un dolce dormir ne' suo' *belli* occhi,
> sendo lo spirto già da lei diviso,
> era quel che morir chiaman li sciocchi.
> Morte *bella* parea nel suo *bel* viso. (*TM* 1.166–72)

> [Not pale, but whiter than the whitest snow
> Quietly falling on a gentle hill,
> She seemed to be aweary and at rest.
>   And that which is called "death" by foolish folk,
> Was a sweet sleep upon her lovely eyes,
> Now that her body held her soul no more;
>   And even death seemed fair in her fair face.]

Is it Petrarch the person or Petrarch the narrator who does the talking? Petrarch the dumbfounded spectator of Death *within* the dream, or Petrarch who *recounts* the dream and therefore has had the time to take in the lesson? For a moment, in fact, the reader may wonder whether the "begli occhi" (lovely eyes) in verse 169 are still those of the living Laura, as recalled in extremis by Petrarch *within* the dream prior to internalizing fully the devastating victory of death. But it is soon clear that there is no difference between memory and dream, since death does not dissolve the woman's beauty but perpetuates it, in the perennial and marmoreal nobleness of a classical sepulchral monument. Once again the poem's general retrogressive structure is confirmed. Once again the vision does not go beyond Petrarchan memory, but saves it.

Triumphus Mortis 2 has stirred up many inconclusive debates. Many see it as an extraneous episode to the poem's overall structure.[18] Others argue it is a fundamental juncture in the architecture of the *Triumphi*.[19] There can be no doubt that the episode narrated in this triumph makes up the generative core of the memorial poetry that is the inspiration for Petrarch's whole vision. It is the night that follows Laura's death, "La notte che seguì l'orribil caso" (The night that followed the dread stroke of fate [*TM* 2.1]). We are taken back, then, to that crucial moment of Petrarchan poetry when the course of time is reversed and the love for a woman of real, living experience is transformed to memory, subject to cyclic reprocessing in the consciousness.

Laura does return in a dream, A vision opens within the vision and Laura *does not* return as Beatrice did to guide the poet in another world, to a point where he could go on *without her* "a terminar lo suo disiro" (*Paradiso* 31.65). In *Triumphi* it is Laura who is the ultimate object of Petrarch's desire. Nor are there other spirits who disrupt the dialogue between the two lovers, maintaining the tone of an intimate and private conversation. Laura, in fact, returns first and foremost for *remembering.* The entire course of Petrarch's love is once again relived and fueled by new flames. To his love, Laura finally joins hers, while insisting on its *duration* (*TM* 2.94, 2.100; 2.155), which extends the memory, breathing new air into it, expanding and enriching the past life instead of leaving it behind and letting it fade away. The present is not modeled on what one wishes to attain in the future, as in the *Divina commedia*, but on what one wishes to relive from the past. In Laura's words, what will be cannot be different from what was (*TM* 2.88–89, 2.139–41, 2.151–53). Time stops in this enchanted, transformed remembering (*TM* 2.176–77). And it is against time that Laura, in *Triumphus Eternitatis*, will fight her last battle, saving both herself and Petrarch's poetry.

An autograph note on *Triumphus Eternitatis* (Vat. Lat. 3196) informs us of the date writing commenced: "1374, dominico ante cenam. 15 Januarii, ultimus cantus" [1374, Sunday before supper, 15 January, the last canto].[20] With death just six months away, Petrarch set about writing the last chapter of the *Triumphi*. The *Canzone alla Vergine* (*Rerum vulgarium fragmenta* 366) had already been written, and the palinodic structure of the collected lyrics had already been set.[21] The transition to the definitive redaction of *Rerum vulgarium fragmenta* follows the author's wish to render it clearer.[22] Yet the dedication with which Petrarch wrote the last triumph makes one suspect that with this "poem in terza rima" he wanted to end a journey that is not less important than the one he had undertaken in *Rerum vulgarium fragmenta*. Before a month had passed, *Triumphus Eternitatis* was finished, as we learn from another of Petrarch's inscriptions in the manuscript, following the last verse: "domenica carnis privii 12 februarii 1374, post cenam" [Sunday of Lent, 12 February 1374, after supper].[23]

In the beginning of the chapter, the awareness of time and its dissolutive power seems to triumph: "e veggio andar, anzi volare, il tempo" ([I] see Time marching, nay more, flying on; *TE* 8). There is no surprise in the direct reference to the feeling of regret that opened the *Canzoniere:* "Ma ben veggio che 'l mondo m'ha schernito" (Well do I see the mockery of the world; *TE* 6). However, the triumph of Eternity is in turn a victory over time, and instead of proposing a palinode, it affirms the poetry with the force of a passionate defense waged on the brink of death.

We note immediately that in the *Triumphi* the encounter with eternity offers a last and radical departure from Dante's model. It is not the absolute that beckons the poet but the poet who lives *within himself* the meeting with eternity. Petrarch, in fact, does not tell us about the encounter with God but about a presentiment of that vision, which he would enjoy fully only after death: "O qual gratia mi fia, se mai l'impetro, / ch'i' veggia ivi presente il sommo bene" (What grace, if I am worthy, shall be mine, / If I may there behold the Highest Good; *TE* 36–37). For this reason, the moment the poet is set to go beyond human limits verbs change from the past (or present) tense to the future, a fully conscious choice as demonstrated by the stark contrast between the preceding triumphs (actually seen) and that of eternity (still to be seen):

> Questi triumphi, i cinque in terra giuso
> *avem veduto*, ed a la fine il sexto,
> Dio permettente, *vederem* lassuso. (*TE* 121–23)
>
> [Five of these triumphs on the earth below
> We have beheld, and at the end, the sixth,
> God willing, we shall see in heaven above.]

Within this unprophetic, personal consciousness Laura rises once again. Eternity appears, according to Augustine's teachings,[24] as the present absolute. This present, however, is not radically different from human life. It is, rather, life itself saved from Death and from Time: the countenances hurt by Death and Time "torneranno al suo più fiorito stato" (will now appear in perfect flowering [*TE* 92]).

The true Petrarchan model of eternity is memory. Like memory, eternity opposes "oblivïon" (*TE* 130); it is a return, a rebirth of that which is

no more. Fame finds redemption by becoming eternal as do other forms of
Petrarchan memory, thanks to the Christian dogma of resurrection of the
flesh[25] which guarantees a full, complete reblossoming of worldly beauty.
In eternity, indeed, the spirits will reunite with their bodies:

> Ne l'età più fiorita e verde avranno
> *con immortal bellezza eterna fama.* (*TE* 133–34)

> [In the full flower of youth they shall possess
> Immortal beauty and eternal fame.]

At the culmination of *Triumphus Eternitatis* it is above all Laura who lives
again, and not only in spirit but again wearing her "bel velo." Developing
concepts already present in the *Rerum vulgarium fragmenta* (302.10–11), Petrarch dedicates the whole conclusion of the work to the triumph of the beloved's beauty, for the last time presented as a form of memory and of poetry:

> Ma innanzi a tutte ch'a rifarsi vanno
>   è quella che piangendo il mondo chiama
> *con la mia lingua e con la stancha penna*
> ma 'l ciel pur di vederla intera brama.
> . . . .
> Amor mi die' per lei sì lunga guerra
> che *la memoria* anchora il cor accenna.
>   Felice sasso che 'l *bel viso* serra!
> Che, poi che avrà ripreso il suo *bel velo,*
> se fu beato chi la vide in terra,
>   or che fia dunque a *rivederla* in cielo? (*TE* 135–145).

[Before them all, who go to be made new,
        Is she for whom the world is weeping still,
Calling her with my tongue and weary pen,
But heaven too desires her, body and soul.
. . . .
Love gave to me for her a war so long
My heart still bears the memory thereof.
        Happy the stone that covers her fair face!
And now that she her beauty hath resumed,
If he was blest who saw her here on earth,
        What then will it be to see her again in heaven!]

And that blaze of the body with which the *Triumphi* ends seems the emblem of humanism in full bloom that creates a new spirituality and a new culture. The triumph of a dematerialized spirituality would have meant the supremacy of theological and mystical knowledge. But the complete recovery of fame and beauty actually signify the ultimate redemption of history and love, of literature and poetry, which become the finest forms of knowledge and worship not only of man but also of eternity.

The kind of memory on which the *Triumphi* as a whole is built is not only a sentimental need, nor is it just a condition of regret and penance as in the *Rerum vulgarium fragmenta* and *De remediis utriusque fortune* ("Such is the condition of things human that the less one remembers, the less reason he has to weep. Where there is no hope for improvement, no place for effective atonement—what else is there but soothing forgetfulness?").[26] With the last canto, the revolutive character of Petrarch's last poem finally acquires cognitive as well as psychological and moral value. It is thanks to historical and literary memory that man constructs his destiny on earth, his individual and collective identity. It is through memory that man rescues from time and death the values of his worldly experience. It is through memory that man consecrates life and in it quests for signs of eternity.

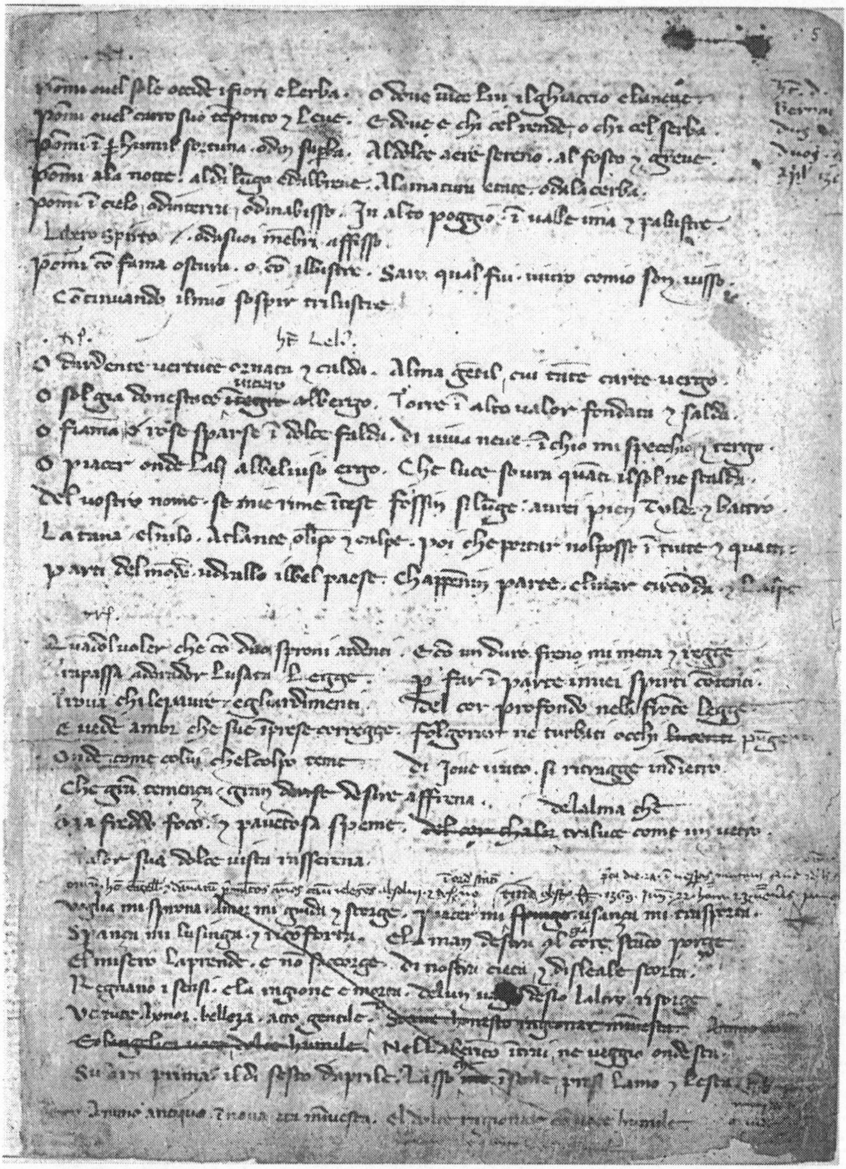

Fig. 2. Petrarch, *Codice degli abbrozzi*. MS Vat. Lat. 3196, fol. 5r (fourteenth century). Biblioteca Apostolica Vaticana, Vatican City.

CHAPTER THREE

PETRARCH'S DAMNED POETRY AND THE POETICS OF EXCLUSION • *Rime disperse*

Justin Steinberg

Compared with other works, Petrarch's uncollected Italian poems, known as the *Rime disperse*, have received little critical attention. This is due no doubt in large part to the ambiguous canonical status of many of the poems. Countless poems, primarily sonnets, are attributed to Petrarch in fourteenth- and fifteenth-century manuscripts, and a large number of these attributions are suspect when not evidently erroneous. With good cause, scholars have therefore concentrated on the poems that we know for certain are Petrarch's, either those included in the *Canzoniere* or those select few that are extraneous to it but have survived in his autograph papers. This conservative approach runs the risk, however, of complicity in the reproduction of Petrarch's authorizing (and deauthorizing) strategies. In other words, what gets lost in the shuffle of unanthologized Petrarchan and pseudo-Petrarchan poems are the motives behind the poet's process of inclusion and exclusion, why he saved certain poems while condemning others to oblivion or at least to "dubious" canonical status. Yet an examination of various extant poems most likely written by Petrarch does reveal one conspicuous reason why he might have dispersed them: their overdetermined contexts. While the linguistic and narrative parameters of the *Canzoniere* aim at transcending any specific time and place, the *disperse* reveal Petrarch's inescapable historicity and the role of his works within a determined political and social arena.

We know from Petrarch's own letters and marginal notes that not all of his vernacular poetry was intended for inclusion in the final version of the *Canzoniere*, the autograph Vaticano Latino 3195. In a letter to Pandolfo Malatesta accompanying one of the public redactions of the *Canzoniere* (*Variae* 9 or version γ of *Seniles* 13.11), Petrarch discusses the process of revision and selection that informs the collection:

I still have here with me, written on ancient slips of paper, numerous other vernacular poems of this kind. Consumed with age, they can be read only with great difficulty. When I happen to have a day of leisure I draw forth from these old slips one component or another, almost as a diversion from work—but rarely. I therefore instructed that ample blank space be left at the end of both parts so that if this should happen, there would be enough space to accommodate these new compositions.[1]

The remnants of this large personal archive of early vernacular poems provides an important source for what we currently refer to as the *disperse*, poems that for one reason or another are not currently included in Vaticano Latino 3195. In large part, exclusion from the *Canzoniere* no doubt depended on constraints of time and space. At a certain point and for a variety of reasons, Petrarch seems to have fixed the number of possible components at 366, although even as late as 1373 he substituted the madrigal "O vedi, Amor, che giovenetta donna" for the excised *ballata* "Donna mi vène spesso ne la mente," thus creating one of the most important *disperse*.[2] And the reference to the importance of blank space mentioned in the letter to Malatesta suggests that a work we typically treat only in its crystallized and final form remained for many years a work-in-progress. In addition to the limits of the human life span and the formal, numerological confines of the *Canzoniere*, many poems seem to have remained archived based on stylistic concerns and questions of content. A marginal note to the sonnet "Voglia mi sprona, Amor mi guida et scorge" (*RVF* 211) in Petrarch's autograph working papers, the so-called *codice degli abbozzi* (Vat. Lat. 3196, fig. 2), illustrates these conscious acts of inclusion and exclusion while suggestively evoking Christian salvation: "Friday, June 22, 1369, 11 at night: Amazing. Rereading by chance this crossed out and condemned poem, after many years, I immediately absolved and transcribed it in order, despite . . . " (here Petrarch inserts an oval intersected by two horizontal lines meeting at an acute angle, apparently the sign for exclusion from the anthology).[3] This nonverbal mark of rejection (fig. 3), this intersected oval separating the damned from the saved, with Petrarch playing confessor to his own confessions, is crucial for understanding the place of the *disperse* among the poet's works. As we shall see, when Petrarch decided to save certain poems or damn others, he automatically changed the function and significance of both.[4]

Besides Petrarch's own guarded papers, another important source for the *disperse* are the poems that were copied, circulated, and anthologized within Petrarch's own lifetime. In the letter sent to Pandolfo Malatesta

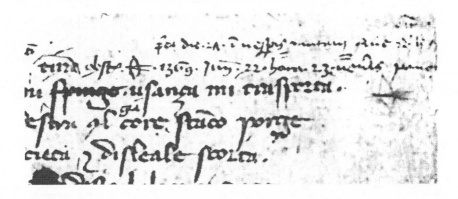

Fig. 3. Petrarch, *Codice degli abbozzi* (detail). MS Vat. Lat. 3196, fol. 5r. Biblioteca Apostolica Vaticana, Vatican City. Detail with Petrarch's symbol of exclusion in right margin of earlier version of "Amor mi sprona" and in an annotation (before date 1369) describing his decision not to reject the poem.

cited above, revised for inclusion in the *Seniles*, the poet adds the following revealing comments about the material public reception of his texts:

> At this age, I confess, I observe with reluctance the youthful trifles that I would like to be unknown to all, including me, if it were possible. For while the talent of that age may emerge in any style whatsoever, still the subject matter does not become the gravity of old age. But what can I do? Now they have all circulated among the multitude, and are being read more willingly than what I later wrote in earnest for sounder minds. How then could I deny you, so great a man and so kind to me and pressing for them with such eagerness, what the multitude possesses and mangles against my wishes.[5]

What is especially striking about this passage is that the formation of the *Canzoniere* at this late date is justified implicitly by the *disperse* themselves, understood broadly as poems circulating in forms that the author would himself reject. It is better to collect and selectively publish these "youthful trifles" (*iuveniles ineptias*) if only to counter their unregulated dissemination and corrupt reproduction. Petrarch's anxiety about the public possession and mishandling of his *rime*—"vulgus habet et lacerat"—is in fact a commonplace in his correspondence. With his peer Boccaccio, he notes in horror in *Familiares* 22.15 how Dante's texts have been corrupted and torn apart by an oral transmission, "scripta eius pronuntiando lacerant atque corrumpunt"[6] while in *Seniles* 5.2 he even cedes authorial rites to those short poems dispersed ("sparsa") among the crowds ("non mea amplius sed vulgi potius facta essent," they are no longer my property but rather belong to the masses). And as is clear from a letter to Giovanni d'Arezzo (*Seniles* 13.4),[7] Petrarch was also well aware of and worried about the written transmission and collection of his texts—especially those unauthorized anthologies of unrevised poems that competed with, and, I would argue, informed his authentic self-anthology. Yet these unauthorized anthologies also created an important tradition of *disperse*, most notably the so-called "raccolta veneta" originating, according to Annarosa Cavedon, in a collection put together by one of Petrarch's most important correspondents, Antonio da Ferrara.[8]

Many of the questions and problems surrounding Petrarch's uncollected poems can be articulated as the tension between these two poles, these two typologies of *disperse:* on the one hand, poems deriving from Petrarch's private archive and autograph papers; on the other, poems attributed to Petrarch in the vast manuscript tradition, a tradition built around a core corpus of authentic poems which circulated in the poet's own lifetime.[9] The problems raised by this division of Petrarch's uncollected rhymes are first and foremost philological and textual, as evident in the standard editions. Angelo Solerti's seminal edition of the *Disperse*, first published in 1909, collects 214 possible compositions. The most recent authoritative edition, by Laura Paulino, includes only twenty-one *Rime estravaganti.* Between these two violently contrasting canons, between Solerti's *Disperse* and Paolino's *Estravaganti*, what is a scholar to do? Although the contributors to this volume have been asked to answer the question, What is it? in relation to Petrarch's work, this cannot be answered without simultaneously asking the very difficult question, Which is it? Textual criticism and literary interpretation are inseparable here as elsewhere.[10]

The all-inclusive nature of Solerti's editorial project in *Rime disperse di Francesco Petrarca* is clear from its subtitle: "o a lui attribuite" (or attributed to him). In fact, the six sections of the edition move from greatest certainty of Petrarchan authorship under the heading "Rime disperse from autographs or apographs" to the least in the last section, "poems by other authors sometimes attributed to Petrarch." Without a more philologically rigorous apparatus, without any sort of manuscript tree, the scholar maneuvers in this sea of often distinctly mediocre poems at his or her own risk. And the various attempts at distinguishing Petrarch from pseudo-Petrarch based on internal evidence have suffered from inconsistencies and arbitrariness.[11] Yet Solerti's edition remains an invaluable resource because it illustrates the omnipresence of Petrarch in fourteenth and fifteenth-century Italy and the power of his name alone to legitimize a poem or collection of poems.

Given the vast and often unreliable manuscript tradition and the ensuing uncertainty of identifying a Petrarch among countless imitators and impostors, most recent critics have limited their investigations to the conservative selection of texts represented in the Paolino edition. The edition relies primarily on two codices, the autograph Vaticano Latino 3196 (*codice degli abbozzi*) and the Casanatense 924, a fifteenth-century deluxe edition of the *Canzoniere* and *Trionfi* in which a sixteenth-century humanist, probably from Pietro Bembo's entourage, has added marginal notes and *disperse* culled from a no longer extant Petrarchan autograph.[12] Paolino's selective canon also includes some of Petrarch's better known correspondences along with a few poems universally attributed to him in early manuscripts, such as the *canzone* to Azzo da Correggio, "Quel ch'à nostra natura in sé più degno."

While the frequent calls for caution in establishing the corpus of uncollected poems are justified, it is important to recognize to what extent our current expectations of authenticity and autograph proof regarding the *disperse* result from the poet's own efforts and innovations. In his autograph pages Petrarch treats these "damned" poems with the same attention to textual and contextual detail as he does the "saved" ones, revising, recopying, cross-referencing, and annotating the date, time, place, and circumstances of their composition and revision. In this way, he turns the very labor of writing, the consecrated presence of the author's hand, into a guarantee of authenticity, and subsequent nonautograph manuscript collections of his work will often reproduce such paratextual elements in order to appear similarly legitimate. As we have seen, even today scholars are wary of accepting any work not stemming from Petrarch's autograph papers, any poem that was out of his direct material control, truly dispersed—a clear mark of Petrarch's success in asserting his vernacular authority.

The tension between private autograph and public manuscript tradition brings us back to the question of why Petrarch excluded certain poems from the *Canzoniere* in the first place, the motives behind that peculiar oval symbol accompanying an early version of "Voglia mi sprona." As I anticipated above, a primary reason for the damnation of the *disperse* seems to be their ineluctable historicity, in particular their occasional nature: the corpus of *disperse* includes a surprising number of sonnet exchanges or *tenzoni* with contemporary minor poets such as Sennuccio del Bene, Antonio

Beccari da Ferrrara, Pietro Dietisalvi, and the count Ricciardo da Bagno. Indeed, a decisive eighteen of the twenty-one poems in the Paolino edition are written to or for others. Two sonnets, "Tal cavalier tutta una schiera atterra" and "Quella che gli animal' del mondo atterra," treating the theme of revenge, appear written at the behest of Petrarch's patron Cardinal Giovanni Colonna ("responsio mea, domino iubente," a reply of mine, the lord commanding, and "alia responsio mea, domino materiam dante e iubente," another reply of mine, the lord providing subject matter and commanding, according to marginal notes). And three sonnets written expressly to fulfill the request of the musician Confortino confirm the poet's contention in *Seniles* 5.2 that his vernacular pieces were sought after and highly marketable.[13]

Even a preliminary examination of the *disperse* reveals a Petrarch surprisingly involved in the exchanges, performances, and contingent and ephemeral functions of poetry that typify the northern courts of fourteenth-century Italy. In these poems, the social and communicative aspects of the poet's lyrics still dominate; he corresponds in them with a poetic community and he appeases his patrons. If the Petrarch of the *Canzoniere* is truly, according to Bosco, "senza storia" (without history),[14] his uncollected poems are undeniably in time, traveling across geographical space to specific intended readers. And the specific dates, locales, and circumstances annotated in the *codice degli abbozzi*—both for actual *disperse* and for those poems that will eventually be "absolved"—stand in sharp contrast with the diegetic and calendrical time of the *Canzoniere*. Indeed, considering the amount of criticism dedicated to the temporal structures of the *Rime sparse*, it is worth considering how the universalizing chronotopes of the *Canzoniere* potentially respond to the historicized time and place of the *disperse*. In the end, the formal and thematic obsession with time in the *Canzoniere* has the odd effect of removing the work from history, at least from the history of what the collection excludes.

At the same time, the border separating the *Canzoniere* from the *disperse* is not always intact. For example, at the time of the so-called Correggio redaction (roughly 1356–58), 38 of the 171 compositions are directed at interlocutors other than Laura, or roughly 23 percent of the entire collection.[15] This form of the anthology is much more choral and communicative, engaged with contemporary historical figures and extratextual events. In a sense, the history of the *Canzoniere* as a book can be expressed as a gradual dilution of the epistolary and historical elements of the Correggio form, a movement away from the occasional nature that also informs the *disperse*. Indeed, if we omit the laments for the dead, of the nearly two hundred poems added to later forms, only four are addressed to external historical figures. Yet despite this steady process of dehistoricization at the level of theme and content, physical redactions of the collection continued to circulate and enjoy a public reception throughout Petrarch's life; as Michele Feo reminds us, many more versions of the *Canzoniere* were published than we are currently aware of.[16] If we only treat the *Canzoniere* as a private, never-changing work, we miss its purchase in time, the significance of its being sent to such important political figures as Pandolfo Malatesta, lord in the Marches, and Azzo da Correggio, lord of Parma. The *disperse* thus help us recover the occasional nature of the *Canzoniere* as well, its status as a contextualized verbal act. Just as Petrarch sent the *dispersa* "Quel ch'à nostra natura" in 1341 to Azzo da Correggio, in 1356 he sent him an early version of the *Canzoniere*.

The *canzone* to Azzo da Correggio is in fact one of the most revealing cases of Petrarch's *disperse*. Written during a period of intense and mutual exchange between the poet and what one historian has labeled "the worst bandit of his era,"[17] the poem unabashedly celebrates Azzo's forceful takeover of Parma from Alberto and Mastino Della Scala in May 1341, depicting it as a republican victory over tyranny and comparing Azzo to Cato in his zeal for liberty. Petrarch's friendship with Azzo likely began in 1337 in Avignon, when, in the presence of Benedict XII and on behalf of Azzo, he defended the forced exile of the bishop of Parma Ugolino Rossi and the illegal seizure of his possessions. In 1341, the two friends and professional allies traveled together to see King Robert of Naples—Azzo to enlist the king's help in conquering Parma, Petrarch in search of the laurel wreath. According to Boccaccio, it was Azzo who facilitated the meeting between king and poet. Azzo accompanied Petrarch to his coronation in Rome, and the two returned to Parma, both victorious in their respective fields. Petrarch's success in this moment, his cherished laurel crown, is inevitably linked to Azzo, and he seems to acknowledge as much in the word play on the latter's name in the *canzone*, expressed as COR REGIO (regal heart), recalling the kind of paronomasia we are used to associating with the name of Laura.

Yet Petrarch excluded the *canzone* to Azzo da Correggio from the Correggio redaction and from all subsequent forms of the *Canzoniere*. Instead, he includes a *canzone* to Italy, "Italia mia" (*RVF* 128). Set in 1344–45, the topic of the poem is, once again, a violent battle for control of Parma among warring aristocratic families, including the Visconti, Este, Gonzaga, and Correggio factions. But in this Dantean lament against the evils of civil strife, Petrarch portrays himself as above the fray, politically neutral, *super partes*.[18] He writes: "per ver dire, / non per odio d'altrui né per disprezzo" (I am speaking to tell the truth, not from hatred or scorn of anyone [128.63–64]). The inclusion of "Italia mia" in the Correggio and the exclusion of "Quel ch'à nostra natura" are often reasonably explained by pointing to Petrarch's new patrons, the Visconti, with whom Azzo had a politically contentious relationship. Yet I would suggest that Petrarch's socially embedded position in the *dispersa*, regardless of its political content, necessitates its exclusion from the anthology. As part of an act of self-fashioning in the northern Italian courts, the *Canzoniere* cannot contradict the humanist trope of Petrarch's intellectual and political independence. Yet while Petrarch did not write "Quel ch'à nostra natura" at the behest of his lord ("domino iubente") strictly speaking, he does little to hide its propagandist elements; instead of originating in literary solitude, this *canzone* to Azzo explicitly boasts of being born away from books and in the midst of arms, "lunge da' libri nata in mezzo l'arme" (113).

Despite the different status, nature, and function of Petrarch's uncollected poems, scholars typically treat the *disperse* as the *Canzoniere*'s ugly little sister, searching for stylistic flaws to explain why the poems didn't make the cut. Certain *disperse* are studied more than others only because they are seen as influences on or early versions of perfected later forms found in the *Canzoniere*. No doubt many poems were further refined for inclusion in Vaticano Latino 3195, but a purely evolutionary perspective risks obfuscating the differentiated social roles of *rime sparse* and *rime disperse*, and why the former were deemed worthy of further refinement while the latter were eventually abandoned or condemned. Especially when they form part of correspondences or exchanges, the uncollected poems obey different rules, norms, and conventions and, as we shall see, are more concerned with participating in a literary conversation than with constructing an authorial lyric voice.[19] The discrete social and generic constraints guiding the uncollected poems should also be taken into consideration when evaluating individual *disperse* for entry into Petrarch's official canon, in order to better understand what might or might not be Petrarch. With these stakes in mind, I will briefly discuss a group of poems that not only challenges the traditional hierarchy between the *disperse* and the *Canzoniere*, but even the potential directionality of influence between them.

The *disperse* "Sì mi fan risentire a l'aura sparsi" and "Quella ghirlanda che la bella fronte" are both written for Sennuccio del Bene, Petrarch's most important poetic correspondent within and without the *Canzoniere*.

Sennuccio's family were high-ranking members in Florence's powerful Calimala (woolworkers) guild, and documentary evidence shows that Sennuccio's father, a wealthy and politically influential merchant, knew and had used the services of Petrarch's father, the notary Ser Petracco.[20] When an exiled Sennuccio arrived in Avignon around 1313, the groundwork for his friendship with Petrarch would have already been laid by family ties and similar political fortunes.

More important for our purposes, Sennuccio was also an accomplished poet in Italian, writing in a late stilnovist vein, and his exchanges with Petrarch form the basis of a sophisticated literary friendship. At least six poems in the *Canzoniere* and three *disperse* are addressed to Sennuccio, and two of Sennuccio's extant poems are addressed to Petrarch.[21] In these poems, Sennuccio emerges as the privileged and almost sole witness to Petrarch's love story, sharing the wondrous vision of Laura at a meeting among the three in "Quella ghirlanda che la bella fronte," asked to intervene with her on his friend's behalf in "Aventuroso più d'altro terreno" (*Rerum vulgarium fragmenta* 108), and asked to wake up Petrarch if he sees Laura first in "Sì come il padre del folle Fetonte." The poetic friendship is sealed by a literary signature distinguishing the poems exchanged between the two, the rare identification of Laura either as the dawn, *l'aurora*, or, even more strikingly, as simply "Laura," sans wordplay or homonym.[22]

Although no response exists for the first *dispersa* in question, "Sì mi fan risentire a l'aura sparsi," the manuscript tradition universally identifies it as directed at Sennuccio:

> Sì mi fan risentire a l'aura sparsi
> i mille e dolci nodi in fin a l'arco,
> che dormendo e vegghiando ora non varco
> che la mia fantasia possa acquetarsi.
>
>   Or veggio lei di novi atti adornarsi,
> cinger l'arco e 'l turcasso e farsi al varco
> e sagittarmi, or vo d'amor sì carco
> che 'l dolce peso non porria stimarsi.
>
>   Poi mi ricordo di Venus iddea,
> qual Virgilio descrisse 'n sua figura,
> e parmi Laura in quell'atto vedere
>   or pietosa ver' me, or farsi rea:
> io vergognoso e 'n atto di paura
> quasi smarrir per forza di piacere.

[So much do the thousands of sweet curls scattered to the horizon resound to me, that sleeping and watching, there is no way that my fantasy can quiet itself.

First I see her adorn herself with a new guise, donning the bow and quiver and moving to a place from which to shoot me with her arrow, then I go so full of love that its sweet burden cannot be measured.

Then I recall the image of Venus, the goddess as Virgil describes her, and I seem to see in her the figure of Laura.

First she shows pity for me, and then she seems cruel; and ashamed and afraid, I almost faint under the force of so much pleasure.]

The image of Laura in the quatrains is characteristic of Petrarch's poetic "grammar" and would not be unfamiliar to contemporaries; she is described as a huntress, with bow and arrow, her hair flowing in the breeze with characteristic wordplay on her name and the breeze, *l'aura*. This visual recollection torments Petrarch's imagination and subsequently triggers, in the *terzine*, a textual recollection of Venus disguised as a huntress as she appears to Aeneas (*Aeneid* 1.318–19). Several scholars have cited the explicitness of this Venus-Laura simile as evidence of the imperfection and immaturity of the poem. [23]

In addition, the heavy-handedness and repetition of the *dispersa* are seen as contributing to its exclusion from the *Canzoniere* in lieu of the similar, but improved sonnet "Né così bello il sol già mai levarsi" (*Rerum vulgarium fragmenta* 144):

> Né così bello il sol già mai levarsi
> quando 'l ciel fosse più de nebbia scarco,
> né dopo pioggia vidi 'l celeste arco
> per l'aere in color' tanti varïarsi,
>
> in quanti fiammeggiando trasformarsi,
> nel dì ch'io presi l'amoroso incarco,
> quel viso al quale, et son del mio dir parco,
> nulla cosa mortal pote aguagliarsi.
>
> I' vidi Amor che' begli occhi volgea
> soave sì, ch'ogni altra vista oscura
> da indi in qua m'incominciò apparere.
>
> Sennuccio, i' 'l vidi, et l'arco che tendea,
> tal che mia vita poi non fu secura,
> et è sì vaga anchor del rivedere.

[I never saw the sun rise so fair when the sky is most free of mist,
nor after a rain the heavenly arc diversify itself through the air
with so many colors,
as on the day when I took on my burden of love, I saw her face
flaming transform itself, which—and I am sparing of words—no
mortal thing can equal.
I saw Love moving her lovely eyes so gently that every other sight
from then on began to seem dark to me,
Sennuccio, I saw him and the bow he was drawing, so that afterward my life was no longer free of care and still yearns to see him
again.]

The two compositions are linked by shared rhymes, the placement of verb
infinitives as verse endings, and the repeated use of *arco* both in rhyme
position and within the verse. As in the *dispersa*, the main theme in "Né
così bello il sol" is the continuing power of an initial vision of Laura. But
in the *Canzoniere* poem the memorial image is pushed farther into the past,
emphasized by the perfect verb tenses, especially the thrice-repeated "vidi,
vidi, vidi" (I saw, I saw, I saw; [lines 3, 9, 12]). The supernatural nature
of Laura, moreover, "nulla cosa mortal" (no mortal thing; [l. 8]) is left to
speak for itself, without the explicit comparison to Virgil's Venus.

If this were all, the two poems could serve, as they often have, as an
interesting example of *variantistica* (the study of textual variants). When
viewed in these terms, "Sì mi fan risentire" would at best lose the stylistic
prize to *Rerum vulgarium fragmenta* 144; at worst it could be reasonably excluded from Petrarch's canon as an inferior, even slavish, appropriation of
some of the most well-known Petrarchan images and phrases.[24] The relationship is complicated, however, when we examine both poems in light of
"Erano i capei d'oro a l'aura sparsi" (90):

> Erano i capei d'oro a l'aura sparsi
> che 'n mille dolci nodi gli avolgea,
> e 'l vago lume oltra misura ardea
> di quei begli occhi ch'or ne son sì scarsi;
>   e 'l viso di pietosi color' farsi,
> non so se vero o falso, mi parea:
> i' che l' ésca amorosa al petto avea,
> qual meraviglia se di sùbito arsi?
>   Non era l'andar suo cosa mortale,
> ma d'angelica forma, et le parole

sonavan altro, che pur voce humana:
    uno spirto celeste, un vivo sole
fu quel ch'i' vidi; et se non fosse or tale,
piagha per allentar d'arco non sana.

[Her golden hair was loosed to the breeze, which turned it in a
thousand sweet knots, and the lovely light burned without measure in her eyes, which are now so stingy of it;
and it seemed to me (I know not whether truly or falsely) her face
took on the color of pity: I, who had the tinder of love in my breast,
what wonder is it if I suddenly caught fire?
Her walk was not that of a mortal thing but of some angelic form,
and her words sounded different from merely human voice:
a celestial spirit, a living sun was what I saw, and if she were not
such now, a wound is not healed by the loosening of the bow.]

In many ways this sonnet has more points in common with either of the
previous poems than they have with each other. Most obviously, "Sì mi
fan risentire" and *Rerum vulgarium fragmenta* 90 seem deliberately linked
by the shared phrasing in the opening lines of each, both referring to the
sweet knots ("i mille e dolci nodi") of Laura's wind-blown hair ("a l'aura
sparsi"). Also of note are the shared *arsi/ ea* rhymes for all three poems;
the image of the beloved as archer-huntress; "color farsi" (90.5) and "color
tanti variarsi" (144.4); and "nulla cosa mortal" (144.8) and "non era l'andar
suo cosa mortale" (90.9). In addition, the imperfect tenses in *Rerum vulgarium fragmenta* 90 reproduce the durative "or . . . or" syntax of "Sì mi fan
risentire a l'aura sparsi" while the single perfect "vidi" in line 13 creates the
same haunting distance from the memorial image as the repeated perfect
verbs of poem 144. Finally and most importantly, in poem 90 the appari-
tion of Laura-deity returns as an unforgettable memorial image, but now
the Venus-huntress simile is fleshed out with all of its implications and distributed throughout the entire sonnet.

    So what is it? Or rather, which is it? Is "Sì mi fan risentire a l'aura
sparsi" the imperfect original source material for *Rerum vulgarium fragmenta*
144 or 90? Or 144, 90, 143 (as has also been claimed), and who knows
how many other poems?[25] What if the relation between the *disperse* and
the *Canzoniere* were not simply one of variants and stylistic evolution? If
we take a step back, for a moment, and recognize the status of "Sì mi fan
risentire" as part of a historicized literary exchange and not just a private
moment of lyric experimentation, is it not possible that one or more of the

poems collected in the *Canzoniere* influenced the *dispersa* and not the other way around?[26] Specifically, could "Sì mi fan risentire a l'aura sparsi" be a self-reflexive gloss on "Erano i capei d'or a l'aura sparsi" played out for the literary relationship of Petrarch-Sennuccio?

This would explain the explicitness of the allusions in "Sì mi fan risentire," perfectly appropriate within the metaliterary conventions of the *tenzone*, in which poets also often appropriate the content and style of their interlocutors. In this case, Petrarch's citation of Virgil's text ("Poi mi ricordo di Venus iddea,/ qual Virgilio descrisse 'n sua figura" [lines 9–10]) in "Sì mi fan risentire" would match Sennuccio's evocation of Ovid ("Chè mai Ovidio o altri non discrisse/ valor di donna tanto affigurata" [lines 9–10]) in the sonnet "Non si potria compiutamente dire." These sorts of direct citations are not uncommon in Sennuccio, who liberally quotes the works of others, including contemporaries Boccaccio and Dante.[27] In fact, critics note that both "Sì mi fan risentire" and "Sennuccio, i' vo' che sapi in qual manera" (*Rerum vulgarium fragmenta* 112) contain strikingly similar passages in Boccaccio and suggest that Sennuccio played a mediating role in either introducing the Italian works of Petrarch to Boccaccio or—more provocatively—those of Boccaccio to Petrarch.[28] While leaving aside the issue of who influenced whom first, it seems clear that Sennucccio does more than mediate; rather, together with his exiled compatriot, he self-consciously reflects upon *auctores* old and new. Petrarch celebrates this literary conversation with Sennuccio in the opening lines of the sonnet that follows "Senuccio, i' vo' che sapi" in the *Canzoniere* (*Rerum vulgarium fragmenta* 113): "Qui dove mezzo son, Sennuccio mio / (così foss'io intero, et voi contento)" (Here where I only half am, my Sennuccio / [would I were here entirely, and you happy]). These lines echo both Horace's description of Virgil as "animae dimidium meae" (half of my soul [*Carmen* 1.3.8]) as well as the choral atmosphere of Dante's "Guido, i' vorrei che tu e Lapo ed io."[29] Horace and Virgil and Dante and Cavalcanti are not only precedents for Petrarch and Sennuccio's literary friendship, their texts (and the ability to recognize allusions to their texts) form the fabric of the latters' poetic exchanges.

This proposed literary conversation/commentary can shed light on the relationship between the *disperse* and the poems eventually finding a place within the *Canzoniere*, a complex relationship in which the former are much more than a prehistory of the latter. In the case of "Sì mi fan risentire," Petrarch appears to be recalling his own poem about the source of his attraction for Laura, the sonnet "Erano i capei d'or a l'aura sparsi," and then citing Virgil as the source of that source. Or, even more drawn out but hardly less suggestive, the typically Petrarchan image in the *dispersa* of

Laura-huntress with her hair in the breeze would set off a chain of intertextual recollections—including the mediation of "Erano i capei d'or"—and
culminate in a return to their source in Virgil in order to contemplate the
relationship between the two representations of Venus—Petrarch's Venus
versus Virgil's Venus. As we know from his own gloss on the Virgilian Venus in *Seniles* 4.5, Petrarch was perfectly capable of moving fluidly between
a passage of his own poetry and literary criticism and even allegoresis.[30]

The potential metaliterary nature of "Sì mi fan risentire" is bolstered by
another *dispersa*, "Quella ghirlanda che la bella fronte," also addressed to
Sennuccio:

> Quella ghirlanda che la bella fronte
> cingeva di color tra perle e grana,
> Sennuccio mio, pàrveti cosa umana
> o d'angeliche forme al mondo gionte?
>   Vedestù l'atto e quelle chiome conte,
> che spesso il cor mi morde e mi risana?
> vedustù quel piacer che m'allontana
> d'ogni vile pensier ch'al cor mi monte?
>   Udistù 'l suon delle dolci parole?
> Mirastù quell'andar leggiadro altero
> dietro a chi ò disviati i pensier' miei?
>   Soffristù 'l sguardo invidïoso al sole?
> Or sai per ch'io ardo vivo e spero,
> ma non so dimandar quel ch'io vorrei.

[That garland that encircled her beautiful brow with a color between pearl and pale yellow, my friend Sennuccio, did it seem to
you a human thing? Or an angelic form come into the world?
Did you see her face and her adorned locks that often gnaw at my
heart and then heal it again? Did you see the beauty that keeps
away every unpleasant thought that afflicts my heart?
Did you hear the sound of her sweet voice? Did you watch those
noble and graceful movements that cause my thoughts to follow
after them?
Did you suffer from that glance that rivals the sun? Then you know
why I live and die and hope, but do not dare ask for my desire.]

To my knowledge, the connection between this sonnet and *Rerum vulgarium fragmenta* 90 in the *Canzoniere* has never been pointed out. Yet in addi-

tion to the shared rhyme words of *parole, umana, sole,* and *sana,* and near identical phrasing such as "cosa mortale/ ma d'angelica forma" (90.9–10) and "cosa umana o d'angeliche forme" (lines 3–4) of the *dispersa,* the poem to Sennuccio is clearly another attempt to involve his friend as an almost evangelical witness to Laura's divinity. Did his friend see (*vedestù*), hear (*udistù*), admire (*mirastù*), and bear (*soffristù*) the superhuman vision as he did? If the *dispersa* "Sì mi fan risentire" teases out the Virgilian implications of poem 90, "Quella ghirlanda" plays on its roots in stilnovism, such as the miraculous effects of the *donna-angelo,* especially her gait, on others; not surprisingly, these traits, echoing Dante's "Tanto gentile," are also frequently found in Sennuccio's poetry.[31] Finally, the entire structure of "Quella ghirlanda" is built around the similar situation and syntax of "Se' tu colui che hai trattato sovente," an exchange between Dante and the ladies in the *Vita nuova* where they share the vision of a grieving Beatrice, evidence, once again, that Petrarch values Sennuccio as both an essential witness and subtle reader.

If *Rerum vulgarium fragmenta* 144 is, after all this, deliberately reminiscent of "Sì mi fan risentire," it is a reminiscence with quite a bit of personal and literary history behind it—and not a small amount of pathos as well. Rather than simply an improved version of the *dispersa,* this poem recalls "Sì mi fan risentire" because the latter poem was part of a formative literary conversation for Petrarch regarding his own poetry and that of his predecessors and influences. But by the time the sonnet was inserted into the *Canzoniere* (at the beginning of the Chigiano section),[32] the original intended recipient of the poem had given way to the implied reader of the anthology. Sennuccio, Petrarch's other half and faithful witness and participant in the younger poet's amorous travails and poetic development, died soon after Laura in 1349. As demonstrated by Laura Paolino,[33] the two deaths are inextricably linked in the notes and drafts of Vaticano Latino 3196. While Sennuccio was the natural recipient of the first redaction of the lament for Laura's death—"altri non v'è che intenda i miei danni" (there is no other who understands my pains)[34]—Petrarch writes in a marginal note that the sonnet on the death of Sennuccio (*Rerum vulgarium fragmenta* 287) and the one on Dawn, *Aurora* (*Rerum vulgarium fragmenta* 291), were the stimulus necessary to finish a new version of the lament for Laura ("Che debb'io far? Che mi consigli, Amore" [*Rerum vulgarium fragmenta* 268]): "28 November 1349, between 6 and 9 in the morning. I now feel in the right mind to finish this [i.e., canzone], on account of the sonnets on the Dawn and the death of Sennuccio, which I have composed in these days and which have elevated my spirits."[35] In the sonnet mourning Sennuccio's

death, "Sennuccio mio, benché doglioso et solo," Petrarch imagines his literary conversation with his friend transplanted in the heavens, as he asks
Sennuccio to greet Laura as well as the poets Guittone, Cino, Dante, and
Franceschino degli Albizzi. It is especially telling that Petrarch links this
poem for his dead friend with *Rerum vulgarium fragmenta* 291("Quand'io
veggio del ciel scender l'Aurora") because the sonnet marks the last time
he refers to Laura by the pun "l'Aurora" and directly as "Laura" (l. 4)—an
elegiac tribute sealing a collective poetic experience.

In some sense, the movement from the *disperse* to Sennuccio to the poems
addressed to Sennuccio in the *Canzoniere* can be described as a movement
from poetic community to isolation, from *tenzone* to ghostly lyric mono-
logue. While the *codice degli abbozzi*, as it now stands, begins with a transcription of Sennuccio's "Oltra l'usato modo si rigira," no one responds in
the *Canzoniere*. The contiguous placement of *Rerum vulgarium fragmenta* 143
and 144 at the beginning of the Chigiano extension—two of the last poems addressed to historical figures to be included in the *Canzoniere*—thus
creates yet another level of distance and isolation. In poem 143 the visual-
textual memorial chain behind the image of Laura is sparked by another
poet's words, "Quand'io v'odo parlar si dolcemente." The poet who speaks
so sweetly, "dolcemente," to Petrarch has been identified as Sennuccio himself.[36] In this light, the perfect tenses in *Rerum vulgarium fragmenta* 144 that
call forth the fateful image of Laura—an image that the author hopes in
vain to see again—evoke the memory of both a complicated series of texts
and a poetic friend ("Sennuccio mio"), with whom Petrarch once could recall this shared community of texts; it is, in other words, a memory about
remembering.

The naming of and apostrophe to Sennuccio in both the *disperse* and the
Canzoniere is one of the last extratextual links of the collection, resurrect-
ing a historical moment of poetic experimentation and poetic collaboration.
From this point on, Petrarch's anthology will become increasingly a closed
system, and this self-referentiality has been the subject of some of the most
influential essays on the *Canzoniere*, as it is heralded as a mark of the poet's striking modernity.[37] Yet it is worth noting that the strategies of exclusion necessary to construct this autonomous lyric self come at a cost, and,
with respect to poems to and about Sennuccio, the loss of reference and
escape from historicity involved seem more compensatory than liberating.
The tone is instead one of mourning for a time when Petrarch was clearly
writing to someone other than Posterity and "Laura" and "Sennuccio" were
more than just a name.[38]

PART II

LITERARY DEBUT, LATIN HUMANISM, AND ORATIONS

CHAPTER FOUR

THE REBIRTH OF THE ROMANS AS MODELS OF CHARACTER • *De viris illustribus*

Ronald G. Witt

To judge from Petrarch's dialogue *Secretum*, the two works on which his hopes for future glory rested were his Latin epic *Africa* and his collection of historical biographies *De viris illustribus* (*On Famous Men*):

> You would rather abandon yourself than your books. I will press my case. To what end I do so remains to be seen, but certainly I do it in good faith. Lay down the great burdens of history. The deeds of the Romans have been sufficiently depicted both by their own reputation and through the ingenuity of others. Abandon Africa and leave it to its own possessors, for there you will acquire no glory, either for Scipio or for yourself. Scipio could not be extolled more highly than he already is, and you are only struggling behind him on an indirect path. Once these things have been put in their place, then finally return yourself to yourself.[1]

In the event, Augustinus's appeal to Franciscus (Augustinus and Franciscus are the two interlocutors) proved unsuccessful. Petrarch worked on both at least sporadically until his last days, but both remained unfinished at the author's death. However, whereas the conception of *Africa* appears to have remained essentially consistent over the years, that of *De viris illustribus* was radically altered at least twice.

Petrarch's contemporaries or near-contemporaries wrote history using three formats: universal history, communal history, and biography. Among Petrarch's acquaintances, two members of the Colonna family, Landolf (d. 1331) and his nephew Giovanni (d. 1340), composed universal histories dealing with human events as a continuum from Adam down to their own day.[2] Both spent many years in Avignon in the period when Petrarch was in residence there.

Communal historiography thrived in northern Italy in the same period. Riccobaldo da Ferrara (c. 1313) composed a Latin history of his native Ferrara. Albertino Mussato's *Historia augusta Henrici VII* (1315), an examination of the ill-fated expedition of Henry VII to Italy (1310–13), was largely limited to its impact on northern Italian communes and especially Padua.[3] About fifteen years after Mussato, Ferreto dei Ferretti of Verona wrote his own version of Henry's three years of campaigning in Italy from the point of view of his own city.[4] These histories had been preceded by a rich tradition of city chronicles in northern and central Italy beginning in the mid-twelfth century.[5]

The biographical tradition was represented by the same Giovanni Colonna who authored his *De viris illustribus* before leaving Avignon for Rome in 1338, and by another of Petrarch's friends, Guglielmo Pastrengo, who wrote two works containing biographies. Pastrengo's *De viris illustribus*, like that of Giovanni Colonna, recounted the lives of famous pagan and Christian writers, while his *De originibus* condensed biographies of many of the same famous men helter-skelter with definitions and etymologies of, among other things, geographical sites, peoples, and stones.[6] Because they dealt with writers and thinkers from all ages, these works were a variety of universal history.

In choosing to follow the *De viris illustribus* format in his first version of the work, Petrarch innovated in four ways. First of all, Colonna's and Pastrengo's biographies were always very brief: those of Colonna in print rarely exceeded 1,400 words and Pastrengo's often only a few sentences. By contrast, although sometimes only three or four pages, Petrarch's could be long: that of Scipio contains 20,000 words and that of Caesar a total of 70,000.[7] Second, while their Latin style was undistinguished, Petrarch's Latin in *De viris illustribus* constituted the most consistent classicizing found in his corpus.[8] Third, while the biographies by the two other authors covered a wide variety of notable individuals, Petrarch concentrated solely on military heroes and civic leaders. Finally, he focused on ancient Romans.

For Petrarch no society in history had equaled that of ancient Rome in the extent of its empire and the greatness of character of its rulers. "What else, then," he asked late in life, "is all history if not the praise of Rome?"[9] Especially disgusted with the weakness and corruption of both secular and ecclesiastical leadership in his own time, he hoped that by eloquently recreating the lives of ancient Roman heroes, he might arouse the hearts and minds of his contemporaries to imitate their example.

Consequently, despite his innovations in the genre, Petrarch, like most medieval historians, composed his biographies for the purpose of enhancing virtuous conduct. As he wrote in what we shall see was the preface to the last version of the work (1371–74), "In my book, nothing is found except what leads to virtues or to the contraries of virtues. For, unless I am mistaken, this is the profitable goal for the historian: to point out to the readers those things that are to be followed and those to be avoided."[10] Given that his stated objective was "to describe the events themselves," Petrarch succinctly outlined his methodology for accomplishing this purpose in the same preface of the work: "I have decided to collect or rather almost to compress into one place, certain illustrious men who flourished in outstanding glory and whose memory has been handed down to us in diverse and widely scattered volumes through the skill of many learned men."[11]

He drew for his materials on ancient Roman historians and poets, principally Lucan, and combined them in his own way so as to attain the greatest moral effect: "For what was lacking in one author I have supplied from another; there were still others whose brevity made them unclear so that I had to make them more lucid. Finally, there were those authors whose sentences were dispersed in other sources and these I have joined together and from the disparate sentences made a whole."[12] Amidst the contradictions found in the ancient accounts, he relied on the verisimilitude of the narrative and on the authority of its author. Although this kind of methodology points to a "cut-and-paste" product, at least in the longer biographies of Scipio and Caesar, Petrarch, through the use of his historical imagination, was able to create distinctively personal accounts of his heroes' lives.[13]

Relative to its importance for Petrarch himself, the *De viris illustribus* appeared in print very late. Not included in the classic four-volume *Opera omnia* published at Basel in 1554, it was first published by Carl Ernst Christoph Schneider over a period of six years in four volumes as *De viris illustribus libri* (Breslau, 1829–34), based on MS IV of the University of Breslau.[14] In this edition the work consisted of a short preface and biographies of twenty-three heroes, of which twenty were Roman from Romulus to Trajan and three ancient foreigners, Hannibal, Pyrrhus, and Alexander. Schneider had previously published a twenty-fourth life, *De vita et rebus gestis C. Julii Caesaris* (Leipzig, 1827), based on a fifteenth-century incunable, which attributed the work to Julius Celsus.[15]

A second edition of the *De viris illustribus* was published forty years later by Luigi Razzolini, who published thirty-five *vitae*, attributing thirty-one to Petrarch and four to Lombardo della Seta.[16] Accompanied by a *volgarizzamento* by Donato degli Albanzani, the Latin edition was largely based on Scheidner's readings of Breslau MS IV, supplemented by the Biblioteca apostolica vaticana, Vaticano Latino 4523.[17]

In 1890, however, Pierre de Nolhac announced his discovery of a new manuscript of Petrarch's *De viris illustribus* in the Bibliothèque nationale of Paris (6069 I) significantly different in character from that heretofore identified with that title.[18] This manuscript did not contain the twenty-three *vitae* of the editions published by Schneider and Razzolini, but instead began with a long preface followed by twelve *vitae* of biblical and mythological figures of which the last, the *De Hercule*, remained incomplete. De Nolhac theorized that these twelve lives were the product of an earlier version of the *De viris illustribus* that preceded the version devoted solely to ancient Roman heroes.[19]

Although this was a departure from previous medieval works that had focused only on men of action and neglected poets and philosophers, this version's concern for completeness reflected a lingering allegiance to medieval encyclopedism. For this reason de Nolhac maintained that the more ecumenical plan of *De viris illustribus* preceded the "Roman" plan and predated *Africa* (c. 1339).[20] Once devoted to composing the Latin epic, de Nolhac reasoned, Petrarch narrowed the scope of *De viris illustribus* so as to use the prose history as a background for the historical poem.

Primarily through the work of Carlo Calcaterra and Guido Martellotti, this chronology of the broader plan preceding a "Roman" plan has now been reversed.[21] According to Martellotti, the first authorial version of the *De viris illustribus* envisaged a series of *vitae* running from Romulus to Titus.[22] As Augustinus remarked in the *Secretum:* "extending now your hand to greater works, you have undertaken a book of history from King Romulus to Titus Caesar, an immense work demanding time and labor."[23] In the light of current debates surrounding the composition of the *Secretum*, this passage may have been written either in 1342–43 or during the revisions of the work in 1347, 1349, or 1353.[24] Petrarch's marginal note in a Suetonius manuscript, which he used between 1338 and 1342, referring to "liber de viris illustribus populi romani" (book of illustrious men of the Roman people) indicates, however, that the "Roman plan" dates at least to 1342.[25]

For Petrarch, the presence of three non-Romans, Pyrrhus, Alexander, and Hannibal, would not have contradicted the "Roman plan."[26] The *vitae* of Pyrrhus and Hannibal were vital to his Roman focus because of their important effects on the history of Rome, whereas by writing a *vita* of Alexander, Petrarch was able to compare his conquests with those of the Romans, as did Livy in a long digression in *De urbe condita* 9.17–19. Like Livy, Petrarch concluded that had Alexander faced the Romans in battle, he would most certainly have been defeated.[27]

Martellotti established that already by 1338 or 1339, before beginning

Africa, Petrarch had written a *Vita Scipionis* to serve as the historical basis for his epic poem. This earliest version of the *vita* was almost certainly
what the character of Scipio's father had in mind when, near the beginning
of *Africa,* he mentions that the hero had been celebrated in another place.[28]
A second, more extensive *Vita Scipionis,* written before 1343, was included
as one of the twenty-three lives in the first edition of the *De viris illustribus* —
the twenty-fourth, *De gestis Cesaris* (*On the Deeds of Caesar*), belongs to the
1360s.[29] Whether or not the other twenty-two lives, those running from
Romulus to Cato, were also finished by 1343 cannot be as securely established. Nevertheless, Martellotti holds that they belong to the years 1342
and 1343, a period of intense work on the *vitae* in the Vaucluse.[30]

Petrarch's second version of *De viris illustribus,* that is, what de Nolhac
considered the earliest version, is currently dated to the period 1351–53,
during Petrarch's last residence in the Vaucluse.[31] The twenty-three lives of
the first edition are preceded, as has been noted, by a preface and twelve
vitae of biblical and mythological figures. The preface clearly limits Petrarch's consideration of heroes to the ancients: "I confess that I should
prefer to write on things seen rather than read, contemporary rather than
ancient, so that posterity would receive from me information about the distant past. However, being tired and desirous of rest, I thank those contemporary princes who free me from this labor, for they contributed material
not for history but for satire."[32]

In assigning this edition to 1351–53, Martellotti relies on what he considers two references to the work in Petrarch's writings at the time. In the
second book of the *Invective contra medicum,* composed in 1353, Petrarch
mentions that he is writing a work entitled *De viris illustribus* dedicated to
those who are illustrious "from every century."[33] An insertion in a letter
actually sent in 1349 but edited as *Familiares* 8.3 in 1351–52 refers to a
work "bringing together illustrious men from all lands and centuries" as
among his current writing projects in the Vaucluse.[34] The letter as sent
omitted this reference. As late as 1354, in a letter to Lelius, he reports that
when recently in conversation with Charles IV at Mantua, he promised the
emperor a place in *De viris illustribus* if Charles showed through his deeds
that it was merited.[35]

My sense, however, is that the preface to the expanded version of *De
viris illustribus* (de Nolhac's Paris 6069 I) indicates that an "ancient heroes"
plan was to be followed in the text, while the references used by Martellotti to establish the dating of this second version reflect an "all-ages" plan.
If we are to accept the dating of these references, then the second version
(Paris 6069 I) belongs at the latest to 1351–52, at which time Petrarch

apparently decided to expand his treatment of heroes to include those of all ages. Because there is no evidence that he tried to implement this design, there is no reason to speak of the project as an edition. At least a return to a plan, whether the "Roman" or the "ancient heroes," seems indicated by his response to Agapito Colonna, who in 1359 had requested that Petrarch include him in *De viris illustribus*. Petrarch explains denying Agapito a place in the book: "And yet had I touched upon illustrious men of our age, I would not say you—that in anger I do not seem to flatter, a thing I do not do when calm—but certainly I would not have passed over your uncle and your father. I have been unwilling, however, for so few famous names, to bear my pen so far and through such darkness. Consequently, sparing subject matter and labor, I have decided to fix a limit to my history long before this century."[36]

The initiative for still another version of *De viris illustribus* came from Francesco da Carrara, lord of Padua and Petrarch's patron, who called on him, presumably about 1368, to suggest famous Romans beginning with Romulus to be depicted in a new room in his palace and to prepare a new edition of *De viris illustribus*.[37] The request inspired Petrarch to take up again the "Roman" *De viris illustribus*. Between 1351–52 and 1366, he had compiled an even more extensive *vita* of Scipio and, in the 1360s, undertook writing a monumental life of Caesar.[38]

Petrarch's plan for a third edition was to extend the *vitae* to thirty-six heroes down to Trajan, but he lived only long enough to touch up twenty-two of the earlier twenty-three biographies, add the third version of the *Vita Scipionis*, along with the *De gestis Cesaris* and a new, shorter preface. By 1379 Lombardo della Seta finished the original design for thirty-six lives with twelve new *vitae* from Titus Quintus Flaminius to Trajan. The work now bore the title *Quorundam virorum illustrium epithoma* (Essay [on the lives] of certain illustrious men), specifically suggesting that the work did not claim to cover the lives of all famous Roman leaders.[39]

Petrarch initiated yet a fourth edition, again at the request of Carrara, perhaps in the very last year of his life, which has become known as the *Compendium*.[40] Following the "Roman" plan again, Petrarch undertook to write condensations of the thirty-six lives that he projected for the Carrara edition.[41] Of the fourteen lives he finished before his death, one, the life of Romulus, is actually condensed, the life of Cincinnatus is thoroughly rewritten, three are identical with those in the third edition, and the remainder are shortened by the omission of a few sentences.[42] In the case of this work as well, Lombardo completed the project by adding the twenty-two left undone by Petrarch.

The critical edition of the first twenty-three lives of *De viris illustribus* by Guido Martellotti published in 1964 in volume 2 of the Edizione Nazionale delle opere di Francesco Petrarch is based on this third version of the work, and includes the first version of the *Vita Scipionis* in an appendix. Martellotti also published the three versions of the *Vita Scipionis* separately.[43] Martellotti died before he could complete the second volume dedicated entirely to the twenty-fourth, the *De gestis Cesaris*.

As regards Petrarch's intellectual development, Petrarch's second version of the *De viris illustribus* (Paris 6069 I), mingling biblical, mythological, and ancient secular figures, has led scholars to seek an explanation for the revision of the initial Roman format of the work. Martellotti has shown that Petrarch's new appreciation of the histories other than of Rome had its literary counterpart in his *Triumphus Famae*, written as well in the early 1350s.[44] Already a draft of the work (ca. 1350) exhibited an enlarged conception of those deserving to be regarded as "illustrious men."[45] In this version Caesar stands at the right hand of the Goddess of Fame while grouped around the two are Augustus, Drusus, Scipio Africanus, Publicus Cornelius Scipio Emilianus, and other republican heroes, together with the line of "good" emperors from Vespasian to Theodosius.[46] Present as well are Hannibal, a host of Greek heroes, and three kings of Israel, David, Judas Maccabaeus, and Joshua.[47] Alexander, King Arthur, and Charlemagne conclude the list.

The definitive version of the work (early 1350s) provides a more organized presentation of the heroes marching in Fame's triumph: (1) Roman heroes down to Marcus Aurelius; (2) Greek, Carthaginian, and Persian heroes; (3) biblical heroes; (4) famous women; and (5) ancient eastern and modern European kings.[48] Scipio Africanus now shares a position equal to that of Caesar in proximity to the goddess. Significantly eleven of the twelve biblical and mythological figures celebrated in the contemporary, second version of *De viris illustribus* are represented in the triumph.[49]

While incorrectly identifying the "all-ages" plan with the "ancient heroes" plan of the second version of the *De viris illustribus*, Guido Martellotti and Hans Baron have interpreted this opening to non-Roman history as the result of a change in Petrarch's vision of history. While recognizing that the growing importance of Petrarch's religious concerns might have led to a growing interest at least in biblical heroes, Martellotti tends to explain the broadening of his historical vision largely as a result of Petrarch's widening knowledge of the sources, his recent acquaintance with Boccaccio, among other scholars, and his appreciation of Christian Rome during his pilgrimage of 1350 as other influences.[50]

Baron prefers to see Petrarch's deepening religiosity, evidenced by the *De otio religioso* and the *De vita solitaria,* as awakening in the middle-aged man a need to integrate his recent readings in Christian literature with his conception of the historically important. This urge led Petrarch to seek the new historical sources emphasized by Martellotti, sources that told him more about the imperial period of Roman history.[51] For Baron the new version of *De viris illustribus* (1351–53), featuring "the traditional conmixture of the biblical and Roman past," serves as one among a number of indications that in these years Petrarch developed a new affinity with medieval thought.[52]

This growing tendency to favor the history of the Empire over that of the Republic led Petrarch to reevaluate his attitude toward monarchy and republican government. Baron and Martellotti have both pointed to *Triumphus Famae* as foreshadowing the laudatory interpretation of Caesar in *De gestis Cesaris* in the following decade. According to both authors, prior to 1350 Petrarch's general assessment of Caesar's character had been largely the negative one found in Lucan's *Pharsalia.*[53] Martellotti tends to ascribe the subsequent reversal of Petrarch's view of Caesar and the empire more specifically to his contact with new texts, the *Historia augusta* and Caesar's *Commentarii* still attributed to Julius Celsus, whereas Baron explains the change as part of a general revision of Petrarch's attitude toward history and politics.[54]

Baron argues that the new sources only became important to Petrarch because he (1) had already been disillusioned with republicanism after the fall of Cola da Rienzo and (2) had come to embrace Augustine's view of Caesar's murderers as motivated by jealousy.[55] For Baron, like the new interest in universal history, Petrarch's shift of preference from republicanism to monarchy indicated a shift of thinking in later life away from ideas heralding later humanist thought.

Both scholars, however, would have to admit that Petrarch's scholarly interests in writing a universal ancient history were short-lived. There is no indication that he continued to work on the text after 1352 when, conceptually, it had become an "all-ages" plan. His third life of Scipio and the *De gestis Cesaris* of the 1360s show that by then he had returned to the earlier Roman focus, and his ambitious outline for the third version of work in response to Carrara's request suggests that to the end of his life he never lost interest in the Roman plan.[56]

As for the two scholars' explanations for Petrarch's exceptionally long biography of Caesar, it should be said, first of all, that Petrarch almost certainly would have included a biography of Caesar had the first version from Romulus to Titus been completed. Second, the newly discovered material, giving him more information about Caesar than he had about any of the other Roman heroes, helps to explain its length. Third, a study of Petrarch's attitude toward Caesar over the course of his life shows that he never fully approved or disapproved of Caesar's career.[57] Even in his later years he remained unconvinced that Caesar had been unjustly slain.[58] Petrarch's ambiguity toward Caesar, moreover, was shared by his medieval predecessors. Consequently, it is difficult to agree with Baron that the *De gestis Cesaris* was inspired by a tendency toward medieval values.

We do not know how Petrarch felt when, with death approaching, he realized that what he had considered the two principal undertakings of his life by which he hoped principally to be remembered were to remain uncompleted. Might he then, in the last days, have found it possible to embrace the counsel of Augustinus: when projects for your work have been "put in their place, then finally return yourself to yourself"?

Fig. 4. Petrarch, *Africa* (Triumph of Scipio). Historiated initial from Lewis M. 48:4. Rare Book Department, The Free Library of Philadelphia.

CHAPTER FIVE

PETRARCH'S PHILOLOGICAL EPIC • *Africa*

Simone Marchesi

The *Africa* is a nine-book epic poem drafted in Latin hexameter, on which Petrarch worked in intermittent bouts of enthusiasm between 1338–39 and 1343–44 and continued revising with increasing skepticism until his death.[1] Perhaps only half-unwittingly reproducing the editorial history of its principal stylistic model, Virgil's *Aeneid*, the work was never finished and never released for publication during the poet's lifetime — except for one, or most likely two, individual sections.[2] Centered on the decisive actions of Publius Cornelius Scipio Africanus the Elder in the Second Punic War, the main narrative line embraces the span of time between the end of hostilities in the Spanish campaign (205 BCE) and the Battle of Zama (202 BCE).[3] The plot is based on Petrarch's close and imaginative reading of the third *deca* (decade) of Livy's *Ab urbe condita libri* (*History of Rome*), starting with Hasdrubal's retreat across the Strait of Gibraltar in 21.61 and culminating with the account of Scipio's triumph that rounds off book 30.[4] Classical rhetoric and style guarantee its generic identity. Structurally, the poem starts in medias res ; it contains an invocation to the Muses (and to the Christian God), a dedication to a specific contemporary addressee (King Robert of Naples), a double proem to the action (on earth and in the heavens), and displays throughout a large number of classical epic similes.[5] Notwithstanding infelicities that the author himself was the first to note, Petrarch's language and meter remarkably approximate ancient models. Finally, the *Africa* contains a traditional, if consistently Christianized, pantheon of epic deities continuously involved in the development of the historical plot.[6]

The scant critical success that the *Africa* has enjoyed since its posthumous publication is potentially misleading if used to gauge Petrarch's authorial investment in the poem. Conceived as the poetic counterpart, possibly even the culmination, of the contemporaneous *De viris illustribus*, the *Africa* was a centerpiece of Petrarch's project of fashioning himself as the leading intellectual and poet-historian of his age. From the circumstances of its conception as narrated and mythologized in the *Posteritati*, to the frequent references and allusions to its existence and progress toward completion that are scattered throughout his various writings, to the carefully constructed bilateral linkage with the coronation ceremony of 1341 (see the signature passage, technically a *sphragis*, in *Africa* 9.236–41), Petrarch makes the poem central to his cultural project of self-promotion. It could hardly have been otherwise. Having been conceived, in scope and nature, as a response to more traditional "medieval" heroic poems, the *Africa* was designed to engage in a harsh, if indirect, confrontation with Dante's *Divina commedia*, a narrative, poetic, and idiosyncratically classicizing giant. Petrarch's attempt to replace Dante's typological work with his own philological epic reflected his strategy to make of himself the initiator of an essentially new kind of classicism.[7]

Elements of the poem that Petrarch might have considered instrumental in fulfilling his ambitious program—the main chapters of his contract with immediate and long-ranging posterity—emerge from a survey of the plot and a closer consideration of the prologue and epilogue, two areas in which the basic outlines of its classicism are most clearly visible. Further philological and cultural questions intertwine around the rehabilitation of Dido's fame and the status of dreams, both amply treated in the narrative. A web of scattered allusions to the text of Dante's works suggests the ambiguous compromise that Petrarch's *Africa* reaches with its most overshadowing antecedent.

1. Orientation: What Is the Poem About?

Petrarch follows closely the major events of the Second Punic War. The first act is centered on Laelius, Scipio's diplomatic envoy, and details his mission to the court of Syphax, a key player in Scipio's strategy of alliances on the continent (books 2, 3, and the very short book 4). After a long lacuna in the narrative, which was probably supposed to have contained an account of Scipio's own visit to the same court, a part of the poem that Petrarch never managed to write, we find the young Numidian prince Massinissa victoriously entering the capital city of Cirta. At this point he has displaced Syphax as the main Roman ally and has just defeated the renegade king. The core of book 5 is devoted to Massinissa's tragic love story with Sophonisba, the wife of Syphax. Strong pathetic tones mark the episode, organized around the moral struggle of the secondary protagonist, who falls in love with the beautiful captive queen, hastily marries her, and is then compelled by Scipio's arguments to break off the marriage. The tragic outcome of Massinissa's double allegiance to the Roman general and to his wife, a double bind of erotic and ethical trust, is Sophonisba's suicide and her descent as an angry shade into Hades (beginning of book 6).

At this point the more strictly "Iliadic" section of the poem begins, overwhelmingly devoted to military matters. Narrative pace quickens: Scipio approaches Carthage and lays siege to it; the Punic Senate summons Mago and Hannibal back from Italy while trying to buy time by sending envoys to Rome with the pretense of a peace offer. Containing the last bits of diplomatic action, book 7 reconstructs the final preparations leading to the clash at Zama, the poem's climax. Hannibal's fleet reaches the shores of Africa, he seeks a parley with his adversary, and the two leaders exchange long and elaborate speeches. Hannibal makes an unacceptable peace offer, immediately rejected by Scipio. After a long digression to an allegorical scene in heaven, where personifications of Rome and Carthage plead for divine assistance before a Christianized council of gods, the battle unfolds in all its phases: from the arraying of the troops, to the two leaders' exhortatory speeches, the accidents of combat (the account of which Petrarch extrapolated from Livy), and the flight of a defeated Hannibal, who seeks refuge away from the battlefield. Book 8, the longest in the poem, chronicles the military and political aftershocks of the epoch-defining battle, both in Rome and in Carthage. The narrative moves back and forth between the two shores of the Mediterranean, framed by a series of episodes related to one another only by temporal sequence; the last bits of warfare intermingle with renewed diplomatic action on both sides. Book 9 (fig. 4) is devoted to the world finally at peace: from the pacified sea across which Scipio's fleet triumphantly returns to Italy, to the general's (and his poet's) triumph in Rome. Its centerpiece is Ennius' from Africa, speech on the nature of poetry, immediately followed by his account of a metaliterary prophetic dream in which both his antecedent Homer and his follower "Franciscus" play a role.

Consistent with its epic models, the *Africa* weaves into the linear progression of the first three books several flashbacks to the early history of Rome and biography of Scipio as well as a few prophetic flash-forwards to the future of both the city and the poem's protagonist. Petrarch employs two distinct grafting methods for connecting the main narrative line of the poem to its extensive analepses and prolepses. The first digressive section, most of books 1 and 2, enters via the fiction of a prophetic dream that Scipio has on the dawn after the last, decisive battle in Spain. The second, which occupies the whole of books 3 and 4, glances backward at the history of Rome and the early biography of the protagonist and is entrusted to the voice of Laelius. During a banquet in his honor, Scipio's right-hand man accommodates a request from the Numidian king to hear an account of Rome's and his leader's greatness. While the second episode exhibits a fully traditional epic pedigree, reproducing similar banquet scenes treated as occasions for retrospective narratives both in the *Odyssey* (books 7–12) and in the *Aeneid* (books 2–3), the principal source of inspiration for the first digressive section is a lineage of prose works that possess an ambiguous rhetorical truth status. Petrarch's "Dream of Scipio the Elder" is based on Macrobius's famed commentary to the *Somnium Scipionis*, Cicero's fictional account of a dream vision ascribed to Scipio Africanus the Younger (the adopted nephew of the protagonist of the *Africa*) in the concluding section of his political treatise *De republica*.[8]

To mark the incipit of his poem as an epic, Petrarch reproduces gestures he found in the Latin canonical works. The first seventy lines contain a triple invocation, to the epic Muse (1–10), to Christ (10–18), and to the first dedicatee of the work, King Robert of Naples (19–70). The series thus constructed appears peculiar, more for the presence of the alternative Christian source of inspiration than for the lengthy address to the earthly ruler—a presence that had been canonized, albeit ironically, in Lucan's treatment of Nero in the prologue to the *Pharsalia* and, probably in a more serious vein, by Statius's evocation of Domitian at the outset of his *Thebaid*.[9] An epic periphrasis preemptively addresses the relationship between the fictional pantheon, which appears on the surface of the poem, and the Trinitarian Christian God, to whose truth it lays claim more explicitly than Dante's invocation to a "good Apollo" (*Paradiso* 1.13):

> Tuque, o certissima mundi
> Spes superumque decus, quem secula nostra deorum
> Victorem atque Herebi memorant, quem quina videmus
> Larga per innocuum retegentem vulnera corpus,
> Auxilium fer, summe parens. Tibi multa revertens
> Vertice Parnasi referam pia carmina, si te
> Carmina delectant; vel si minus illa placebunt,
> Forte etiam lacrimas, quas (sic mens fallitur) olim
> Fundendas longo demens tibi tempore servo. (*Africa* 1.10–18)

[Thou too, Who are the world's / securest hope and glory of the heavens, / Whom our age hails above all gods supreme / and victor over Hell; Whose guiltless flesh / we see scarred by five gaping wounds, O come, / all-highest Father, bear me succor here. / Full many a reverent verse shall I bring back / to Thee—if verses please Thee—from the crest / of high Parnassus. If they please Thee not, / then Thine shall be the guerdon of those tears / which long since I might fittingly have shed / save that my wretched blindness checked their flow.][10]

The invocation is noteworthy for two reasons. First, its visualization of the body of Christ as a crucifix confirms the mythologized account of the circumstances of the poem's original inspiration as provided in the *Posteritati* and connects its genesis to Good Friday of 1338. Second, again by the force of the calendrical allusion that associates it to the eleventh-anniversary sonnet *Padre del ciel* (*Rerum vulgarium fragmenta* 62), the work is presented as a potential alternative to the love poems in the author's intellectual autobiography. The now "pia carmina" that Petrarch promises in exchange for divine inspiration are a sign of the "più belle imprese" to which *Rerum vulgarium fragmenta* 62.6 alludes. Similarly, the tears evoked in the Latin text as a substitute for all-too-human poetry are deemed more fittingly shed for the passion of the Christ than for the persisting earthly passion for Laura. The irresolute author of the *Rerum vulgarium fragmenta* has been replaced by a poet with programmatic ethical resolution. The proem of the epic presents the text as a successful product of a postconversion author—a poet who has solved, if not the fundamental dilemma of poetic versus penitential expression, at least the theoretical problem of choosing between erotic and Christian inspiration.[11]

Like a bridge spanning the entire work, Petrarch's attempt at unambiguously establishing the status of the poem reappears in the concluding metapoetic section that occupies the center of book 9. In Ennius's long conversation with Scipio, two questions Petrarch's dialogue addresses deserve particular attention: the truth value of poetry, which is discussed in lines 90–105;[12] and the ungenealogical nature of poetic lineage, which is explored in a dream sequence comprised between lines 133 and 289. In the latter, Homer appears to his successor Ennius, the first bard to recount Scipio's heroic actions, and then Ennius is in turn afforded a vision of his successor Petrarch, the ultimate singer of the general's glory.[13] The poem transfers from authorial direct discourse to an authoritative character in the plot, Ennius, the task of defining the relation between poetry and truth. In keeping with the Augustinian notion that Scripture invites interpretation of its difficult parts because a truth that is achieved through interpretive labor is more appealing than one that requires no effort on the part of the reader,[14] Petrarch's theory culminates in the assertion that the true poet is the historian-poet—someone who is able to take as his theme historical, moral, or natural truths and disguise them under the veil of a pleasant fiction. For the light it may shed on the inspiring principles of the epic, Petrarch's retrospectively programmatic statement deserves to be quoted in full:

> Non illa licentia vatum est
> Quam multis placuisse palam est.
> Scripturum iecisse prius firmissima veri
> Fundamenta decet, quibus inde innixus amena
> Et varia sub nube potest abscondere sese,
> Lectori longum cumulans placidumque laborem,
> Quesitu asperior quo sit sententia, verum
> Dulcior inventu. Quicquid labor historiarum est
> Quicquid virtutum cultus documentaque vite,
> Nature studium quicquid, licuisse poetis
> Crede: sub ignoto tamen ut celentur amictu,
> Nuda alibi, et tenui frustrentur lumina velu,
> Interdumque palam veniant, fugiantque vicissim. (*Africa* 9.90–102)

[The warrant of a bard / does not pertain to those who openly / would please the multitude. For, mark you, first, / one who would plan a poem must lay down / a firm foundation of the truth whereon / he then may build a cloud-like structure, sweet / and varied, veiling the foundation. Thus / he will prepare for those who choose to read / a lengthy, tranquil, and rewarding labor. / So, as the meaning harder is to seek, / the sweeter is the finding. All such things / as trials that history records, the ways / of virtue, lessons taught by life, / or Nature's secrets—all such matters are / a poet's substance, not to be exposed / as elsewhere, but to be disguised beneath / a covering cloak, or better, a light veil / which tricks the watcher's eye and now conceals / and now discloses underlying truth.]

According to Petrarch, "fiction" should be limited to the elocutionary sphere of the poet's activity; the essence of the poem, its underlying *inventio*, should remain firmly grounded in history. The *Africa* conforms to the principle, both in the accuracy with which it reproduces the historical plot preserved in Livy and in the moral message entrusted to the unwaveringly exemplary figure of Scipio. With a jab aimed more at the inventive fictions of his immediate past than at the classical examples of poetic vatic excess, Petrarch concludes:

> Qui fingit quodcumque refert non ille poete
> Nomine censendus, nec vatis honore, sed uno
> Nomine mendacis.

> [One who invents what he relates should not / be honored by the title of a poet, / nor deemed a seer, but rather called a liar.]

If we keep this pronouncement on poetics in mind, it is not hard to see why the poem will align itself with other Petrarchan texts in the polemic against the poetic—that is, antihistorical—treatments of the Dido story.

2. Correction: The Displacement of Dido

In a poem that makes the causes of the Punic wars one of its themes (*Africa* 1.71–114), Petrarch could not avoid dealing with the traditional epic version of the conflict's prehistory. As the last menacing words of Dido suggest in *Aeneid* 6.622–29, the opposing shores of the Mediterranean were never to enjoy peace, and the two opposing peoples could never be joined by any stable treaty because she had been betrayed by Aeneas. The curse that the forsaken queen cast on Rome even contained the prophecy of *Africa*'s coprotagonist Hannibal as the natural historical avenger of Dido's honor, when it predicted that a son of Carthage was going to wreak havoc on Italy in a distant future. On the other hand, in keeping with his guiding principle of historical truthfulness, Petrarch could not allow himself to entertain such absurd fabrications as Virgil, who had perverted the chronology of Rome's legendary history and made Dido a contemporary of wandering Aeneas in order to mythologize the conflict's origin. After all, Petrarch was involved in vindicating the fame of the historical Dido in all his Latin and vernacular writings, turning the rehabilitation of the Carthaginian queen into one of his favorite philological and poetic battle cries.[15]

In the *Africa*, Petrarch tackles the question of Dido in two distinct episodes that may be read as part of a coherent strategy. In book 3, while imitating from a distance the Virgilian episode of Iopa's singing at the banquet in Carthage (*Africa* 1.740–47—implicitly eliding it with a Homeric reference in lines 375–77), Petrarch has Syphax's court minstrel recite snippets of the history of North Africa. The poem's stance is unmistakable.

The content of the unnamed performer's song includes a section devoted to Dido: developing numerous historicizing glosses that circulated along with the *Aeneid* (and Dante's *Divina commedia*) and the polemical statements against Virgil's fictionalized account available in such central texts as Augustine's *Confessions* and Macrobius's *Saturnalia*, Petrarch sides with the philological party and defends the queen's reputation.[16] Undeterred by the *post-factum* prophetic nature of the statement (as he will be for the prophecy about himself in book 9), Petrarch has the singer allude proleptically to Virgil's creative rewriting of the plot in harsh, if justifiably nationalistic, terms:

> Iniuria quanta
> Huic fiat, si forte aliquis—quod credere non est—
> Ingenio confisus erit, qui carmine sacrum
> Nomen ad illicitos ludens traducat amores! (*Africa* 3.424–27)

> [What cruel injustice will be done to her—/ but who will believe it?—if yet should be / that some detractor, trusting in his art, will, in his verses, tarnish her fair name / with taint of shameless passion!]

In Petrarch's words, the author of the *Aeneid* is overconfident (*ingenio confisus*) and animated by less than serious intentions (*ludens*). Such a dismissive attack might be surprising in the context of this most Virgilian poem, but surprise decreases if we entertain the possibility that Petrarch was targeting medieval associations of Dido with *libido* more than the *Aeneid* itself. He takes issue with a tradition that had submitted her story to a process of exemplary moralization, culminating recently with Dante's Dido, a figure of lust by antonomasia (*Inferno* 5.85).[17]

Petrarch's second redeployment of the *materia Didonis* is the justly famous episode of Massinissa and Sophonisba, which takes Virgil's text as the paradigm to be imitated rather than as an object of polemical reprisal. The poetic shadow of the Virgilian Dido is central to the doomed love story that occupies the bulk of books 5 and 6 as Petrarch simultaneously preserves and reorients the narrative, displacing it from fiction to history. In Petrarch's allusive rewriting, mechanisms of condensation and substitution are at work, affecting principally the characters and the value system that had attached to the Virgilian narrative. Sophonisba's suicide recalls Dido's for virile courage in the face of death and her curse on Scipio (*Africa* 5.719–66); love-torn Massinissa is modeled on the unsteady, wavering Aeneas; and Scipio's counsel shares both the poise of Virgil's Jove and the eloquence of his envoy Mercury. Yet Petrarch rearranges this material in two fundamental ways. First, he transfers to Massinissa the burden of erotic passion, Dido's prerogative in the *Aeneid*, by projecting onto him the familiar features of a soliloquy-prone Petrarchan lyrical subject, torn between attachment to his passions and knowledge of right conduct.[18] In the *Africa*, it is he (not Sophonisba) who is inflamed by love and in whose mind erotic and ethical principles clash. Dido's tragedy had arisen from the contrast between her duty as queen to the people of Carthage and her pursuit of individual happiness (most evidently in *Aeneid* 4.86–89); in Massinissa's case, the struggle is between his duty as a Roman ally and his erotic desire for Sophonisba. The displacement even reaches the lexical level when Massinissa recites one of Dido's most recognizable lines. Resolved to order Sophonisba's suicide, he bemoans his destiny, crying: "O utinam Libicum nunquam transisset in orbe! / O utinam Latiis semper mansisset in oris!" (Would he [Scipio] ne'er had come / into the Libyan land, would he had stayed forever / on the Latin shores!). Dido had expressed the same wish in her suicide oration at *Aeneid* 4.657–58: "felix, heu! nimium felix, si litora tantum / numquam Dardaniae tetigissent nostra carinae!" (Happy, alas, too happy / if only the Dardanian keels had never / beached on our coast [trans. Fitzgerald]).

By alluding to Virgil's line, Petrarch locates his imitation at a busy crossroads of literary influence, tradition, and canon formation. Ovid's Dido had struck the same chord in the *Heroides*, echoing with Virgil the feelings and language of the Nurse in the memorable opening lines of Euripides' *Medea*, a fragment Catullus appropriated for the lament of Ariadne, which had been independently preserved by Cicero's *De oratore* and Macrobius in the *Saturnalia*.[19] Petrarch's imitative transformation, his "mellification" of this one key element concerning Dido, perfectly conforms to the theory he set out in *Familiares* 23.19, according to which the task of the poet is not to reproduce verbatim one model but to combine elements deriving from different sources in order to produce a new and better text, as bees take nectar from many flowers to make honey.[20] In its redistribution of traditional cultural associations, however, Petrarch goes one step further than his own theory might have suggested and produces a counter-text.

Petrarch also intervenes in his exemplary model for this episode's second protagonist, Sophonisba. By distancing the vanquished queen from the powerful but love-stricken Dido and turning her into an object at the mercy of Massinissa, Petrarch strives to disambiguate her character. The shift in the power relation between male and female protagonists is, however, not the only new feature Petrarch introduces into the Virgilian model. In his high-pitched rhetorical response to Scipio's reproach in book 5, the defeated Syphax shifts all the blame for his decision to switch sides and enter a suicidal war with Rome onto his ex-wife, who had seduced, disempowered, and eventually forced him to join the battle inauspiciously (*Africa* 330–70). The same material will recur later in the plot, in the lament Syphax performs while bidding farewell to his land from the ship that is taking him into captivity. Now playing the role of a living and retrospectively outraged Sichaeus, he again accuses his wife and seductress of driving him to break his allegiance with the Romans, which ultimately caused his demise (*Africa* 6.272–77). The combined import of the two episodes redefines Sophonisba as an eloquent and conniving schemer who has already taken advantage of her seductive power with her first husband and who is now ready to maneuver the enamored Massinissa to her political advantage.[21] The *Africa* dispels any potential sympathy its readers might have entertained for this new character Sophonisba. Unlike the *Aeneid*, Petrarch's poem resolutely and almost exclusively advances what one may call "the reasons of epic."

If the author's allegiance to his virtuous subject matter has been clear from the proem, when the poet had taken preemptive measures against any erotic interference with his poem, this does not mean that the *Africa* will consistently reject all the pathetic *topoi* of the elegiac tradition. Not even the exemplary moral perfection of Scipio is totally immune from them, for erotic language subtly interferes with military matters as well. A brief passage in book 5 depicts Scipio pondering his next move in the campaign against Carthage, transferring to him the topical "quid faciam?" (what shall I do?) dilemma that Latin epic and elegy had traditionally attached to the figure of the abandoned heroine. The rhetorical structure is unmistakable: "Scipio . . . per noctem singula secum / ancipiti mente rotat: num . . . an . . . an . . ." (But Scipio . . . through the long night lay sleepless, pondering. . . . Should he . . . or . . . or should he first . . . ? *Africa* 487–94). As it was true for Dido's lament shifted to Massinissa, so in the background of Scipio's dilemma readers are asked to perceive the presence of similar soliloquies by Virgil's Dido (*Aeneid* 4.325–30 and, more extensively, 534–46), Ovid's Ariadne (*Heroides* 10.59–66) and Catullus's archetypal version of this deserted heroine (64.177–87).[22]

A parallel passage guarantees the pertinence of the intertextual gloss. The same night that sees Scipio sleeplessly debating with himself sees Massinissa just as sleepless and uncertain about the future of his liaison. A hero who is about to forsake his own heroine, he, too, ponders the "quid faciam?" question for about seventy lines and allows the tradition of the erotic lament to resurface (*Africa* 5.510–83). It might not be by chance that the pathetic episode has enjoyed some success with Petrarch's audiences. These leftover areas of rhetorical, if not moral, ambiguity counteract, at least in part, what even classically trained readers come to experience as the inhuman perfection of the poem's protagonists and the inexorably moralizing mechanisms of its narrative.

3. Revision: The Role of Dream-fiction

Petrarch, like Virgil, uses the intervention of *Fama* as the hinge around which Massinissa's and Sophonisba's love story revolves—turning from a happy, if ominous, beginning to a tragic, if ethically appropriate, end. Just as it had been true for the relationship between Dido and Aeneas, so also between Massinissa and Sophonisba fame brings about their fall, by relating to Scipio news of their marriage—news that is partly distorted but proves no less worrisome to him (*Africa* 5.273–84).[23] A further element that the *Africa* develops in conscious parallel with the *Aeneid* is the pair of mutually responding, prophetic dreams experienced by the two couples of protagonists. The terminology that the two authors use to designate the nocturnal visions of their characters can serve to introduce a discussion of the status of Scipio's dream—the dream writ large in the early books of the *Africa*.

In the *Aeneid*, Dido dreams first. She mysteriously sees herself chased by Aeneas through a deserted landscape, having been abandoned by all her people—a hallucination that Virgil likens to the experience of Pentheus or a stage Orestes (*Aeneid* 4.465–73). In response to Dido's nightmare Aeneas has a dream, in which someone who looks like Mercury reiterates almost verbatim Jove's command to leave Carthage, adding that now the time to do so is imminent, while the queen has not yet changed her attitude from love-stricken to wrathful and has not yet barred the Trojans from setting sail toward Italy (*Aeneid* 4.554–70). Taking his cue from Virgil, Petrarch, too, grafts two mutually reinforcing dreams into the narrative, but in so doing he explores with more care—the care of a post-Macrobian writer— the relationship that they entertain with factual truth.[24]

The first to dream is Sophonisba, immediately on the night of her wedding, and her dream contains the foreboding of her demise: she sees herself being separated from her second husband and then taken away to the peak of a mountain. Suddenly a second and mightier mountain crashes against the one on which she is enthroned, two gelid rivers pour down the peak, the smaller mountain gives way, and she falls into Tartarus (*Africa* 5.262–72). What she sees is the truth of her future, veiled by a series of images that require interpretation. While the protagonist does not possess the key to uncover the real meaning of the prophetic nightmare, the reader will soon be able to establish a precise series of correspondences between each element of the dream and the unfolding of the plot. In her experience, a veil of ambiguous images covers a core of prophetic truth.[25] The chronological order between the facts and the oneiric experience that alludes to them is inverted in the case of Massinissa's dream. From the beginning, he had intuited that the white doe he saw in his dream represented Sophonisba. Now, after Scipio's intervention has taken place, Massinissa also knows who the shepherd is and why the doe was to be taken away from her second mate. What he yet refuses to acknowledge is that the dream maintained its truthfulness and coherence even in the last part, which implied the death of Sophonisba. His attempt to recategorize the experience as an insignificant "visum" is futile (*Africa* 5.604–611).

Unlike the two lover-dreamers who are caught in the failed interpretation of the initially obscure oneiric material presented to them, both Scipio, in the first two books of the poem, and Ennius, in the last, are attentive and receptive readers of the visions they receive. In both cases, however, Petrarch points out that the natural tendency of all characters is to dismiss their visions as pure fictions. In both cases, a choice should be made to interpret the dreams as endowed with oracular truth. At the beginning of book 2, it is Scipio's own father who introduces the possibility that the vision that his son has been granted will be obliterated by the coming of the day or misread as an insignificant dream:

> Ambigue subito tibi somnia noctis
> Omniaque implicite vanescent visa quietis:
> Si qua animo memori vestigia forte manebunt,
> Somnia vana tamen, mentemque errasse putabis. (*Africa* 2.7–10)

> [Soon these dubious visions of the night / and all the things you've seen while wrapped in sleep / will fade and vanish from your waking eyes, / and, if some shreds of memory remain / you'll deem them fancies of a wandering mind.][26]

The task of the dreamer is not to dismiss the vision but rather to apply its teachings (mainly of philosophical and historical nature) in future actions. On the validity of the dream will depend, first of all, the amount of comfort that Scipio might derive from knowing that the outcome of the war will favor him. Yet there is more. The correct perception that Scipio (and the poem's readers) should have of Rome's glorious past, the certainty of virtue being rewarded, the strenuous future of Rome, and the eschatological destiny of all things human are also conveyed by the dream in its oracular form.[27] The philosophical truth hidden in the dream, together with the authority of the dreamer and the controlled conditions in which it takes place, validate both the experience itself and the fiction that transmits it.

As often happens in medieval dream fiction, the question of the belief that should be granted to the vision has a final, not unrelated, corollary. The dream is prophetic insofar as it is metapoetic.[28] A crucial point in the prophetic account that Scipio receives from his father is concerned with the role that Petrarch himself and the poem that is being composed will eventually play in the perpetuation of his fame:

> Cernere iam videor genitum post secula multa
> Finibus Etruscis iuvenem qui gesta renarret,
> Nate, tua et nobis veniat velut Ennius alter.
> Carus uterque michi, studio memorandus uterque:
> Iste rudes Latio duro modulamine Musas
> Intulit; ille autem fugientes carmine sistet;
> Et nostros vario cantabit uterque labores
> Eloquio, nobisque brevem producere vitam
> Contendet; verum multo michi carior ille est
> Qui procul ad nostrum reflectet lumina tempus. (*Africa* 2.441–50)

[Far down the centuries to come I see / a youth, Etrurian born, who will narrate / your splendid story; he shall be, my son, / for our renown a second Ennius. / I hold both dear, for both of them possess / a memorable ardor. One of them / brought rustic Muses, in rough fashion clad, / to Latium, and the other with his notes / detains them as they flee. And each will sing / in manner of his own of our exploits, / thus striving to prolong our lives' brief course. / Dearer I count him who in distant years / will backward cast his glance upon our age.]

Petrarch's own inscription in the history of Scipio as a belated singer of Rome and its general, is a move that initially only contributes to authenticate him as a member of the authorial canon of epic poets rapidly sketched in the prologue. Virgil, Statius, and Lucan (*Africa* 1.50–55)—and now also Petrarch—have sung world-historical wars of the past and have thus occupied, for material and stylistic merits, a relatively secure position in the pan-chronic system of cultural history. In the eternal synchronicity (if not the eternal present) of the canon thus formed, the envisioned relationship of authors and texts is one of collaborative cohabitation in and mutual reinforcing of the tradition. The closest mythopoetic equivalent to the cultural dynamics envisioned by Petrarch seems to be Dante's "bella scola" (fair school) of poetry, the quintet of poets by the noble castle who engage in technical conversation that the poem refrains from relating (*Inferno* 4.104–05 and *Purgatorio* 22.10–18).

In the second major visionary episode of the text, Ennius's dream of Homer in book 9, the prophecy of Petrarch's own successful writing of the work reappears, and it is again connected to the issue of credibility. Still somewhat skeptical—or at least cautious—about the veracity of any dream, Scipio states he is ready to suspend disbelief and accept the prophetic nature of the vision Ennius relates to him. It is a confirmation of what he has already heard from his ancestor, and as such it is endowed with proper authority. Nevertheless, some degree of uneasiness remains. Scipio concludes his praise with an unsettling distich about Petrarch, which might reflect authorial worries about the possibility of becoming the successful author of the *Africa* and thus providing with an actual poetic body the "empty name" of his promised epic: "Promissumque mihi gemino sponsore profecto / diligo, quisquis erit; si nullus, diligo nullus" (He is mine / by warrant of this double sponsorship. / Whoever he may be I cherish him, / and if an empty name, why then I'll cherish / an empty name, *Africa* 9.302–7).

The attempt to prophesy a "complete Petrarch" in visionary form offers an alternative structuring of the epic lineage, one that differs from the more traditional canon surveyed above in two major elements. First, the *Africa* here moves from Homer to Ennius to Petrarch, strategically bypassing Virgil and his immediate successors. Secondly, as a medley relay of ghostly poetic inspiration, the lineage is deeply marked by the passage of time. Whereas in book 1, Petrarch had claimed a spot in the inclusive canon of epic alongside Ennius, in the concluding dream, the author of the *Africa* envisions his work as part of a distinctly chronological order of succession:

> Hic ego—nam longe clausa sub valle sedentem
> Aspexi iuvenem–: "Dux o carissime, quisnam est,
> Quem video teneras inter consistere lauros
> Et viridante comas meditantem incingere ramo?"
> . . . .

"Ille diu profugas revocabit carmine Musas
Tempus in extremum, veteresque Elicone Sorores
Restituet, vario quamvis agitante tumultu;
Franciscus cui nomen erit; qui grandia facta,
Vidisti que cunta oculis, ceu corpus in unum
Colliget: Hispanas acies Libieque labores
Scipiadamque tuum: titulusque poematis illi AFRICA" (9.216–19,
230–36)

[There in the distance I could see a youth / seated within a valley
closed by hills. / I asked: "O cherished guide, disclose, I pray, /
who is it I behold taking his rest / under the tender laurel? . . . That
youth in distant ages will recall / with his sweet notes the Muses,
long exiled, / and though by tribulations sorely tried / he'll lure the
venerable sister back / to Helicon. He will be called Franciscus; /
all the glorious exploits you have seen he will assemble in one
volume—all / the deeds in Spain, the arduous Libyan trial; / and he
will call his poem *Africa*."]

Authorized by the epic forefather Homer and by Ennius's own direct
vision, the *Africa* is not designed to collaborate with its immediate model,
the *Annales* that Ennius is about to write. Homer's words insist on both the
unity finally accomplished in the new epic poem and on its stylistic merit in
terms that suggest emulative challenge more than imitative distance. Echoing the guiding principle for Petrarch's work of collecting and systematiz-
ing the scattered fragments of his soul (in the *Secretum*) and of his rhymes
(in *Rerum vulgarium fragmenta* 1.1), the prophecy characterizes Petrarch's
work in terms of absolute thematic unity: the young Franciscus will assemble in one volume (*corpus in unum colliget*) the fragmentary matter of Scipio's
deeds.

To be sure, the new epic will also reproduce the work of Ennius himself,
the first to bring the Muses to Latium (according to Scipio's first dream),
and yet, in so doing, it will also replace it. By stepping in for the stylistically inadequate epic of the *Annales*, a philologically shipwrecked poem
that survived only in fragments, the *Africa* will appropriate Ennius's hero
(*Scipiadam . . . tuum*) and provide him with the ultimate praise he deserved.
It will, however, also supplement and erase its antecedent.[29] Instead of contributing to the formation of a balanced and exhaustive constellation of canonical works, each new epic poet who appears in the final vision displaces
and replaces his forerunner. As the traditional tag *alter Homerus* suggested,

Ennius is a second and different (inadequate) Homer; in his turn, Petrarch is *alter Ennius*, a different (more competent) singer of Scipio. The lineage is neither genealogical nor, as had been for Ennius (the author), is it due to a process of reincarnation, in which a core noetic identity is preserved beyond the contingency of each individual life. Rather, the prophetic authorization may exist only thanks to a process of differentiation in which each individual's identity is historically determined. In sum, the tradition Petrarch envisions is grounded on the philological notion of discontinuity.[30]

At the plot level, the historical speaker in the *Africa* is doubly isolated in his position as failed intermediary between the unbridgeable past of Greek epic and Petrarch's present-day writing. On the one hand, Ennius re-evokes Homer as ghastly and alien—more a figment of his literary-historical mind than an agent of poetic inspiration.[31] On the other, Scipio's first bard is prevented from speaking directly to the prophesied young Florentine poet. In both cases, Franciscus's presence is to be blamed for the disrupting and muting effect it has on the attempt to construct a genealogical tradition. In two interdependent moments, Petrarch's text depicts a situation in which no real communication may occur across the strict boundaries of philology. At first, the overwhelming desire that Ennius has to talk to the young poet elicits in him the incredible wish that Homer be silent (*Africa* 9.268–71); then Franciscus raises his gaze to meet Ennius's and disrupts the dream, just before any word might be uttered by the younger poet or before any word from the elder one might be recorded in the text (284–85). Through this double ellipsis Petrarch replaces the simultaneous conversation of texts and authors that he found in his classical source (and in his Dantean antecedent) with a chain of philological discontinuity.[32]

4. Inflection: The Ideology of Language

Since medieval cultural *translatio* is seldom severed from considerations of linguistic translation, a question of linguistic unity might be at work in Petrarch's uncanny dream of epic transference. One could always argue an opposite interpretation to the one given above, and the intermediary role that Ennius plays in Petrarch's text might be read as an essentially felicitous moment in the passing of the epic crown across historical and linguistic barriers. Yet, there is a small, historically accurate, detail in the account of Hannibal's final preparation of the battle at Zama that suggests the ideological care with which Petrarch's poem posits the question of its exclusive linguistic choice.

Whereas in the case of Scipio's last harangue to his army Petrarch concentrates on the stylistic merits of his rhetoric, for Hannibal's speech he crosses into linguistics. Hannibal's multifarious army requires its leader to employ a multiplicity of languages:

> Haec ubi disposuit, quoniam sibi castra coacta
> Gentibus ex variis fuerant et dissona linguis,
> Nunc interpretibus, proprio nunc ore cohortes
> Accendit stimulatque, suo non segnior hoste. (*Africa* 7.856–60)
>
> [When his battalions are arrayed he too exhorts them, speaking now with his own voice, / now through interpreters, since his array / includes mixed races of divergent tongues. / With zeal as eloquent as Scipio's / he strives to rouse his men.]

Even if the detail will play no further role in determining the outcome of the battle (or, perhaps, precisely because it remains an isolated remark), the plurilingualism of the historically defeated host invites commentary. Presented as a collection of all vices in the poem's polarized moral system, Hannibal's camp is characterized by a linguistic multiformity that is axiologically charged. In extradiegetic terms, the language of Petrarch's epic must be one, and that one language must be Latin because Latin is the language of the Roman unifying power—a power that, in turn, is providentially ordered. Preempting the necessity of any translation and making its best bid to cultural endurance, the *Africa* vindicates its nonvernacular uniformity against the multiform otherness of other poems that include and invite translation through historical times and across geographical spaces. Its inferiority having been established on linguistic even earlier than military grounds, Hannibal's army also represents a defeated poetic option.[33]

If indeed it is liable of a metapoetic interpretation, the linguistic inferiority predicated on Hannibal's glottological strategy is a nonspecific charge, under which all vernacular epic attempts may be reunited. That it was most likely the example of Dante's poem that Petrarch had in mind when he characterized Hannibal's harangue as polyglot is confirmed by a singular allusion to the text of the *Commedia* hidden in a surprisingly oblique context. While deprecating before the Roman Senate the terrible consequences of Carthage having fallen prey to its fascination with Hannibal, the old Hasdrubal describes the young general's victories in Spain and Italy as a raging fire rapidly spreading through the continent:

Ivit
Assuevitque malo imperio et feralibus armis;
Et magnam tenui flammam accendente favilla,
Quanta per Ausonium ruerint incendia mundum
Vidistis. (*Africa* 8.729–33)

[He went to Spain and quickly learned the use / of evil power
and death-dealing arms. / That tiny spark brought forth a mighty
flame, / and you have seen what fires have spread abroad / to rav-
age the Ausonian world.]

In the form of a gnomic commonplace, but with a distinct Dantean ring
to it, Hasdrubal's metaphor of the tiny spark igniting a mighty flame allu-
sively connects the poem's villain to the successful writer of *Paradiso*, who
had expressed his confidence in an eventual poetic lineage by stating that
a great flame may follow the smallest of sparks in the line *poca favilla gran
fiamma seconda* (*Paradiso* 1.34).[34]

Displaced from Dante to Hannibal and from poetics to politics, the
threat of a different poem and of a different poetic lineage haunts Petrarch's poem. The original context of the fragment that Hasdrubal re-
cycles, Dante's invocation to the "good Apollo," was particularly close to
Petrarch's own mythological imagination. Not surprisingly, it elicited a
strong, if subtle, response from him. It was in that passage opening the *Paradiso* that the author of the *Commedia* had made his highest bid to the laurel
crown and in so doing, he had come closest to leaving no room in the epic
canon, no poetic alternative to his successors but to follow in his footsteps.
In particular, by linking "the triumphs of Caesars and poets" to the laurel
crown, Dante had anticipated Petrarch's most exclusive poetic and auto-
biographic myth, the same connection of political and poetic reward on
which the *Triumphi* are based and that rounds off action in the *Africa*. As
Dante's ambiguous canonization through the incriminating allusion suggests, however, Petrarch's most difficult antecedent—and the greatest men-
ace to his poem's eventual success—resisted all efforts to exorcise them
from the text.

CHAPTER SIX

THE BEGINNINGS OF HUMANISTIC ORATORY • Petrarch's *Coronation Oration* • *Collatio laureationis*

Dennis Looney

"Sed me Parnasi deserta per ardua dulcis / raptat amor" (But a sweet longing urges me upward over the lonely slopes of Parnassus).[1] With these lines from Virgil's *Georgics* 3.291–92, Petrarch opens his best known oration, commonly referred to as the *Collatio laureationis* (*Coronation Oration*), delivered when he was crowned poet laureate at the top of the Capitoline Hill in Rome on Easter Sunday in 1341.[2] Ernest Hatch Wilkins passionately argues for the importance of the speech: "The oration delivered by Petrarch on the occasion of his coronation on 8 April 1341 illuminates more clearly than does any other existing document the gradual transition from the Middle Ages to the Renaissance. With all its mingling of elements old and new it is the first manifesto of the Renaissance. Yet it is almost unknown."[3] Some fifty years after Wilkins made his claim, the oration still suffers in relative obscurity, its overt literariness, its extreme artificiality, and its occasional nature making it difficult for readers to evaluate. The very reason Wilkins gives for its value, namely, "its mingling of elements old and new," which establish "the first manifesto of the Renaissance," creates interpretative difficulties that may account for why many readers have given it short shrift if they haven't ignored it altogether.

The *Collatio laureationis* is one of only six speeches that constitute Petrarch's body of oratorical works. It does not appear in the *Opera omnia* (Basel, 1554); in fact, it did not see the light until 1874 in Attilio Hortis's edition of *Scritti inediti*, in which four of Petrarch's six speeches were first published.[4] Petrarch's rigorous cultivation of the life of solitude didn't put him in a position to engage in public oratory on a regular basis, as he himself notes in the dedicatory letter to *Familiares* 1.1. During his years in Milan in service to the Visconti government he was called upon to speak publicly as an ambassador and spokesman four times, and he made one additional speech near the end of his life on behalf of Francesco da Carrara of Padua. Nevertheless, the title page to the 1554 edition of his works refers to Petrarch as a philosopher, orator, and poet, in that order. While "orator" in that context suggests more a master of prose eloquence rather than precisely a public speaker, the term does connote eloquence on display in the public arena. Despite his limited engagement in actual public oratory, Petrarch's reputation emphasized his oratorical skill. As part of his self-fashioning in this regard, in numerous passages he suggests ways in which his cultivation of eloquence is inspired by Cicero's example.[5] In addition, he compares himself to Demosthenes in *Invective contra medicum* (1.40), claiming that he is like the Athenian orator in defending himself at great length.[6] Francesco Nelli, Petrarch's principal correspondent, refers to the master reciting in front of his followers and surpassing Cicero in his oratorical prowess.[7] Leonardo Bruni states that Petrarch wrote invectives so that he would be considered an orator as well as a poet.[8]

In addition to the six specific orations, there are numerous hortatory letters in Petrarch's epistolary corpus that share many of the rhetorical characteristics of a public speech.[9] The reader first coming to Petrarch's epistles may be surprised to discover that even the most intimate letters read as if they were written with a view to future publication. All the more striking, perhaps, is that a surprising number of these compositions sound as if they were meant to be delivered.[10] The official diploma that Petrarch received at his coronation, *Privilegium laureationis*, which has his imprint all over it, "as a whole, has the character of a speech delivered, rather than the character of a document prepared for reference only."[11] And as Leonardo Bruni observed, his *Invective* are very much oratorical performance pieces.

The *Collatio laureationis* is a programmatic piece that articulates Petrarch's humanistic ideas, specifically his understanding of the relationship between past and present as mediated by a body of canonical texts to which he would add his own. The setting for the oration, delivered in Petrarch's contemporary Rome with the remnants of the ancient city all around from the vantage point of the Capitoline Hill, emphasizes this movement between past and present. Analogous to the classical fragments strewn before them, the audience will hear literary fragments from the Roman past that fill the *Collatio laureationis*, as Petrarch has signaled with his opening citation from the *Georgics*. The piece focuses on poetry and its possible role as mediator between then and now, raising the crucial issue of the role of poetry and of the classicizing poet in the modern city. With the papacy in Avignon and Rome's civic fabric torn by the ongoing strife between the Colonna and Orsini families, the city was suffering from a lack of political leadership. Several years later, Cola di Rienzo would maneuver politically to try to fill the vacuum with his dreams of a new Rome. In the meantime Petrarch dared to imagine, for his part, the role of poetry and the poet in restoring the ancient polis at the center of a unified Christian republic at the center of the Holy Roman Empire. Inspired by Cicero, his restoration of the obsolete civic ritual of recognizing a victor's excellence by crowning him with a laurel wreath was nothing less than an attempt to restore the values of classical Rome and to place the poet at the center of a new Roman civic and political life. Albertino Mussato had been crowned with ivy and myrtle in Padua in 1315. Dante, invited to receive the honor in Bologna, had refused, hoping in vain to be crowned in Florence, as he sings plaintively in *Paradiso* 25.1–12. For Petrarch, however, the most fitting model was Statius, whom he believed erroneously had been crowned poet laureate in the first century C.E. on the same spot, the Capitol of triumphal Rome.[12] Rome was the focus of Petrarch's enterprise.

The *Collatio laureationis* also records the author's obsession with literary fame. But unlike several of Petrarch's other works that deal with the power of letters to project one's presence in the future, this work is complete. Moreover, it is one of the few works in Petrarch's corpus, as far as we can tell, that the poet did not submit to his typical process of extensive and obsessive revision.[13] The *Africa* and the *Epistola posteritati* (*Letter to Posterity*) both provide important statements on Petrarch's thinking about the rewards of literary fame, but they are incomplete. The *Collatio* sets forth a program in 1341 that subsequent works seek to fulfill and comment upon. While the *Africa* is written in part before the *Collatio*, the author continues to tinker with it post-1341, trying to finish it (which he never does) to bring it in line with the humanistic program articulated in the *Collatio*.[14] The *Posteritati*, which covers the events in Petrarch's life up to 1351 and which he was working on as late as 1371, is an end piece in relation to the oration. In the *Posteritati*, also left unfinished, Petrarch comments at great length on being crowned poet laureate, a narrative "occupying a disproportionate part of the story."[15]

Examining the *Collatio laureationis* and the *Posteritati* as part of a broader literary continuum in which Petrarch not only fashions himself but also critiques the very process of self-fashioning shows much that is typical of Petrarchan poetics. To the grandiose, hyperbolic optimism of the *Collatio*, the *Posteritati* provides a corrective. I use the word "corrective" to make a point, for the letter presents itself as a text that corrects several of Petrarch's earlier ones, a text that sets the record straight. At the same time, it documents the poet's growth over the approximately three decades from the time of the *Collatio* in 1341 to the final rewriting of the *Posteritati* in 1371, depending heavily on the image of the self as a corrupted text in need of authorial intervention and correction. In the *Posteritati*, he deliberately and carefully uses the vocabulary of authorship and textual criticism to describe his career, literary and moral, with the narrator figured not merely as the author of a potentially corrupt and incomplete manuscript but also, strikingly, as that text itself. This paradoxical duality, so familiar to readers of Petrarch, is anticipated in various ways in the *Collatio* where, for example, Petrarch makes the case that he is deserving of the laurel crown even though, in truth, he hasn't written enough to have really earned it. Moreover, as we shall see, Petrarch imagines himself not only as Cicero the defender of poetry but also as Archias, the poet at the center of the storm who deserves to be recognized for his potential value to the city.

The *Collatio* is ostensibly on the art of poetry, specifically Petrarch's command of that art, for which he has earned the right to be crowned poet laureate, a title he would continue to use throughout his life. But by the fall of 1340, when Petrarch received the invitation to be crowned, one may question whether or not he had actually written enough to have earned the designation. Fifteen Latin poems had circulated among his friends, most of them in metrical epistles, and there was the unfinished *Africa*. It is unlikely that his vernacular lyric production would have been taken into account in assessing his merits as poet. Not surprisingly, then, the *Collatio* focuses more on the profession of the poet than on the product of his art, as Douglas Biow has argued.[16] Noted by scholars from Burckhardt to Greene, this move is a consistent feature of Petrarch's modus operandi, for once he has a forum and has captured the audience's attention, he turns away from the nominal subject of the speech, poetry, to focus on himself. But as Giuseppe Mazzotta has shown, Petrarch moves easily among many different worlds, and so to shift the focus to himself is not merely the exercise in vain self-indulgence it may seem.[17] One of his selves is that of the humanist, the scholar devoted to the recovery, study, and promulgation of texts in the classical tradition. If Petrarch is deserving of the award for poet laureate, it is more for his accomplishments as a humanistic scholar devoted to the cultural recovery of antiquity than for what he has actually done up to this point in his poetic career.

Speaking in the Senatorial Palace at the top of the Capitoline Hill, Petrarch begins with a classical text that is about, in a manner of speaking, scaling the tops of hills: "But a sweet longing urges me upward over the lonely slopes of Parnassus."[18] He intones the passage from the *Georgics* and then begins his careful and extended explication of it as a church father might treat a passage from the Bible. Like a speaker trained in homiletics, Petrarch delivers a speech that is similar in its form to that of a medieval sermon, dramatizing his encounter with the passage, weighing every word, considering every possible meaning, calculating its impact on the audience. The speech's opening sentence concludes with a commentary on this sort of close reading: "and I have therefore taken my text from a poetic source" (300). He has taken it, in the Latin original, "ex poeticis scripturis," literally "from poetic writings," a word in which one also inevitably hears the Latin for "scriptures." For Petrarch, poetry, even classical poetry and perhaps especially Virgilian classical poetry, constituted a new category of scriptural text. A classical text treated with the reverence due scripture: this habit of reading becomes one of the markers of Petrarch's humanism. In a sense, this way of reading recalls Dante, the unnamed presence that looms over so much of Petrarch's production, but we are following the more modern author into different territory. The guide, however, is still Virgil, although no longer merely the author of the *Aeneid*. The bucolic Virgil commands Petrarch's attention no less than the epic poet. In this bucolic mode, Virgil is devoted to the work of the farmer, making the *Georgics* an appropriate point of reference in Petrarch's meditation on the labor of the poet. Moreover, as quickly becomes clear in the *Collatio*, Cicero, too, is one of Petrarch's guides, as he sets out on a different path from that of Dante and earlier figures. Shortly before his death, Petrarch reflects on the importance of Cicero and Virgil in his intellectual formation in *Seniles* 16.1, a letter written to papal secretary Luca da Penna, on April 27, 1374. He recounts how his father threw all his books into a fire "like heretical books . . . I recall that my father, seeing me so sad, thereupon quickly grabbed two books, already nearly burned by the fire, and, holding a Virgil in his right hand and Cicero's *Rhetoric* in his left, handed both to me." Of course, this dramatic recreation of cultural recovery reflects how Petrarch, not his father, rescued two authors from the flames of medieval fundamentalism, two authors who are assigned pride of place in the *Collatio*.[19]

In his opening remarks, Petrarch seizes the audience's goodwill while establishing the generic boundaries for his speech. He promises that there will be none of "those hairsplitting distinctions that are usually to be found in theological declamations" (300), previewing the sort of anti-Scholastic comments he will make later in life in *De sui ipsius et multorum ignorantia* (*On His Own Ignorance and That of Many Others*) and elsewhere. Instead he offers the speech as a *collatio*, "a loose oratorical form . . . closely connected to communal monastic life [and] conceptualized as a sort of conversation" that "might seem improvisational, yet it was intellectually rigorous."[20] Petrarch also declares that he will be brief, a claim that he repeats eight times in the speech. He then ends the opening *captatio* by invoking the Virgin Mary. But from the beginning of the speech, Petrarch makes it clear that he is marking out a new tradition for the poet in the city. He is not promoting the prophetic voice of religious poetry, sounded by Dante among others, but something altogether different: a politically engaged new poetry inspired by the classical examples of Cicero and Virgil.

The citation from Virgil takes pride of place in Petrarch's *Collatio*, even preceding the invocation of the Virgin Mary, which the Virgilian verse frames when repeated. Virgil, however, is but one of many classical sources cited in the piece. There are references to fifteen authors and citations from nearly two dozen different classical works. If Petrarch accords Virgil's lines from the *Georgics* a kind of scriptural status with his opening invocation and subsequent explication, he strikes a similar note when he refers to Cicero "with the fervor," according to de Nolhac, "one might use in praying to a saint of the Church."[21] Petrarch refers repeatedly to Cicero, at one point going so far as to claim erroneously that Cicero spoke in the same hall where he is delivering the *Collatio*. The references to and overt parallels with Cicero lead one to conclude that this classical author in particular is closely connected with the occasion of Petrarch's coronation.

The *Collatio* depends heavily on Ciceronian rhetoric in general and on one speech in particular, the *Pro Archia*, which Petrarch had come upon in Liège in 1333. In *Seniles* 16.1, to the papal secretary Luca da Penna, he remembers with nostalgia the discovery of Cicero's work:

> [W]henever, in my desire to travel (which I would often do at that time), I set off for faraway places, if I happened to see a monastery in the distance, I would immediately turn aside and say, 'Who knows if there is something I want here?' When I was about twenty-five, I was hurrying through Belgium and Switzerland; but when I reached Liège, hearing that there was a good supply of books, I stopped and kept my companions waiting until I could copy one of Cicero's orations by a friend's hand, and another by my own, which I circulated afterward throughout Italy. To make you laugh, in that fine uncivilized town it was a real chore to find ink, and at that [the only ink I could find was] nearly the color of saffron. (*Seniles* 2: 604–5)

Petrarch's remarks allude to many of the steps in the humanist project that he was beginning to define and clarify for his ever-increasing group of followers. Always on the lookout for forgotten or unknown texts, he identifies a potential source on the road. Once there he comes upon Cicero's *Pro Archia*, which he employs a friend to copy, while he copies another unidentified work of the orator, while still other friends bide their time as they wait for the pair of copyists to finish their job. This scribal camaraderie suggests the communal endeavor involved in Petrarchan humanism. Moreover, he states outright that he saw to it that Cicero's *Oration* "circulated afterward throughout Italy," sharing the fruits of his discovery and transcription with a wider public of humanistically inclined readers.[22] Italy is, indeed, a rather wide market for distribution, but the grandiosity of Petrarch's claim is in keeping with his image as promulgator of the classics. Finally, the last comment on the difficulty of finding good ink suggests the challenges the dedicated humanist had to overcome on a daily basis. Liège, "fine uncivilized town" though it be, harbors many wonders, and Petrarch is able to locate them and literally package them for the cultured minority south of the Alps.[23]

Cicero's *Pro Archia* presents the case made in 62 BCE in defense of the poet Archias, a Syrian Greek from Antioch, whose right to Roman citizenship had been challenged under the Lex Papia. Cicero knew Archias well, and he undertook his friend's defense in a case tried before the orator's brother, Quintus Cicero, then praetor. It was not difficult to contest the charge and to prove Archias's claims to citizenship. The better part of the speech, then, becomes an occasion for the orator to reflect on literature and to allude to its potential role in the community, raising the ultimate question: should poetry itself be considered an alien as the accusers had tried to do with Archias? Veiled and strange as it is, should poetry nevertheless be accorded a legitimate status in the city? Underlying Cicero's query is another even more venerable question on the status of the poet elaborated in Plato's *Republic:* should the poet be banned from the city?

In the *Pro Archia*, Petrarch had discovered a work from Roman antiquity in dialogue with other classical works that provided arguments for the value and validity of his own work nearly 1,400 years later. The modern author does not shy away from showcasing his discovery. Petrarch refers directly to Cicero's oration several times in his speech, at its beginning and end with the references forming a kind of Ciceronian frame to the entire piece. As he first prepares to explain the opening point in the argument, namely, the difficulty of being a poet, he turns to Cicero.

> The inherent difficulty of the poet's task lies in this, that whereas
> in the other arts one may attain his goal through sheer toil and

study, it is far otherwise with the art of poetry, in which nothing can be accomplished unless a certain inner and divinely given energy is infused in the poet's spirit. Take not my word for this, but Cicero's, who in his oration for Aulus Licinius Archias has this to say of poets: "We have it upon the authority of the most learned men that . . . the poet attains through his very nature, is moved by the energy that is within his mind, and is as it were inspired by a divine inbreathing . . ." (*Collatio laureationis* 301)

Petrarch's main source for the argument, then, is from a text of Cicero that he had personally brought back to light. Repeatedly in the *Collatio laureationis*, Petrarch will say of poetry what Cicero says of it, the modern author finding his voice in the words of the classical *auctor*.

In addition to these direct allusions to *Pro Archia*, the *Collatio laureationis* bears a general Ciceronian imprint throughout. In the opening section, which constitutes roughly the first third of the speech, Petrarch claims that there are three things that make his task as poet difficult: 1) one needs a divine gift; 2) he has suffered misfortune; and 3) people tend not to like poets and poetry nowadays.[24] But there are three counterpoints to these positions that enable Petrarch to continue in his goal to be a worthy poet: 1) the honor of Rome motivates him; 2) fame in general inspires him; 3) the need to establish a program of cultural renewal in Italy with himself as guide spurs him on. These classicizing ideals of honor, fame, and—I will call it for what it is—renaissance, enable him to overcome the various impediments that block his way. "As to the third point, namely the stimulation of the activity of others . . . I am venturing to offer myself as guide for this toilsome and dangerous path; and I trust that there may be many followers" (*Collatio laureationis* 306). No sooner does he articulate the project of Petrarchan humanism in this way than he thanks God for his talents, "that God who may rightly be called, in the words of Persius, 'Magister artis ingenique largitor' (Master of the arts and bestower of genius)." Liberated by Cicero, Petrarch immediately sets to work recontextualizing the classics. It is no longer enough to liken God to Jupiter, as Dante had done; now the humanist can call on the actual words of a Roman satirist to describe the Christian deity. Again, the humanist-poet finds his voice in the words of another, speaking through and like a classical *auctor*.

In the middle section of the piece, Petrarch comes to the crux of his argument and addresses the issue of poetry as a profession. What exactly does the poet do? His answer, like so much of the speech (one quarter of which is made up of citations), is drawn from an ancient source. He invokes Lactantius, the Christian Cicero, one of the few non-classical Roman authorities in the *Collatio laureationis*.[25] According to Lactantius, the poet composes with figurative language ("obliquis figurationibus") to restate historical truths: "For the office of the poet consists in this, that he should take things that have really come to pass and transform them by means of figurative language into things of a different sort. To make up all that one writes is to be a fool and a liar rather than a poet" (*Collatio laureationis* 306). After the definition of the poet's task in the words of this Christian apologist, Petrarch—claiming that he is too short on time to give the definition its due—recasts that charge with an appropriately veiled poetic image: "[T]he difference between a poet on the one hand and a historian or a moral or natural philosopher on the other is the same as the difference between a clouded sky and a clear sky, since in each case the same light exists in the object of vision, but is perceived in different degrees according to the capacity of the observers" (*Collatio laureationis* 307). Petrarch is advocating a serious role for poetry in the newly instaurated city and by calling upon the Christian Ciceronian Lactantius, he sanctifies that role, signaling a desire to combine the ethos of the ancient republic with that of the Holy Roman Empire.

Only in the final section of his speech does Petrarch come to the occasion for it: his own impending triumph. He turns again to Ciceronian themes from the *Pro Archia* to state that his reward will be threefold if he is granted the recognition he seeks. First, he will have personal glory. Second, his name and the names of those he celebrates will gain immortality. Third—and here he leaves Cicero and moves into his own private mythology—he specifically deserves the laurel crown for a list of reasons connected with the laurel's properties, which he then enumerates.

At the mention of laurel, the *Collatio laureationis* ends with Petrarch choreographing the final moment of his crowning. He turns to Orso dell'Anguillara, the senator charged by Robert of Anjou, king of Naples and Sicily, to present the crown. Robert had tested Petrarch's intellectual skills having read from the *Africa* and he heard him recite from it during the poet's stay in Naples en route to Rome. Petrarch's final comment concerns the Roman people: "To you, [Orso], . . . there have been conveyed the requests . . . of the most illustrious King . . . , by whose high and profound judgment I, though unworthy, have been approved—to whom, moreover, by ancient custom the power of approval has been entrusted by the Roman people" (*Collatio laureationis* 313). The people of Rome, the potential beneficiaries of the classical revival Petrarch hopes to bring about, have the last word in their authorization of the symbolic act.

In his final letter to Boccaccio, *Seniles* 17.2, of April 1373, Petrarch responds to his friend's praise that he has "perhaps equaled Virgil in poetry and Tully in prose" by lamenting "that laurel crown, woven with immature leaves came to me when I was not ripe for it in age and in mind. Had I been any more mature I would not have wanted it . . ." (*Seniles* 2:652). Nor, it turns out, were the Roman people ready for a republic, let alone one with room for a poet. Cola di Rienzo, Petrarch's idealistic contemporary who fantasized reviving a republican form of government inspired by his study of ancient history, fell short in the years following 1341, and Rome would have to wait half a millennium for Mazzini and others to revive and in some ways to achieve the Petrarchan dream alluded to in the *Collatio laureationis*. In the meantime, however, Petrarch had established a foundation for the revival of oratory that would characterize the humanist movement in cities and courts across central and northern Italy in the second half of the fifteenth century. And in so doing, to return to the opening comment from Wilkins, he had indeed articulated a manifesto that marks a crucial transitional moment in the move from medieval culture to that of the Renaissance.[26]

CHAPTER SEVEN

PETRARCH THE COURTIER • Five Public Speeches • *Arenga facta Veneciis, Arringa facta Mediolani, Arenga facta in civitate Novarie, Collatio brevis coram Iohanne Francorum rege, Orazione per la seconda ambasceria veneziana*

Victoria Kirkham

Petrarch's five public speeches postdating the *Collatio laureationis* express a side of the poet that posterity has pushed into shadows.[1] It is inconvenient, discordant with the man in his own sleeker self-portraits and our mythic conceptions. This is Petrarch the courtier, whom his Colonna, Correggio, Visconti, and Carrara patrons supported in a style that gave him leisure to write, counting on him in return for services that allowed them to reap benefits as rulers from the talents of their house celebrity. Orations by assignment were among those services, which ran a gamut from dining at the lord's table to improvising occasional poetry, performing as humanist secretary, and traveling as ambassador. Petrarch's acceptance of secular patronage supplemented income he accumulated from ecclesiastical benefices, making him a man of wealth who could hire his own copyists, enjoy in later years the elegant, spacious quarters of the home on land from the Carrara at Arquà, and in his *Testamentum* bequeath luxuries of a materially comfortable life, such as his painting by Giotto, horses, and a lute.[2] Five times the courtier was called on to orate publicly, all during the last two decades of his life, when his renown had spread through Europe, and all for occasions representative of the princely life: a suit for peace between warring republics (November 8, 1353, before Doge Andrea Dandolo and the Venetian senate), the death of a ruling lord (October 7, 1354, in Milan for Giovanni Visconti), the conquest of a territorial rival (June 19, 1358, at Novara for the Milanese triumph over Monferrato), a dynastic marriage sealed by a dowry to replenish royal coffers (January 13, 1361, at Paris before King John II of France), and reconciliation after a military rout and Francesco da Carrara's defeat (October 2, 1373, before the Venetian doge and senate).

Financial assistance from wealthy benefactors, whose names evoke families at the summit of influence in fourteenth-century Italy, began flowing Petrarch's way as early as 1325. First among those who took him into their service were Stefano Colonna the Elder and his son Giacomo, a friend from Petrarch's university years at Bologna, cut short when Ser Petracco passed away. Left at Avignon with a paternal inheritance that soon ran out, Petrarch committed to the clerical life and in 1330 entered the household of Giacomo's brother, Cardinal Giovanni Colonna, whom he served for seven years, intermittently continuing the association for another ten thereafter.[3] Officially he was the cardinal's chaplain; unofficially, his poet on call. A pair of playful sonnets on Love's lethal tactics as a warrior and a basilisk, banished from *Rerum vulgarium fragmenta,* survive as evidence of a pen available to the patron.[4]

Repugnance for the corrupt papal curia—Babylon on the Rhone, Petrarch called it—drove him away from Provence.[5] After the pivotal journey to Naples and Rome for the laurel crown, he accepted an invitation to stay in Parma with Azzo da Correggio, a friend to whom he sent his collected lyric poetry and to whom he dedicated *De remediis utriusque fortune.* The arrangement, which provided Petrarch with a peaceful country house near Selvapiana, would stretch at intervals across a decade (1341–51).[6] When Azzo da Correggio rode into Parma, feted as its liberator from Veronese tyrants, Petrarch arrived freshly laureated, a trophy guest of rising fame. Alongside serious literary pursuits (*Africa, De rerum memorandarum libri,* and possibly the *Triumphi*), he found time there for ephemeral verse. To flatter the conquering hero he devised the whimsical conceit of a talking tower. Not just Azzo's subjects, but the city's very stones echo with admiration. This particular landmark happens to be fluent in Latin hexameters:

> Imperiosa situ victrici condita dextra
> turris ad astra levor, spectabilis intus et extra.
> Corrigie splendor, fulget quo principe Parma,
> bellipotens Azo me vult munimen ad arma.
> Me videat securus amans hostisque tremiscat:
> subdere colla iugo, vel poscere federa discat.
>
> [Imperious tower, built for a manly victory,
> I rise to the stars a marvel within and without.
> Azzo, splendor of the Correggio,
> the prince who makes Parma shine,
> as a warlord wants me for defense in battle.

May friend see me safely, and may foe tremble,
and learn to yield to the yoke or entreat pacts of peace.][7]

When he moved in 1353 to Milan he was criticized by his Florentine friends, especially Boccaccio, for sacrificing principle to expediency; he served eight years at the courts of Giovanni, Bernabò, and Galeazzo II Visconti.[8] Rhetoric was the coin that paid for his keep. Named godfather to Bernabò's son Marco (b. 1353), a little boy dubbed Golden Knight at two months and affianced at the age of three, Petrarch drafted a suitable metrical epistle. Rivers throughout the Visconti lands welcome the child's arrival in a grand confluence behind their king, the Po. Counting smaller relatives, from the Ticino to Reno, they parade as an epic catalog of exactly ten named waterways. Petrarch's gift of a golden "patera" (cup) can wait for use until Marco grows older, when he might delight in its donor's verse. Then, in a tour de force on the baby's Christian name, this adulatory epistle expands into a gallery of great men from Marcus Tullius Cicero to Saint Mark the Evangelist, worshipped in the great temple at Venice.[9]

Prose letters, too, left his secretarial desk, like one for Bernabò, said to have bred 5,000 dogs to support his fanatical hobby of boar hunting. The epistle (1359) thunders against Jacopo Bussolari, an Augustinian monk who had seized Pavia from its Milanese overlords and, during a brief rule as tyrant, not only expelled from his besieged city the women, children, infirm, and aged, but the poor in Christ as well. If that weren't bad enough, Bussolari planned to destroy all its dogs, too. Bothered at such treatment of the canines, Bernabò instructs Jacopo to send to Milan a goodly number of the condemned animals so that they not perish, being creatures obedient and faithful to man. "If they could speak," the letter concludes, "they would much rather serve us or (if that be their destiny) fall to the fangs of the peccary than die of hunger or by the sword."[10]

Although Petrarch always claimed that he preserved his personal freedom and preferred to dwell by himself quietly in the country, the Bussolari business betrays a picture more ambiguous. His own later editorial choices define the shifting line he walked—the letter for Bernabò he excluded from his collections, but the hexameters on Marco find a niche in his *Epystole*. A personage to be put on enviable display, he graced Visconti banquets and processed with his lords in ceremonial pomp, small bites into his time. More costly, though, was an arduous mission to Prague as a Visconti emissary for colloquies with Charles IV. Years later in a letter to the emperor's courier Sagremor de Pommiers, he recalls how they traversed bandit-infested forests with swords drawn and ringed by a bodyguard, arbalests at the ready. In compensation, the emperor bestowed on him the honorific title of Count Palatine.[11]

When service demanded, Petrarch summoned his talent for oratorical performances. On November 8, 1353, he represented Giovanni Visconti with an *Arenga facta Veneciis* (*Speech Made to the Venetians*), addressing the doge and senate. The poet carries a plea to end triangular hostilities involving Milan in its relationship with Genoa and Venice, twin rivals who had warred for maritime supremacy in the Mediterranean. Genoa was the loser. Giovanni Visconti had cut access for supplies to the Genoese, who finally capitulated to their Milanese oppressor. He then sent a legation to Venice, urging them to reconcile with Genoa—implicitly, with him, risen to formidable strength on the Italian peninsula. After requisite protestations of inadequacy, Petrarch sets his talk in motion with a biblical quotation, Psalm 45:9–10: "Come and behold the works of the Lord, the astonishing things he wrought upon the earth. He makes wars cease even unto the end of the earth, he destroys the bows and breaks the spears, and burns the shields with fire." The "lord" who brings peace is, of course, Giovanni Visconti. Although Visconti had strangled Genoa, Petrarch's declamatory logic not only paints him white, but adds a further euphemistic twist, staging the defeated Ligurians as gratefully calling on the foreign despot to take control of their city.

A smattering of classical citations enhance the message as the orator explicates scripture in the prescribed political key. To help make his point—that nothing is more salubrious than peace, which is the reason for fighting in the first place, he calls on Cicero, Livy, and Virgil. From the last, he cites Anchises' prophecy to Aeneas in the Elysian Fields: "Remember, Roman, to rule the peoples with your power—these shall be your arts—and to impose peace and actions with civility."[12] Unspoken but anticipated by a cultured audience is the line directly following these verses (*Aeneid* 6.851–52), a favorite from the poet's stockpile: "to spare the humbled, and to subdue the proud." In this, the shortest of all his speeches, Visconti's spokesman failed to convince Venice. As he later reproached Doge Dandolo, he had won only applause for his words, but not senatorial votes (*Familiares* 18.16): "neither our eloquence nor perhaps that of Cicero could open your tightly closed ears or move your obstinate spirits."[13]

Whether we have only half or all of another oration is not quite clear. It is the *Arringa facta Mediolani* (*Speech Made in Milan*) on October 7, 1354, a short panegyric for Archbishop Giovanni Visconti, dead from a neglected carbuncle on the eyelid.[14] A reluctant prelate, this "Bonaparte of Italy" proved a most able tyrant whom Petrarch harshly criticized before moving to Milan but later counted a friend. Rule was now passing to Giovanni's three nephews, Matteo II, Bernabò, and Galeazzo II. In praising the deceased, who cast a giant shadow, Petrarch had to strike a delicate balance between past and future, avoiding the suggestion that the coming to power of the next generation could bode political decline.[15] So the tactful message is "We mourn one and welcome three."

As in his first Venetian speech and later orations at Novara and Paris, Petrarch hangs this Milanese eulogy on a scriptural quotation, using the preacher's technique for constructing a sermon. His chapter and verse for the day is Psalm 37:11–12: "My heart throbs quickly, my strength has left me, and the very light of my eyes fails me."[16] In characteristically eclectic fashion, he mingles examples from antiquity with the Bible. Here a case that comes to mind is Plato, at whose death the sun seemed to fall from the sky. So, too, with the passing of Giovanni Visconti, light of the orator's eyes. Did Petrarch complete his eloquent tribute? Anxious that transfer of power take place at precisely the most propitious moment, a court astrologer stopped the speech halfway through. Ten years later the frustrated speaker recalls for Boccaccio what awkwardness that disruption caused in a letter rife with ridicule for the ignorance of soothsayers (*Seniles* 3.1). Petrarch, in fairness, pardons the one who had silenced him, as a likable personal acquaintance who was just doing his job in order to support a large family.

On June 19, 1358, Galeazzo made a ceremonial entry into Novara, freshly reconquered from the Marquis of Monferrato. In his company was Petrarch, who orated to the populace at sunset next to the cathedral, pronouncing the *Arenga facta in civitate Novarie* (*Speech Made in the City of Novara*). Again he builds his discourse on a Psalm (72:10): "Convertetur populus meus hic" (my people return to them), deftly explicating each part of the quotation with copious textual examples. Probing the noun "populus," Petrarch explains that it refers not just to any group, like a band of pirates or marauding mercenaries, but defines a law-abiding polity, bound together as Cicero writes in *De republica* and Augustine in *De civitate dei* by common law and purpose. Why the possessive "my people"? Novara had belonged to the Visconti in past, a long line of loving rulers going back to the thirteenth century—Matteo I, an earlier Galeazzo, Azzone, and Archbishop Giovanni of fond memory. Now the living Galeazzo Visconti is a new David, to whom the "populus" that had strayed by lending allegiance to Monferrato returns. Many scriptural passages illustrate the orator's points: Jeremiah 50:6 on a flock led astray by its shepherds (i.e., Monferrato); Matthew 3:17 ("This is my beloved Son"); John 1:12 on the new baptism; and Paul's letters to the Galatians (3:26), to the Romans (8:14), and to the Ephesians (1:5). Other authorities rise and parade for the occasion from the arsenal of a court speaker steeped in patristic and humanistic writings: Augustine's commentary on Psalm 118, Boethius's *De consolatione Philosophiae*, Virgil in *Aeneid* 6 speaking of Caesar Augustus, Terence in *Andria*, Seneca to Lucillus, Cicero's *Tusculanae disputationes* 4, *De clementia* 2, *Pro Ligario*, *Pro Marcello*, Aristotle in the *Rhetoric*, Sallust on the Cataline conspiracy, Livy on Scipio, Servius on Virgil. Aimed at reassuring Novara of Visconti clemency, they hammer on the ideas of mercy, forgiveness for wrongdoing, and echo of *Aeneid* 6 to convey the ruler's intention. He will spare the humbled and subdue the proud. By the end, the orator has transmuted Visconti from David the Psalmist to the Lord God, and the Novaresi to His Chosen People, quoting Tobias 3:14 "To thee, Lord, I turn my face . . . my eyes"; and Deuteronomy 26:18, "the Lord hath chosen thee this day to be his . . . people." The speaker, apologizing for having kept his audience for too long, closes on a note at once conciliatory and monitory. "I pray God that he illuminate your lord and illuminate you too, granting that he govern with justice and wisdom and you live submissive in fidelity and obedience, without wanting any other state or *signoria*, without forcing him to love another people more than you."[17]

The most famous poet, philosopher, and orator of his day—"oracle of Europe," Sismondi called him—Petrarch plied his skills as far away as Paris. There in the *Collatio brevis coram Iohanne Francorum rege* (*Brief Oration in the Presence of John, King of the French*), on January 13, 1361, he celebrated John II's release from English captors in the Hundred Years' War and his daughter's betrothal to Gian Galeazzo Visconti.[18] That king, a ruler ruinous for his country but ironically surnamed "the Good," had been taken captive at the battle of Poitiers (1356). After four years the English released their royal hostage for a dizzying ransom of 3,000,000 gold crowns. Timely help flowed into the French ruler's coffers when Galeazzo Visconti, offering a dowry package toward the first installment of 600,000 florins, brokered a prestigious marriage between his son Gian Galeazzo, then eight, and the eleven-year old princess Isabelle of Valois.[19] Shutting out entirely a background of wartime devastation visited on France, graphically described by Petrarch in a letter to his friend Pierre Bersuire (*Familiares* 22.14), the orator's sleight-of-voice publicly transforms King John and his realm into models of good fortune triumphant. Again the speaker's hook is scriptural, a reference to the return home of King Manasseh from exile in Babylon (2 Chronicles 33:13): "he heard his prayer, and brought him again to Jerusalem into his kingdom."[20]

Ceremony trumps honesty throughout the *Collatio brevis*. Unfolding as a masterpiece of flattery, it collects some fifty quotations that come tumbling one after another in a pastiche of breathless rhythms. With the first draft of his *De remediis utriusque fortune* just recently completed, Petrarch considers how John has been subject to Fortune, first bad and now good. A sixteen-line passage from Seneca's play *Thyestes*, culminates with a resonant chord: "Res deus nostras celeri citatas / turbine versat" (The god turns in a whirling vortex these things of ours); then Isaiah side by side with Virgil asserts the upswings that follow spirals into adversity. As the speaker develops his scriptural text, he likens Paris to Jerusalem, the king's subjects to Israel. In the end, he does not forget the marriage that will unite the two houses and surely be a happy match if the children follow Seneca's advice: "si vis amari ama" (if you wish to be loved, love). Finally, he presents the king with two rings that Visconti has sent, and closes on a pair of Psalms whose message holds promise for eternal peace and prosperity to those who dwell in Jerusalem (Psalms 124:1–2; 127:5).[21]

To the same Great Council Chamber where he had first declaimed on behalf of Giovanni Visconti Petrarch would return on October 2, 1373, his death less than a year away. Again he delivered a diplomatic speech before the ruling nobles of the Adriatic Queen, *Orazione per la seconda ambasceria veneziana* (*Oration for the Second Venetian Embassy*) to represent his last patron, Francesco da Carrara of Padua, thumpingly defeated in his war of aggression on Venice 1372–73). Now Francesco dispatches his son Francesco Novello, with Petrarch in tow, to swallow terms of peace dictated by the more powerful victor. The conflict had forced Petrarch himself to flee his home at Arquà and return for refuge to Padua in mid-November 1372. A friend, quixotically hopeful that rampaging soldiers would spare the poet's home if it were marked as his property, receives a letter from Petrarch, serenely resigned to the upheaval:

> I returned to the city the day before yesterday, and today or tomorrow at the latest I expect my little retinue, left behind in the country. The books I had there I have taken with me. Christ will watch over the house and the rest, since He has cared for me and watched over me from childhood, or rather from my mother's womb, though I am unworthy and undeserving. If nonetheless, it is destined to be burned, God's will be done; besides, the grave, my final home, is enough for me. What love dictates and what you write about inscribing my name on the very threshold of the house shows devotion rather than adjustment to the circumstances and the times. Mars does not respect the names of scholars.[22]

Only a sixteenth-century Paduan dialect summary survives of the speech Petrarch made about a year after this evacuation. Attributed to Nicoletto d'Alessio da Capodistria, chancellor of the Carrara and Petrarch's friend, it preserves in Latin the opening quote, "Amantium ire re(d)integracio amoris est," roughly, "Lovers' anger restores love."[23] From a comedy by Terence, for whom the admiring and philologically astute Petrarch had by 1359 composed a scholarly *Vita*,[24] this line has the aphoristic quality he found so appealing in language well wrought. Pursuing the idea that a quarrel makes two people love each other all the more afterwards, the orator develops his reassuring theme of reconciliation. Closing, the chronicler recreates pageantry of the ritual and bows to the venerable elder who orated:

> With our magnificent Messer Francesco Novella da Carrara there went to Venice a great retinue of noble knights and doctors of law and other men in large number, among whom was the most noted poet, a man of lofty and celebrated fame worthy of being remembered always, Messer Francesco Petrarca, Tuscan by birth. He was charged by the aforesaid magnificent lord with the duty of speaking in that place, and so he did in the form above indicated, although because of his old age and an infirmity that he had had and from which he was not yet recovered, his voice trembled a little.[25]

The Carrara were Petrarch's last princely patrons. Their patriarch Jacopo had coaxed him to come in spring 1349, with a lucrative canonry, establishing his warm ties with the family and their city. It was in Padua two years later that Petrarch entertained Boccaccio for the first of the visits that were high points of their treasured friendship. At Padua, he continued revising *De viris illustribus*, dedicated in its "Roman" form to Francesco da Carrara, whom he advised for a great corresponding fresco cycle of *uomini famosi*. Francesco, in a final honoring gesture, would be personally present at his funeral. How great the orator's gratitude was toward them lies sealed in his will (April 4, 1370). There he bequeaths to Francesco his most precious possession, a portrait of the Madonna by Giotto, but first he stipulates that

> if I should die in Padua where I am now, I should wish to be buried in the church of S. Agostino, which the Dominicans now hold. For not only is this place dear to my soul but it is also there that that man lies who loved me very much and who, through his de-

voted entreaties, brought me to these parts, Jacopo da Carrara of most illustrious memory, sometime Lord of Padua.[26]

Petrarch's biographers have always wrestled with the difficulty of reconciling the meditative poet who claimed he loved peace and personal freedom with the courtier who chose to reside in close company of rulers blackened by reputations for ruthless territorial aggression, tyranny, treachery, cruelty, violence, and bloody murder, even of their own kinsmen. Yet Petrarch befriended them, not only in seeming sincerity but apparent admiration. Responding to Boccaccio's censure, he writes on April 27, 1373 with a scolding, defensive edge:

> I wasted a good part of my time in the service of princes. . . . I was with the princes in name, but in fact the princes were with me; I never attended their councils, and very seldom their banquets. I would never approve any conditions that would distract me even for a short while from my freedom and from my studies. Therefore, when everyone sought the palace, I either sought the forest or rested in my room among my books. . . . Once I was sent to Venice to negotiate the reestablishment of peace between that city and Genoa, and I used up a whole month of the winter; later, in behalf of peace in Ligura, three summer months far away from civilization with the Roman prince [Charles IV] . . .; finally, three more winter months to congratulate King John of France, who had then been freed from an English prison. . . . I call them lost days, although on my last one, while returning to Italy, I dictated an enormous letter. . . . There, then, are the seven months I lost in the service of princes.[27]

Yet the truth is not quite so simple, the time not so minimal or neatly contained. Occasional verse, correspondence, smaller embassies and errands, conversations laced with advice to the lord—these too occupied the poet in his relationship with the princes. Nor was it a negative experience from the mature Petrarch's perspective.

His vision, anticipating the ideal Italian Renaissance union of courtier and humanist, emerges in a mirror of princes addressed to Francesco da Carrara, the model ruler (ca. 1370–73): "you showed yourself not only an outstanding prince to your own people but a model for princes in other cities."[28] What qualities must such a man possess? Above all, he should be loved, not feared or hated (as Machiavelli allowed). "If you wish to be loved, love," writes Petrarch, reprising the Seneca that had seasoned his words to Good King John.[29] The prince must provide his subjects with victuals and water, protect them with city walls, be merciful and generous. There is, however, a higher order of civic business, reached in the writer's peroration:

> you should honor outstanding men and make them your closest friends. . . . I call outstanding those whom some excellence has distinguished from the common herd, whom unusual justice and holiness, alas, rare in our age, or experience and training in strategy, or resourcefulness in literature, and knowledge of things has made unique.[30]

As tokens of such honor, a host can give "horses, clothing, arms, plates, money, houses, farms, and the like."[31] The list points to the kind of payments Petrarch received. In fact, he built his house at Arquà on land donated to him by Francesco da Carrara. His will names two legatees with instructions that they divide by lot his horses.

Think, he exhorts Francesco, of Augustus Caesar, whose retinue counted Cicero, Virgil, and Horace. Peerless poets, Petrarch calls them—not so subtly implying the one obvious contemporary comparison. The prince must surround himself with illustrious men, like those Romans whose portraits ringed the great Paduan council chamber in the cycle (with a monumental *Petrarch in his Study* at one end) inspired by *De viribus illustribus:*

> What, I ask you, can be more attractive to deserving, exceptional men than to spend their lives under a just and kind prince who is also a favorable judge of merit? . . . while men at arms can be useful to you at the moment, and perform timely services, men of letters can provide timely advice and a lasting name, as well as show you the straight path to heaven.[32]

By the end of this long letter in the *Seniles,* we understand that this man of letters is not only thanking his Carrara patron. He is describing himself. He is the man we see in the mirror.

CHAPTER EIGHT

THE UNFORGETTABLE *BOOKS OF THINGS TO BE REMEMBERED* • *Rerum memorandarum libri*

Paolo Cherchi

The *Rerum memorandarum libri* (*Books of Things to Be Remembered*) is unique among Petrarch's works, not because it is incomplete—so are several of his other works—but because its subject matter and organization are unique in the poet's oeuvre.[1] It is distinct, moreover, by virtue of the fact that Petrarch never revised it, never published it, never made mention of it, or circulated any of its chapters or sections as he almost always did with his other works before publishing them. It seems that well along in the second year of its redaction, he decided to truncate it because he must have become so dissatisfied with it that he did not even bother to destroy it, preferring instead to erase it from his memory. Yet if Petrarch chose to forget it, the book proved unforgettable to his immediate posterity. Contrary to his own judgment, this turned out to be one of his most influential works in the later humanistic period and most especially in the Renaissance. Paradoxically, the features Petrarch must have disliked the most turned out to be the ones that made the work popular and quite important two centuries later. Such a drastic decision on the author's part cannot be attributed to fatigue (the plan of the work, as we shall see, required many years of research) or to other external factors. Most likely a series of important elements prompted the dropping of the project, elements that amount to a sort of conversion, to a sudden realization that the subject, the structure, and the message of the work were no longer interesting. In fact, they must have seemed to stand as an impediment for the writer, eager to breathe new air. Thus it is important to identify these elements, to establish their nature, and to understand their role first in inspiring the *Rerum memorandarum libri* and then in the author dropping it, and finally in seeing how they contributed to its later and greatest success. We must proceed on two separate and yet complementary lines of investigation, starting by describing

151

the subject matter, the sources, the structure of the work, and the cultural conjuncture in which it was conceived; then the intellectual and existential crises that caused Petrarch to abandon it, and finally, look at its later reception, although this part, for obvious reasons, will be dealt with in a summary way.[2]

The *Rerum memorandarum libri* was planned as many books, but only four were completed. The first was meant to contain a general introduction, while the others were supposed to illustrate the four cardinal virtues. Considering that the three books completed are devoted to "prudentia," we can calculate that the entire work would have consisted of twelve books (three per virtue) besides the introduction. The missing parts are so substantial that it is impossible even to guess how Petrarch would have filled the gap. What he did finish, however, gives a quite clear idea of how the planned books would have been organized because the model set at the beginning was to be followed throughout in order to convey the particular view of history that Petrarch intended to present.

The books completed deal with "prudentia," or "sapientia," as others would say, namely, with the first of the four cardinal virtues. Petrarch wrote only the first paragraph (actually just the title) of the fifth book, which was dedicated to "temperantia," the second cardinal virtue. Then he came to a full stop, a sort of sudden death. The silence that Petrarch kept concerning the existence of this work makes it more of a miracle that it even survived. The autograph was found in 1378 by Tedaldo della Casa, who transcribed it and made it known perhaps against the deepest wish of its author, who then had been dead for nearly a decade. Petrarch composed it in the years 1343–1345, which means that he invested a considerable effort in it, a fact that makes his sudden and irreversible change of mind even more dramatic and wanting an explanation.

The title would suggest that Petrarch intended to write a work in the style of the *Noctes Atticae* by Aulus Gellius, a collection of curiosities, concerning historical anecdotes, linguistic problems, natural history as well as anthropological data. Works of this kind flourished in the thirteenth and fourteenth centuries, both in Latin—such as the *Otia imperialia* (*Recreation for an Emperor*) of Gervaise of Tillbury and the *Mare historiarum* (*Sea of Histories*) of Guido delle Colonne, an acquaintance of Petrarch's—and in the vernacular—such as the *Fiorita di varie storie* (*Bouquet of Various Stories*) by Armannino da Bologna, the *Fiorita* by Guido da Pisa and the *Libro di varie storie* (*Book of Various Stories*) by Antonio Pucci. However, Petrarch did not collect "curiosities" simply to entertain his readers, and he never composed a book lacking a clear purpose or a well-written structure. For him the "res" (things) to remember were strictly concerned with "humanitas," and any other subject was extraneous to his curiosity.

Let us then look for other models. Once we peruse the work and see that it deals primarily with virtues and the lack thereof, we might imagine that the *Rerum memorandarum libri* is similar to some sections of medieval encyclopedias, such as *De rerum proprietatibus* (*On the Properties of Things*) of Bartholomaeus Anglicus or the *Speculum morale* (*Moral Speculum*) of Vincent of Beauvais, or to works on vices and virtues by authors like Peraldus or Bono Giamboni. But then again we are unable to find any close similarities with the *Rerum memorandarum libri*, either in the taxonomic principles that guide these works or in their subject matters. The *Rerum memorandarum libri* presents some encyclopedic features—for example, the compiling and cumulative techniques—but it would be wrong to classify it among the medieval encyclopedias because it lacks any encyclopedic taxonomy (be that based on the order of the liberal arts or that of the seven days of Creation or any other arrangement found in medieval encyclopedias), and it is not a book of "virtues and vices" either, or at least it is not so in the primary intention of Petrarch. Thus the *Rerum memorandarum libri* would seem an original work without any models; yet it does have one, which turns out to be extremely influential concerning some crucial points of its organization. We will identify it as we look deeper into the content of the *Rerum memorandarum libri*.

This content consists of the following topics. The general introduction deals with "otium" (leisure), the "vita solitaria" (solitary life), and with studying and learning, all activities and qualities that are considered to be the prelude to virtue. The second and third books deal with memory and intelligence, the fourth with "providentia" (foresight). However, it is better to be more specific for reasons that soon will be clear. Fortunately, Petrarch himself helps us in this task since he gave a table of contents to these four books, so it is easy to view at a glance how he divided the materials.

Book 1: "De otio et solitudine" (On leisure and solitude); "De studio et doctrina" (On study and learning).
Book 2: "De memoria" (On memory); "De ingenio et eloquentia" (On disposition and eloquence); "De facetiis ac salibus illustrium" (On humor and witticisms of illustrious people); "De mordacibus iocis" (On biting retorts); "De ingenio paupertatis" (On lack of talent).
Book 3: "De solertia et calliditate" (On shrewdness and artfulness); "De sapientia" (On wisdom).
Book 4: "De providentia et coniecturis" (On foresight and predictions);

"De oraculis" (On oracles); "De sibillis" (On Sibyls); "De vaticiniis furentum" (On prognostications by mad persons); "De presagiis morientium" (On predictions by dying people); "De sompniis" (On dreams); "De aruspicum et augurum disciplina" (On the art of soothsayers and diviners); "De ominibus et portentis" (On omens and portents); "De caldeis mathematicis et magis" (On magicians). Of this last chapter only the title exists.

Book 5: the first of the books devoted to "temperantia" and contains only two anecdotes, one concerning Tiberius and the other Augustus.

Note the correspondence between some of its titles and some titles found in the *Factorum et dictorum memorabilium libri IX* (*Nine Books of Memorable Deeds and Sayings*) by Valerius Maximus. This suggests that Valerius Maximus was the inspirational model for the *Rerum memorandarum libri*. This finding goes far beyond the usual discovery of "a source," which essentially brings to light the debt of an author towards another insofar as themes and subject matters are concerned. In this case the presence of Valerius in the background sheds light on the particular new method of approaching history presented for the first time in the *Rerum memorandarum libri* through the unusual way of arranging the anecdotes on the pattern that had been unique to Valerius and then expanded by Petrarch. The success of the *Rerum memorandarum libri* among humanists and Renaissance writers owes a great deal to the particular use Petrarch made of his model. Thus it is necessary here to focus on Valerius and his presence in Petrarch's library.

Valerius Maximus appears in the list of *auctores peculiares*, his "preferred authors," that Petrarch compiled between the years 1330–40; specifically he appears in the first place among the historians: Valerius Maximus, Livy, Justin, Florus, Sallust, Suetonius, Festus, and Eutropius. Certainly this list is not based on any hierarchic principle, but Valerius Maximus's inclusion is nonetheless significant. For us Valerius is hardly a historian, certainly not comparable to Livy or Sallust and not even to the epitomizers Justin and Florus, found in this list. This may be the reason for his particular afterlife: he was widely read and excerpted throughout the Middle Ages but never glossed as other authors like Ovid, Statius, and Virgil were, at least, not until the middle of the fourteenth century, when he was made the object of commentaries of a quality reserved for the great classics.[3] When Petrarch included him in his canon of historians, Valerius was just being rediscovered in the protohumanist circles where Petrarch moved, and where the *Dictorum factorumque memorabilium libri* were read in their entirety rather than in sections and selections of anecdotes as was

the case through the many *florilegia* that were fairly common in the previous centuries. At the root of this revival was an appreciation for Valerius's Latin style, and in general the attention of Dionigi da Borgo San
Sepolcro—the first commentator of Valerius Maximus[4]—and of the translator Antonio Lancia and many protohumanists of their caliber, or even
of early humanists like Guarino Veronese. All of them attached great importance to the exemplary value of the anecdotes, their historical nature
(which was sufficient to distinguish them from the typical medieval *exempla*), and Valerius's fascinating narrative, which isolated them from any historical context, making them timeless. Petrarch surely appreciated those
values, but he distinguished himself from these early admirers by paying
particular attention to the way Valerius arranged his narrative and to his
unique method of "comparing" or "pairing"—or even better, "paralleling"—
histories, or his way of "bringing together stories sharing similar traits."
Valerius was a historian of a different kind from the ones found among Petrarch's "auctores peculiares." He did not write history in the annalistic or
the political mode, nor did he write biographies in the manner of Suetonius,
nor did he epitomize other historians. What he did was to cull anecdotes
from various authors and arrange them in a thematic way. These themes
cover a vast range of subjects, including many of those seen in the *Rerum
memorandarum libri*. Within that thematic arrangement there was another
device, a very important one at that. Valerius divides each set of anecdotes
into two parts: the first contains stories or data taken from Roman history;
the second, deeds and sayings of foreign people, mostly Greeks, grouped
under the heading of "externi." This was a new way of writing history, and
Petrarch took to imitating it.

   In his imitation Petrarch disregarded all subjects touching upon civic
and juridical institutions, to which Valerius had paid some attention mostly
in the first two books, and he focused exclusively on the "human" aspects,
that is, on the anecdotes that cast light on the greatness or baseness of the
human soul, as shown through deeds and sayings. Valerius's thematic arrangement appealed to him since it provided a sort of check against potential dispersion in this kind of narrative, and most of all, it strengthened
the presentation of a virtue by showing the variety of its facets or minor
virtues. For example, wisdom, one of the cardinal virtues, can take the
form of "memoria" (memory), "intelligentia" (discernment, understanding),
and providentia" (foresight). Not less important was a complementary and
to some degree opposite element, namely, the "distribution" of virtues and
vices across different latitudes and times. This latter element was shown
in the division and similarities between the Romans and the "externi." For

Petrarch this approach represented a great novelty in writing history: not a history of wars or conquests, of empires or republics, but rather tales of men who present behavior for which at least one or more parallel instances can be found in Roman history as well as in other regions or civilizations far from Rome. It was possible not just to write a history of men and mankind but to write about some universal human elements in history.

Petrarch adopted this innovation, but he modified Valerius Maximus's system by adding a section of "moderni" to the Romans and to the "externi." Such an updating was of the utmost importance because it added a diachronic element to the "synchronic" method of Valerius, and this element establishes a chain of continuity between ancients and moderns. Without this bridge it would be more difficult to understand how the ancient world can teach anything to moderns. This link stresses the fact that man retains his human nature and qualities through the ages, and it gives sense to our studies of antiquity since they would be totally useless unless modern people shared some traits with the ancients. The section of "moderni" constitutes a proof that antiquity was exemplary because it could be and was imitated in modern times, although not as frequently as Petrarch would have wished. These are the major theses implied in the structure and in the diachronic organization of the *Rerum memorandarum libri*.

An important insight into the work is gained by considering the period in which the *Rerum memorandarum libri* was written. The years when it was composed, 1343–45, coincide with the period in which Petrarch's "infatuation" or cult for the Roman world was beginning to fade away and his existential crisis was showing its first signs. Petrarch had spent many years working at *De viris illustribus*, a set of biographies of illustrious ancient Romans, and perhaps this work was still in the making when the model of Valerius Maximus suggested another way of approaching antiquity, and rather than focusing on the "life" of a few great people Petrarch wanted to write on many qualities and faults of all sorts of people, including the moderns and even his contemporaries. Valerius's method covered a wider range of cases and persons and offered a comparative view of ancient and modern worlds. This outlook was refreshing and gave Petrarch a sort of respite from the very engaging and laborious biographical genre. Take, for example, the relatively brief chapter devoted to leisured and solitary life ("De otio et solitudine.") Here, after a few introductory paragraphs devoted to the notions of "otium" and "solitudo," we find five anecdotes under the heading "Romana" (Scipio, Scipio Africanus, Cicero, Mutius Scaevola, Augustus), three in the "externa" section (Epaminondas, Achilles, Socrates), and just one representing the "moderna" (King Robert of Naples). Another example on "De sollertia et calliditate," taken mostly from Valerius 7.3, "Vafre dicta aut facta" (Clever sayings and deeds), contains twenty-eight anecdotes (fifteen Roman, twelve "externi," and one modern), about the same number as those recorded by Valerius (twenty). Still another example is from "De mordacibus iocis" (On biting jokes), a subject somewhat related to the previous one. In this section the majority of the twenty-two jokes (fifteen Roman, four "externi" and three modern") are drawn mostly from the second book of Macrobius's *Saturnalia*, and from *Vitae duodecim Caesarum* (*Lives of the Twelve Caesars*) of Suetonius, and this time Petrarch's selection significantly reduces the number of the anecdotes found in the sources. As one can see, the variety of cases is great and the transition from one to the other presents no problem since each anecdote is autonomous, although a common theme binds them together. These factors give an agility to the work, which can be read just opening any page and starting from any point and jumping from this to any other one. These are features that the *Rerum memorandarum libri* shares with works in the style of Aulus Gellius.

The variety of subject and the agility of the presentation is enhanced by the narratives, which are most often quite brief. Just one example from the chapter on dreams gives an idea of these anecdotes:

> The rest of Cassius of Parma, a strong supporter of Anthony, was equally sad and frightening, and did not have a happier conclusion. When Anthony was defeated in the battle of Actium, in total despair Cassius sought refuge in Athens. While he was asleep at night, he had the impression that a huge man, who was dark as an Ethiopian and unusually ugly, came into his room. Stunned by this vision, Cassius asked him who he was. The man answered with a ghastly roaring that sounded like Greek. Awakened by fear, terrified Cassius woke up his servants and asked them about that man who had broken into his bedroom. Since they firmly denied that anyone had entered it, he went back to sleep not feeling well. But when the same horrific vision woke him again, he ordered his servants, who had come in with some light, to stay by him. A day of suffering followed a night of fear. During those very days, he was in fact executed by order of Augustus. Unhappy with ordinary invectives, Cassius had previously provoked him with particularly harsh insults.[5]

This episode in the life of Gaius Cassius, one of the murderers of Cesar, is taken from Valerius Maximus, from the chapter "On prodigies":

> What follows outdoes the dire aspect of this dream. After M. Antony's power had been broken at Actium, Cassius of Parma, who had followed his party, fled to Athens. As he was lying in bed there at dead of night deep in sleep after his anxieties and cares, he thought that a man of huge proportions, black in color, with unkempt beard and hair hanging down, visited him and when asked who he was, replied, "Your bad angel." Alarmed by the horrible sight and the fearful name, he called his servants and inquired whether they had seen anyone of that appearance entering or leaving the room. They answered that nobody had come that way. So Cassius gave himself up again to rest and sleep; and the same apparition came before his mind. So with sleep put to flight he ordered a light brought in and the slaves not to leave him. Between that night and his execution by Caesar's order very little time intervened.[6]

Petrarch's closeness to his source highlights his way of rewriting it. Space does not permit an analysis of how he renders the ancient authors (Valerius, Cicero, Macrobius, Seneca, or Pliny, among the most frequent sources) each one with his own style (a thorough comparison should be done on the original texts); however, Petrarch remains close to their succinct way of telling an anecdote. The majority of the anecdotes in *Rerum memorandarum libri* are as brief as the one just quoted. Some are even briefer; only rarely are they longer, and then they are mostly "modern," such as the case of "Rex Robertus" (King Robert of Anjou), in which Petrarch exceptionally inserts some personal memories. This stylistic feature together with the thematic variety makes the work highly and easily readable; and its new approach to history seems quite promising.

However there were problems and pitfalls with this new approach. The variety could cause dispersion and make it difficult to set limits to collecting anecdotes as well as in establishing firm criteria for selecting those deemed worthy of being remembered. Briefness in the long run could cause boredom. But above all variety and shortness sacrificed character with a consequent loss of exemplariness and study of ethical values. With this method history ceased to be "magistra vitae" (a teacher about life). What could a work like *memorandarum libri* really teach, except many witticisms and many deeds that show character but often do so at the cost of distorting history since character is shown in constant behavior rather than in a sporadic saying or deed? What was its audience? The lack of clear answers to these questions must have been one of Petrarch's main reasons for interrupting this work. Billanovich suggests two reasons: one was Petrarch's sudden departure from Parma in February 1345, where he left the manuscript; another could be the fact that in Verona Petrarch discovered Cicero's letters and devoted all of his time to transcribing them.[7] Some maintain that the immense bulk of materials was the primary cause for abandoning the project.[8] These reasons are certainly important, yet there must have been other fundamental reasons of an existential nature. Around the years of its composition Petrarch was still looking for "character," for those great and exemplary personalities of the ancient world, but it was becoming imperative for him to look for his own character and care less or not at all about the great souls of the past. It was the period in which Petrarch, following the exhortation of Augustine recorded in the *Secretum* (the latitude of the dates proposed for the composition of the *Secretum* can include the later period of the composition of the *Rerum memorandarum libri*), begins the conversion into his own interiority, into his own conscience, and abandons the study of antiquity and moves into his own self. He did go back to the *De viris illustribus* when he planned to include some illustrious Christians next to the great Romans, but he never went back to the *Rerum memorandarum libri*.

Greatness has in itself a high degree of exemplariness, whereas an accumulation of anecdotes does not; and Petrarch must have suddenly realized that *Rerum memorandarum libri* was an immense project with little value for his own self-knowledge. In other words, it presented materials that could not be used at an autobiographical level. From this point on Petrarch tends to use literature and history only insofar as they help him to understand himself. Petrarch was not a historian in the strict sense, but he was an avid reader of historians, and he even edited Livy. He saw in history a great source of moral inspiration, a lesson of how man achieves greatness. In other words he looked for a way of translating history into experience, into persuasive models of life. The *Rerum memorandarum libri* represented a departure from this way of reading history: he moved to broaden the stage in all directions because he understood through Valerius that there are many other human events, be they virtues or vices, that are "memorable" besides the moral greatness of a few especially gifted persons. Memory is, after all, the main function of history itself. But this was as much as Petrarch could do at this point in his intellectual life. When he discovered that this approach to history would not work as a tool of intimate persuasion and did not leave him any room for a personal presence, he abandoned the project. The crisis of 1348, the year of the plague and Laura's death, as well as of many of Petrarch's close friends, closed forever that kind of historical and moral writing.

Paradoxically, the lack of exemplarity and of autobiographical elements contributed to the fortune of the work. *Rerum memorandarum libri* had a great impact on the literary culture of Italy and Europe. The reasons were twofold. Once the criteria of greatness and exemplarity in the medieval sense were removed to make room for all sorts of "memorable" things, the boundaries of history were broadened to limits hitherto unknown, and the sources of all histories and of all times yielded a wealth of materials previously neglected. Bringing to the fore the "memorable" factor was not sufficient: it was important to see its durability through repetition, through the comparison with similar cases, and this was the second reason why *Rerum memorandarum libri* became a textbook of sorts for later generations. It was Valerius's principle of "concordances of history," or "le concordanze delle storie" as Anton Francesco Doni, a sixteenth-century writer, would say. This technique of grouping ancients and moderns according to some attributes (e.g., illustrious birth) or virtues (e.g., endurance against pain) or other qualities (e.g., prophetic gift) transformed history into rhetoric since it did not "narrate" lives or political events, but rather extrapolated data that are "predicabilia," that is, those accidental elements that tell of individuals and their historical specificity, and at the same time provide the bases for a link with other individuals. This is a somewhat complicated problem, but it is easy to understand if we say that history was seen as a depository of "commonplaces," as an inexhaustible "topica" (set of topics). In this way the emphasis falls on the "humanity" that can reveal itself in a variety of situations and on a variety of people from all periods. In this way history is not narrated in the typical sequence of events studied in their causes and effects or in the abstract way of mediaeval *exempla*, but through a series of anecdotes that in their "concordance" or repetitiveness predicate human traits in a concrete historical fashion. Their exemplarity or persuasive power, as well as their possibilities of embracing larger parts of history, are far superior to those attained through the presentation of great characters who tend to be unique and unrepeatable. A serial list of anecdotes implies the possibility that any reader may fit into one or into several of those chains of anecdotes, just because he or she is human and may have some or all the traits presented in the anecdotes, regardless of the degree in which he possesses them. This reduction of history to rhetoric was the greatest achievement of the *Rerum memorandarum libri*. Petrarch, as we have seen, embraced this new way of understanding history, but then he rejected it. But this novelty was not lost on generations that followed. They found very appealing an approach to history capable of bringing to light an infinite number of characters and cases, not for writing about them but for using them in all sorts of writing.

In many ways the *Rerum memorandarum libri* presents a synoptic and simultaneous vision of history of the kind found in the *Divina commedia* and in Boccaccio's *Amorosa visione* (*Amorous Vision*) and *De casibus virorum illustrium* (*Falls of Illustrious Men*), and, of course, in the *Triumphi* of Petrarch himself. These "visioni" of conflated histories were a literary genre invented in Italy, a genre that became immensely influential especially during the quattrocento in numerous allegorical poems in many vernaculars of Western literatures. There are, of course, differences between the *Rerum memorandarum libri* and the *Commedia* and the works of Boccaccio, but they are beyond the scope of this discussion. I can only say that the *Rerum memorandarum libri* began to be fully appreciated when those allegorical visions were dying out and humanistic "topics" were taking their place. Its full potential became clear toward the end of the quattrocento and at the beginning of the cinquecento in the midst of the great rhetorical and pedagogical reforms, which looked for ways of combining history and rhetoric and for teaching the use of history in literary studies. The names of Lorenzo Valla, Rudolph Agricola, Desiderius Erasmus, and Philipp Melanchton give an idea of the level of engagement in these areas. Speaking in general terms we see the need for breaking down large categories of classification into more reduced commonplaces called "tituli," that is, "titles" that referred to a series of anecdotes bearing some resemblance to each other: for example, "men who died because they were bitten by snakes" or "incestuous women." Headings such as these could absorb endless events of "microhistory" that may be present in the history of all times and periods. The role played by Valerius Maximus through Petrarch's adaptation in the *Rerum memorandarum libri* in this great revolution was a seminal one, as I showed in an essay of 2002.[9] Concordances of histories under *tituli* appeared everywhere and especially in the works of Volaterrano (Raffaello Maffei), Battista Fregoso, and finally, in Ravisius Textor, whose fortunate *Officina* contains over three hundred fifty *tituli*, many of which are taken directly from Valerius and Petrarch. Most of them follow the pattern of making "concordances of histories." In all these works and in many others that were meant to be great tools for literary *inventio*, the anecdotes always combine but keep separated Romans and *externi*, ancients and *moderni*. The influence of these manuals on the culture of the cinquecento was immense, as I tried to show in a study on the fake erudition of the Italian writers in the cinquecento.[10] I can say now that Petrarch was at the origin of this peculiar "concordanze delle storie" with a work that he rejected. He must have dropped it because there was no room for his own self in it, but this lacuna appealed to the humanists who saw the *Rerum memorandarum libri* as a work of pure erudition, which set ancient histories next to modern ones in an agreement that made it possible to combine history and rhetoric.

PART III

CONTEMPLATIVE SERENITY

CHAPTER NINE

PASTORAL AS PERSONAL MYTHOLOGY IN HISTORY • *Bucolicum carmen*

Stefano Carrai

The revival of the bucolic literary genre in fourteenth-century Italy, first achieved in an exchange of eclogues between Dante Alighieri and Giovanni Del Virgilio, reached its apex with Petrarch's *Bucolicum carmen*, soon after imitated by his great disciple and emulator Boccaccio.[1] Petrarch began planning a collection of eclogues while residing in Vaucluse, between 1346 and 1347. Ten years later, with the exception of a few details that he later retouched, it was complete, and in 1357 in Milan the author transcribed the eclogues into the codex now referred to as MS Vaticano Latino 3358. The outcome of this long effort was a book fascinating both for its formal elegance and for its moral and autobiographical implications, ingeniously concealed beneath the pastoral allegory. Petrarch's twelve eclogues actually trace a journey through the fundamental stages of personal and social history during the decade he was composing them, from his brother Gherardo's entry into a Carthusian monastery to the death of Robert of Anjou, from Cola di Rienzo's attempted political reform to the poet's resignation from service to cardinal Giovanni Colonna, from the Black Death of 1348 to the Hundred Years' War.[2] From a summary of each eclogue's essential content there emerges an overarching image of this complex work.[3]

In the first eclogue, entitled *Parthenias*, the shepherd Monicus, who represents Petrarch's brother Gherardo, sings the praises of David's Psalms and invites Silvius—that is, Francesco—to draw his inspiration from them rather than the Latin classics.[4] Although Silvius cannot deny the virtues of the biblical songs extolled by his interlocutor, he proclaims his intention of continuing to follow the Homeric-Virgilian genealogy to which he is devoted. This dialogue reflects Petrarch's spiritual crisis, which culminated around the mid-1340s, and the strong impact on him of his visit to his brother at the Chartreuse of Montrieux in 1347.

In the second eclogue, "Argus," Petrarch shifts his attention to contemporary political issues. He focuses on a trio of shepherds: the poet, once more as Silvius, and two of his friends, Giovanni Barrili and Barbato da Sulmona, as Idaeus and Pythias, respectively. These three personages eulogize Robert of Anjou, the "Argus" of the title, mourning his death and deploring the political turmoil occasioned by the strained succession that followed in the Kingdom of Naples.[5]

Temporarily moving away from politics, Petrarch takes up the subject of love in his third eclogue, whose subject its title announces. "Amor pastorius" (The amorous shepherd) is a dialogue between Stupeus and Daphne. He sings of falling in love with her, but like Ovid's nymph and Laura in the *Rerum vulgarium fragmenta*, this Daphne evades his advances. Stupeus, a name loosely translatable as "Wonderstruck," is Petrarch, as a passage from the third book of his *Secretum* confirms. In this dialogue Augustinus, speaking to Franciscus of the latter's first meeting with Laura, declares, "You were seized with wonder, and your eyes were dazzled with extraordinary brilliance. Wonder indeed is said to be the beginning of love." The eclogue stages a perfect *interpretatio nominis*, when the lovestruck shepherd acts out ("interprets") his own name, "Stupui" (I marveled, *Bucolicum carmen* 3.87).[6]

The fourth eclogue, entitled *Daedalus*, returns to a theme seeded in the first, the art of poetry. It features a conversation between Tyrrhenus ("Tuscan") and Gallus ("Frenchman"), recognizable as Petrarch and the French musician Philippe de Vitry, respectively. The musician expresses his admiration and envy of Petrarch's poetical skills, and the latter replies that his Parnassian talents are a gift bestowed upon him from birth by Daedalus, the most celebrated artist of antiquity. Invoking the famed mythological craftsman in this way, the author connects himself with the classical past and, at the same time, suggests the divine nature of poetic inspiration.[7]

Italian politics come once again to the fore in the fifth eclogue, "Pietas pastoralis" (The shepherds' filial piety), as Martius and Apicius, representing the Colonna and Orsini families respectively, discuss the miserable condition of Rome. While Martius is eager to remedy the many ills facing the once-great metropolis, Apicius remains passive and unconcerned. Soon afterwards, a third shepherd, Festinus, joins them to announce that someone else (implicitly, Cola di Rienzo) has begun to take action to resolve the city's problems and restore its former grandeur.[8]

The next two eclogues hold up the Church and its officials as targets of a scathing attack. In the sixth, entitled *Pastorum pathos* (*The Shepherds' Suffering*), Pamphilus—meaning "all-loving" and probably a pastoral mask for the first pope, Saint Peter—challenges the guilty conscience of Mitio ("the fat one"), alter ego of Pope Clement VI, who in the poet's view was driving the Church to the brink of collapse with his greed and corruption.[9] The seventh eclogue, "Grex infectus et suffectus" (The infected and replenished flock), features Mitio once again, joined this time by his spouse Epy. With a name allusive to the Epicurean life, she stands for the corrupted Church.[10]

Petrarch appears once more in the eighth eclogue, "Divortium" (Separation), this time in the guise of the poor shepherd Amiclas, who explains to Ganymede (that is, Cardinal Giovanni Colonna) why he is quitting his service.[11]

A tragic tone dominates eclogues 9–12, which all confront catastrophe and loss. In the ninth, called *Querulus* (*Lamentation*), Philogeus and Theophilus describe the sorrow and devastation caused by the Black Death in its spread from Sicily, up the Italian peninsula, and then throughout Europe in 1348.[12] As their names imply, Philogeus ("Lover of Earthly Goods") is concerned about the plague's devastation in the physical world, whereas Theophilus ("Lover of God") invites him to look beyond, toward life eternal.[13] In the tenth, titled *Laura occidens* (*The Fallen Laurel*), Petrarch as Sylvanus speaks to Socrates, his friend Ludwig van Kempen.[14] Sylvanus relates the sad story of his long and patient care for the laurel tree and its destruction by furious winds, patently alluding to Laura's passing.[15] In the eleventh, "Galatea," it is the duty of three nymphs—Niobe, Fusca, and Fulgida, representing the sorrow-stricken, the resigned, and the faith-enlightened soul, respectively—to seek the grave of Laura, alias Galatea, and to sing the praises of the deceased.[16] The twelfth and last eclogue, "Conflictatio" (The Conflict) presents Multivolus ("Wanting Much") and Volucer ("Swift Messenger"), who describe the onset of the conflict between Pan (the ruler of France) and Arthicus (the English monarch) that developed as the Hundred Years' War.[17]

This overview, although succinct, should suggest the cohesive design of the collection, which Petrarch conceived with a programmatic aim of disguising under pastoral allegorical veil key events, chronologically arranged, in his personal life and in European history during the decade spanned by the book's composition. He clearly rejected the numerical structure of Virgil's *Bucolica*, comprised of ten eclogues, choosing instead another canonical Virgilian number, that of the twelve-book *Aeneid*. The care Petrarch took in outlining the macrotext can help explain, for example, the particular position of his anti-Avignon diptych, eclogues 6 and 7 with Mitio ("fat" Pope Clement VI) as its main character, exactly at the midpoint of the series.

The polemic against the corrupt Avignon church, which returns in letters of the poet's *Liber sine nomine* and certain sonnets of the *Rerum vulgarium fragmenta*,[18] proves indeed central both structurally and conceptually to *Bucolicum carmen*. It is no coincidence that the pastoral collection opens with the presentation of Petrarch's monastic brother Gherardo (Monicus). Pope Clement VI, who should act as a "good shepherd" to the Christian flock, constitutes instead a morally negative model, in open contrast with Saint Peter, the first pope, who represents the early, uncorrupted Church. This very Peter, as Pamphilus in the sixth eclogue, is the mouthpiece for a dramatic invective against Clement (Mitio), whom the saint denounces as an unfaithful servant to his good lord, that is, God. It culminates as Pamphilus rails:

> Cross after fetters and iron after rods—such
>   treatment would suit you—
> No—it would be too little. Say, rather, to
>   match your merit,
> Torment unending in durance eternal—unless
>   there's some worse thing.
> Ingrate! Evasive servant, untrue to a
>   kindly master![19] (6.121–24)

With these verses, allusive to Christ's martyrdom as a model for every true Christian, Petrarch means to say that he who does not fear his Lord and is not devout will be justly punished by the eternal pain of Hell, compared to which the brief suffering of death on the cross or from the breast-piercing lance is far preferable.

The allegorical representation of the Church as a whore, arrogantly averse to evangelical spirituality and Christianity's ailing flock, seems in sum to constitute the center of the *Bucolicum carmen* as a whole. "Fat" Mitio himself declares the pope's foolhardy behavior and that of other contemporary church officials, all absorbed in worldly goods and pleasures of the material life, oblivious to eternity, speaking in tones so unbefitting that they sound blasphemous and pagan. In the seventh eclogue he, the pope, urges his wife Epy, a personification of the Church, to partake freely of earthly enjoyments with him:

> Nothing of man endures; we also must die,
>   being mortal.
> Therefore I counsel pleasure; of this time that is
>   passing let us

Waste not an hour but rather dismiss all
   fruitless and idle
Worries—unless, my darling, you are of a
   different opinion.[20] (7.82–85)

The overall conceptual framework of the *Bucolicum carmen* is firmly rooted in a medieval worldview and in Christianity's historical situation. This orientation is evident from the very start since the theme of monasticism that dominates the first eclogue sets the tone for the rest of the volume, replaying the great medieval *de contemptu mundi* motif (on contempt for the world).

Within the work's decidedly medieval Christian frame of reference, however, a reader can discern the poet's affinity with the Virgilian eclogues that are his primary model.[21] For example, even in Petrarch's first eclogue, with its ascetic subject matter, a correspondence may be seen with the first of the Mantuan poet's *Bucolica*. The dialogue between Petrarch's characters, Monicus and Silvius, is partly based on that between the shepherds Tityrus and Meliboeus. Virgil's eclogue opens with Meliboeus reproaching Tityrus for his secluded and sedentary way of life, while the speaker must depart from his home and wander throughout the world. Meliboeus declared,

You, Tityrus, lie under your spreading beech's covert, wooing the woodland Muse on slender reed, but we are leaving our country's bounds and sweet fields. (Virgil *Eclogues* 1.1–3)[22]

Similarly, in the initial lines of Petrarch's eclogue, Silvius comments on Monicus's reclusive lifestyle, hidden away as he is in a cave, detached from such earthly matters as tending to his herds and fields:

Monicus, hidden away alone in your
   quiet cavern,
You have been free to ignore the cares of the
   flock and the pastures;
I, hapless vagrant, go straying o'er thorny hills
   and through thickets.[23] (*Bucolicum carmen* 1.1–3)

Petrarch borrows another image from Virgil's first eclogue for his second, that of fields laid waste by the shattered peace. In both cases, lightning-struck trees disrupt pastoral tranquility. Virgil's Meliboeus laments the poor condition of his flocks and lands: "this mishap was foretold me, had not my wits been dull, by the oaks struck from heaven" (*Eclogues* 1.17–18). Likewise, in Petrarch's "Argus," Idaeus recalls how the sudden darkening of the sky and a violent thunderstorm that uprooted a mighty cypress signaled the death of King Robert:

> . . . all of a sudden
> Phoebus's light was snuffed out behind a dark cloud-
>   bank and swiftly
> Night with no warning descended upon us. A
>   terrible hailstorm
> Shook the blind air as great gales in clashing
>   contention and tempests
> Raged in their fury while lightning flashed through
>   the fissured welkin.
> Struck by a thundering bolt, the lofty cypress
>   fell headlong,
> Shaking the hills and the fields. . . .[24] (2. 7–13)

Moreover, when in this same Petrarch an eclogue the shepherds prepare to intone their epicedium, or elegy, for Argus (King Robert), they allude to the dirge in Virgil's fifth bucolic for the Roman emperor Augustus, heralded there as "Daphnis." Idaeus proclaims,

> ". . . If once the shepherds sang
>   only of Daphnis,
> Now it behooves your song to tell of
>   magnanimous Argus."[25] (2.62–63)

Again, Virgil's fifth eclogue, which rises to a climax with verses envisioning the emperor's deification, sets the example for Laura's glorification as Galatea in Petrarch's eleventh. Both poets describe the birth of an eternal cult commemorating the deceased—for Virgil public ritual, for Petrarch private devotion cultivated in the heart.

Let these examples suffice to demonstrate the Virgilian echoes discovered, as one would expect, in each of Petrarch's eclogues, both in their general narrative framework and in the occasional integration of specific fragments of Virgil's text. One must not, however, view Petrarch's eclogues as a simple recycling of the earlier poet's achievement. Rather, Petrarch develops motifs of his own by blending Virgilian elements with echoes of other classical authors. It is no accident, for instance, that traces of Ovid's tale of the Cyclops Polyphemus and his love for the sea nymph Galatea[26] work their way into Mitio's erotically charged appeal to his wife Epy (Pope Clement VI speaking to his Church) at the opening of the seventh eclogue.

> Sweeter you are, than these pleasant groves, sweeter than the
>   grasses,
> Welcome more that the grottoes, welcome more than the
>   murmuring river;
> Come to me, please, while I sit here alone; come join me, dear Epy.
> (*Bucolicum carmen* 7.1–3, trans. Bergin, modified to highlight
>   parallels with Virgil)[27]

Clearly, these Petrarchan verses are modeled upon the words of Ovid's Polyphemus as he woos Galatea with sensuous advances:

> O Galatea, whiter than snowy privet-leaves, more blooming than
> the meadows, surpassing the alder in your tall slenderness, more
> sparkling than crystal, more frolicsome than a tender kid, smoother
> than shells worn by the lapping waves, more welcome (*gratior*)
> than the winter's sun and summer's shade, more goodly than or-
> chard-fruit, fairer than the tall plane-tree, more shining-clear than
> ice, sweeter (*dulcior*) than ripened grapes, softer than swan's down
> and curdled milk, and, if only you would not flee from me, more
> beauteous than a well-watered garden. (*Metamorphoses* 13.789–98,
> trans. Miller)[28]

From Ovid's lengthy catalog of similes, Petrarch selected the words "dul-cior" and "gratior" to which he calls attention through the rhetorical device of repetition, thus strongly alluding to his source without overtly reproduc-ing it entirely. It is certainly not by chance that, out of the vast mosaic that makes up the *Metamorphoses*, Petrarch chose to reproduce a single pair of small tiles from a passage with such an elaborate pastoral soliloquy.

For his *Bucolicum carmen* Petrarch draws on material from nonpastoral sources as well. The name "Mitio," for example, actually comes from Ter-ence's play *Adelphoe*. In fact, the sixth eclogue produces a theatrical moment when Pamphilus, speaking for Saint Peter, addresses Mitio, the corrupt, neglectful Pope Clement VI, using obscenity reminiscent of Roman com-edy. He sarcastically asks his interlocutor, "Tu michi quid servas, nisi cor-nua dempta iuvencis?" (What are you saving for me, aside from horns taken

from oxen?" *Bucolicum carmen* 6.61). In other words, Mitio, the protagonist of this central eclogue, is insulted as a cuckold (cf. Italian "cornuto").
Taking yet another jab at the Avignon papacy, Petrarch here refers to the
whorish nature of Pope Clement's first spouse, symbolically the Church
that he has allowed to grow corrupt under his negligent stewardship.[29]

This comic dialogue pointing to Terence is but one of myriad examples
of Petrarch's receptivity to other texts and genres, from which fragments
pass into his own. Among them, the medieval *tenso* figures significantly as
a model for the kind of dialogic exchange and debate in the eclogues with
more than one voice.[30] The *tenso* was, in effect, a poetic dialogue in two or
more voices, often strongly polemical to the point of bordering on reciprocal invective, which had been launched in grand style on Europe's poetic
stage by the troubadours, that is, the poets of Provence, where Petrarch
had grown up and received his early education. In their wake the first Italian poets in Sicily and Tuscany had made the *tenso* into a genre that enjoyed
much success among readers. Whether the debate was purely fictitious or
represented a true and proper discussion, poets imaginatively conceived it
as a way of dynamically rendering different or even opposing points of view.
This evocative grafting of a debate among shepherds to the type of the *tenso*
is a brilliant intersection of a modern genre with the bucolic tradition.

Such heterogeneous borrowings distance Petrarch from strict adherence to Virgilian bucolics. Overall, the extent to which Petrarch diverged
from the classical pastoral model was proportionate to his adherence to the
moral eclogue tradition, established in the Middle Ages and legitimized by
Servius's commentary on Virgil.

In the letter to his brother explaining his first eclogue (*Familiares* 10.4),
Petrarch wrote that bucolic poetry "is incomprehensible unless explained
by the author." Speaking with reference to this Petrarchan affirmation, the
early commentator Benvenuto da Imola confirms, "it is impossible to understand pastoral verse if the author does not explain it."[31] The identities of
the shepherds in the *Bucolicum carmen*, as well as the events to which they
allude in their conversations, would remain unknown or unexplained—that
is exactly what happens with other texts—without help from past commentators and what Petrarch himself wrote in his correspondence with persons connected to those events, such as his brother Gherardo (*Familiares*
10.4), and Barbato da Sulmona and Cola di Rienzo (*Lettere disperse*, 7, 11]).
Thanks to these sources of information, a full understanding of Petrarch's
painstakingly crafted allegories, both personal and historical, is possible.
He interweaves allusions to the Church's Avignon captivity or to Cola di

Rienzo's attempt at republican reform with references to his separation from Cardinal Giovanni Colonna and the spiritual tragedy he suffered with the loss of Laura. The reference to Cola goes so far as to open a cross-section of style midway between epic and prophetic, where recourse to the topos of the animal kingdom living in complete harmony, liberated from all struggle and aggression, expresses the poet's vision of a world pacified under the tribune's able governance (*Bucolicum carmen* 5.116–33).

Pastoral poetry is born therefore of suggestions from literary tradition as well as stimuli from a personal historical reality that the poet hides behind the rustic screen. Even if the allusiveness and programmatic obscurity of the poetic text make it difficult, if not impossible, to comprehend or pinpoint the bucolic scene's context, the depiction still may refer to autobiographical or period reality.

It is highly significant, moreover, that Petrarch's pastoral cycle closes with an eclogue dedicated precisely to that bloodiest of conflicts, the Hundred Years' War—a tremendously disruptive chapter in Christian history—and that this twelfth and final eclogue ends with a hopeful line delivered by Multivolus (the populace) in the final line. He instructs Volucer, "Go now, and put certain hope in matters of happier promise."[32] Thus the *Bucolicum carmen* at its finale sounds a note that invokes one of the theological virtues, hope, which for a faithful Christian signals the ultimate hope of eternal life.

The tenth eclogue constitutes another focal point of the collection, magisterially analyzed by Guido Martellotti.[33] Sylvanus-Petrarch, under the veil of an imaginary voyage he has taken through the world, reviews the entire history of Western poetry, concluding with a celebration of his deceased beloved, now risen to a symbol of poetry itself. Sylvanus opens this story metaphorically, recalling his amorous cultivation of the laurel plant:

> . . . I cultivated my laurel in spite of
>   its thorny
> Site 'mongst the crags. Nor did I rely on my
>   own skill only,
> But, going forth into the world, I sought counsel
>   of alien farmers.
> Neither my journey's extent nor the times,
>   which were unpropitious,
> Nor yet the arduous task deterred me. . . . (*Bucolicum carmen*
>   10.36–40)[34]

The fondness and devotion with which the poet cultivated the plant, symbol both of his lady and of poetry,[35] harks back to the narrative of the third eclogue and foreshadows the great sorrow occasioned by the tragic, sudden uprooting of the plant by furious winds, alluding figuratively and metaphorically to Laura's death:

> But with malevolent glance did Fortune observe
>   my contentment.
> While I had chanced to go off to visit the ancient
>   woodlands
> Pestilent Eurus on one hand swept in, and
>   rain-swollen Auster
> Struck from the other. And felling trees far and
>   wide they uprooted
> My joy and delight, my laurel. They buried its
>   savagely shattered
> Boughs and its fair-crested leaves forever under
>   the earth's surface. (*Bucolicum carmen* 10.379–84)[36]

In the eclogue's finale, the speaker's friend Socrates (that is, Ludwig van Kempen in pastoral garb) consoles the mourner over the death of the laurel-Laura, allowing him to glimpse the possibility of a poetic and Christian sublimation for the plant that represents the beloved lady:

> . . . In truth, neither Eurus nor Auster
> Ravished your sacred tree. Immortal powers
>   have transplanted
> It to God's blessed grove; the corruptible cortex
>   has perished,
> But firmer than ever before the roots are living
>   and thriving,
> And the new seed of your laurel makes fecund
>   the fields of Elysium. (10.399–403)[37]

Although the pastoral genre implies here a reference to the pagan deities and the Elysian fields of antiquity, the laurel's translation to a happier realm would have unequivocally alluded, in the eyes of a medieval reader, to the Christian paradise. The fact that the poet can take solace in his beloved's death squares with the frame of mind he openly declares in the third book of the *Secretum*, when Augustine in dialogue with Francesco

reproaches him for having loved Laura's body. The finale of this tenth eclogue is thus in line with the palinode registered so unequivocally in that
chapter of the *Secretum*. There Petrarch has Augustine say that he should
have loved the beautiful creature insofar as she was God's creature and
therefore as a vehicle for redirecting his love toward the Creator. Thus in
the eclogue the poet consoles himself with the realization that only Laura's body has died, while her soul, the proper object of his love, dwells in
paradise.

This same theme undergoes further development in the next eclogue,
the eleventh, wholly dedicated to the apotheosis of Laura, celebrated under
the name Galatea. As it opens, Niobe laments the death of so beautiful a
nymph, pronouncing solemn words before Galatea's tomb:

> What a small dwelling, alas! too somber for so
>   much glory!
> This is your home, Galatea?—you, whom the
>   sun beholding
> Saw in its wonder a splendor like to its own
>   but greater
> And its amazement endured till slowly it sank
>   in the ocean. (11.18–21)[38]

In the eclogue's conclusion, however, Fulgida forcefully elaborates the
theme, barely hinted at by Niobe, of the consolation that must come from
the separation between the body, lying underground, and the soul that lives
with God (11.78–80).

Fulgida's speech clearly voices the Christian doctrine of the soul that
pulls itself free from the imprisoning body and ascends back to the bosom
of God, thereby allowing those who mourn the deceased to accept the departure as a passage into true, eternal life.

Such moral and personal allegory, obviously, is of great importance in
Petrarch's pastoral poems, yet at the same time, they bend away from their
middle-Latin background, not only at the level of style and language but
also with respect to the themes that run through the collection. Petrarch
assimilates his own personal mythology into the bucolic genre so that the
dirge over the severed laurel merges with grief over Laura's death and also
with loss of any possibility for ever again composing true poetry:

> Alas, whither now shall I turn, being weary?
>   What sheltering refuge

Will solace my pain? At my age to whom shall I
venture to offer new songs?" (10.385–86).[39]

Even the poet's own childhood and his peregrinations are evoked in what
has by now become a mythical aura. Speaking of fortune as a force that
controls all worldly things, the shepherd Amyclas, who represents Petrarch, tells Ganymede, a figure of Cardinal Colonna, how he was uprooted as a child from the land of his ancestors and exposed to the dangers
of a marshland:

> . . . Hither in childhood, outcast in
>   exile, my father
> Brought me, away from the land of my forebears,
>   and left me abandoned
> Here on this marshy shore. . . . (8.85–87)[40]

The language of this declaration, legendary in its tone, connects with the
first letter of Petrarch's *Familiares*, addressed to Ludwig van Kempen.
There, comparing his wanderings to those of Ulysses, the poet recalls how
he was begotten and born in exile, a birth so difficult for his mother that
the midwives and doctors thought at first it had killed her:

> Arezzo, not an ignoble city of Italy, recalls all of this. It was there
> that my father, expelled from his native city, fled with a large num-
> ber of good men. From there, in my seventh month I was taken and
> carried throughout Tuscany on the arm of a strong young man.
> Since I enjoy recalling for you these first labors and dangers of
> mine I might add that he carried me hanging at the end of a rod af-
> ter having wrapped me in a linen cloth so as not to hurt my tender
> body just as Metabus had done with Camilla. (*Familiares* 1.1)[41]

These personal and metapoetic aspects of the text, coupled with its formal elegance, must have greatly appealed to Petrarch's contemporaries, at-
tracting their attention and that of his immediate posterity. We can well
understand why Boccaccio so quickly understood that Petrarch had elevated the bucolic style to an exceptionally high level. Boccaccio's epistle
to the Augustinian monk Fra Martino da Signa with the author's key for
decoding hidden meanings in his own eclogues, inspired by Petrarch's,
begins with a brief history of the genre. Theocritus invented it, but without writing allegorically. "After him Virgil composed in Latin, and he did

hide under the cortex certain meanings. . . . After him others wrote, but they were ignoble and completely negligible, except for my supreme master Francesco Petrarca, who lifted the style somewhat above its wont, and in accordance with the matter of his eclogues continually put meanings behind the names of his interlocutors."[42] What he particularly admired about Petrarch's pastorals was their style and their allegory, the serious "real" meaning concealed beneath ostensibly banal surface events. In his passionate defense of poetry at the culmination of his *Genealogies of the Gentile Gods*, Boccaccio asks:

> Who would be so foolish as to believe that Francis Petrarch, that most illustrious and Christian man . . . spent so many vigils, so many holy meditations, so many hours, days, and years, as we can reasonably supposed he did spend—if we measure the gravity of the verse in his *Bucolicum carmen* and the exquisite ornate elegance of the words—only to imagine and represent Gallus who asks Tyrrhenus for his bagpipes, or Pamphilus and Mitio having an argument, and the like ravings of other shepherds?" (*Genealogie deorum gentilium* 14.10.4)[43]

The Certaldan himself had already advanced tradition in his vernacular works, opening still further avenues for exploring and restoring the genre with his *Ninfale fiesolano* (*Nymphs of Fiesole*) and *Comedia delle ninfe fiorentine* (*Comedy of the Florentine Nymphs*, or *Ameto*), the latter explicitly an allegory of the seven cardinal virtues.[44]

Petrarch's encyclopedic digression on the ancient poets in "Laurea occidens" (*Bucolicum carmen* 10) is a seminal example of humanistic writing. This eclogue's motif of the poet traveling to Asia, Greece, and back to Italy to converse with classical authors, reminiscent of the beginning of Dante's *Divina commedia*, is taken up again in the fourth chapter of *Triumphus Cupidinis* and anticipates the literary history outlined a century later in Angelo Poliziano's *Nutricia* (*Things for My Wetnurse*).[45] Indeed, the philosophy of poetry is one of the principle themes of the *Bucolicum carmen*. As his fourth eclogue conveys talk about the nature of poetic inspiration, Petrarch sees poetry as a link to the eternal, a precious gift bestowed by God. This in fact becomes an important theme among critics and poets during the Renaissance, when pastoral poetry is a much more successful genre, both in Latin and in Italian, thanks to the revival of the fourteenth century and especially the examples of Petrarch and Boccaccio.

CHAPTER TEN

"YOU WILL BE MY SOLITUDE" • Solitude as Prophecy • *De vita solitaria*

Armando Maggi

I know a man, I am not speaking as Paul, but an actual man in the flesh who is confirmed in the solitary life (*in solitudine constitutum*), content with his rude subsistence and his studies and who, though he lack much of a blessed life, at least has this considerable compensation for his solitude, that his whole year passes happily and peacefully as though it were a single day, without annoying company, without irksomeness, without anxieties.[1]

This passage from the first book of *De vita solitaria* (*The Life of Solitude*) is Petrarch's powerful self-portrait as a new Saint Paul (cf. 2 Cor. 12:2), to whom a life of solitude has granted an essential insight on the true nature of man. Giving his expression a legal connotation (solitude has confirmed or constituted him), the poet claims that solitude gives birth to a new spiritual man, as Paul underwent a radical transformation after his ascent to the third heaven. Similarly, in *Rerum vulgarium fragmenta* (*Fragments of Vernacular Matters*) the poet writes that love "gives wings to [his followers] to make them fly to the third heaven" (*Rerum vulgarium fragmenta* 177.3–4).[2] Whereas the poetic formulation is metaphorical (love grants wings to lovers to fly up to the third heaven, that is, the planet of Venus), in his compelling treatise on solitude Petrarch speaks of "a man . . ., an actual man in the flesh." As he openly states in a crucial passage of *De vita solitaria*, for Petrarch solitude has a prophetic character. We could argue that the ultimate theme of this challenging text is not the pleasure of solitude per se but rather, in the poet's words, the "holy" nature of human identity, which finds in solitude its fullest realization.

In the vast corpus of Petrarch's works, *De vita solitaria* "best represents his most intimate inspiration."[3] Petrarch is the "first historian of solitude" and is the first to theorize a solitude that is both lay and religious.[4] The entire European meditation on the meaning of solitude, from Montaigne to

Pascal, Schopenhauer, Kierkegaard, and Tolstoy finds in Petrarch's treatise its first representative. During the fourteenth and the fifteenth century, *De vita solitaria* along with *De remediis utriusque fortune* (*Remedies for Fortune Fair and Foul*) was Petrarch's most transcribed text. It survives in more than 120 manuscripts from that period. One splendid copy, made on vellum in Lombardy for the Visconti family (ca. 1460–70), provides our volume's frontispiece.[5] Today this fundamental work is usually seen as a lengthy and erudite catalog of classical and Christian stories about solitude, a sort of immense warehouse of facts and figures from the past that the humanist Petrarch strives to link to his own personal experience through a series of interesting musings on this subject.[6] In Etienne Gilson's words, in *De vita solitaria* Petrarch "does not limit himself to gathering some literary reminiscences . . . he makes use of all his sources."[7]

In truth, *De vita solitaria* lies at the core of Petrarch's thought. For him solitude does not mean isolation, which he identifies with the love experience (Laura), but rather intimate dialogue with a friend who pursues the same intellectual and spiritual ideals. Dialogue is a key concept in Petrarch's "new" solitude.[8] As we will see in detail later, the physical or symbolic presence of the friend merges the two seemingly opposite facets of Petrarch's solitude: its religious character that recalls the monastic experience and the classical *otium* (leisure). Petrarch argues that if a human being's life is in a constant dialogue with Christ, who lives in the deepest recesses of our soul, a friend symbolizes both the neighbor in the Christian sense, that is, the other through whom Christ presents himself to us, and the intellectual's special interlocutor, as the Latin philosophers Cicero and Seneca recommend. In a key passage of *De vita solitaria* Petrarch writes that "You," Philippe de Cabassoles, its addressee, "will be my solitude." Philippe de Cabassoles was bishop of Cavaillon. His diocese included Vaucluse, where Petrarch resided.

As *De vita solitaria* eloquently shows, Petrarch's solitude is in fact densely populated. In his view, this dialogical solitude corresponds to the highest manifestation of human nature. We will see that at the end of *De vita solitaria* the poet imagines that nature enthusiastically responds to his insight. Not merely erudite addenda, the long lists of exemplary figures participate in the poet's concept of solitude.[9] The numerous *exempla* evoke an imaginary geography of solitude, an ideal and well-structured map of the world based not on its political contours but rather on its historical rapport with solitude. Petrarch places himself and Vaucluse at the center of this almost oneiric atlas of universal solitude. For Petrarch to live in the solitary nature of Vaucluse is an act of memory. If the "world" ("secol noioso," as he writes in the *Triumphi*) is an "unnatural" landscape in that it fosters decadence and oblivion, Vaucluse is a hymn to that pristine nature revealed by the early Christian thinkers but already sensed by some classical philosophers, such as Cicero and Seneca.[10] But the atlas of solitude is not founded only on memory. I have defined Petrarch's solitude as "oneiric" because, like a dream, it is both remembrance and desire. It is a project that the "friend," the solitary man's alter-ego, blesses and validates.

Petrarch composed *De vita solitaria* during the Lenten season of 1346, as he writes in one of his *Seniles* (6.5). The first version took him only a few months.[11] The poet continued to work on this text for some years, between 1353 and 1366, when he finally sent it to its dedicatee, the bishop of Cavaillon.[12] In 1371, Petrarch wrote an additional segment for his treatise on solitude. This addendum is called "Supplemento Romualdiano" because it concerns the life of the Saint Romuald, whose love for solitude was not mentioned in the previous versions of the text.[13] *De vita solitaria* is divided into two parts, plus the dedicatory epistle to Philippe de Cabassoles. For a general definition, we could say that book 1 debates the topic of solitude from a philosophical and theological standpoint, whereas book 2 deploys a universal atlas of solitude through an extensive number of *exempla* from classical and Christian history.

The primary inspiration for *De vita solitaria* is Augustine's *De vera religione* (*The True Religion*, 391 C.E.), which Petrarch used as "a sort of manual of Augustinian doctrine."[14] Together with the *Confessions*, it is for Petrarch Augustine's most influential work.[15] A brief introduction to this text is essential for our understanding of *De vita solitaria*. *De vera religione* opens by emphasizing the necessity of healing the soul so that it can contemplate the atemporal beauty of God.[16] The contemplation of divine beauty is in reality man's most natural desire, even though many doubt its existence. The theme of divine beauty as the "intrinsic order of nature" (*intimis naturae terminis*) returns in the second part of the tract, where Augustine reiterates that each element of the created world responds to an "immutable law of harmony."[17] Only Christianity can cleanse man of his spiritual disharmony and lead him to the perception of the inner rule of nature. Augustine contends that the wise men of the classical past would convert to Christianity if they lived now.[18] The opposition between the past of a false knowledge and the present enlightenment is a key theme of Augustine's treatise. Augustine holds that the Christian faith has imposed itself "all over the world," and that after a long period of persecution churches are being built now in "every inhabited part of the world."[19] The contrast between the past and the present is also present in *De vita solitaria*, but in a reversed order. Citing Augustine almost verbatim, Petrarch argues that the current world has lost the purity of the past. Both Augustine and Petrarch, moreover, describe the tension between decadence and faith as the distinction between a worldly and a spiritual man. Augustine speaks of the "old, external, and earthly" man (*vetus, exterior, terrenus*), who only cares for the flesh.[20] The worldly man's behavior is, in Petrarch's view, against the order of nature itself.

Augustine's insistence on the unbridgeable contrast between the "world" and "nature" is what most impressed Petrarch when he first read *De vera religione,* as he explains in the *Secretum.* For Petrarch, the world-versus-nature opposition mirrors the body-versus-soul conflict. Speaking of the innumerable sinful and confusing images that creep into the soul through the bodily senses, in the *Secretum* Petrarch introduces the healing effect of his first encounter with *De vera religione.* To read this book was like leaving his homeland because of his desire to see (*quam qui videndi studio peregrinatur a patria*) and finally entering a new famous city.[21] Petrarch, reminiscent of Augustine's *City of God,* opposes two cities, that is, man's "homeland," the land of the body and of the chaotic images that overwhelm the imagination, and the new city of the spirit, the city of God where nature and solitude coexist. The city of solitude is a place of a new and cleansed sight. In Petrarch's words, he came to *De vera religione* in his desire "to see." We could go so far as to say that *De vita solitaria* is an enthusiastic hymn to the "new" sight only solitude can grant. The sight of solitude heals the wise man of his "distress" (*aegritudo*), Petrarch's "pernicious illness of the soul" according to Augustine in the *Secretum.*[22]

Petrarch's image of the opposing cities recalls a passage from Cicero's *Tusculanae disputationes,* which in *De vita solitaria* Petrarch defines as a main source of Augustine's *De vera religione.*[23] Cicero contends that "[t]he seeds of virtue are inborn in us and, if they were allowed to ripen, nature's own hand would lead us on to happiness of life."[24] We depart, however, from nature (*natura*) as soon as we "are acknowledged" by our fathers; that is, as soon as we enter society or, as Augustine and Petrarch call it, the "world." As we also find in Augustine and Petrarch, Cicero visualizes "our revolt from nature" and thus also our return to it, as a journey. And like Augustine and Petrarch, Cicero argues that the "world" perverts our sight.[25] How did the concept of the netherworld arise in popular culture? The populace that rushed to theaters, Cicero holds, could not envision the souls of deceased people without visualizing some sort of bodily figure: People could not see anything in their mind; "everything was brought to the test of eyesight."[26]

Petrarch's concept of solitude evokes the inner sight or foresight of a prophetic knowledge. The implicit apocalypticism of *De vita solitaria* finds in the *Triumphus Eternitatis* the following poetic rendition:

> . . . . I at last beheld
> A world made new and changeless and eternal.
>   I saw the sun, the heavens, and the stars
> And land and sea unmade, and made again
> More beauteous and more joyous than before. (*TE* 20–24 trans.
>   Wilkins)[27]

The final dissolution of the world, a recurrent biblical theme (e.g., Rev. 21:1; 2 Peter 3:10–13) leads to the birth of a new Jerusalem character-ized by a firm and perennial nature, which is exactly what the solitary man seeks away from the *saeculum* or world.[28] It is worth noting how in his apocalyptic description of the end of time Petrarch first mentions the eternity and stability of the new world and then the destruction of the four elements (fire, air, earth, and water), as if the longing for the forthcoming and spiritual reign caused the annihilation of our physical and corrupt-ible condition. In terms similar to the opening verses of T. S. Eliot's *Four Quartets*, Petrarch's new Jerusalem is described as the quintessential place of solitude, a deserted ("herma") space "with no grass" ("d'erbe ignuda") dominated by an eternal present where words like "shall be," "has been," "ne'er," and "before" mean nothing.[29]

In *Familiares* 3.5, Petrarch argues that "eloquent writers have written on [the solitary life], none in my opinion has hitherto praised such a life suffi-ciently."[30] *De vita solitaria* is meant to fill this grave gap. However, the open-ing paragraph of the dedicatory epistle to the bishop of Cavaillon shows that the real issue at stake in *De vita solitaria* is not solitude but rather the pursuit of "immortal . . . truth" (*immortalis veritas*) in sharp contrast to the "falsity" (*fictio*) and "deceit" (*mendacium*) of the world.[31] Paraphrasing Saint Paul, Petrarch sees solitude as a synonym for revealed truth: "every secret is in time disclosed; the shadows depart" (cf. 1 Cor 4:5: "The Lord will bring to light everything that is hidden in darkness").[32] Solitude evokes an apocalyptic expectation. Revealed truth, nature, and solitude are three terms defining one and only one experience.

It is worth noting that this initial praise of the solitary life is directly linked to a warm celebration of friendship, although what Petrarch writes to Philippe could sound contradictory at first. On the one hand the poet states that, given his popularity, he cannot experience solitude: "Whether I go out into the open or remain sitting at home, I must still be in the public gaze."[33] He cannot live alone in silence any longer because he has become a public figure. On the other hand, Petrarch also reminds Philippe that in the past the two of them tasted solitude together for a couple of weeks. What seems inconsistent in reality reveals the essence of *De vita solitaria*. For Petrarch solitude is both memory (the past intimacy with Philippe) and dream (an ideal project denied by reality). Philippe is an essential element of Petrarch's concept of solitude for a variety of reasons. In Petrarch's words, the bishop validates the poet's *otium*, the leisure time he spends reading and writing, and thus his literary identity tout court: "Clearly, should I not have been a thoughtless steward of my time (*otium*), if I did not have regard to one whom I consider the first admirer of my literary talent?"[34] In these initial pages, Petrarch claims that he writes because of his friend's constant and ideal presence. But the bishop also corroborates his view of solitude, since they shared it in the past even if for a short time. Like writing, solitude is a project whose success remains hypothetical. Like writing, solitude is a disposition of the soul. It is a longing.

Solitude as an unappeasable yearning is the first topic examined in *De vita solitaria*. One could find it ironic that this lengthy text on solitude opens by denying the possibility of experiencing a truthful solitude: "I believe that a noble spirit (*generosum animum*) will find repose nowhere (*nusquam*) save in God, in whom is our end, or in himself, and his private thoughts, or in some intellect united by a close sympathy with his own."[35] Petrarch introduces solitude as an impossible place, a utopia (a "nowhere" place). The paradox behind this treatise becomes even more apparent if we keep in mind that, according to Petrarch, the fundamental topic of *De vita solitaria* is indeed the "place" of solitude. In book 2 the poet argues that there are three kinds of solitude: solitude of place, "with which my present discourse is especially taken up"; solitude of time; and solitude of the soul, which corresponds to a state of contemplation.[36] Petrarch believes that only Saint Francis of Assisi was able to practice all three sorts of solitude. One could thus infer that, for Petrarch, the *poverello* of Assisi embodies the perfect example of solitary man. How could Francis receive the celestial revelation of the stigmata had he never left Assisi? Petrarch's emphasis is less on the ultimate place of solitude, which does not exist, than on the departure from the familiar place or places of one's biography, from the world. Petrarch's innate restlessness is well known and is even reflected in his *Testamentum* where he imagines seven different places for his burial. Among the innumerable names of solitary figures in the history of Western culture mentioned in *De vita solitaria*, Petrarch underscores the uniqueness of Saint Paul's and Saint Francis's experience. In both cases, solitude coincides with a revelation. Solitude literally transformed and marked them (the stigmata; the physical ascension to the third heaven).

The impossibility of the "noble spirit" to attain the place of solitude and repose finds a paradoxical parallel in Petrarch's initial distinction between two hypothetical men, one whose life is led by nature (*natura duce freti*) and the other who lives according to the populace's base addictions. Although the poet identifies the "occupatus" (busy man) with a man who stifles his natural desire for solitude by juggling infinite job and family tasks, we cannot help but see an essential similarity between this restless and unhappy man and the noble spirit's inability to rest in solitude. The concrete impossibility of solitude is the common denominator of the two seemingly opposite human beings. This opening discussion on the "occupatus" versus the "solitarius," which has received considerable critical attention, can be only understood if read in the light of *De vera religione*.[37] As I briefly mentioned at the beginning of this essay, in chapter 26 Augustine depicts two men with contrasting ways of life, the "old and exterior and worldly man" versus the "new and interior man."[38] If the first man follows "what common people define as happiness" and only longs for worldly goods, the "new" man experiences an inner "rebirth." Augustine holds that this spiritual rebirth undergoes a seven-stage process, which starts off with the nourishment of positive examples. Accordingly, the entire second book of *De vita solitaria* is a barrage of positive *exempla*, or models of behavior, from classical and patristic sources. Augustine explains that, if in stages two through four the "new" man witnesses the marital sweetness springing from the unity of soul and mind, in the fifth stage he experiences an ineffable wisdom. The sixth "age" corresponds to the total oblivion of temporal life. The final "age" is eternal tranquility (*beatitudo perpetua*).[39]

Augustine's distinction between two men is in fact a process of conversion within the same man. Unlike Augustine, Petrarch sees these two hypothetical men not as two moments in the same process of transformation but rather as two irredeemably opposed human beings. Nobility of the soul is for Petrarch an immutable, almost ontological condition. However, following Augustine's insistence on the private conversion granted by solitude, Petrarch insists that his treatise is based on his personal experience of both his present solitary condition and the remembrance of his previous, worldly life.[40] The Italian poet contends that his writing has nothing to do with existing books on this subject. Like a new Saint Paul blessed with the experience of solitude, he relates a new and unique event. Petrarch mentions only one book that might serve as a possible source, Pseudo-Basilius's *Laus eremiticae vitae* (*Praise of the Eremitical Life*). From this treatise he claims to have taken only the title, although we know that in fact some passages of *De vita solitaria* echo Pseudo-Basilius. It is worth asking why Petrarch reports this title only to distance himself from the rest of the work.[41] The *Laus eremiticae vitae*, actually the final chapter of Saint Peter Damian's eleventh *Opusculum*, is a lyrical praise of the "eremus" (life of the hermit).[42] An easy answer would be that such an isolated life of self-denial is not what Petrarch has in mind. Yet the long list of *exempla* that open book 2 of *De vita solitaria* to a large extent derives from another literary source, the *Historia lausiaca* (*Lausiac History*), which exalts the eremitical life.[43] The second sentence of Pseudo-Basilius's *Laus eremeticae vitae* defines the "solitaria . . . vita" as the "discipline of divine arts." The difference between Pseudo-Basilius's eremitical life and Petrarch's *De vita solitaria* is the concept of "testis" or witness. For Pseudo-Basilius, the "cella" (cell) is the witness to the monk's progress toward enlightenment.[44]

Augustine's *De vera religione* enlightens Petrarch's initial query on the necessity of having a "witness" (*testem*) to our solitude.[45] What does it mean to hypothesize a witness to our solitude and, conversely, what does it mean to witness another's solitude? In this initial section of his book, Petrarch insists that Christ witnesses every moment of our existence, whereas the ancients posited a number of different hypothetical bystanders (for instance, Seneca mentions Epicurus, Cato, or just "someone"), which reflected, in Petrarch's view, their remoteness from the sole "natural" religion, Christianity.[46] Augustine stresses that in the classical era only isolated men, like Socrates, perceived the presence of the divine in those "works of nature" (*opera naturae*) that were "produced thanks to divine providence," and avoided the temples of false gods.[47]

By now we should be aware of the complexity of *natura* in Petrarch's text on solitude. Although in the *Rerum vulgarium fragmenta* nature at times seems to be an entity distinct from God (for instance, RVF 251.7, "Or già Dio et Natura nol consenta"), in *De vita solitaria* nature is God's manifestation through the created world, including human beings' "qualities, tendencies, [and] instincts."[48] To live according to nature means to achieve one's full humanity, as Saint Paul and Saint Francis confirm. Given that God is both within and without us, nature is at once the "place" (*locus*) in which we live and the true identity of our soul. As Cassirer puts it, for Petrarch, "landscape becomes the living mirror of the Ego."[49]

There is a problem, however, with this analysis of nature and solitude. We have seen that for Petrarch the natural place of solitude is less an actual landscape than a longing. Critics often stress that the solitude described in *De vita solitaria* is very different from that analyzed in *De otio religioso*. An accurate exam of the former, however, brings to the fore the deeply religious nature of Petrarch's "lay" solitude. *De vita solitaria* exalts a universal vocation for a solitude that is at once intellectual and inherently religious. As Petrarch's treatise underscores, the sacred does not necessarily reside in monasteries but rather lies at the core of every human being's identity. The dialogue with a friend, which mirrors the dialogue between the subject and Christ, blesses and ritualizes the layman's quest for solitude.

How should one interpret the "encyclopedia of solitude" that constitutes most of the second part of *De vita solitaria* and that finds in the *Historia lausiaca* its first and most abundant source?[50] Contrary to a widespread critical belief, the innumerable stories in *De vita solitaria* are not lumps of citations loosely connected to each other. They chart a historical geography of solitude, which finds its center in the Italian peninsula. Italy is the holy land of Petrarch's "new" solitude.

Petrarch loots the *Historia lausiaca*, but to his own ends. For instance, he tends to deemphasize references to supernatural occurrences. His goal is evoke the figure of a humanist-like hermit who would foreshadow Petrarch's modern ("new") solitude. It is revealing that the life of Isidorus, the very first biography in the *Historia lausiaca*, is absent from Petrarch's lengthy list. Isidorus, who is praised for his great knowledge of the Scriptures, was a mystic who frequently experienced an "excessus mentis" (literally, an excess of the mind, a mystical condition) that silenced him even when he was at dinner with his brothers.[51] In the first two selected biographies from the *Historia lausiaca* Petrarch reveals the parameters of his choice. After a fleeting reference to Dorotheus, who lived in a "spelunca" for sixty years,[52] the Italian poet focuses on the hermit Amon. The first event of his life recorded by Petrarch is the fact that Amon abandoned his wife, with whom he had lived in chastity for some twenty years, to pursue solitude. Petrarch fails to say that it was his "blessed" wife (*illa beata*), who suggested that he live elsewhere to nourish his "virtus philosophiae" (virtue of philosophy).[53] Moreover, Petrarch doesn't consider it necessary to mention the mystical qualities that this man had acquired. We read that an angel carried Amon over a river while he was in ecstasy.[54] An additional crucial element of Petrarch's selective criteria is the insistence on a hermit's scriptural and literary knowledge. This aspect is apparent in his third extensive reference to the *Historia lausiaca*, the life of Ammonius, which corresponds to the twelfth chapter of the hagiographic collection. Petrarch reports that, because of his profound "study and knowledge of the sacred literatures" Ammonius was asked to become bishop, but he cut off an ear to make himself unsuitable for this social position.[55] Although in the *Historia lausiaca* we do find an initial reference to Ammonius as "doctus" (learned), we also understand that this quality was related to his pursuit of religious perfection ("summum pietatis ac religionis"). In Ammonius, Petrarch reads a reflection of his own biography, torn between social duties and fame on the one hand, and the pursuit of knowledge through solitude on the other. Another eloquent example concerns the hermit Didymus. Petrarch defines this holy man, who became blind at the age of four and received no formal education, as "literis clarum" (famous for literary learning), even though the *Historia lausiaca* says that his "spiritual knowledge" was exclusively a gift of divine grace.[56] It is thus evident that Petrarch's idea of solitude summons the image of a prototypical humanist-like hermit, a sort of Petrarch's alter ego. With his "new" concept of solitude, Petrarch brings to completion a long spiritual process that originated in the classical era and later was transformed in the light of Christianity. The Italian poet posits himself as a new referential figure, a new Saint Paul, who inaugurates a new era of solitude.

After the desert fathers, Petrarch selects "less famous exempla that are scattered in the recesses of the scriptures."[57] What follows is actually a list of familiar biblical figures, including Adam, Moses, and the prophets Elijah and Jeremiah. Why does Petrarch move in reverse chronological order, from the desert fathers back to the Old Testament? The biblical sources add a teleological, prophetic connotation to Petrarch's initial portrait of a protohumanist hermit. Petrarch reminds us that, speaking of the "public calamity" brought about by the moral corruption of Judah, the prophet Jeremiah invoked the redeeming power of solitude and penance.[58] Petrarch directly links solitude to prophesy. In his words, the solitary life is a "life of philosophy, of poetry. [It is] a holy, prophetic life." Let us recall that Petrarch compares himself to a new Saint Paul ascended to the third heaven. In his definition Petrarch does not oppose two sets of intellectual practices (lay versus religious culture) but rather uses the adjectives "holy" and "prophetic" to define "poetry" and "philosophy." His focus is on the two highest areas of intellectual investigation, which in Petrarch's new solitary man reveal their sacred essence.

After the biblical exempla, Petrarch turns to modern figures of solitary men who lived in Italy. In Italy, Petrarch writes in reference to the third book of Gregory the Great's *Dialogues*, solitude works miracles ("solitudinis Italie congesta miracula").[59] Italy lies at the center of Petrarch's universal atlas of solitude. In Italy solitude manifests its sacredness. Echoing the story of the desert father Ammonius, Petrarch reminds us that Ambrose, the bishop of Milan, fled into the woods whenever he was free from his social duties.[60] Imagining that Ambrose composed the "sweet flowers of his books" in this solitary setting, Petrarch reproduces a long quotation from an epistle from Ambrose to Sabinus. Ambrose stresses that a solitary man is not alone if he keeps a friend "close to [him]" and writes having his friend in his mind, as the classical philosophers suggested that the solitary man always keep a hypothetical interlocutor.[61] Petrarch transcribes the beginning and the ending of this letter, but he leaves out its central part in which Ambrose speaks of God's own solitude in heaven and states that to meditate upon the Gospel is like walking alone in heaven. Both sections enumerate holy figures who lived alone. In the first part of the letter, Ambrose mentions the Virgin Mary, Peter, and Adam. Petrarch interrupts the citation when Ambrose mentions that Adam lost his solitude because of a woman and thus became unable to fulfill his "celestial duties."[62] Instead, Petrarch inserts a tirade about women's negative influences on men's search for solitude, backing up his accusations with a citation from Virgil's *Georgics:* "For the sight of the female slowly inflames and wastes his strength, nor, look you, does she . . . suffer him to remember woods or pasture."[63] Virgil speaks of bulls and horses, but Petrarch applies this comparison to men. For the Italian poet, woman is the name of man's exile from nature, whereas "friend" signifies man's residing in his own nature.

Italy, the holy land of solitude, mirrors Jerusalem.[64] *De vita solitaria* recalls the *Itinerarium ad sepulchrum domini nostri Yhesu Christi* (*Itinerary to the Sepulcher of Our Lord Jesus Christ*), where Petrarch sketches the hypothetical itinerary of his friend Giovanni Mandelli's journey to the Holy Land.[65] In book 2 of *De vita solitaria*, the trajectory of Petrarch's solitude starts from Milan (Ambrose, Martin, Augustine) and then moves down to Rome. The first exempla about Rome, however, describe holy people who left Rome for the Holy Land. This is true of Jerome, the first Roman example, who "moved away from Rome" to live in Bethlehem.[66] Gregory the Great is the first name of a holy man who lived in Rome, although, Petrarch adds, he regretted it often.[67]

Petrarch considers three levels of "foreign solitudes" vis-à-vis Italy, the holy land of solitude.[68] The first is "Gallia," the closest country to Italy both from a geographic and a spiritual perspective.[69] In the second area are all the other Christian countries more distant from Italy. The third zone is made of those northern and Asian continents where Christ's message has not yet arrived, although these ignorant populations are naturally drawn toward solitude. Returning to Italy from his digression on foreign solitudes, Petrarch mentions Saint Peter Damian and Pope Peter Celestine V, whose refusal of papal power Petrarch regards as the highest dedication to solitude. From Italy, Petrarch goes back to France, apparently only because of a mental association. The above two Peters reminded him of Peter the Hermit, who lived in France and claimed that Christ had ordered him to gather military forces for the First Crusade.[70] "No one fights to regain the residence of Christ," Petrarch says in a new long invective, aimed against the rulers of his day.[71]

Petrarch's geography of solitude does not photograph a static landscape, as we usually see in an atlas. It is projected onto the future of a possible, apocalyptic retrieval of a past configuration. As the place of solitude is more a restless longing than an actual location, the poet's geography is the febrile tension between the remembrance of an ideal past, the present of its dissolution (the destruction of the ancient boundaries of natural solitude), and the future of a religious expectation. The Holy Land in the hands of the infidels reflects a larger process of decadence involving Christian Europe in its entirety.[72] Petrarch reminds his reader that, in the *Confessions* (1.14.23), the African Augustine writes that he cannot read Homer well because Greek is a foreign idiom for him, but he has no problem with Virgil, because Latin is his language. If in your mind you travel through Africa now, Petrarch remarks, you will find no one who knows or loves Latin, "unless he is a traveler, a merchant, or a prisoner."[73] Petrarch associates the loss of the Latin culture to the loss of faith in Christ. As Petrarch points out, in *De vera religione* Augustine contends that in every region of the world the Christian rituals are known and respected. Petrarch reiterates that, if you traverse those African lands in your imagination now, you will find no one who believes in Christ, "unless he is a traveler, a merchant, or a prisoner." The encroaching corruption of European Christianity's roots affects our pursuit of solitude, for we do not seek but rather are "sought out" by solitude. Solitude is a calling from Christ.[74]

The final two lists of exempla concern those people who geographically or temporally live outside the boundaries of Christian solitude. At the close of his inventory of Roman leaders, Petrarch makes a key narrative transition toward his final disclosure on the nature of solitude. At this point Petrarch examines his concept of "otium." While reviewing the major leaders of Latin antiquity, the Italian poet recalls that, after their war enterprises, the two Scipio Africanuses used to leave the celebrations in Rome and rested in solitary places "alone with a friend."[75] As Ronald Witt has explained, in *De vita solitaria* Petrarch "set[s] pagan *otium* . . . within a Christian context where it [becomes] the way of salvation."[76]

Petrarch points out that, according to Cicero's *On Duties*, for Scipio Africanus "otiosus" and "solus" are synonyms, although "solus" paradoxically means "alone with someone."[77] Petrarch also mentions that, in *De officiis ministrorum* Ambrose held that, long before Scipio, numerous biblical prophets had experienced *otium* and "had been accompanied in their solitude."[78] This theological dispute allows Petrarch to introduce a new brief series of biblical exempla, whose real meaning is to support his concept of solitude as dialogical companionship. As I have already stressed, in book 2 of *De vita solitaria* biblical exempla work as transitional reinstatements of the key ideas expressed in a previous catalog of exempla. How could we think that the prophets were inactive (*otiosi*) if Moses defeated legions of enemies and Elijah resuscitated a man?[79] The prophets' solitude, similar to Scipio's but enlightened by divine revelation, leads Petrarch to this final, paradoxical definition: "I want a non-alone solitude" (*volo solitudinem non solam*).[80] After offering a concise look into the activities of this solitude (reading, leisure endeavors, physical recreation), Petrarch states that his solitude includes the crucial presence of a friend.[81] His oneiric solitude (a solitude that is both project and remembrance) finds in the friend its "home," so to speak. The ultimate "place" of solitude is the friend.

At this pivotal point *De vita solitaria* reintroduces its original addressee and becomes an epistle directed at the bishop of Cavaillon (*Tibi, pater*), thus unequivocally linking the closure of the text to its dedicatory epistle.[82] The beginning and the ending complement and clarify each other, as if all that is written after the dedicatory epistle and before the ending were an explanatory amplification. In his analysis of the prefaces to Latin rhetorical treatises, Tore Janson recognizes some recurrent features that are common to all prose treatises: "[D]edication, request from the dedicatee, the unwillingness of the author due to a lack of time or self-confidence, and his final submission to the dedicatee's requests."[83] The striking difference between this topos and Petrarch's proemium is based on the unique relationship between his addressee and *De vita solitaria*. First of all, no expression of lack of self-confidence is detectable in the proemium. Second, Petrarch does not write his treatise as a timid response to the bishop's request. On the contrary, he offers his atlas of solitude to his friend as a necessary reading.

Petrarch can compose his self-portrait in solitude because the bishop ("you, beloved father") will see "as in a mirror" the complete image of Petrarch's identity reflected in his treatise.[84] Petrarch's solitude is founded on this mutual mirroring between two friends who live their "not-alone solitude" in the name of Christ, who "loved this kind of life." The rhetorical connection between the proemium and the closing reveals that *De vita solitaria* is in fact a hortatory epistle to the bishop of Cavaillon. Returning to the theme of the proemium, in the conclusion Petrarch reminds Philippe de Cabassoles of the latter's special interest in his writings, which the bishop favors over the classics, Cicero and Plato included.[85] The bishop's conversion to solitude may occur as a response to the "novelty" (*novitas*) of Petrarch's text, as Augustine's *De vera religione* had offered Petrarch a unique insight into the meaning of solitude.[86] The sharing of the book leads to an identification between author and addressee, between the one who has already converted to solitude and the friend who is encouraged to embark on the same journey of conversion.

Petrarch invites the bishop to come to his refuge of "Clause Vallis" (Vaucluse), where his new view of solitude originated. Vaucluse is like a new Garden of Eden, where the original peace and purity of Adam's solitude might be restored and preserved only if shared with another. Petrarch invites his friend Philippe to cross the symbolic river that still separates him from solitude: "Like one who has crossed a dangerous torrent I call from the opposite bank and bid you pass over boldly: there is not the slightest danger. Where I first set foot everything was slippery and uncertain; here I can report everything is safe and pleasant . . . I may take you by the hand . . . and lead to these places."[87] A similar image is also present in *Triumphus Eternitatis*, the last part of the *Triumphi*, where it signifies the passage from mortal to eternal life:

> Happy indeed is he who finds the ford
> to cross the torrent, mountainous and swift
> that is called life, to many men so dear! (*Triumphus Eternitatis*
> 46–48, trans. Wilkins, 109)[88]

In a previous part of this essay I showed how in *Triumphus Eternitatis* the perennial present of the new Jerusalem, which Petrarch sees as a silent desert following the annihilation of the world, echoes the perfect solitude he hypothesizes in *De vita solitaria*. The act of wading ("il guado") a perilous river signifies both the encounter with the friend who is expecting us in the land of solitude and the passage from life to death. The solitary man indeed dies to the world, whereas "the blind and common folk" (*la volgare e cieca gente*) remain in the space of vain appearances, as Cicero also says in the *Tusculanae disputationes*.[89]

It is fascinating to see that Petrarch uses a similar image at the beginning and the conclusion of *De otio religioso*, his treatise on monastic solitude dedicated to his brother Gherardo, who lived in the monastery of Montrieux. *De otio religioso* opens with the poet being escorted by the monks up to the boundary allowed by their strict religious order.[90] After his visit to his brother, the poet returns to his solitude (*in solitudinem propriam regressum*). If in the opening section of *De otio religioso* it is Petrarch who turns around and keeps walking away from the monastery toward his solitude, in the final paragraph of this lengthy treatise the poet invites the monks to continue their path of monastic solitude and, unlike Lot's wife, not to turn around.[91] Unlike *De vita solitaria*, *De otio religioso* emphasizes a departure, not an arrival. *De otio religioso* is written in the form of an exhortation directed at the monks so that they pursue a monastic solitude, as if they had paradoxically left for the monastery only after listening to Petrarch's long recommendation. If in *De vita solitaria* Vaucluse might become the perfect place of solitude only with the friend's arrival, in *De otio religioso* the monastery indicates an essential distance between the others, the monks, on the one hand, and the poet and his solitude on the other. Petrarch's solitude lies in this unbridgeable distance. The world (*saeculum*) and the monastery lie at an opposite but equal distance from Petrarch's solitude. Vaucluse embodies a new place of solitude in that the new community it advocates is "distant" from every recognizable social construction.

Petrarch envisions solitude as a "'holy'" communion of two friends in Christ. The other, the friend, is solitude itself. In Petrarch's words, "you will be my solitude" (*solitudo mea eris*). The poet emphasizes that "to be the other's solitude" does not simply mean to share a state of solitude. The presence of Philippe as the witness of Francesco's solitude is the "pledge of judgment" about Francesco's writing, which does not falsify the nature of things.[92] This is what the ancients failed to accomplish. The "luminosity of the[ir] words" was not enlightened by the light of Christ's presence.[93] To be the other's solitude in Christ brings forth the luminosity of nature, as if nature itself could express its truthfulness thanks to this "not-alone solitude." Every branch fluttering from a gust of wind, Petrarch writes, every spring murmuring around his refuge seems to be saying, "[Y]ou speak the truth."[94] These are the last words of *De vita solitaria.*

A linguistic and thematic similarity exists between the final image of *De vita solitaria* and *Rerum vulgarium fragmenta* 142, a sestina that most critics believe is contemporary to *De vita solitaria* (1345–47).[95] The expression "omnis impulsarum vento frondium fragor" (each fluttering of leaves due to a gust of wind) in the final section of *De vita solitaria* echoes the "frondi" (branches or leaves), the word-rhyme repeated seven times in this poem, and in particular the second verse of the second stanza: "né mosse il vento mai sì verdi frondi" (nor did the wind ever move such green leaves).[96] No other poem of the *Rerum vulgarium fragmenta* presents such insistence on this image or on the term "frondi." The sestina opens as follows:

> To the sweet shade of those beautiful leaves
> I ran, fleeing a pitiless light
> That was burning down upon me from the third heaven.
>   (*RVF* 142.1–3)[97]

Both this sestina and *De vita solitaria* speak of an act of conversion. The poem opens with a reference to the third heaven, Venus, from which emanates a noxious influence. We have seen that in *De vita solitaria* Petrarch portrays himself as a new Paul ascended to the third heaven. If in the sestina the negative effects of a carnal love descend from the third heaven, in *De vita solitaria* the poet ascends to solitude.

The sestina details a three-step inner transformation. The past encounter with the "frondi" (leaves) that have been "mosse dal vento" (moved by the wind, v. 8) coincide with the poet's withdrawing from lust and embracing a more noble desire (the laurel/Laura):

> The world never saw such graceful branches
> nor did the wind ever move such green leaves,
> as showed themselves to me in that first season.
>   (*RVF* 142.79)

The poem, however, concludes with the reference to "altre frondi" (other leaves) that at the present moment invite the poet to follow "altr'amore . . . et altro lume" (another love . . . and another light; *RVF* 142.37). Abandoning the laurel branches that had revealed to him the power of spiritual love, Petrarch now feels compelled to follow new branches, a new and more truthful nature, which is identified with the love for Christ. If the "fron-dium fragor" (noise of the branches) of the conclusion of *De vita solitaria* voices the truthfulness of Petrarch's "new" discourse on a not-alone soli-tude, this sestina confirms that the poet's "holy" solitude is "prophetic" in that it reflects the natural order of the created world.

Fig. 5. Petrarch, *De otio religioso* (in an Italian translation). Cod. Guelf. 86.8 Aug. 2°, fol. 1r. Herzog August Bibliothek, Wolfenbüttel.

CHAPTER ELEVEN

A HUMANISTIC APPROACH TO RELIGIOUS SOLITUDE • *De otio religioso*

Susanna Barsella

etrarch's treatise dedicated to religious meditative activity, *De otio religioso*, has been traditionally considered an anomalous work, apparently in contradiction with Petrarch's humanism and a step back into medieval exaltation of monastic spirituality. In opposition to this interpretation, the present essay argues that *De otio religioso* presents a humanist approach to religious solitude and introduces a new perspective on monastic spiritual activity. The uniqueness of this treatise cannot be fully understood without placing it in context with the other works Petrarch wrote between 1347 and 1357, particularly *De vita solitaria* (*The Life of Solitude*). The reading presented here takes these works into account to show an ideological coherence that would otherwise be missing were *De otio religioso* taken as an isolated piece of literature.

A debatable commonplace about *De otio religioso* is that it praises the religious life in opposition to secular life. Analysis of previous works dealing with this theme, however, reveals that Petrarch considered religious life a privileged but not a unique way to God. In medieval culture, another route existed that did not involve rejection of human experience but built on it to offer moral guidance aimed at the edification of the Christian society. Only individual inclinations determined which of the two paths to take, but both were conceived within a Christian perspective and equally dignified.

Petrarch wrote his treatise on monastic activity as a man of secular letters who had chosen the second path, and thus saw in the very act of writing a form of participation in the Christian work of salvation. As a humanist, he approached religious solitude by using classical literature to illustrate and support his arguments, and focused on themes such as the dignity of man, which would become central to quattrocento humanism. This chapter discusses the main elements that characterize Petrarch's approach to religious solitude and shows his innovative contribution in the field of practical moral theology.

In early 1347, Petrarch visited for the first time his brother Gherardo at the Carthusian cloister of Montrieux.[1] As a sign of gratitude for the monks' hospitality, Petrarch addressed to them *De otio religioso*, a treatise in epistolary form on religious solitude that is a commentary on verset 11 of Psalm 45, "Vacate et videte / quoniam ego sum Deus" (Be still and see that I am God).[2] Although he probably wrote the treatise during Lent in 1347 at Vaucluse, over the following years he continued to revise it simultaneously with his treatise on lay solitude, *De vita solitaria*.[3] A completed version of the treatise reached Gherardo and the monks of Montrieux in 1357.[4] Based on newly discovered manuscripts, Rotondi hypothesized the existence of two editions of *De otio religioso*. Martellotti, who continued his work, maintained that these were simply two versions: a shorter and less elaborated one, which appears in all printed editions of the fifteenth century; and a longer and more refined one, contained in fewer and lesser-known manuscripts.[5] According to Martellotti, the second version expanded the numerous, briefly annotated quotations of the first one with the intention of making the text flow like a sermon. Recently, however, Giulio Goletti has produced new evidence in favor of Rotondi's hypothesis.[6]

Although not usually considered among the most renowned works of Petrarch, *De otio religioso* was a relatively widespread textbook for the novices entering coenobitical orders. Even if the information on the circulation of this text is not exhaustive, Rotondi's research proved that it was present in the libraries of Italian and European monasteries.[7] Its presence as a reference text in Jean Mombaer's *Rosetum*, the first important text on methodical meditation of the late fifteenth century (1494) attests to this. Lay circles too knew it, evident in a vernacular copy (fig. 5) for the Strozzi family.[8]

It is still undecided whether Petrarch dedicated his book to Gherardo, the community of Montrieux, or the brethren of the Carthusian order.[9] The codex Vat. Urb. Lat. 333, on which Giuseppe Rotondi based the most accurate extant edition of *De otio religioso*, contains a dedication to Gherardo. The treatise, however, opens with Petrarch's address to the "fortunate servants of Christ" (*felix Cristi familia*), and seems to have a broader purpose. Gherardo and his order represented the monastic form of solitude, the alternative to the lay solitude Petrarch celebrated in his works and letters.[10] The theme of solitude and the comparison between these forms recurred in Petrarch's writings and was crucial to his identity as a man of letters. As a poet interested in the moral reformation of society, Petrarch shared with the monks their love for solitude, but rather than seeking sanctity in a religious order, he chose to exert a positive influence in the world through his writings.

The epistolary genre Petrarch chose for his treatise suited well his ideological intent to redefine religious solitude in terms of classical *otium* (active leisure) and casts special light on its interpretation. In choosing this genre, Petrarch pursued two objectives: on the one hand, he wanted to make his work immediately recognizable as belonging to the canon of religious literature; on the other, he wished to treat the theme of religious solitude with the mode of a friendly but persuasive conversation rich in examples and anecdotes, in which he could introduce his innovative views on relevant aspects of monastic leisure. In addition, the epistolary structure allowed Petrarch to stage a fictional dialogical interaction between "external" and "internal" voices, thus innovating on the Augustinian model of soliloquy: "Indeed, I shall control my pen so that my letter to those who are distant may be for me something like a conversation with those who are present."[11]

Like *De vita solitaria*, *De otio religioso* has the appearance of neither a doctrinal treatise nor of a systematic theological exposition. It was a book of practical moral theology written in the monastic rather than Scholastic literary tradition. An important antecedent and a likely model for the *De otio religioso* was Guillaume of Saint-Thierry's *Epistola ad fratres de Monte Dei* (*A Treatise on Solitary Life*), written after he visited the Carthusian monastery of Mont-Dieu in 1145.[12] Saint-Thierry, like Petrarch, addressed it to the brethren of the monastery. The circumstances that led Petrarch to write *De otio religioso* are remarkably similar to those that inspired Guillaume of Saint-Thierry's *Epistola*. Attributed to Saint Bernard, Saint-Thierry's admired friend, the *Epistola* was a basic textbook used in monasteries and convents. In content and structure, however, Saint-Thierry's work was, like Petrarch's, a treatise on practical moral theology whose main objective was to encourage the novices to pursue virtue as a necessary step toward mystical contemplation.

Saint-Thierry instructed the monks on "moral conversion" (*conversio mori*), the passage from vice to virtue necessary to achieve the final stage of ascetical perfection, the contemplation of the "face of God." Saint-Thierry, like Petrarch later, emphasized the importance of intellectual activities aimed at rendering the *conversio mori* effective. Unlike Petrarch, however, he did not include among his sources the works of ancient authors. According to Saint-Thierry, the monks should concentrate exclusively on the Scriptures and the writings of the fathers and the doctors of the Church. Although not all schools of mysticism shared this anticlassicist position, it prevailed in the monastic orders strictly obeying the Benedictine rule such as the Carthusians and the Camaldulese. Similarly, in *De otio religioso* Petrarch suggests that the monks meditate on the Scriptures but limits the theological writings to those of early fathers such as Basil, Gregory, Jerome, and Augustine. He does so, however, by continuously interlacing the authorities of sacred literature with examples and passages from the works of the pagan poets and philosophers. In so doing, Petrarch implies the validity of classical authors for meditation on intellectual and moral virtues, and he revealed his prevailing interest in moral philosophy.[13] The ancient authors, according to Petrarch (and Boccaccio's) "poetic theology," although without revelation, received divine enlightenment on the truths concerning natural and moral spheres and achieved excellence in the knowledge of human nature.[14] Moreover, they provided the rhetorical skills necessary to make moral discourse against vices persuasive. Although their study could not produce any spiritual effects without the intervention of Grace and they were inferior to the Christian writers in doctrine, ancient poets created illustrious examples in a language so refined as to inspire true love for virtue.[15] In dotting the prose of *De otio religioso* with excerpts from ancient literature, Petrarch illustrated the vital role that classical poetry, cast in Christian perspective, may have in religious solitude and Christian *otium*.[16] Christian theology could build on the foundations of classical ethics and use the heritage of antiquity so that we may not only know but also love virtue:

> Although our ultimate goal does not lie in virtue, where the philosophers placed it, yet the straight path toward our goal passes through the virtues, and not through virtues that are merely known, I say, but loved. Thus the true moral philosophers and valuable teachers of virtues are those whose first and last purpose is to make their students and readers good. They not only teach the definitions of virtue and vice, haranguing us about virtue's splendor and vice's drabness. They also instill in our breasts both love and zeal for what is good and hatred and abhorrence of evil.[17]

Consistent with his vision, Petrarch significantly departed from Saint-Thierry in making his sources visible. Like most medieval authors, Saint-Thierry rarely quoted his authors, especially if they were pagan. Nonetheless, classical rhetoric shaped his prose, for ancient authors remained in the Middle Ages authoritative examples of rhetorical dexterity, and even those who condemned secular studies had received an education in the liberal arts, like Saint-Thierry and Peter Damian.

If Cicero, Seneca, and Horace were relevant models of persuasive rhetoric, Saint Paul and the literature of the early fathers were not of lesser relevance for Petrarch, particularly Augustine's *De vera religione,* not only for
the content of their writings but also because they represented a synthesis
of doctrine and eloquence, an equilibrium that Petrarch tried to achieve in
all his writings.[18] Quite significantly, Petrarch in *De otio religioso* privileged
the early fathers over Scholastic authorities, which he never mentioned.[19]
Likely, this was because their pre-Scholastic (or anti-Scholastic) theology had not yet assimilated Aristotelian logic and metaphysics in a dog-
matic form, and Petrarch shunned the rational approach of Scholastics to
the mystery of divine truths.[20] The only type of medieval thought present
in the treatise is from the mystical tradition rather than from Scholastic
systematic theology. The core notion Petrarch appropriated from mystical theology and applied to virtue was the notion that man cannot know
God but can only love Him: "Thus greatly err those who spend their time
in studying rather than acquiring virtue, but even greater error perform
those who study God instead of loving him, for in this life of ours knowing
God is impossible, while it is possible to love him with all our devotion and
ardor."[21]

The canonical form of the epistle was for Petrarch a safe structure to
express an innovative message, for he made a "paradoxical" use of Saint-
Thierry's *Epistola:* on the one hand, he followed his model; on the other,
he adapted it to serve a different function. As Edward F. Cranz argued,
this was an intellectual and rhetorical operation not unusual to Petrarch,
who systematically subverted the notions he took from authorities such as
Augustine, Cicero, or Seneca.[22] If the authoritative doctrine of these models was Petrarch's launching pad, the changed historical and philosophical
contexts of the trecento induced him to adapt their truths to a new vision
of human identity, which was no longer heaven-centered. Thus, by adapting ancient forms to new contents, Petrarch promoted at once innovation
and continuity with tradition.

Beyond Saint-Thierry and the classical authors, other sources are of no
lesser importance for *De otio religioso.* The influence of Biblical commentaries and homiletic and hexaemeral genres is visible in the structure of
the treatise, which is organized in two books commenting on verset 11 of
Psalm 45: "Vacate et videte / quoniam ego sum Deus" (Be still and see that
I am God). Psalm 45 is a hymn to Jerusalem, which, freed after a siege, became a stronghold for his inhabitants. It symbolizes the spiritual strength
of those who live in the grace of God and suggests a parallel with the monastery, the defensive citadel where the monks fight against the lures and

dangers of the secular world. Traditionally, this verset was used by the theologians to exhort to contemplation. The *Vetus Itala* version found in Augustine's *De vera religione*, another of the main sources of *De otio religioso*, enlightens the meaning Petrarch gave to the term "vacate" (be still) of the Vulgate. In the *Vetus Itala* this term is "Agite otium," which translates the word "scholasate" of the Greek Septuagint.[23] In this translation of the Bible God's direct exhortation to His people says literally, "work your leisure."[24] The *Vetus Itala* version, through the authoritative comment of Augustine, significantly connects verset 11 of Psalm 45 to the classical ideal of "otium," a theme pivotal to Petrarch's entire literary production.[25]

"Otium" had two different but related meanings in classical and medieval religious traditions. While in antiquity it indicated a speculative pause in active life, in Christianity it was associated with contemplation and "vacatio" that, connected to "videre," indicated physical and mental alacrity aimed at moral perfection in view of salvation.[26] Petrarch stressed the necessity of a continuous activity of the mind during contemplative rest by explicitly recalling the *Vetus Itala* version: "Indeed you do not need a leisure which is relaxed and indolent and which weakens your minds, but one which is strong and, especially in view of your unique character, religious and dutiful. . . . Where Jerome's translation of the Bible says, 'Take time,' an older translation said 'Be active in your leisure.'"[27]

Leisure is activity; a work (*opus*) to be accomplished, and not a mere state of emptiness and suspension in waiting for future bliss. Petrarch's interest in "Agite otium," which suggests a synthesis of both meanings of "otium," is visible not only in the title of *De otio religioso* but also in its opening metaphor, in which monastic activity appears as the earthly mirror of angelic alacrity.[28] As the angels incessantly move around the source of their beatitude, so the monks constantly work to produce the honey of exemplary sanctity. The metaphor of the bees, recurrent in medieval hagiography, had its matrix in Virgil's *Georgics*, and the synthesis of classical and Christian sources perfectly suited Petrarch's philological interpretation of "vacate."[29]

In patristic and mystical traditions, verset 11 of Psalm 45 was usually associated with the exhortation to set the mind free from worldly occupations in order to prepare it for the atemporal experience of heavenly beatitude. Origen, Ambrose, Augustine, and mystics such as Bernard of Clairvaux contributed to this prevailing interpretation of "vacate et videte." Literally, however, Psalm 45 does not exhort us to seek God's face in the heavens. Rather, it urges us to turn our eyes toward the marvels of creation and discover in them the existence of God.[30] Verset 11 contains, according to the etymological perspective of "vacatio," an exhortation to "become free" from inane occupations so as to be able to "engage in" activity of physical and intellectual contemplation, to which the "videte" of the verset alludes. The relation between the material and the spiritual acts of seeing—of paying attention to the world instead of forgetting it—surfaces in Petrarch's comments on the verset:

> For what else is "take time and see"? "take time": this means there should be quiet in the present; "see" it means there will be eternal quiet. Take time on earth, and you will see in heaven. Even on earth the eye is able to see, insofar it is pure and cleansed, but still carnal.[31]

Spiritual and material vision, knowledge and experience interact in guiding the itinerary to God through the world. The claim that meditation on experience is essential to the knowledge of truth, that this experience is individual and is a journey of the mind in the self constitutes a characteristic trait of Petrarch's humanism. From this perspective, Petrarch in *De otio religioso* focuses on the necessity to speculate not only on heavens but also on Earth, and to pursue not only theological but also moral virtues. The shift in attention from the heavens to Earth that marks the treatise thus retrieves, at the macrotextual level, the literal meaning of Psalm 45.

Consistent with Petrarch's interpretation of the Psalm, *De otio religioso* focuses on the theoretical necessity of pursuing virtue, even when conducting a life of sanctity, for freedom from the temptations of the mind and of the flesh are never completely assured. Moreover, if virtue is a precondition to meditation and contemplation, its attainment cannot be confined to the preparatory stages of religious life as novices, but must remain at the core of the monks' meditation during their lives: "Virtue is the path, God is the goal seen on Zion."[32] By indirectly recalling the Aristotelian distinction between intellectual and moral virtues, Petrarch discusses intellectual fallacies that may lead one astray from the truths of faith and moral vices, referring to the traditional capital sins. Challenging the commonly shared view that a life dedicated to prayer and contemplation protected monks from temptations, Petrarch contends that the monks who live in the safe harbor of a monastery are in fact more exposed to the attacks of vice than those who live in the city. The more the isolation of the monastery induces a feeling of safety, the higher are the risks of temptations. For virtue responds better to the assaults of bad fortune than to the caresses of good fortune.[33]

You should not think yourself safe because you live in the camp of Christ, for although you may fight under the best leader and your camp may be very well fortified and very strong, nevertheless no place must be considered completely safe, for sleepless wild enemies make noise on all sides.[34]

The martial metaphor suggests an image in contrast with that of serenity and peace traditionally associated with the monastery. Like real soldiers, *militia Cristi*, the monks are incessantly under the attacks of enemies, especially those inside their minds and bodies. Temptations and disquiet, Petrarch affirms, are useful and should be blessed for "freedom from worry is suspect and may impede not only our spiritual, but also our worldly journeys."[35] Vice, heresy, lack of faith, and lack of moral strength put the monks under siege and keep them spiritually alert, forcing their eyes to look down on the world around and inside them.

With all your watchfulness protect your heart, and with constant determination beware those things which you recognize as ruinous. This will be easy for those who have experienced in the world what has been treacherous, violent, and especially threatening to your way of life. Cautiously avoid those things which you have understood to be more harmful: anger tortured one man, lust another; pride exalted one man, melancholy depressed another; greed, gluttony, and grievous jealousy aroused one man to a frenzy. Each man should recognize his own particular enemy in the battle, and then he should be especially aware of where the greater danger lies.[36]

To fight the attacks of vices effectively the monks should know their enemies and be conscious of their strength. To this end, Petrarch exhorts them to meditate on their past experience in the world and to rely on the possibility that incarnation had granted to all men. Petrarch departs here from a purely negative consideration of human nature and stresses man's capacity to restore his prelapsarian condition through cooperating Grace, which, by acting on the will, induces men to seek virtue. Schools of different mystical orientations shared this idea of "paradise restored," including Guillaume of Saint-Thierry and Hugh of Saint-Victor.[37] Although still heaven-oriented, this idea embedded in embryonic form the positive vision of human nature that animated Petrarch's conception of *otium*.[38]

In the passages of book 1 dedicated to this theme Petrarch criticized the medieval contempt for human nature and invites the monks to abandon a

religious vision based on the celebration of the misery of man, thus anticipating the humanistic theme of the dignity of man.[39]

> What an indescribable sacrament! To what higher end was human-
> ity able to be raised than that a human being, consisting of a ratio-
> nal soul and human flesh, a human being, exposed to our mortal
> accidents, dangers, and needs, in brief, a true and perfect man,
> inexplicably assumed into one person with the Word, the Son of
> God, consubstantial with the Father and coeternal with Him. To
> what higher end was humanity able to be raised than that this per-
> fect man would join two natures in Himself by a wondrous union
> of totally disparate elements?[40]

The sporadic passages that resound with accents suitable to the literature
of *contemptum mundi* (contempt for the world) illustrate the traditional topic
of human weakness and should be interpreted in the light of the essentially
humanist vision of Petrarch that irreversibly distances him from his medieval models.

Petrarch's attention to the human world emerges also in his discussion
of the practical knowledge necessary to achieve the goal of virtue, seen as
a prerequisite for achieving the quiet of mind. Thus in book 2 Petrarch
insists on the necessity of contemplating the cities where the vestiges of the
past invite meditation on the caducity of earthly goods. It is an invitation
to consider not only the marvels of nature but also the works of men, and
meditate on the eternity of creation and the volatility of human art to learn
the best course to take in this life to prepare for the other. In the same way,
the monks should not forget their individual experience as human beings
but instead learn from it. Revealing once more the distance between medieval and humanist approaches, Petrarch affirms that religious solitude
should be neither rejection nor oblivion of the world.

By using classical authors to discuss in an educative perspective the
main themes concerning religious solitude, and by affirming that defeat-
ing vice was a primary goal also in monastic life, Petrarch implicitly questioned a well-established and revered medieval institution: the *"curriculum"*
of monastic meditation. His treatise represented a sort of intrusion of a
man of letters in a field that used to be the exclusive terrain of the religious.
Moreover, by discussing and giving advice to the monks in matters such as
asceticism and moral education, the poet implicitly granted lay Christians
a status comparable to that of the clergy.[41] This theme was central to Petrarch, who argued for the dignity of secular solitude in other texts such as

De vita solitaria, The Ascent to Mount Ventoux (Familiares 4.1), and *Parthenias,* the first eclogue of *Bucolicum carmen. De otio religioso* represented a particular moment in Petrarch's attempt to redefine and interpret the social role of the man of letters, and for this reason it should be read along with *De vita solitaria,* also written as an epistle in two books.[42] *Seniles* 5.2 shows that Petrarch conceives of the two treatises as belonging to the same project: "I got the idea of writing during Lent for two years two short books befitting the holy season and that place of yours, and partly my condition too: one was on the solitary life, the other on religious repose."[43]

While the *De otio religioso* attempted a redefinition of religious solitude in terms of *otium,* the *De vita solitaria* endeavored to define literary *otium.* If the former showed that a religious curriculum may include the *humanae litterae* (human literature), the latter contended that the program of study of the lay solitary should include the *sacrae litterae* (divine literature).[44] The two treatises complement each other, bringing to the surface the common traits of secular and religious forms of solitude. Since the solitary and the monk had the common goal of virtue, then religious and secular *otia* could not differ in principle: both must be dedicated to parallel study and meditation on secular and Christian scriptures, where Christian ideals and ethical values enlightened each other. Together, the two treatises questioned two main tenets of medieval monastic thought: that seclusion from the world was the only possible way to God, and that the only knowledge useful to the Christian was that of the Scriptures.[45] Thus, Petrarch's works on solitude provided the theoretical basis for that ideal combination of Christian and pagan traditions Petrarch sought in his works and that was central to his humanism.

Petrarch's redefinition of Christian "vacatio" in terms of *otium* indicates that a rethinking of the social function of the *literatus* (man of letters) was already in progress in the second half of the fourteenth century.[46] In his humanistic view of society, as monastic and secular *otia* were similar and complementary, so were the functions of the monk and the man of letters, for both were committed to the moral perfection of earthly experience. While monks testified to a perfect spiritual life through their sanctity, philosophers, poets, and princes were the moral and political guides to the edification of Christian society.

Although ethical goals were common to secular and religious solitudes, a crucial difference existed in Petrarch's new intellectual perspective. While the monks sought virtue as a way of anticipating celestial beatitude on earth, the literate sought in virtue the blossoming of human nature. While monks aimed at becoming examples of sanctity that may guide others, poets preserved, transmitted, and created works to inspire virtue in their readers. Their goals were different but connected; in both the action of the will to direct the soul toward virtue was crucial.

Petrarch wrote *De otio religioso* in a period of intense moral and spiritual meditation. Other works written in this period treated similar themes and cast light on the interpretation of the treatise.[47] Relevant among these were book 1 of the *Rerum memorandarum libri* (literally "Books on things to be remembered"), dedicated to "Leisure and Solitude," and book 4 of *Contra medicum*, in which Petrarch rejected the common opinion that solitude was sterile, affirming its social utility.[48]

Very important in this connection was the *Ascent to Mount Ventoux* (*Familiares* 4.1), addressed to Dionigi da Borgo San Sepolcro.[49] Petrarch wrote this letter a few years before the parallel revisions to the two treatises on solitude. The letter narrates Petrarch and his brother Gherardo's ascent of Mount Ventoux, and symbolically illustrates the equivalence of religious and secular Christian lives. While Gherardo takes the straight and steep path leading quickly to the peak, Francesco follows a meandering path, often interrupted and sometimes leading back to the valley, passing through the woods, but finally reaching the peak where his brother is waiting for him. A way to salvation passing through worldly experience is possible. It unfolds through self-investigation and does not linger in the abstract speculation of the causes, but researches the principles of human actions so that they may be useful to others.

Connected to the theme of the two equivalent paths was also *Parthenias*, the first eclogue of the *Bucolicum carmen*, and *Familiares* 10.4 to Gherardo, which expounds the allegorical meaning of the eclogue.[50] As in *Familiares* 4.1, the two protagonists, Monicus (Gherardo) and Silvius (Petrarch), represent two different attitudes toward solitude. Monicus seeks estrangement from the world to sing divine chants.[51] On the contrary, Silvius's solitude leads to an introspective journey. Like Franciscus in *Secretum* (*The Secret*), he longs for glory. Nevertheless, his decision to leave Monicus has moral implications, for Silvius applies to singing the exemplary deeds of the Roman hero Scipio in *Africa*. The message contained in these narrations is consistent with the exposition of *De otio religioso*: all poetry committed to inspire love for virtue has Christian value.

Petrarch's positive vision of man and of human experience leads him to stress man's ability to pursue salvation through virtue. This virtue, however, must not just be understood, but loved; for love only can direct the will to desire it. As the sweetness of Davidic chant conveyed the word of God more effectively than any sermon, so ancient poetry did elicit that love without which virtue cannot be attained.[52] This can be considered the essence of the message contained in *De otio religioso,* a message addressed not only to the monks but also to all Christians. In it, moral philosophy intertwined with a moral theology that does not descend from Scholasticism but from patristic and mystical theology. This vision of the role of poetry and rhetoric places *De otio religioso* among the works that anticipated the later developments of quattrocento humanism.

PART IV

JOURNEYS INTO THE SOUL

Fig. 6. Petrarch, *Secretum*. Brugge, Grootseminarie. MS. 113/78 fol. 1r. Made in 1470 for Jan Crabbe, Abott of Ter Duinen (1457–1488). From left to right: Petrarch, *Veritas* (Truth), Augustine, and Abbot Crabbe, with two attendants. Reproduced with the kind permission of the Archief van het Grootseminarie, Brugge. Photograph: H. Maertens.

CHAPTER TWELVE

THE BURNING QUESTION • Crisis and Cosmology
in the *Secret* • *Secretum*

David Marsh

or nearly fifty years, the *Secretum* (*The Secret*) has been probably the most widely read, studied, and taught of Petrarch's Latin works.[1] Yet despite the apparent clarity of its structure and debate, it continues to defy definitive interpretation, as if its meaning, like its title, remains a "secret." Petrarch's *Secretum* is structured in the conventional format of three books, which correspond to three days of discussion, and are introduced by a proem. Petrarch sets the scene using an allegorical framework in which late classical and medieval elements predominate.[2] In a dream-like reverie, the author is confronted by Veritas (Truth), a distant kinswoman of Philosophia in Boethius's *Consolation;* and just as Dante's Beatrice had summoned Virgil, so Veritas introduces a venerable authority, Augustine, to counsel Franciscus in his distress (fig. 6).[3] But after the discussion has been launched by this allegorical booster rocket, it falls away. When the debate begins in book 1, with Augustinus reproaching Franciscus as a little man (*homuncio*),[4] Veritas remains silent; and the dialogue ends without any reference to the opening scene.

I have called the work a dialogue, but that is not the author's term for it. Petrarch calls it a *familiare colloquium*, a "conversation with a friend."[5] Although modern readers may view Augustine more as a doctrinal superego than as a boon companion, we should recall that Petrarch, like many humanists after him, spoke in his letters of "conversing" with correspondents both ancient and modern.[6] Indeed, although the strict limits of geography and time form an important topic of the dialogue, the interlocutors Franciscus and Augustinus transcend such boundaries and are more "familiar" with each other's lives and works than, say, Dante and Virgil in the *Divina commedia.* This sort of intertextual penetration is not limited to the *Secretum;* in the *Africa,* Homer appears to Ennius and prophesies about the epic that Petrarch would write in the future. Later in life, Petrarch would use the dialogue form to offer moral guidance that was less personal in nature, although he did not call the chapters of his *De remediis utriusque fortune* "dialogi."[7] All the same, *dialogi* is the title of a hagiographic classic that Petrarch knew well and commended to his brother Gherardo, the consolatory dialogues of Gregory the Great.[8] Not surprisingly, we find that Gregory's opening scene anticipates that of Petrarch's *Secretum*. Here Gregory describes his retreat (*secretum locum petii*) and, like Petrarch, calls himself a little man (*homuncio*):

> One day, when I was overwhelmed with the excessive troubles of secular affairs, which often force us to pay debts that we clearly don't owe, I sought out a more private place for my companion grief, where everything unpleasant in my tasks would be openly revealed, and all those things that generally caused me pain would freely appear before my eyes. Now, after I had sat there greatly afflicted and silent for some time, my most beloved son Peter the deacon arrived; and seeing that I was tormented by a grave malady of the heart, he asked, "Has something new happened to cause you to suffer more grief than usual?" . . . "If I were only to tell you, Peter, what I have learned, as one little man, about perfect and laudable individuals, either through the witness of good and true men or through my own studies, I think the day would end before my talk was done."[9]

We should not rule out Gregory as a source for Petrarch. Book 2 of *De vita solitaria* is filled with lives of saints similar to those narrated in the *Dialogi*, and Gregory's commentary on Ezekiel is quoted in *Invective contra medicum*.[10]

At the same time, the *Secretum* also purports to record the "conflict of my personal worries," and it is clear that Franciscus and Augustinus represent the author's own contrasting viewpoints, rather than the historical Petrarch and Augustine. Indeed, Petrarch possessed a peculiar gift for dramatizing his inner struggles through dialogue—a literary habit that would markedly shape the writings of Leon Battista Alberti.[11] In Petrarch's Latin poetry, for example, several of the *Epystole*—most notably 1.6, 1.14 ("Ad seipsum"), and 2.18—employ the question-and-answer technique of soliloquy to dramatize the poet's inner conflicts. Similarly, the *Bucolicum carmen* uses exchanges between shepherds to illustrate contrasting ways of life. Thus the first eclogue, *Parthenias*, finds clear parallels in Petrarch's epistles to his brother Gherardo.[12] And in an extreme example of self-dramatization, the epic poem *Africa* casts the poet in three separate incarnations—as Ennius, as Homer, and as the prophesied Tuscan celebrant of Scipio Africanus.[13]

From the very beginning of book 1, the *Secretum* abounds in the literary conventions of ancient genres. For a central model of dialogue as a therapeutic treatment of grief and depression, we need only cite Cicero's *Tus-culanae disputationes*; Seneca's consolations *Ad Helviam*, *Ad Marciam*, and *Ad Polybium*; and Boethius's *Consolatio Philosophiae*. Moreover, given Petrarch's obsession with love, it is hardly surprising to find that the *Remedia amoris* of Ovid—later cited in book 3 by Augustinus—offers parallels that refer to the key words *secretum* (secluded withdrawal) and *colloquium* (conversation):

> You do not need seclusion, for seclusion
> Makes madness grow; but crowds will do you good
>
> . . . .
>
> Flee not from conversation, and keep your door unlocked.[14]

Yet if Ovid considers seclusion a danger, Petrarch regards it as conducive to moral improvement. In his treatise *De vita solitaria* 1.4, he quotes approvingly a passage in which Quintilian lauds solitude (*secretum*) as essential to study: "If we come to them rested and restored, night studies are the best kind of seclusion. Of course, silence and withdrawal and a completely unhampered mind, while greatly to be desired, cannot always be found . . . so in a crowd, on the road, and even at banquets our thoughts can create their own seclusion."[15]

Once the proem has set the scene, the three books of the *Secretum* proceed, according to the norms of ancient dialogue, to record three days of conversation. As book 1 begins, Augustinus assails Franciscus with a series of reproaches, but the discussion soon develops into a debate on the question, can a person be unhappy against his will?[16] The arguments for voluntarism presented by Augustinus draw on a number of sources from ancient Stoic tenets and Cicero's *Tusculanae disputiones* to Augustine's *De vera religione*.[17] Book 2 takes a decidedly Christian turn as Augustinus gradually examines Franciscus for all seven of the deadly sins, beginning with pride. But instead of Augustinian confessions, Franciscus seems only to offer Petrarchan concessions about his spiritual shortcomings. In book 3, Augustinus fires a double-barreled accusation against Franciscus: he fails to seek salvation because he is fettered by two chains—love and glory.[18] These charges in fact recall the chains that fettered the saint's will before his conversion:

> The adversary held my will, and made it a chain to bind me. For when our will is perverted, lust is created; and when we become slaves to our lust, habit is born; and when we don't resist habit, compulsion arises. Thus, as if by interconnected links—which is why I have called it a chain—harsh servitude held my will in bonds. But

my new will, by which I had begun to wish to worship and enjoy you freely, O God, who are our only certain pleasure, was not yet capable of overcoming my old will, grown strong through many years. Thus, within me two wills—one old and one new, one carnal and one spiritual—battled each other, and their discord weakened my soul.[19]

First, using Cicero's *Tusculanae disputationes* and Ovid's *Remedia amoris* as his principal texts, Augustinus urges Franciscus to abandon his love and the poetry it inspires. Then he addresses the problem of Franciscus's love of glory, which means his quest for winning literary fame, especially by his Latin writings. The second half of book 3, which forms the culmination of the *Secretum*, addresses the spiritual crisis of Petrarch as author and poet.[20] In particular, Augustinus challenges the two literary projects that celebrate ancient Rome, the prose compilation *De viris illustribus* and the verse epic *Africa*. By dedicating himself to these massive and unfinished projects, Franciscus has forgotten himself. For the goal of his salvation, he has substituted the short-sighted aim of achieving glory.

It is easy to understand the poet's doubts about his epic poem. This projected masterpiece was responsible for Petrarch's coronation in Rome in 1341, and the speech he delivered on that occasion extols the role of glory in inspiring poetry.[21] If it was easy to deliver that speech, it was not easy to deliver the finished masterpiece. Petrarch's principal model, Virgil's *Aeneid*, portrays the legendary Trojan past as paving the way toward the grandeur of Augustan Rome. But instead of prophesying the advent of a successor to Scipio Africanus, the *Africa* envisions the coronation of a Tuscan poet who will celebrate the Roman hero 1,500 years later.[22] Like Walt Whitman, Petrarch could boast, "I celebrate myself." Yet now that he has been crowned, the poet must answer this "burning question": will the finished epic justify his laurel wreath, or should he consign it to the flames?

Recalling the transience of human life, Augustinus warns that both of Franciscus's planned masterpieces remain unfinished and that death may unexpectedly claim the writer at any moment.[23] This observation causes Franciscus to shudder as he recalls how during a recent illness he in fact contemplated burning his unfinished *Africa*, rather than leaving it incomplete. As Franciscus describes it, the episode is laden with irony. By alluding to Virgil's deathbed wish to burn his *Aeneid*, Franciscus both celebrates the supremacy of his poetic model and mocks the imperfections of his own work. He also puns on the name of his epic: just as Africa is continually burned by the fiery tropical sun and once was put to the torch by its Roman conquerors, so his poem nearly perished in flames lit by its author.[24]

Augustinus now challenges Franciscus's literary ambitions, which he says can win no lasting or widespread fame; for human glory must appear insignificant in the vastness of God's creation:

> Augustinus. What great thing do you think you will achieve?
> Franciscus. Truly a splendid, rare, and outstanding work.
> Augustinus. . . . This splendid work will neither be widely known nor last a long time, for it is restricted by the narrow confines of place and time.[25]

At this point, Franciscus bursts out angrily. "I recognize that ancient and trite fable of the philosophers," he says. "The whole world is like a tiny point, a great year consists of thousands of years, and a man's fame cannot even fill either this point or this year. . . . But in my experience such sayings are more attractive to relate than they are truly beneficial."[26]

What provokes this vehement denunciation of "the philosophers"? Clearly, Augustinus has hit a nerve. In order to condemn the ambitious projects of Franciscus based on the history of Rome, Augustinus has appealed to a philosophical reflection that deflates Roman virtue and fame by viewing them *sub specie aeternitatis*. The phrase *angustie locorum* ("confines of place") echoes a locus classicus dear to Franciscus and thus appropriate to his Roman projects—book 6 of Cicero's *De republica*.[27] While most of the work is lost, the concluding scene, known as the *Somnium Scipionis* (*Dream of Scipio*), was preserved with a commentary by Macrobius, and its cosmological vision thus survived to inspire numerous generations of Latin authors.[28] In the passage, Scipio Africanus and his grandson view the earth from the heavens, and this vantage point allows them to envision the pettiness of the world. The celestial perspective reveals that human fame is insignificant because human life is so short compared to eternity, and because people inhabit only a small part of the earth, which itself is only a tiny point compared to the universe. Evidently, Petrarch found this Ciceronian passage deeply persuasive, for he echoes it in three passages of his *De remediis utriusque fortune*, composed between 1354 and 1366.[29]

The *Somnium Scipionis* was of course inspired by the conclusion of Plato's *Republic*, and in turn it inspired the commentary by Macrobius which preserved it for posterity. Franciscus's allusion to the fiery tropical sun of Africa had demonstrated his familiarity with classical notions of geography; but when Augustine begins to lecture him on the subject, Franciscus denounces it as something that doesn't move him. Augustinus is surprised, for he himself has discussed the earth's geography in his *De civitate dei* (*City of God*).[30] "Is this a fable," he asks, "when it uses geometrical demonstrations to describe the narrow confines of the whole earth?"[31]

But Augustinus is a clever advocate of his case and knows how to win over the recalcitrant Franciscus. He turns from science to poetry and cites four passages from Franciscus's epic *Africa* that both prove his point and flatter the author. Of course, there is a classical precedent for Petrarch's quotations of his own Latin verse. In book 2 of Cicero's *De natura deorum*, Quintus Lucilius Balbus quotes at length from the translation of Aratus's *Phaenomena* that Cicero had made as a young man.[32] The first quotation repeats the thematic adjective *angustus* that Petrarch had used in describing the petty world:

> The globe, restricted by confining boundaries,
> Is but a tiny island in extent, which Ocean circles
> In its winding curves. . . .[33]

Soon Franciscus changes his tune and confesses an urge to reject his old ways:

> Augustine. You have heard my opinion of glory . . . unless perhaps all
> this still strikes you as fairy tales.
> Franciscus. Not at all. Your remarks have not moved me like fairy
> tales, but have rather given me a new desire to reject my old ways.[34]

Paradoxically, Augustinus succeeds in persuading Franciscus by citing a work—the epic poem *Africa*—which he has relentlessly denounced as a futile endeavor. For it is evident that Franciscus finds poetry (especially his own) far more persuasive than science or logic. And we should note that the "science" in this case—namely, the five-zone model of the earth—was first made canonic by Aristotle's *Meteorologica*.[35]

But is Aristotle the only figure whose authority must be exorcised? While Augustinus plays the role of Petrarch's Latin, or African, superego, Franciscus is by birth and profession primarily a Tuscan writer. Small wonder, then, that the invocation of the *Somnium Scipionis* in book 3 evokes Dante's *Commedia* as a literary subtext. If we review the highlights of the *Secretum*, we note that the work begins by presenting Franciscus with authoritative guides who reincarnate the Beatrice and Virgil of the first cantos in the *Inferno*.[36] Then, in book 2, when Augustinus examines Franciscus's conscience, we retrace the steps of Dante's gradual ascent-through-confession in the *Purgatorio*. And book 3 now culminates by invoking the heavenly vision of the earth's insignificance that Dante describes in *Par-*

adiso 22.133–35, creating an indelible image that would inspire the final
scene of Chaucer's *Troilus and Criseyde:*

> My face I turned again toward all the spheres,
> All seven, and I beheld our globe so small,
> I smiled at its abject appearance.[37]

This "poetic cosmography," to borrow Vico's expression, must have appealed to Petrarch.

Nevertheless, behind the open dialogue of the *Secretum* there looms an
ominous specter, an alternative Dante whose intellectual horizons included
the mundane as well as the celestial. Returning to terrestrial geography,
we recall that Dante embraced Aristotelian cosmology in his treatise *Convivio.*[38] Even more to the point, in 1320 he composed the *Questio de aqua et
terra*, a Scholastic disputation that discusses geography in terms of the
mathematical demonstrations rejected by Petrarch:

> For as is shown by mathematical theorems, the regular circumfer-
> ence of a sphere must always rise up with a circular contour from
> either a plane or a spherical surface, such as a surface of water
> must be. And that the earth rises up in a form like a half-moon is
> made clear by the natural scientists who discuss it, by the astrono-
> mers who describe the climatic zones, and by the cosmographers
> who assign the earth's regions through all its parts. For as is com-
> monly recognized by everyone, the inhabitable earth extends lon-
> gitudinally from Cadiz, which lies where Hercules set his bound-
> aries, to the mouth of the river Ganges, as Orosius writes.[39]

Clearly, Dante's disputation, with its frequent citations of "the Philosopher"
(Aristotle), falls into the category of the *ludibria* (ludicrous trifles) mocked
in Petrarch's *Collatio laureationis* (*Coronation Oration*).[40] Thus, by embracing
Dante's poetic adaptation of Cicero while rejecting his profession of Aristotelian cosmology, Petrarch hints at the pointed contrast between poetry and
science that would resurface in his *Invective contra medicum* and *De ignorantia.*

Now that Franciscus has expressed a desire to change, Augustinus attempts to dissuade him from continuing his literary projects. He tells him
to embrace virtue and to "leave *Africa.*"[41] Franciscus again objects, and the
dialogue ends with a sense of unresolved conflict. But Petrarch took Augustine's advice. He abandoned the *Africa* and, following in the footsteps of
the saint, sought out Saint Ambrose in Milan.

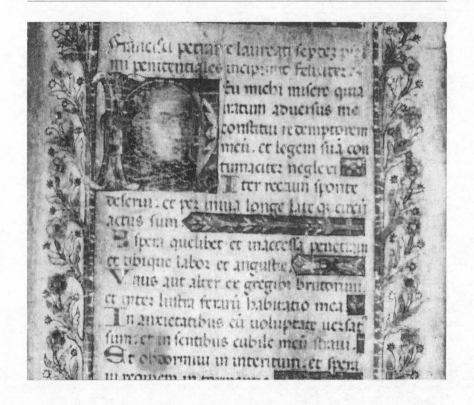

Fig. 7. Petrarch, *Psalmi penitentiales* (title page). Sondersammlung Handschriften und alte Drucke, S. 20, 4°. Zentral- und Hochschulbibliothek, Lucerne.

CHAPTER THIRTEEN

PETRARCH'S PERSONAL PSALMS •
Psalmi penitentiales

E. Ann Matter

The Book of Psalms[1] was perhaps the most important part of the Bible for medieval Christians. The hundred and fifty Vulgate Psalms played a crucial daily role for religious people of all walks of life. After the institution of Benedictine monasticism in the sixth century, members of religious communities had an intimate relationship with the Psalms, since the office established by the Benedictine *Rule* included the chanting of the entire Psalter, all hundred and fifty psalms, every week. Nonmonastics, too, were well acquainted with the Psalms through their use in various liturgical formats, including the prayers of the Books of Hours. Two subcollections of psalms had special liturgical functions: the fifteen Gradual Psalms or "Psalms of Ascents"—Psalms 119–33 (120–34)—were originally intended, scholars think, for holiday pilgrimages to Jerusalem, while the seven Penitential Psalms—Psalms 6, 31 (32), 37 (38), 50 (51), 101 (102), 129 (130), and 142 (143)—all poems that reflect the cries of a remorseful soul, were used liturgically in penitential rituals, especially during Lent.

The voice of the Penitential Psalms, a soul crying out in sorrow over sin, was understood by the tradition to be King David lamenting especially his sin of adultery with Bathsheba, the story related in 2 Samuel 11. In fact, this shows a creative reading of the Penitential Psalms by the Christian tradition, since not all of the seven Penitential Psalms are officially attributed to David in the biblical text. Five of them, Psalms 6, 31 (32), 37 (38), 50 (51), and 142 (143), do carry attributions to David, but the other two are more generic. Psalm 101 (102) is the prayer of the anxious *pauper* who pours out his lament to God, and Psalm 129 (130), the *De profundis*, is only identified as one of the Gradual Psalms.

Nevertheless, these seven psalms, taken in the order in which they appear in the Hebrew Bible, have long been placed together as a minicanonical collection because of their shared subject matter. From a literary point of view, the collection can be understood as one voice because the seven psalms have an overarching structure that actually links them together rhetorically and metaphorically. The first three of the series, Psalm 6, 31 (32), and 37 (38), all ask God to turn away his anger; a similarity underlined by the fact that the texts of Psalms 6 and 37 (38) begin with the same phrase: *Domine, ne in furore tuo arguas me*, that is, *O Lord, rebuke me not in your anger.* In the last three of the seven, Psalm 101 (102), 129 (130), and 142 (143), the speaker asks God to hear him. Here again, there is a rhetorical link, since Psalm 101 (102) and 142 (143) both begin *Domine, exaudi orationem meam*, that is, *O Lord, hear my prayer.* That leaves the central psalm of the seven, Psalm 50 (51), the magnificent "Miserere," as an emotional centerpiece for the minicanon. The following schematic representation of the first lines of the seven Penitential Psalms will show the rhetorical and emotional progression of this collection, from "do not be angry" to "have mercy" to "hear me":

Psalm 6 *Domine, ne in furore tuo arguas me* (O Lord, rebuke me not in your anger)

Psalm 31 (32) *Beati quorum remissae sunt iniquitates* (Blessed are they whose sins are forgiven).

Psalm 37 (38) *Domine, ne in furore tuo arguas me* (O Lord, rebuke me not in your anger).

Psalm 50 (51) *Miserere mei, Deus, secundum magnam misericordiam tuam* (Have mercy on me, O Lord, according to your great mercy).

Psalm 101 (102) *Domine, exaudi orationem meam* (O Lord, hear my prayer).

Psalm 129 (130) *De profundis clamavi ad te Domine* (From the depths I cry to you, O Lord).

Psalm 142 (143) *Domine, exaudi orationem meam* (O Lord, hear my prayer).

Since the sixth century, the Penitential Psalms have been recited in litanies of penance. In the thirteenth century, Pope Innocent III ordered them recited during Lent; in the sixteenth century, Pius V refined this by establishing them as part of the Friday Office of Lent.[2] We know of several medieval Latin commentaries on the Seven Penitential Psalms, one by Alcuin, Charlemagne's schoolmaster in the ninth century,[3] one widely attributed to both Pope Gregory the Great in the sixth century and Pope Gregory VII (Hildebrand) in the eleventh,[4] and later medieval commentaries of uncertain authorship, but attributed to the formidable twelfth-century Pope Innocent III.[5] Exegetical fascination with these poems continued into the Reformation period: Martin Luther also wrote a commentary on the Penitential Psalms.[6]

Between the thirteenth and the sixteenth centuries, the Penitential Psalms seem to have entered into the piety of lay people, as they formed the basis of the Book of Hours, the abbreviated Office developed for the laity. Perhaps because of the expanded social context of this lay devotional tradition, the seven Penitential Psalms came to be translated into European vernacular languages. They exist in Italian in a version attributed to Dante,[7] and were paraphrased in Italian by Laura Battiferra degli Ammannati, Pietro Aretino, Luigi Alamanni, and others in the sixteenth century.[8] The Penitential Psalms were translated into English into the sixteenth century in the context of the English Catholic-Protestant struggles, with English commentaries, paraphrases, and poetic translations by John Fisher, Thomas Wyatt, Mary Sidney, Anne Lock, and Henry Howard, Earl of Surrey, among others. In the seventeeth century, George Chapman actually did a loose English translation of Petrarch's *Psalmi.*[9]

Given this rich cultural and literary heritage, it is not surprising that Petrarch was also the author of seven "psalms" entitled *Psalmi penitentiales*, but the work itself does surprise. Petrarch's *Psalmi*, strangely, are not overtly connected to the seven Penitential Psalms of the Bible; not even, like Thomas Wyatt's English poems, as vernacular paraphrases of the biblical poems. Instead, these seven compositions are Latin works, seven poems written in a type of poetic prose reminiscent of Hebrew. Petrarch's *Psalmi* immediately raise the question I would like to address in this essay: are they related to the biblical Penitential Psalms? It is a difficult question because Petrarch's *Psalmi penitentiales* have not been subjected to much scholarly scrutiny, at least in comparison to Petrarch's other works, even his Latin works, but when they have been studied, they have managed to provoke controversy. I will approach the question by first discussing the problems surrounding the text, especially since there is still no critical edition, and then making some comments about the poems, including a comparison to the biblical Penitential Psalms.

The official critical edition of Petrarch's *Psalmi penitentiales* was originally entrusted to Don Giuseppe de Luca as part of the systematic editing of Petrarch's works for the Commissione Reale per l'edizione critica delle opere di F. Petrarca. As Donatella Coppini has shown, from 1938 on there was increasing dissatisfaction on the part of the editors with the slow pace of de Luca's work.[10] De Luca had been working on this edition since the 1920's, and had identified, as he says in his notes to the project, 92 manuscripts, of which Coppini, as of 1993, could identify 88.[11] The dilatory progress of de Luca left the door open for the publication in 1929 of an edition by Henry Cochin based on one manuscript from Lucerne, Switzerland.[12]

Cochin argued that this manuscript (fig. 7) was copied for the court of a very young Gian Galeazzo Visconti; therefore, since it had a special importance in the history of transmission, it was able to stand for the original manuscript tradition. Modern scholars have accepted his argument (rather elaborate, actually, based on the reconstruction of a partially effaced ex-libris and coat of arms)[13] but have not been satisfied with an edition that represents only one manuscript out of eighty-eight. Modern editors have shied away from taking on the critical edition but have tried to give more representative readings. In an edition of four of the psalms (1, 4, and 6), Guido Martellotti added some readings from manuscripts at the Laurenziana and Riccardiana libraries in Florence; while the popular (but complete) edition of Roberto Gigliucci uses Cochin's edition but reprints Martellotti's variant readings.[14] There is still no complete critical edition, but Gigliucci's is the best version currently available.[15]

When de Luca reviewed Cochin's edition of the *Psalmi penitentiales*, he did so anonymously (under the name of "Odoskopos") and harshly.[16] That much could be expected, of course; but what is more surprising is exactly what aroused de Luca's criticism, that is, Cochin's interpretation of the poems. Cochin's edition created a rather romantic vision of the *Psalmi penitentiales* in two ways: first, the preface by the noted man of letters Pierre de Nolhac placed the poems in the period of Petrarch's spiritual crisis and his infatuation with Laura, classifying the work as a series of love poems.[17] Cochin's introduction also related these psalms to "the central crisis of his moral life."[18] In the discussion of the manuscript and the edition, Cochin goes to some length to place the manuscript at Gian Galeazzo's court soon after his betrothal to Isabelle de Valois in 1360.[19] Even though a connection is also made here between the Psalms and Francesco's brother, the Carthusian monk Gherardo, in Cochin's edition, Petrarch's *Psalmi penitentiales* become love poems.

To de Luca's taste, this interpretation was a terrible misunderstanding, a sort of tone deafness to the period and the author. He says:

> The trecento, and Petrarch himself, have decidedly other accents for religious poetry, either sweet or terrible (*o dolci o tremendi*). The *Salmi* are a devout exercise, perhaps not insincere. By sending them, Petrarch takes upon himself a sort of improvisation, and it seems that he speaks truthfully.[20]

Coppini suggests that this dispute with Cochin was the reason that de Luca gave up the critical edition. Perhaps so. What is clear is that it does raise for us an important question: what is Petrarch's *Psalmi penitentiales*? Is it a set of love poems or a religious work in the penitential mode? Could it be both things at once?

Recent scholarship has come to see the *Psalmi* as a product of a slightly later period of Petrarch's life than the presumed crisis of 1342–43, placing their final redaction around 1347, or a bit later, at the time of the writing of the *Secretum*.[21] The importance of this change could be that the implied human interlocutor (as distinguished from God, to whom all seven psalms are addressed, at least on the literal level) would be Augustine (the interlocutor of the *Secretum*) rather than Laura. It is interesting to note, though, that this later dating would also place the *Psalmi* right around the time of Laura's death in 1348, and so in and of itself does not remove all possible connections to Petrarch's longing for his impossible love, nor his guilt over that longing. But all we really know for sure about the dating is the description Petrarch gives in a letter to Sagremor de Pommiers, sent in 1367 or 1368, in which he speaks of the "Psalmos septem," he is sending as works "et me multos ante annos, luce una nec integra dictasse" (works I dictated many years ago in less than one complete day).[22] The semipopular edition and translation of Roberto Gigliucci piously repeats this claim to haste, but Pacca says that it is certainly an exaggeration and that in fact, Petrarch's letter to Sagremor de Pommiers suggests that the *Psalmi* had been worked on over several decades.[23]

It is not clear whether the *Psalmi penitentiales* had been published prior to this letter, but it is known that they were sent to Francesco's brother Gherardo. This is significant because it was Gherardo, a Carthusian monk who, in the guise of "Monicus" in Petrarch's Eclogue 1, argued with the classicizing "Silvius" in defense of the superior, if rhetorically rough, poetry of the *Psalmi*.[24] This makes it all the more interesting that the *Psalmi* were circulated in collections of Carthusian piety, connected to the writings of Ludolph the Carthusian (Ludolph of Saxony, author of the late medieval best seller and spiritual guide, the *Vita Christi*). In fact, the first printed edition by Albert Stendal in Venice, 1473, is attached to Ludolph's *Vita Christi*. There is a 1514 edition of this combination of texts (Ludolph plus Petrarch), printed in Paris by Betholdo Rembolt and Johnannes Paruo, in the Annenberg Rare Book Library of the University of Pennsylvania.[25] It is in this printed edition that the title *Septi psalmi poenitentiales* appears for the first time. A further connection to Gherardo is suggested by Coppini, who points out that the seven psalms could be based on the seven hours of the monastic Office rather than the seven Penitential Psalms.[26]

But, of course, the question, What is this text? is best answered by looking at the *Psalmi* themselves. In this regard, it is worth pointing out that Petrarch himself calls them "Seven Psalms," if not "Seven Penitential Psalms." Indeed, from a literary point of view, they are more accurately called "psalms" rather than "poems" or "songs," or even "hymns," for several reasons. For one thing, these are prosaic poems, in the style of Hebrew poetry, in a Latin that mimics the Hebrew poetic forms of repetition and alliteration that mark the shift from prose to poetry. For another, they are addressed to God. This is absolutely clear in each of the seven psalms, since the word "Deus" (God) or "Dominus" (Lord), the most common name for the Divine in the Psalter, appears in each poem. Finally, the liturgical use of the Psalter is echoed by the Doxology that ends each Psalm, the formula found at the end of biblical Psalms when they are used in various Christian liturgies:

> Gloria Patri et Filio et Spiritui sancto
> Sicut erat in principio, et nunc, et semper
> Et in secula seculorum.
> Amen.[27]

So, if these are literary works that their own author calls psalms, if they are clearly addressed to God, and end with the Doxology, then why is there even any question about whether or not they are religious poems?

The more scholarly answer to this question has to do with language and sources. There is an unmistakable literary feel to the *Psalmi*. In Psalm 1.8, for example, Petrarch describes his beaten-down state in an elaborate simile of shipwreck:

> Et factus sum naufrago simillimus, qui, mercibus amissis, nudus enatat, iactatus ventis et pelago.
> [I have become like a shipwreck, having lost all my goods, swimming away naked, beaten by the wind and the waves.][28]

Indeed, Petrarch's *Psalmi penitentiales* are enormously literary and full of allusions: to Cicero, Horace, Juvenal, Virgil, Ovid, Seneca, Plautus, Terence, even Catullus. Christian authors also abound: Cassiodorus of course, since he was the author of a famous and influential commentary on the Psalter,[29] Gregory the Great, the archpoet of the *Carmina Burana*, Thomas Aquinas, and, of course, many references to Augustine. There are also many allusions to other books of the Bible apart from the Psalms, and self-referential allusions to Petrarch's own works.[30] The biblical resonances of language are so strong that many scholars have noted that Petrarch seems to be trying here to reproduce a certain sort of biblical language, the "prose-poetry" of Hebrew verse found most strikingly in the Psalms, a type of poetic form known for alliteration, repetition, and mirrored vocabulary.[31] Ariani's analysis of this poetic language recalls the "rough" characterization of Psalms by "Monicus" in the *Parthenias*: "They are little verses of a prose type with which Petrarch attempts to invent a 'rough' and 'harsh' Latin poetry on the model of Jerome's [Vulgate] translation."[32]

And the *Psalmi* also give evidence of a careful crafting to emphasize certain ideas. The great scholar of medieval Italian religious literature Giovanni Pozzi has suggested an overarching framework for Petrarch's *Psalmi penitentiales* that in important ways echoes the rhetorical structure of the seven Penitential Psalms.[33] According to Pozzi, Psalms 1 and 5 speak of being beaten down, shipwrecked, "abbattuto del dolore; e rimorso." Psalms 2 and 6 are poems of contrition, seeking reconciliation with God. Psalms 3 and 7 are about God's pardon. That leaves Psalm 4, the central psalm, which is, in a wonderful contrast, a hymn of praise. Just a comparison of the first lines will show how this overall structure fits together like a set of boxes encompassing the central Psalm 4:

1. *Heu mihi misero, quia iratum adversus me constitui redemptorem meum, et legem suam contumaciter neglexi* (Alas, I am miserable, for I have raised the wrath of my redeemer against me, and obstinately I neglect his law).

2. *Invocabo quem offendi, nec timebo; revocabo quem abieci, nec erubescam* (I will invoke the one I have offended, nor will I fear; I will call again on the one I have cast off, nor will I be ashamed).

3. *Miserere dolorum meorum, Domine; satis superque volutatus sum, et in ceno peccatorum meorum marcui miser* (Have mercy on my suffering, O Lord; enough and more than enough have I wallowed, and in the mud of my sins I languish miserably).

4. *Recordari libet munerum tuorum, Deus, ut sit mihi confusio ante oculos, et rubor in genis meis* (Gladly do I remember your gifts, O Lord, since they bring confusion before my eyes and a blush on my cheeks).

5. *Noctes meae in merore transeunt et terroribus agitant innumeris. Conscientia concutit insomnem et male michi est* (My nights are passed in sorrow and innumerable terrors disturb me. My conscience shakes me, insomniac, and evil is with me).

6. *Circumvallarunt me inimici mei, perurgentes me cuspide multiplici* (My enemies surround me, tormenting me with their many spears).

7. *Cogitabam stare, dum corrui; vae michi, quia duriter nimis allisus sum* (I thought I was standing, while I collapsed; woe is me, for I have been thrown down violently).

What is most remarkable about this arrangement is both its similarity to and difference from the overall structure of the Penitential Psalms that I have already articulated. For the Penitential Psalms, the larger form is threefold, with the first and third sections further divided into three, in an a-b-a sequence: "do not be angry" (three psalms, a-b-a) to "have mercy" (one psalm) to "hear me" (three psalms, a-b-a). Petrarch's *Psalmi*, instead, have a perfectly symmetrical overall structure: a-b-c-d-a-b-c. Although the structures are obviously different, in each case, there is a framework of common themes that serves to emphasize the message of the central poem. But the messages of these central psalms are very different. While Psalm 50 (51), the "Miserere," is a wallowing in sin, including the famous verse 7, the essence of an Augustinian concept of sin:

> Ecce, enim in iniquitatibus conceptus sum
> Et in peccatis concepit me mater mea.
> [Behold, I was conceived in sin,
> And in iniquity did my mother conceive me.]

Petrarch's Psalm 4, the centerpiece of his *Psalmi penitentiales*, tells a very different story. This is a hymn of praise and thanksgiving, beginning with the opening line:

> Recordari libet munerum tuorum, Deus, ut sit mihi confusio ante
> oculos, et
> rubor in genis meis.
> [Gladly do I remember your gifts, O Lord, since they bring confusion before my
> eyes and a blush on my cheeks.]

And it continues with a litany of the things God has made for him, Francesco: the sky, the stars, the seasons; the sun, the moon, days and nights, light and darkness, air, earth, water, mountains and seas, and all placed under the feet of men, because God loves us. Petrarch's Psalm 4 ends with a lament for human ingratitude, but it is a far cry from the desolation of Psalm 50 (51), the "Miserere."

So is Petrarch's *Psalmi penitentiales* a religious work? I would say yes, absolutely. But it is also a work in progress, the spiritual musings of a sensitive soul who is in conversation, if not in conflict, with the Christianity he has inherited. Did Petrarch's personal sorrows, perhaps his unrequited love for Laura, have a role in this work? Very likely, since the sincere personal laments of the *Psalmi* speak of regret for foolishness, falling down when he felt strong, obstinacy in sin. Everything in Petrarch's personal life would be filtered through the moral consciousness of Augustinian theology, especially in the period in which he was writing his great imagined dialogue with the bishop of Hippo. In this way, the *Psalmi penitentiales*, like the *Secretum*, is Franciscus speaking with Augustinus.

CHAPTER FOURTEEN

THE PLACE OF THE *ITINERARIUM* ·
Itinerarium ad sepulchrum domini nostri Yhesu Christi

Theodore J. Cachey, Jr.

You express the desire to hear about my state; yet if the word state derives from
standing still, man does not have here on earth a single state but perpetual motion
and slipping, and ultimate collapse. Nevertheless, I do understand what you wish:
not how my affairs stand but how they are evolving, whether happily or unhappily.

—*Familiares* 19.16, "To Guido, archbishop of Genoa, a detailed
account of his state of affairs" (spring–summer, 1357)[1]

Within the topographical system of Petrarch's life's work taken as a
kind of map, what is the place of Petrarch's *Itinerarium ad sepulchrum
domini nostri Yhesu Christi* (*Itinerary to the Sepulcher of Our Lord Jesus Christ*),
and what are its distinguishing characteristics as constituting a textual
territory within the author's oeuvre? Given the work's relative obscurity
within the Petrarchan canon, in order to motivate the attempt to situate the
work more precisely in the spatial rather than thematic or linguistic-stylistic
terms proposed in this chapter, a preliminary word about the occasion of
its composition and its contents is first in order.

Petrarch composed the *Itinerarium*, by his own report, in three days'
time during the spring of 1358 at the request of a Milanese nobleman at
the Visconti court named Giovanni Mandelli, who was about to depart on
a pilgrimage to the Holy Land. Mandelli invited Petrarch to join him on
the journey, but Petrarch demurred. The poet feared shipwreck, he wrote,
and especially the risk of "slow death and nausea, worse than death itself,
not without reason but from experience."[2] In his place Petrarch sent to his
friend an erudite "familiar" letter that was delivered to its dedicatee on
April 4, 1358, according to the colophon at the end of an apograph manu-

229

script of the work that has survived (Cremona, Biblioteca Statale, Deposito Libreria Civica, MS BB.1.2.5):

> Nevertheless, I shall be with you in spirit, and since you have requested it, I will accompany you with this writing, which will be for you like a brief itinerary. You have followed the usage of lovers, asking of me, whom you will miss, the image with which you will be able to console yourself during your absence, not the image of the face that changes daily but rather the more stable effigy of my soul and my intellect, which however small it may be, is surely the best part of me.[3]

Despite its conventional and commonplace nature, Petrarch was evidently attracted to the pilgrimage genre because it presented him a unique opportunity to indulge in the subgenre of the autobiographical itinerary, which characterizes several signature moments in his Latin prose epistolary, including the dedicatory letter to the *Familiares*, the *Posteritati* (*Seniles* 18.1), and the autobiographical letter to Guido Sette (*Seniles* 10.2).[4] In fact, these are just three of the more prominent literary expressions of what for Petrarch was an ongoing need to situate himself through his writings in relation to an itinerary of places (among others, Arezzo, Pisa, Carpentras, Montpellier, Avignon, Bologna, Vaucluse, Naples, Parma, Selvapiana, Milan, Padua, Venice, and Arquà). Writing his life as the itinerary of a journey represented a literary means of addressing his spatially deracinated status, that is, the fact that Petrarch was the son of a Florentine exile born in exile. The *Itinerarium* satisfied, albeit in a somewhat more indirect way, the same fundamental need to situate the self in space as did these other more prestigious writings in the Petrarchan canon. The intrinsic spatiality and location of the work within the canon are thus important for the interpretation of the *Itinerarium*'s deeper resonances, which belie its brevity and its relatively marginal status in the critical bibliography.

Petrarch's highly personal contribution to the medieval pilgrimage genre takes Genoa rather than the more usual Venice as its point of departure. This route offered the opportunity to revisit Petrarchan literary sites along the same Tyrrhenian coast where Mago had famously expired in the only passage from Petrarch's *Africa* (6.885–916) that was published in the author's lifetime. Petrarch recalls that the beauty of those shores "inspired me to describe these places in a passage of my *Africa*" and patronizingly reassures the pilgrim that if he does ever manage to finish the poem and Mandelli is lucky enough to read it, then he will be able to remember these places that he is about to see firsthand (*Itinerarium* 5.1). The ports of call along the Tyrrhenian coast that Petrarch rehearses and variously illuminates with tidbits of erudition largely correspond to those found in the contemporary portolan maps that he must have had in mind if not spread out on his table when he composed the letter, including Capo di Monte, Portofino, Rapallo, Sestri, Portovenere, Lerici (although some such as Luni, Sarzana, Avenza, Rio Freddo, and Massa derive from Petrarch's firsthand knowledge of the area). Mention of Elba and Giglio on the other hand stirs memories of a famous "shipwreck" sonnet from *Rerum vulgarium fragmenta* 69. Rome gets only passing mention here: "If I had the intention of speaking of it in a brief space I would show myself to be intolerably too bold" (*Itinerarium* 8.0).[5] Ports along the coasts of Lazio, including Anzio and Astura, and Circeo ("a mountain of a certain height to which it is believed the sorceress Circe, powerful for her incantations gave the name" [*Itinerarium* 8.1]),[6] are clearly less inspiring to Petrarch's imagination than the Neapolitan regions, especially for their Virgilian associations (the Mantuan's tomb). Naples itself receives special attention, and the *Itinerarium* establishes numerous links and cross-references with the reports of Petrarch's biographical journeys there (*Familiares* 5.3–6). The *Itinerarium* weaves together geographical places he visited and wrote about to form a self-referential fabric that achieves the author's expressed intention of offering an itinerary that is tantamount to a self-portrait, "the more stable effigy of my soul and intellect."

Departing Naples, the journey resumes and we encounter in rapid succession Vesuvius, Capri, and Salerno, at which point Petrarch hopes that his correspondent "will reach the ends of Italy as easily brought by favorable winds and smooth sailing, as I am by a simple and swift style" (*Itinerarium* 12.0).[7] In fact, leaving behind Scalea on a course "due south to Reggio," the pilgrim's pace noticeably accelerates as he passes between Scylla and Charybdis, leaves behind Mount Etna in the distance to the right, passes around the heel of the "boot" (as Petrarch was first to fashion it),[8] past Squillace, Crotone, and Taranto and crosses "under full sail" to the first cape of Achaea. Continuing east through the Greek archipelago with Crete on the right and Euboea on the left, the pilgrim runs up against Asia Minor. In front of Cilicia is Cyprus and opposite Cyprus in the farthest corner of the sea is hidden Lesser Armenia. At this point, Petrarch writes, you may disembark at any one of the available coastal cities (Tortosa, Tripoli, Beirut, Tyre, Caesarea, Jaffa, Ascalon); if you travel by land to the north you can see Damascus. Nevertheless, Petrarch recommends landing further south: you will miss many sites, but since the destination of the journey is Jerusalem, it is better to disembark closer to it. At which point we have arrived at the Holy Land.

Petrarch's guide makes little or no attempt to provide any practical information about travel in the Holy Land. In fact, he never traveled there. This part of the text, which takes its sources primarily from the Bible and coeval pilgrimage literature, has less of a guidebook character than the Italian portion and appears more designed to assist the pilgrim in his meditations. Nevertheless, the uniquely Petrarchan point of view is unmistakable, emerging clearly in the mix of classical and sacred references and particularly in some of the more idiosyncratic treatment of the sites. The most noteworthy of these is the supplementary excursion to the tomb of Alexander that concludes the *Itinerarium*. Petrarch makes a point of retelling the same Suetonian tale about Augustus Caesar, who asked to see the tomb of King Alexander, that Petrarch had also related in *De viris illustribus*. Caesar, when asked if he would also like to see Ptolemy's tomb, declined. Thomas Greene insightfully related its occurrence there to Petrarch's vindication of "his right to select his own material as biographer. . . . Augustus refuses the conventional tour and refuses the conventional title of king to the late Ptolemy. The true sovereign chooses to divert his attention to another true sovereign."[9] The same anecdote functions in the *Itinerarium* as a kind of implicit concluding justification for the author's unconventional pilgrimage journey and is of a piece with the author's closing boast that he completed in three days the pilgrim's journey of three months.[10]

Since Pierre de Nolhac's classic study *Pétrarque et l'humanisme*, Petrarch's *Itinerarium* has always been considered a more or less interesting expression of Petrarch's geographical erudition, which had long been considered a characteristic aspect of his humanism. This reception can be updated somewhat by viewing Petrarch from an anthropological perspective as a kind of "long-distance specialist." In fact, according to M. W. Helms, those few members of traditional societies who were able to become familiar with geographically distant phenomena and with geographical knowledge in general were often accorded an aura of prestige and "awe" that approached "the same order if not always the same magnitude as that accorded political-religious specialists or elites in general."[11] But clearly, as even a brief sketch of its contents reveals, there is more to the *Itinerarium* than the simple display of geographical and historical erudition. More important than its ostensible geographical content is the spatial self-portrait of the poet at a crossroads in his career, and this aspect of the text merits closer examination.

So what then is the place of Petrarch's *Itinerarium*? In his chapter on Petrarch for the Salerno *Storia della letteratura italiana*, Marco Ariani made a first gesture in exploring this question by connecting the pilgrimage guide directly with the *Canzoniere*. As we have already noted, Petrarch explicitly stated in the proem to the *Itinerarium* that the work was intended to stand in the place of its author. The *Itinerarium* thus had, according to Ariani, "the specific function of healing an absence according to the 'fashion of lovers,' which is singularly evoked as presiding over the writing of the text itself. The humanistic faith in the erudite apparatus as a substitute for experience connects the *Itinerarium* to the imaginative world of the *amor de lonh* upon which Petrarch was constructing, precisely in those years, the book of lyric fragments, as the sign of a philology that was perfectly capable of constituting complete universes of sense independent of any obligation or correspondence with empirical reality."[12]

In seeking to develop further this line of inquiry, it is important to recall that the book of lyric fragments had reached a particular state in its evolution in the same year that Petrarch wrote the *Itinerarium*, that is, according to the fiction of the final form of the *Canzoniere*, in that same spring of 1358. The philological evidence and critical consensus concerning the dating of the first publication of the work, the "Correggio" form (1356–1358), corresponds to the explicit dating of the end of the affair from the retrospective viewpoint of the last dated poem of the book in its final form: "Tennemi Amor anni ventuno ardendo, / lieto nel foco, et nel duol pien di speme; / poi che madonna e 'l mio cor seco inseme/ saliro al ciel, dieci altri anni piangendo" (Love held me twenty-one years gladly burning in the fire and full of hope amid sorrow; since my lady, and my heart with her, rose to Heaven, ten more years of weeping [*RVF* 364.1–4]).[13] In his *Life of Petrarch*, Wilkins, ingenuously but nonetheless suggestively for our purposes, discussed the composition of the last of the dated poems of the *Canzoniere* immediately following his account of the composition of the *Itinerarium*, taking *Rerum vulgarium fragmenta* 364 to have been written on April 6, 1358, the tenth anniversary of Laura's death and the thirty-first anniversary of Petrarch's "'enamorment,'" as he calls it.[14] In fact, Petrarch's *Itinerarium* had been delivered to its dedicatee just two days before, according to the explicit statement of the Cremona apograph manuscript, April 4. As Santagata, among others, has pointed out, the explicit date given in *Rerum vulgarium fragmenta* 364 cannot automatically be taken to correspond to the effective date of composition, and the poem does not in fact enter the collection until the last stages of the Vaticano 3195, between 1373 and the author's death on July 18, 1374. Nonetheless, Santagata is probably right in his surmise that Petrarch dates here the end of his "love story" to 1358, because that was the year in which he first published the *Canzoniere* "—the book, that is, which, for the first time, had told that story."[15]

There is, in fact, some trace of Petrarch's first publication of the *Canzoniere* in the important "detailed account of the state of his affairs," *Familiares* 19.16, written in the spring–summer of 1357, from which was taken the epigraph cited at the beginning of this chapter:

> Once the storms of youth were bridled and that flame was extinguished thanks to the maturity that comes with age—oh, what am I saying when so many lecherous and foolish old men can be seen everywhere a shameful spectacle and example for the young— after the fire was extinguished, rather, by celestial dew and Christ's assistance, the tenor of my life has nearly always remained constant, nor have I altered it despite my frequent changes in location. (*Familiares* 19.16)[16]

This reference to the bridling of the storms of youth and the extinction of his passion would be incongruous at this late date and in this context (didn't he get over Laura, according to the *Posteritati*, around his fortieth year?), except for the fact that Petrarch was at this time preparing the first published form of the book of lyric fragments for his friend and patron Azzo da Correggio. One can observe that the passage also punctually reinforces the palinodic ethical structure of the "Correggio" form as explicated by Santagata among others, which ended with what proved to be a not quite definitive farewell to the love lyric: "Or sia qui fine al mio amoroso canto: / secca è la vena de l'usato ingegno,/ et la cetera mia rivolta in pianto" (Now here let there be an end to my song of love; dry is the vein of my accustomed wit, and my lyre is turned to weeping [*RVF* 292 12–14]).[17]

Closing the book on the "Correggio" *Canzoniere* and taking three days to compose a pilgrimage guide for his friend Mandelli were not the only things that preoccupied Petrarch toward the end of the 1350s. Ensconced in the literary otium afforded him by the Visconti of Milan, Petrarch was enjoying one of his most productive periods, as important and in many ways complementary to the time between 1347 and 1353 when he first conceived the major works of his maturity. These had included the *Canzoniere* and the epistolary collections in both prose and verse. Both projects had emerged as the literary response to a kind of "place panic" experienced by a patron-less Petrarch during the uncertain and itinerant period following the deaths in 1348 of Laura and (just as importantly) of Giovanni Colonna, when he was still shuttling back and forth between France and Italy. At the end of the 1350s, well into his eight years in Milan, Petrarch found himself instead "under spreading beech's covert" (*sub tegmine fagi*, in Virgil *Eclogues* 1.1), sheltered by his Milanese patrons, between the tranquil suburbs of the city and the charterhouse at Garegnano. In terms of literary territorialization, however, we find our author during this period always between coming and going, shuttling, if you will, between finishing works, reopening old ones and beginning new ones. We might say along with Wilkins, in his understated style, that during the late 1350s "Petrarch did much writing, turning now to one work and now to another," and that this period of relative physical stasis was characterized by restless, not to say frenetic mobility in the literary realm.[18] Petrarch "finished" the first *Canzoniere* between 1356 and 1358, "completed" the *Bucolicum carmen* in the fall of 1357,[19] reopened and made additions to the ten-year-old *De otio religioso* (including a long interpolation about the Basel earthquake, whose devastation he had witnessed on his return from Prague in 1356), added verses to his twelfth eclogue, sent to Barbato the first of his eclogues, *Parthenias*, copied in his own hand, along with a revised proemial letter (originally written in 1350); and, between 1357 and 1359, he composed the last three letters addressed to Nelli that make up the *Sine nomine* (*Sine nomine* 18 was written in April or May of 1358, around the same time as the *Itinerarium*). And finally, Petrarch completed around 1360 *De remediis utriusque fortune*, the last and longest of his major works in Latin.

Concerning Petrarch's compositional practices, Wilkins once observed how "Petrarch never felt constrained to finish one work before beginning another one. There was indeed in his nature a certain restlessness—frequently shown in his changes of residence and his thoughts of still other changes—that manifested itself, in his literary activity, in a turning from one to another of the works that he had on hand at a given time, or in the undertaking of an entirely new work."[20] Wilkins never developed this intuition of the existence of a link between Petrarch's biographical restlessness and his movements back and forth between his works in a systematic way. Nevertheless, it is evident that the constitutionally unsettled spatial state of this son of an exile who was "begotten and born in exile," as he reports in the dedicatory letter to the *Familiares*, expressed on the one hand a profound awareness of man's ultimate irremediable homelessness, and on the other a no less compelling biographical need for dwelling, for some form of temporary shelter. The epochal and epic embodiment of this irresolvable tension is at the heart of Petrarch's intellectual history and produces as its effect in writing not only the place of Petrarch's *Itinerarium* but the entire corpus and eventually the place or what has recently been termed "the site of Petrarchism."[21] Long before Theodor Adorno so poignantly expressed it, Petrarch exemplified the fact that "for the man who has no home, writing becomes a place to live."[22] His restless movements between his works during his residence at Milan reflected his pursuit through writing of an unstable equilibrium between the desire for stability or permanence of state in the world and life's perpetual motion and slippage. It was by means of this practice that he also sought to defer "ultimate collapse," or, to adopt Petrarch's favorite trope for this "ruina," the inevitable shipwreck of this life.

Thus, at a juncture when so many books and projects were coming to their (albeit provisional) conclusions, including and in particular the book of vernacular fragments, Petrarch instinctively found the need for new beginnings. As he wrote to Lelius at the beginning of 1359: "Today I seem to have begun for the first time; the wise man's words (*Ecclesiastes* 18.1) are literally being realized in me: 'When man brings his work to an end, then will he begin, and when he has completed it, then will he be beginning'" (*Familiares* 20.14.1). And it was in the arena, or better, the *aringo*, to use a term of Dante (*Paradiso* 1.18), of vernacular poetry where Petrarch undertook at this time his most important new challenge in the *Triumphi*, which would engage him from the late 1350s forward. In fact, the earliest surviving manuscript datings for the poem, which was written in Dante's own "*terze rime*," begin in 1356. Following a relatively intense period of work on the *Triumphus Cupidinis* 1 and 3 between 1356 and 1360, they extend intermittently over the rest of the poet's life culminating in the autograph of the *Triumphus Eternitatis*, whose final "hoc placet" (Vat. Lat. 3196) dates from the last year of the poet's life.[23]

The enthusiasm in connection with a fresh start on the *Triumphi* is expressed in the same *Familiares* 19.16 from which we departed and which also contained the allusion to the provisional closure of the *Canzoniere* previously discussed. Ariani has called attention to the following passage, which he no doubt rightly takes to be a clear allusion to the project of the *Triumphi* which Petrarch had taken up again in earnest during 1357:

> In the interim, I sigh, keep vigil, sweat, see, and struggle against adversity, and the thicker the hedge of difficulties, the more eagerly I faced them, aroused and driven onward by their very novelty or arduousness. My labor is certain, the results uncertain, an evil held in common with others who enter this contest. (*Familiares* 19.16)[24]

Moreover, Ariani considers the *Triumphi* to be one of the "inaccessa" (inaccessible things) Petrarch speaks of in the famous letter on imitation to Boccaccio written in 1359 (*Familiares* 22.2), at which time, work on the poem was at a peak:

> I do want a guide who leads me, not one who binds me to him, one
> who leaves me to use my own sight, judgment, and freedom; I do
> not want him to forbid me to step where I wish, to go beyond him
> in some things, to attempt the inaccessible, to follow a shorter or,
> if I wish, an easier path, and to hasten or stop or even to part ways
> and return. (*Familiares* 22.2.4)[25]

What does all this have to do with the place of the *Itinerarium* within the topography of the author's life's work? Paradoxically, viewed from the spatial and structural perspective outlined here, one finds that Petrarch's foray into the most conventional and anonymous of medieval literary genres reveals itself to be vitally related to the same innovative and experimental movement that informed the *Triumphi* at the end of the 1350s. The *Itinerarium* emerges as an effect of the same impulse toward new beginnings behind the vernacular poem at a crucial juncture in the journey of Petrarch's life and works, and provides a gloss on the point of transition between the book of lyric fragments on the one hand, which was already tending in its first published form toward a circular (and ultimately calendrical) macrostructure, and on the other, the linear narrative trajectory of the *Triumphi*.

But what is most important for understanding the why and wherefore of the *Itinerarium* is the place of the work itself within the topography of Petrarch's oeuvre, for besides signaling forward motion at this crucial juncture in the context of Petrarch's life's work, the pilgrimage guide provided a congenial space in which Petrarch could address issues he was confronting at the same time in the *Triumphi*, including, most significantly, his relationship with Dante, which went to the heart of his inspiration in that vernacular poem.

It is remarkable that the structural-spatial analogy between the pilgrim's progress and the triumphal procession should have remained unnoticed, despite a fair bit of commentary on the distinctive spatial characteristics of the "Triumph" as genre.[26] Both works illuminate the same point in Petrarch's artistic evolution, a point when he was sanguine about overcoming what had represented for him throughout his career a particular challenge or limitation, one which in fact he never overcame, as the unfinished and "fragmentary" state of the *Africa*, the *Rerum memorandarum libri*, the *De viris illustribus,* and ultimately the *Triumphi* reveals.[27] Having reached some form of provisional closure on the side of the book of lyric fragments, Petrarch was inspired to attempt again the challenge of a long poem, utilizing this time the macrostructure of the triumphal march or parade, and this time in the vernacular. In its modest but nevertheless illuminating way the structure of the pilgrimage guide expresses the same aspiration to overcome, by traveling expeditiously through an itinerary of places, what Marziano Guglielminetti termed long ago Petrarch's *Erlebnis* (experience) of the fragmentary.[28] At opposite ends of the generic spectrum within Petrarch's works and within the system of late-medieval literature, Petrarch's pilgrimage guide and his most radical and innovative poetic experiment share at bottom the same creative preoccupation, which is manifested in the same progressively itinerant rhythm that characterizes both works, in the passage from one vignette or exemplum to the next in the Italian poem and the progression from one locus to the next in the pilgrim's guide.

One's sense of a deeper ideological relationship between the two works is only heightened by several intertextual contacts between them, most prominently in those parts of the Italian poem that describe the journey to Cyprus in the *Triumphus Cupidinis* 4 and then to Scipio's Literno and to Rome in the *Triumphus Pudicitie.* While the terrain is unstable here, since there are no dated annotations for these parts of the *Triumphi,* such correspondences support the idea that Petrarch was working on these Mediterranean sections of the *Triumphi* at the time that he wrote the pilgrimage guide.

One idea worth considering in this context for its possible connection to Dante is between *Itinerarium,* 9.1, in which is recounted some mythological background on Ischia, and two narratively and structurally crucial similes in the *Triumphus Cupidinis* (4.154–56) and the *Triumphus Pudicitie* (112–14):

> In any case, before your eyes will be Inarima, which will present itself right in front of you: an island noted for the praise of poets that the people today call Ischia, beneath which, it is said, the giant Typhoeus was buried by the will of Jupiter. The clouds of vapor that rise there, which bring to mind those of a gasping man, give credit to this legend, as do the flames that are used to rising from there as upon Mount Etna. (*Itinerarium* 1.9)[29]

The similes from the *Triumphi* compare the effects of the eruptions of the same Mediterranean volcanic islands that are mentioned here in the *Itinerarium* to the frustrated rage of the captive lover in the *Triumphus Cupidinis* 4 and to the frustrated rage of Love conquered by Chastity in the *Triumphus Pudicitie:*

> cotale era egli [Amor], e tanto a peggior patto,
> che paura e dolor, vergogna ed ira
> eran nel volto suo tutte ad un tratto.
> 　　　Non freme così 'l mar, quando s' adira,
> non Inarime, allor che Tipheo piagne,
> né Mongibel, s' Enchelado sospira.

[So now was love, but in still worse a plight, / Since fear and grief and shame and wrathfulness / Were all together written on his face: / Greater his rage than that of the angry sea, / Or that of Ischia when Typhoeus weeps, / Or Aetna's when Enceladus laments.][30]

The *Itinerarium*'s reference to the fact that the flames rise over Inarima (Ischia) as upon Etna parallels another passage linking the two volcanoes from *Sine nomine* 18, written between April and May 1358, where the sufferings of the world during the Babylonian captivity are compared to those of Enceladus beneath Etna and Typheus under the island of Ischia ("quasi Etnam Eneceladus aut Typheus Inarimen pati potest").[31]

Petrarch's insistence on the pairing may have to do with the fact that in placing Typheus beneath Ischia (consistent with Horace *Carmina* 3.4.53–58; Seneca *Hercules Oetaeus* 1155–59; Lucan 5.99–101; Claudian *De raptu Proserpinae* 3.183–87), he was departing from the "authority" of Dante (*Paradiso* 8.67–70; cf. *Inferno* 31.124) who followed Ovid (*Metamorphoses* 5.346–58) in placing Typheus beneath Etna, a departure that had stimulated one of Petrarch's only three explicit mentions of Dante in his writings, in an unfortunately undated postil in the margin of a passage of Pomponius Mela describing the marvels of Cilicia and locating Typheus there (1.13.76): "Nota contra Dantem."[32] Petrarch betrays here an unusual preoccupation with Dante's opinion regarding the point, considering the fact that, when it came to locating Typheus beneath Ischia rather than in Sicily, there were numerous and greater authorities than Dante, including Virgil and Ovid, from whom Petrarch is distancing himself. However, while the question of Petrarch's philological-geographical investment as "long-distance specialist" in locating the burial sites of Enceladus and Typheus merits further study, for our more immediate purposes it serves to raise the issue of how the *Itinerarium* can provide some perspective on Petrarch's evolving attitude toward Dante expressed at this time in the *Triumphi*.

For finally, the place of the *Itinerarium* in the network of places constituting Petrarch's works is perhaps most significant for the light it sheds on Petrarch's complex relationship with Dante, most explicitly, in a key passage towards the end of the pilgrimage guide that radically revised Dante's Ulysses:

> But what are you thinking now? Hasn't the desire to see us again taken you yet; hasn't the desire to return to your home, your fatherland, and friends entered your soul yet? I believe so and am sure it could not be any other way. But there is no greater stimulus than virtue. Virtue inspires the generous soul to overcome every difficulty; it does not suffer one to remain in one place, nor that one should look back; it forces one to forget not only pleasures but also just duties and affections; it does not allow one to choose anything but the ideal of virtue and it does not allow one to desire or think of anything else. This is the stimulus that made Ulysses forget Laertes, Penelope, and Telemachus, and now keeps you far from us, I am afraid, longer than we should like. (*Itinerarium* 17.0)[33]

Petrarch here praises the same Ulysses Dante had condemned in the *Inferno* for, among other things, abandoning his family: "neither fondness for my son, nor reverence for my aged father, nor the due love which would have made Penelope glad, could conquer in me the longing that I had to gain experience of the world and of human vice and worth" (*Inferno* 26.94–9). The passage from the *Itinerarium* anticipates by little more than a year a more famous passage from Petrarch's letter to Boccaccio about Dante (*Familiares* 21.15),[34] in which Petrarch again praised Dante for the very same reasons that Dante had condemned Ulysses:

> (Dante) resisted and began devoting himself all the more vigorously to his literary pursuits, neglecting all else and desirous only of glory. In this I can scarcely admire and praise him too highly when nothing—not the injustice suffered at the hands of his fellow citizens, not exile, poverty, or the stings of envy, not his wife's love or his devotion to his children—diverted him from his course once he had embarked upon it, when many other great talents, be-

ing weak of purpose, would be distracted by the least disturbance. (*Familiares* 21.15.8)[35]

It is worth noting that Petrarch's utilization of Dante's Ulysses in the *Itinerarium* as a positive model for "going beyond the bounds" in pursuit of virtue and in his letter to Boccaccio, where he delivers an implicit criticism of Dante for his Ulysses-like pursuit of glory, necessarily and characteristically involved the suppression or at least the deferral of Dante's shipwreck of Ulysses.[36] And Petrarch's suppression of or swerve around Ulysses' shipwreck in the *Itinerarium*, suggests that perhaps the threat of shipwreck at the beginning of the *Itinerarium* that kept him from undertaking the physical journey of the pilgrimage was something more than just an example of Petrarch's famous fear of the sea, but was ultimately related to issues of poetic identity. How else to explain the presence of Petrarch's arguably most important and revealing utilization of the Ulysses figure in such a minor and marginal position within his works? Dante was very clearly on Petrarch's mind when he wrote the *Itinerarium*, as early as the proem where he uncharacteristically used the expression "second death" (Pr. 4) in the patently Dantean sense of damnation rather than in the usual Petrarchan meaning of fame's passing as representing a "second death." What the *Itinerarium* adds to our understanding of the relationship between Dante and Petrarch, once we have a clearer notion of its place in the oeuvre, has therefore to do with the way in which it expresses in its forward movement ("[virtue] does not suffer one to remain in one place, nor that one should look back") the *vis polemica* of the project of the *Triumphi* in which Petrarch sought to go beyond his predecessor Dante in the arena of vernacular eloquence and "to attempt the inaccessible." Petrarch's revision of Ulysses and swerve in the *Itinerarium* around the rock or *scoglio* of Dante's shipwreck of the Greek hero expressed his aspiration at that crucial juncture in his career to move beyond Dante and to establish his own place in the realm of vernacular poetry vis-à-vis the *Divina commedia*.[37]

PART V

LIFE'S TURBULENCE

CHAPTER FIFTEEN

ON THE TWO FACES OF FORTUNE •
De remediis utriusque fortune

Timothy Kircher

Petrarch composed the majority of *De remediis utriusque fortune* (*Remedies for Fortune Fair and Foul*) between 1354 and 1360, dedicating it to his volatile friend Azzo da Correggio, onetime lord of Parma. He completed the treatise in a second redaction prior to the autumn of 1366, and noted soon afterward the acclaim his contemporaries granted the work.[1] While the *De remediis* remained very popular in succeeding centuries, undergoing translations into vernacular European languages, the modern era has witnessed its neglect.[2] Klaus Heitmann in 1958 published the only monograph analyzing its qualities, and just several years ago Christophe Carraud established the first modern Latin edition, though this work is based on incunabula, not on manuscripts.[3]

An overview of the contents of the *De remediis* suggests its appeal to Renaissance readers. The work consists of two parts. The first part is devoted to discussing remedies against good fortune, or against the dangers implicit in prosperity. The second part addresses the cures for the blows of bad fortune. Together both parts contain 254 conversations or dialogues concerning various cases of fortune, in which the persona of Ratio (Reason) responds to the personae of Gaudium, Spes, Dolor, and Metus (Joy, Hope, Sorrow, and Fear, respectively). Petrarch may derive these emotional interlocutors from *Aeneid* 6.730–734, which he cited in his earlier dialogic work, the *Secretum;*[4] and he may well have had in mind a passage from one of his favorite philosophical treatises, Cicero's *Tusculan Disputations*, where Cicero notes how four different emotions resist the guidance of reason.[5] As its model Petrarch's work refers explicitly to the small set of dialogues entitled *De remediis fortuitorum* (*Remedies against Happenstances*) which he believed Seneca wrote, but which is now attributed to the sixth-century bishop Martin of Braga.

In Martin's work Sensus argues with Ratio over a limited number of misfortunes, mainly concerning one's own death, poverty, or the deaths of friends and family.[6] Petrarch would organize and amplify this desultory model, composing a first part on the perils of plenty and setting the meditation on death as the coda to the entire discussion. He constructs an overarching formal arrangement among the various dialogues, however casual the actual sequence of dialogues sometimes appears. There are many internal cross-references among the dialogues.[7] These imply that Petrarch anticipated that the reader would follow the conversations sequentially towards the telos (goal) of the contemplation or commemoration of death, a theme he also knew well from his readings of Cicero, Seneca, and Augustine, among others.[8]

Petrarch's collection of conversations on fortune goes beyond the pseudo-Senecan treatise and other antecedents not only in the detailed attention to the perils of prosperity but also in the scale of the project: it is, for example, replete with citations of authors and heroes both *antiqui* and *moderni*. And unlike the contemporary mendicants with their penitential *summae*, which resemble the *De remediis* in their encyclopedic scope, Petrarch operates without an explicit Christian design. The work focuses on one's response to the accidents of fortune, and in the second volume Ratio distinguishes between the distress caused by external misfortune and the sorrow over voluntary sin.[9] The contributions of Heitmann and Charles Trinkaus have underscored the treatise's uneasy syncretism of Christian doctrine with classical dicta. Heitmann has shown how Petrarch revises at times the Stoical philosophy he otherwise admires by presenting Platonic, Peripatetic, and Christian concepts.[10] Trinkaus especially has recognized the significance of the dialogue 2.93, on human dignity, for later humanist compositions on this subject.[11] I would point out another innovation of the work in the history of ideas. Bearing in mind the form and sequence of dialogues, one encounters a fundamental skepticism in the work. This skepticism is deeper than the Academic or Ciceronian viewpoint, for it questions the moral supremacy of reason prized by classical philosophy and by many Christian writers as well, including Petrarch himself.[12]

The quiddity of the *De remediis* is the nature of Fortune and her ills.[13] The allegorical personae of these dialogues, Ratio and the various emotions, provide both the unifying framework as well as the richness of expression Petrarch desired. We therefore approach the work's treatment of Fortune not only by analyzing its moral-philosophical logic but also by tracing the poetic avenues it presents in addressing his readers. The two aspects of this treatment together compose a complex response. The view of Fortune as moral malady appears initially simple and traditional: Fortune, understood as the accidental or external circumstances of life, sparks the passions that derail one's progress in virtue, and it is reason's role to extirpate or bridle the passions. Fortune's fair and foul faces may incite overconfidence or despair; these two faces require that it be either resisted with temperance or suffered in patience, as the Stoic and Christian sages recommend.[14] But the work compromises and complicates this view through its poetic sensibility that defies stasis. This restless sensibility shows Fortune to be not merely a moral opponent of virtue, but moreover an existential figure representing the flow of history and time. The existential face of Fortune in the *De remediis* is not the Stoic Fatum or Christian Providentia, to which one must submit. It is a more dynamic force inherent in the human condition, which overcomes static conclusions and demands that one recognize the temporal flux of one's awareness. What is missing in Petrarch's sources of classical philosophy and Christian dogma, the work suggests, is the category of the existential. This category is only acknowledged by a poetic sensibility, one disclosed primarily by the form of the treatise.[15]

Examining the work's moral-philosophical logic, we uncover consistent distinctions scattered throughout the dialogues. In a discussion of fishponds, Ratio tells Joy that "if the mind were submissive or obedient to reason, it would lead you to a better end by a straighter way, and would reveal to you why you should scorn many things you now desire."[16] Ratio's claim in *De remediis* 2.75 on "mental discord" is clearer still. Citing "the philosophers," Ratio advances a tripartite division of the mind, the highest and ruling part heavenly and serene, the lower ones filled with anger and impulse, lust and desire. Ratio tells Sorrow to "coax, by advice or by force, the vile parts to obey the superior one."[17] Ratio replicates its counsel in its own actions, since it attempts to persuade the emotions to follow its guidance. For Petrarch, as philosopher and poet, the conceptual intertwines with the rhetorical. On the conceptual level, Ratio distinguishes between higher and lower spheres, reason and emotion, mind and body. No surprise then when Ratio declares that the body is perishable, transitory, and a house for deceptions,[18] which the emotions generate and invigorate. Towards the conclusion of the second part, when Fear tells Ratio it fears to die, Ratio defines humanity as rational and mortal. The things of the higher mind, especially virtue, shall persist, while the baser desires and the physical body must pass away into corruption.[19]

What are the practical consequences of this moral anatomy, what is its ethical force? Petrarch, in his prefatory letter to Azzo da Correggio, writes that above all he concerns himself with the human spirit, striving to curb its pride and alleviate its weariness.[20] Knowledge and speech find their end in action. Ratio expresses the dictum that moral probity is of greater value than learning or eloquence, so all its wit must serve the aim of goodness.[21] Ratio emphasizes the vicious effect of greed and material wealth on virtue.[22] Since virtue by definition demands effort, it finds better comfort in work and poverty, indeed in adversity itself.[23] Ratio tells Sorrow at the outset of part 2 that virtue gains glory only in battle against Fortune's wiles.[24] These difficult conditions liberate the mind to discover the true nature of things; in accord with the Stoics, Ratio asserts that only the sage is authentically free and genuinely rich.[25] Near the close of the work Ratio engages in a protracted debate with Sorrow over the power of physical pain. Ratio employs a careful analysis of free will to demonstrate that it lies in the hands of every person, and not merely of people of unusual character, to combat the temptation to surrender to Fortune's devices.[26]

The dialogues provide an elaborate, extended psychomachia or spiritual struggle of Ratio counseling and cajoling unsteady emotions to follow the path of virtue, and this psychomachia correlates with the idea of conscience in the individual soul. The idea of conscience occupies in fact the central place in authorizing and validating Ratio's counsel. For where else can virtue be recognized and glorified, unless in the mind of the individual self? Certainly not in the voice of the crowd, the insignia of institutions, or in the mirror of one's desires.[27] Find your own reputation within you, Ratio proclaims; there is virtue's true reward.[28]

Petrarch's moral teaching, based as it is on traditional metaphysics— of the stability of reason and the fluctuation of passion in the body— circumscribes the *agon* between virtue and Fortune. But as this struggle is ineluctable and never-ending, the reader asks when Ratio will gain mastery over the emotional netherworld and whether any degree of mental calm signifies virtue's reward, or only a greater degree of self-deception. Ratio warns Joy that inner tranquility may be fraudulent, just as peace between rulers simply permits them to prepare for war.[29] Man should be, by definition, a political and social animal, but he is not, being continually at odds with his neighbors.[30] Ratio therefore explains to both Joy and Sorrow that full inner liberty is found only in death, when one departs the mortal coil.[31] Do you not see, Ratio tells the jilted lover, how not only one's material goods, but "[m]an himself is being whirled about, does not stand still but, as it is written: 'cometh forth like a flower, and is destroyed, and fleeth as a shadow, and never continueth in the same state.'"[32]

This citation from Job (14:2) indicates how Petrarch's logic moves from describing what a person should be to what a person actually is; it makes Fortune both an existential figure as well as a moral opponent of virtue.

Fortune not only seduces one from virtue; she marks the track of time itself that all mortals must traverse. Virtue can, Ratio claims, provide a sort of halt to time's flow, just as virtue overcomes Fortune.[33] But in the end one's larger fortune is to be temporal as part of one's very nature, like the flowers of Job. Virtue's task is never finished, yet one's own fortune is to vary, fluctuate, and pass, in the existential sense of Petrarch's term. With this view of Fortune the *De remediis* moves beyond its precedents in classical and medieval philosophy.[34]

Petrarch's pendular movement between the moral and existential features of Fortune follows from yet complicates his view of Ratio's relation to the emotions. Virtue alone can provide inner serenity, but virtue shines only in adversity. Little wonder that Petrarch prizes the statement of Heraclitus, "Everything exists by strife."[35] In the oscillation between the moral and the existential spheres, the moral philosopher in Petrarch meets the poet. While the moral philosopher searches for inward order and stasis, aiming at who a person should be, the poet, even through the mouthpiece of Ratio, assesses who a person is: the human condition is temporal, involved in emotion. Time, Ratio asserts, must flow, and it alters one's opinion and judgment about things as one travels from youth to age:

> SORROW: I have grown old very fast.
> REASON: I have been telling you that time flies; now you are beginning to believe it. I never can quite fathom the difference in opinion that exists not only among several persons but even within one and the same person alone! The youth, who has his whole life before him, thinks it is very long. But when, as an old man, he looks back, life seems to have been exceedingly short.[36]

This awareness of strife and change explains the diversity of subjects in the dialogues, as well as the rhetorical variety of the work. Yet this variety and diversity qualifies Ratio's demand for moral stasis.

Ratio's attempt to "coax" the passions into obedience takes various avenues of feeling and tone, disclosing a richer intention in the work than a recasting of Stoical precepts, such as those found in Cicero.[37] Ratio forays into the psychological, for example, when it warns against the arrogance of learning or when it lists the causes of ingratitude as envy, pride, and greed.[38] That these psychological mainsprings remain obscure to both the rational analyst and the emotional analysand makes the cure all the more negotiable. The haste of Sorrow leads it to false perceptions, and Ratio itself, when speaking of the joys and perils of adopting a child, states that humanity is "a dark and uncertain commodity."[39] As a measure against distress Ratio urges Sorrow to turn its complaints against others back against itself, and use them as a fulcrum for self-examination. In this way personal conscience is found as the still, secret center of moral judgment, identifying and preventing what we now call the phenomenon of projection, of castigating one's own faults in other people.[40]

The method of self-accusation (*deprecatio*) is one way of changing one's perspective toward one's lot. Another is the poetic device of metaphor. The roundness of coins, Ratio states, conveys the instability of wealth, since they roll away so easily.[41] Just as the body is a prison of the mind, so those physically incarcerated or tortured should remember their spiritual chains and lashes of desire, those shipwrecked that the sea is less perilous than the foundering of passion.[42] Exiles should remind themselves that the whole world, indeed heaven itself, is their true home.[43]

But the voice of Ratio plies the folds of emotional memory in another way by speaking in axioms with Senecan *brevitas:* "Man is a most stupid animal, forever longing for what is worst for him";[44] or, at the close of part 1: "People rarely strive as vigorously to be saved as they strive to perish."[45] In these tones we discover most clearly Petrarch's choice of the impersonal persona of Ratio. It allows the author to make general statements about the human condition without committing himself to a specific, individualized voice. Nonetheless the emotional charge of these statements belies the rational mask, as the rhetoric permeates and alters the moral logic of the work.

Indeed, Ratio cannot resist climbing into the pulpit at times and declaiming against human foolishness in tones more impassioned than cerebral. These tones underscore Ratio's appeal to the will, eliciting conviction prior to comprehension. Consider the peroration against kingship in *De remediis* 1.96: "Therefore, awake now, ye mortal men, open your eyes, cease to be forever blinded by false glitter. Measure and weigh your wretched carcasses, look about you in your narrow confines, cease to ignore the geometers and the philosophers. The entire earth is a mere dot. . . . When you think you are going up, you are going down; when you seem to stand firm, you are falling precipitously. Nor is there any other animal more unaware of its capacities; yet, often, you worms, though half-dead, dream of kingship and empire!"[46]

To assist its arguments, Ratio has many classical authorities and *exempla* at hand: an abstemious Caesar, a drunken Alexander, impoverished but virtuous Romans, a loyal Scipio.[47] Ratio includes Christian or contemporary examples, such as the valiant sufferings of Jesus or the perseverance of Stefano Colonna.[48] Larger trecento events also infiltrate the work, such as Florentine factionalism, the rebellion of Cola di Rienzo, and the Basel earthquake of 1356.[49]

But these *exempla antiqua et moderna* do not suffice in the work's rhetorical enterprise. Petrarch inserts in the second part *exempla* from fable or of his own invention. This one told by Ratio answers Sorrow's lament, that he has discovered the child he is raising is by another man:

> They say that not far from the ocean shore facing the coastline of Britain there lived, not many years ago, a woman who was poor but strikingly attractive and remarkably lustful. She had twelve little boys, by as many men, each of them one year older than the next. When the hour of her death approached, she had her husband called to her bedside, and said, "This is not the time to fool you any longer. None of these children is yours, save the oldest—because, during the first year of our marriage, I lived chastely." It so happened that at that moment all twelve boys sat on the floor, around the fire, eating, as is customary in the country. The husband was shocked, and the boys listened anxiously as she proceeded to name the father of each of them. The youngest, who was three years old, put down the bread he had in his right hand and the turnip in his other hand, and, trembling with excitement, extended his arms, as if in prayer, and cried, "Please mother, give me a good father!" And when, at the end of her list, she named some famous, rich man as the father of the youngest, he picked up his food again: "Good," he said, "I have a good father."[50]

Ratio calls the tale "silly" but "not altogether pointless." But Ratio's point is not obvious. Is it to show Sorrow's foolish preoccupation over female fidelity or over a child's paternity? Or to satirize the common system of values represented by the child, namely, that a father's goodness derives from his wealth and social status? Ratio ends the story without explanation, and the reader may suspect that traces of *Decameron*-ian creativity enter the work at this moment. The jesting, ironic persona of Ratio here is almost a different narrator from the moralist declaiming against kingship. Petrarch in the course of the work loosens the reins of Ratio, allowing the persona to voice a wider variety of inflections, tones, and modes of discourse. This demands more active, engaged readers who must draw their own conclusions.

From the beginning of the work, Ratio addresses diverse situations, sometimes with ambivalence. Ratio admits statuary and music convey delight but impair one's pursuit of virtue if not enjoyed in moderation.[51] The most glaring discrepancy comes to the fore in Ratio's assessment of the human condition. Ratio, to counter Sorrow's sadness, praises the dignity of God's creation;[52] yet she also responds to Joy's happiness by claiming "no one is happy until he moves out of this vale of miseries."[53] Thus the multiplicity of human fortunes requires Ratio to shift her own perspective, and let moral precept yield to concrete predicament. And as the weight falls upon the individual condition, the maxim can lose its gravity.

In contrast to Cicero, who adhered to the regulatory role of reason as the "mistress of all" (*domina omnium*),[54] Petrarch heightens the tension toward the end of the work between an individual situation and general precept in a way that threatens the command of Ratio over these conversations. The greatest challenge to Ratio's preeminence arises in dialogue 2.114, on severe pain. When Ratio declares that physical pain cannot be an ill, since virtue is the only good, Sorrow rejects this "philosophical babble" or rather "these inanities that you call philosophical." Sorrow seeks to "trust remedies more useful and better designed for my state than the inhuman and stony opinions of the Stoics—although, by now, I distrust trusting anybody."[55]

The work revises here Cicero's sentiments. Although Cicero, like Sorrow, claimed that the Stoics dismiss pain with a mere "flood of words" (*copia verborum*), he counseled the sick to meet their distress with patience and perseverance, affirming the Stoic position that virtue is the greatest good: the abhorrence of moral weakness should prevent physical suffering from marring one's character.[56] The *De remediis* at this late phase has reached a crisis, where logic and rhetoric collide over the hard fact of actual existence. Sorrow trusts its immediate senses, not universal moral dicta; the authorities and *exempla* cited by Ratio are too far removed from Sorrow's experience. Their virtue is exceptional, constitutional. Preoccupied with how every person should be, Ratio has overlooked how a specific person is.[57] Ratio goes on to examine in the final fifteen dialogues the fear of death, a condition reflecting the facticity of existence, one's larger fortune, the end of one's personal, historical time on earth. The moral counsel is inflected with more overt religious tones and symbols, as if to recognize the shortcomings of the rational enterprise of classical moral philosophy.[58]

"The most harmful of human ills is to forget about God, yourself, and death," Ratio counsels Fear. "These three are so intimately connected that one can hardly consider them separately."[59] To overcome the grief over a shameful death Ratio presents the example of the Crucifixion.[60] Dialogue 126 confronts the terror of dying in sin. Ratio counsels repentance and adds: "No sin of man can be greater than the mercy of God." The resurrected Christ stands by one's bed, aiding one's entrance into a new life.[61]

If Petrarch's contemporaries warmly regarded the *De remediis*, we have had occasion to consider its inconsistencies. Despite his conscious intention, Petrarch is not always clear about critical terms: Fortune may indicate accidental circumstance, which virtue may overcome, or it may indicate time itself that carries with it change and strife. We may from a systematic requirement regard this lack of clarity as a failure. But this failure makes the work more complex and interesting, moving both Petrarch and his readers to confront the intersection, the harmony and discord, between the moral and existential faces of Fortune. Virtue may subdue Fortune's accidents, but not her temporal essence. The task of virtue, while never complete, shifts with the changes in one's character over time: hence the enormity of the task, and also the inherent sense of incompletion and fragmentation. The work's rhetorical variety and poetic sensibility color its logical consistency; the restlessness of the poet himself imbues the voice of Ratio with a different quality. Poetry and rhetoric contribute however to the work's philosophical resonance. They demarcate the boundaries of rational moral philosophy and appreciate the power of emotions that reason would restrain, and of time and history that no one can escape.

CHAPTER SIXTEEN

THE ART OF INVECTIVE · *Invective contra medicum*

Stefano Cracolici

The *Invective contra medicum* (*Invectives Against a Physician*) present a set of four polemical discourses with a strong ethical connotation regarding the art of poetry and the art of medicine.[1] Petrarch openly denigrates something and somebody in order to praise something and somebody else, with an engaged intellectual allegiance to the liberal art of rhetoric against the mechanical art of medicine, to the sacred dimension of poetry against the barren dimension of Scholastic dialectics, to the peaceful life of the countryside against the turbulent life of the city.[2] This strong polemical engagement enables Petrarch to provide a graphic account not only of what he understands as poetry and medicine, but, more importantly, of what he regards as intellectual freedom, promoted here, as elsewhere, as the necessary condition for embarking on a process of moral perfectionism.[3]

Petrarch himself triggered this harsh polemic. Its origin can be traced to a letter addressed to Pope Clement VI, who was recovering from a serious illness in the winter of 1351, now to be read in the fifth book of his *Familiares*.[4] Petrarch advises Clement to avoid in such difficult situations the contentious verdict of the doctors mobbing around his sickbed and to rely exclusively on the recommendations of a single experienced physician, "outstanding not because of his eloquence," he maintains, "but because of his knowledge and trustworthiness."[5] This letter, written in March 1352, irritated one of those doctors, who hurriedly addressed a pungent response to Petrarch, prompting from the latter an acid and yet elegant reply, hastily written within the same month. This reply is now read as his first invective.[6] The controversy spread quickly in the intellectual circles around the Curia, and, at the beginning of the following year, the unknown doctor replied in turn with a little book, unfortunately lost like his previous letter, in which he praised medicine to the detriment of rhetoric and poetry. Petrarch finally brought the dispute to its conclusion, adding to his first invective three more against those mechanical artists who sought with their alleged mastery of logic and dialectics to exert their hegemony over every field of knowledge. According to Petrarch, not only had they forgotten the real purpose of medicine, which ought to be mute and tend only to the body, while rhetoric speaks and attends to the soul, but they had also failed to grasp the "vera philosophia," the true philosophy, which for Petrarch is nothing more and nothing less than an inspired contemplation of death, for

> to meditate about death, to arm oneself against it, to prepare oneself to disdain and accept it, to meet it when necessary, and to exchange with sublime resolve this brief and wretched life for eternal life, for blessedness, and for glory—all these things are true philosophy, which has been simply described as the contemplation of death.[7]

The composite work, which we now rather arbitrarily call *Invective contra medicum*, is in fact the result of incessant revisions, written in a turbulent moment of Petrarch's life, from 1352 to 1353, while the poet was still in Avignon. This unremitting revision spans a lengthy period of time, from the early fifties far into the sixties, when Petrarch was already in Milan and had definitively abandoned the city of Avignon.[8] The custom of returning to his works to emend, polish, and redress what he had previously written for different contexts and different circumstances certainly constitutes a distinctive feature of Petrarch's working habit.[9] But it is rather peculiar to see the same investment of time and care devoted to a text, like the *Contra medicum*, that not only was written in a particular context but that also in his later revisions still remained deeply bound to a specific biographical occasion. All this bespeaks a more general import for Petrarch's *Invective*. The *vis polemica*, which so characteristically informs this work, appears therefore as somehow detached from the historical episode that justified it. Its relentless revision ultimately transforms the contingent episode into a literary genre, a genre that we ought to understand as a cultural or intellectual attitude rather than merely a rhetorical form, for presenting an argument more vividly, in a strong polemical manner.

It is true, as has often been repeated, that the specific import of the *Invective* relies on a thematic cluster that Petrarch himself treasured as particularly crucial in his intellectual career. But these themes, as well as his harsh polemics against the medical profession, are certainly not new in Petrarch's work.[10] What is new here, and what the polemicist likes to keep in this form in his later revisions, is the rancorous acrimony conveyed by the genre of the invective, which impresses upon his discourse the mark of a profound indignation. The heart of the matter is not to read this strong emotional and intellectual commitment in a formal way, offering a reading of the *Invective* to illuminate a portrait of Petrarch as the protohumanist primarily interested in revitalizing some ancient oratory genres by possibly detailing his debt to Cicero, Sallust, Jerome, and whoever else one could consider as a possible rhetorical model for his *Invective*.[11] What I suggest we do here is ponder the function, the quality, and the target of Petrarch's intellectual acrimony, considering not only his literary antecedents as the primary source of his inspiration but also his actual anger. This implies a study of literary genres with regard to a functional rationale rather than merely a formal one, a new approach to literary genre that acknowledges the epistemological power of literature within both its cognitive and affective dimensions.[12]

The pamphlet by the poet's anonymous detractor certainly represented a direct attack against Petrarch's public image. Petrarch must have felt provoked to enter the arena of Scholastic philosophy in order to justify his critical position. The art of invective, which he reenacts on the basis of ancient models, allows him to present his position from the vantage point of his intellectual freedom, confirming once more his personal detachment from any form of institutionalized knowledge. What Petrarch vigorously presents here is not a competing theory of the moral life but rather a dimension or a tradition of the moral life with which he identifies not only the writings by Augustine, Seneca, and Cicero, but also a violated idea of medicine, a forgotten idea of philosophy, an endangered idea of the self, which spawns in his heart an authentic sense of indignation and makes his humanistic enterprise sound anachronistic or even utopian. This latter more controversial engagement relies on a vigorous reaffirmation of the sacred and secret connection of body and mind, staged as the reciprocal interplay of immanent and transcendent forces.[13] Petrarch cannot distinguish the sense of his culture's decline from his concerns with managing his public image in a way that might contribute to halting or reversing that decline; his idea of culture and cultivation is not restricted to the territory of a specific discipline, but rather presented as a form of life, as poetry as a form of life. It is this fusion of both emotional and intellectual concerns that constitutes the functional aspect of his intellectual acrimony, striking the reader of the *Invective* still today.

To describe the quality of Petrarch's acrimony it is profitable to go back to the letter that originally provoked the quarrel:

I know that your bed is besieged by doctors, this is the first reason for my fear. They all disagree purposely, each considering it
shameful to suggest nothing new or to follow upon the footsteps
of another. "There is no doubt," as Pliny says elegantly, "that all
of them strive for a reputation with some kind of novelty and they
regularly use our souls as an item of trade . . . and it happens only
in this profession that whoever professes to be a doctor is immediately believed although it is impossible to imagine a more dangerous falsehood. We do not, however, reflect about this because
everyone is flattered by the pleasure of his hope for himself. Furthermore, there is no law to punish this dangerous ignorance, and
no example of such a wrong being punished. They learn by sub-
mitting us to dangers and they experiment unto death itself. Only
for the doctors is there maximum impunity for murder." More
merciful father, look upon their multitude as if it were a battle line
of enemies.[14]

The point of the contention is formulated, in a terse and cogent manner,
by borrowing a passage from Pliny's *Natural History*, which in Petrarch's
time still constituted a rarity. Pliny, who in the twenty-ninth book of his
encyclopedia had summarized the history of medicine and harshly criticized the doctors, allows Petrarch to present his point as a long-established
institutional rivalry, while evoking, at the same time, a sense of estrangement in his audience.[15] The target of his attack is not medicine as such, as
he later repeatedly asserts in his *Invective*, but more pertinently a particular
form of professional rivalry that Petrarch regards as inherent to the medical profession.[16] The profession of medicine portrayed here had danger-
ously become a locus of intellectual action, in which an increasing number
of contenders competed for the expansion of their own sphere of influence.
What doctors were hazardously reproducing in defining their profession
seems to Petrarch utterly similar to the hoary disputes that had plagued
the field of philosophy, more precisely, Scholastic philosophy.[17] Doctors
are now, Petrarch maintains, crossing their disciplinary boundaries and
spreading their contentious habit also to the fields of rhetoric and poetry:
"And while their patients are dying, they knit the Hippocratic knots with
the Ciceronian warp; they take pride in any unfortunate event; and they
do not boast of the results of their cases but rather of the empty elegance of
words."[18]

The indignation that led Petrarch to write this letter was not of a super-
cilious kind or simply an indirect attack against Scholastic philosophy, as

has been purported, but rather the expression of his personal and sincere indignation over the degeneration of medicine as the result of the ambition of the medical establishment striving to develop and expand its reputation by dressing its discourse in philosophical clothes.

For the sake of a more structured exposition, it may be useful to qualify the acrimony at stake by considering the three kinds of intellectual hostility that sociologist Randall Collins has described in one of his most recent studies: acrimony as a "career rivalry," which concerns those intellectuals who feel squeezed out from a certain attention space; acrimony as "border-crossing intrusion," which concerns those intellectuals who invade a disciplinary field traditionally considered alien to their sphere of competence; and acrimony as "intellectual fortress," which concerns long-lasting, institutionalized rivalries among different intellectual networks.[19] In the eyes of Petrarch, we could say, the speech of the unknown doctor ultimately embodies all three kinds of intellectual hostility described so far: he could be portrayed as a "career rival" when he acts like a liberal artist and challenges the epistemological validity of poetry; he could be charged as a "border-crossing intruder" when, as inhabitant of the field of medicine, he unlawfully colonizes the field rhetoric; and finally, he could be accused of perpetuating the ancient quarrel among doctors that Pliny had already criticized in his *Natural History*.[20] Petrarch himself abstained from taking these forms of academic antagonism seriously, with the result of provoking in his detractor an even stronger sense of hostility. His discursive strategy makes an extensive use of so-called *irrisio* ("derision" or "mockery"), one of the most powerful prerogatives of the rhetoric of blame, in general, and of the genre of the invective, in particular. Mockery allows Petrarch to steer his discourse away from the argumentative web of Scholastic philosophy, while at the same time demolishing the rhetorical apparatus of his antagonist.

As for the hostility that Petrarch shows here, it cannot be simply reduced to the classification of intellectual acrimony provided by Collins. The style of this particular form of acrimony is certainly exuberant and sometimes even excessive, for quite often his irony collapses into sarcasm. But it rarely attains the level of brutality and vulgarity of the later humanist's invectives, which could indeed be considered as a form of career rivalry.[21] To indulge momentarily in an issue of formal concern, we could profitably apply to Petrarch's style what sometime later the humanist Leonardo Bruni stated in the preface to his Latin translation of Demosthenes (1421), qualifying the style of the Greek orator as possessing a "gravitas quaedam nervosa" (a certain nervous gravity), significantly opposed to a bad form of style designated as "inanitas verbosa" (verbose emptiness) which may characterize the alleged style of the unknown physician.[22] The quality of Petrarch's acrimony is of an ethical, not academic, nature.

If the quality of Petrarch's ethical acrimony can be qualified as a *gravitas nervosa*, its target is identified with the devastating outcome of the corrupted deontology of the medical profession. The time when Petrarch wrote his *Invective* was one in which the plague had taken a heavy toll of victims, including Laura and Giovanni Colonna, of course, but also Franceschino degli Albizzi, Senuccio del Bene and later, in the wake of the second onslaught of the disease, also Angelo di Pietro, Stefano dei Tosetti, Francesco Nelli, Ludwig van Kempen, and even more tragically Petrarch's own son Giovanni. Given the circumstances, it is quite difficult to reduce his attack on medicine merely to a form of intellectual hostility.[23]

The plague not only had demonstrated the inevitability of death, not only had proven the operative inefficiency of medicine, but, more gravely, had also shown the degradation of a concept of medicine as caring practice, where immanence and empathy should cohabit with transcendence and divinity.[24] What Petrarch is implicitly lamenting in the *Contra medicum* is not just the verbose and quarrelsome consequences inherent in the professionalization of a discipline that was striving to acquire a stable and respected academic endorsement, but more importantly the dangerous outcome of an instrumental medicalization of pain, attacked as a process that ultimately disregards and undermines the sacred dimension of the body:

> But suppose—I shudder to think it!—that the pope had paid his debt to nature. Even the vicar of immortal God is mortal. What great and unresolved discord there would have been among you concerning his pulse, his humors, his critical day, and his medications! Ignorant of the real cause of his illness, you would have filled heaven and earth with dissonant cries. Wretched are the sick who trust in your aid! But Christ, who holds all human salvation in his hands, saved him despite your ignorance. I pray that Christ may do all that is necessary for him and the Church he governs.[25]

During the twelfth century, through a long series of councils and ultimately through the *Super specula*, the decree pronounced by Honorius III in 1219, the regular and secular clergies were prohibited from the practice of medicine, giving rise to the professionalization of health care and the introduction of medicine in the academic curriculum.[26] The idea of medicine that Petrarch aims at restoring, then, may indeed sound anachronistic, a form of medicine that would bring us back to the High Middle Ages, where medicine was seen as a gift from God and where the ill person, portrayed as *tacitus* (silent) like Christ during the stages of his passion, needed to be treated with silent reverence and awe.[27] "I did write a brief letter to the Roman pontiff," admits Petrarch in his first invective, "dictated by my fear and devotion when he was seriously ill."[28] Suffice it here to remember that these texts were written close to his ascetic and moral works, *De vita solitaria*, *De otio religioso*, and *De remediis utriusque fortune*, where the patristic and monastic way of life participated in the foundation of a new system of ethical values.[29] The loss of the sacred dimension of pain and distress, which for Petrarch basically equates with the human condition ("this brief and wretched life"), is rescued through a new conception of poetry as a form of *egrotantis cura* ("a patient's care"), a form of poetry as medicine.[30]

In the medieval period, literature and poetry in particular fall within the province of ethics, for "to define ethics in medieval terms is to define poetry, and to define poetry is to define ethics," as Judson Boyce Allen rightly maintains.[31] According to a classification provided by the medieval encyclopedic tradition, which Allen however doesn't quote, we can distinguish between an *ethica docens* or *ethica absoluta* ("theoretical ethics"), on the one hand, which concerns the events of the human being in general and where the boundaries between philosophy and theology are practically only a matter of captious distinctions; and, an *ethica utens* or *ethica relativa* ("practical ethics"), on the other, which concerns the events of the human being in particular, where physiology and ethology, with their cultural and social implications, converge with politics.[32] The moral and intellectual perfectionism Petrarch has in mind certainly implies an elitist theory of the moral life, good for the intimate improvement of the state of one's soul, a dimension that actually places a tremendous burden on personal relationships and on the possibility or necessity of experiencing a form of harmonic connectedness with society and the world in general. In the *Invective*, Petrarch formulated his theory of poetry as a form of theology. But in a passage from the fifteenth chapter of his *Genealogie deorum gentilium*, Boccaccio explains Petrarch's famous definition of poetry as theology in these terms:

> No more is there any harm in speaking of the old poets as theologians. Of course, if anyone were to call them sacred, the veriest fool would detect the falsehood. On the other hand there are times, as in this book, when the theology of the Ancients will be seen to

exhibit what is right and honorable, though in most such cases it
should be considered rather physiology or ethology than theology,
according as the myths embody the truth concerning physical nature or human.[33]

It is difficult to say whether Boccaccio is explaining or rather rectify-
ing Petrarch's definition of poetry.[34] This would certainly make the latter's recommendation to read Pliny's *Natural History* more plausible for the
doctors, a recommendation that from a strictly medical point of view must
have initially sounded rather absurd. But it is through this kind of specifi-
cation that the ethical dimension of poetry can move from theory, from its
qualification as *docens*, to practice, to its qualification as *utens*, and finally
become medical.[35]

CHAPTER SEVENTEEN

THE ECONOMY OF INVECTIVE AND A MAN IN THE MIDDLE · *De sui ipsius et multorum ignorantia*

William J. Kennedy

*D*e *sui ipsius et multorum ignorantia* (1367–70) is, by genre, an invective, but it is a singularly self-effacing one.[1] Not just impugning those who have accused him of ignorance, Petrarch assents to their charges and represents himself as willfully ignorant in the name of ancient wisdom and Christian piety. And he does so *con brio* with playful wit and gamesome paradox, droll sarcasm and lip-smacking one-upsmanship. There is ironic caricature and wry self-regard: "I have become a poor peddler of learning (*mercator inops literarum*)," Petrarch opines, but "what has been lost cannot be lost again, . . . [and] nothing can be less than nothing (*minus nichilo, nichil est*)."[2] There are sublime yet surprisingly jaunty comparisons, as of the author's madness to "the madness (*insania*) of Saint Paul" upon embracing the doctrine of Jesus: "I console myself," writes Petrarch, "for I am in the company of great men (*magnis comitibus*)" (238–39). And so he concludes: "I am the greatest ignoramus of all (*et ego omnium ignorantissimum me*), but"—here skipping a beat—"I except perhaps four others (*imo quattuor fortassis excipiam*" (346–47). *De ignorantia* scarcely attains the ludic energy, satiric thrust, and Lucianic ebullience of, say, Erasmus's *Praise of Folly*, with which it compares in some ways. But in its good-natured, yet pungent and provocative manner, Petrarch's treatise allows its author to overcome his opponents' charge of inferior attainment, a charge so wounding at first that he seems to have removed it from his consciousness and replaced it with what Sigmund Freud calls "an 'economy' of verbal wit."[3]

By invoking Freud's *Jokes and Their Relationship to the Unconscious* (1905) as I have just done, I want to draw attention to the psychic energy that infuses Petrarch's invective against those who have accused him of ignorance. Civilization, writes Freud, has taught us to repress instinctual urges and egotistic impulses in the name of safeguarding the larger community and guaranteeing some degree of social order. But in finding such renunciation very difficult, the human psyche turns to verbal wit to regain what has been lost. "Strictly speaking," notes Freud, "we do not know what we are laughing at," precisely because we have so deeply repressed the feelings and emotions that we are seeking to liberate through jocularity and witty repartee.[4] The problem for *De ignorantia* would be to ask what censored thoughts, what worried associations Petrarch might be seeking to protect. My discussion of the text will argue that *De ignorantia* deals stringently with the author's anxieties about human friendship, the rational and irrational faith upon which all human friendship is based, and the social and economic order that in turn is based on such faith. Petrarch emerges as a "man in the middle," neither part of the established social institutions that might proclaim his scholarly and intellectual competence, nor part of an emergently mercantile commercial order that might reward him with material wealth, communal prestige, and strategic influence. He is not even sure of his place within a small circle of friends, four of whom have maligned him in public. And therein lies the initial source of his anxiety.

Though Petrarch's invective refers in passing to some contemporaneous philosophical schools and issues, its deeper focus aims elsewhere. It certainly exonerates the University of Padua, which Petrarch visited periodically during his residence in Venice (1362–68) and where he had friends such as the rhetorician Pietro da Moglio, the grammarian Lombardo della Seta, and the renowned polymath Giovanni Dondi, the last a member of the faculty of medicine and astronomy who would serve as Petrarch's physician and a quondam poet who shared his humanist aversion to narrowly defined Aristotelian natural philosophy.[5] Nor does it aim specifically at other universities such as Paris, Oxford, or Bologna, with their Averroist, Ockhamite, and emergently materialist science, respectively, though it refers in passing to clownish exaggerations of such teachings.[6] Its immediate target is four men who had maligned the author in 1365, each a public figure and self-proclaimed intellectual who lived and worked in Venice, none currently affiliated with any university or scholarly institution.[7] They include two Venetian noblemen: Leonardo Dandolo, a member of the military elite and son of the late doge Andrea Dandolo (who had been a friend of Petrarch); and Zaccaria Contarini, scion of a distinguished family that had produced a yet earlier doge, and himself a senator with connections to Venetian bankers. The third was Guido da Bagnolo, a nobleman from Reggio-Emilia, who had been educated in medicine (likely at Bologna) and who had served as personal physician as well as political counselor to King Peter I of Cyprus. The fourth was Tommaso Talenti, a naturalized

Venetian citizen of Florentine origin and a prosperous silk merchant who had collected a library of over a hundred volumes and whose testament of 1347 would endow a chair of logic and philosophy in his adoptive city.[8] These four shared with Petrarch certain interests in classical thought but were to diverge from him in their distinct preference for Aristotelian natural philosophy. Among them, the poet emerges quite conspicuously as an intermediate figure, betwixt and between, distinctly lower in his social origins, aspiring higher in his intellectual pursuits. Three of his accusers were noble-born; all were wealthy individuals, well connected with the military, diplomatic, merchant, and medical elite; each was representative of an ascendant governing, professional, or commercial class energizing and progressively enriching Venetian society.

The bad-mouthing by these four men paradoxically affirms their admiration of him. It stems from "sacred friendship (*sancta amicitia*)" because friendship sets up expectations of equality that their varying public renown maliciously defeats. The object of their envy cannot be his material wealth (*non opes certe*), especially since theirs "exceeds mine (*me superant*)" (230–31). Here Petrarch refers to his resources as "modest (*mediocres*), shared with others (*comunicabiles*), . . . not sumptuous but humbly lacking in pomp or ostentation," so much so that his defamers "wish me even greater wealth (*maiores optant michi*)" (230–31). They cannot even envy his eloquence, he concludes, because eloquence is something that they "despise as our modern philosophers do, and reject as unworthy of learned men" (232–33). Petrarch views this assault upon friendship all the more grievously because his attackers had formed their opinion of him while enjoying his hospitality and catching him off-guard: "It is quite easy to trick a trusting soul (*fidentem*)" who entertained them "with a happy face and even happier spirit" in a give-and-take that he believed a "faithful sharing (*fidelis participatio*) of all the rest, including our knowledge" (262–63).

Here it is worth noting that in his dedicatory letter to Donato Albanzani, a Venetian grammarian born at Casentino in the Tuscan Appenines, Petrarch considers the material quality of this book, its physical shape and visual appearance, a testimony to his friendship with its recipient.[9] It is a "small work on a vast subject (*librum paruum de materia ingenti*)" (222–23), hardly a book but rather a "colloquium" that recalls "my fireside chats on winter nights (*me ante focum hibernis noctibus fabulantem*)" (222–23), a trifle offered as "it is customary for friends to beguile each other" (222–23). It is moreover "laced with numerous additions and corrections, and all of its margins crammed with notes" (224–25), but its deformities constitute a material sign of friendship between giver and receiver, as long as the latter accepts them with good will, and trusts the former's best intentions.[10] The insertions amount to some 200 lines, representing about 8 percent of the complete text. As it happens, the ink and pen strokes of two existing manuscripts, one the autograph presentation copy for Donato (begun in May 1367 and completed in June 1370, now at Berlin's Staatsbibliothek), and the other Petrarch's personal copy (dated from Arquà on June 25, 1370, now at the Vatican Library), reveal four layers of insertions and revisions incorporated between 1367 and 1370. Most of these layers amplify the treatise's midsection on the ancients' (particularly Cicero's) thinking about religion, but a good number of them affect later sections of the treatise, where they introduce metacritical reflections on their own roles in exemplifying topics of friendship and calculation.

These two topics prove important to Petrarch's sustained argument about knowledge and ignorance, as we shall see. Friendship, assurance, faith, and trust all constitute the moral basis of civil society, the ground upon which economic transactions and exchanges might operate. Without such a basis, there would be no commerce, trade, or professional institutions such as we know them. Petrarch can feel only dismay as his four friends, representatives of the social, political, professional, and mercantile hierarchy of Venice violate the very bond upon which their prosperous society depends. And he locates his dismay in a series of economic figurations when he avers that the objects of their envy, his learning and eloquence, are themselves so impoverished: "What a small amount (*quantulum*) is even the greatest knowledge (*quantumcunque*)" (250–51). No matter how vast the accumulation of human knowledge, one's possession of it is "always slight in itself (*semper exigua*)," a claim strengthened by Saint Paul's account of things that "we now know in part (*qua ex parte nunc scimus*)" (250–51, referring to 1 Cor. 13:9).

Certainly the locale against which the writer plays off his *ignorantia* ("I sadly and silently acknowledge my ignorance," 250–52) opposes material wealth to intellectual poverty in palpable ways. The site of conflict is Venice, a patrician republic built upon its wealth and economic abundance, as Petrarch notes sporadically in this "great and beautiful city" (260–61), a commercial "maritime city (*nautica civitate*)," (256–57), home of "seamen (*naute*)" and long-distance merchants (342–43).[11] Here his accusers have dabbled in philosophy as a secondary leisure activity, in effect commodifying it as a hobby or entertainment adjacent to the pursuit of wealth and recognition: "They think they are great (*magnos*) and indeed they are all rich (*sunt plane omnes diuites*), which is the only greatness mortals have today" (236–37). The author by contrast had negotiated his own formal education in squalid Montpellier, Bologna, Toulouse, and Padua. In an idealized Naples he received public recognition from the philosopher-king Robert, to whom he was "no match (*tanto impar*) for his fortune" (254–55). The "greater . . . and most studious part" of his life has so far unfolded amid the opulence of papal Avignon. But for his studies and meditation, only the humble "trans-Alpine Helicon" (256–57) of Vaucluse has afforded him the quiet, solitude, and simplicity that he needed for genuine scholarly work.

Petrarch belongs to neither the patriciate of Venice, nor to a courtly entourage at Naples or Avignon, nor to a university *collegium* at Padua, Bologna, Montpellier, or elsewhere.[12] He had always charted an independent career and had based it not on academic collaboration or clubbish camaraderie, but (in a threefold repetition of the verb *legere*, "read," with an extra *lego*, "I read," added in the margin) on acts of reading that bind him to the language of religion, law, poetry, and philosophy: "I still read the books of poets and philosophers, and above all the works of Cicero" (272–74). Here he avers that of all Cicero's texts, the one that has fired him "most powerfully" is *De natura deorum* (272–73). This dialogue in three books written around 45 BCE imagines a conversation among three prominent Romans on the topic of divinity in Platonic, Epicurean, and Stoic philosophy.[13] For Petrarch, it provides a model of civilized discourse, intellectual tolerance, and reasoned disagreement among philosophizing friends.[14] The author's lengthy quotations from it (about 140 lines, representing 5 percent of *De ignorantia*) complicate his own humanist enterprise with their concrete examples of Ciceronian style and eloquence. Weaving whole passages into his own composition, Petrarch attempts to mesh his style with Cicero's.

This citational strategy exposes Petrarch to the charge that he is simply emulating Cicero as slavishly as his opprobrious friends emulate Aristotle. In his tacit defense, the author reverts to economic figurations. On the one hand his borrowings amount to a bookish theft, an openly confessed literary plagiarism: "Even now I am carried along (*raptus*) by the unusual charm of Cicero's subject and style. . . . I cram my little works (*opuscula*) with another's words" (284–85). On the other, he has suffered the theft of his own name and reputation through an attack by friends, an attack more reprehensible since he considers himself a mere vehicle of transmission for writing perhaps greater than his own, a kind of commercial agent who has been defrauded by those whom he sought to help: "I have become a poor peddler of learning (*mercator inops literarum*), robbed (*spoliatus*) of my knowledge and fame by these four brigands (*predonibus*). Now that I have nothing of my own (*michi proprium*), poverty (*paupertas*) must excuse my importunity and impudence in begging from others (*si aliena mendicem*)" (284–85).

The etymology of the key term "mercator inops" seals this identification. The noun *mercator* derives from the archaic Latin *merx*, a shortened form of the name Mercury, which Petrarch had etymologized in his *Contra medicum* as *mercatorum kyrios*, "lord of merchants."[15] This god of commerce and communication is a deity whose quicksilver wit lubricates profitable transactions and exchanges, but who, when assimilated to the Greek Hermes, also invented the lyre (for which Apollo bestowed divine powers upon him) and served as messenger of the gods, a transmitter of wisdom from the deities to humankind. The adjective *inops* derives from the name of the indigenous Roman deity Opis, wife of Saturn, "the sower" and goddess of the August harvest (both later assimilated to the Greek deities Rhea and Chronos).[16] Signifying abundance and prosperity, the substantive noun *ops* in turn generates *opus*, "productive work," and, as Varro had erroneously postulated, *oppidum*, "a fortified town," a center of commercial activity and prosperity. The conflation of all these elements in the phrase "mercator inops"— abundance, prosperity, productivity, wealth, the invention of song, and the transmission of divine wisdom—points to the censored thoughts and worried associations that the author is trying to protect in *De ignorantia*.

These associations concern the appropriation of intellectual capital and the contingencies of making positive and productive use of it. Petrarch spells out his concerns through an economic figuration when he invokes the historical personage of Averroes, the Arabic conduit of Greek thought to the Christian middle ages. Averroes, he claims, exaggerated Aristotle's net worth when he spent the major part of his career in writing a commentary upon Aristotle's work: in Petrarch's words, "It all comes down to the old adage, 'Every merchant praises his own merchandise (*mercatores omnes suam mercem solitos laudare*)'" (322–23). Commentators, in another economic figuration that extends the argument to general academic practice, resemble craftsmen or artisans who peddle their own wares, and the greater the master-text such as Peter Lombard's *Sentences*, the more "it has suffered at the hands of a thousand such workmen (*opifices*)" (322–23). Petrarch, on the other hand, would fashion the value of his own career in more generous economic terms.

These terms summon the author's continued investment in faith, trust, and candor. Confidence in the word of another is the basis for all human transactions and exchanges, subtending every legal, commercial, economic, institutional, and professional relationship. Since such activities depend upon verbal compacts, they depend upon how words are used, which is to say that they depend upon style or verbal eloquence. In this context, Petrarch's apparent digression on style loops back to one of his dominant questions: "How might a Christian man of letters (*homo literatus*) appear to those who say that Christ was an ignoramus?" (300–301). Right from the start, Petrarch contrasts such a plain-speaking person with latter-day Aristotelians whose "greatest glory is to make some confused and baffling statement (*confusum aliquid ac perplexum*) which neither they nor anyone else can understand" (302–3). In the ancient world, as he points out, Augustus Caesar "made it his chief aim to express his thoughts as clearly as possible," and he "laughed at his friends who collected unusual and obscure words (*insolita et obscura*)" (302–3).[17] The hallmark of effective style is its "clarity (*claritas*), the supreme proof of one's understanding and knowledge" (302–3), which enables a sharing of mind, a *com-mentum* or commentary on truth that articulates, if not absolute ineffable truth, at least such a responsive, shared approach to it as is humanly possible. And insofar as this style enables such a sharing of mind, it exemplifies *amicitia* in its highest form, the act of relating to another person as to one's own self.

Petrarch explores this proposition with unsettling consequences for his argument. Referring to his critics' assault on him, he cites Macrobius's remark about Aristotle (in *Somnium Scipionis* [*Scipio's Dream*], 2.15.18): "It seems to me that such a great man could not have been ignorant of anything" (310–11). The remark proves troublesome because its author's possible irony, "whether he wrote in jest or in earnest (*sive ioco, sive serio*)" (310–11), sets no logical limit to understanding the intent: does Macrobius mean what he says, or does he mean the exact opposite? Petrarch's exploration of *metaphrasis*, "change in phrasing," slips into a demonstration of *antiphrasis*, "irony," as it confronts the problem of double meaning. In response, he pressures his own writing to register a transparent statement of his attitude: "It seems to me just the opposite (*prorsus contrarium*) is true" (310–11). In a straightforward effort to specify a reason for his friends' attack, he avers that overtly they lacerate him for rejecting Aristotle, but the real reason is that covertly they envy his fame: "For this they harass me; and although the root of their envy is something else [viz. their desire for Petrarch's fame], this is the cause they allege: that I do not worship Aristotle" (310–11).

The problem with his accusers' argument—again Petrarch expresses the concept through economic figurations—is that the "poverty (*inops*) of their intelligence or of their language (*vel intellectus vel sermonis*)" (312–13) limits their understanding. The task is not to suppress rhetorical nuance but to heighten it, not to flatten out one's style but to empower it, not to diminish the verbal palate but to enhance its iridescence. And the compelling motivation to fashion such a style is grounded as much in *caritas* as in *claritas*, in the Christian commitment to serve one another, in friendship as a means to attain it, and finally in the faith that words powerfully articulated convey truth. On these grounds, Petrarch faults Aristotle for a defective style: "I must confess now and admit that I take no great pleasure in the style of the famous man as it comes down to us" (312–13). And a page later he repeats the claim: Aristotle "teaches us the nature of virtue. But reading him offers us none of those exhortations, or only very few, that goad and inflame (*stimulos ac verborum faces*) our minds to love virtue and hate vice" (314–15).

The argument reveals Petrarch's own wounding defect. Without having directly experienced Aristotle's style in the original Greek text, he can only surmise that its translators have rendered as "harsh and rough (*durus scaberque*)" what Cicero and other ancients have declared to be "sweet, copious, and ornate in his own tongue (*in sermone proprio et dulcem et copiosum et ornatum*)" (312–13). The author recurs to the humanist tenet that we can fully understand a text only in its original language. But in this case, it is a tenet that he cannot observe, "since Greece is deaf to our speech (*quoniam Gracia nostris sermonibus surda est*)" (314–15), or, more properly through antiphrasis: We are deaf to Greek speech. Here, in a moment of stunning self-exposure, Petrarch's focus on rhetoric foregrounds his most censored thought. His strongest claim reveals his greatest weakness and his besetting ignorance: he cannot read Greek. Subsequently, the author bases his long peroration in praise of Plato to the detriment of Aristotle (325–35) on the material evidence of possessing Plato's written words in physical form: "I have in my home at least sixteen of Plato's books" (328–29). And he finesses the powerful countercharge that he cannot effectively read these words because the death of his teacher in Greek, Barlaam the Calabrian, "cut short this noble undertaking" (328–29).[18]

His friends' attack on him amounts to a breach of trust, with regard both to their faith in God, which philosophy should reinforce, and to their support of the author, for whom *amicitia* means "loving another as oneself" (338–39). The consequences of this breach play out in a quantified economic context. His accusers "love me wholeheartedly, but not all of me (*non totum me*)" (338–39). Friendship should thrive on parity, but his accusers "seek equality in our friendship (*in amicitia pares esse*)" as they detract from his merits so that "we are all obscure (*simus omnes obscuri*)" (340–41). Petrarch seeks to defuse their assault by handing over his property to them: "I leave my spoils (*exuuias meas*) to these dear brigands (*raptoribus caris*), . . . if fame can be given to a robber as money (*pecunia*) is snatched from its owner. . . . I shall be happier and richer (*ditior*) . . . than they are with their proud spoils (*superbiis spoliis*)" (342–43). Such wealth and fortune ought to impress his friends, since they inhabit Venice, a "most noble and excellent city (*urbem nobilissimam atque optimam*)" distinguished by "the magnitude and manifold variety of its populace (*populi magnitudinem multiplicemque uarietatem*)" (344–45). Its citizens enjoy "great liberality in many things (*multa enim rerum omnium libertas*)," referring to the scope of its coffers, but also to the extent of its cultural capital, "including an excessive freedom of speech, which I would call its only or its greatest evil (*uerborum longe nimia est libertas*)" (344–45).

Such liberality, registered in a syntax in which the single noun *libertas* governs both physical *rerum* and cognitive *uerborum*, has invited the penury of small-mindedness, envy, and grudge. Envy, after all, focuses not on any solid truth but on the prestige of an "empty name (*uani nominis*)" (348–49). Petrarch appears troubled by this predicament. On the one hand, he construes the bulk of his textual revisions in *De ignorantia* as a sign of the care that he has taken in presenting his case. One marginal insertion calculates human knowledge in terms of economic magnitude: "Those who are thought rich (*ditissimi*) are themselves truly paupers (*uere inopes*)" (350–51). In yet another marginal insertion, this "dire lack of knowledge (*scientie inopia*)" can only generate "a great discrepancy of opinions (*quanta opinionum contrarietas*) . . . a number of factions and differences (*sectarum numerus que differentie*)" (350–51). The upshot is a profusion of Scholastic energies, a paradoxical multiplication of schools with endless dialogue and debate, "uncertainties about things (*rerum ambiguitas*), . . . perplexity about words (*uerborum perplexitas*)" (350–51), a situation in which "we may argue with equal force on both sides of any question (*ad utranque partem*)" (350–51).[19] But at least the participants in these sophistic exercises, the members of schools and academic institutions, hold something that Petrarch does not possess: they belong to recognized faculties and they share at least some collegiality, however chaotic it might be. The four friends whose breach of confidence had motivated this invective did not formally belong to such schools. But as scholars whose interests were amateur, they enjoyed the support of other institutional structures beyond Petrarch's purview associated with the Venetian nobility, the merchant class, and the medical establishment.

By contrast, the author construes the tangle of his revisions as a sign chiefly of his intimacy with Donato Albanzani, to whom he sends his blotted manuscript: "For you'll understand how special a friend you are to me when I write in this way, hoping that you regard my additions and corrections as so many tokens of our friendship and affection" (224–25). For

Petrarch, writing amounts to a colloquium with the self and is shared by friends. It is above all a colloquium with the texts that one reads, linking other readers to a past that cannot be fully retrieved or entirely grasped.[20] One function of the schools and academic institutions that Petrarch disparaged is that they provide a social framework and collegial support for work in the disciplines they embrace. Petrarch enumerates successive generations of teachers in rhetoric and philosophy who had nurtured their disciples in agreement with or opposition to such principles: from Arcesilas, Gorgias, Hermagoras, and Hypias to Epicurus, Metrodorus, Chrysippus, and Zeno. The last boldly insulted Socrates with invective, "using the Latin word *scurra* ('buffoon, trifler, know-it-all,' as Cicero recounts in *De natura deorum* 34.94]," in order, as Petrarch speculates, "to give the jibe more bite" (358–59).[21] As Petrarch further points out, Cicero's rivals turned the same taunt against him because of "the remarkable wit (*festivitatem*) of his tongue" (358–59). This lesson, registered in the treatise's penultimate insertion, is not that such scholars are cruel or uncharitable but that they use such invective to unite their adherents in defending "the equal validity (*paritas*) of great men's views, which inspires divergent judgments in their followers" (358–59).

This idea of bonding within academic communities, though often a source of dissention, contrasts with Petrarch's forbearing dismissal of his friends' attacks on him. Compared with earlier invectives, "all the stinging barbs of my judges are easily tolerated jests (*ludi*), to be borne with a serene mind (*equissimo animo*)" (360–61). But this forbearance itself hardly conceals the writer's wound, one smarting in his sense of being exceptional, unique, and alone. A man in the middle with no recognizable or at least conventionally defined institutional affiliations, no stable forms of economic protection, and few firmly established networks of cultural support, Petrarch perceives his scholarly career as adrift in the evolutionary sea change of late fourteenth-century communal, economic, and commercial relations. His final marginal addition to the text recalls from *De natura deorum* 1.33.93 an invective that "a Greek woman named Leontium, whom Cicero calls a prostitute (*meretricula*), dared to write against the great philosopher Theophrastus" (360–61). Using this gendered figure of the *meretricula* to evoke the selling and buying of commodified bodies in a public marketplace, Petrarch locates his own career in a comparable environment. "Hearing this," he writes, "how could one be indignant when attacked, when such figures were attacked by such critics" (360–61). His four accusers live in a world where social hierarchy, material wealth, and commercial activity mean so much to so many. Petrarch sees himself on the margins of this world, tugged by the competing claims of a quite different medieval *caritas* and *communitas* on the one hand, and on the other an emergent but narrow scholarly public and literary professionalism, to which the commercial revolution of the mid-fourteenth century is both complementary and antithetical.[22]

Petrarch called his collected letters to friends and associates *Epistolae familiarum*, as though in addressing the latter he were part of an extended community that embraced them all, a *familiaris* among *familiares*, each serving one another's material needs and spiritual interests. This title projects a vision of *caritas* and *communitas*, imbued with more than a classical tinge of the political *amicitia* that has brought them together. But even as his letters multiply, Petrarch expresses the pain of separation, of a drift backward and forward as old identities are destroyed, new identities are taken on, boundaries are transgressed, and familiar categories are breached. In this respect he is exquisitely aware of his involvement in multiple zones of readership with diverse rules for diverse audiences, for which his sense of the distinctive otherness of the past serves as a beacon. In his incipient humanism, Petrarch gravitates toward an unfamiliar environment where bonds of faith, trust, and loyalty impel new divisions of labor in the world of literature, philosophy, thought, and letters, shadowing new divisions in the world of politics, trade, and public commerce. Such may be the censored thoughts that find their utterance in the wordplay of *De ignorantia*.

PART VI

PETRARCH THE EPISTLER

CHAPTER EIGHTEEN

A POETIC JOURNAL · *Epystole*

Giuseppe Velli

Some fundamental philological data are essential for a correct understanding of Petrarch's epistles in verse. Their true title is *Epystole*;[1] this is the title Petrarch chose, the one his immediate followers, including Giovanni Boccaccio, knew. The choice of this title was motivated by the nature of its contents, a "real" poetic correspondence, obviously stylistically elaborated, and by the purposeful recall of the *Epistulae* of Horace, a recall imposed by the almost religious devotion the early Petrarch had for the classics. Hence the necessity for the writer to select a different title for his prose letters, *Rerum familiarium libri*.[2]

Petrarch published this work in 1364, possibly just before the death of its dedicatee Barbato da Sulmona, a statesman as well as a man of letters, whom he had met on the occasion of his brief Neapolitan sojourn in preparation for his Roman coronation. The *Epystole* contain sixty-six letters, divided as follows: fourteen in the first book, eighteen in the second, and thirty-four in the third. Through publication Petrarch intended to provide a text that he controlled and approved. He endeavored to stop the unauthorized circulation of arbitrary and uncorrected copies of individual letters, which is attested by the manuscript tradition. These individual letters were the primary source of the writer's fame in the late thirties and early forties and consequently of his coronation as a poet in Rome. The publication of *Epystole* proceeded in phases:

1. selection of letters already composed and sent;
2. harmonization of content;
3. stylistic revision.

The three phases are typical Petrarchan techniques, already present in the *Rerum familiarium libri* and *Rerum vulgarium fragmenta*. The final result of this process shows that the significance of the work in its entirety is much greater than the meaning resulting from the sum of its individual pieces. The global message exceeds the occasions that justified the actual letters; it has become a literary message that has its own structure and reasons. Reality is only the point of departure for this Petrarchan work. Its conclusion implies important consequences: first of all, a strong reduction, if not a total cancellation, of the chronological gaps among the single letters, returning the material to the writer's emotional and intellectual conditions at the time the collection was born; to the time, that is, of the dedication to Barbato, whose date, for reasons that are both internal and external, is 1350. After the great public and private losses in 1348 (the plague caused the death of friends, patrons, and Laura), with greater determination Petrarch draws the balance of his life and of his literary work. In this regard, it is important to consider the textual affinities between the introductory letter to Barbato (*Epystole* 1.1) and the prefatory sonnet of the *Rerum vulgarium fragmenta*, with which the first epistle of the *Familiares*, given its overall mood, also has a certain affinity. Let us begin with a few extracts from the first *epystola:*

> . . . Memor ergo precum, dilecte, tuarum
> institui exiguam *sparsi* tibi mittere partem
> *carminis,* exacte percurrens otia vite. (*Epystole* 1.1.29–31)

> [. . . mindful, therefore, dear one, of your prayers,
> I have decided, looking back on the leisure hours of my past life,
> to send you a small portion of my *scattered poems.*]

A similar opposition between a past condition of inner turmoil and the present peacefulness returns in a later passage.

> . . . Veteres tranquilla tumultus
> mens horret, relegensque *alium* putat ista locutum. (*Epystole*
> 1.1.64–65)

> [. . . my mind now at peace trembles at
> the old turmoil of love and in reading them over feels that
> *a different man* has spoken.]

> [Musa] Prodeat impexis ad te festina capillis
> . . . *veniam*que precetur
> non laudem. . . . (*Epystole* 1.1.73–75)

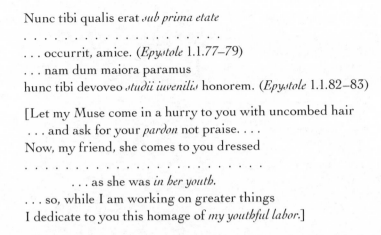

Nunc tibi qualis erat *sub prima etate*

. . . .

. . . occurrit, amice. (*Epystole* 1.1.77–79)

. . . nam dum maiora paramus

hunc tibi devoveo *studii iuvenilis* honorem. (*Epystole* 1.1.82–83)

[Let my Muse come in a hurry to you with uncombed hair

. . . and ask for your *pardon* not praise. . . .

Now, my friend, she comes to you dressed

. . . .

            . . . as she was *in her youth.*

. . . so, while I am working on greater things

I dedicate to you this homage of *my youthful labor.*]

Let us read now the opening verses of *Rerum vulgarium fragmenta:*

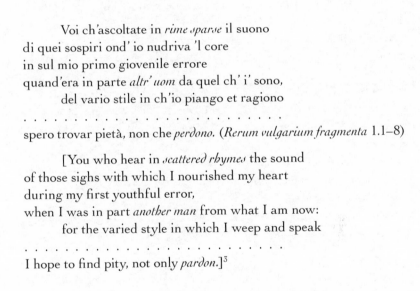

        Voi ch'ascoltate in *rime sparse* il suono

di quei sospiri ond' io nudriva 'l core

in sul mio primo giovenile errore

quand'era in parte *altr' uom* da quel ch' i' sono,

        del vario stile in ch'io piango et ragiono

. . . .

spero trovar pietà, non che *perdono.* (*Rerum vulgarium fragmenta* 1.1–8)

        [You who hear in *scattered rhymes* the sound

of those sighs with which I nourished my heart

during my first youthful error,

when I was in part *another man* from what I am now:

        for the varied style in which I weep and speak

. . . .

I hope to find pity, not only *pardon.*][3]

Once we have accepted the preeminence of the "'ideal'" over the actual chronology, is it possible to trace the guidelines governing the author's strategies of organization? I think it is. The profound meaning of the conclusion of the last letter of *Epystole* (3.34) has not escaped attentive critics. Its admonition to his correspondent Guglielmo da Pastrengo to leave his home, to free himself even from his family ties, and to go on a pilgrimage to Rome with Francesco as his companion is undeniably charged with strong moral and literary implications:

Cuncta tibi calcanda sunt; pulcherrima merces
proposita est . . .
Mene, oro, comitem refugis? Comes esse volenti
institui meliore via. Iam mundus, et omne
quod placuit iuveni, domita vix carne, valete.[4] (*Epystole*
3.34.38–40)

[You have to trample upon everything. A most beautiful
reward is ready for you. . . .
Are you refusing me as a companion? I decided to embark, if you
take me, on a better path. Now I take leave of you, o world, of all that
I have loved in my youth, the strength of my flesh barely tamed.

Here we encounter the author's signature, which signals the completion
of his work.[5] Moreover, he obliquely but clearly speaks of a journey away
from the world, from its allurements, and the constraints of the flesh toward the heavens.

Other correspondences can be detected. The last of the *Epystole*, 3.34,
has parallels in the final letters of the first and second book, 1.14 and 2.18.
The former (*Ad se ipsum*, "To himself," 1.14) is a lucid, yet desperate analysis of Petrarch's moral predicaments as he is facing the tragedy of the
plague. The "I," the speaking character, is perfectly aware that a radical
turnabout in his life is necessary more than ever, even though he is unable
to enact it:

Sepe ego premetuens animamque amplexus inertem
cogito si qua via est medius auferre per
corporeasque unda lacrimarum extinguere flammas,
Sed retinet mundus. . . . (*Epystole* 1.14.47–50)

[Often in fear, taking in my arms my sluggish soul,
I seek a way to save it through the fire
and to extinguish the flames of the flesh with a wave of tears.
But the world is holding me back.]

Later the poet emphasizes the "swift steps" of time:

Nonne vides volucri labentia secula cursu?
Impellunt momenta levem successibus horam;
illa diem noctemque fugat. . . . (*Epystole* 1.14.88–90)

[Don't you see how time slips away with swift
steps? Moments push away the short hour;
it flees day and night. . . .]

"Your day has passed for the most part," the poet concludes:

Preteriitque tue tibi iam pars magna diei,
iam ruit eterne prenuntia vespera noctis.
Tu longum senior curas extendis in evum,
tu dormis, moriture . . .

. . . .
. . . male perdita tempora defle,
dum licet, ac patriam versus vestigia volve,

. . . .
vixisti in pelago nimis irrequietus iniquo
in portu morere. . . . (*Epystole* 1.14.110–14, 116–20)

[Your day has passed for the most part.
Evening, harbinger of the eternal night, hastens up;
You, old man, are prolonging your pains.
You, who are doomed to die, are asleep . . .

. . . .
. . . weep upon time vainly spent,
while you can, turn your steps towards home.

. . . .
You lived restlessly in the iniquitous sea,
die in the harbor!. . . .]

I will not insist on the at times literal contacts with crucial nuclei of *Rerum vulgarium fragmenta*, particularly with canzone 264, *I' vo pensando et nel penser m'assale*, which begins the section "in morte" (in death) of Laura, nor on the thorny problem of the chronology of the various pieces of the puzzle.[6] I would like to stress, however, the importance of the position of the letter at the end of the first book, where we find fear, nausea for the world, and uncertainty concerning his final destiny. The last verses, with their Senecan tone, are highly meaningful:

. . . exitus ipse docebit
quis fuerim vere . . . (*Epystole* 1.14.142–43)
[. . . the end will show the man I really was].

In contrast, at the opposite end of the work, we find that a decision, however conditional, has been made:

> . . . iam mundus, et omne
> quod placuit iuveni, domita vix carne, valete. (*Epystole*
> 3.34.39–40)
>
> [. . . Now I take leave of you, o world; of all
> that I have loved in my youth, the strength of my flesh barely
> tamed.]

The end of the last letter of the second book (*Epystole* 2.18) could be de-
ceiving. This letter is about the construction of Petrarch's house in Parma;[7]
it shows the writer's wavering psychological attitude toward this task, a
clear symptom of a deeper malaise. Its conclusion is striking. The metaphor
of a shipwreck, much loved by the poet, comes to the fore but, surprisingly,
the poet is not part of it. Petrarch sees others (*vulgus ineptum*) in a much
worse state. Petrarch is indeed aware of his condition, of his irremediable
inadequacy. His mind is tossed *inter fluctus*—"among the waves"; but "the
inept populace" is hurled in bigger billows, without rudder, menaced by a
universal wreck. All in all, he laughs at himself and at everything mortal
in this world:

> . . . Tandem omnia librans,
> rideo meque simul mortali quidquid in orbe est. (*Epystole*
> 2.18.60–61, ed. Rossetti, 2.19)
>
> [. . . Finally, all things considered,
> I laugh at myself, and everything mortal in this world.]

The line connecting the conclusions of the three books now appears clear:
from anguished uncertainty to scornful detachment, and finally to the resolute relinquishment of all worldly things, since the poet is now free of all
possible illusions. This is the moral portrait the author intends to convey.
The choice of a better path—the path toward salvation—implies awareness
and control of one's internal contradictions.

Moreover, it should not escape the reader's attention that Petrarch has
shrewdly prepared the final triumph of his will by placing, immediately
before *Epystole* 3.34, letters 32 and 33, the former to his Socrates (Ludwig
van Kempen, early companion of Petrarch's youth in Provence), the latter
to Simonide (Francesco Nelli), his new Italian and Florentine friend. Let-

ter 32 is an obsessive catalog of all the possible vain ambitions and occupations of those intent solely on worldly matters, unmindful of heaven—a true
contemptus mundi (contempt for the world); letter 33 is a personal "acknowledgment" of the truth of the general, abstract paraenesis. Somehow the two
friends summarize the whole parable of the writer's existence from his time
in Provence to his residence in Italy, motherland of his affections and intellect. In *Epystole* 3.34, Rome, seen as the mystic city every Christian yearns
for, is the final destination of another couple, Guglielmo and Francesco.
Assured voluntarism is an essential part of the dialectics of Petrarch's entire work: *to be* and *ought to be.* It is important that the *Epystole* be implicated
in such a dialectics. They are not a haphazard heap of preexisting material, as was the general opinion that, with reservations and nuances, still
holds today. Preexisting literary material, a fruit, as the poet says, of his
youth (cf. 1.1.43: *tenero . . . in evo*), is screened by a keen moral and literary consciousness never resigned to the disorderly, chaotic flux of "reality."

Now this general structure encompasses minor thematic units carefully
distributed along the apparently casual flow of the epistolary discourse,
actually obeying a skilled strategy of parallels, contrasts, and balance. Let
us focus on a few instances. It is not a coincidence that the death lament
for the poet's mother (*Epystole* 1.7), possibly the first piece of his Latin poetry, is inserted between an anguished confession of his tormenting love
(*Epystole* 1.6 and 1.8), which expresses the fear that his passion might be
rekindled. Furthermore, the death motif in 1.7 is picked up with greater
resonance both in 1.13 (a *planctus* or poem of "weeping" for the death of
his older friend Dionigi da Borgo San Sepolcro) and in 1.14 (*Ad se ipsum*).
Similarly, the decreasing frequency of the love motif is paralleled, in opposition, by the massive presence of the poetry theme. The love motif is
present in two letters in the first book, totally absent in the second, reappears in the third in letter 3 to Guglielmo da Pastrengo (an elegant and
mundane badinage on the love affair of his friend) and, almost at the center
of the book but in a deprecatory manner, in two more letters (15 and 16),
addressed to the musician Floriano da Rimini. In opposition to the abating
love motif in the above letters, the theme of poetry (its practice, its meaning and its value) becomes more insistent in the second book (letters 2, 3,
and 4 to the Cardinal Bernard d'Aube, a failing but aspiring poet); 10 and
17 to Zoilus, a nickname for Brizio Visconti, Bernabò's powerful son. The
organic character of the *Epystole* cannot therefore be doubted.

These letters offer a wide panorama—geographic, cultural, and affective. The historical past of the various regions and cities touched upon by
Petrarch, with its cultural and symbolic import, is brought to the fore with

strong emotional participation expressed either with longing or with hortatory and polemic force (Avignon, Vaucluse, Italy with her cities: Naples
and her Virgilian memories; Rome with her classical and Christian heritage; Parma, Milan, Padua). The intellectual, cultural and emotional dimensions are not separated neatly. The first prevails when the writer is motivated by ethical and political reasons (letters such as 1.2 and 5, addressed
to Benedict XII; and 2.5 to Clement VI, stressing the necessity for the pope
to return to Rome, his "natural" residence). The second occupies the lime-
light when the poet moves from external reality to his rich inner life, his
restlessness, his discontent, his fears, his love, his solitude in the company
of his best friends, and books. There we find the often great Petrarch of the
Rerum vulgarium fragmenta.

Variously dated by scholars but certainly belonging to the period
1337–39, *Epystole* 1.4 is a charming invitation to Dionigi da Borgo San
Sepolcro to visit Petrarch in his remote residence at Vaucluse. It is a description of his "transalpine Helicon," a place that the frequent mythical
references and the pregnant literary allusions raise to a different sphere,
a reality immune to natural contingencies, existing solely in the realm of
literature. This is what will become Petrarch's personal "myth." Vaucluse
is again the general background of *Epystole* 1.6, which is addressed to his
friend and confidant Giacomo Colonna—perhaps antecedent, but placed
after *Epystole* 1.4 solely for structural reasons insofar as it occupies almost
the center of the first book. It is the landscape of his unrequited love and
the serene happiness of the humanist. Laura occupies the first half of the
letter, all her attempts to escape are in vain. Her features are always before
the narrator's eye:

> . . . per avia silva
> dum solus reor esse magis, virgulta tremendam
> ipsa representant faciem truncusque reposte
> ilicis et liquido visa est emergere fonte,
> obviaque effulsit sub nubibus aut per inane
> aeris aut duro spirans erumpere saxo
> credita suspensum tenuit formidine gressum. (*Epystole* 1.6.146–51)

> [. . . when I think
> To be alone in pathless forest shades,
> I see the face I fear, upon the bushes
> Or on an oaken trunk; or from the stream

She rises; flashes on me from a cloud
Or from clear sky; or issues from a rock,
Compelling me, dismayed, to hold my step.][8]

But here we find Petrarch's other aspect as the companion of the ancients,
with whom he converses through their books. The passage to the second
part of the letter strikes the reader with its abrupt, almost impatient brake:
Hactenus hec (Enough of this, v. 156). In this second part, we have what
we could safely call the original manifesto of humanism, which the poet
expresses with unsurpassed forcefulness and eloquence. Petrarch's "secret
friends," his books, are the trustees and "transmitters" of mankind's memories, the depository of men's highest and most precious accomplishments:

Nunc hos, nunc illos percontor; multa vicissim
respondent, et multa canunt et multa loquuntur.
Nature secreta alii, pars optima vite
consilia et mortis, pars inclita gesta priorum,
pars sua, preteritos renovant sermonibus actus. (*Epystole* 1.6.188–92)

[Now these, now those I question, and they answer
Abundantly. Sometimes they sing for me;
Some tell of the mysteries of nature;
Some give me counsel for my life and death;
Some tell of high emprise, bringing to mind
Ages long past. . . .][9]

Conversing with books is certainly a classical motif, but its constant recurrence in Petrarch's works, with ever new expressive formulations, from
Epystole to *Familiares* to *De vita solitaria*, renders his reformulations particularly cogent, as is shown by their echoes in his immediate circle (Boccaccio, Zanobi da Strada) and also in later writers. A close analysis of the
texts demonstrates that Petrarch's usage is primarily responsible for the
renewed life of the motif. When Machiavelli in his famous letter to Francesco Vettori of December 10, 1513, writes:

dove io non mi vergogno *parlare* con loro [i grandi uomini antichi di cui i libri sono testimoni] della ragione delle loro actioni; et
quelli per loro humanità mi *rispondono.*

[where I am not ashamed *to speak* with them (the great men of antiquity to whose lives books are witness) to ask them the reason for their actions; and they in their kindness *answer me.*][10]

he literally takes up (because he "translates") Petrarch's *Epystole* 1.6.188–89: "Nunc hos, nunc illos *percontor;* multa vicissim / *respondent.*"[11] It is important to note that at such an early date (1338), before his coronation, Petrarch establishes with such passionate strength the fundamental moment (the meeting with books) in which "tradition" begins to live: the past is brought back to nourish the future.

If Vaucluse is the transalpine Helicon for Petrarch, Selvapiana is the Italian one. After his Capitoline triumph (April 1341) the newly laureated poet, accompanied by Azzo da Correggio, repaired to Parma where he remained, guest of her lords, until January 1342. In the woods of Selvapiana, not far from the city, he was suddenly taken by a renewed enthusiasm for his unfinished *Africa*, as he states in his *Posteritati*[12] and in *Epystole* 2.16 of 1343 (vv. 19–23), addressed to Barbato da Sulmona, to whom the entire work was to be dedicated.[13] The description of the strikingly suggestive landscape stands out in the epistle, an equivalent in Latin of the intense lyricism of the *Rerum vulgarium fragmenta*. In this description, we also encounter the emblematic image, the "myth" of the man of letters who brings back to life neglected poetry after centuries of oblivion. I quote vv. 36–46:

> Florens in medio torus est, quem cespite nullo
> erexit manus artificis, sed amica poetis
> ipsa suis natura locum meditata creavit.
> Hic avium cantus fontis cum murmure blandos
> conciliant somnos; gratum parat herba cubile,
> fronde tegunt rami, mons flamina submovet Austri;
> horridus hunc metuit pedibus violare subulcus,
> rusticus hunc rastris digitoque hunc signat et alto
> silvarum trepidus veneratur ab aggere custos.
> Intus odor mirus statioque simillima Campis
> Elysiis profugisque domus placidissima Musis. (*Epystole* 2.16.36–46)

[In the middle there is a flowery seat, not built with turf
by a craftsman, but created by nature herself, the friend of poets.
Here the birds' singing, along with the murmur of a fountain,

induce a peaceful slumber; the grass offers a pleasant bed;
the branches a covering, the mountain keeps off Auster's blowing.
The uncouth swineherd is afraid of violating it with his feet,
the peasant with his rake, and the forester
points to it and in awe from a mound reveres it.
Inside, a wonderful scent and an abode quite similar to the Elysian
fields, a most pleasant home for the exiled Muses.]

This is a sacred place. It is the Elysium of poets, fashioned not by man but
by nature herself. The holiness is subconsciously felt and acknowledged
by unholy beings: the swineherd, the peasant; for the forester, the specific
verb *veneratur* is even used. The tone is exalted and indeed is appropriate
to a religious hymn. The later, great *canzone* of the "visions" (*Rerum vulgarium fragmenta* 323) takes up the motif again in the same terms (*Epystole*
2.16.37–48):

> Chiara fontana in quel medesmo bosco
> sorgea d'un sasso, et acque fresche et dolci
> spargea, soavemente mormorando;
> al bel seggio riposto, ombroso et fosco,
> *né pastori appressavan né bifolci,*
> ma nimphe et muse a quel tenor cantando.
> Ivi m'assisi, et quando
> piú dolcezza prendea di tal concento
> et di tal vista, aprir vidi uno speco,
> et portarsene seco
> la fonte e 'l loco: ond' ancor doglia sento,
> et sol de la memoria mi sgomento.

> [A clear fountain in that same wood
> welled from a stone, and fresh and sweet waters
> it scattered forth, gently murmuring;
> to that lovely, hidden, shady, and dark seat
> neither shepherds came nor ploughman,
> but nymphs and muses, singing to that burden.
> There I seated myself, and when
> I took most sweetness from that harmony
> and that sight, then I saw a chasm open
> and carry away with it

the fountain and the place, whereat I still grieve,
and I am stricken with fear by the very memory.][14]

The connection between the two descriptions is clear. The *canzone*, how-ever, reverses the optimistic, assertive impetus of the epistle: Laura's death will signify the death of poetry.

Placing next to each other the two instances of ekphrasis, which are dis-tant from one another both in time and in orientation, allows us to discover the genetic paths of Petrarch's Latin and vernacular poetic writing. As for the *canzone*, the fourth stanza has in itself and in the light of the entire structure (six visionary images, all founded on a positive-negative opposi-tion) a nightmarish warning sign. Imperfect tenses *sorgea, spargea, appres-savan, prendeva* (welled up, scattered forth, came, took) turn into the perfect tenses *m'assisi, vidi* (I sat, I saw). Consider also the second verb *vidi* in line 45, which irremediably breaks the enchanted atmosphere. From a thematic standpoint, that nightmare echoes the *horror* in Lucan's *De bello civili* (*Pharsalia*) 3.399–425 (a description of the forest of Marseille), which suggests with its *cavas . . . cavernas* (*De bello civili* bk. 3, v. 418) Petrarch's *lo speco* (chasm) that devours *la fonte e 'l loco* (the fountain and the place).[15]

As for epistle 2.16, it is an exceptional document of the creative *imitatio* Petrarch theorizes in *Familiares* 23.19 to Boccaccio. Poets, like bees, visit many flowers to make the "honey" produced by intimate appropriation of classical texts. A few examples of such mellification suffice:

> . . . *si* dextra favebunt
> sidera, tum *tandem* incipiet secura vagari
> Africa *per* Latium studio redimita supremo
> Scipiadesque meus. . . . (*Epystole* 2.16.58–61)

> [If the stars will be favorable, then at last
> *Africa* and my Scipio will securely travel
> through Latium, perfected by my last labors.]

These verses are a remake of Virgil *Catalepton* 14.1–4:

> *Si* mihi susceptum fuerit decurrere munus
> O Paphon, o sedes quae colis Idalias,
> Troius Aeneas Romana *per* oppida digno
> Iam *tandem* ut tecum carmine vectus eat

[If it be granted me to complete the charge I have undertaken,
o lady of Paphos and Idalian groves, and the day will come
at last when, borne with you in worthy songs, Trojan
Aeneas shall travel through Roman towns.][16]

By avoiding a literal appropriation, the poet retains only the conditioning elements of the passage (*si, per, tandem*), hence that notion of the "similar / dissimilar" proposed by Petrarch as the goal of *imitatio*.[17] But the writer can also choose not to avoid literal appropriation, achieving an Alexandrian inlay elsewhere in the same epistle. The verses

Hic avium cantus fontis cum murmure blandos
conciliant somnos (*Epystole* 2.16.39–40)

[Here the birds' singing, along with the murmur of a fountain, induce a peaceful slumber.]

come from juxtaposing Ovid's *Remedia amoris* 177, *Aspice labentes iucundo murmure rivos* (Watch the streams gliding with cheerful sound),[18] with Claudian's *In Rufinum* 1.214,[19] *Hic avium cantus, labentis murmura rivi* (Here is song of birds and the murmur of the gliding stream).[20] Intelligent use of his readings is accompanied by a refinement of style wherein the syntactical balance, the never mechanical *Wortstellung*, the smooth elegance of the verse, and the discreet phonosymbolism make Petrarch's Latin form something new. To perceive and appreciate this novelty, let us take, for instance, *Epystole* 2.16.41–43:

horridus hunc metuit pedibus violare subulcus,
rusticus hunc rastris digitoque hunc signat et alto
silvarum trepidus veneratur ab aggere custos.[21]

[The uncouth swineherd is afraid of violating it with his feet, the peasant with his rake, and the forester points to it and in awe from a mound reveres it.]

Only if we keep in mind these poetic results, will we understand why Petrarch, the Latin poet of the *Epystole* (and *Africa* and the *Bucolicum carmen*), became a model for humanist Latin poetry and later, in the sixteenth century, after Bembo, when the Latin and the vernacular "lines" combined, entered the mainstream of the great Italian literature of the Renaissance.

There is perhaps no higher example of this phenomenon than Torquato Tasso's poetry. In *Gerusalemme liberata* 13.3.1–8 (the description of the Saron forest), Tasso goes back to Lucan, the original source, and turning the "horror" of the classical author into the fruit of sorcery, recaptures both of Petrarch's passages (*Epystole* 2.16.42–44 and *Rerum vulgarium fragmenta* 323.40–42). With his new reformulation, Tasso bequeaths to tradition what had been a "unity" in Petrarch's inspiration:

> Ma quando parte il sol, qui tosto adombra
> notte, nube, caligine ed orrore
> che rassembra infernal, che gli occhi ingombra
> di cecità, ch' empie di tema il core;
> né qui gregge od armenti a' paschi, a l' ombra
> guida bifolco mai, guida pastore,
> né v' entra peregrin, se non smarrito,
> ma lunge passa e la dimostra a dito.[22]

> [But as the sun departs, there dwell at once
> dark night and clouds and horridness of mist,
> which quite resemble hell, and charge one's eyes
> with blindness, and makes every soul afraid.
> There is not one shepherd, not one herdsman comes
> with flock or herd to look for shade or grass;
> he who comes by, bewildered, does not linger,
> but fast goes on, and points it with his finger.][23]

We can only marvel at the pervasive, propulsive strength of Petrarch's poetry. His *Epystole* deserve deeper and wider critical attention and appreciation. Furthermore, their fortune in Renaissance literature, greater than suspected and eloquent proof of their vitality, has still many surprises in store.

CHAPTER NINETEEN

THE BOOK WITHOUT A NAME • Petrarch's Open Secret • *Liber sine nomine*

Ronald L. Martinez

A few years after the Jubilee of 1350, while still looking about to uproot himself from both Avignon and Vaucluse, Petrarch assembled thirteen prose epistles attacking the Avignon papacy and lamenting its effects on Rome.[1] Between about 1353 and 1359, after his removal from Provence, and while living in Visconti Milan, he added six more and a preface; this final collection includes twenty distinct pieces.[2] Marco Ariani has fairly summed up the work: "the density of the citational impasto (biblical and classical), and the insistent virulence of the antipapal invective, place the *Sine nomine* on the most inventive and experimental tangent of the Latin Petrarch."[3] This inventive, experimental tangent will be the focus of my remarks in this essay.

One criterion for determining what something is, *Quid sit*, is its title. In the case of a book without a name, the task is at once problematic and intriguing. The manuscript tradition delivers an overwhelming majority opinion in favor of the *titulus* of *Sine nomine liber* (*The Book without a Name*), or *libellus* (booklet), preferable to *sine titulo* (without title), the name used in the first printed Basel edition, and to the attested *contra clericos liber* (book against clerics), which assimilates the collection to the genre of anticlerical satire, of which more presently.[4] Since there is no autograph, *Sine nomine* lacks full authority, but the choice of title likely took a cue from the preface to the collection, where Petrarch, who begins by citing the Terentian *sententia* that truth gives birth to hatred, goes on to claim that he will spare his addressees danger and opprobrium: "I have deliberately concealed their names, which, if they came to light, would bring harm to the recipients if still alive or hatred if they were dead, as if I had preferred to write to those I knew would be most willing to hear."[5]

Although Michele Feo rejects the association of the title *Sine nomine* with the suppression of named addressees, such an association seems warranted

by further references to the omission of names within the collection. Concluding the eleventh letter, Petrarch notes that he has not affixed his name,
nor his seal, nor the date and place, omissions of what were for medieval epistolary art canonical parts of an epistle.[6] Since a letter by definition consists of thoughts written down and expedited to a recipient remote
in space, letters that omit to name both sender and addressees are really
not missives at all. Although Petrarch notoriously wrote to addressees who
could not read his words—Cicero, Seneca, Livy, Horace, Homer, and the
other dead Latin authors of the last book of the *Familiares* spring to mind—
his spotlighting of technical anomalies in the *Sine nomine* alerts readers to
reflect on what truncated epistles might signify. For example: truncation
reflects, as Petrarch wrote elsewhere, that the letters had been uprooted
(*scripta . . . avulsa*) from their intended locations in the evolving collection
of the *Familiares*, which Petrarch was bringing to a first stage of completion
while finishing the revision of the *Sine nomine*;[7] truncation also resonates
with the rhetorical violence, the mordant invective of the entire enterprise.
In this light, the account in the second letter of how Cola di Rienzo's messenger was abused by papal officials, resulting in the scattering of his dispatches, serves as a *mise-en-abîme* of the risk run by the whole collection:
its clandestinity is justified because it travels in fear.[8] Ugo Dotti calls attention to the closely related passage in *Familiares* 21.1, where Petrarch acknowledges sometimes suppressing material "propter metum Judaeorum,"
quoting the Gospel phrase for the apostles' "fear of the Jews."[9] In fact, the
preface to the *Sine nomine* anticipates that some readers will wish to destroy
the letters; the collection is thus expected to bear the brunt of censorship
so that the larger collection might be spared, making the *Sine nomine* a kind
of preemptive literary lightning rod or scapegoat.[10] That Petrarch's caution was not wholly misplaced was verified when portions of Pier Paolo
Vergerio's Italian rendition of some of the *Sine nomine* were placed on the
Vatican's Index of Forbidden Books for the years 1559 and 1560.[11] Yet the
collection also circulated widely before the Catholic Reformation with no
doubt as to its author, whose fame did indeed speak for itself.[12]

For if Petrarch omitted names to spare his correspondents, he also
spared himself. In his preface, anticipating a future readership after he is
comfortably dead, he paraphrases Juvenal in deducing that if it is safe for
the living to speak of the dead, it is even safer for the dead to speak of the
living. In this way, Petrarch positions his authorial voice as speaking from
beyond the cesura, or one could say the truncation, of death.[13] In this respect, the truncation of the letters is a fertile literary strategy that magnifies Petrarch's voice and enhances his authority. Suppression throughout

the collection of all but a few contemporary proper names allows Petrarch to shift his frame of reference at will to the ahistorical plane of apocalyptic, where the names of historical individuals fade in the clamor of cosmic events. The imagined audience of the letters is reoriented, in the case of the sixth letter explicitly, toward that posterity of which Petrarch was always thinking. Not by accident, in this same letter Petrarch presents himself as a scribe following the dictation of truth.[14] At the same time the poet can claim, as in the eleventh letter, that his letters need no signature, as their distinctive style and tone—*vox loquentis*—are sufficient to identify him; while in the last letter, addressing the unnamed emperor (Charles IV), Petrarch exclaims, "[W]hat use are words, where the things themselves speak out?"[15] These gestures identify Petrarch with his own unmistakable reputation, the enduring *fama* for which he strove, and align his voice with the truth of history itself.[16]

As almost invariably in Petrarch's slowly evolving works, the mutations of the collection over time, especially the order of the pieces, is crucial to both their form and content. In the case of the *Sine nomine*, not only their protracted elaboration but also their implicit narrative, Petrarch's slow self-extraction from Avignon and Vaucluse, parallels that of several other major works during the productive period between 1350 and 1359. The first version, framed at both beginning and end by letters to and about Cola di Rienzo, constructed the collection by opposing a corrupt papal Avignon to Rome, the city destined to be renewed under the visionary leadership of Cola after his resumption of the long-abandoned ancient Roman office of the tribunate. Given the historical irrelevance of Cola, ignominiously dead by 1353, Petrarch's additions and revisions of the late fifties revise these earlier priorities. By shifting to the beginning of the new collection the letters to and about Cola found near the end of the first version, Petrarch makes them, and Cola with them, the past tense for a new, implicit autobiographical narrative.[17]

Although Ernest Hatch Wilkins claimed that chronology determined the second arrangement, the core of the second collection, letters five through thirteen, although all written in 1351–52, are not in strict chronological order, and other criteria, both verbal and rhetorical, are likely to be in play in Petrarch's arrangement of them.[18] Letters five to seven are linked to the letters concerning Cola that precede them, because they formulate the attack against Avignon in Roman or Italian terms—in the fifth, a happier Italian Helicon is juxtaposed to that of Vaucluse, unfortunately close to Avignon's "Babylon"; in the sixth, the Pope is a tyrant like Nero or Domitian and Petrarch boasts his subject matter could furnish a corpus of Senecan tragedies. In the seventh letter, speaking of the relief of Rome, Petrarch exclaims, "O that I might be a part of such a great task, of such glory!"[19] Avignon-as-Babylon appears first, briefly, in the fifth letter, heralding the rise to dominance of this topic in the eighth.[20] Petrarch emphasizes his personal stakes in Avignon as Babel by signing the following letter, the ninth, from the place of exile, "by the waters of Babylon," *super flumina Babylonis*, and then calls attention, in the incipit of the tenth letter and central piece of the collection, to this centrally placed and telling *subscriptio*.[21] From the eighth to the thirteenth letter the subject of Avignon-as-Babylon alternates or coincides with that of Avignon as a labyrinth, and with Nembroth and Semiramis, king and queen of Babylon, as the enciphered pope and his possible consort. After this sequence these three subjects all but disappear, but then recur in the last three letters (17–19).[22]

The group of letters from 1351–52, which in the earlier order inchoately broached the idea of departure from Avignon, serve in the new order to prepare the narrative breakthrough of the second version. Letters 8–9 are closely linked by the idea of Petrarch's shame at his own lack of resolve, one that parallels the submission of Italy itself, "for in our time Italy groans under the burden of persecution."[23] In the *subscriptio* of letter 9 referred to in letter 10, Petrarch attests to his crisis of conscience regarding his prolonged submission to a Babylonian captivity. A Petrarchan retreat from Avignon to Vaucluse, marking a gesture of active separation ("an escape [*fugam*] which, you see, is a relief to me, freeing my eyes from such a sorrowful sight"), is registered in letter 13, the place in the order where the first collection left off, and which remains a major articulation in the new collection.[24] This leaves the six letters added in Milan between 1353 and 1359 to explore the theme of departure from both Avignon and Vaucluse — the departure that Petrarch achieved in 1353.

In the *Sine nomine* the departure is achieved not, however, in terms of Petrarch himself, but through proxies: the fourteenth concludes with an invitation to its addressee to visit Italy, after escaping Avignon; in the fifteenth, Avignon is a version of Hell, and only divinity can free its prisoners; while the sixteenth letter celebrates "your return, for to go to the homeland (*patriam*) is to return."[25] The last three concern an official journey Nelli makes to the papal city, and the last of all, the nineteenth, crystallizes the achieved return with the four dramatic perfect-tense verbs beginning the letter: *evasisti, erupisti, enatasti, evolasti* ("you escaped, broke out, swam free, flew away"). Borrowed from Cicero's second Catilinarian oration where they refer to Catiline's flight into exile, the string of perfects is given a positive resonance that Petrarch warrants with other literary allusions.

References to flying, like Daedalus, out of the Cretan labyrinth (*evolasti*) signify Nelli's (and, retrospectively, Petrarch's) escape from Babylon;[26] with *evasisti* and *erupisti* Petrarch suggests that Nelli has escaped from a prison or indeed Hell, the Avignon that Petrarch calls "the Hell of the living."[27] If the governing literary model is clearly Virgil's Sybil warning Aeneas about the difficulty of retracing steps out of Hell,[28] the example of Dante, the most famous refugee from Hell in recent literary history, whose pilgrim had, in Cato's words, "fuggita la pregione etterna" (fled the eternal prison; *Purg.* 1.41), is unmistakable as well. Moreover, in fusing these two distinguished predecessors Petrarch enlisted allusive and rhetorical forces developed in meditating on his own oft-expressed desire to escape from his attachment to Laura. He had long since cast his love for her as a bondage from which only Christ's victorious arm could free him—that is, he had cast his imagined escape as that harrowing of Hell represented for medieval readers by the *descensus* portion of the Gospel of Nicodemus and in the liturgical Latin of the Office of the Dead.[29] In this light, as anticipated above, Christ's Harrowing of Hell, the escapes of Aeneas and Dante from the underworld and of Nelli from Avignon, serve as prologues to Petrarch's self-uprooting from the snares of Babylon, including even the *locus amoenus* of Vaucluse where his devotion to Laura had first flourished.

We can gauge the overall historical and political distance traveled from the first collection by noting that where that version began with a letter to the Romans appealing for assistance on behalf of Cola, who had been delivered as a prisoner to Avignon by Charles IV, the final letter of the new collection addresses the same Charles IV as a liberator, who "has the power to pluck out (*eruere*) the bride of Christ from filth and fetters."[30] The appeal to Charles is made in concert with those of the second half of the *Familiares* (ten direct appeals in books 10–23) and recalls once more the kinship between the uprooted *Sine nomine* and the parent trunk, the much greater collection dedicated to Ludwig van Kempen, Petrarch's "Socrates." Petrarch's self-congratulatory narrative of his escape from Avignon to Italy can be traced in the greater collection as well, where the symbolic break is made in books 10–12, with the turn to Charles as a potential savior of Italy and with the Roman Jubilee of 1350.

The unusual title of the collection may also yield clues to its literary genre. Forced to choose a defining genre for the *Sine nomine*, we would have to opt for satire, or speaking more broadly, invective, a genre Petrarch worked assiduously during his career.[31] This is warranted by Petrarch's reliance on Juvenal, the *satiricus* by antonomasia, as he warns in the first satire about the dangers of speaking plainly; while Horace's casualness about whether his *Satires* are verse or prose might have emboldened Petrarch to think of himself as *satiricus* even in prose, out of hexameter.[32] But it would be a mistake to stop there.[33] Readers have long observed that the nineteen prose epistles are in their subject matter cousins to a sheaf of lyrics against Babylon collected in the *Rerum vulgarium fragmenta* and to three contemporary *Epistole metriche*—among the last Petrarch wrote, two of them to Nelli—that treat of the labyrinth of Avignon, suggesting that Petrarch kept an open mind regarding the best generic avenue for his attacks on Babylon.[34] One of the reasons I earlier suggested might have driven the choice of name for the collection is Petrarch's apparent wish to use a collection of pseudo-letters to experiment with a wide range of genres. The opening *sententia* from Terence's *Andria* introduces Latin comedy to the collection, a context that Petrarch mines directly in the penultimate letter rounding off his tale about a lecherous cardinal with the formula ending Latin comedies, *Plaude, fabula acta est* ("Clap, the play is done").[35] In the same preface, Petrarch compares the anonymity of his collection to the enigmatic encipherment of historical figures in his own *Bucolicum carmen*, which he calls a "poem of ambiguous kind."[36] Now, the same description suits the *Sine nomine*, if Petrarch's *ambiguus* is taken in the sense of "uncertain." Indeed, that the generic profusion set loose in the preface is no accident emerges when Petrarch returns in the sixth letter to propose other possible generic shapes for his material: as we saw, he has enough matter to furnish the corpus of Senecan tragedy or fill histories dense as the annals of Rome.[37] Nor are we limited to classical literary genres: we find reference to the Scholastic *quaestio* in letter 3,[38] as well as examples of scriptural laments and petitions to God in letters 7 and 12,[39] and a passage arguably imitated from a contemporary meditation on the Passion in letter 17.[40] In the breadth of genres and discourse types invoked we see Petrarch's experimental tendencies in full force.

Petrarch's gestures toward a broad variety of genres associated with satire is not done without support from classical authors and from rhetorical tradition. Horace, Juvenal, and Persius repeatedly trade on the kinship of their form to comedy, mock-heroic and mock-epic. Petrarch was, moreover, surely aware of traditions that understood satire to denote, yes, the vehement reproof of vice expressed in a middle level of style, but also one that was miscellaneous or varied, after the idea of a the *satura lanx*, heaping plateful of varied foods, and that was energetic and often scurrilous because of its kinship to the classical satyr-play. This much Petrarch could have taken from Isidore of Seville alone.[41]

Still, as Ugo Dotti insists, it is Juvenal, famed as the most splenetic of the satirists, who must be honored as the godfather of the collection.[42] Juvenal's obsession with the transgressions of Roman matrons in the notorious sixth satire underwrites Petrarch's vision of the papal curia as a hotbed of sexual escapades.[43] If we survey Petrarch's borrowings from the first satire alone, Juvenal, like Petrarch in the sixth letter, keeps an eye cocked toward the opinion of posterity. Regarding the prudence of addressing satire safely to the dead—Petrarch's point of departure in his preface, Juvenal furnishes as well the idea of keeping one's mouth shut ("curb your lip with your finger"), an idea Petrarch adapts for his conclusion to the collection, though he veils it with a citation from Job: "I shall put my hand over my mouth."[44] Juvenal's view of his work as a wide-ranging miscellany (he calls it a *farrago,* a mishmash) warrants Petrarch's generic experiments in the letters; and it is Juvenal's first satire that is cited in letter 6 when Petrarch introduces the notion of his collection as tending toward tragedy and history. In fact, Juvenal begins his first satire by mocking the tedium of tragedies and dropping several mock-heroic references, including Daedalus's flight from the Cretan labyrinth, the flight that becomes, as we saw, central to Petrarch's conception of Avignon as a place from which he must and does escape.[45]

Juvenalian *indignatio* also undoubtedly lends acid to the tone of Petrarch's collection. Appearing as the force behind the words—*facit indignatio versum*—in the very first satire, the term typically characterizes the satirist's bile in the tradition of *accessus* and commentary, and accordingly appears in seven of Petrarch's twenty pieces.[46] But indignation and outrage are in fact outpaced in the collection by expressions of sorrow for neglected Rome and servile Italy—twelve pieces include expressions of woe and lamentation. That both *conquestio* (complaint) and *indignatio* might be oratorically combined is typically Ciceronian, but the scriptural stamp displayed by Petrarch's version of this mixture argues his close attention to the significant expressive use by Dante of such a combination in texts from *Purgatorio* 6 to the Latin political epistles, texts whose persistent importance for Petrarch has been noted by Giuseppe Velli.[47] That *Purgatorio* 6 itself draws on the Provencal genre of plaint mixed with satire, *planh-sirventes,* as shown by Maurizio Perugi, confirms these underlying continuities in Latin and vernacular rhetorical traditions.[48] We know, too, that Dante's language for his laments over servile Italy and desolate Rome—and his sardonic attack on Florence—rely conspicuously on biblical Lamentations, a text that medieval commentary from the *Glossa ordinaria* onward saw fit to equip with a preface in which the categories of *indignatio* and *conquestio* were equipped with more than a dozen apposite figures of speech apiece.[49]

Thus filtered through Dante's political utterances and through commentary, Lamentations is an important intertext for the *Sine nomine*. In the
second letter a series of rhetorical variations on *Roma* as a former *domina*
presently subject to her former servant, Provence, that is *Provincia*, yields
a pointillist fragment of the first verse of Lamentations ("facta est quasi
vidua *domina* gentium, princeps *provinciarum* facta est sub tributo").[50] Petrarch also tucks Dante's opening apostrophe to "serva Italia" into the text
of the ninth letter, writing that "under this burden of persecution, a servant
(*serva*) in these times, Italy (*Italia*) sighs (*suspirat*)."[51] Examples could be
multiplied; an important point is that Petrarch preserves the nuptial metaphor, drawing on Dante's laments for Rome widowed of pope and emperor
to fuel his indignation against the pope's illicit espousal of Avignon.

Having touched, in *Sine nomine* 18, the rhetorical climax of indignation
by apostrophizing the whore of Babylon herself,[52] Petrarch is true to his
plan of generic admixture in concluding the eighteenth letter with a brief,
comic *novella*. The tale is presented as a scene from a comedy, a *fabula;* the
adaptations of Horace, Terence, Plautus, and Apuleius in Petrarch's text
have been deftly analyzed by Ezio Raimondi.[53] The tale works as more
than a virtuoso insertion, however, for it complements the parodic, adulterous nuptials of Clement VI, Nimrod, and Semiramis, the personified *Ecclesia Avinionensis*.[54] In the tale, the lecherous cardinal can embrace the girl
procured for him only when he covers his bald pate with his cap (*pileum*)
and cries out, "Cardinalis sum, Cardinalis sum, ne timeas, filia" (I am a
cardinal, I am a cardinal, lest you fear, my daughter). The mock-epic touch
of having the Furies sponsor the coupling—another hint from Juvenal—
makes it clear that the spousal allegory in the collection remains in force,
indeed, becomes explicit with Petrarch's comparison of the assignation to
the marriage of Cupid and Psyche, of Love and the Soul.[55] And in fact the
cardinal's embrace is both adulterous and incestuous. He, a spouse of the
church, couples with one not his spouse who is a daughter of the baptismal
font, thus in a sacramental sense his own daughter—as he unwittingly recognizes with the words that precipitate his success.[56]

Thus Petrarch's satirical vocation coordinates a biting and realistic
comic style with underlying patterns of allegory and apocalyptic, while
Petrarch's authorial voice, garbed in anonymity and aimed at posterity,
is elevated to suprapersonal status as the solitary defender of *nuda veritas*.
Both Petrarch's emphasis on satire as tolerant of generic admixture and the
problem of authorizing the poet's voice on the world stage may reflect Petrarch's keen awareness during the 1350s, after his post-Jubilee exchanges
with Boccaccio, of the hot breath of Dante's example. Over the course of

the trecento, from Guido da Pisa to Benvenuto da Imola, the classification of Dante's generically anomalous *Divina commedia* was debated, with several writers attributing to the *sacro poema* a full suite of labels: tragedy, comedy, and satire.[57] It has long been recognized that Petrarch's prose satires of Avignon, his most "comic" and realistic work, represent his closest approach in Latin to Dante's muscular vernacular. It might follow that the miscellaneous genre of medieval satire afforded Petrarch, on his chosen ground of Latin prose, his best chance of coming up to Dante's daunting example.

CHAPTER TWENTY

THE UNCOLLECTED POET · *Lettere disperse*

Lynn Lara Westwater

P etrarch wrote to Roman tribune Cola di Rienzo two months after Cola
had taken power to issue the leader a warning:

> do not think that the letters that come to us from you remain only
> in the hands of their addressees. Everybody copies them imme-
> diately with great industry and they are circulated in the Curia
> with such zeal that it almost seems they were not sent by a member
> of the human race but by one of the gods or an inhabitant of the
> antipodes.[1]

Such assiduous collection and dissemination also became true of the poet's
letters. His correspondents greedily gathered and saved not only the letters
addressed to them by Petrarch himself but also those they succeeded in
copying from elsewhere. One of his correspondents and friends, the distinguished humanist Barbato da Sulmona, informed him in a letter from late
1362 or early 1363 that "I seek, wherever I can, not only your long letters,
but also small bits of your eloquence."[2] Some seven years earlier, Petrarch
had already noted Barbato's tireless efforts:

> the same power of friendship drives you with assiduous enthusi-
> asm to collect my writings, which you tell me you have solicited
> from innumerable people, different in country, custom, and pro-
> fession. . . . [M]y admiration for such perseverance springs anew
> each day, since time, which erodes everything, subtracts nothing
> from your affection.[3]

Petrarch here expresses appreciation for Barbato's efforts to gather his
scattered writings. But Barbato's diligent collecting and that of many oth-

ers also worked against one of the poet laureate's greatest impulses, that of carefully crafting the image of himself that he would transmit to posterity.

Central in this process of self-construction were the prose epistolary collections that Petrarch organized, and particularly the major collections, the *Familiares* and the *Seniles*.[4] As numerous critics have noted, the writer carefully structured these works and revised the letters they contained to promote his cultural agenda and to convey an idealized self-portrait. Petrarch himself did not pretend his letter collections contained the actual letters he sent. He acknowledged in fact in his dedication of the *Familiares* that, in order to construct a cohesive collection, he needed to eliminate contradictions, repetition, and uninteresting personal details. But the changes he made went far beyond these: Vittorio Rossi describes the "work of balancing, adapting, ordering . . ., expanding, abbreviating, dividing or combining" that Petrarch carried out when transforming a letter into its definitive version for a collection.[5]

The evidence of the changes that Petrarch made to letters comes from the survival of the letters that Petrarch actually sent instead of those that appeared in the collections, or of a version that in any case predated the definitive ones.[6] The survival of an original letter, termed *transmissiva* or version γ, or of an intermediate version, is one result of the drive to gather and save Petrarch's writings.[7] Another result of this impulse is the survival of some seventy-six prose letters that did not enter into his collections. These missives, gathered together over the centuries from scattered sources, are today known as the *Lettere disperse*.[8] Since they were not selected, edited and ordered by Petrarch into literary exemplarity, these letters allow the reader to experience what is rarely available to Petrarch's audience: texts that escaped the poet's tight control.

But even though they were not subject to endless revision, his scattered letters cannot be read as sincere or unconstructed reflections. An intense awareness of the reader characterizes letter writing in general,[9] and it is heightened when the writer knows the epistles will be circulated. Such was the circumstance, as Giles Constable observes, in the Middle Ages, when letters were "for the most part self-conscious, quasi-public literary documents . . . often intended to be read by more than one person even at the time they were written."[10] Although he broke in significant ways with medieval epistolary practice,[11] Petrarch necessarily maintained, even in his everyday letter writing, a similar consideration of a public audience, a consideration intensified by his awareness of the fervor to disseminate his works and his ongoing concern for his public image. Petrarch's expectations of audience for the original missives were nevertheless different from those he assumed for his planned collections. As he reworked the letters for these, he both rewrote the past and tried to sculpt his image for the future. The scattered letters, subject neither to retrospective revision nor to the heavy pressure from posterity, bear instead a more direct relationship to their immediate contemporary audience.

Beyond issues of audience, the scattered letters certainly have a different status than those Petrarch sanctified by including them in his planned collections. It is impossible to read the *Lettere disperse* without an eye to this difference and to the questions of inclusion and exclusion that such a reading elicits. This is not to ignore the warning of Alessandro Pancheri, the editor of the modern version of the *Lettere disperse*, against considering *all* the letters as the result of a "meditated gesture of repudiation."[12] But many of the most compelling *disperse* do in fact raise, more or less directly, the question of their exclusion. Indeed, the *Lettere disperse* are often interesting precisely for the light they shine on the editorial and artistic decisions that went into preparing the planned collections from which they were excluded. The lens of exclusion also brings into focus certain aspects of Petrarch's self-presentation and its alteration over time. The *Lettere disperse* might be read as part of Petrarch's messy first draft of his life, circulated in installments. In this lacuna-filled virtual manuscript—most interestingly read next to the completed manuscripts of his planned collections—we glimpse the ongoing and public process of Petrarch's self-fashioning.

For certain *disperse*, we have direct evidence that Petrarch intended to include them in his letter collections and then for various reasons eliminated them. These letters allow us to trace with a degree of specificity some of the editorial decisions that Petrarch made. We have access to such letters in the codex Marciano (M).[13] A preliminary attempt to order books 20 through 23 of the *Familiares*, prepared in the mid-1360s under the direct supervision of Petrarch,[14] the codex contains seven letters that were later excluded from the collection.[15] The apparent motivations for this exclusion were various: in one case, Petrarch seemingly eliminated a letter that was too repetitive of a nearby letter of the *Familiares*;[16] in other cases, it appears that he finally chose to eliminate certain letters or a series of letters because events that postdated the letters' composition outdated or contradicted the letters' content.[17] These *disperse* shed light on the extraordinary attention Petrarch brought to his planned collections.

In addition to the deliberate exclusion we can deduce based on manuscript evidence, we can more conjecturally propose such exclusion for certain letters based on their content. Petrarch may have chosen, for example, to exclude letters that cast him in an imperfect light. Some such letters date from his controversial eight-year stay in Milan (1353–61) as guest of the Visconti family where he wrote letters on behalf of the brothers Galeazzo and Bernabò. In the six of these letters that figure among the *Lettere disperse*, Petrarch succeeds with disturbing ease at becoming the mouthpiece for the repressive family. Such unflattering *disperse* hold a special interest since they show Petrarch as he allowed himself to be seen at certain way-stations in his life as a public intellectual. In *Lettere disperse* 36, for instance, Petrarch writes in the name of Bernabò and Galeazzo[18] to Markwart von Randek, bishop of Augsburg and imperial vicar, who as head of an anti-Viscontean league had sent a threatening letter to the brothers. Answering Markwart's threats, Petrarch railed:

> As far as we can understand it, you seem to want to terrorize us at any cost with thunder made just of wind and with the clatter of empty words, since you probably think that you're just dealing with children. But we . . . disparage your threats and all that you say, since we shiver neither at the buzzing of gnats nor at empty saber rattling.[19]

The letter brims with such violence, against a bishop and imperial representative, moreover, that some earlier critics denied it was Petrarch's; the attribution is maintained, however, by more recent scholars.[20] *Lettere disperse* 39 is similarly unsavory. In it Petrarch, writing on behalf of Bernabò, berates the friar Jacopo Bussolari, who had rallied the population of Pavia against a first and then a second Viscontean siege. Petrarch's letter acknowledges the suffering of the citizens but blames it on the friar's cruelty and not on the siege.[21] Moreover, the letter highlights not the citizens' suffering but that of the city's dogs, which Bussolari had, because of the desperate circumstances, ordered killed.[22] Some of Bussolari's actions were certainly extreme,[23] but the *dispersa* shows Petrarch rejecting the cause of the people and ignoring their suffering.[24] In the midst of his Milanese years, he assumed the position quite publicly, since this propaganda (like any) needed to be circulated widely. Retroactively, however, Petrarch chooses a different representation. The long letter to Bussolari included in the *Familiares* (29.18), though it contains perhaps harsher invective, has an extremely different overall tone because it presents itself as an exhortation to peace and is interwoven with religious and classical citations. The contrast here between the *Lettere disperse* and the *Familiares* gives us some sense for the kinds of traits Petrarch tried to highlight or downplay as he rewrote his life for posterity.

Petrarch's Milanese tenure dismayed many of the poet laureate's intellectual friends, a distress the *Lettere disperse* record by reflection as Petrarch attempts in varying ways over time to justify his choice to them.[25] In *Lettere disperse* 19, written to friends at the beginning of his stay in Milan, Petrarch explains that he was seduced into coming to Milan by the insistent pleas of Archbishop Giovanni Visconti. But he expresses ambivalence about this situation, saying that, in accepting this position, "I submitted my unaccustomed neck to the yoke."[26] In *Lettere disperse* 24, probably written a couple of months later,[27] Petrarch answers the versed appeal of Gano da Colle,[28] transmitted by a *giullare*, or minstrel, "that he leave the tyranny of the Milanese lords and move to a free land."[29] In his response, Petrarch does not justify his choice or express any ambivalence about it, but asserts that "a confusion of the facts deceives even the greatest minds."[30] He instead expresses dissatisfaction with his situation in *Lettere disperse*, from 1354,[31] where he thanks Philippe de Cabassoles for his efforts to help him return to Provence:

> you are working in fact to secure me not a common thing but the
> supreme joys of life: freedom, solitude, leisure, quiet; you are work-
> ing to secure me rest from troubles, tranquility of the mind, and fi-
> nally, to restore you and me to myself.[32]

Petrarch here obliquely but surely expresses how his Milanese life rankled him. A 1355 letter to Neri Morando (*Lettere disperse* 28)[33] hints at a similar feeling of constraint, when Petrarch asks his friend not to emulate the style of the works he is forced to write since

> When I am forced to deal with low and plebeian tasks, which I
> don't think worthy of my pen, I do not reject plebeian forms, nor
> do I devote more thought to the words than the content merits.[34]

But *Lettere disperse* 40 to Giovanni Boccaccio, written probably in 1357,[35] strikes quite a different tone. Referring to letters written to him by Zanobi da Strada and many others, all of which "intend to show that my having settled here is not in keeping with the rest of my life,"[36] Petrarch says he composed a short treatise of response.[37] He writes:

> with this I believe that it will be demonstrated to that friend (not
> to mention to those who admire me, those who love me, those who
> attack me, and those who openly want to tear me apart) how my

actions have been, I say not irreprehensible or praiseworthy, but at least tolerable and justifiable.[38]

Here Petrarch does not complain of his Milanese tenure, nor does he unambiguously embrace it, but he instead speaks of it pragmatically.[39] Differing audiences and passing time led Petrarch to discuss the issue of his Milanese years with notable variability in the *Lettere disperse,* quite in contrast to the universal perspective that the poet brought to the episode in his *Familiares.* Dotti shows, for instance, how in *Familiares* 16.12 to his dear friend Francesco Nelli, in which Petrarch responded to Nelli's and others' criticism of his Milanese stay,[40] Petrarch does not focus on the particulars of his situation but instead universalizes the discussion to talk about truth versus popular opinion. This letter, Dotti observes, acts as a sort of introduction to *Familiares* 17.10, his last discussion of the issue in the letter collection. He here vaults beyond the question of his Milanese residence to create "an exemplary moment in the life of the spirit." Framing the issue in terms of interior conflict and contrasted will and amply citing from Augustine, Petrarch "removes any possibility of bringing the discussion back to the real, but now belittled, issue. . . . Petrarch's rhetorical ability made even this biographical episode an exemplary case."[41] The interior conflict in the *Familiares,* where time is telescoped, is synchronous; in the *Lettere disperse,* which lack this temporal uniformity, the conflict emerges more unevenly from the contrasts *between* the letters, which show Petrarch's ongoing attempts to explain his Milanese life.

The shifting effects of time on Petrarch's self-presentation can be felt even more acutely in the *disperse* addressed to Cola di Rienzo. In the four *disperse* to the tribune, Petrarch avers unequivocal support of Cola's endeavors and expresses the enormous if fleeting hope for the revival of republicanism that Cola's revolution offered. The first of these (*Lettere disperse* 8) was written as soon as Petrarch received the news of Cola's ascension to power. The longest of any *dispersa,* the letter voices forceful support of the tribune's mission and elation at his success:

> But, again, what words can express a joy that is so sudden and so unexpected? With which wishes can I express the commotion of my exulting mind? I disdain the ways that have been used and I dare not find new ones.[42]

The subsequent *disperse* warn Cola of the dangers of his undertaking but express only confidence in the tribune himself, whom Petrarch terms "liberty's only champion."[43] The letter to Cola that appears in the *Familiares* (7.7), on the other hand, is a rebuke and a plea to reform after Petrarch had heard of Cola's abuses of power.[44] Petrarch questions: "Will the world then see you move from a leader of good men to a follower of reprobates?.... Yours will be eternal glory or eternal infamy."[45] This letter shows Petrarch tending toward the side of history, as he warns the Tribune against betraying the people. The letters from the *Lettere disperse*, which lack this retrospective element, show the poet swept along with the revolution's early promise. Petrarch clearly considered his original letters to Cola very public documents, given the fervor that surrounded Cola's enterprise and his own high-profile support of it; the first *dispersa* to him in fact is addressed also to the Roman people. Broadly circulated as the events were still unfolding, Petrarch designed the letters as instruments of persuasion to help the tribune to succeed.[46] The need to persuade also characterizes the letter included in the *Familiares*, but the audience to convince becomes posterity, and for this public, Petrarch distances himself from Cola's doomed endeavor and veils his own past naïveté.

In contrast to the historically significant *disperse*, the most notable temporal aspect of other *disperse* is their ephemerality. Such is *Lettere disperse* 49, to Leonardo Beccanugi, the only surviving letter of Petrarch's in Italian.[47] The affair he treats is mundane—he asks the businessman to anticipate the payment on books his representative will acquire—and his everyday register befits the matter.[48] Both its language and its commonplace subject matter made it inappropriate for the planned collections. *Lettere disperse* 23 instead seems to embody some of the transcendent and classicizing elements that Petrarch sought for the planned collections. Basing himself on the model of Horace,[49] Petrarch recounts to his friend Nelli the unwelcome visit of a garrulous friar.[50] He vivaciously sketches the visitor's verbal assault, so tiring that the poet could have gone to bed after "supping just on idle chatter."[51] He finishes the letter dispatching the duty the friar had given him: to have Nelli inform the friar's family that he had traveled safely. Petrarch quipped: "I can testify that, as far as his tongue went, he arrived here quite unharmed."[52] Petrarch's playful tone and the obvious pleasure he takes in narrating the friar's verbal excess make this perhaps the most purely entertaining of the *Lettere disperse*.[53] This letter is quite similar to *Familiares* 22.8, to Socrates, which even includes the same quote from Horace. The repetition perhaps led to this lively *dispersa*'s exclusion from a formal collection.

The *Lettere disperse* were written over thirty-five years (1338–72), and because the letters were not revised retrospectively like those for the *Fa-*

miliares or *Seniles*, they are more disjointed temporally. In many other ways the letters are *varie*, or various, as Giuseppe Fracassetti originally termed them. The *Lettere disperse* are addressed to forty-one different men,[54] quite distinct in their position and rank. Among the most powerful addressees are those Petrarch wrote on behalf of the Visconti brothers: the dauphin Charles of Valois; Cardinal Gui of Boulogne, uncle of the queen of France; Louis of Tarentum, king of Jerusalem and Sicily; and Aldobrandino III D'Este, lord of Modena and vicar of Ferrara. Other powerful addressees whom Petrarch wrote independently include Pandolfo Malatesta and Ungaro Malatesta and Pope Urban V.[55] The *Lettere disperse* also address the influential intellectual figures Johann von Neumarkt, Imperial chancellor, and Benintendi Ravagnani, grand chancellor of Venice. In contrast to these eminent men, other figures are considerably more humble, like the minstrel Malizia. Most frequent among the *Lettere disperse* are, unsurprisingly, letters to Petrarch's close friends or fellow intellectuals, including Guglielmo da Pastrengo (three letters); Giovanni Barrili (one, and a probable second); Barbato da Sulmona, dedicatee of the *Epystole*, his letters in verse (six, and a probable seventh); Nelli (three), dedicatee of the *Seniles;* Zanobi da Strada (one letter, and a probable second); Giovanni Aghinolfi (one); Boccaccio (two); Azzo da Correggio (one);[56] Ludwig Van Kempen, Petrarch's Socrates and dedicatee of the *Familiares* (one); and Francesco Bruni (six).

A handful of the addressees of the *Lettere disperse* receive a relatively large portion of these letters: the grammarian Moggio Moggi, who taught Petrarch's own son and was chancellor to Azzo da Correggio, is the addressee of seven of the letters,[57] and Barbato and Bruni, as mentioned, each of six;[58] these nineteen letters to just three individuals together constitute a quarter of the *Lettere disperse*. The efforts of at least two of these addressees to retain the correspondence from Petrarch—testified by Moggi's manuscript L, with nine autograph *disperse* or fragments thereof,[59] as well as by Barbato's avowed passion for collecting Petrarch's writing[60]—likely contributed to their heavy representation. In addition to the diligence of individual correspondents, many *disperse* probably survived because of the prominence of the individuals they addressed or the notability of the situations they discussed. Such was likely the case at least with the Viscontean letters and those addressed to Cola di Rienzo. Whether so clamorously public or more quietly so, each *dispersa* has survived to testify to what Petrarch revealed of himself to contemporaries but chose to exclude, or neglected to include, in his letters destined for posterity.

CHAPTER TWENTY-ONE

PETRARCH'S EPISTOLARY EPIC • Letters on Familiar Matters • *Rerum familiarum libri*

Giuseppe F. Mazzotta

The 350 letters composing the *Rerum familiarum libri*, or *Familiares*, were written between 1325 and 1366.[1] The event that led Petrarch to think of assembling them in one volume occurred in 1345, when he rediscovered in the Cathedral Library of Verona the corpus of letters Cicero had written to Atticus, Quintus, and Brutus. These letters, along with Seneca's *Epistles to Lucilius* gave him the impulse to compose the *Familiares* in a volume. It was meant to be taken mainly as a book of instruction for daily living.

Much like Cicero and Seneca, Petrarch throughout dispenses prescriptions about questions of ethics: the value of moderation and chastity, the rewards of friendship, rules for dining, care about the condition of faraway friends, tranquility of mind, how to contain feelings of anxiety about the flight of time, praise of the solitary life, cultivation of body and soul, appeals to peace, on how to bear grief, how to exercise virtue in the face of fortune's adversity, avoid suffering, offer consolation for death, and so forth. But because a book of ethics, a term to be understood as the art of living, can only emerge out of the texture of one's life, Petrarch includes in his collection accounts of what he himself has actually lived through. The slices of his life range from an experience, such as mountain climbing, taking walks among the ruins of the Roman Forum, or countering malevolent gossip about his personal reputation (especially the general suspicions about his purported envy toward Dante). On occasion he treats subjects that belong to the arena of politics or public discourse, such as Cola di Rienzo's quest for power that ended tragically, defenses of poetry and oratory, the need for reform of the papal Curia, or even reflections on time-honored topics such as the desirable form of the education of the prince.

Such a fluid multiplicity of topics may produce the effect of an organized incoherence, a sort of deliberate reflection of the randomness of the concerns of daily life, but it does not really forfeit the volume's rhetorical unity. For all his ramblings, Petrarch's thoughts are so intimately woven together that it is difficult to remember where one letter ends and the next begins. Several of them are stitched around a rubric (for example, the educational practices of his time, the value of eloquence or grammar). Over time, Petrarch freely rearranged many of them (by putting in the last book, say, the letter to Cicero he had written on discovering his manuscript in 1345) in order to generate connections or relationships that are not simply fortuitous or contingent. And he counters the digressiveness or apparent disconnectedness of the volume by giving it an epic framework or design. We know that originally Petrarch had conceived of writing twelve books of letters. In 1359, however, after reading through the partial translation of the *Odyssey* by Leonzio Pilato, he settled on twenty-four books. With that discovery, an epistolary epic is born, and, as such, it is marked by a number of peculiar stylistic and thematic features.

In the dedicatory letter (1.1) to the *Familiares*, which he sends to his friend Socrates (the pseudonym for Ludwig Van Kempen, a Flemish musician he had met in Avignon), Petrarch admits to a stylistic pluralism as the dominant trait of his letters. The reason for the lack of unification or for the inconsistencies of style, he says, is to be attributed to the variety of his correspondents. They are dead or alive, drawn from antiquity or contemporary life, and they include Socrates; Cicero; Seneca; Homer; Cardinal Giovanni Colonna; Robert, king of Sicily; the emperor Charles IV; Boccaccio; the doge of Venice (Andrea Dandolo); the grammarian Zanobi; the archbishops of Genoa and Prague; Guido Sette, the seneschal for the kingdom of Sicily; and his brother Gherardo, among others. They constitute a panoply or elite corps of impressive individuals, though unequal in rank. Petrarch writes,

> Indeed, the primary concern of a writer is to consider the identity of the person to whom he is writing. Only in this way can he know what and how to write, as well as other pertinent circumstances. The strong man must be addressed in one way, the spiritless one in another, the young and inexperienced one in still another, the old man who has discharged his life's duties in another, and in still another manner the person puffed up with good fortune, the victim of adversity in another, and finally, in yet another manner must be addressed the man of letters renowned for his talents and the ignoramus who would not understand anything you said if you spoke in even a slightly polished fashion.[2]

This self-conscious commonplace from what sounds like a primer of the rhetoric of letter writing sheds light on the economy of the whole volume. Petrarch draws attention to the mixed styles he deploys and urges us not to discuss them as a mere idiosyncrasy. They do not fit together in one over-arching style, and the multifariousness of the styles he exhibits makes him appear "inconsistent" and even "self-contradictory." Inconsistency, how-ever, turns into a virtue. For one thing, it signals that his styles entail a careful evaluation of or perspective on the character, power, and status of his many correspondents. By addressing them and drawing them into his confidence, they are bound to feel that they are his privileged interlocu-tors to whom he seems to open up the intimate recesses of his mind. To be sure, they are never given a voice in the text, and yet Petrarch coaxes them and coopts them as agents or coplayers in the epic battles he fights—and they are to fight with him—against his own personal detractors, his "hos-tile critics," and more generally, against the cultural and spiritual deca-dence of their times. Together, they are to join forces against their common enemies.

Petrarch calls his "inconsistency" an "expedient" that allows him to come to terms with the "infinite . . . varietates hominum" and their minds (*Familiares*, ed. Dotti, par. 29). The inconsistency he claims for himself in dealing with all sorts of people leads him to a carefully calculated writ-ing posture. His (self-consciously) ambiguous posture—a mixture of can-dor, need for complicity, and careful distance, which is appropriate to self-confessions—involves even his Socrates. Petrarch asks him not to share with anybody else the letters he sends him. They are to be kept hidden from the intrusive, "lynx-like eyes" of his other friends. Each friend is to have access to a part or fragment and not to the whole. By keeping letters and friends separate from one another, Petrarch achieves one aim: none can claim to know or to understand him completely. Only he is to enjoy an omniscient, transcendent viewpoint encompassing all styles, as well as his cohorts' partial perspectives. The outcome resembles a musical orchestra-tion where all players are assigned specific roles under his sole direction. He ranks and arrays them in an epochal war that largely takes place in his mind (in every sense of the phrase).

As befits an epic, the *Familiares* recounts a war in which the author's arguments are nothing less than weapons, and his ruses of styles are strat-egies against the enemy and friends alike. Life on earth, so does Petrarch say, is "not only a military service but like actual warfare" (*Familiares*, trans. Bernardo, 1:8–9.) Rhetoricians, when they are at their most skil-ful, act like military leaders, who, in their rhetorical strategies, know how to fight and when to retreat or conceal themselves. The overt analogy between rhetoric and war (which goes back to the *Phaedrus* and its claim that Ulysses was the inventor of rhetoric during the leisure hours of the Trojan War) surfaces but is quickly submerged as Petrarch accounts for the design of his letter collection: "as the rhetoricians and military leaders are want to place their weakest parts in the middle, so I shall give the work both a beginning and an end consisting of the most manly advice" (*Familiares*, trans. Bernardo, 1:13–14).

It may well be that the reason for such highly controlled tactics in the letters has to do with Petrarch's generalized and particular sense of danger. It prevents him from really opening himself up even to his trusted friends especially, as he adds in one apparently self-ironic aside that may betray his real thinking, when one is "unsure of how many true ones" there are. His predicament highlights his conviction that he is the lonely, beleaguered hero in a war he wages on many fronts. His heroic life, worthy of an epic hero, will be warmly recalled both like an old man's distant war memories and dark presages of new storms lying in ambush on his life.

One war, common to him and his reader, is fought against time, which, as if it were sand flowing in the hourglass, "has slipped through our fingers" (*Familiares*, trans. Bernardo, 1:3). Another war must be seen as a triumph against death. The starting point of the dedicatory letter is 1348, the year of the plague, which, of course, also triggered the writing of the *Decameron*. Against this tragic background, "which subjected us to irreparable losses" (*Familiares*, trans. Bernardo, 1:3), Petrarch longs to begin anew, to dispel the shadow of death, and to free himself from the tyranny of his own past. He tosses to the fire a pile of these writings in which he can no longer recognize himself. Like the plague, the fire destroys and yet purifies his purposes, and both show him that to destroy is the precondition for producing a new work, or using his own imagery, to embark on a new voyage.

The voyage, which is the central figure organizing the movement of the *Familiares*, can be called more an adventure than a project. Petrarch has not settled on a clear course nor does he journey "home." He has no home. If anything, the collection closes, as if in a circle, with a letter to his friend Socrates (*Familiares* 24.13), and the circular structure he imparts to the work suggests that "home" is identified by Petrarch as the ideal realm of a friendship enduring across time and space. In his intellectual biography, this last letter is not a "conclusion": it preludes the *Seniles*. In point of fact, he lives in perpetual exile, displaced, as his father was displaced from Florence, along with Dante, in 1302, neither of whom were ever allowed to return. His birth in exile (Arezzo), his continual travels among many people and through many towns (Pisa, Avignon, Bologna, Verona, etc.), and the present impossibility of reaching land cast him as the epic hero Ulysses:

> I have spent all my life, to this moment, in almost constant travel. Compare my wanderings to those of Ulysses. If the reputation of our names and of our achievements were the same, he indeed traveled neither more nor farther than I. He went beyond the borders of his fatherland when already old. . . . I experienced danger even before being born and I approached the very threshold of life under the auspices of death. . . . my father, expelled from his native city, fled with a large number of good men. From there, in my seventh month I was taken and carried throughout Tuscany . . . Our Tuscan wanderings ended in Pisa, whence I was once again snatched, this time at the age of seven, and transported by sea into France. We were almost shipwrecked by winter winds not far from Marseilles and once again I was not very far from being denied a new life on its very threshold. . . . As for how many kinds of dangers and fears I have encountered on my trips no one knows better than you except myself. I have enjoyed recalling some of this for you . . . provided I have now grown old and that even more painful things are not reserved for me in my old age.[3]

This autobiographical account, the journey of life ranging from birth to the present, signals that the *Familiares* aims at telling a coherent story of Petrarch's life and ordeals as they mirror the life of his mind. In this sense, the letters' underlying purpose is to bring literature as close to life as possible, to contain and document it. More to the point, this autobiography is couched as an epic journey or quest: just as Augustine casts his autobiographical *Confessions* as the *Aeneid* of the heart, so Petrarch's experience of homelessness comes through as an existential *Odyssey*. Like Ulysses, he visits the land of the dead (the shades of Homer, Cicero, Seneca) who turn out to be the oracles of history. Like Ulysses, companionless at the end, he faces inner demons and monsters. One term, "errores," joins the two of them. The word, etymologically from *iter*, journey, conveys the sense of the circuitousness and aimlessness of their shared misadventures, the iterative and random patterns of their minds.

Petrarch's Ulysses in the *Familiares* is neither the hero of either the Neoplatonists' *nostos* (return home) nor of the Neoplatonic Christian fathers (Saint Ambrose, Augustine's *De beata vita* [*On the Blessed Life*]) for whom the Greek hero's round trip to Ithaca figures as the allegory of the flight of the soul back to its homeland. It resembles somewhat Seneca's version of Ulysses as the emblem of the troubled mind tossed around by the winds and ills of life (*Epistle* 78.7). In addition, in Petrarch's version, Ulysses sets out from his homeland in his old age ("Ille patriae fines iam senior excessit," *Familiares*, ed. Dotti, par. 22) and, in this sense, he recalls the errors of Dante's representation of the hero.

There are two reasons, one extratextual and one textual, for this suggestion. In 1352 Boccaccio writes his biography of Dante, *Trattatello in laude di Dante*, which he dedicates to Petrarch. Boccaccio even hand delivers a copy to him in Padua as well as another one to Dante's daughter, Sister Beatrice, in Ravenna. He had met both of them in 1350, when he went to Ravenna to give ten gold florins to the nun and when, in the month of October of the same year, Petrarch visited Florence. Boccaccio paid special attention to both Petrarch and Sister Beatrice because he had something of a dream. He wanted to bring back to Florence the children of the exiles of 1302 and, to this end, he even argued that reparations be paid for the property confiscated from their parents. In the biography, Dante's peregrinations are described as if they reenact those of Ulysses.[4] Petrarch appropriates the emblem to himself. He recalls his personal odyssey and the dangers he experienced "even before being born" (*Familiares*, trans. Bernardo, 1:8). As he also recalls his father's exile from Florence (which "he fled with a large number of good men"; *Familiares*, trans. Bernardo, 1:8), he raises a pointed objection to Boccaccio's version of the myth of Ulysses. Petrarch moves in the wake of Dante's representation of the Greek hero, and in the process he gives a complex, more equivocal conception than either Dante or Boccaccio did.

Like Dante, Petrarch casts Ulysses' quest as if it were Aeneas' open journey toward the unknown. As in Dante's version, Ulysses went beyond the borders of his fatherland when already old. The conjunction between Ulysses and Aeneas (as well as Virgil and Homer) can be traced to other texts by Petrarch. See, for instance, sonnet 186 in the *Rime sparse* or *Familiares* 9.13 to Philippe de Vitry: "You who are now the sole French poet, have pity on this Ulysses or Aeneas of yours . . ." (*Familiares*, trans. Bernardo, 2:40). And if Dante makes Ulysses a rhetorician supremely aware of style, one who speaks both eloquently and covertly, but at the same time distances himself from the viciousness of the hero, Petrarch displays his own polytropic powers as he brings to the forefront of his reflections the question of style's simulations in the way the Greek hero addresses his companions. Yet, unlike Dante, for whom Ulysses dies tragically, Petrarch silences this central feature of the Dantesque myth. He gives no hint that Ulysses dies after traveling beyond the Pillars of Hercules.

Does Petrarch's silence about the deadly outcome of Ulysses' journey toward "virtue and knowledge" constitute a morality of hypocrisy or is it ignorance or just an outright rejection of Dante's reading of Ulysses? When Boccaccio equates Dante and Ulysses he knows what he is doing: he condemns both. He makes no bones that Dante, from a political perspective, was a tragic failure in that he was an exile and not a citizen. The same question can be stated differently in this manner: grandiloquence or epic narcissism about oneself aside, why does Petrarch choose to view Ulysses as the emblem of his own life?

The most direct answer is that Petrarch, for whom literature is the prism through which he looks at and understands the world, likes Ulysses because he is a literary figure. Above all, he likes him because, as a literary figure, Ulysses appears steadily in the most contradictory, shifty light. Ulysses is, at one and the same time, the multifarious, polytropic hero: both a sage under the protection of Athena and a crafty dissimulator in words and deeds. As Dante's representation in *Inferno* 26 shows, Ulysses speaks covertly, forever hidden in the tongues of fire, and yet his language attains sublime heights of rhetoric; he is the bearer of a secret knowledge (the secret of self-knowledge) but remains unknown to others, and, in the Homeric version, he keeps his identity concealed even from his wife Penelope.[5] The tradition—from Homer to Augustine, from the Neoplatonists to Seneca and Cicero (*De finibus*), to Dante and Boccaccio—has appropriately represented him in ever inconsistent ways, each account at odds with another, and each account often at odds with itself. For his part, Petrarch in his *Familiares*, where he is engaged in a literary creation of his own self in the form of a confessional self-revelation, has chosen Ulysses as a figure of himself exactly because he is both a recognizable hero and yet he remains a stubbornly enigmatic, elusive character. He is forever on his way, forever displaced, never to be fixed in time or space.

This rhetorical move is bound to puzzle us. For, in spite of his openly staged inability to live according to his best judgment and in spite of his divided will, Petrarch wants to come through, indeed he must appear to his friends as an ethical, morally reliable character. It is his only way to give credibility to his role as a moral and spiritual counselor. After all, the strong disapproval he voices of Cicero and Seneca is developed around the question of their moral inconsistencies. On the one hand, Petrarch acknowledges their moral precepts and rhetorical exemplarity for the *Familiares*. On the other hand, Cicero's letters to Atticus allow Petrarch to peek into the moods of his soul and into the unprincipled political conduct whereby he is led to disapprove of Cicero's lack of commitment to either the Roman Republic or to Octavian. By the same token, the letter Petrarch writes to Seneca (*Familiares* 24.5) praises him for his philosophical pedagogy of Lucilius and for turning philosophy into a daily practice of Stoic self-governance. At the same time, he points out that Seneca's cultivation of self never gets out of the exclusive, narrow circle of vain self-centeredness. His tragedies (pace the earlier Paduan humanists' cult of Seneca and Mussato's *Ecerinis*, who are deliberately Petrarch's polemical target) stage the failure of Senecan philosophy to lead Nero on the same path of Stoic self-knowledge treaded by Lucilius. Petrarch sees in both his authors, Cicero and Seneca, an inconsistency between the way they lead their lives and the moral claims they advance in their literature.

All the models—philosophical, rhetorical, and literary—Petrarch deploys in the *Familiares* share a selfsame fate, one on which, however, he does not dwell. Dante's Ulysses leads himself and his companions to disaster; Cicero died a death unworthy of a philosopher—his tongue and arms were cut off by Mark Antony's henchmen in his villa at Formia; Seneca was forced to commit suicide by the passions of his disciple, the tyrant Nero. Dante, as a man, is pitied for his radical political failures culminating in exile, while in the *Triumphi* these failures are retrieved as a form of visionariness and power as a love poet.

The dissimulated knowledge (or feigned ignorance) of the tragic fate of these fictional and real figures is flanked by the explicit acknowledgment of exile as the harsh punishment arbitrarily inflicted by Florence's democratic government on his own father and on himself even before being born. It expresses itself as fear of the tyrants who rule the cities. It comes through openly as a "war" to be waged against his critics, and even as a fear that his own friends may not be altogether trusted with his shadowy secrets. Such a historical background—of future fears and memory of wrongs he has suffered—triggers in Petrarch the need for a politics of writing, which is dramatized as a care in subjecting his letters to a prudent rhetorical discipline whereby he both reveals and veils his deeper purposes. From this point of view, the *Familiares* marks the birth of what later will be known as a practice of simulations and dissimulations.[6] One image from an Ovidian fable in *Familiares* bends the intrinsically double discourse of literature into the horizon of a hazy, intellectually ambivalent political discourse. Letter 1.1 dramatizes Petrarch's strategy through the image of the spider. This is the context of the reference. In a mock-epic tone, Petrarch describes how, as he was searching through his dusty writings, "a spider enemy of Pallas attacked me for doing the work of Pallas" (*Familiares*, trans. Bernardo, 1:3). The reference is clear. In book 6.5–145 of the *Metamorphoses*, Ovid tells the artistic contest between Minerva and Arachne. Arachne rejects the tyrannical rule of the gods and weaves on her tapestry the stories of their impieties (especially Jupiter's disguises and trickeries). Pallas Minerva (or Athena), the goddess of weaving and of the mighty intellect, first, disguises herself as an old woman to appeal to Arachne's piety and, later, punishes Arachne's transgression of undermining the authority of the gods. Minerva turns Arachne into a spider doomed forever to spin its fragile threads. For Petrarch, Ovid's narrative weaves an esthetic-political tale that he keeps in mind (though, ironically in terms of his own safety from Augustus and future exile on the Black Sea, Ovid himself did not).

Petrarch begins by siding with the tyrannical goddess Pallas against the enemy-spider. By the end of the letter (which is predictably described as a coming ashore) he wishes farewell to his Socrates and recalls once again the fable of Arachne. He shifts his perspective and expresses the desire that he were Arachne: "these letters, therefore, woven with multi-colored threads, if I may say so, are for you. However, if I were to enjoy a steady abode . . . I would weave on your behalf a much more noble and certainly a unified web or tapestry" (*Familiares*, trans. Bernardo, 1:14).[7] No doubt, the myth of Penelope, the artful weaver and the stable center of the *Odyssey*, looms behind the myth of Arachne. Penelope is the object of Ulysses' quest, and so, her oblique recall gives a formal coherence to the epic structure of the *Familiares*. One might add that the figure catches the distinctive trait of Petrarch's voice: he casts himself as simultaneously the subject and the object of his own quest, simultaneously as Ulysses and as Penelope. He is both the starting point and the point of arrival of his reflections. But because Petrarch highlights the tragic fate of Arachne (and silences Penelope), the passage also shows Petrarch's genuine concerns, his sense of the necessity to speak with a double voice. The issue for him is not, as it was for Ulysses, to come home. It is to take cover from the possible violence of the gods of the city, be they popes, the despots and the tyrants who are his patrons and who are likely to have the principles of their own authority violated by the poet's sovereign claims.

The desire to speak with one voice, to live a coherent life, and to weave a seamless story lingers on even as he ends up acknowledging that tyrannical gods and artists alike disguise themselves. They speak the truth, as it were, by lying. The gods hide their misdeeds. The artist, such as Arachne, tells the truth about the gods through art and, unlike the goddess, she loses her life but retains her art. By the end of the letter, Petrarch, who began by siding with Pallas, ends up in Arachne's camp. He will lie to protect his life, his status, and his power, and his power fantasies from the gods of the city—and he knows that only by creating himself as a character in fiction will he really survive in every sense.

All this talk about simulation and lies does not mean that Petrarch is not an authentic artist. To be authentic, we might say by a spin on Dante's etymology of "auctor" from "autentin" (to be worthy of faith; *Convivio* 4.6.3–6), is to be the author of one's own acts.[8] The *Familiares* is an authentic work, a way for Petrarch to imagine the possibility that kings, lords, teachers, poets, chancellors, and cardinals will heed his advice; that he, like an epic hero, could throw his very friends to the fire; and that his subterfuges, like Penelope's secret steady weaving and unweaving to hold at bay her suitors, will circumvent the harassment of his patrons. Petrarch is authentic in that he can imagine a world alternate to the existing one and he can conceive a grand project of culture, such as the one dreamed up by his real model, Varro, who was Caesar's librarian.

The empire of culture Petrarch envisions is, in its universalizing impulse, Roman, but it is not Rome. The final twenty-fourth book of the collection takes us to the familiar territory of the classical Roman tradition. Introduced by a letter to Philippe, bishop of Cavaillon (*Familiares* 24.1), made of distant echoes and aphorisms on the existential sense of time, on time and mortality as inward dimensions of life, the book shifts its focus and records letters to Cicero, Seneca, Varro, Quintilian, Livy, Asinius Pollio, Horace, Virgil, and Homer (which contains a quick reference to Penelope and Ulysses and, more importantly, a quite traditional comparison between Virgil and Homer in favor of Virgil). The book ends, as stated above, with a letter to Petrarch's friend, Socrates. Taken in its entirety, the book, which contains an eloquent summing-up of his understanding of the deeper elements of the classical tradition, is governed by its own inner logic.

Against the background of time as a subjective experience of ruptures (and the casting of the self through Horace's self-transparent figure of Postumus), the classical tradition, toward which he acknowledges his indebtedness, provides the framework of a continuity transcending and countering the radically timebound limitations of the self. Roman culture was established and founded by this series of thinkers as much as by the power of Rome's armies. But this history of Roman culture is never idealized. It is now damned to a ghostlike existence. And it is marked by tensions and rifts, such as the one between Quintilian and Seneca, who, in spite of their common origin, hate each other, or the one between Caesar and

Varro, respectively the figure of political power and the intellectual, or the relation between poets (Virgil and Homer), in which the successor fails to acknowledge the decisive import of his predecessor. Seen in this light, the final letter to Socrates clarifies Petrarch's strategy: it defines him in his existential solipsism, inexorably part of the world of devouring time. The idea of time's rifts triggers in him the conviction that the fate of present culture depends on him.

The empire of culture he conceives, incarnated in the classical and Christian branches of the tradition, needs no geographical boundaries and yet is run in his name by his tight circle or international intellectual elites. It is the empire of culture as he articulates it in his *Collatio laureationis*. From this standpoint, the *Familiares* remains the key text in Petrarch's canon because it introduces us to his extraordinarily lucid and self-conscious plan and yet shadowy, secretive project of cultural politics. This cultural project comes through by necessity under the cover of an ethical text. But the veil is subtle. It is so subtle that it did not keep Machiavelli from seeing with his sharp, lynx-like eyes the politics underlying Petrarch's ostensible discourse. Like a true kindred spirit, he does not fail to acknowledge Petrarch's poetry as he closes off the *Prince*.

CHAPTER TWENTY-TWO

LETTERS OF OLD AGE • Love Between Men, Griselda, and Farewell to Letters • *Rerum senilium libri*

David Wallace

It was in 1361, as his fifty-seventh birthday came and went, that Petrarch conceived of two further epistolary collections to complement his *Epistole familiares*, or "letters on familiar matters." The first would gather together letters already written (a plan never systematically realized, although many letters survive outside the two main collections); the other, consisting of letters not yet composed, would take its name from Petrarch's advancing old age. The *Seniles*, as this collection is called, consists of 128 letters (as compared to the 350 of the *Familiares*); *Seniles* 16.3, written in 1372, tells us that Petrarch has excluded a thousand other letters from his two collections for want of room.[1] Letters of the *Seniles* are artfully disposed in eighteen books (seventeen plus the concluding *Letter to Posterity*). Nine letters written after 1361 were actually assigned to the *Familiares*, and three letters written before this date were assigned to *Seniles*.[2] Once a particular letter was chosen as a candidate for *Seniles*, it was subjected to polishing and revision that ranged from minor amendment to wholesale rewriting. In seven instances it is possible to compare the final *Seniles* form of a letter with its earlier state as routine missive. *Seniles* 6.6, for example, reworks a letter originally sent to Zanobi da Strada in 1358. The earlier form denounces Zanobi for abandoning the life of letters (he was crowned laureate at Pisa in 1355, much to Boccaccio's disgust) to become a papal secretary. The later form treats him more gently (actually suppressing his name); Zanobi had in any event died in 1361.[3] Some letters in *Seniles* were very likely written for the collection itself (that is, never sent out to a particular addressee). Some longer letters were split up, and other, shorter letters were fused together. *Seniles* does in general observe a chronological order of composition, with book 1 assigned to 1361–62 and book 17 to 1373–74, but chronology within books is less consistent.[4] *Seniles* 13 contains the greatest number of letters (18), whereas *Seniles* 7 (addressed to Pope Urban V) stands dramatically alone.

Seniles bears witness to an extensive and intricate network of correspondence, spanning much of Europe and attesting to Petrarch's status as the preeminent scholar and cultural personality (much courted by princes) of his age. It has proved a difficult text to study, given the absence of a complete modern edition; the manuscript tradition is complex, and it is still necessary to refer to the first complete printed edition of 1501 (and its derivatives).[5] Matters are just now set to improve, however, given the critical edition of Elvira Nota (which began appearing in 2002).[6] Many of the themes explored in free-standing treatises—such as the benefits of country living, and the need for solitude—are rehearsed in the letters; there are glimpses of great figures (such as painter Simone Martini, 1.6), animadversions on the follies of jousting ("we never read that Scipio or Caesar went in for this," *Seniles* 11.13), and a chillingly classicizing account of Tartar slaves at Venice.[7] There is a continuous sense of the vagaries of warfare and especially of plague (treated in quick succession in *Seniles* 13.10 and 11), with accompanying concern for the welfare of friends. In 1364 Petrarch had written to his friend Luchino dal Verme on behalf of the doge of Venice, urging him to assume command of Venetian forces and crush a rebellion on Crete. Luchino complied, and victory was won (*Seniles* 4.1 and 4.2); Petrarch was subsequently obliged to sit through several days of celebratory jousting at Venice. In 1366, Petrarch wrote again to Luchino, urging his return from another military expedition—this time "against the Assyrians" (that is, the Turks: *Seniles* 8.4). Petrarch professes "a strange, unwonted fear" and proves prophetic when Luchino dies at Constantinople; the next letter in the *Seniles* sequence, written to his son Giacomo, expresses profound regret. The pain of physical absence is expressed most eloquently by the brief *Seniles* 8.4: "return to us and please hurry," Petrarch implores Luchino, "every day of waiting is longer than a year. To the eyes of those who love you," he pleads, "give back the light we are yearning for" (289). Absence is, of course, the enabling condition of every letter; "the urge for friendship" is, as Nicholas Mann suggests, "perhaps the most salient characteristic of the correspondence and the man behind it."[8] The man Petrarch loved most, and to whom he dedicates most letters in the *Seniles*, is Giovanni Boccaccio.

Eighteen letters in *Seniles* are addressed to Boccaccio; they run as follows: 1.5, 2.1, 3.1, 3.2, 3.5, 3.6, 5.1, 5.2, 5.3, 6.1, 6.2, 8.1, 8.8, 15.8, 17.1, 17.2, 17.3, and 17.4.[9] As Petrarch himself observes to Boccaccio, the most important things tend to come first and last (17.3; p. 655); Boccaccio leads off five of the first eight books as addressee and rounds off the eighth. After *Seniles* 8.8, however, Boccaccio fades from the scene: no further letters are addressed to him until *Seniles* 15.8 (from the period 1369–73). For some of the intervening period, Boccaccio and Petrarch have actually been together (so no letters could be expected): but the long absence of the *primo amico* from the heart of *Seniles* makes the resumption of *Seniles* 15.8 seem all the more poignant. Why, Boccaccio wants to know, has Petrarch not written? "Well," Petrarch responds, "health left me along with you; I was never well after that, and I have a feeling I shall never again be well" (582). These hints of a lover suffering *amor hereos* (lovesickness) in the absence of his beloved[10] are reinforced by the perhaps-tearful reproach of the concluding lines:

> I must add that, as I was saddened and put out with you for sneaking away, and reproaching myself and perhaps weeping too, I congratulate you upon returning safe and sound. Farewell. (583)

In book 17 of *Seniles*, however, Boccaccio makes a grand and definitive return. Every letter in the book is addressed to him and responds to his work—both his own epistles, and his history or tale of Griselda. Yet this return is poignant. The Petrachan Griselda story can be read, I shall argue, as a farewell to imaginative writing, and as a door closing on the most intense and sustained relationship of Petrarch's life: his liaison not with Laura but with Boccaccio. The Griselda story has been much studied outside Italy, most notably because of its translation (with the help of French intermediary texts) to Chaucer's *Canterbury Tales*.[11] Chaucer merits mention in this volume because he honors Petrarch as Petrarch would want to be honored: as he who, "with his rethorike sweete/ Enlumyned al Ytaille of poetrie."[12] This essay, however, brackets out Chaucer as far as possible to consider quite how Petrarch's Latin tale reads within the general economy of Petrarch's life and writing. More specifically, Petrarchan Griselda is read as part of the penultimate book of *Seniles*: the book where, indeed, Petrarch bids adieu both to letter writing and to the friendships it has long sustained. Fittingly, then, having taken the Griselda story from the end of Boccaccio's greatest vernacular work, the *Decameron*, he will use it to make an end to his own epistolary oeuvre; his *Posteritati* will follow as book 18, and the rest is silence.

The Griselda story, which ran and ran through centuries of European storytelling, poetry, drama, opera, painting, matrimonial advice manual, and pageant, has been exhaustively analyzed as a rolling confabulation all about women (or one exemplary woman) and her sufferings at the hands of despotic, marital, masculine authority. Here, however, I read this *his-*

toria or *fabula,* as Petrarch tells it, as a text between men. Of course, relations "between men" (following Eve Sedgwick's famous formulation) have long been negotiated through traffic in women.[13] In such an arrangement, a woman may feature as ostensible love object, but her narrative function is to forge greater bonds (excite greater love) between the men competing over her; mere female presence generally keeps intense male-male relations within heterosexual bounds. Such triangles may be deployed to grandly allegorical (yet still erotic) effect. Most famously, Boccaccio's much-imitated tale of Roman Titus and Greek Gisippus "solves" the love of Rome for Greece—thus confirming the translation of Greek culture to Rome—by having a woman, Sofronia, pass between them.[14] Petrarchan Griselda, however, operates a little differently: for she is not so much a woman moving "between men" (although famously "translated," she is yet more than a go-between) as she is protagonist of a narrative designed to exclude women altogether.[15]

Decameron 10.10, appearing in the *lingua materna,* is expressly framed for the reading pleasure and possible censure of women; *Seniles* 17.3, however, is not. In concluding his tale, Petrarch deliberately claims that he has elected to retell Boccaccio's story in "stilo alio": another style. Possibly, as in a handful of manuscripts (including, it seems, Chaucer's) this might read "stilo alto," "high or elevated style"; in both cases, this means Latin.[16] Petrarch claims that his tale has no designs upon the women of modern Italy, makes no demand for amendment of wifely behaviors.[17] His words are entirely addressed to *legentes* (readers [330]) who presumably share the masculine gender of the five historical men already implicated in the tale-telling itself: these are (we learn from *Seniles* 17.4) Boccaccio, author of the source tale and addressee of the Petrarchan revision; Petrarch himself; a Paduan friend of both these men, who proves to be a weepy reader; a friend of this friend, who carries on reading when he breaks down; and another friend ("just as we have other things in common," Petrarch tells Boccaccio, "so we have friends") from Verona.[18] Since men are the only anticipated readers of and commentators upon this tale, men or males (as upon the Elizabethan Shakespearean stage) play all the parts. There are female characters, most famously Griselda, but the high walls of Latinity and of highly restricted textual circulation tacitly invite these learned men to occupy every subject position within the tale world; and also, I would suggest, to move from one subject-position to another, to be by turns Walter, Griselda, and sometimes, almost, God, the all-seeing purveyor of *historia,* the *auctor* behind or before every *auctor.*[19]

In taking up Petrarch's claim that *Seniles* 17.3 makes no claim for feminine attention I am not suggesting that his famous letter makes no difference to, has no implications for, the lives of historical women. The studied exclusion of Petrarch's male-networked, Latinate narration performs powerfully gendered, social work. Chaucer, in effect, points this out by undoing the Petrarchan strategy, revernacularizing Griselda and dialoguing her *makere*, an Oxford clerk, against the mightiest of all mother tongue rhetors, the Wife of Bath.[20] Here, however, I wish to consider *Seniles* 17.3 within its own, very particular, textually localized parameters: the *hortus inclusus* of humanist Latin. My contention is that the Petrarchan Griselda story is indeed all about love, loyalty, and the trials and tribulations of marriage: chiefly those of his lifelong liaison with Giovanni Boccaccio and the shared pleasures of narration.

At the beginning of *Seniles* 17, in the first, short letter, Petrarch makes it clear to Boccaccio that he is only able to write the letter immediately following (he is only able to indulge in narrative dilation) because a space for *otium* or leisure has unexpectedly opened up: a friend has taken pity on him, relieving him from the task of copying out a previous letter ("crawling with erasures"), and so he snatches up his pen again, "more on impulse than reflection" (643). It is 1373: Petrarch is in his seventieth year, and old age is much on his mind. Or rather, upon Boccaccio's mind, since Giovanni has suggested, in an earlier letter, that the ageing laureate should slow down a bit. *Seniles* 17.2 takes vigorous issue with this suggestion. Petrarch and Boccaccio thus go at it, within the closeted intimacy of epistolary space, like an old married couple. "If just one bed is our bedroom," Petrarch says, "it would easily accommodate two beings of one mind, and be a trusty mediator of our sleep and our worries" (646). And yet Boccaccio has said things to Petrarch, Petrarch says a bit later, "which, unless you loved me a great deal, and unless I knew that you were truly another me, would make me believe I was being fooled and mocked. But now I feel that it is not I being fooled by you," he continues, "but you by love" (647). The register shifts again, a bit later, when Petrarch, the Wife of Padua, returns to berating Boccaccio for thinking of him too highly: "I thought there was never anyone who knew me better than you did"; and I, Petrarch adds (hilariously) am "rudis homuncio," an uncultured weakling of a man.[21] Eventually they come to the favorite topic of ageing married people: who gets to die first. "I wish to die while you are alive and well," Petrarch says, "and to leave behind some in whose memory and words I may live, by whose prayers I may be helped, by whom I may be loved and missed."[22] It is not, I think, extravagant to consider Petrarch and Boccaccio toiling, sparring, and loving one another in bonds suggestive of matrimony: for as

Alan Bray demonstrates in his wonderful book, *The Friend*, suggestions of marriage between men, and the imagining of the various ritual forms and casual expressions that this might take, formed a relaxedly familiar part of medieval consciousness.[23] Familiar and public: for the *Seniles* project is designed to address a discerning, internationalized society of initiates. As Bray remarks, "the principal difference between the friendship of the modern world and friendship I describe in this book is that . . . friendship was significant in a public sphere" (2).

Petrarch, we know from annotations in his personal copy of the text, was a sympathetic and sometimes convulsed reader of Abelard's *Historia calamitatum*. At a point where Abelard describes falling off his horse, Petrarch writes "et me, nocte."[24] There is much mysterious noting of dates and sorrowful exclamation in this volume, perhaps to be associated with Petrarch's own struggles with, as he saw it, sins of the flesh.[25] The letter exchange between Abelard and Heloise is famously that between hard logic and humane letters (although Abelard does suggest, in opening his *Historia*, that he is shifting to Heloise's softer discursive ground).[26] Chaucer, we have noted, commends Petrarch as he who illuminates all Italy with his "sweet rhetoric"; and Petrarch, famously, had limited patience for logicians. In *Seniles* 17, however, Petrarch assumes the harder-edged gendered position in countering Boccaccio's arguments: he plays Abelard to Boccaccio's Heloise, a division of roles supported by the oft-remarked obesity of the ageing Giovanni.[27] *Seniles* 17 casts Boccaccio, like Heloise, as fleshly, querulous, jealous of his beloved's time, worried about his beloved's health, vainglorious about his beloved's ever-spreading fame. The Boccaccio-Petrarch relationship, beginning at midlife, proves lifelong, and life-changing: for just as the *Decameron* is bringing Boccaccio to the very peak of his artistic powers, Petrarch induces Boccaccio to renounce this world of vernacular fiction by inclaustrating himself (not to strain the Heloise parallel too far) in the more austere, world-fleeing environment of Latin encyclopedism. In later years, long after the famous meeting of 1351, Boccaccio and Petrarch sustain their relationship through the highly tactile medium of epistolary exchange. By the end of *Seniles* 17, however, Petrarch is looking to end both this long liaison through letter writing and the kind of writing for pleasure that he still definitively associates with Boccaccio.

Seniles 17.3, the Griselda story, follows immediately after (logically enough) 17.2, the epistle setting forth Petrarch's refusal to slow down in old age, as Boccaccio has requested. "Farewell," that letter ends, "remember me, and live happily, and persist *manfully*" (654; "Tu vale, mei memor, et vive feliciter ac *viriliter* persevera," 1158, emphasis added). *Seniles* 17.3

opens with Petrarch remembering the *Decameron,* that "book you produced in our mother tongue long ago, I believe, as a young man."[28] The last story in particular, Petrarch says, has long delighted him—"it nearly made me forget myself"—and he has decided (again, following a momentary impulse) to translate it, "something I would not readily have undertaken for anyone else. I was drawn by love for you," Petrarch says, "and for the story" (656).[29] The story itself begins with extended geographical description, ranging over chains of mountains, the course of a mighty river and its numerous tributaries, and the disposition of a "lovely plain" and its surrounding hills and mountains. None of this was to Chaucer's liking: his Clerk of Oxenford calls it "a thing impertinent," a pointless delay of the business of storytelling. But this too, I would suggest, forms part of the Petrarch-Boccaccio complex and of "my love for you" that Francesco has just expressed to Giovanni: for Boccaccio is famous as, precisely, a Latinate geographer, author of works such as the exhaustively titled *De montibus, silvis, fontibus, lacubus, fluminibus . . . maribus.*[30] Geography is an issue of more particular importance in this letter, however: for the space mapped out neighbors Lombardy, the territory upon which Petrarch served Visconti princes, or despots, during the most intensive phase of his political life.[31] Such service is clearly on Petrarch's mind in this penultimate book of the *Seniles:* in 17.2 he actually tots up all the months he "lost" (Petrarch's word) "at the princes' bidding" (650).[32] Boccaccio, as lifelong loyalist to the Florentine Republic, did not spend a day in the service of Lombard despots (or, in Florentine parlance, tyrants); the northern tyrant of *Decameron* 10.10 is given short shrift as the perpetrator of (in his treatment of Griselda) "una matta bestialità."[33] Petrarch's treatment of the same tyrannous tale is altogether more ambivalent, reflecting both those lyrical paradoxes and ambivalences for which he is famed and his awkward status as celebrity-in-residence at the Visconti court. For in *Seniles* 17.3 Petrarch seems at once, or by turns, to be both the protagonists, Walter and Griselda. He is Walter in that he *invents* Boccaccio's mother tongue tale as Walter finds Griselda (remembering that "invention" retains the Latinate kernel of *invenire,* to come across). Petrarch then translates Boccaccio's tale to the world by (as he says) "changing its garment" (to something more beautiful) much as Walter translates Griselda from peasant hovel to princely palace, revealing her inner beauties to the world—visible only to him, as a man of extraordinary insight—by laying gorgeous clothes and ornaments upon her.[34] In all this, then, Petrarch implicitly claims a kind of parity with the Lombard princes he served, consigning Boccaccio to the Griseldian subject position. In the previous letter, Petrarch had boldly claimed that "I was with the princes in name, but in fact the princes were with me" (650).[35] He also takes occasion to remind Boccaccio that "we are not equal in merit" (646).[36] Elsewhere in his epistolary oeuvre, however, Petrarch was pleased to imagine himself into Griseldian positions. Had it not been for one great prince grabbing his bridle at just the right minute, he says in one letter, he would have fallen right over a cliff to perdition.[37] And at the foundational moment of his seduction into Visconti patronage, he found his own powers of volition quite flooded out, surrendered to the will of the prince: "I blushed and remained silent," he says in *Familiares* 16.12; "and by doing so I consented or seem to have consented. There was nothing, or at least I could find nothing, to say against it."[38]

Such a position of surrendered will returns us to Griselda and those moments at which her very acceptance of abject circumstances is to be appreciated as formidable strength. In *Seniles* 17.2, Petrarch had censured Boccaccio for his ceaseless whining about being poor, urging him to think of someone exemplary who enters princely service and is not at all deterred by harsh and vicious treatment. When we first glimpse Griselda in 17.3 she is living a life of eclogue-like simplicity, eating scraps of food, always hard up, knowing no pleasure, expecting no luxury or ease: but enclosing within "her maiden heart . . . a brave and wise spirit" (658). The Latin is worth attending to here: "sed virilis *senilis*que animus virgineo latebat in pectore" (302; emphasis added). The qualities to be discerned, publicized, and imitated in Griselda, then, are not just manlike, but senile: or, translating more sympathetically, those qualities of mature wisdom that the Petrachan *Seniles* are attempting to gather. And, like the ever-industrious Petrarch of *Seniles* 17.2, the virtuous Griselda is determined never to "tire" (quoting from 17.3) "or to slow down, as long as there is any breath left in me" (666).[39]

The urge to allegorize such a complex tale leads inevitably to profusion and confusion: multiple moralizings (as at the end of Chaucer's "Clerk's Tale"), and no final sense of what *that* was all about. The tale's resistance to allegoresis stems in part from the inadequacy of one-to-one identifications: Walter is God; Walter is a tyrant; Walter is a trecento humanist employed by despots. Within the restricted, all-male environs of this tale world, I am suggesting, any one man can play all the parts, imagine himself into all the subject positions: Petrarch is Walter and Boccaccio, Griselda; Galeazzo Visconti is Gualtieri di Saluzzo and Petrarch is simple-hearted, poor-living Griselda, and so on. All this becomes clearer, I think, when the tale is read within the run of letters in *Seniles* 17 and, of course, within the greater span of Petrarch's life and work. To complete this span, however, we need to see what happens in *Seniles* 17. 4 and to note the heavy curtain that descends as *Seniles* 18.

In 17.4, the ringing resolution never to tire, sounded by Petrarch to Boccaccio in 17.2 and by Griselda to Walter in 17.3, finally loses conviction. For whereas Griselda may conceal senile virtues in her young maiden breast, Petrarch (now, in 1373) actually *is* old, inside and out. Petrarch's letters to Boccaccio, it seems, are not getting through: they are being intercepted by border guards, anxious to find any scrap of praise with which to flatter the "aures asininas," the "donkey ears" of their political masters.[40] "Of course, to this annoyance," Petrarch tells Boccaccio, "is added my age and weariness (*aetas et lassitudo*) with almost everything, and I have not only had my fill of writing, I am sick of it" (670). All this means, Petrarch tells his "dear friend," that this letter represents "a last farewell, in order that flimsier scribblings (that is, letters like the ones they have long shared) "not to the end hinder me, as they have long done, from more worthwhile study." Petrarch then adds, as an afterthought: "if ever I need to write to you or to others, I shall write so as to be understood but not to amuse myself" (671). Which is to say: *Seniles* 17.3, the Griselda story, stands as the last example of recreational or amusing narrative that Petrarch intends to write; his translation of *Decameron* 10.10 (pinned firmly on Boccaccio as "auctor") marks the end of pleasurable storytelling. It also marks the end of the long liaison, the love affair, with Boccaccio: for in *Seniles* 18, Petrarch imagines himself already dead, speaking to us directly from beyond the grave: "Francesco Petrarca. Posteritati. Salutem."[41]

Petrarch's strategy of bringing his lengthy and varied corpus of writing to an end records that of another writer active in Italy in this same year of 1373: Geoffrey Chaucer. In Fragment 9 of his *Canterbury Tales*, Chaucer takes leave of fiction making with a short tale of Apollo and his caged, mellifluously talkative bird (clearly a surrogate poet figure);[42] in fragment 10 he invites us to scrub up nice with the *Parson's Tale*, a prose treatise on the seven deadly sins. The Paduan scholars who located and disseminated the *Seniles* after Petrarch's death found seventeen books in good order, with the promise of "Posteritati" to come: but this last, heavy curtain letter—written in large part before 1350—lay among Petrarch's foul papers, covered in amendments and erasures and not yet ready to see the light.[43] The true and considered leave-taking of *Seniles*, most appropriate for this volume at its finale, is thus the very last paragraph of *Seniles* 17.4. Here we learn, finally, that Petrarch's resolution to give up speaking with his much-loved Boccaccio, and with us, has been achieved only with the greatest wistfulness and regret. The concluding passage of this letter is every bit as self-questioning and tumultuous, until the invocation of Cato finally calms things down, as anything in Petrarch's lyric poetry. "I recall," he tells Boccaccio,

> . . . that in a certain letter of this series that I had promised from now on to be briefer in my letter writing, prompted by the lack of time, which is running out. But I did not want to keep the promise; and, as I am given to understand, it is much easier to be silent with friends than brief. So great is the zest for conversing, once we have begun, that it would be easier not to have begun than to curb the onrush of a conversation that has begun; but I did promise. Yet, is not a promise kept when one does more than was promised? When I promised, I believe, I had forgotten those words of Cato in Cicero which are widely known, to the effect that old age is more loquacious by its very nature. Farewell, friends. Farewell, letters.[44]

PART VII

EPILOGUE

CHAPTER TWENTY-THREE

TO WRITE AS ANOTHER:
THE TESTAMENT • *Testamentum*

Armando Maggi

I, Francesco Petrarca, have written this, who would have drawn up a different
testament if I were rich, as the mad rabble believes me to be.[1]

This is the final sentence of Petrarch's *Testamentum* (*Testament*). Its "jarring" tone and hypothetical, convoluted phrasing is a revealing commentary on the entire text.[2] Rather than celebrating in the name of Christ
a conclusive reconciliation with those he despised throughout his life (the
"vulgus"), Petrarch posits his irredeemable and resentful difference as
the mark of his identity. This disconcerting conclusion also alludes to a
hiatus between imagination and reality, between hypothetical and objective beliefs. Along with the testament he has just penned, the poet could
have written another testament, if he had been another person, the wealthy
intellectual the populace wrongfully believes he is. The poet seems to be
inviting those who will read his text to imagine a second and radically
different will, which reflects an alternative, and inexistent, Petrarch. The
dialogue between two opposite identities, between memory and imagination, informs the entire *Testamentum*.

Far from being only a brief legal document the poet wrote before departing for a demanding journey, the *Testamentum* is Petrarch's final and
truly unforgettable self-portrait according to the medieval model of *imitatio
Christi*. Essential motifs of this religious tradition such as the condemnation of the body and the embracement of complete poverty and humility
converse with some of Petrarch's other recurrent themes, such as his fierce
denigration of the "vulgus" (populace) in opposition to the private dialogue
with "learned" friends. As we shall see, its ideal nature becomes even more
apparent if we compare it to Boccaccio's sparse and modest will, which
he wrote on August 28, 1374. Unlike Petrarch's, Boccaccio's testament expresses the writer's heartfelt concern for his family members, friends, and

his faithful servant. If, as Jacques Chiffoleau argues in his seminal work on medieval and early modern death rituals, a will also serves to protract the deceased's presence in his family and to maintain its peace and cohesion, Petrarch's *Testamentum* speaks of a man isolated in his ideal self-construction, which for better or worse mediates all his human relationships.[3]

The original of the *Testamentum* is lost. As Mommsen explains in the introductory essay to his edition, the text "must have been presented as evidence in the course of the protracted litigation between the cathedral chapter of Padua and Francescuolo da Brossano which concerned the endowment of Petrarch's anniversary mass."[4] Apart from a fifteenth-century copy now held at the Biblioteca Civica of Trieste, none of the subsequent printed versions claims to be a faithful reproduction of the original. Its *editio princeps* was published in Venice by Bernardino De' Vitali circa 1499/1500. Lodovico Dolce first translated the text into Italian in his edition of *Il Petrarca* in 1557.

The poet composed his *Testamentum* in Padua on April 4, 1370, only four years before his death. He wished to travel to Rome to celebrate the return of Pope Urban V to the Eternal City. Although the pontiff had reestablished his residence in Rome three years earlier, Petrarch's physical condition had prevented him from embarking on this journey until the first months of that year. It turned out, however, that his health was still very precarious, because shortly after his departure for Rome at the end of April 1370, he fell seriously ill in Ferrara. His doctors suggested that he return to Padua, whence he informed the pontiff of his health problems. In his famous epistle to Urban V, Petrarch offers a dramatic account of his sudden malady or "syncope":

> I started out with such alacrity as had never, I believe, marked the beginning of any other journey. But my alacrity was of the spirit only. My body was still weak and ill, and I put my faith in the help of Heaven. And so it happened that on the way my desire to reach your presence led me to make greater haste than was fitting for my lack of strength and for my age; and suddenly death halted me . . . Nor was it merely illness, but true death. Others may say that only through poetic fiction or through undue exaggeration could one give the name of death to a malady or a syncope . . . All I can say is that for more than thirty hours I was unconscious.[5]

A seemingly modest writing, his *Testamentum* corresponds to one of the most arduous and painful moments of the poet's life. Its composition actually preceded a first "true death," since, as Petrarch writes to the pope, he lay unconscious "for more than thirty hours." We will see that in the *Testamentum* Petrarch imagines multiple deaths and multiple burials. His attempt to dominate his own death in order to turn it into the final chapter of his ideal self-portrait is apparent in this epistle, where death "halted" him while he was trying to reach the pontiff. Petrarch's rendition of that unfortunate incident hints at the final battle between the forces of evil (death) and his soul's deep longing for the sacred (the pontiff). And again, like the "mad rabble" at the end of his will, "others" may deny him this first death experience and, as a consequence, would also question the religious significance he saw in it. Petrarch is aware of the tension between brute reality (what "others" see) and his ideal reading, which is "fictional" only if we fail to read it within the larger scope of the poet's ideal biography. The act of composing his testament evidently responded to the sense of emergency that accompanies a terminally ill person, even if the fatal illness is nothing but advanced age and the imminent risk is a laborious journey from northern Italy to Rome.

The *Testamentum* is a short text. In his edition, Theodor Mommsen divides it into thirty-three succinct paragraphs, which open with a fairly long prefatory section (para. 1) followed by an introductory sentence where the poet peremptorily announces his conscious decision to lay out his last will ("Volo igitur hanc meam ultimam voluntatem ordinare," I want, therefore, to draw up this last will of mine), and ends with the above final commentary on the other testament he would have written had he been another person.[6] The uniqueness of this will appears from the first sentence of the preamble: "I have often reflected on a matter concerning which no one can reflect too much and only a few reflect enough, namely, the last things and death." The insistence on the verb "to reflect" (*cogitans, cogitant*) exceeds the formulaic expressions typical of fourteenth-century testaments. Samuel Cohn traces how in the late Middle Ages "the testamentary preambles changed over time."[7] By the late trecento wills often include clichéd Latin expressions about the incertitude of life in opposition to the certainty of death ("Cum nichil sit certius morte et nil hora mortis repariatur incertius") and the importance of composing a will while still in good mental health, given that no one can foresee the moment of one's death. These two basic themes are also present in the opening section of Petrarch's *Testamentum*, but they are inserted in an infinitely more personal formulation. Petrarch shifts the emphasis from these basic themes to the act of "reflecting" upon them, that is, on his individual appropriation of their urgent significance. The second sentence of the preamble reiterates the crucial value of "such reflection" (*cogitatio*) because "just as death is certain for all men, so the hour of death is uncertain."

The preamble of Boccaccio's testament opens by repeating a similar concept twice ("Since nothing is more certain than death and more uncertain than the time of one's death and since, according to Gospel, it is necessary to be vigilant because it is impossible to know the day and hour of a man's death").[8] These statements remain clichéd expressions typical of many late medieval testaments. Petrarch, on the contrary, transcends the strictures of this bureaucratic style and places his will within the genre of classical Stoic treatises on the finitude of human existence, as he read in Seneca or Cicero's *De senectute* or *Tusculanae disputationes*, which speak in closely related language about the certitude of one's death and the incertitude of the day of its occurrence.[9] In the *Seniles* Petrarch repeatedly broaches the soothing and enlightening power of letters for an aging man. See, for instance, the epistle he wrote to Boccaccio in 1362:

> The life of all mortals is short, and the life of old people shortest . . .
> Indeed the life we live here is only smoke, a shadow, a dream, an illusion, in short, nothing but a threshing floor for grief and toil . . .
> If the letters are harbored in a good soul, they arouse a love of virtue and either remove or lessen the fear of death.[10]

Petrarch transforms his testament into a "reflection" on the meaning of his own death. What the poet bequeaths to his heirs and readers is first of all the testament itself, the document detailing his final reckoning with death. Petrarch intends his testament as an exemplary *vade mecum* in which each aspect of his biography (his possessions, his acquaintances and friends, the cities he visited, the possible locations of his tomb) turns into significant chapters of a universal experience. Even the formulaic reference to the present soundness of mind versus a possible imminent fatal sickness, which appears in the preamble of many late fourteenth-century wills, acquires a much deeper resonance when Petrarch, still in the preamble, uses it to reinforce the concept of the inexorable supremacy of "vicissitudes" over man's self-determination, one of the most familiar themes of Petrarch's oeuvre.

As a memento of an exemplary biography that also posits itself as a model for others, Petrarch's will recalls Francis of Assisi's powerful *Testamentum*, which the saint likewise defines as "recordatio" (memory), "admonitio" (admonition), and "exhortatio" (exhortation) that he directs to "you, my blessed brothers" (*vobis fratribus meis benedictis*) so that, by observing it as a "rule" (*regulam*), they may live "in a more catholic manner" (*melius catholice*).[11] It is worth noting that in his will Petrarch requests to be buried in a Franciscan church, if he happens to die in none of the seven possible cities mentioned in his will. In the case of Francis, "Testamentum" primarily means "final desires" or "last wishes," since he has nothing material to leave.[12] As for Petrarch, the fundamental gift bequeathed by the saint's will is the will itself. Like Petrarch's, Saint Francis's testament opens with the "testator" sharing with the reader the biographical experiences that led to its composition. Both texts originate from a crucial insight that molds the rest of the testator's life. In both cases, this revolutionary perception revolves around the Christian experience of death. Both authors present themselves as models of Christian virtue, but whereas Petrarch sees bodily death as the foundation of all philosophical inquiry in the tradition of classical thought, for Saint Francis death means a radical withdrawal from the world. For the *poverello*, "to die to the world" is a pivotal event that is much more extreme and significant than bodily death. Petrarch comes to grips with his physical extinction by positing himself as an isolated and idealized emblem of Christian perfection, whereas at the beginning of his *Testamentum* the *poverello* makes clear that his spiritual death signified his self-effacement, his disappearing as subject and his becoming pure service to others. Francis's spiritual death is not a private event, but rather a gift from the lepers he used to spurn. It is useful to remember that Petrarch's will closes with a harsh reference to the "vulgus" he detests so vehemently. In Petrarch's idealized self-portrait no reconciliation is admissible. He is virtuous insofar as he hates the populace. On the contrary, Francis "left the world" (*exivi de saeculo*) after the Lord led him to the lepers ("Dominus conduxit me inter illos") so that they could "do mercy" together (feci misericordiam cum illis) and what was bitter ("amarum") later became "spiritual and physical sweetness" (*dulcedinem animi et corporis*).[13] To "do mercy" with others means that Francis experienced his conversion as a communal act.

Petrarch's testament recounts no conversion and no transformation. His self-portrait is a static representation that appropriates the legal formulas typical of contemporary wills and turns them into highly literary expressions of his idealized autobiography. After the clichéd introduction stating his decision to write a testament to avoid possible "litigation concerning what little property I have," the poet places his soul at the top of his properties. In late trecento wills it was common to declare the superiority of the soul over the body and then call for the intercession of God, the Virgin Mary, and saints.[14] In this initial section of his text Petrarch in effect reproduces the standardized form of the time. The so-called *commendatio anime* usually followed an opening formulaic prayer, which in Petrarch's text is the initial long philosophical musing on "the last things and death," and it preceded the choice of funeral and place of burial, as we also read in Petrarch's testament.[15] In the poet's will, the *commendatio anime* and the choices regarding his funeral and burial are not two distinct sections of the testament but rather two moments of the poet's final return to God, to whom all creatures belong. Through his highly effective rendition of a merely legal discourse (where he would like to be buried and what kind of funeral he desires) Petrarch stages his ultimate and complete abandonment to divine mercy.

The poet's *commendatio* is more than a mere invocation. It recalls the *Confiteor*, the opening prayer in the sacrament of confession. Chiffoleau emphasizes the distinct sacramental undertone of late medieval testaments.[16] Before finding its exact formulation in the fourteenth-century *Ordo Romanus XIV* by Cardinal James Cajetan, the *Confiteor* was present in the Middle Ages in a variety of versions. In the Canonical Rule of Saint Chrodegang of Metz (d. 743), for example, we find a formula that is similar to Petrarch's *commendatio:* "First of all prostrate yourself humbly in the sight of God . . . and beseech the Blessed Mary with the holy Apostles and Martyrs and Confessors to pray to the Lord for you."[17] Petrarch writes:

> In the first place I humbly commend (*recommendo*) to Jesus Christ my soul . . . With the genuflection of this very soul I prostrate myself before Him and beseech Him that He may protect that which was created by Him and redeemed through the price of his most precious blood and that He may not allow it to fall into the hands of His enemies. For this also I implore . . . the aid of the most blessed Virgin, His mother, and of the blessed Archangel Michael and of the other saints.[18]

Throughout his oeuvre Petrarch manifests a deeply Christocentric spirituality that in this passage reaches its most visual and most intense expression. Rather than a simple prayer to the incarnate Word, the poet evokes a spiritual encounter in which his soul "'prostrates'" herself before her Lord the risen Christ, whose source of redemption is His own sacrificial death. Petrarch's *commendatio anime* is both prayer and intimate revelation. In the act of commending his soul to Christ, the poet beseeches Him that "He may not allow it to fall into the hands of His enemies" (*nec permittat ad suorum manus hostium pervenire*). In a similar fashion, in the third of his *Penitential Psalms* Petrarch begs the Lord that He snatch him away from his slavery condition to the enemy ("Eripe me servitio hostis tui") and free him from eternal suffering ("Libera me de supliciis eternis").[19] What is absent from Petrarch's *Penitential Psalms* is the significant presence of the Virgin Mary, whose aid the poet first implores at the moment of leaving his soul to the Lord and in two other subsequent passages. Although Mary is traditionally mentioned in the *commendatio anime* after Christ and before the archangel Michael, Mommsen underscores the particular significance of the Virgin in the *Testamentum* and relates it to Petrarch's special devotion to the cult of Mary during the last years of his life, as the epistle *Seniles* 10.1 confirms.[20] Let us remember that the *Canzoniere* ends with canzone 366 to the Virgin ("Vergine bella che di sol vestita"), whose initial apocalyptic portrait recalls *Revelation* 12.[21] As in the last verses of the final canzone of *Rerum vulgarium fragmenta*, in the *Testamentum* Petrarch asks Mary to intercede with Christ so that his soul may be granted peace.[22] In the *Testamentum* the same request acquires a particularly solemn tone, because to the Virgin the poet adds the archangel Michael and the saints as his intercessors. The poet's strong and intimate attachment to Mary is confirmed in a later passage of the *Testamentum*, where Petrarch mentions as one of his possible burial places the chapel that he wished to build in honor of the Virgin.

After his soul, Petrarch surrenders his body to its destiny. In his study of Sienese death rituals, Cohn explains that instructions regarding the funeral became frequent only after the plague in 1363.[23] Similarly, references to the burial, already mentioned before the plague, increased significantly after the pestilence. In his will Petrarch vigorously stresses that his body must "return to the earth . . . and this [is] to be done without any pomp but with utmost humility." He begs his heir Francescuolo da Brossano, who had married Petrarch's illegitimate daughter Francesca in 1362, and his friends not to ignore his request for a humble burial.[24] "This request," Petrarch writes, "befits me so well and I wish it to such a degree that if they were to act against it . . . they ought to be held responsible to God and to me on the day of Judgment." Moreover, no one is supposed to weep at his funeral. People should rather pray to Christ for Petrarch's soul and give alms to "the poor of Christ" (*Christi pauperibus*). This is the passage of the *Testamentum* where the poet most strongly evokes the ideal image of *alter Christus* through his symbolic abandonment of man's most personal property, his soul and his body. In the final section of the long letter from *Seniles* 14.1 directed at Francesco da Carrara, ruler of Padua, he expresses his strong opposition to all forms of "exaggerated mourning" (*dolor immodi-*

cus).[25] The conclusion of this important epistle is a meditation on death that closely recalls his testament. The poet states that he thought of exhorting his friend Francesco "to reform [his] people's ways."[26] Although he is aware that his request is impossible, Petrarch confesses that "there is one custom" of the Paduan people he cannot fail to mention: their attitude toward death and funerals. Francesco da Carrara, of course, knows expressions such as "moriendum esse certum est: et id incertum an hoc ipso die" (death is certain; uncertain is the day of one's death), which Petrarch also mentions at the beginning of his will. The poet continues by criticizing people's (noble and poor people alike) costume of excessive mourning and weeping (*dolor immodicus atque ingens fletus*).[27] In particular, he asks Francesco da Carrara to forbid women's (*matrone*) noisy mourning in public spaces, especially roads and squares.[28]

Although he claims that he is not concerned with his "burial place" because he will be content to rest wherever Christ wants him to, in his *Testamentum* Petrarch adds a list of seven possible cities where he may pass away, specifies the churches where he would like to be buried, and in some cases explains the reasons for his choice.[29] Contrary to his alleged disinterest in the location of his tomb, Petrarch visualizes seven different possible deaths and seven different burials. The poet's innate "restlessness," as Nicholas Mann puts it, shows also in his testament.[30] Petrarch, who saw himself as a constant wanderer or pilgrim, is unable to envision a place of eternal rest.[31] Being alone and uprooted is the very core of his identity. Let us remember that at the beginning of his will, after the traditional brief invocation to God and the Virgin Mary, Boccaccio mentions only Florence and Certaldo as possible places of his burial.[32] The choice of seven potential cities for Petrarch's interment is not a merely autobiographical reference. It also corresponds to a literary topos that Boccaccio mentions more than once in reference to Homer's burial. In *Genealogie deorum* (14.19) he cites Cicero's *Pro Archia* as a source of this topos, and in *Trattatello in laude di Dante* he speaks of the "real or fictional" burial that may have taken place in one of seven possible cities.[33] Interestingly, in the same chapter of *Genealogie deorum* Boccaccio also writes a long praise of the "divine" (*celestis*) Petrarch, whom he aligns next to Homer and Virgil for his poetic accomplishments and whose perfect honesty and spirituality is, according to Boccaccio, an example for all who know him.[34]

In his *Testamentum* Petrarch multiplies his death according to the memories he has of each given place he may find himself at the end of his life. In particular, if he dies in Padua, he would like to be buried in the Dominican Church of Saint Augustine, because "it is a place dear to my soul" but also because he would join his friend Jacopo da Carrara, "who loved me very much" (*qui me plurimum dilexit*) and first invited him to those parts. When he was the lord of Padua, Jacopo had arranged for Petrarch to receive a canonry in the cathedral of Padua, so that the poet would be encouraged to visit his friend more frequently.[35] Only two years after his generous gesture, Jacopo was assassinated and Petrarch was asked to write the epitaph for his tomb.[36] After Jacopo's death, the lordship of Padua passed to his son Francesco. To be buried in Padua would signify the realization of an eternal communion with a beloved friend. This first reference to a possible interment in Padua also summons an essential topos of Petrarch's thought. Jacopo da Carrara "brought" (*attraxit*) Petrarch to this city through his generosity and kindness. A burial close to his friend recalls Petrarch's essential concept of a dialogical solitude, what he calls a non-alone solitude (*solitudinem non solam*) in the second part of *De vita solitaria*.[37]

It is useful to remember that in the late Middle Ages the most indigent could not afford to be buried in churches. For them, only cemeteries were available.[38] If he dies in Arquà, his "country place," Petrarch would like to be laid in the small chapel dedicated to the Virgin Mary he intends to build. If he dies before the construction of this holy place, he would like to rest somewhere close to the parish church. Petrarch did not succeed in completing the construction of this chapel. He was buried outside the parish church of Arquà in a monument that was completed six years after his death. For the other five possible places (Venice, Milan, Pavia, Rome, and Parma) of his burial, Petrarch goes so far as to identify the exact location within or close to his selected churches. To specify an exact location of one's tomb is not unusual in fourteenth-century testaments.[39] In Milan, Petrarch would like to be buried "in front of the Church of Saint Ambrogio near the outer entrance which faces the walls of the city." Before detailing his seven possible burial places, Petrarch had written that his body had to be returned to the earth that had produced it.

Rather than abandoning his body to the earth as something borrowed for a limited time, Petrarch seems very attached to the "heavy burden for noble souls" (*nobilium gravem sarcinam animorum*). The body may be a "burden" as a long Neoplatonic and Christian tradition asserts, but it is through this cumbersome weight that the poet imagines the survival of memory, the enduring contact with the places that saw him alive.[40] Aware of the obvious contradiction between his supposed indifference vis-à-vis the destiny of his corpse and the meticulous description of exact locations for his tomb, at the end of this list of hypothetical burials the poet acknowledges that his lengthy remarks are not suitable for "a learned man" (*virum doctum*). They should be read as if coming from an "unlearned man" (*indocto*).[41] In other words, this digressive part of his testament is not really his, but it rather belongs to someone else, an imagined individual who unlike Petrarch is still fettered to the allurements of the world. This man is, again, Petrarch's hypothetical alter ego, the wealthy and self-satisfied individual who would have written a radically different testament, as the poet states at the beginning of his text. We have seen that this alien presence within the poet's text comes from the populace, the "vulgus," Petrarch's vicious enemy in all his Latin and Italian works.

The distinction between Petrarch as a "learned" man and Petrarch as an "unlearned" member of the "vulgus" introduces the second part of the *Testamentum*, in which the poet details the "disposal of those things which men call goods, although frequently they are impediments to the soul." The first items mentioned are directed at religious institutions. Boccaccio's succinct will follows a similar structure. After the place of burial, Boccaccio draws up a series of four telegraphic "He bequeaths" (*reliquit*), all regarding religious institutions and the construction of the walls of Florence. In Petrarch's text, the first donation takes up more than one page in Mommsen's edition. Petrarch mentions the "small piece of land" he was determined to purchase for the Cathedral of Padua, which had already received the "oral permission" of his friend Francesco da Carrara, and the "twenty ducats" he donates to the church where he will be buried, and one hundred ducats to the "poor of Christ."[42] Petrarch has already used this expression when speaking of his funeral. Who are the "poor of Christ"? This is a recurrent expression in medieval wills. It is difficult to determine "whether these 'poor of Christ' were always the lay poor."[43] Maybe they were also the members of the mendicant orders or wandering monks. Bequests to the poor, however, were usually of a very modest amount. Petrarch insists that nobody should "receive more than a single ducat."

The first of "the other possessions" is the "panel or icon" (*tabulam meam sive iconam*) of the blessed Virgin Mary, "a work of the eminent painter Giotto," that Petrarch had received from Michele de Vanni. The poet bequeaths this precious painting to his friend and lord of Padua Francesco da Carrara, so that "the blessed Virgin herself may intervene with her son Jesus Christ on his behalf."[44] This was not only an item that could suit a prince, it was also the poet's most meaningful possession, given his dedication to the Virgin Mary. This priceless gift, which is also Petrarch's most intimate expression of love for "my lord" (*domino meo*), is accompanied by a renewed attack against the "vulgus," those ignorant people (*ignorantes*) who are unable to appreciate the beauty of Giotto's work.[45] Once again

Petrarch envisions friendship as a spiritual bond forged through the rejection of others, those inferior men who do not deserve to participate in the friends' intimacy.

Given the deeply different structures of the two testaments, a brief look at the corresponding section of Boccaccio's will is of great relevance for a clearer understanding of Petrarch's text. Boccaccio cites two images of the Virgin Mary, but these articles are not the first in the testament. After his gifts to three religious institutions plus a bequest for constructing the walls of Florence, each of them introduced by the verb "He bequeaths," Boccaccio adds a new "He also bequeaths" to specify the first "lay" bequest. The first person to be mentioned is Bruna of Cianco, who "has lived with him for a long time." What this servant receives is simply "the bed she used to sleep in." A characteristic of Boccaccio's testament is the detailed descriptions of its modest articles, which gives this text a truly moving tone. Whereas each of Petrarch's possessions has an idealized and almost symbolic connotation in agreement with the universal meaning of his will, Boccaccio strives to identify his poor objects as unique items of his biography. He describes this bed (*lectum*), the first nonmonetary gift of his testament, as if he tried to make us see it and thus remember it. The bed is made of a wooden frame, with a small feather blanket, a pillow, and another white blanket. Along with her bed, Bruna will also receive a couple of sheets and a bench that is usually placed at the end of that bed. She will also get a small chestnut table where she can have her meals. The first image of the Virgin, a "small alabaster image of our Lady," is mentioned at the beginning of a long list of religious items (among them a small cushion for an altar and a tin jar for holy water) Boccaccio bequeaths to the employees of San Giacomo di Certaldo.[46] In a subsequent part he mentions a small picture of the Virgin. It shows on one side the portrait of our Lady and on the other "the skull of a dead man." This image goes to lady Sandra, now married to Francesco di Lapo Buonamici. Boccaccio's library is the most precious part of his will. We know that Petrarch was interested in it because in *Seniles* 1.5 (written in 1362), where he also exalts the healing powers of Letters, he offers to buy it. Instead Boccaccio leaves his books to his "venerable master" Martin of the Eremitical Order of Saint Augustine and of the Convent of Santo Spirito in Florence.

Compared to Boccaccio's truly humble testament, Petrarch's insistence on the paucity of his property could sound preposterous. Petrarch introduces the rest of his bequest by apologizing for his modest assets, thus reiterating his faithfulness to the ideal of Christian poverty. We read that his horses will go to Bonzanello da Vigonza and Lombardo della Seta, who will also receive the poet's round cup made of silver and gilded.[47] As Petrarch states in a later section of his will, Lombardo, a minor humanist who played a major role in the posthumous editing of the poet's works, would also become his new heir if Francescuolo da Brossano died before the poet.[48] Petrarch also specifies that the priest Giovanni a Bocheta will get the breviary he purchased in Venice, and that his friend Boccaccio will receive fifty Florentine gold florins "for a winter garment to be worn by him while he is studying and working during the night hours."[49] Petrarch tactfully and affectionately apologizes for his modest gift, although Boccaccio's real poverty was not a secret. The same amount goes to the famous physician Giovanni dall'Orologio, who was on friendly terms with Petrarch, despite his vocal resentment against doctors' arrogant ignorance in *Invective contra medicum*.

Before two final addenda, Petrarch indirectly expresses his paternal care for his daughter Francesca. "Of all my movable and immovable goods," he writes, "I institute as the heir general Francescuolo da Brossano, son of the late Lord Amicolo da Brossano, citizen of Milan."[50] The poet specifies that Francescuolo will have to divide "into two parts whatever money he find in my possession." He will keep one part, whereas the other will go "to the person to whom he knows I wish it to go" (*alteram numeret cui scit me velle*).[51] Francesca is the *innominata* of her father's testament. Being an illegitimate daughter, Francesca exists in the protective shadow of her husband, whom Petrarch trusts. Her father's reticence makes Francesca a unique figure within this unique text of Petrarch's oeuvre. She is also the sole woman to be a recipient in the poet's testament and only through the silent accord between two men.

The first of the two final additions (*addenda*) to the *Testamentum* evoke the beloved land of Vaucluse, the poetic setting of so many of Petrarch's works. "The little piece of land which I own beyond the Alps," the poet writes, will become the property of the local hospital and will be used for the "poor of Christ." If this transfer cannot be made, he adds, it will go to the two sons of Raymond of Clermont, "commonly called Monet," the man who faithfully served Petrarch for many years, as he says in *Familiares* 16.1. To remember his good servant by his nickname in an otherwise official document seems to synthesize the affection the poet has for the land that preserved his solitude and fostered his studies. It is again through the name of a friend, in this case the modest and faithful "Monet," that Petrarch expresses his attachment to a place, as he had done in a previous section of his testament, when he had spoken of the lord of Padua Jacopo da Carrara, "who had loved me very much." The last person to be mentioned in his *Testamentum* is his brother Gherardo, the Carthusian monk for whom Petrarch composes *De otio religioso*, the second treatise on the essential subject of solitude. After his death, Petrarch writes, his heir will have to notify his brother and ask him "whether he wishes to receive one hundred florins [at once] or five or ten florins annually, as he may please."[52]

These final affectionate expressions of care and memory (his daughter Francesca, his deceased servant Monet and his sons, his brother Gherardo) are in stark contrast with the "jarring" tone, according to Mommsen's definition, of Petrarch's final sentence. The poet would have written a different testament had he been a different person, a wealthy man, as the "mad rabble" (*vulgus insanum*) seems to believe. This puzzling statement points to the poet's obsession against those indistinct and "unlearned" presences who question both his values and his self-portrait. As he clearly states in the *Testamentum*, these unlearned and despicable people worry about their burial places and are unable to perceive the importance of Giotto's art. The obsessive leitmotif of the poet's will is the insistence on the modesty of his financial means. His hatred toward the indistinct populace in fact springs from a doubt that the poet carries inside of himself. The concept of the "vulgus" in opposition to the enlightened man is something Petrarch found both in the Church Fathers and the Latin classics. As I explain in my essay on *De vita solitaria*, Petrarch's great interest in Augustine's short *De vera religione* also comes from its initial insistence on the radical dichotomy between a worldly and a religious man. But Petrarch's disgust for the "vulgus" exceeds Augustine's remarks. The "vulgus" threatens Petrarch's most forceful attempt to construct a stable and untouchable monument to himself as the modern embodiment of classical and Christian values. His restlessness, his view of life as a perennial pilgrimage, and his deep sense of nonbelonging affect also his final and most official document. Petrarch's *Testamentum* is indeed an "apprehensive" text in that not only does it blend a variety of literary genres (stoic treatise on last things; Christian confessional text; memoir), it also harbors two contrastive forces. The despicable "vulgus" is inside the text, not outside. The "vulgus" is the implicit voice that undermines the poet's belief in his idealized self-image as his longed-for "homeland."

Students of early modern European culture have been debating at length whether Petrarch's opus depicts a modern subject "characterized by a distinct singular interiority" or summons a still medieval concept of personhood through a dense weaving of classical and patristic *auctoritates*.[53] Does the last sentence of his testament allude to a post-medieval and self-contradictory subjectivity reminiscent of Montaigne? Petrarch ends this official document by emphasizing two main issues. First, *if* he were another person he would have written a different text. Second, even though this is only a totally hypothetical possibility, it triggers a resentful attack against the "mad rabble" (*vulgus insanum*) who is convinced that Petrarch is different from what he really is. If we accept that the "vulgus" is also an inner presence and not only an objective entity, we could infer that the harsh contrast between the poet and the populace dramatizes a clash between real and ideal self-perception. If on the one hand Petrarch purports that his written self is inherently identical to his real and biographical one, on the other hand the "vulgus" denies such identification and thus also the salvation the poet incessantly seeks through the writings the essays of this volume have analyzed.

A first unique aspect of the *Testamentum* within Petrarch's oeuvre is its incontestably practical purpose. Unlike his epistles, whose goals and even addressees are highly questionable, Petrarch's testament seems to respond to a concrete concern, the division of his goods after his death. As Mommsen points out, "of all the writings and letters belonging to this period of Petrarch's old age his testament . . . may rightly be called one of the most personal documents."[54] It is paradoxical that this alleged personal touch is present in the most external, least private and literary of his texts. In reality, like all his other writings, Petrarch's *Testamentum* works also as *exemplum*, and as such it defies its strictly legal format. The *Testamentum* is at once ideal self-portrait, legal document, and manifestation of a truly individual self. Maybe, rather than trying to locate Petrarch's exact position on the hypothetical axis that runs from the Middle Ages to the Renaissance, we could envision Petrarch and his literary, philosophical, and spiritual legacy as both medieval and early modern, thus concluding that in this contradiction lies his persistent appeal.

NOTES

A Life's Work

1. For text and discussion of this important letter, see Petrarch, *Senile V 2*, ed. Monica Berté (Florence: Le Lettere, 1998). Petrarch's scribe, who attaches the date "August 28," seems to have dictated it in 1364, but Boccaccio didn't receive it until 1366. It was one of three letters (*Seniles* 5.1–3) stolen and kept as souvenirs of their famed author by the messenger charged with their delivery. Petrarch recovered them and asked his trusted friend Donato Albanzani to carry them to their destination. See the commentary by Ugo Dotti in Petrarch's *Lettres de la vieillesse. Rerum senilium*, ed. Elvira Nota (Paris: Les Belles Lettres, 2003), 2:529, n. 42. For the English, see Petrarch, *Letters of Old Age. Rerum senilium libri I–XVIII*, trans. Aldo S. Bernardo, Saul Levin, and Reta A. Bernardo (Baltimore: Johns Hopkins University Press, 1992).

2. Petrarch tries to soothe Boccaccio by recalling Seneca, who ranked Cicero second after Virgil among Latin writers, followed by Asinius Pollio, and then Livy. The flattering implication is that Boccaccio is "one up" on Livy. In an earlier letter to Boccaccio (*Familiares* 21.15), Petrarch cringes to think of Dante's plebian public—fullers, tavern keepers, and woolworkers. He acknowledges, however, Dante's superiority in the vernacular. See Petrarch *Familiares* 21.15.24 in *Le familiari*, ed. Vittorio Rossi and Umberto Bosco (Florence: Sansoni, 1926–42), 4:99: "in vulgari eloquio quam carminibus aut prosa clarior atque altior assurgit"; for the translation, *Letters on Familiar Matters. Rerum familiarium libri XVII–XXIV*, trans. Aldo S. Bernardo (Baltimore: Johns Hopkins University Press, 1985), 206: "[Dante] rises to nobler and loftier heights in the vernacular than in Latin poetry or prose."

3. *Petrarchino* describes an edition of Petrarch's lyric poetry in small editorial format. The fashion for such objects expresses *Petrarchismo*, mania for reading and imitating his vernacular poetry. From left to right in figure 1 the subjects are Marsilio Ficino, Cristoforo Landino, Petrarch, Boccaccio, Dante, and Guido Cavalcanti. The panel, today in the Minneapolis Institute of Arts, was commissioned by Luca Martini, a cultured gentleman who served Cosimo I de' Medici as the ducal administrator in Pisa. In his portrait by Agnolo Bronzino (Pitti Palace), Martini holds a map of the swamps he drained around that city. Martini, a poet in his own right, was an eager amateur *Dantista*. For commentary, see Edgar Peters Bowron, "Giorgio

Vasari's 'Portrait of Six Tuscan Poets,'" *Minneapolis Institute of Arts Bulletin* 60 (1971–73): 43–54; Deborah Parker, "Vasari's *Portrait of Six Tuscan Poets:* A Visible Literary History," in Deborah Parker, ed., "Visibile parlare: Images of Dante in the Renaissance," special issue, *Lectura Dantis* 22–23 (Spring–Fall 1998): 45–62.

4. See p. 7 for Petrarch's career as a cleric, or member of the secular clergy. His book of poetry is today often called *Canzoniere* (*Songbook*) or *Rime sparse* (*Scattered Rhymes*). He attached to it a Latin title, *Rerum vulgarium fragmenta* (*Fragments of Vernacular Matters*). Throughout his correspondence, he refers both to his epistles and his love poetry for the lady called Laura as "nugae," that is, "trifles," "bagatelles," or in Ugo Dotti's Italian translation of the letters, "cosucce" (thinglets). See, for example, *Familiares* 1.1, 12.6.

5. Arturo Graf's classic essays of 1888, "Petrarchismo" and "Antipetrarchismo," in *Attraverso il Cinquecento* (Turin: Giovanni Chiantore, 1926), 1–70, open with an aphorism that amusingly captures the persistent addiction to the vernacular lyric poet: "Petrarchism is a chronic illness of Italian literature." A gallery of portraits whose sitters hold a *Petrarchino* has been assembled with illustrations by Novella Macola, "I ritratti col Petrarca," in *Le lingue del Petrarca,* ed. Antonio Daniele (Udine: Forum [Società Editrice Universitaria Udinese], 2005), 135–57.

6. See, e.g., Dino Cervigni, ed., "Petrarch and the European Lyric Tradition," special issue, *Annali d'Italianistica* 22 (2004); Valeria Finucci, ed., *Petrarca: Canoni, esemplarità* (Rome: Bulzoni, 2006); Leonard Forster, *The Icy Fire: Five Studies in European Petrarchism* (Cambridge: Cambridge University Press, 1969); William J. Kennedy, *Authorizing Petrarch* (Ithaca: Cornell University Press, 1994); Christopher Kleinhenz and Andrea Dini, eds., *Approaches to Teaching Petrarch and the Petrarchan Tradition* (New York: Modern Language Association, 2009); Amedeo Quondam, *Petrarchismo mediato: Per una critica della forma antologia* (Rome: Bulzoni, 1974); studies on women Petrarchists published in the University of Chicago Press "Other Voice" series, e.g., Laura Battiferra degli Ammannati, *Laura Battiferra and Her Literary Circle: An Anthology,* ed. Victoria Kirkham (Chicago: University of Chicago Press, 2006). I would like to thank Mary W. Gibbons for a patient reading of this introduction and for suggesting mention of these sibling volumes.

7. See, e.g., the manuscript note connected with one such exchange, in which Petrarch (or his correspondent?) writes via the poem he sends how "sweet" it was to have heard the other person and talked with him. Giuseppe Frasso calls attention to the jotting, which may relate to poem 17a in *Rime estravaganti,* ed. Laura Paolino, in Petrarch, *Trionfi, Rime estravaganti, Codice degli abbozzi,* ed. Vinicio Pacca and Laura Paolino, 2nd. ed. (Milan: Mondadori,

2000), 726. See Frasso, "Minime divagazioni petrarchesche," in *Il genere "tenzone" nelle letterature romanze delle Origini*, ed. Matteo Pedroni and Antonio Stäuble (Ravenna: Longo, 1999), 159–63.

8. Edward H. R. Tatham codified the epithet in the title of his classic two-volume biographical study, *Francesco Petrarca: The First Modern Man of Letters* (London: Sheldon Press, 1925–26). Dante had spoken of the "maternal tongue" learned by nursing infants in his *De vulgari eloquentia* 1.1.2: "vulgarem locutionem appellamus eam qua infantes assuefiunt ab assistentibus, cum primitus distinguere voces incipiunt; vel, quod brevius dici potest, vulgarem locutionem asserimus, quam sine omni regula nutricem imitantes accipimus" [we call vernacular speech that to which infants are accustomed by those at their sides when they first begin to recognize words, or since it could be said more briefly, I assert that vernacular locution is what we take in without any rules at all, imitating the woman who nurses us]. By *nutrix* is meant "mother." Dante Alighieri, *De vulgari eloquentia*, ed. and trans. Aristide Marigo, 3rd ed. edited by Pier Giorgio Ricci (Florence: Le Monnier, 1968), 7. Cf. *De vulgari eloquentia* 1.14.7 with reference to "materno . . . vulgare."

9. On his boyhood in Provence, see Ernest Hatch Wilkins, *Life of Petrarch* (Chicago: University of Chicago Press, 1961), 3–4; Ugo Dotti, *Vita di Petrarca* (Bari: Laterza, 1987), 7–16; Marco Ariani, *Petrarca* (Rome: Salerno Editore, 1999), 19–27. Petrarch's Virgil is now at the Ambrosiana Library in Milan (MS A 79 inf.). See the description from the *Enciclopedia Virgiliana* in Michele Feo, *Petrarca nel tempo: Tradizione lettori e immagini delle opere* (Pontedera: Bandecchi and Vivaldi, 2003), 496–99.

10. Wilkins, *Life of Petrarch*, 179. For the Latin, see Ernest Hatch Wilkins, *Petrarch's Later Years* (Cambridge: Mediaeval Academy of America, 1959), 8: "Ioannes noster, homo natus ad laborem, ad dolorem meum, et uiuens grauibus atque perpetuis me curis exercuit, at acri dolore moriens uulnerauit, qui, cum paucos letos dies uixisset in uita sua, obiit anno Domini 1361, etatis sue XXV, die Iulii X seu IX medio noctis, inter diem Veneris et Sabbati. Rumor ad me Paduam xiiij° mensis, ad uesperam. Obiit autem Mediolani in illo publico excidio pestis insolito, queue urbem illam hactenus immunem talibus malis nunc tandem reperit atque inuasit."

11. The eulogy is *Epystole* 1.7; cf. *Seniles* 10.2. For the text, see *Panegyricum in funere matris*, ed. Carlo Muscetta, reproduced by P. Blanc in "Petrarca ou la poétique de l'Ego: Éléments de psychopoétique pétrarquienne," *Revue des Études Italiennes*, n.s., 29, nos. 1–3 (1983): 124–69, with an appended document, 180–83. On the commonplace tradition of the Pythagorean Y as a symbolic road branching to virtue on the right and vice on the left, see Janet Levarie Smarr, "Boccaccio and the Choice of Hercules," *Modern Language*

Notes 92, no. 1 (1977): 146–52. Although Wilkins dates the panegyric to Eletta's death (*Life of Petrarch*, 5–7), Blanc, who reproduces the text, dates it to ca. 1325, but without any other evidence than the absence of Laura, who supposedly didn't enter Petrarch's life until 1327. This eulogy must postdate, at least by a few years, the loss it mourns since Petrarch would at that time have been only about fourteen years old.

12. Elena Giannarelli, "Fra mondo classico e agiografia cristiana: Il *Breve panegyricum defuncti matri* di Petrarca," *Annali della Scuola Normale di Pisa* 9, no. 3 (1979): 1099–118, identified many of the sources, an inventory revisited by Blanc in "Petrarca ou la poétique de l'Ego." See further on Petrarch's deeply affectionate memories of his mother and the maternal aspects of Laura in the *Canzoniere*, in Kristen Ina Grimes, "A proposito di *Rvf* 285: Petrarca tra Laura e Monica," *Atti e Memorie dell'Accademia Galileiana di Scienze, Lettere ed Arti già Ricovrati e Patavina* 117 (2004–5): 273–95.

13. Feo, *Petrarca nel tempo*, fig. 155, pp. 479, 481. The manuscript is Paris, Bibl. nat., Lat. 2201, fol. 58v, "Libri mei peculiares." Cf. Wilkins, *Life of Petrarch*, 15.

14. Wilkins, *Life of Petrarch*, 16, touches on Petrarch's reconstruction of Livy.

15. Petrarch *Familiares* 2.7.5 (ed. Rossi; trans. Bernardo, 93): "Meministi, credo, in *Philologia* nostra, quam ob id solum ut curas tibi iocis excuterem scripsi, quid Tranquillinus noster ait: 'Maior pars hominum expectando moritur.'"

16. Giovanni Boccaccio, *Vita e costume di Messer Francesco di Petracco, di Firenze*, ed. Renata Fabbri, in *Tutte le opere*, ed. Vittore Branca, vol. 5, part 1 (Milan: Mondadori, 1992), 910–11; Dotti, *Vita di Petrarca*, 59–60. Wilkins, *Life of Petrarch*, 15, dates it to his Avignon period in the 1330s. Dotti speculates that he might have burned it, judging that he could not equal the great comic playwright of ancient Rome, Publius Terentius Afer. Guido Martellotti, "Sulla *Philologia*," in *Scritti petrarcheschi*, ed. Michele Feo and Silvia Rizzo (Padua: Antenore, 1983), 360–61, finds appealing the suggestion advanced by G. Bernardi Perini that the play derives from Martianus Capella's *Marriage of Philology and Mercury*. Feo, *Petrarca nel tempo*, 312, mentions it under "Carmina latina varia."

17. In one, after a 1347 visit to his brother Gherardo at Montrieux, Petrarch apparently asks for an arrangement that would allow him to live with his friend Socrates close to the Cistercian monastery "propter germanum suum" (because of his brother). Nothing came of this proposal. See Ernest H. Wilkins, "Petrarch's Ecclesiastical Career," *Speculum* 28, no. 4 (1953): 754–75. The one other document in which traces remain of Petrarch's hand dates from 1348 and pertains to that "assai pingue Benefizio" (very fat benefice), the archdeaconate of Parma. See also Feo, "Suppliche," in *Petrarca nel tempo*, 455.

18. J. B. Trapp published richly informed studies on Petrarch visualized. See

"The Iconography of Petrarch in the Age of Humanism," *Quaderni Petrarche-schi* 9–10 (1992–93): 11–73, and idem, "Petrarch's Laura: The Portraiture of an Imaginary Beloved," *Journal of the Warburg and Courtauld Institutes* 64 (2001): 55–192. For further portraits of Petrarch, sometimes confused with Boccaccio (also a cleric), see Victoria Kirkham and Jennifer Tonkovich, "How Petrarch Became Boccaccio: A Bronze Bust from the Morgan Library," *Studi sul Boccaccio* 33 (2005): 269–98.

19. Francesco il Vecchio da Carrara, dedicatee of the last two versions of the *De viris illustribus*, also commissioned the closely related frescos in the "hall of famous men" in his palace. Although some have suggested that Petrarch himself composed the *tituli* for that fresco cycle (e.g., Dotti, in his commentary on *Seniles* 14.1 [ed. Nota, 4:578]), the attribution was rejected by Theodor E. Mommsen, "Petrarch and the Decoration of the *Sala virorum illustrium* in Padua," *Art Bulletin* 34, no. 2 (June 1952): 95–116.

20. Boccaccio's more medieval *De casibus virorum illustrium*, a dream vision in nine books, lays out the universal trajectory of human events as an endless struggle between good and evil. As in Dante's *Inferno*, shades crowd before the author to tell their mournful fates. Adam and Eve lead the procession, which continues through the ages with notables up to the fourteenth-century Sicilian washerwoman who rose to control the throne of Naples. When inspiration flags, the author imagines that his "excellent and venerable master" Petrarch makes a visionary appearance to rouse him. Man, argues a laureated Franciscus in Boccaccio's eloquently scripted speech, was born to strive for fame (8.1). This spur to finish *De casibus virorum illustrium* seems to date from the two men's visit at Milan in March 1359. See Victoria Kirkham, s.v. "Giovanni Boccaccio: Latin Works," in *Encyclopedia of Italian Literary Studies*, ed. Gaetana Marrone (New York: Routledge Taylor and Francis, 2007), 1:255–60. For an English translation, see Boccaccio, *The Fates of Illustrious Men*, trans. Lewis Brewer Hall (New York: Frederick Ungar, 1965).

21. The text, indebted to Livy *Ab urbe condita libri* 9.17–19, 35.14.5–12, is preserved as MS Lat. 7 in the Annenberg Rare Book and Manuscript Collection of the University of Pennsylvania. For a facsimile, see Petrarch, *Collatio inter Scipionem, Alexandrum, Annibalem et Pyrhum*, ed. with an intro. by Guido Martellotti (Philadelphia: University of Pennsylvania Libraries, 1974). Martellotti's introduction, which appears in an English translation by Enzo U. Orvieto, was published originally in the *Library Chronicle* 28 (1962): 109–14. Cf. Martellotti's annotated edition in *"La Collatio inter Scipionem, Alexandrum, Hanibalem et Pyrrum,* un inedito del Petrarca nella Biblioteca della University of Pennsylvania," in *Classical, Mediaeval, and Renaissance Studies in Honor of Berthold Louis Ullman,* ed. Charles Henderson, Jr., 2:145–68 (Rome: Edizioni

di Storia e Letteratura, 1964), which also appears in Guido Martellotti, *Studi petrarcheschi*, ed. Michele Feo and Silvia Rizzo (Padua: Antenore, 1983), 321–46. Vinicio Pacca, *Petrarca* (Rome and Bari: Laterza, 1998), 43–44, mentions it as a spinoff of the Hannibal *vita* in *De viris illustribus*.

22. Petrarch, *Africa*, ed. Nicola Festa (1926; repr., Florence: Le Lettere, 1998), 9.233–34.

23. Contrast Boccaccio, who in his *Filocolo* (5.97) will attach Dante to the classical canon of Virgil, Lucan, Statius, and Ovid, saving "sixth" place for himself as Dante had done in *Inferno* 4. See Victoria Kirkham, *Fabulous Vernacular: Boccaccio's 'Filocolo' and the Art of Medieval Fiction* (Ann Arbor: University of Michigan Press, 2001), 149.

24. Attilio Hortis, *Scritti inediti di Petrarca* (Trieste: Tipografia del Lloyd Austro-Ungarico, 1874), 311–28.

25. Ernest Hatch Wilkins, "The Coronation of Petrarch," in *The Making of the 'Canzoniere' and Other Petrarchan Studies* (Rome: Edizioni di Storia e Letteratura, 1951), 9–12, identifies thirty-one passages or compositions by Petrarch that bear on the coronation. For a history of the editions and a facsimile of the earliest manuscript, see Feo, *Petrarca nel tempo*, 17 and plate M4.

26. Petrarch, *Africa*, ed. Festa, 9.238–42 (trans. Bergin and Wilson [New Haven: Yale University Press, 1977], 9.325–31): "Hic tandem ascendet Capitolia vestra, nec ipsum / Mundus iners studiisque aliis tunc ebria turba / Terrebit quin insigni florentia lauro / Tempora descendens referat comitante Senatu. / Hinc modo tantus amor, tanta est reverentia lauri."

27. Wilkins, "Coronation of Petrarch," 53–61, provides an extensive discussion of the *Privilegium*. First published in the seventeenth century, its most recent editor is D. Mertens, "Petrarcas *Privilegium laureationis*," in *Litterae Medii Aevi: Festschrift für Johanne Autenrieth zu ihrem 65. Geburtstag*, ed. Michael Borgolte and Herrad Spilling (Sigmaringen: Jan Thorbecke Verlag, 1988), 225–47. For other editions, see Feo, *Petrarca nel tempo*, 17.

28. Petrarch, *Rerum memorandarum libri IV*, ed. Giuseppe Billanovich (Florence: Sansoni, 1945), 1.37.11: "O vox vere philosophica et omnium studiosorum hominum veneratione dignissima, quantum michi placuisti!" Robert is "prince of philosophers and kings" (ibid., p. lxxxiii).

29. Cicero, *The Speech on Behalf of Archias the Poet*, in *Pro Archia, Post reditum ad quirites, Post reditum in senatu, De domo sua, De haruspicum responsis, Pro Plancio*, trans. N. H. Watts (1923; repr., Cambridge: Harvard University Press, 1979). Petrarch shared this Ciceronian text with Boccaccio, probably at their Paduan visit in 1351, and Boccaccio adapted it to the panegyric on poetry at the center of his *Trattatello in laude di Dante* (*Life of Dante*). See Victoria Kirkham, "The Parallel Lives of Dante and Virgil," *Dante Studies* 110 (1992): 233–53.

30. Petrarch, *Rerum memorandarum libri* (ed. Billanovich), 2.1. He invites the reader reverently to enter with him the doors of the "religiosissimi . . . templi," where Prudence stands at the threshold. Petrarch announces the project in *Familiares* 5.7. Incomplete, it didn't circulate until after his death, when Tedaldo della Casa, a scribe of scrupulous accuracy, copied it from the autograph. A letter from the Florentine chancellor Coluccio Salutati dated July 13, 1379 requests a copy from Lombardo della Seta, Petrarch's literary executor. The first person who knew *Rerum memorandarum libri* (probably only by title) was a poet from Pistoia, Zenone Zenoni, who composed a funerary tribute to Petrarch in terza rima, *Rerum memorandarum libri*, introduction by Billanovich, xi–xii.

31. On the total of forty souls in Dante's *Inferno* 4, a society ruled by the four pre-Christian virtues, see Victoria Kirkham, "A Canon of Women in Dante's *Commedia*," *Annali d'Italianistica* 7 (1989): 16–41.

32. The opening chapter of book 1 of *Rerum memorandarum libri*, the treatise on Wisdom, is entitled "De otio et solitudine." Cf. Valerius Maximus, *Fatti e detti memorabili*, trans. Luigi Rusca (Milan: Rizzoli, 1972), bk. 8, chap. 8.

33. Ernest Hatch Wilkins, "Peregrinus Ubique," in *The Making of the 'Canzoniere' and Other Petrarchan Studies* (Rome: Edizioni di Storia e Letteratura, 1951), 1–8. Although relying on a conversion theory now challenged, Giles Constable brings valuable work to Petrarch's inward turning ca. 1342–52, in "Petrarch and Monasticism," in *Francesco Petrarca Citizen of the World*, ed. Aldo Bernardo (Padua: Antenore, 1980), 53–99.

34. Giuseppe Billanovich compellingly argued the fictitious date of the letter, which had to have been written after Petrarch's brother Gherardo entered a Carthusian monastery in 1342 (and after the death of its destinee, Dionigi), in "Petrarca e il Ventoso," *Italia Medioevale e Umanistica* 9 (1966): 389–401. See further, Robert M. Durling, "The Ascent of Mt. Ventoux and the Crisis of Allegory," *Italian Quarterly* 18, no. 69 (Summer 1974): 7–28; Bortolo Martinelli, *Petrarca e il Ventoso* (Milan: Minerva-Italica, 1977); and Carolyn Chiappelli, "The Motif of Confession in Petrarch's 'Mt. Ventoux,'" *Modern Language Notes* 93, no. 1 (Jan. 1978): 131–36.

35. For more on the numerology of *Familiares* 4.1 in the context of reciprocal influences between Petrarch and Boccaccio, see Kirkham, *Fabulous Vernacular*, 54–60.

36. Petrarch, *Secretum*, in *Opere latine*, ed. Antonietta Bufano (Turin: Unione Tipografico-editrice Torinese, 1975), 1:94: "cupidissime perlegi: haud aliter quam qui videndi studio peregrinatur a patria, ubi ignotum famose cuiuspiam urbis limen ingreditur, nova captus locorum dulcedine passimque subsistens, obvia queque circumspicit," ibid., 1:102–4: "Lectio autem ista quid

profuit?. . . . Quanquam vel multa nosse quid relevat si, cum celi terreque ambitum, si, cum maris spatium et astrorum cursus herbarumque virtutes ac lapidum et nature secreta didiceritis, vobis esti incogniti?" For the English translation, see *The Secret by Francesco Petrarch with Related Documents*, ed. Carol E. Quillen (Boston: Bedford/St. Martin's, 2003), 72.

37. Petrarch *Secretum* (trans. Quillen), 52, connects Petrarch's dialogue with *Aeneid* 9.641, which makes virtue a "path to the stars." Cf. note 11 above on the Pythagorean Y, of which Petrarch speaks in the panegyric to his mother. It returns in *Secretum* (trans. Quillen), bk. 3, 113–14.

38. Petrarch *Secretum* in *Opere latine* (ed. Bufano, 1:258; trans. Quillen, 147): "sparsa anime fragmenta recolligam."

39. That task has fallen to Donatella Coppini, who as of 1993 had found 88 manuscripts. Her count has now swelled to 138, an accumulation that marks their great popularity.

40. Feo, *Petrarca nel tempo*, 447–48, and color reproduction of the *rotolus* for Gian Galeazzo, 452–53.

41. An apocryphal tradition associated Petrarch's psalms with another version by "Dante," cited by Matter: *I sette salmi penitenziali di Dante Alighieri e di Francesco Petrarca* (Bergamo: Mazzoleni, 1821; reprint, Florence: Società Tipografica, 1827). The title is still listed in Edward Moore, *Tutte le opere di Dante*, 3rd ed. (Oxford: Oxford University Press, 1904); but cf. Wilkins, "An Introductory Dante Bibliography," *Modern Philology* 17, no. 11 (March 1920): 624, who called the attribution spurious. For a more recent assessment, see Salvatore Floro Di Zenzo, *Studio critico sull'attribuzione a Dante Alighieri di un antico volgarizzamento dei Sette salmi penitenziali* (Naples: Laurenziana, 1984).

42. Dotti, *Petrarca*, 155–57, assigns the *Psalmi penitentiales* to 1348 and on the authority of Francisco Rico, the *Secretum* (set in 1342) to 1347, with revisions in 1349 and a final version in 1353. Nicholas Mann concurs in his very readable monograph *Petrarch* (Oxford: Oxford University Press, 1984), 23.

43. Petrarch, *Orationes contra tempestates*, in *Scritti inediti* (ed. Hortis), 367–72.

44. Ibid., 399: "Salus mea hriste ihesu si te ad misericordiam inclinare potest humana miseria: adesto mihi misero et preces meas benignus exaudi, fac peregrinationem meam tibi placitam et gressos meos onmes dirige in viam salutis etterne, dignare michi in exitus mei die et in illa suprema hora mortis assistere. Neque reminiscaris iniquitatum mearum, sed egredientem ex hoc corpusculo spiritum, placatus excipias, ne intres in iudicium cum servo tuo domine. misericordiarum fons misericorditer mecum age. cause mee faveas. et deformitates meas contege in die novissimo, nec patiaris hanc animam opus manum tuarum ad superbum tui et mei hostis imperium pervenire, aut predam fieri spiritibus inmundis et famelicis canibus esse ludibrio, deus meus

misericordia mea. per te salvator." I thank Ann Matter for working with me on the English translation.

45. Cachey refers to William Kennedy, *The Site of Petrarchism: Early Modern National Sentiment in Italy, France and England* (Baltimore: Johns Hopkins University Press, 2004).

46. Petrarch, *Les remedes aux deux fortunes, De remediis utriusque fortune: 1354–1366*, ed. and trans. Christophe Carraud (Grenoble: Millon, 2002), 1:xxiv, 2:lviii, on the *sic et non* of presenting a case; for the text, 1:320–21; "De multiplici spe," 1:520–23: "*Spes.* Spero longam vitam./*Ratio.* "Diuturnum carcerem. . . ./*Spes.* Laudationem funeri./*Ratio.* Philomenam surdo./. . ./*Spes.* Gloriam post mortem./*Ratio.* Lenes auras post naufragium."

47. Petrarch, *De remediis* (ed. Carraud), Liber secundus, Praefatio, 530: "Omnia secundum litem fieri," 1:549.

48. "De morte," "De morte ante diem," "De morte violenta," "De morte ignominiosa," "De morte repentina," "De moriente extra patriam," "De moriente in peccatis," "De studio fame anxio in morte," "De moriente sine filiis," "De moriente qui metuit insepultus abici."

49. Petrarch, *De remediis* (ed. Carraud, 1:1147; trans. Conrad Rawski, *Petrarch's Remedies for Fortune Fair and Foul* (Bloomington: Indiana University, 1991), 3:338): "*Metus.* Insepultus abiciar./*Ratio.* Age res tuas. Curam hanc linque viventibus."

50. Ovid's *Remedia* may also lurk in the background. Ariani, *Petrarch*, 144.

51. Boccaccio hits similar notes, more humorously, in his contemporary characterization of Maestro Simone. See Victoria Kirkham, "Painters at Play on the Judgment Day (*Decameron* VIII 9)," *Studi sul Boccaccio* 14 (1983–84): 256–77, reprinted in *The Sign of Reason in Boccaccio's Fiction* (Florence: Olschki, 1993), 215–35.

52. For useful information, see Steven A. Walton, "An Introduction to the Mechanical Arts in the Middle Ages," Association Villard de Honnecourt for Interdisciplinary Study of Medieval Technology, Science and Art, University of Toronto, 2003, available at http://members.shaw.ca/competitivenessofnations/2.%20Articles.htm.

53. Petrarch, *Invective*, in *Invectives*, trans. David Marsh (Cambridge: Harvard University Press, 2003), 189.

54. *Invective* (trans. Marsh), 209.

55. *Invective* (trans. Marsh), 196–99: "Non dat Fortuna mores bonos, non ingenium, non virtutem, non facundiam. Unde hec qua nescio quid anserinum potius quam cycneum strepis, non eloquentia, ut dicebam, sed loquacitas tua est."

56. *Invective* (trans. Marsh), 218–19: "ad nundinas Simonis, non ut serus, sic et

piger mercator accesseris." Petrarch alludes to the Acts of the Apostles 8:18, as Marsh notes in his commentary (504).

57. *Invective* (trans. Marsh), 282–83: "non quasi philosophum loquentem, *sed apostolum.*"

58. *Epystole* 3.30, in *Petrarch at Vaucluse: Letters in Verse and Prose*, trans. Ernest Hatch Wilkins (Chicago: University of Chicago Press, 1958), 39–40. For the Latin, see *Epystole metrice* at http://www.bibliotecaitaliana.it. He begins his *Collatio brevis coram Johanne Francorum rege* by apologizing for not speaking French, but the stance is rhetorical.

59. "Natura autem Galli sunt indociles," quoted by Gianfelice Peron, "Lingua e cultura d'oïl in Petrarca," in *Le lingue del Petrarca*, ed. Daniele, 11–32. Petrarch claims not to speak French in the speech he made at Paris in 1361 for Galeazzo Visconti before King John II of France. In a fourteenth-century didactic strain of thought, he judged negatively other French romances—Arthurian tales and legends of Alexander the Great—because as fiction (*fabulae*) they lack the authority of history (*historia*). Cf. William Paden, "Petrarch as a Poet of Provence," *Annali d'Italianistica* 22 (2004): 19–44, with rich bibliographical references. For the intractability of the French, see Petrarch *Invective* (trans. Marsh), 440–41.

60. *Invective* (trans. Marsh), 370: "a feritate morum Franci olim dicti," literally, "[French] were once called Franks from their feral manners." Disclaiming responsibility for his insult, Petrarch says he merely follows the historians and cosmographers, who all called the French "barbaros Gallos."

61. *Invective* (trans. Marsh), 379; cf. for other insults that beastialize Hesdin (387, 399, 427, 445).

62. *Invective* (trans. Marsh), 375, 385.

63. See the classic discussion by Giuseppe Billanovich, "Dall'*Epystolarum mearum ad diversos liber* ai *Rerum familiarium libri XXIV*," in *Petrarca letterato. 1. Lo scrittoio del Petrarca* (Rome: Edizioni di Storia e Letteratura, 1947), 1–55.

64. Petrarch to his new friend, Francesco da Siena, a teacher of logic and medecine, *Seniles* 16.3. Cf. *Familiares* 1.1.9 (ed. Rossi 1: 5): "mille, velo eo amplius, seu omnis generis sparsa poemata seu familiares epystolas . . . Vulcano corrigendas tradidi" [I committed to Vulcan's hands for his correction at least a thousand and more of all kinds and variety of poems and friendly letters; trans. Bernardo, 5]. Bernardo applies the epithet "born-again ancient" in the introduction to his translation of the *Seniles* (1:xix). Wilkins, *Life of Petrarch*, 52, connects this Verona visit to Petrarch's acquaintance with Pietro Alighieri, a recipient of one of his *Epystole*.

65. Ariani, *Petrarca*, 168, for Petrarch's "grafomania." On the comparative quan-

tity of Petrarch's letter writing, see Wilkins, *Life of Petrarch*, 150; also quoted by Bernardo in his introduction to the *Seniles*, xix.

66. Petrarch speaks of both projects in his letter dedicating the *Familiares* to Socrates. On the date of the dedicatory epistle (*Familiares* 1.1), suppressed in the text, see Wilkins, *Life of Petrarch*, 87; Ariani, *Petrarca*, 68. Petrarch mourns the death of Socrates in a letter ca. 1361–62 to Nelli (*Seniles* 1.3).

67. There is one letter to a woman. See Petrarch *Familiares* 21.8 (ed. Rossi, 4: 61): "Ad Annam imperatricem, responsio congratulatoria super eius femineo licet partu et ob id ipsum multa de laudibus feminarum" [To Empress Anna, felicitations on the birth of a child, though a girl, and the occasion it affords to express many thoughts in praise of women; trans. Bernardo, 175]. Anna is the only female addressee in all of Petrarch's letter collections. Even writing on the death of his grandson (*Seniles* 10.4), he does not name the child's mother. Neither does he write to his daughter Francesca or name her in his will, which designates her husband, Francesco da Brossano, as Petrarch's universal heir. For the phases of composition of *Seniles*, see Wilkins, *Life of Petrarch*, 152. The very last letter, like the first, is to Socrates. Probably fictional, it closes the anthology in a ring structure.

68. Petrarch *Familiares* 24.13.6–7 (ed. Rossi, 4: 265; trans. Bernardo, 251–52): "hic liber satis crevit nec, nisi iusti voluminis meta trascenditur, plurium capax est, que huius quidem generis scripta iam superant, his avulsa extra ordinem alio quodam, que scribenda autem, siquid tale nunc etiam sum scripturus, ab etate iam nomen habitura, rursus alio venient claudenda volumine."

69. For a thumbnail sketch of Nelli's life, see *Rai International Online*, s.v. "Francesco Nelli" at http://www.italica.rai.it/rinascimento/parole_chiave/schede/136nelli.htm. Petrarch mourned his death in a letter to Boccaccio (*Seniles* 3.1). Nelli receives twenty-seven letters in the *Familiares*.

70. Petrarch, *Seniles* (ed. Bernardo), xix. Bernardo quotes from his article, "Petrarch's Autobiography: Circularity Revisited," *Annali d'Italianistica* 4 (1986): 50.

71. Petrarch *Seniles* 10.2: "incolarumque colluvie exundans" (ed. Nota, 3: 243; trans. Bernardo, 360); "concursantes et coactas ibi concretasque totius orbis sordes ac nequitias" (ed. Nota, 3: 251; trans. Bernardo, 360, 363). The letter dates from 1367. Carpentras lies about twenty kilometers from Avignon.

72. As Stefano Carrai writes of the *Bucolicum carmen* in this volume: "He clearly rejected the numerical structure of Virgil's *Bucolica*, comprised of ten eclogues, choosing instead another canonical Virgilian number, that of the twelve-book *Aeneid*." So, too, for *Familiares*, Petrarch chose an "epic" num-

ber, as Giuseppe Mazzotta writes (see below): "We know that originally
Petrarch had conceived of writing twelve books of letters. In 1359, however,
after reading through the partial translation of the *Odyssey* by Leonzio Pilato,
he settled on twenty-four books. With that discovery, an epistolary epic is
born."

73. See Carlo Calcaterra's classic chapter "Feria sexta aprilis," in *Nella selva del
Petrarca* (Bologna: Cappelli, 1942).

74. Petrarch *Secretum* in *Opere latine* (ed. Bufano, 1:166; trans. Quillen, 102):
"Ego vero numerum ipsum ternarium tota mente complector; non tam quia
tres eo Gratie continentur, quam quia divinitati amicissimum esse constat.
Quod non tibi solum aliisque vere religionis professoribus persuasum est,
quibus est omnis in Trinitate fidutia, sed ipsis etiam gentium philosophis, a
quibus traditur uti eos hoc numero in consecrationibus deorum: quod nec
Virgilius meus ignorasse videtur ubi ait: *numero Deus impare gaudet.*" The Virgil Petrarch cites is *Eclogues* 8.75. In the Pythagorean-Neoplatonic system,
odd numbers are superior to even numbers, and the first odd number that
"counts" is 3. For a discussion in the context of Boccaccio's rich numerology,
see Kirkham, *Fabulous Vernacular*, 159. Petrarch again plays on the number 3
in the preface to his *De remediis*, which opens with an allusion to the three
parts of Prudence (memory, understanding, and foresight) and then comments that man, endowed with wisdom unlike the beasts, "must continuously
wrestle with threats as menacing as a three-headed Cerberus" (trans.
Rawski, 1:3).

75. Hence the *Divina commedia* has 10 × 10 cantos and a cosmology with ten
heavens, while Dante's infernal funnel pierces earth through nine concen-
tric circles. So, too, Boccaccio's woeful cases of the fallen mighty, *De casibus
virorum illustrium*, form an encyclopedia in nine books. Boccaccio probably
designed his *De casibus* in nine books to echo the number of circles in Dante's
Hell. See Victoria Kirkham and María Rosa Menocal, "Reflections on the
'Arabic' World: Boccaccio's Ninth Stories," *Stanford Italian Review* 7, nos. 1–2
(1987): 95–110.

76. Paul Piur, *Petrarcas 'Buch ohne Namen' und die päpstliche Kurie* (Halle: Max
Niemeyer, 1925), "laruarum ac lemurum domus est," 194, "civitas confu-
sionis," 198, "laberinthum Rodani," 221, "populum . . . militantem Satane,"
221, "Nulla ibi preterea lux, nullus dux, nullus index amfractuum, sed caligo
undique et ubique confusio, ne parum uera sit Babilon ac perplexitas rerum
mira," 216, and for the city's denizens, see, e.g., 193–94; trans. Norman Zacour, *Petrarch's Book Without a Name* (Toronto: Portifical Institute of Medieval
Studies, 1973), 68, 71, 72, 91, 93, 99).

77. Piur, *Petrarcas 'Buch ohne Namen'*: "Hec tibi raptim Hierosolymitanus exul

inter et super flumina Babilonis indignans scripsi," 196 (trans. Zacour, 71). Martinez calls attention to the sole subscription "signature" in his essay in this volume, *The Book without a Name:* Petrarch's Open Secret." Jersualem here stands for Rome and Italy.

78. For a schematic presentation of the dates and dedicatees of the letters, see Ernest Hatch Wilkins, *The "Epistolae metricae" of Petrarch: A Manual* (Rome: Edizioni di Storia e Letteratura, 1956). See Feo, *Petrarca nel tempo*, 292–302, on the textual history. Eight of the metrical epistles find an elegant English translator in Ernest Hatch Wilkins, *Petrarch at Vaucluse: Letters in Verse and Prose* (Chicago: University of Chicago Press, 1958). Scholars have also created a category of "epistole metriche varie." See Wilkins, *"Epistole metrichae" di Petrarca*, 16–17. For the current thinking on what pieces legitimately belong there, including two recent discoveries, see Feo, *Petrarca nel tempo*, 309.

79. Petrarch *Familiares* 1.1.21 (ed. Rossi, 1: 7; trans. Bernardo, 8): "Ulixeos errores erroribus meis confer."

80. Mazzotta ends linking Petrarch's name to Machiavelli's. It is not a farfetched comparison. Cf. Dotti, *Vita di Petrarca*, 449, who refers to Umberto Bosco's intuition "Già sentì nello scrittore un cenno del futuro 'principe' del Machiavelli" [He sensed in the writer a future sign already of Machiavelli's "prince."]

81. Petrarch *Secretum* 1:250–52 (trans. Quillen, 144; *cf. Petrarch's Testament*, ed. and trans. Theodor E. Mommsen (Ithaca: Cornell University Press, 1957), 3–4: "incipe tecum de morte cogitare, cui sensim et nescius appropinquas. Rescissis velis tenebrisque discussis, in illam oculos fige. Cave ne ulla dies aut nox transeat, que non tibi memoriam supremi temporis ingerat."

82. Petrarch, *Poesie minori*, ed. Domenico Rossetti (Milan: Società Tipografica de' Classici Italiani (1829–34), "Epigraphe" 4.7, vol. 2 (n.p.): "Vix mundi novus hospes iter, vitaeque volantis/Attigeram tenero limina dura pede./Franciscus genitor, genitrix Francisca; secutus/Hos de fonte sacro nomen idem tenui./Infans formosus, solamen dulce parentum,/Nunc dolor; hoc uno sors mea laeta minus./Caetera sum felix, et verae gaudia vitae/Nactus et aeternae, tam cito, tam facile./Sol bis, luna quarter flexum peragraverat orbem:/Obvia mors, fallor, obvia vita fuit./Me Venetum terris dedit urbs, rapuitque Papia:/Nec querar, hinc coelo restituendus eram." Among his other surviving epitaphs are those he composed for himself, for Pope John XXII, and for his dog Zabot. See Feo, "Carmina latina varia," in *Petrarca nel tempo*, 312.

83. Petrarch, *Invective* (trans. Marsh), 384–85: "Nec videtur audivisse, civili cautum lege, ut is locus, ubi non dicam liberi, sed servi etiam corpus, nec corpus modo integrum, sed pars corporis humo condita est, religiosus habeatur";

466–67: ". . . Parisius insignium choros ecclesiarum sic confertas bustis et cadaveribus peccatorum, quodque est fedius peccatricum, ut vix quisquam possit ibi se flectere vixque iter pateat ad altare."

84. Vittore Branca, "Francesco Petrarca," *Dizionario critico della letteratura italiana* (Turin: Unione Tipografico-Editrice Torinese, 1986), 3:419–32.

85. Giosuè Carducci, *Ai parentali di Giovanni Boccacci in Certaldo* (Bologna: Zanichelli, 1876).

86. Wilkins, "Peregrinus ubique," reckons that Petrarch was in eighty-three cities: Abano, near the Adda, the Adige valley, Aix-la-Chapelle, the Ardennes forest, Arezzo, Arquà, Avignon, Baia, Basel, Bergamo, Bologna, Bolsena, Capranica, Carpentras, Carpi, Cavaillon, Cave of Ste-Beaume, Mt. Cenis, Cologne, the Enza river valley, Ferrara, Florence, Lake Garda, Garignano, the Garonne valley, Genoa, Ghent, Imola, near Lavenza, near Lerici, Liège, L'Incisa, Lombez, Lonigo, Lyons, Malaucene, Mantua, Milan, Modena, Monaco, Monpellier, Montrieux, Monza, near Motrone, Naples, Narni, Nice Novara, Oriago, Padua, Palestrina, Paris, Parma, Pavia, Perugia, Peschiera, Piacenza, Pisa, Porto Maurizio, Pozzuoli, Prague, near Reggio, Rimini, Rome, Saint Maximin, San Colombano, Scandiano, Selvapiana, Siena, Suzzara, Todi, Toulouse, Treviso, Valserena, Vaucluse, Mt. Ventoux, Udine, Verona, Venice, Vicenza, and Viterbo.

87. "[N]obilibus non ultima pestis ingeniis," Petrarch *Seniles* 5.1 (ed. Nota, 2:123), cited and trans. James Harvey Robinson, with Henry Winchester Rolfe, *Petrarch: The First Modern Scholar and Man of Letters* (New York: Putnam, 1898), 27. Translated by Bernardo as "not the least of the plagues that we noble minds endure" (1:115).

88. Timothy J. Reiss, *Mirages of the Selfe: Patterns of Personhood in Ancient and Early Modern Europe* (Stanford: Stanford University Press, 2003), chap. 11 ("Multum a me ipso differre compulsus sum"), 303.

89. Francesco De Sanctis, *Storia della letteratura italiana* ed. Paulo Arcari (1870–71; Milan: Fratelli Treves, 1925), 1:211: "Così sorsero i primi puristi e letterati in Italia, e capi furono Francesco Petrarca e Giovanni Boccaccio" [Thus arose the first purists and men of letters in Italy, and the leaders were Francesco Petrarch and Giovanni Boccaccio], and 1:213: "Questo sentimento delle belle forme, della bella donna e della bella Natura, puro di ogni turbamento è la Musa del Petrarca" [This sentiment of formal beauty, of female beauty, and of natural beauty, purified of all disturbance, is Petrarch's Muse].

90. The so-called conversion was said to have occurred in 1342–43, when his brother became a monk and his second daughter was born. Dotti, *Petrarca*, 447–48, cites Bosco: "The period in which he was in large part other than

what he later became either didn't exist except as the poet's illusion, or else it has left no appreciable literary traces." Dotti agrees: "the complex problem of relations between classical and Christian culture should be approached taking into account an elementary truth: that Petrarch is reflected the same way in all his works."

91. Giosuè Carducci, "Ad Arquà, presso la tomba del Petrarca," in *Prose scelte*, ed. Emilio Pasquini (Milan: Biblioteca Universale Rizzoli, 2007), 225–26.

92. See the introduction by Manlio Pastore Stocchi to Petrarch, *Opere latine*, ed. Bufano, cited by Branca, *Dizionario critico*, 3:423.

93. Petrarch *Seniles* 17.2 in *Epistole* (ed. Dotti, 856): "Multum . . . adhuc restat operis multumque restabit; nec ulli nato post mille secula preciditur occasio aliquid adhuc adiciendi." Cited by Robinson, *Petrarch*, 418.

Chapter One

1. The title in the autograph is *Francisci petrarche laureati poete Rerum vulgarium fragmenta* (*Fragments of Vernacular Matters of Francis Petrarch Poet Laureate*). The title *Rime sparse* (*Scattered Rhymes*), with its Italian analogue to the Latin *fragmenta*, is taken from the first verse of the first poem: *Voi ch'ascoltate in rime sparse il suono*. The title *Canzoniere* is traditional and derives from the Italian noun *canzoniere* or collection of lyric poems. I will refer to the *Rerum vulgarium fragmenta* at times as *Fragmenta*, and I will use the acronym *RVF* in citation.

2. See Aristotle, *Physics*, in *The Basic Works of Aristotle*, ed. Richard McKeon, trans. R. P. Hardie and R. K. Gaye (New York: Random House, 1941). Dante's *Convivio* is cited in the edition of Cesare Vasoli, in *Opere minori*, vol. 5.1, part 2 of La letteratura italiana: Storia e testi (Milan: Ricciardi, 1988).

3. This position is set out more fully in Teodolinda Barolini, "Petrarch as the Metaphysical Poet Who Is Not Dante: Metaphysical Markers at the Beginning of the *Rerum vulgarium fragmenta*," in *Petrarch and Dante*, ed. Zygmunt Baranski and Theodore Cachey (Notre Dame: Notre Dame University Press, 2009). The common view is that Petrarch rejected metaphysics along with Scholasticism and other forms of the medieval mindset: "In place of speculative metaphysical systems, of scientific, especially medical, investigation, of legal codification, he puts grammar, rhetoric, poetry, history, moral philosophy" (Peter Hainsworth, *Petrarch the Poet: An Introduction to the "Rerum vulgarium fragmenta"* [London: Routledge, 1988], 4). While not without elements of truth, this commonplace requires considerable nuancing.

4. On the critical issues surrounding the division, see Teodolinda Barolini, "Petrarch at the Crossroads of Hermeneutics and Philology: Editorial Lapses,

Narrative Impositions, and Wilkins' Doctrine of the Nine Forms of the *Rerum vulgarium fragmenta*," in *Petrarch and the Textual Origins of Interpretation*, ed. Teodolinda Barolini and H. Wayne Storey, Columbia Series in the Classical Tradition (Leiden: Brill, 2007), 21–44.

5. According to Petrarch's handwritten note, sonnet 211 was originally excluded from the collection and added very late, in 1369; see note 31 below. Lyric poets in this period did not title their poems, but referred to them by their incipits, or first verses; because the incipits are often syntactic fragments, I have not provided translations.

6. Citations of the *Rerum vulgarium fragmenta* are from Marco Santagata's edition: *Canzoniere* (Milan: Mondadori, 1996, rev. 2006). The translations, with occasional modifications, are by Robert M. Durling, *Petrarch's Lyric Poems* (Cambridge, Mass. and London, England: Harvard University Press, 1976). In this instance I have written out the numbers in poem 336 as Durling does in poem 211.

7. For elaboration of these views, see Teodolinda Barolini, "Notes toward a Gendered History of Italian Literature, with a Discussion of Dante's *Beatrix Loquax*," *Dante and the Origins of Italian Literary Culture* (New York: Fordham University Press, 2006), 360–78.

8. The constructed nature of this tension comes more clearly into focus if we consider that in the year 1327 Good Friday actually fell on April 10, not on April 6.

9. *Confessions* 8.9, emphasis added. Augustine's *Confessions* are cited in the translation of R. S. Pine-Coffin (London: Penguin, 1961), 172. For the importance of Augustine in the *Rerum vulgarium fragmenta*, see Nicolae Iliescu, *Il "Canzoniere" petrarchesco e Sant'Agostino* (Rome: Società Accademica Romena, 1962); Kenelm Foster, *Petrarch: Poet and Humanist* (Edinburgh: Edinburgh University Press, 1984); and Sara Sturm-Maddox, *Petrarchan Metamorphoses: Text and Subtext in the "Rime sparse"* (Columbia: University of Missouri Press, 1985), chapter 5.

10. Foster lists a set of "penitential poems," referred to as such in the appended chart "Metrical and Thematic Sets in the *Rerum vulgarium fragmenta*," in *Petrarch: Poet and Humanist*, 60.

11. Peter Hainsworth claims "some eighteen political, moral or occasional poems which are not love-poems in any obvious sense" (*Petrarch the Poet*, 51) but does not list the poems he includes in this count. Classification is difficult because the categories overlap. For instance, there are five poems to Sennuccio del Bene, the last on his death (108, 112, 113, 144, 287), which could be classified as occasional, but they are also love poems. I have construed

"occasional" broadly in appendix 1, and have included all poems addressed to friends even if they are love poems, arriving at a group of 31 poems.

12. The fifteen anniversary poems are 30, 50, 62, 79, 101, 107, 118, 122, 145, 212, 221, 266, 271, 278, 364. See Dennis Dutschke, "The Anniversary Poems in Petrarch's *Canzoniere*," *Italica* 58 (1981): 83–101.

13. Hainsworth, *Petrarch the Poet*, 135.

14. See Ernest Hatch Wilkins, *The Making of the "Canzoniere" and Other Petrarchan Studies* (Rome: Edizioni di Storia e Letteratura, 1951). Wilkins's methods and findings are currently being challenged and updated by philologists working with contemporary technologies; see, for instance, Dario Del Puppo and H. Wayne Storey, "Wilkins nella formazione del canzoniere di Petrarca," *Italica* 80 (2003): 295–312. Unfortunately, over the last decades many of Wilkins's interpretations have been disseminated as philological fact. For a study that critiques our acceptance of Wilkins's doctrine of the nine forms, and emphasizes the existence of only two forms, see Barolini, "Petrarch at the Crossroads of Hermeneutics and Philology."

15. *Rerum vulgarium fragmenta. Codice Vat. Lat. 3195, Edizione in fac-simile* (vol. 1 [2003]) and *Commentario* (vol. 2 [2004]), ed. Gino Belloni, Furio Brugnolo, H. Wayne Storey, and Stefano Zamponi (Rome: Antenore, 2003–4).

16. Malpaghini's work was continuous, unlike Petrarch's (Wilkins, *Making of the "Canzoniere"*, 137); he stopped work on April 21, 1367 (Wilkins, *Making of the "Canzoniere"*, 139). Malpaghini transcribed 244 poems, 189 in part 1 and 55 in part 2; Petrarch transcribed 123 poems, including one retranscription, 75 in part 1 (the retranscription is number 121) and 48 in part 2. See Wilkins, *Making of the "Canzoniere"*, 75–76.

17. To see tabulated the last 31 poems of Vat. Lat. 3195 both according to the position in the manuscript and according to Petrarch's added marginal numerals, see table 1 in Wilkins, *Making of the "Canzoniere"*, 77.

18. On this topic, see H. Wayne Storey, "Doubting Petrarca's Last Words: Erasure in MS Vat. Lat. 3195," in *Petrarch and the Textual Origins of Interpretation*, ed. Teodolinda Barolini and H. Wayne Storey, Columbia Series in the Classical Tradition (Leiden: Brill, 2007), 67–88.

19. "These sonnets [259–263] were his last additions to the collection. He presumably intended to add still other poems—otherwise he would hardly have inserted a full duernion at the end of Part I. But he never did so: Part I of the *Canzoniere* is therefore, in a sense, incomplete. I find no evidence, internal or external, to indicate that Petrarch ever thought of 263 as a terminal poem for Part I, or that he was ever concerned to bring the total number of poems in the *Canzoniere* to three hundred and sixty-six" (Wilkins, *Making of*

the "Canzoniere",186–87). Dependent on the intentionality of the total of 366 poems are all arguments like Thomas Roche's, "The Calendrical Structure of Petrarch's *Canzoniere,*" *Studies in Philology* 71 (1974): 152–72.

20. For a discussion of the properties of the lyric sequence as a genre, see Teodolinda Barolini, "The Making of a Lyric Sequence: Time and Narrative in Petrarch's *Rerum vulgarium fragmenta,*" *MLN* 104 (1989): 1–38; now in *Dante and the Origins of Italian Literary Culture,* 193–223.

21. The passage is the beginning of *Familiares* 24.1, which treats "de inextimabili fuga temporis," in the translation by Aldo S. Bernardo, *Letters on Familiar Matters: Rerum familiarium libri XVII–XXIV* (Baltimore: Johns Hopkins University Press, 1985), 308.

22. Citations from the *Secretum* are from *Prose,* ed. Enrico Carrara (Milan and Naples: Ricciardi, 1955), quotation on 210.

23. Wilkins, *Making of the "Canzoniere",* 145.

24. The formulation "canzoniere come genere letterario e canzoniere come genere codicologico (il repertorio 'antologico')" belongs to Del Puppo and Storey, "Wilkins nella formazione del canzoniere di Petrarca," 306.

25. In "Medieval English Literature and the Idea of the Anthology," Seth Lerer seeks the "controlling literary intelligence" of the anonymous medieval English Harley 2253 manuscript; see *PMLA* 118 (2003): 1251–67, quotation on 1255.

26. Along with the Chigi form of the *Rerum vulgarium fragmenta,* Chigiano L V 176 contains Dante's *Vita nuova,* fifteen of Dante's lyrics, Boccaccio's *Vita di Dante,* his poem to Petrarch *Ytalie iam certus honos,* and Cavalcanti's *Donna mi prega.* See the facsimile of the Chigiano with introduction by Domenico De Robertis (discussion of the date on 12), *Il codice chigiano L. V. 176, autografo di Giovanni Boccaccio* (Rome: Archivi edizioni, 1974).

27. Olivia Holmes, *Assembling the Lyric Self: Authorship from Troubadour Song to Italian Poetry Book* (Minneapolis: University of Minnesota Press, 2000) champions Guittone, claiming that "the elaborate formal disposition of Guittone's texts serves as evidence of an original authorial ordering" (47). However, in the absence of an authorial codex we cannot claim to be witnessing "original authorial ordering."

28. The full title of the Chigi collection as given by Boccaccio is *Francisci petrarce de Florentia Rome nuper laureati fragmentorum liber* (*The Book of Fragments of Francis Petrarch of Florence Lately Crowned in Laurel at Rome*). Still extremely helpful on the Chigi form is the study by Ruth Shepard Phelps, *The Earlier and Later Forms of Petrarch's "Canzoniere"* (Chicago: University of Chicago Press, 1925).

29. Of course canzone 264, *I' vo pensando,* was not number 264 in the earlier

Chigi collection, but number 175, because the Chigi collection consists of a total of 215 poems, 174 in part 1 and 41 in part 2.

30. The contents of Vaticano Latino 3196 are easily accessed through the edition of Laura Paolino in *Trionfi, Rime estravaganti, Codice degli abbozzi*, ed. Vinicio Pacca and Laura Paolino (Milan: Mondadori, 1996).

31. The notation to *Voglia mi sprona* reads in part: "Mirum: hunc cancellatum et damnatum post multos annos, casu relegens, absolvi et transcripsi in ordine statim, non obstante . . . 1369 iunii 22, hora 23, veneris" (Amazing, rereading by chance after many years this [sonnet] which had been crossed out and condemned, I absolved it and transcribed it in order immediately, in spite of [having rejected it], on Friday, June 22, 1369, at the 23rd hour). The text is from *Trionfi* (ed. Pacca and Paolino), 809–10; the translation is Peter Hainsworth's, *Petrarch the Poet*, 46.

32. For Petrarch's sequential count, see Wilkins, *Making of the "Canzoniere"*, 122.

33. On sonnet 34 as the original number 1, see Wilkins, *Making of the "Canzoniere"*, 147.

34. Given the cancellation of time carried out in this sonnet, it is interesting that verse 8, "ove tu *prima*, et *poi* fu' invescato io" (emphasis added), echoes very precisely the Aristotelian definition of time in Dante's *Convivio*: "numero di movimento, secondo *prima* e *poi*" (*Convivio* 4.2.6; emphasis added). For Petrarch's handling of the Apollo/Daphne myth, see P. R. J. Hainsworth, "The Myth of Daphne in the *Rerum vulgarium fragmenta*," *Italian Studies* 34 (1979): 28–44.

35. The form *pentere*, for *pentire*, is unusual; Hainsworth points out that the irregularity "was muted in many editions by replacing the unusual 'pentersi' with the more usual 'pentirsi'" (*Petrarch the Poet*, 180).

36. Thus, the comment to poem 1 in the Carducci-Ferrari edition: "Proemio; e dovrebb'essere epilogo" (The proem, but it should be the epilogue [3]). The words "breve sogno" are from *Voi ch'ascoltate*'s celebrated last verse, "che quanto piace al mondo è breve sogno" (whatever pleases in the world is a brief dream).

37. Hainsworth, *Petrarch the Poet*, 151.

38. Petrarch wrote next to 366 "in fine libri ponatur" (to be placed at the book's end); see Wilkins, *Making of the "Canzoniere"*, 177.

39. I would suggest as a model Augustine, who structures his *Confessions* so that the conversion experience occurs at roughly two-thirds of the way through the text.

40. For the use of narrativity as a means of injecting temporality into the *Rerum vulgarium fragmenta*, see Barolini, "Making of a Lyric Sequence." On time as

a thematic (rather than structural) presence in the *Rerum vulgarium fragmenta*, see Gianfranco Folena, "L'orologio del Petrarca," *Libri e documenti* 5, no. 3 (1979): 1–12, and the two contributions of Edoardo Taddeo, "Petrarca e il tempo: Il tempo come tema nelle opere latine," *Studi e problemi di critica testuale* 25 (1982): 53–76, and, on the *Rerum vulgarium fragmenta*, "Petrarca e il tempo," *Studi e problemi di critica testuale* 27 (1983): 69–108. See also Giovanni Getto, "*Triumphus Temporis:* Il sentimento del tempo nell'opera di Francesco Petrarca," in *Letterature comparate: problemi e metodo. Studi in onore di Ettore Paratore* (Bologna: Patron, 1981) 3: 1243–72, Marianne Shapiro, *Hieroglyph of Time: The Petrarchan Sestina* (Minneapolis: University of Minnesota Press, 1980), and Marco Santagata, *I frammenti dell'anima: storia e racconto nel "Canzoniere" di Petrarca* (Bologna: Il Mulino, 1993).

41. Wilkins adopted as his principles of construction for Vaticano Latino 3195 those adduced by Ruth Shepard Phelps for the Chigi collection in her book *The Earlier and Later Forms of Petrarch's "Canzoniere."* Although Wilkins was explicit in acknowledging the contribution of "Miss Phelps" (93), her fundamental work has been largely overlooked.

42. Wilkins's desire to account for all textual decisions in terms of chronological order is one of the most dated aspects of his analysis. With respect to variety of form, Wilkins notes that the intermixture of sonnets, canzoni, *ballate*, and *madrigali* constitutes "a major innovation" (156). Variety of content is achieved by the inclusion, alongside love poems, of poems of "friendship, politics, religion, etc.," so distributed "as to prevent the existence of long series of love poems" (156).

43. Although the verse in question is probably Guillem de Saint-Gregori's, according to Contini Petrarch certainly attributed it to Arnaut; see Gianfranco Contini, ed., *Canzoniere* (Turin: Einaudi, 1964). Petrarch felt a particular affinity with Arnaut, the troubadour who invented the sestina.

44. If Dante wrote the *Fiore,* he wrote an extended version of the kind of *corona* of sonnets practiced by poets like Folgòre da San Gimignano (for which see Marco Santagata, *Dal sonetto al Canzoniere: Ricerche sulla preistoria e la costituzione di un genere* [Padua: Liviana, 1979]). This operation does not entail collecting previously written lyrics and transcribing them in a newly significant order but composing sonnets with the express purpose of telling a story. The *Fiore*'s sequence of 232 sonnets condenses and retells the *Roman de la rose* in a mode that is less philosophically digressive and hence, if anything, more dedicated to narrative thrust than the octosyllabic original. In fact, this sequence of sonnets (which, if Dante's, would constitute a pre–*Vita nuova* example of Dante's experimentation with lyric/narrative *contaminatio*), in no way eschews narrativity. It is best compared not to Petrarch's lyric sequence,

in which the *contaminatio* is so delicately balanced, but to a work like the *Filostrato;* the sonnets take the place that in Boccaccio's work will be taken by octaves. In other words, although made of lyrics, the work is a narrative. See Barolini, *"Cominciandomi dal principio infino a la fine:* Forging Anti-narrative in the *Vita nuova,"* in *Dante and the Origins of Italian Literary Culture,* 175–92, esp. pp. 190–92.

45. For *Giovene donna* belonging to two contradictory sets, see Barolini, "Making of a Lyric Sequence," 205; this essay also offers interpretive guidelines to some of these categories, in particular, the marking of a beginning, middle, and end, the canzoni series 70–73 and 125–129, the anniversary poems, the sestine, and the "death sequence."

46. The word *istoria/historia* appears only in canzone 127.7 and in sonnet 343.11. It is worth noting that canzone 127, *In quella parte dove Amor mi sprona,* with its first use of *istoria,* is followed by the "historical" political canzone, *Italia mia.*

47. The idea that part 1 can be divided into two sections is not new: for instance, in *Petrarch the Poet* Hainsworth writes of the "second half of Part 1" (61) and considers the series 125–29 to be the "turning-point" (61), although he also uses poems 140 and 133 (the exact midpoint) as divisions (59). There are other possible implicit endpoints in this vicinity. Much was made by Wilkins of sestina 142 as a poem that "would have made a dignified and appropriate ending" to an earlier version of part 1 (97). Whichever of these endpoints is chosen, the effect is to create an implicit tripartite structure to counteract the explicit bipartite structure.

48. For the importance of the number 6, reflected in my numerological note to appendix 2, see Carlo Calcaterra, *Nella selva del Petrarca* (Bologna: Cappelli, 1942), chapter 7.

49. The Latin text of the *Confessions* is from the Loeb Classical Library edition, 2 vols. (Cambridge: Harvard University Press; London: Heinemann, 1976). For discussion of these passages from the *Confessions,* which influenced greatly both Dante and Petrarch, see Teodolinda Barolini, *The Undivine Comedy* (Princeton: Princeton University Press, 1992), chapter 7.

50. Because Laura here possesses an "angelica forma," the reflex has been to suggest that we must be in the presence of stilnovist themes—in the presence of theologized courtliness. Indeed, the formulaic rigidity that has calcified the Italian critical tradition is such that the mere presence of the word "angelic" is taken to signal a stilnovist pedigree. But the echoes of stilnovism that we find in the concluding sextet of the sonnet *Erano i capei d'oro a l'aura sparsi* are interesting precisely because they do *not* constitute a homage to the transcendent.

51. For these different intertexts, see Sturm-Maddox, *Petrarchan Metamorphoses.*

52. This quintessentially Petrarchan focus on (lack of) self and identity was painstakingly achieved through the lengthy process of revision of canzone 23. The earlier version of this verse is courtly and Dantean. "Però con una carta et con enchiostro/Dissi: accorrete, donna, al fedel vostro!" (Therefore with a paper and ink I said: run, lady, to your faithful servant!) became "ond'io gridai con carta et con incostro: Non son mio, no. S'io moro, il danno è vostro" (so I cried out with paper and ink: I am not my own, no; if I die the fault is yours). For the development of the canzone, see Dennis Dutschke, *Francesco Petrarca: Canzone XXIII from First to Final Version* (Ravenna: Longo, 1977).

53. This is the limitation of the gender analysis in Nancy Vickers, "Diana Described: Scattered Woman and Scattered Rhyme," *Critical Inquiry* 8 (1981): 265–79; the analysis does not account for the fact that particularizing description and bodily fragmentation are applied to the male lover/poet as well as to Laura (for instance, in the many references to his hair).

54. This synthesis is from Barolini, "Making of a Lyric Sequence," 222.

Chapter Two

1. The text cited for *Rerum vulgarium fragmenta* is Petrarch, *Canzoniere*, ed. Marco Santagata (Milan: Mondadori, 1996); and for *Triumphi*, Petrarch, *Trionfi, Rime estravaganti, Codice degli abbozzi*, ed. Vinicio Pacca and Laura Paolino (Milan: Mondadori, 1996). Translations of the *Triumphi* are from *The Triumphs of Petrarch*, trans. Ernest Hatch Wilkins (Chicago: University of Chicago Press, 1962), occasionally modified to retain a more literal reading. All emphases in the quotes are added. Other translations, unless attributed, are my own. On Petrarch's debt to the *Divina commedia*, see Claudio Giunta, "Memoria di Dante nei *Trionfi*," *Rivista di Letteratura Italiana* 11 (1993): 411–52. For the more complex triangular interaction among Petrarch, Dante, and Boccaccio, see Vittore Branca, "Intertestualità fra Petrarca e Boccaccio," *Lectura Petrarce* 14 (1994): 359–80; and Carlo Vecce, "La 'Lunga Pictura': Visione e rappresentazione nei *Trionfi*," in *I Triumphi di Francesco Petrarca (Gargnano del Garda, 1998)*, ed. Claudia Berra, 299–315 (Milan: Cisalpino, 1999).

2. Marina Ricucci, "L'esordio dei *Triumphi*: Tra *Eneide* e *Commedia*," *Rivista di Letteratura Italiana* 12 (1994): 313–49.

3. Although the text of the *Triumphi* is in Italian, its titles are in Latin.

4. Emilio Pasquini, "Il Testo: Fra l'autografo e i testimoni di collazione," in Berra, ed., *I Triumphi di Francesco Petrarca*, 11–37.

5. Dante Alighieri, *La Commedia secondo l'antica vulgata*, ed. Giorgio Petrocchi (Turin: Einaudi, 1975), *Inferno* 1.1; *The Divine Comedy*, trans. by Charles S. Singleton, 6 vols. (Princeton: Princeton University Press, 1970–75).

6. Victoria Kirkham, "Dante's Polysynchrony: A Perfectly Timed Entry into Eden," *Filologia e Critica* 20 (1995): 329–52.

7. Teodolinda Barolini, *The Undivine Comedy: Detheologizing Dante* (Princeton: Princeton University Press, 1992), 3–16.

8. Guido Martellotti, "Il Triumphus Cupidinis in Ovidio e nel Petrarca," in *Scritti petrarcheschi* (Padua: Antenore, 1983), 517–24.

9. Giovanni Ponte, "La decima *Egloga* e la composizione dei *Trionfi*," in *Studi sul Rinascimento: Petrarca, Leonardo, Ariosto* (Naples: Morano, 1994), 63–90; and Claudia Berra, "La varietà stilistica dei Trionfi," in Berra, ed., *I Triumphi di Francesco Petrarca*, 175–218.

10. Paola Vecchi Galli, "I Triumphi: Aspetti della tradizione quattrocentesca," in Berra, ed., *I Triumphi di Francesco Petrarca*, 343–73; Tateo, "Sulla ricezione umanistica dei Trionfi," ibid., 375–401; Corsaro, "Fortuna e imitazione nel cinquecento," ibid., 429–85; and Konrad Eisenbichler and Amilcare Iannucci, eds., *Petrarca's Triumphs: Allegory and Spectacle* (Toronto: Dovehouse, 1990).

11. "Illustres itaque viros, quos excellenti quadam gloria floruisse doctissimorum hominum ingenia memorie tradiderunt, eorumque laudes." Petrarch, *De viris illustribus*, ed. Guido Martellotti (Florence: Sansoni, 1964), prohemium.

12. Wolfgang Iser, *The Act of Reading: A Theory of Aesthetic Reponse* (Baltimore: Johns Hopkins University Press, 1978); Susan Suleiman and Inge Crosman, eds., *The Reader in the Text: Essays on Audience and Interpretation* (Princeton: Princeton University Press, 1980); Robert C. Holub, *Reception Theory: A Critical Introduction* (London and New York: Routledge, 1984); and Elizabeth Freund, *The Return of the Reader: Reader-Reponse Criticism* (London and New York: Methuen, 1987).

13. Johannes Bartuschat, "Sofonisba e Massinissa. Dall'*Africa* e dal *De viris* ai *Trionfi*," in *Petrarca e i suoi lettori*, ed. Vittorio Caratozzolo and Georges Güntert (Ravenna: Longo, 2000), 109–41.

14. Petrarch, *De viris illustribus*, prohemium: "Si vero forsan studii mei labor expectationis tue sitim ulla ex parte sedaverit, nullum a te aliud premii genus efflagito, nisi ut diligar, licet incognitus, licet sepulcro conditus, licet versus in cineres, sicut ego multos, quorum me vigiliis adiutum senseram, non modo defunctos sed diu ante consumptos post annum millesimum dilexi."

15. Petrarch, *Secretum,* ed. Enrico Carrara (Turin: Einaudi, 1977), 188.

16. Petrarch *Seniles* 3.9.15 in *Lettres de la vieillesse. Rerum senilium,* ed. Elvira Nota (Paris: Les Belles Lettres, 2002).

17. Francisco Rico, *El sueño del humanismo: De Petrarca a Erasmo* (Madrid: Alianza Editorial, 1993).

18. See Petrarch, *Die Triumphe,* ed. Carl Appel (Halle an der Saale: Niemeyer,

1901); *Il Canzoniere e i Trionfi*, ed. Andrea Moschetti (Milan: Vallardi, 1908); Carlo Calcaterra, *Nella selva del Petrarca* (Bologna: Cappelli, 1942).

19. See Petrarch, *Triumphi*, ed. Marco Ariani (Milan: Mursia, 1988); Emilio Pasquini, "Il testo: Fra l'autografo e i testimoni di collazione," in Berra, *I Triumphi di Francesco Petrarca*, 11–37.

20. Angelo Romanò, *Il codice degli abbozzi (Vat. Lat. 3196) di Francesco Petrarca* (Rome: Bardi, 1955), 282, 284.

21. Marco Santagata, *I frammenti dell'anima: Storia e racconto nel Canzoniere di Petrarca* (Bologna: Il Mulino, 1992), 290–91.

22. Santagata, *I frammenti dell'anima*, 295–343.

23. Romanò, *Il codice degli abbozzi*, 283.

24. Edoardo Taddeo, *Petrarca e il tempo e altri studi di letteratura italiana* (Pisa: ETS, 2003).

25. Mario Petrini, *La risurrezione della carne: Studi sul Canzoniere* (Milan: Mursia, 1993); and Maria Cecilia Bertolani, *Il corpo glorioso: Studi sui Trionfi del Petrarca* (Rome: Carocci, 2001).

26. Ea est rerum conditio humanarum, ut qui pauciora meminerit, minor illi fletuum causa sit. Ubi nec emendatio, nec penitentia utilis locum habet, quid superest aliud quam oblivionis auxilium? *De remediis utriusque fortune* bk. 2, chap. 101 (ed. Carraud, 1:988).

Chapter Three

1. "Sunt apud me huius generis vulgarium adhuc multa, et vetustissimis cedulis, et sic senio exesis ut vix legi queant. E quibus, si quando unus aut alter dies otiosus affulserit, nunc unum nunc aliud elicere soleo pro quodam quasi diverticulo laborum, sed perraro; ideoque mandaveram quod utriusque partis in fine bona spatia linquerentur, ut, si quando tale aliquid accidisset, esset ibi locus horum capax." Latin text from the new version edited by Michele Feo, "'In vetustissimis cedulis.' Il testo del postscriptum della senile XIII 11 γ e la 'forma Malatesta' dei *Rerum vulgarium fragmenta*," *Quaderni Petrarcheschi* 11 (2001): 148.

2. Poems from the *Rerum vulgarium fragmenta* are cited from Petrarch, *Canzoniere*, ed. Marco Santagata (Milan: Mondadori, 2004); English translations from idem, *Petrarch's Lyric Poetry: The Rime sparse and Other Lyrics*, ed. and trans. Robert M. Durling (Cambridge: Harvard University Press, 1976). The *disperse* are based on Petrarch, *Trionfi, Rime estravaganti, Codice degli abbozzi*, ed. Vinicio Pacca and Laura Paolino (Milan: Mondadori, 1996); English translations from idem, *Rime disperse*, ed. and trans. Joseph A. Barber (New York: Garland, 1991). Translations unless otherwise attributed are my own.

3. "Mirum, hunc cancellatum et damnatum, post multos annos casu relegens
    absolvi et transcripsi in ordine statim, non obstante . . . [oval symbol]. 1369
    iunii 22, hora 23, veneris." Transcription from Vaticano Latino 3196 in Pe-
    trarch, *Trionfi, Rime estravaganti, Codice degli abbozzi*, 809–10.

4. Aldus Manutius, in his 1514 edition of the *Canzoniere*, already justifies the in-
    clusion of a short appendix of *disperse* by pointing to what these poems might
    reveal about Petrarch's anthologizing strategies: "Se non in altro, in questo al
    meno vi seranno utili: che da qui potrà ognuno conoscere a che regola driz-
    zava il Petrarca le cose che per sue volea che si leggessero, e se drittamente di
    sé medesimo giudicava" [If nothing else these (poems) will at least be useful
    to you: that anyone will be able to know through them by what rule Petrarch
    corrected what he wanted to be read as his own, and whether he was a cor-
    rect judge of himself]. Cited in Petrarch, *Rime disperse di Francesco Petrarca o a
    lui attribuite*, ed. Angelo Solerti (1909; repr., Florence: Le Lettere, 1997), 38.

5. Petrarch *Seniles* 13.11: "Invitus, fateor, hac etate vulgari iuveniles ineptias
    cerno, quas omnibus—mihi quoque, si liceat—ignotas velim. Etsi enim
    stilo quolibet ingenium illius etatis emineat, ipsa tamen res senilem dedecet
    gravitatem. Sed quid possum? Omnia iam in vulgus effusa sunt legunturque
    libentius quam que serio, postmodum, validioribus annis scripsi. Quomodo
    igitur negarem tibi, sic de me merito tali viro tamque anxie flagitanti, que,
    me invito, vulgus habet et lacerat?" English translation based on Petrarch,
    Letters of Old Age/ Rerum senilium libri, trans. Aldo S. Bernardo, Saul Levin,
    and Reta A. Bernardo (Baltimore: Johns Hopkins University Press, 1992),
    2:500; Latin from *Librorum Francisci Petrarche annotatio impressorum* (Venice,
    1501), 2:177.

6. Petrarch, *Le familiari*, ed. Vittorio Rossi and Umberto Bosco (Florence: G. C
    Sansoni, 1933–42), 4:141.

7. "You say you have many of my letters. I should like you to have all of them,
    particularly in a corrected text, but it will never be up to me, and I should
    like the same about other things too. Besides you hope you have collected
    all my vernacular writings and my poetry, but that is hard for me to believe.
    You realize, however, that they more than other writings require the most
    exact corrections, since I suppose you have begged them from various peo-
    ple who did not even understand them." Petrarch, *Letters of Old Age*, 2:486.
    "Dicis te habere epystolas meas multas: velim omnes et maxime correctas
    habeas, neque unquam per me steterit idque ipsum et de aliis velim. Ad hec
    cunta nostra vulgaria et siquid est poeticum collegisse te speras, sed id michi
    difficile est creditu. Ceterum illis ante alia necessariam esse correctionem
    exactissimam sentis, que a diversis, ut auguror, iisque nec intelligentibus
    mendicasti." *Seniles* 2:151.

8. See Annarosa Cavedon, "Intorno alle 'Rime estravaganti' del Petrarca," *Revue des études italiennes*, n.s., 29 (1983): 86–108, and especially idem, "La tradizione 'veneta' delle 'Rime estravaganti del Petrarca,'" *Studi Petrarcheschi* 8 (1976): 1–73.

9. Paola Vecchi Galli has proposed using different terms to refer to the two categories, *estravaganti* versus *disperse:* "Per una stilistica delle 'disperse,'" in *Le lingue del Petrarca*, ed. Antonio Daniele (Udine: Forum, 2005), 110.

10. For a summary of the textual question of the *disperse*, see the excellent *postfazione* by Paola Vecchi Galli in the reprint of Petrarca, *Rime disperse di Francesco Petrarca*, 325–401, as well as her entry "Rime disperse" in *Petrarca nel tempo: Tradizione lettori e immagini dell opere*, ed. Michele Feo (Pontedera [Pisa]: Bandecchi & Vivaldi, 2004), 159–68. See also on the same subject, Alessandro Pancheri, *"Con suon chioccio": Per una frottola 'dispersa' attribuibile a Francesco Petrarca* (Padua: Antenore, 1993), 3–22.

11. For a critique of past attempts at establishing a canon of *disperse* based on impressions of Petrarch's stylistic or psychological development, see Vecchi Galli's comments in Petrarch, *Rime disperse di Francesco Petrarca*, 332–35 and 344–45.

12. Even several of the texts of the Casanatense are of questionable attribution. Three sonnets found in Solerti's edition, "L'ora, le perle e i bei fioretti e l'erba"; "In cielo, in aria, in terra, in fuoco, e in mare"; and "O pruove oneste, ligiadrette e sole" (*Rime disperse*, ed. Solerti, 12, 13, and 14) are now excluded from modern editions because of their distinctly Venetian linguistic traits.

13. On the poems written for Confortino, see Alessandro Pancheri, "Pro Confortino," in Cesare Segre and others, *Le varianti e la storia: Il canzoniere di Francesco Petrarca* (Turin: Bollati Boringhieri, 1999), 49–59.

14. Umberto Bosco, *Francesco Petrarca* (Bari: Laterza, 1968), 10.

15. The Correggio is the name given to the form of Petrarch's *Canzoniere* at the time he prepared a fair copy for Azzo da Correggio, as evident in a marginal note in the *codice degli abbozzi*. Since no manuscript exists, its exact content and order are not certain, although scholars have largely reconstructed it from Petrarch's autograph notes. Although no longer unquestioned, the starting point for the history of the forms of the *Canzoniere* remains E. H. Wilkins, *The Making of the "Canzoniere" and Other Petrarchan Studies* (Rome: Edizioni di Storia e Letteratura, 1951). See also, especially for the choral aspects of this form, Marco Santagata, *I frammenti dell'anima: Storia e racconto nel Canzoniere di Petrarca* (Bologna: Il Mulino, 1992), 159–60.

16. Feo, "'In vetustissimis cedulis,'" 144.

17. Irene Affò, cited by Giorgio Montecchi in the entry s.v. "Correggio, Azzo da" in the *Dizionario biografico degli Italiani* (Rome: Istituto della Enciclopedia

Italiana, 1960), 425–30. Most of what follows on Azzo derives from this entry.

18. See Santagata, *Frammenti dell'anima*, 162–63.

19. For a general treatment of poetic exchanges in late medieval Italy, see Claudio Giunta, *Versi ad un destinatario: Saggio sulla poesia italiana del Medioevo* (Bologna: Il Mulino, 2002).

20. For biographical details on Sennuccio and his family, see the introduction to Daniele Piccini, *Un amico del Petrarca: Sennuccio del Bene e le sue rime* (Rome and Padua: Antenore, 2004), xi–xlii, as well as Giuseppe Billanovich, "L'altro stil nuovo: Da Dante teologo a Petrarca filologo," *Studi Petrarcheschi*, n.s., 11 (1994): 1–98.

21. "Oltra l'usato modo si rigira" responds to *Rerum vulgarium fragmenta* 266 in the name of Giovanni Colonna; and "La bella Aurora nel mio orizonte" responds to the *dispersa* "Sì come il padre del folle Fetonte." The text for Sennuccio's poems is based on Piccini, *Un amico del Petrarca*.

22. For a survey of Petrarch's poetic exchanges with Sennuccio, see Joseph A. Barber, "Il sonetto CXIII e gli altri sonetti a Sennuccio," *Lectura Petrarce 2* (1982): 21–39.

23. See for example, Barber, "Il sonetto CXIII," 33–36.

24. In "Per una stilistica delle 'disperse,'" Paolino, while making exception for "Sì mi fan risentire," generally cautions against the canonicity of poems echoing too closely Petrarch's language and imagery. Similar conclusions and cautions about later imitators of Dante and Petrarch are in Emilio Pasquini, "'Minori'in bilico fra le 'due corone,'" in *Le botteghe della poesia: Studi sul Tre-Quattrocento italiano* (Bologna: Il Mulino, 1991), 331–51.

25. For the various claims about the influence and critical place of "Sì mi fan risentire a l'aura sparsi," see Barber, "Il sonetto CXIII," 33–35; Rosanna Bettarini, "Perché 'narrando' il duol si disacerba (Motivi esegetici dagli autografi petrarcheschi)," in *La critica del testo: Problemi di metodo ed esperienze di lavoro, Atti del Convegno di Lecce, 22–26 ottobre, 305–20* (Rome: Salerno, 1985), 309–10; Dante Bianchi, "Intorno alle 'rime disperse' del Petrarca: Il Petrarca e i fratelli Beccari," *Studi Petrarcheschi* 2 (1949): 131–33; Solerti's note in Petrarch, *Rime disperse di Francesco Petrarca*, 112; and Carlo Pulsoni, *La tecnica compositiva nei Rerum vulgarium fragmenta: Riuso metrico e lettura autoriale* (Rome: Bagatto Libri, 1998), 110–12.

26. Laura Bellucci suggests a similar reversal in the direction of influence between the *Canzoniere* and the *disperse* in her analysis of an exchange with Antonio da Ferrara. See "Palinodia amorosa in una 'dispersa' di Petrarca," *Studi e problemi di critica testuale* 2 (1971): 117.

27. Of the many possible examples noted by Piccini in *Un amico di Petrarca*, at

least one is worth mentioning: "a nullo amato amar perdona" from "Amor, tu ssai ch'i' son col capo cano" (line 70). This is clearly a conscious citation of *Inferno* 5.103 and not simply a mark of Dante's influence on Sennuccio.

28. For Petrarch's influence on Boccaccio, see Wilkins, *Making of the Canzoniere,* 300–1; Armando Balduino, *Boccaccio, Petrarca e altri poeti del Trecento* (Florence: Olschki, 1984), 231–347; and Giuseppe Billanovich, *Petrarca letterato I. Lo scrittoio del Petrarca* (Rome: Edizioni di Storia e Letteratura, 1947), 81–83. For Boccaccio's influence on Petrarch, see Marco Santagata, *Per moderne carte: La biblioteca volgare di Petrarca* (Bologna: Il Mulino, 1990), 246–70; and Giuseppe Velli, ""La poesia volgare del Boccaccio e i *Rerum vulgarium fragmenta.* Primi appunti," *Giornale Storico della Letteratura Italiana* 169 (1992): 183–99.

29. For the relationship between *Rerum vulgarium fragmenta* 113 and "Guido i' vorrei," see Pulsoni, *La tecnica compositiva,* 136–39.

30. For a recent discussion with relevant bibliography, see Enrico Fenzi, "L'ermeneutica petrarchesca tra libertà e verità," *Lettere italiane* 54 (2002): 170–209.

31. See for example, "Tu se' tal maraviglia a chi ti vede/alto valor sovr'ogni umanitade/che discese dal ciel ciascun ti crede" [You are such a marvel to anyone who sees you, that each believes you are a lofty power descended from heaven] from "L'alta bellezza tua è tanto nova" (lines 12–14); "o angiola discesa in questa vita/ di tal bellezza e di vertú vestita" [O angel descended among us, dressed in such beauty and virtue] from "O salute d'ogni occhio che ti mira" (lines 6–7); and "chi per la tua via corre/ disposto a bene amare e qui si sprona" [whoever runs across your way is spurred to be disposed to love well] from "Amor, tu ssai ch'i' son col capo cano" (lines 68–69).

32. The Chigi or Chigiano form (1359–1363) refers to Boccaccio's transcription of the *Canzoniere,* now MS Vaticano Chigiano 50.5.176.

33. Laura Paolino, "'Ad acerbam rei memoriam': Le carte del lutto nel codice Vaticano latino 3196 di Francesco Petrarca," *Rivista di letteratura italiana* 11 (1993): 73–102.

34. Petrarch, *Trionfi, Rime estravaganti, Codice degli abbozzi,* 856 (line 82). In the original draft, the incipit reads "Amore, in pianto ogni mio riso è vòlto" and is accompanied by the marginal note "non videtur satis triste principium" [the beginning does not seem sad enough].

35. "1349 no[ve]mbr(is) 28, inter primam et tertiam. Videtur nunc animus ad hec exp[ed]ienda pron[us], propter sonitia de morte Sennucii et de Aurora, que his diebus dixi et erexerunt animum." Petrarch, *Trionfi, Rime estravaganti, Codice degli abbozzi,* 850.

36. For recent discussions and further bibliography, see commentary in Petrarch,

Canzoniere, 692; and Bettarini, "Perché 'narrando' il duol si disacerba," 309–11.

37. See at least the groundbreaking essays of John Freccero, "The Fig Tree and the Laurel: Petrarch's Poetics," *Diacritics* 5 (1975): 34–40; and Giuseppe Mazzotta, "The *Canzoniere* and the Language of the Self," *Studies in Philology* 75 (1978): 271–96.

38. See the last line of "Quand'io veggio": "né di sé m'à lasciato altro che 'l nome" [nor has she left me anything of herself besides the name]. Analyzing Petrarch's exchanges with Sennuccio, Giuseppe Billanovich argues that Laura was in fact only a name: "Laura fantasma del *Canzoniere,*" *Studi Petrarcheschi,* n.s., 11 (1994): 149–58.

Chapter Four

1. "Te ipsum derelinquere mavis, quam libellos tuos. Ego tamen officium meum peragam; quam feliciter, tu videris, at certe fideliter. Abice ingentes historiarum sarcinas: satis romane res geste et suapte fama et aliorum ingeniis illustrate sunt. Dimitte Africam, eamque possessoribus suis linque; nec Scipioni tuo nec tibi gloriam cumulabis; ille altius nequit extolli, tu post eum obliquo calle niteris. His igitur posthabitis, te tandem tibi restitue." Petrarch, *Secretum,* ed. Enrico Carrara, in Petrarch, *Prose,* ed. Guido Martellotti, Pier Giorgio Ricci, Enrico Carrara, and Enrico Bianchi (Milan and Naples: Ricciardi, 1955), 206. The translation is taken from *The Secret,* ed. and trans. Carol E. Quillen (Boston: Bedford/St. Martin's, 2003), 144.

2. For fragments of Landolf's *Brevarium,* see Giuseppe Billanovich, *La tradizione del testo di Livio e le origini dell'Umanesimo,* vol. 1, *Tradizione e fortuna di Livio tra medioevo e umanesimo,* vol. 1.1, Studi sul Petrarca, 9 (Padua: Antenore, 1981), 129, n. 1. The contents of Giovanni's work, *Mare historiarum,* are described by Stephen L. Forte, "John Colonna, O.P., Life and Writings (ca. 1298–1340)," *Archivum fratrum praedicatorum* 20 (1950): 394–402. Among other Italian contemporaries writing universal histories were (1) Riccobaldo da Ferrara (d. 1318): *Pomerium* (unpublished), *Historiae* (unpublished), and *Compendium romanae historiae.* The last is edited by A. Teresa Hankey, *Riccobaldi ferrariensis. Compendium romanae historiae* (Rome: Istituto Storico per il Medioevo, Fonti per la Storia d'Italia, no. 108 in 2 pts., 1984). Despite its title, the *Compendium* is a summary of world history with a concentration on Roman history. (2) Giovanni Matociis (Mansionarius, d. 1337): *Historia imperialis* (unpublished). (3) Benzo da Alessandria (d. 1333): *Cronica.* Joseph Berrigan has published the first of three parts of this work: "Benzo d'Alessandria and the Cities of Northern Italy," *Studies in Medieval and Renaissance History* 4 (1967): 125–92. (4) Giovanni da Cremenate (d. 1344): *Historia Johannis de*

Cremenate, notarii mediolanensis, ed. L. A. Ferrai, Fonti per la storia d'Italia pubblicate dall'Istituto storico italiano per il Medio Evo, 2 (Rome: Forzani E. C. Tipografi del Senato, 1889).

3. Riccobaldo da Ferrara's *Chronica parva Ferrariensis* has been edited by Gabriele Zanella (Ferrara: Deputazione Provinciale Ferrarese di Storia Patria, 1983). See the important observations on the work by A. Teresa Hankey, *Riccobaldo of Ferrara: His Life, Works and Influence* (Rome: Istituto storico italiano per il Medio Evo, 1996), 4–5 and 78–92. For Albertino Mussato, see *Historia augusta Henrici VII caesaris et alia quae extant opera,* ed. Laurentii Pignorii vir. Clar. Spicilegio necnon Foelici Osia et Nicolae Villani, etc. (Venice: Ducali Pinelliana, 1636), separately paginated.

4. Ferreto dei Ferretti, *Historia rerum in Italia gestarum,* in *Le opere di Ferreto de' Ferreti vicentino,* ed. Carlo Cipolla, Fonti per la storia d'Italia, 42–43 (Rome: Forzani, 1908–20).

5. For a discussion of earlier Italian city chronicles, see my forthcoming *The Italian Difference: The Two Latin Cultures of Medieval Italy (800–1250).*

6. On Giovanni's work, see Braxton W. Ross, "Giovanni Colonna, Historian at Avignon," *Speculum* 45 (1970): 533–63; and G. M. Gianola, "La raccolta di biografie come problema storiografico nel *De viris* di Giovanni Colonna," *Bullettino dell'Istituto storico italiano per il Medio Evo e Archivio muratoriano* 89 (1991): 509–40. Pastrengo, *De viris illustribus et de originibus,* ed. G. Bottari, Studi sul Petrarca, 21 (Padua: Antenore, 1991), has a long introduction. Cf. Rino Avesani, "Il preumanesimo veronese," *Storia della cultura veneta* (Vicenza: Neri Pozzi, 1976), 2:126–29. Bottari in Pastrengo, *De viris illustribus,* xxxi–xxxii and xciii, acknowledges Colonna's influence on the alphabetical order followed by Pastrengo and the latter's decision to deal both with pagan and Christian authors. Doubtless well known to these authors was Saint Jerome's *De viris illustribus* that briefly discussed the life and works of Christian writers from Simon Peter to his own time.

7. These are the calculations of Ernest Hatch Wilkins, *Petrarch's Later Years* (Cambridge: Medieval Academy of America, 1959), 284 and 287.

8. I have analyzed a passage from the *Vita Scipionis* in my *"In the Footsteps of the Ancients": The Origins of Humanism from Lovato dei Lovati to Leonardo Bruni* (Leiden and New York: Brill, 2000), 271–72.

9. "Quid est enim aliud omnis historia, quam Romana laus," *Invectiva contra eum qui maledixit Italie,* in Petrarch, *Invective,* ed. and trans. David Marsh, I Tatti Renaissance Library (Cambridge: Harvard University Press, 2003), 417.

10. Petrarch, *De viris illustribus,* ed. Guido Martellotti, Edizione nazionale delle opere di Francesco Petrarca, no. 2, pt. 1 (Florence: Sansoni, 1964), 4: "Apud me nisi ea requiruntur, que ad virtutes vel virtutum contraria trahi possunt;

hic enim, nisi fallor, fructuosus historicorum finis est, illa prosequi que vel sectanda legentibus vel fugienda sunt." The translation is from Benjamin Kohl, "Petrarch's Prefaces to the *De viris illustribus,*" *History and Theory* 14 (1974): 143. On history as teaching by example, see especially Eckhard Kessler, *Petrarca und die Geschichte: Geschichtsschreibung, Rhetorik, Philosophie im Übergang vom Mittelalter zur Neuzeit* (Munich: W. Fink, 1978).

11. *De viris illustribus,* 3: "Illustres quosdam viros quos excellenti gloria floruisse doctissimorum hominum ingenia memorie tradiderunt, in diversis voluminibus tanquam sparsos ac disseminatos . . . locum in unum colligere et quasi quodammodo stipare arbitratus sum." For a translation, see Kohl, "Prefaces to the *De viris illustribus,*" 142.

12. *De viris illustribus,* 3: "Namque . . . quedam enim que apud unum desunt ab altero mutatus sum, quedam brevius, quedam clarius, quedam que brevitas obscura faciebat expressius, quedam que apud alios carptim dicta erant coniunxi et ex diversorum dictis unum feci." Kohl, "Prefaces to Petrarch's *De viris illustribus,*" 143. The earlier preface (1351–52) contains the same ideas similarly expressed: Petrarch, *Prose* (ed. Martellotti et al.), 218–27.

13. I illustrate this in "Petrarch's Conception of History," in *Petrarca: Canoni, Esemplarità,* ed. Valeria Finucci (Rome: Bulzoni, 2006), 211–18. I suggest a degree of parallel between Petrarch's and Dante's focus on Rome and their capacity to recreate ancient personalities.

14. Martellotti describes the codex in his edition of Petrarch, *De viris illustribus,* xxxvii–xxxviii.

15. On the early publication history of this *vita,* see Domenico Rossetti, *Petrarca, Giulio Celso e Boccaccio, illustrazione bibliologica delle Vite degli uomini illustri del primo, di Cajo Giulio Cesare attribuita al secondo e del Petrarca scritta dal terzo* (Trieste: G. Marenigh, 1828), 154–75.

16. *Le vite degli uomini illustri di Francesco Petrarca,* ed. Luigi Razzolini (Bologna: Collezione di opere inedite o rare dei primi tre secoli della lingua, 1874–79).

17. Martellotti in *De viris illustribus,* xx–xxi, describes Vat. Lat. 4523. The manuscript, representing the *De viris illustribus* as completed by Lombardo della Seta, contains thirty-six lives, not the thirty-five attributed to it by Razzolini, *Le vite degli uomini illustri,* xvi–xvii.

18. Pierre de Nolhac, "Le *De viris illustribus* de Pétrarque," in *Notices et extraits des manuscrits de la Bibliothèque nationale et autres bibliothèques* 34, no. 1 (1891): 91.

19. Because the twenty-fourth biography included in 6069 I, the *Vita Cesaris,* was composed at least toward the end of Petrarch's life, a scribe would have had to add it to the second version of the *De viris illustribus* (1351–53) at a later time. For the dating of the *De gestis Cesaris,* see below, n. 38.

20. This wider plan has usually been referred to as "the all-ages plan." See, for

example, Kohl, "Prefaces to the *De viris illustribus*," 33. See, however, below, pp. 107–8.

21. Scholars commonly cite Carlo Calcaterra, "La concezione storica del Petrarca," *Annali della cattedra petrarchesca* 9 (1939–40): 3–25; republished in his collection of articles, *Nella selva del Petrarca* (Bologna: Cappelli, 1942), 415–33, breaking with de Nolhac by placing the "Roman" plan prior to the version discovered by the French scholar. But in fact, in this article of 1939, Calcaterra ("La concezione storica del Petrarca," 7–8) accepts de Nolhac's chronology. He rewrites these pages and reorders the versions only when including the essay in his collection three years later (*Nella selva*, 418–19). Martellotti offers a detailed description of the development of *De viris illustribus* following Calcaterra. See Martellotti, "Linee di sviluppo dell'umanesimo petrarchesco," *Studi Petrarcheschi* 2 (1949): 51–80; also in *Scritti petrarcheschi*, ed. Michele Feo and Silvia Rizzo, Studi sul Petrarca, 16 (Padua: Antenore, 1983), 131. Henceforth all citations from this and Martellotti's other articles will be to *Scritti petrarcheschi*.

22. In Petrarch *Africa* 2.274–76, ed. Nicola Festa, Edizione nazionale delle opere di Francesco Petrarca, no. 1 (Florence: Sansoni, 1926), 40. Petrarch has Scipio end his prophesying with the reigns of the Emperors Vespasian and Titus: "Ulterius transire piget; nam sceptra decusque/ Imperii tanto nobis fundata labore/ Externi rapient Hispane stirpis et Afre."

23. Petrarch *Secretum* 192: "Ideoque manum ad maiorem iam porrigens, librum historiarum a rege Romulo in Titum cesarem, opus immensum temporisque et laboris capacissimum, agressus es."

24. The dating of the *Secretum* and, consequently, that of the reference to the *De viris illustribus* has been the subject of intense debate. Traditionally the work had been assigned to 1342–43 on the basis of Franciscus's remark that he had known Laura for sixteen years at the time of the colloquy with Augustinus (*Secretum*, 136). Interpreting the marginal note "modo 3, 1353, 1349, 1347" on the final page of the manuscript copied by the meticulous scribe Tedaldo della Casa from Petrarch's original (Biblioteca Laurenziana, Florence, 26 sin. 9 [formerly Santa Croce 696], fol. 243) as indicating three versions of the *Secretum*, Francesco Rico, *Vida u obra de Petrarca: Lectura del Secretum*, Studi sul Petrarca, 4 (Padua: Antenore, 1974), 471, concludes that the current version is the product of "una refundición íntegra" of the work done by Petrarch in 1353. Hans Baron, *Petrarch's Secretum: Its Making and Its Meaning* (Cambridge: Medieval Academy of America, 1985), 20–21, accepts Rico's interpretation of the three dates as indicating three versions of the text, but he argues for an initial composition in 1347 with some revisions in 1349 and 1353. Several scholars remain convinced that the date given by

Petrarch was in fact the date when the work was initially composed:
B. Martinelli, "Sulla data del *Secretum* del Petrarca. Nova et vetera," *Critica letteraria* 13 (1985): 431–82 and 643–93; and Giovanni Ponte, "Nella selva del Petrarca," *Giornale storico della letteratura italiana* 167 (1990): 1–63. Ponte points out, for example, that the preface to the *Secretum* refers to the *Africa* as containing a description of the palace of truth, a passage belonging to a version of the poem dated before 1341–42 and replaced, probably in 1344, by a description of the palace of Syphax: Petrarch *Africa* 3.88–3.264 (ed. Festa, 54–62). The discussion of dating is important for an understanding of the development of *De viris illustribus* in that specialists generally have agreed that between 1351 and 1353 Petrarch was following an "all-ages" plan for the *De viris illustribus* (see below and my discussion of the 1351–53 dating). If, as Rico contends, the work was totally revised in 1353, Petrarch's description of the *De viris illustribus* in book 3 as following the "Roman plan" ill accords with the 1351–53 dating. In his work of 1974 (*Vida u obra*, 386–88, n. 478) Rico identifies a passage in book 2 of the work as referring to the "all-ages" plan (*Secretum*, 72): "Si, cum omnis evi clarorum hominum gesta memineritis, quid vos quotidie agitis non curatis?" This passage would consequently be dated 1351–53. However, in his "Ubi puer, ibi senex": Hans Baron y el *Secretum* de 1353," *Il Petrarca latino e le origini dell'Umanesimo. Atti del Convegno internazionale Firenze 19–22 maggio 1991, Quaderni Petrarcheschi*, 9–10 (Florence: Nistri-Lischi, 1996), 228–29, Rico identifies the reference to the "Roman plan" as an "eco del pasaje de Livio (XX III 43, 6) en que Escipión afirma que es propio de un espíritu grande compararse 'cum omnis aevi claris viris.'" Consequently, the latter phrase was not meant to designate a particular version of the *De viris illustribus*. In this article Rico appears to endorse the opinion of Guido Martellotti expressed in the latter's review of Rico's book according to which the reference to the "Roman" plan, "deve riportarsi senza anacronismi alla data fittizia [1342–43]; sicchè le testimonianze relative agli inizi del poema e dell'opera storica conservano il loro valore documentario." "Sulla data del Secretum," *Scritti petrarcheschi*, 493. For Baron, who denies that the text was completely rewritten in 1353, the reference to the "Roman" plan would have been included in 1347 or 1349, before Petrarch's decision to reconcepualize the work in 1351–53, *Petrarch's Secret*, 130–31.

25. The marginal note is discussed in Giuseppe Billanovich, "Uno Suetonio della Biblioteca del Petrarca (Berlinese Lat. Fol. 337)," *Studi Petrarcheschi* 6 (1956): 29.

26. Petrarch *De viris illustribus* 58–92.

27. Ibid., 70; Martellotti, "Linee di sviluppo dell'umanesimo petrarchesco," 131. Martellotti, "La *Collatio inter Scipionem Alexandrum Hanibalem et Pyhrrum*. Un

inedito del Petrarca nella biblioteca della University of Pennsylvania," *Scritti petrarcheschi*, 324–26, points out that in this brief work Scipio's superiority as a general is recognized by the other three.

28. Petrarch *Africa* 2.449–54 (ed. Festa, 54–62). On this passage and the earliest *Vita Scipionis*, which Martellotti labels γ, see "Sulla composizione del *De viris* e *l'Africa*," 9.

29. Martellotti, "Il *De viris* et *l'Africa*," 13, effectively argues that the second edition of the *Vita* Scipionis (ß) was written before 1343 because it makes no mention of the death of Magone, an incident celebrated in the fragment of the *Africa* sent to Barbato dal Sulmona in 1343. The original twenty-three lives recur in all revisions of the work. They are the following: Romulus, Numa, Tullus Hostilius Ancus Martius, Junius Brutus, Horatio Cocles, Lucius Quintius Cincinnatus, Marcus Furius Camillus, Titus Manlius Torquatus, Marcus Valerius Corvus, Publius Decius, Lucius Papirius Cursor, Marcus Curius Dentatus, Fabritius Lucinius, Alexander, Pyrrhus, Hannibal, Quintus Fabius Maximus Cuntator, Marcus Claudius Marcellus, Claudius Nero, Livius Salinator, Publius Cornelius Scipio, and Cato Censor. The second edition contains twelve lives of biblical and mythological figures: Adam, Noah, Nimrod, Ninus, Semiramis, Abraham, Isaac, Jacob, Joseph, Moses, Jason, and Hercules.

30. According to Martellotti, "Il *De viris* et *l'Africa*," 15: "quanto si è visto finora intorno all'attività del Petrarca ci permette di datare più precisamente il testo ß della Vita di Scipione al 1342; e a quell'epoca risale pressappoco tutto lo stadio ß dell *De viris*. Il poeta attendeva allora alacremente alla sua opera storica, ordinandola e completandola, col proposito di presentarla a Roberto di Napoli insieme con *l'Africa*. La morte del principe interruppe bruscamente il lavoro, che solo più tardi doveva esser ripreso." In a later article, published in 1949, "Linee di sviluppo dell'umanesimo petrarchesco," 128, he writes that "lo studio critico della tradizione manoscritta indica alla fine del '42 o ai primissimi del '43 un alacre lavoro intorno al *De viris*. Sappiamo che subito dopo il Petrarca ne abbandonò la composizione per dedicarsi a quella dei *Rerum memorandarum*, e in quest'opera infatti egli parla del suo *De viris* come di qualche cosa che sia già lontana nel tempo." The *Rerum memorandarum* has been definitively dated by Giuseppe Billanovich as written between 1343 and 1345: *Rerum memorandarum libri*, ed. Giuseppe Billanovich, Edizione nazionale delle opere di Francesco Petrarca, 5 (Florence: Sansoni, 1945), cix–cxx. Martellotti divides the manuscript tradition of ß into two families, "s," presumably reflecting the work as it was in 1343, and "u," showing later modifications by Petrarch: *De viris illustribus*, lxi–lxii. That the "s" family dates from 1343, however, cannot be proven.

31. De Nolhac, "Storiografia del Petrarca," *Scritti petrarcheschi*, 482–83.

32. Petrarch, *De viris illustribus*, ed. Guido Martellotti, in Petrarch, *Prose*, ed. Guido Martellotti, Pier Giorgio Ricci, Enrico Carrara, and Enrico Bianchi (Milan and Naples: Ricciardi, 1955), 218: "Scriberem libentius, fateor, visa quam lecta, novat quam vetera, ut sicut notitiam vetustatis ab antiquis acceperam ita huius notitiam etatis ex me posteritas sera perciperet. Gratiam habeo principibus nostris, qui michi fesso et quietis avido hunc preripiunt laborem; neque enim historie sed satyre materiam stilo tribuunt." The translation is from Kohl, "Petrarch's Prefaces to *De viris illustribus*," 138.

33. Petrarch, *Invective contra medicum*, in *Invectives*, 51: "Scripsi aliqua, nec desino, aut unquam desinam, dum hic digitus calamum feret. Sed, omissis aliis, ne me rursum de me ipso magnifice loqui dicas, scribo de viris illustribus. Que non ausim dicere: iudicent qui legent; de quantitate pronuntio: haud dubie magnum opus multarumque vigiliarum et, si non ab auctore, certe a subiecta materia nominandum. Nichil ibi de medicis nec de poetis quidem aut philosophis agitur, sed de his tantum qui bellicis virtutibus aut magno reipublice studio floruerunt, et preclaram rerum gestarum gloriam consecuti sunt. Illic, si tibi debitum locum putas, dic ubi vis inseri; parebitur; sed verendum est ne quos ex omnibus seculis illustres, quantum hac ingenii paupertate licuit, in unum contraxi adventu tuo diffugiant, teque ibi solo remanente, mutandus libri titulus, neque *De viris illustribus* sed *De insigni fatuo* inscribendum sit."

34. Martellotti, "Linee di sviluppo dell'umanesimo petrarchesco," 128–30. The edited version is found in *Le familiari*, ed. Vittorio Rossi and Umberto Bosco, Edizione Nazionale delle Opere di Francesco di Petrarca, 10–13 (Florence: Sansoni, 1933–), 2:160: "Ex omnibus terris ac seculis illustres viros in unum contrahendi illa michi solitudo dedit animum."

35. Petrarch *Familiares* 19.3 (3:314–15), cited from Baron, *Petrarch's Secretum*, 151–52, n. 72.

36. "quanquam si illustres evi nostri viros attigissem, non dicam te–ne tibi, quod placatus non soleo, iratus adulari videar–at certe nec patruum nec patrem tuum silentio oppressurus fuerim. Nolui autem pro tam paucis nominibus claris tam procul tantasque per tenebras stilum ferre; ideoque vel materie vel labori parcens longe ante hoc seculum historie limitem statui ac defixi." Petrarch *Familiares* 4:28–29.

37. As Petrarch writes in the last lines of his preface to *De viris illustribus* dedicated to Carrara (5): "ab illo igitur, ad quem rogatus stilum vertere paro, Urbis Romanae conditore Romulo nam sic volentis desiderium impellit, inchoandum iter assumo." The first lines of the preface to Carrara also make it clear that the work was undertaken "rogatu tuo" (at your request). For a

discussion of Carrara's relationship to the composition, see the discussion of Wilkins, *Petrarch's Later Years*, 285–86, and 300–1.

38. On the third *Vita Scipionis*, see Umberto Bosco, "Il Petrarca e l'umanesimo filologico," *Giornale storico della letteratura italiana* 120 (1942): 84–92; and Martellotti, "Storiografia del Petrarca," 483–84. Martellotti's edition of the *De viris illustribus* (see above, n. 10) contains the earliest *vita* as an appendix (327–54). Whereas Martellotti ("Petrarca e Cesare," 78–79), believes that the lives of Caesar were conceived of as independent works, Wilkins (*Petrarch's Later Years*, 290–91) holds that Petrarch continued to see it as part of *De viris illustribus*. Furthermore, whereas Martellotti maintains that the *De gestis Cesaris* was completed before Carrara made his request for a new edition in 1368 (79–89), Wilkins holds that "the Life of Caesar may have been begun either before or after Petrarch's receipt of Francesco's request" (291). He argues that, because the first twenty-three lives were already completed before Carrara's request, were *De gestis Cesaris* already finished by then, we must assume that, having written a dedicatory preface to Carrara for the *De viris illustribus*, that Petrarch "never did anything toward its completion." I agree with Wilkins on both issues.

39. Wilkins, *Petrarch's Later Years*, 294–95, points out that Petrarch's own references to the work throughout most of his life indicated that he thought of the work as encompassing all the major Roman heroes not merely certain ones, but Petrarch's description of the work in his preface to Carrara (see above, n. 11) as "illustres quosdam viros" suggests that Lombardo reflected Petrarch's own sense of the subject of the *De viris illustribus* at this time. In his "Storiografia del Petrarca," 485, Martellotti suggests that *epithoma* in the title *Quorundam virorum illustrium epithoma* "sembra significare 'sezione' dell'opera intera, 'saggio' o qualche cosa di simile." Also see his extensive analysis of the terms *epitome* and *compendium* in "Epitome e compendio," *Scritti petrarcheschi*, 50–66.

40. Wilkins, *Petrarch's Later Years*, 292, cites from the first edition of the Latin works of Petrarch (Basle, 1496), fol. 362v: "Iussisti enim multa et maxima quorundam virorum illustrium facta: prius quodam Epitomate neque prolixo neque artato: sed mediocri stilo declarari: nunc quodammodo (ut ita dixerim) eadem stipare compendiosius imperas: ut cognitioni tradantur . . . Hoc enim idem et celeberrimo Petrarchae commiseras invictissimae eloquentiae viro: qui cum desiderio tuis satisfacere lucubraret: terris elatus evanuit rediturus ad astra."

41. Martellotti, "Storiografia del Petrarca," 485. Cf. Wilkins, *Petrarch's Later Years*, 292–93.

42. Martellotti, "Epitome e compendio," 58.

43. Petrarch, *La vita di Scipione l'Africano,* ed. Guido Martellotti (Milan: Ricciardi, 1954).

44. Marco Santagata, in *Trionfi, Rime estravaganti: Codice degli abbozzi,* ed. Vinicio Pacca and Laura Paolino (Milan: Mondadori, 1996), xlviii, concludes his extensive discussion of the dating of the *Trionfi* by assigning the whole work to the early 1350s.

45. The date 1350 is that given by Martellotti, "Linee di sviluppo dell'umanesimo petrarchesco," 126, n. 24. Santagata, in *Trionfi, Rime estravaganti* (ed. Pacca and Paolino), xxxii, concludes only that this draft "sta anteriore al 1352–53." The draft is published, ibid., 555–85.

46. Santagata, in *Trionfi, Rime estravaganti,* 558–70 (vv. 22–102). Petrarch's decision to celebrate Trajan, Hadrian, Antonius Pius, and Marcus Aurelius was probably motivated by contact with *Historia augusta,* a work he possessed from 1356, but which he could well have known earlier: Martellotti, "Linee di sviluppo dell'umanesimo Petrarchesco," 119, and especially n. 15.

47. Petrarch *Trionfi TF* 1a 120–56, 1a 157, and 1a 160–63 (ed. Pacca and Paolino, 574–83).

48. I am using for reference *Triumphus Fame I* and *Triumphus Fame II* in the edition of Pacca and Paolino (pp. 353–428). The subdivision of the categories are as follows (1) *TF* I, vv. 1–129 (353–86); (2) *TF* II, vv. 1–51 (393–406); (3) vv. 52–87 (406–12); (4) vv. 88–120 (412–18); and (5) vv. 121–62 (418–28).

49. Martellotti, "Linee di sviluppo dell'umanesimo petrarchesco," 126–27.

50. Ibid., 126–27.

51. Hans Baron, "The State of Petrarch Studies," in *From Petrarch to Leonardo Bruni: Studies in Humanistic and Political Literature* (Chicago: University of Chicago Press for the Newberry Library, 1968), 30–31 and 44–45.

52. Ibid., 23–27.

53. Martellotti traces the changing attitude of Petrarch toward Caesar in "Petrarca e Cesare," 77–89. He regards what might be considered as a somewhat positive reference in book 8 of *Africa* as a later interpolation (83) and maintains that the decisive change in attitude came with a close reading of the *Commentarii* in the 1360s. Two years later in "Linee di sviluppo dell'umanesimo petrarchesco," 119, Martellotti finds the change taking place in the first version of the *Triumphus Fame* and here he tends to credit *Historia augusta Henrici VII* for giving Petrarch a more positive attitude to the emperors: see above, p. 109.

54. Martellotti, "Linee di sviluppo dell'umanesimo petrarchesco," 139–40.

55. Baron, *From Petrarch to Bruni,* 37–40.

56. Baron, *From Petrarch to Bruni*, 45, suggests that Petrarch returned to the original Roman plan because Carrara insisted on it. If the beginning of the *De gestis Cesaris* cannot be firmly dated before 1368, when Carrara made the request, that is not the case with the third biography of Scipio. This new biography indicates that Petrarch's interest in the Roman plan preceded Carrara's request.

57. See my "The *De tyranno* and Coluccio Salutati's View of Politics and Roman History," *Nuova rivista storica* 53 (1969): 445, republished in Ronald G. Witt, *Italian Humanism and Medieval Rhetoric* (Aldershot and Burlington: Ashgate/ Variorum, 2001).

58. Ibid., 443–50.

Chapter Five

1. In general, a twofold philological question surrounds the poem's composition and publication. Nicola Festa, who produced the first and only critical edition of the work in 1926, focuses on Petrarch's reluctance to publish in his *Saggio sull'Africa* (Palermo: Sandron, 1926)—to date still the most complete discussion of the poem. Festa's introduction to his edition also carefully maps the complicated and delayed editorial process that lead to Pier Paolo Vergerio's first edition in 1396. On the question, see the sparse notes in Giuseppe Billanovich, *Petrarca letterato. I. Lo scrittoio del Petrarca* (Rome: Edizioni di Storia e Letteratura, 1952), 228–30, 251–52, 286–99; and Ernest Hatch Wilkins, *Studies in the Life of Petrarch* (Cambridge: Medieval Academy of America, 1955), 248–50. See also Vincenzo Fera, *La revisione petrarchesca dell'"Africa"* (Messina: Centro di Studi Umanistici, 1984); and most recently, Enrico Fenzi, "Dall'*Africa* al *Secretum:* Il sogno di Scipione e la composizione del poema," in *Saggi Petrarcheschi* (Fiesole: Cadmo, 2003), 305–64. On the compositional unity of the proem, see Giuseppe Velli, "Il proemio dell'*Africa*," *Italia medioevale e umanistica* 8 (1965): 323–32.

2. The published excerpts from the poem are the lament of Mago from book 6 (on which see *Seniles* 2.1 to Boccaccio) and, most likely, what is now the description of the palace of Syphax (*Africa* 3.87–262)—an extended ekphrastic piece probably intended for a different episode (known to Petrarch's friend Pierre de Bersuire as early as 1339–40: see Enrico Fenzi, "Di alcuni palazzi, cupole e planetari nell'*Africa* del Petrarca," in *Saggi Petrarcheschi* (Fiesole: Cadmo, 2003), 233–35. For Virgil's strategy of reluctant publication of the *Aeneid*, see the so-called *Vita Donati*, which attests the recitation to Augustus of books 2, 4, and 6 in their entirety and of other fragments to larger audiences.

3. Interwoven with the drafting of the *Africa*, Petrarch also composed a biogra-

phy of Scipio that was to occupy the central position in the *De viris illustribus*. Three progressively enlarged versions of this biography survive dating from 1338–39, 1343, and probably 1353. For a study of the three redactions, see Guido Martellotti, *La vita di Scipione l'Africano* (Milan and Naples: Ricciardi, 1954). A survey of Scipio in Petrarch's works may be found in Aldo Bernardo, *Petrarch, Scipio and the "Africa": The Birth of Humanism's Dream* (Baltimore: Johns Hopkins University Press, 1962).

4. On the importance of Petrarch's philological work on Livy—and in particular on this *deca*—see the seminal contributions by Giuseppe Billanovich, "Petrarch and the Textual Tradition of Livy," *Journal of the Warburg Institute* 14 (1951): 137–208; *La tradizione del testo di Livio e le origini dell'umanesimo: Tradizione e fortuna di Livio tra medioevo e umanesimo* (Padua: Antenore, 1981); and the summation of his findings in "Tito Livio, Petrarca, Boccaccio," *Archivio Storico Ticinese* 97 (1984): 3–10. Petrarch's involvement with Livy is reflected in his Caesarian sonnets, *Rerum vulgarium fragmenta* 102–4.

5. For the three episodes the *Africa* most clearly inherits from classical pretreatments (Scipio's dream, Sophonisba's suicide, and the council of the Gods in book 7), see Tamara Visser, *Antike und Christentum in Petrarcas "Africa"* (Tübingen: Gunter Narr Verlag, 2005), with comprehensive bibliography. On classical similes, see Franz Friedersdorff, "Die poetischen Vergleiche in Petrarcas *Africa*," *Zeitschrift für Romanische Philologie* 20 (1896): 471–91; 21 (1897): 58–72; and 22 (1898): 9–48.

6. Petrarch, unlike Lucan, does not eliminate supernatural agency from the historical poem. For the peculiar status of Lucan as historian-poet, see Isidore of Seville's definition at *Etymologiae*, 8.7.10: "Unde et Lucanus in numero poetarum non ponitur, quia videtur historias composuisse, non poema" ["Lucan too, thus, should not be listed among the poets, since he appears to have written books of history, not a poem"—my translation]. See *Etymologiarum sive originum libri XX*, ed. W. M. Lindsay (Oxford: Clarendon Press, 1911). On the direct influence of Lucan's *Bellum civile* on precise episodes in Petrarch, see Richard T. Bruère, "Lucan and Petrarch's *Africa*," *American Journal of Philology* 56 (1961): 83–99.

7. For Dante's presence in the *Africa*, see Giuseppe Velli, "Il Dante di Francesco Petrarca," *Studi Petrarcheschi* 2 (1985): 185–99.

8. Cicero's work was, in its turn, a historicizing remake of the so-called "Myth of Er," a similar dream vision with which Plato brought to a close his own treatise on the state, also known in the Latin West as *De republica*.

9. See Lucan *Bellum civile* 1.33–66; Statius *Thebaid* 1.18–40, and (in a minor key) *Achilleid* 1.14–19. On the thorny question of the potentially ironic tone of Lucan's dedication to Nero, see Michael Dewar, "Laying It on with a Trowel:

The Proem to Lucan and Related Texts," *Classical Quarterly* 44 (1994): 199–211. See also Gian Biagio Conte, "Il proemio della *Farsalia*," *Maia* 18 (1966): 42–53; and the problematizing position of Alessandro Barchiesi, *Speaking Volumes: Narrative and Intertext in Ovid and Other Latin poets* (London: Duckworth, 2001), 75–76.

10. All citations are from Petrarch, *L'Africa*, ed. Nicola Festa (Florence: Sansoni, 1926). The English version cited here and throughout is from *Petrarch's "Africa,"* translated and annotated by Thomas G. Bergin and Alice S. Wilson (New Haven: Yale University Press), 1997. The line numbers refer to the Latin text. For a new critical edition, which appeared too late to be incorporated into this essay, see *L'Afrique/Affrica*, ed. and trans. with introduction and notes by Pierre Laurens (Paris: Belles Lettres, 2006), cxxix–cxliv.

11. On the issue, see J. Christopher Warner, *The Augustinian Epic: Petrarch to Milton* (Ann Arbor: University of Michigan Press, 2005), 20–50.

12. In the same passage, Petrarch also stresses the connection of poetry with the active life and expounds on the theme by connecting poetic and military valor through their shared signifier, the laurel (lines 109–23).

13. For the stylistic issues involved in Petrarch's relationship with Ennius, the epic poet whose *Annales* were a "ruvido carme" (rough poetry) in praise of Scipio, see *Rerum vulgarium fragmenta* 186.12–14. From the brief review of the Latin epic canon, which Petrarch phrases as options for imitation in *Africa* 1.45–55 (Virgil, Statius, Lucan), Ennius is left out as the author of an epic on contemporary matters surviving only in fragments and as having potentially exhausted the last heroic subject available to the new epic poets. Silius Italicus's *Punica*, a poem containing a few episodes uncannily similar to those we find in Petrarch's, remained most likely outside of the philological scope of the available models, its text having been recovered only in the fifteenth century by Poggio Bracciolini. See Guido Martellotti, "Petrarca e Silio Italico: Un confronto impossibile," in *Scritti Petrarcheschi* (Padua: Antenore, 1983), 563–78; and Carlo Santini, "Nuovi accertamenti sull'ipotesi di raffronto tra Silio e Petrarca," in *Preveggenze umanistiche di Petrarca*, ed. Giorgio Brugnoli and Guido Paduano (Pisa: ETS, 1993), 111–39.

14. For the notion that the balance achieved in Scripture between difficult and easy passages is designed to counteract both the readers' despair of achieving understanding and their potential satiety with an all-too-available meaning, see the key passage in Augustine's *De doctrina christiana* 2.6.7–.8—a textual locus with which Petrarch's argument deeply resonates.

15. The vicissitudes of the late-antique and medieval interpretation of Dido are complex. I have tried to assess the centrality of the problem for Petrarch's first disciple, Boccaccio, in Simone Marchesi, *Stratigrafie decameroniane* (Flor-

ence: Olschki, 2004), 67–85. For the best philological account in English of the two Didos, see Arthur Stanley Pease, *Publi Vergili Maronis Aeneidos. Liber quartus* (Cambridge: Harvard University Press, 1935), 3–79; for a more recent discussion of the story's medieval redeployments, see Marilynn Desmond, *Reading Dido: Gender, Textuality, and the Medieval "Aeneid"* (Minneapolis: University of Minnesota Press, 1994), 23–73.

16. For the historicizing glosses to Dido, see Servius's commentary *Ad Aeneidem* 1.267, 1.343, and 4.36. For Augustine, see the famous passage in *Confessiones* 1.13; for Macrobius *Saturnalia* 1.17.

17. For a discussion of the Petrarchan *loci* on the Dido question, see Giuseppe Billanovich, *Restauri boccacceschi* (Rome: Edizioni di Storia e Letteratura, 1947), 137–38. The list of relevant passages ranges from *Triumphus Pudicitiae* 10–12 and 154–59 (particularly bent on rebuffing Dante's treatment of Dido in *Inferno* 5), to *Familiares* 13.8 and *Seniles* 4.5.

18. Chaucer' *Troilus and Criseyde* 1.400–20 takes advantage of the "mixed style" (*Rerum vulgarium fragmenta* 186.4) that Petrarch had experimented with for his Massinissa. On the episode's peregrination across genres and languages, see Johannes Bartuschat, "Sofonisba e Massinissa: Dall'*Africa* e dal *De viris* ai *Trionfi*," in *Petrarca e i suoi lettori*, ed. Vicenzo Caratozzolo and Georges Günthert (Ravenna: Longo, 2000), 109–41.

19. That there was a literary Medea-Dido connection that allowed circulation of such poetic material was a commonplace ever since Servius had prefaced his commentary to *Aeneid* 4 indicating that Virgil depended on Apollonius' portrayal of Medea in love in his *Argonautica;* for the lament, see Euripides, *Medea*, prologue 1–2; Catullus 64.171–72; and Ovid *Heroides* 7.139–40. For the transmission of Catullus's wording, see Cicero *De oratore* 3.214; and Macrobius *Saturnalia* 6.1.42.

20. On Petrarch's imitation theory, see Thomas M. Greene, *The Light in Troy: Imitation and Discovery in Renaissance Poetry* (New Haven: Yale University Press, 1982), 98–99.

21. The Dido connection is stressed by the ring composition of the lament: at its onset, Syphax evokes Dido as the origin of all of Africa's misfortunes (*Africa* 6.225–30), and he then closes his set speech with the denigration of Sophonisba. In the triangular scheme Massinissa-Sophonisba-Syphax, Syphax plays a role not unlike that of the deceased husband, who appears satirically in Boccaccio's *Corbaccio* dream vision to denounce to the lover the wickedness of his wife.

22. For the rhetorical soliloquy of the forsaken woman in the Latin tradition, see Barchiesi, *Speaking Volumes*, 29–48.

23. The Virgilian corresponding passage may be found at *Aeneid* 4.173–4.195.

Petrarch appears more reluctant to associate "rumor" with his own narrative: his Fama is more accurate than Virgil's and she does not "sing" as in Virgil's poem.

24. The text through which the Middle Ages conceptualized the experience of dreaming was Macrobius' *Commentary on the Dream of Scipio*, a treatise conceived as an extended gloss to the last book of Cicero's *De republica*, which contained a preliminary discussion of dreams (1.3.1–1.3.11). For the reception of Macrobius's theory and text, see Macrobius, *A Commentary on the Dream of Scipio*, trans. William H. Stahl (New York: Columbia University Press, 1962), 39–55; and Albrecht Hüttig, *Macrobius im Mittelalter: Ein Beitrag zur Rezeptionsgeschichte der "Commentarii in Somnium Scipionis"* (Frankfurt am Main: Peter Lang, 1990), 147–73.

25. In perfect correspondence with the fivefold division elaborated by Macrobius (*somnium, visio, oraculum, insomnium, visum*), the text labels her dream as "somnium" and associates the technical verb "visa est" (she seemed to see) with her experience.

26. The Elder Scipio here echoes a passing remark that he had made at the beginning of the dream, forewarning the dreamer that he must lend credit to the vision and preserve it in his memory: "Put fear aside and with attentive mind / take in my words. For God, who reigns on high, / lord of Olympus, grants us one hour, / brief but yet promising great joy, if you / but waste it not" (*Africa* 1.170–72).

27. The three classes of subjects of instruction in the curriculum taught to Scipio are evidently heterogeneous. A difference in the time of composition might account for the difference in tone between the section on the past history of Rome and the one on its future. In *Dall'Africa al Secretum*, Fenzi notes that the second, more eschatological and pessimistic part of the dream was probably composed later in Petrarch's life (1350s), in conjunction with the new project of meditation on time and eternity addressed in the Latin dialogue.

28. Macrobius is the starting point, for instance, of the *Roman de la rose* and Chaucer's *House of Fame;* even Dante's *Divina commedia* is open—ever so briefly—to the dream option (*Inferno* 1.10–12), which will become the absolute framing device for Boccaccio's *Amorosa visione*. See the background study by Patricia Cox Miller, *Dreams in Late Antiquity: Studies in the Imagination of a Culture* (Princeton: Princeton University Press, 1994), 1–123.

29. Cf. an earlier passage, in which Ennius evokes together Achilles, Alexander, and Scipio as a lineage of the epic protagonists who had received praise from stylistically different poets (9.50–64). The situation is the same as in *Rerum vulgarium fragmenta* 187.1–4.

30. The argument has been first advanced by Theodor Mommsen, "Petrarch's

Conception of the 'Dark Ages,'" *Speculum* 17 (April 1942): 226–42; most recently, see Andreas Kablitz, "Das Ende des Sacrum Imperium: Verwandlung der Repräsentation von Geschichte zwischen Dante und Petrarca," in *Mittelalter und Frühe Neuzeit*, ed. W. Haug (Tübingen: Niemeyer, 1999), 499–549.

31. Several disconcerting elements mark Homer's dream-apparition to Ennius. His visitation is admittedly an escape from the "prison of Dis," not a descent from the starry heaven (*Africa* 176–77); despite the ecstatic tone, he is the literary repository of little more than geographical-poetic expertise (*Africa* 147–48 and 189–95). For Petrarch's geographical praise of the coast between Genoa and Rome in the *Africa* (6.839–84), as it is echoed in the most geographically based of his later works, see Theodore J. Cachey, *Petrarch's Guide to the Holy Land: Itinerary to the Sepulcher of Our Lord Jesus Christ* (Notre Dame: University of Notre Dame Press, 2002).

32. The principle of discontinuity here enforced is surprising, as it contradicts Petrarch's habit of conversation with the ancients. For the paradigmatic case of Augustine in the *Secretum*, and for the character's reconsideration of the *Africa*, see the essay by David Marsh in this volume.

33. The point Petrarch makes here through an allusion ultimately derives from Virgil's ekphrastic depiction of the Battle at Actium (*Aeneid* 678–84 vs. 685–88; and 698–700 vs. 704–6). It will not be lost on Tasso, as demonstrated by Sergio Zatti's seminal study *L'uniforme cristiano e il multiforme pagano: Saggio sulla "Gerusalemme liberata"* (Milan: Il Saggiatore, 1983).

34. The lexical association of *favilla* and *flamma* is, to my knowledge, not common in classical poetry. The purest example of the maxim may be found in Curtius Rufus, *Historia Alexandri* 6.3.11 (often cited for Dante's line, but not fully coincident with Petrarch's): *Parva saepe scintilla . . . magnum excitavit incendium.* Parallels that are closer in language may be found in Ovid, *Metamorphoses.* 7.80–81, and *Tristia* 5.12.62–66, but the notion is also biblical; see Isaiah 1.31.1–3 and James 3.5.

Chapter Six

1. I follow the Latin text in Carlo Godi, "La 'Collatio laureationis' del Petrarca nelle due redazioni," *Studi Petrarcheschi,* n.s., 5 (1988): 1–58. In an e-mail message to me on April 1, 2004, Italo Pantani, who is editing and translating the work for the Edizione Nazionale delle Opere del Petrarca, reports that he doesn't anticipate major changes to Godi's text. But see Silvia Rizzo's suggestions for improving it in Michele Feo, ed., *Codici latini del Petrarca nelle biblioteche fiorentine* (Florence: Le Lettere, 1991), 322–30. *Codici latini*, ed. Feo contains a beautiful reproduction of the opening page of the *Collatio*, folio 57r, from the only manuscript of the complete work, Biblioteca Nazionale

Centrale, Firenze, 2.8.47 (plate 34). I follow the translation of Ernest Hatch
Wilkins in "Petrarch's *Coronation Oration*," *Studies in the Life and Works of
Petrarch* (Cambridge: Mediaeval Academy of America, 1955), 300–13, which
is based on Attilio Hortis's 1874 edition.

2.   Its full title is *Collatio edita per clarissimum poetam Franciscum Petrarcam Florenti-
num, Romae in Capitolio, tempore laureationis sue*. Wilkins's essay, "The Coronation of Petrarch," in *The Making of the "Canzoniere"* (Rome: Edizioni di storia e
letteratura, 1951), 9–69, remains the essential starting place for studying the
oration.

3.   Wilkins, "Petrarch's *Coronation Oration*," 300.

4.   In addition to Pantani's edition of the *Collatio*, the Edizione Nazionale will
also include new editions of Petrarch's five other orations, two of which will
be edited by Michele Feo (speech at Novara and second Venetian speech
of 1373), with the remaining three to be edited by Giacinto Namia. In the
bibliography I provide information on the editions of these works that we
must depend on for now. The first four of these speeches date from Petrarch's
period in Milan when he served the Visconti. They include: *Arenga facta
Veneciis* (Speech delivered to the Venetians, November 8, 1353), delivered by
Petrarch as ambassador for the Visconti court before the Venetian Senate
on ending the Third Genoese War; *Arenga facta Mediolani* (Speech delivered
to the Milanese, October 7, 1354), a funeral oration on the death of Archbishop Giovanni Visconti, which we have only in a late sixteenth-century
Italian translation; *Arenga facta in civitate Novarie* (Speech delivered in the city
of Novara, June 19, 1358), a speech made against the rebellious citizens of
Novara; and *Collatio brevis coram Iohanne Francorum rege* (Brief oration in the
presence of John, king of the French, January 13, 1361), a speech delivered
in Paris in honor of King John the Good, celebrating both his release from
English captors in 1360 and the betrothal of his daughter Isabelle to Gian
Galeazzo Visconti. Petrarch's last official oratorical work, *Orazione per la
seconda ambasceria veneziana* (Oration for the second Venetian embassy,
October 2, 1373), was a speech delivered before the Venetian Senate as an
ambassador for Francesco da Carrara of Padua, suing for peace between
Venice and Padua, of which we have only a summary in Paduan vernacular made by an anonymous contemporary chronicler. See Rossella Bessi's
annotations on all the oratorical works in Feo, *Codici latini*, 332–33, as well
as, *Petrarca nel tempo. Tnadizione lettori e immagini delle opere*, edited by Michele
Feo (Pontedera: Bandecchi and Vivaldi, 2003), 435–42. I am grateful to the
anonymous reader for the Press for additional bibliographical information on
current editions.

5.   See Petrarch *Familiares* 18.16, where he refers to having used Cicero's words

before the Venetian Senate in 1353; and 24.4, where he emphasizes Cicero's eloquence as a public speaker but without claiming explicitly to follow the Roman model in his own speaking. Ronald L. Martinez presents a full list of passages in which Petrarch acknowledges his debt to Cicero in "Petrarch's Lame Leg and the Corpus of Cicero: An Early Crisis of Humanism?" in *The Body in Early Modern Italy*, ed. Julia L. Hairston and Walter Stephens.

6. Petrarch depicts Demosthenes playing second fiddle to Cicero in *TF* 3.13–24. Given Petrarch's devotion to Cicero, one wonders if the comparison of himself to Demosthenes is an admission of some degree of inadequacy.

7. See Francesco Nelli, *Un ami di Pétrarque: Lettres de Francesco Nelli à Pétrarque*, ed. Henry Cochin (Paris: Champion, 1892), 206: "But, to sum up those gestures better in a word, I noticed that your habits were such as neither Cicero would have better formulated as precepts nor himself have more fittingly put into practice." I thank Ronald L. Martinez for this reference and Mark Possanza for advice on translating it.

8. "[S]cripsit etiam *Invectivas*, ut non solum poeta, sed etiam orator haberetur" [He also wrote *Invective* so that he would be considered not only a poet but also an orator]. Leonardo Bruni, *Ad Petrum Paulum Histrum Dialogus*, in *Prosatori latini del Quattrocento*, ed. Eugenio Garin (Milan and Naples: Ricciardi, 1952), 72.

9. Ronald G. Musto points out that in general "the medieval letter followed the rules of oratory," in *Apocalypse in Rome: Cola di Rienzo and the Politics of the New Age* (Berkeley: University of California Press, 2003), 41.

10. One example among many: Petrarch *Familiares* 12.4, to Francesco Nelli.

11. Wilkins, "Coronation of Petrarch," 58–59. Edward H. R. Tatham, who gives a spirited reconstruction of the events surrounding the coronation, argues that the *Privilegium* was composed by a scribe consulting the *Collatio;* see *Francesco Petrarca: The First Modern Man of Letters* (London: Sheldon Press, 1926), 2:145–46.

12. Petrarch makes two errors: victors in the Capitoline contests of ancient Rome received crowns of oak leaves, and Statius never won in those contests; but see Wilkins, "The Coronation of Petrarch," 17–20, for the medieval tradition of Statius's laureation. See also Michelangelo Picone, "Il tema dell'incoronazione poetica in Dante, Petrarca e Boccaccio," *L'Alighieri* 25 (2005): 5–26, esp. 14–20, for comments on the theme of coronation in Petrarch's lyrics.

13. Hans Baron makes this point in *From Petrarch to Leonardo Bruni: Studies in Humanistic and Political Literature* (Chicago: University of Chicago Press, 1968), 15. In "La 'Collatio laureationis,'" Godi contradicts this claim, without, however, referring to Baron's comments (1). Although the changes seem rel-

atively minor (e.g., "deportasse" > "reportasse" at 6.1), Godi is emphatic that Petrarch does elaborate some changes in his text.

14. Stephen Murphy explores the *Africa*'s ties to the *Collatio* in *The Gift of Immortality* (Madison, Teaneck: Farleigh Dickinson Press and Associated University Presses, 1997), 74–127.

15. Nicholas Mann, *Petrarch* (Oxford: Oxford University Press, 1984), 108. For a detailed list of the various passages in Petrarch's writings that refer to the coronation, see Marco Ariani, *Petrarca* (Rome: Salerno, 1999), 39–40.

16. In Douglas Biow, *Doctors, Ambassadors, Secretaries: Humanism and Professions in Renaissance Italy* (Chicago: University of Chicago Press, 2002), 27–44.

17. Mazzotta uses the image of "worlds" both as a metaphor for the different realms in which Petrarch fashioned his self-image (literature, history, politics, philosophy, theology, etc.) and as a synonym for the literary works he created while passing through these realms. The fragmented assemblage of varied works is shaped by the unifying presence of the singular Petrarch.

18. For Petrarch's understanding of Roman monuments including those on the Capitoline Hill, see Maria Accame Lanzillotta, "Le *antiquitates romanae* di Petrarca," in *Preveggenze umanistiche di Petrarca* (Pisa: ETS, 1993). See also J. B. Trapp, "The Poet Laureate," in *Rome in the Renaissance*, ed. P. A. Ramsey (Binghamton: MRTS, 1982), 101–7.

19. For the epistle to Luca da Penna, see *Letters of Old Age* (trans. Bernardo et al.), 2:601. Consider also *Seniles* 12.2, where Petrarch lambastes Arabic authorities to fall back again on Virgil and Cicero; see Gian Carlo Garfagnini, "Note sull'uso degli *Auctores* nelle *Seniles*," *Quaderni Petrarcheschi* 9–10 (1992–93): 676–77.

20. In Biow, *Doctors, Ambassadors, Secretaries*, 32. Contrast the discovery announced by Godi ("La 'Collatio laureationis,'" 2) of a heretofore-unknown manuscript copy of an excerpt from the *Coronation Oration*, Vat. Pal. Lat. 1552, which refers to the work as an *oratio* rather than *collatio*, "Oratio Francisci Petrarche." But see Michele Feo's rebuttal of Godi's discovery in "Note petrarchesche. I: Petrarca e Enrico da Iernia. II: Le 'due redazioni' della *Collatio laureationis*," *Quaderni Petrarcheschi* 7 (1990): 186–203.

21. Pierre de Nolhac, *Pétrarque et l'humanisme*, 2 vols. (Paris: Champion, 1907), 2:213.

22. Petrarch was a great disseminator of Cicero's works: "Once in Petrarch's hands, *Pro Cluentio* spread quickly, not only in Italy but also in France," in M. D. Reeve and R. H. Rouse, "[Cicero's] Speeches," in *Texts and Transmission: A Survey of the Latin Classics*, ed. L. D. Reynolds (Oxford: Clarendon Press, 1983), 87. See also Petrarch *Familiares* 13.6 where he describes sending the *Pro Archia* to friends in Florence.

23. Petrarch's involvement with the complex process of restoring the Ciceronian corpus included, among other innovations, the separation of the speeches as a body of work from other works by Cicero (Reeve and Rouse, *Texts and Transmission*, 94).

24. I follow Wilkins's helpful division of the speech into three large sections. Godi, "La 'Collatio laureationis,'" 17, regrets not having followed Wilkins's design, a situation one hopes Pantani will correct in his edition.

25. "At the Renaissance, Lactantius, the most classical of all early Christian writers, comes to be known as the Christian Cicero," in *Oxford Classical Dictionary*, ed. Simon Hornblower and Antony Spawforth, 3rd ed. (Oxford: Oxford University Press, 1996), 811.

26. Several recent critics have agreed with Wilkins's position: Godi, "La 'Collatio laureationis,'" 1; and Riccardo Fubini, review of Douglas Biow in *Renaissance Quarterly* 56 (2003): 1152–53.

Chapter Seven

1. Petrarch's speeches, six all together, go by three kinds of titles that are synonymous in meaning. First is the classical Latin "collatio" (oration), used for *Collatio laureationis* (*Coronation Oration*), and *Collatio brevis coram Iohanne Francorum rege* (*Brief Oration before John, King of the French*). Second is the medieval "arenga" or "arringa" (from Old German "hring"), which survives in modern Italian ("arringa") and is cognate with English "harangue." This identifies talks he gave in Venice and Milan. Third is the Italian "orazione," used to designate the final discourse, before the Venetian senate in 1373, which survives only in a chronicler's vernacular summary. Except for this last talk, all are preserved only in single copies. For basic information on their transmission and editorial history, as well as facsimile reproductions of the first folios, see Michele Feo, *Petrarca nel tempo: Tradizione lettori e immagini delle opere* (Pontedera: Bandecchi and Vivaldi, 2003), 435–42.

2. Giuseppe Frasso, *Itinerari con Francesco Petrarca* (Padua: Antenore, 1974), the catalog of an exhibit at the sixth centenary of the poet's death, includes photographs of the house at Arquà, near Padua, and of many places he lived or visited. For the will, see Theodore E. Mommsen, *Petrarch's Testament* (Ithaca: Cornell University Press, 1957) and Armando Maggi's epilogue below.

3. Ugo Dotti, *Vita di Petrarca* (Bari: Laterza, 1987), 28–47, documents the poet's service as "capellanus continuus commensalis" in the Colonna family. See further, by the same author, *Petrarca a Parma* (Reggio Emilia: Diabasis, 2006), 22–23, for their financial assistance from 1325. Petrarch speaks of Cardinal Giovanni Colonna as a "father" or better, "brother," in his autobio-

graphical letter to Posterity. See Petrarch, *Posteritati*, ed. Gianni Villani (Rome: Salerno, 1990), 48–49.

4. Petrarch *Rime estravaganti* (ed. Paolino), nos. 6–7 (674–81). They answer a proposing sonnet from an unknown poet. In the manuscript that preserves them, Petrarch's Vatican autograph 3196, his notes introducing the first read: "Responsio mea, domino iubente" (My answer, at my lord's command), and explaining the second, "Alia responsio mea, domino materiam dante et iubente" (Another response of mine, at the command of my lord, who gave the material).

5. Avignon as Babylon is a recurrent motif in Petrarch's *Liber sine nomine*. See, for example, letters 10 and 17 and the essay in this volume by Ronald L. Martinez.

6. Dotti, *Petrarca a Parma*, reconstructs the chronology and literary activity of the three Parma sojourns: May 23, 1341, to June 1342; late December 1343 to February 23, 1345; and intervals between March 1348 and June 1351. Petrarch sent the "Correggio" redaction of *Rerum vulgarium fragmenta* (ca. 1356–58) to Azzo, a friend until his death in 1362.

7. Latin text reproduced from Dotti, *Petrarca a Parma*, 16, translation mine. A mannered canzone fabricated for the same occasion highlights Azzo's family name: "COR REGIO fu, sì come suona il nome, / quel che venne sicuro a l'alta impresa" (REGAL HEART it was, as the name sounds, / that came sure to the high task). See Petrarch *Rime estravaganti* (ed. Paolino), no. 21, vv. 49–57. Halting rhythms, banal formulas, and dated content—signs of enforced poetic activity, sent this vernacular exercise into the discard bin of dispersed rhymes. See further the essay by Justin Steinberg in this volume.

8. Giovanni Boccaccio *Epistole*, ed. Ginetta Auzzas, no. 10, "A Francesco Petrarca," in Boccaccio, *Tutte le opere*, 5.1: 574–83. Petrarch's first Visconti patron was the archbishop of Milan, Giovanni, who came to power with his brother Luchino after the death of their predecessor in 1339. They ruled together until Luchino's death in 1349, after which Giovanni recalled three nephews exiled by Luchino and sons of another brother of theirs, Stefano, to join in administration of the duchy: Matteo II, Bernabò, and Galeazzo II. They inherited rule from Giovanni (d. 1354). Matteo died, perhaps simply from a life of excesses or possibly from poisoning by his siblings (as their mother is said to have suspected) in 1355. The two survivors partitioned rule. Milan became the residence of cruel Bernabò (d. 1385); Pavia became headquarters to Galeazzo (d. 1378), a constructive ruler and diplomat, who married his son Gian Galeazzo to Isabelle of Valois, daughter of the king of France, and his daughter Violante to the son of England's King Edward III.

9. "In ortu M. Vicecomitis," (*Epystole* 3.29), in *Poesie minori del Petrarca sul testo*

latino ora corretto volgarizzate da poeti viventi o da poco defunti, ed. Domenico
Rossetti (Milan: Società Tipografica de' Classici Italiani, 1831), 2: 158–69.
Hyperbole magnifies the infant in this metrical epistle, which begins "Magne
puer" (Great boy). Petrarch's company in the family reveals something of
his status: godfathers to little Marco's brother's were the marchesi of Ferrara, of Mantova, and the republic of Bologna. Marcello Simonetta offers
some astute pages on the poet's ambiguous situation at the court of Milan,
"L'antenato dei segretari: Petrarca e i Visconti," in *Rinascimento Segreto: Il
mondo del Segretario da Petrarca a Machiavelli* (Milan: FrancoAngeli, 2004),
25–36.

10. Petrarch, *Lettere disperse varie e miscellanee,* ed. Alessandro Pancheri (Parma:
Guanda, 1994), 39.65: 312–14: "si humano ore loqui possint, natura ipsa
fatebitur; vel si ita sors tulerit, aprorum dentibus quam fame vel gladio
perituros." A manuscript of the letter at Bergamo ends with a note saying
Petrarch wrote it for Bernabò: "Franciscus Petrarca pro domino Bernaboue
Vicecomite Mediolani etc. domino generali." Francesco Novati, "Il Petrarca
e i Visconti," in *Francesco Petrarca e la Lombardia* (Milan: Hoepli, 1904), 9–84,
esp. 36–39, exonerates Petrarch by reading the letter as a masterpiece of
sarcasm; Ernest Hatch Wilkins, *Petrarch's Eight Years in Milan* (Cambridge:
Mediaeval Academy of America, 1958), 197–98, takes a more neutral stance.
Dotti, *Vita di Petrarca,* 334, finds the episode "mean-spirited and miserable."
Petrarch had earlier, on March 25, 1359, written an angry but honest letter
to Bussolari, urging him to abandon politics and return to a life of prayer
(*Familiares* 19.18). Attilio Hortis, *Scritti inediti di Francesco Petrarca* (Trieste:
Tipografia del Lloyd Austro-Ungarico, 1874), gives detailed historical back-
ground in his discussion of Petrarch's letters to this temporary tyrant, whom
one local historian called "the Savonarola of Pavia," 175–81, esp. 179, n. 1.
Such was Bernabò's notoriety for outrageous villainy that it generated a
collection of scurrilous *novelle.* See Piero Ginori Conti, *Novelle inedite intorno
a Bernabò Visconti* (Florence: Fondazione Ginori Conti, 1940). I thank David
Wallace for this last reference.

11. In *Seniles* 10.1, to Sagremor de Pommiers congratulating him on becoming
a Cistercian monk, Petrarch mentions the frightening journey they made
together through Switzerland and Germany to Prague in 1356. Shortly after
his return, in the fall of that year, Basel was destroyed by an earthquake, an
event that deeply impressed Petrarch (*De remediis* 2.91; *Seniles* 10.2). He had
earlier traveled from Milan to Mantua to meet in person with the emperor,
when the latter came to Italy in fall and winter of 1354–55. See Wilkins,
Petrarch's Eight Years in Milan, 142–44, and further, 152–53, on the northern
journey. Petrarch recalls being made a member of the Counts Palatine in a

thank-you letter to the emperor's chancellor, the bishop of Olmütz (*Familiares* 21.2).

12. For the text, see Petrarch *Scritti inediti* (ed. Hortis), 329–33, *Arenga facta venecijs 1353, octauo die Nouembris super pace tractanda Inter commune Janue et dominum Archiepiscopum Mediolanensem ex una parte, et commune veneciarum ex altera per dominum franciscum petrarcham poetam et ambasiatorem supradictum;* and for the words quoting Virgil, 331: "Tu regere Imperio populos romane memento, hec tibi erunt artes pacisque imponere morem et res." An electronic version of Petrarch's text is available at the University of Rome's "La Sapienza" site Biblioteca italiana, under the rubric *Arringhe* and the title *Super pace tractanda*. The same site also offers the speeches on the death of Giovanni Visconti and to the conquered Novarese.

13. Ps. 46:9–10: "Venite et videte opera Domini, quia posuit prodigia supra terram auferens bella usque ad fines terre archum conteret et confringet arma et scuta conburet igni." Petrarch's role was ceremonial; he didn't participate in the official peace negotiations. For an account of the political situation and the Latin text of this brief oration, *Arenga facta veneciis* (*Speech to the Venetians*), see Hortis, *Scritti inediti*, 107–126, 329–33. Here and throughout scripture is cited in the Douay version. For the letter to Dandolo, see Petrarch, *Le famiari*, ed. Rossi, 18.16.9, vol. 3, p. 304: "Sed aperire aures obseratas et obstinatos animos movere non nostri, nescio an vel ciceroniani esset eloquii"; *Letters on Familiar Matter* (trans. Bernardo [1985]), 70.

14. Hortis, *Scritti inediti*, 131, reports on the manner of Giovanni Visconti's sudden death on October 5, 1354. Hortis first published the panegyric from the only surviving version, ibid., 335–40. A late sixteenth-century copy in Italian, gives the date of the oration as October 7, 1354; so too Feo, *Petrarca nel tempo*, 435, noting that the biographical tradition erroneously puts it on October 17, 1353.

15. Hortis, *Scritti inediti*, 66–67, terms Giovanni Visconti the greatest prince of his age and quotes Thomas Campbell's *Life of Petrarch* on the epithet "Bonaparte of Italy." Giovanni controlled extensive territories in Lombardy and beyond from a court resplendent with pageantry and patronage (54–63).

16. "Cor meum conturbatum est, dereliquit me virtus mea, et lumen ocularum meorum et ipsum non est mecum" (trans. Douay).

17. *Petrarca a Novara* (Novara: Interlinea Edizioni, 2004), 39: "deum oro ut dominum ut uos illuminet et sibi ea iusticia ac consilio preesse vobis ea fide atque obsequio subesse tribuat ne aut vobis alium statum seu dominum optare aut sibi alium populum plus amare conveniat." The 2004 edition reprints the text in Latin and Italian from *Francesco Petrarca a Novara e la sua aringa ai novaresi,*

trans. Carlo Negroni (Novara: Fratelli Miglio, 1876). Negroni reproduced the *arenga* in Latin from Hortis, *Scritti inediti*, 166–74. Hortis gives extensive historical background. The speech is about 3,000 words.

18. Agriculturalist, economist, political scientist, and historian, Jean Charles Léonard Simonde de Sismondi (1773–1842) published his *Histoire des républiques italiennes du moyen âge* in the second decade of the nineteenth century. Hortis quotes him, *Scritti inediti*, 155–56.

19. For a sense of proportions, we can recall that Petrarch in his *Testamentum* bequeathed fifty gold florins to his friend Boccaccio, for the purchase of "a winter garment to be worn by him while he is studying and working during the night hours," and his entire bequest to his brother Gherardo was 100 florins. Mommsen, *Petrarch's Testament*, 82–83: "pro una veste hiemali ad studium lucubrationesque nocturnas"; and for the bequest to Gherardo, 92–93.

20. Petrarch *Familiares* (ed. Rossi), 22.14.3, vol. 4, p. 138: "sic ubique solitudo infelix et meror et vastitas, sic ubique horrida et inculta arva, sic dirute deserteque domus nisi que, cincte arcium menibus aut urbium, evasissent, sic demum locis omnibus Anglorum mesta vertigia, et recentes fedeque cicatrices cladium extyabant"; (trans. Bernardo), 242: "Everywhere were dismal devastation, grief, and desolation, everywhere wild and uncultivated fields, everywhere ruined and deserted homes . . . everywhere remained the sad vestiges of the Angli and the recent, loathsome scars of defeat." The biblical text is 2 Chron. 33:13: "Exaudivit orationem eius reduxitque eum in Ierusalem, in regnum suum." For the text of the oration and an Italian translation, see Petrarch, *Opere latine*, ed. Antonietta Bufano (Turin: Unione Tipografico-Editrice Torinese, 1975), 2: 1285–1309.

21. For a concise description of this mission see Wilkins, *Petrarch's Eight Years*, 220–25.

22. Petrarch *Seniles* (ed. Nota), 13.16, vol. 4, pp. 217–19: "Ego ad civitatem redii—iam tertius dies est—et familiolam meam rure dimissam hodie vel, ad tardius, cras expecto. Libellos quos ibi habui mecum abstuli; domum et reliqua conservabit Cristus qui solicitus est mei quique a pueritia, imo ab utero matris mee, licet indignum et immeritum, me custodit. Que si tamen omnino destinata esset incendio, fiat voluntas Dei; michi de cetero satis est sepulcrum, domus ultima. Nam quod amor dictat et tu scribis de inscribendo nomen meum ipso domus in limine, pium magis quam accommodatum est rebus atque temporibus: studiosorum nomina Mars non curat" (trans. Bernardo, 519), dated Nov. 17 [1371], to Gasparo [Squaro dei Broaspini] di Verona, introduced to Petrarch by Coluccio Salutati. Books surviving from Petrarch's library, in and of itself the subject matter for many books, preserve numerous

marginalia and annotations constituting another family of his writings, but beyond the scope of this volume. A useful starting point is the catalog "La biblioteca. 1. I codici postillati," in Feo, *Petrarca nel tempo*, 457–95.

23. Feo, *Petrarca nel tempo*, 442. Background on the war, Petrarch's role in the embassy, and the surviving vernacular summary of his oration can be found in Vittorio Lazzarini, "La seconda ambasceria di Francesco Petrarca a Venezia," in *Miscellanea di studi critici pubblicati in onore di Guido Mazzoni dai suoi discepoli*, ed. Arnaldo Della Torre and P. L. Rambaldi (Florence: Successori B. Seeber, 1904), 1:173–83. Cf. Wilkins, *Life of Petrarch*, 240–41.

24. In this *vita*, which circulated widely after he died, Petrarch distinguishes between two ancient men of the same name, the playwright and a senator. On Petrarch and Terence, see Pierre de Nolhac, *Pétrarque et l'humanisme*, rev. ed. (Paris: Honoré Champion, 1907), 1:187–93; Feo, *Petrarca nel tempo*, 377; and for further bibliography, Ariani, *Petrarca*, 64.

25. Lazzarini, "La seconda ambasceria," 183: "Con lo qual magnifico Signor messier Francesco nouello da Carrara andò a Venesia una gran comitiua de nobili caualieri et doctori de lege et de altri homini in numero assai, intro i quali fo el notissimo poeta, homo da alta et celebre fama degno de farne sempre memoria, messier Francesco Petrarca, per nation toschano. Al quale, per lo predicto magnifico Signore, in quella parte fo commesso lo officio de douer dir le parole, et così fe' in la forma che da soura è dicto; ben che per la soa uechieça et per una infirmità la quale ello hauea habuda et de la qual ello no era ancora guarido, le vose ie tremò un pocho."

26. Petrarch, *Testamentum* (ed. Mommsen), 73, 79–80. For Petrarch's last years at Padua and Arquà, see Dotti, *Vita di Petrarca*, 401–39, and for his funeral, 439.

27. *Seniles* 17.2, in Petrarch *Prose*, ed. G. Martellotti, P. G. Ricci, E. Carrara, E. Bianchi (Milan: Ricciardi, 1955, 1446–48: ["Huc etiam illud effers:] bonas me partes temporum sub obsequio principum perdidisse. . . . Nomine ego cum principibus fui, re autem principes mecum fuerunt. Numquam me illorum consilia et perraro convivia tenuerunt. Nulla michi unquam conditio probaretur, que me vel modicum a libertate et a studiis meis averteret. Itaque cum palatium omnes, ego vel nemus petebam vel inter libros in thalamo quiescebam. . . . semel Venetias pro negotio pacis missus inter urbem illam et Ianuam reformande, hibernum in hoc mensem integrum exegi; inde ad romanum principem in extrema barbarie . . . tres estivos menses; denique ad gratulandum Iohanni Francorum regi, britannico tunc carcere liberato, alios tres hibernos. . . . perditos dies voco; quamvis in ultimo, . . . epystolam ingentem dictavi. . . . Ecce ergo: menses septem sub obsequio principum amisi."

28. *Seniles* 14.1 (ed. Nota), 4:235: "non civibus tantum tuis egregium te rectorem, sed exemplar aliarum urbium rectoribus exhiberes"; (ed. Bernardo), 523.

29. *Seniles* 14.1 (ed. Nota), 4: 247; (ed. Bernardo), 528.

30. *Seniles* 14.1 (ed. Nota), 4: 299–301: "[reor, quod] viros egregios ut honores tibique familiarissimos efficias. . . . Egregios autem viros dico, quos e grege hominum vulgarium aliqua abstraxit excellentia, et vel iustitia insignis ac sanctitas—quod, heu, nostra etate perrarum est—vel rei militaris experientia ac doctrina, vel literarum copia, rerumque notitia, singulares fecit"; (ed. Bernardo), 549.

31. *Seniles* 14.1 (ed. Nota), 4: 285: "equi, vestes, arma, vasa, pecunie, domus, agri, et que sunt eiusmodi"; (ed. Bernardo), 543.

32. *Seniles* 14.1 (ed. Nota), 4: 305; (ed. Bernardo), 551."Nam quid, oro, benemeritis et insignibus viris potest esse iocundius quam sub iusto et miti principe ac favorabili extimatore meritorum vitam agere? . . . Armati enim tibi ad horam utiles esse possunt et temporale obsequium prestare, literati autem et temporale consilium et mansurum nomen; insuper ascendendi ad superos rectum iter ostendere."

Chapter Eight

1. All references are to Petrarch, *Rerum memorandarum libri,* ed. Giuseppe Billanovich, Edizione nazionale delle opere di Francesco Petrarca, 5 (Florence: Sansoni, 1945). Billanovich's edition is the only modern one. English translations from this source are my own.

2. The *editio princeps* was published at Louvain in 1485, and other editions appeared in the complete *Opera* of Petrarch published at different dates. The *Rerum memorandarum libri* has no translation in English or in any other language, except for a German one by Stefanus Vigilius, published in three editions in the sixteenth century: at Augsburg in 1541, at Frankfurt am Main in 1566, and at Frankfurt am Main in 1591. For notice of this version, see *Catalogue of the Petrarch Collection in Cornell University Library,* intro. by Morris Bishop (Millwood: Kraus-Thomson Organization, 1974), 92. Petrarch enjoyed a vast *Rezeption* in Germany, on which see Frank L. Borchardt, "Petrarch: The German Connection," in *Francis Petrarch Six Centuries Later,* ed. Aldo Scaglione (Chapel Hill and Chicago: North Carolina University Press and Newberry Library, 1975), 418–31. Borchardt recalls that Herman Schedel "went to the trouble of compiling an index for an early imprint of Petrarch's *Rerum memorandarum liber*" (426). In general the *Rerum memorandarum libri* has not enjoyed much attention on the part of Petrarch scholars, who at the most devote some paragraphs to it in general works while dealing with Petrarch's Latin production; on the other hand, given the "erudite" nature of

the work, there have been occasional notes on philological details—see Joseph G. Fucilla, *Oltre un cinquentennio di scritti sul Petrarca (1916–1973)* (Padua: Antenore, 1982), 213—such as one by Pier Giorgio Ricci, "Una citazione del Petrarca," in *Rinascimento* 3 (1952): 372. On the same line of research, see Paolo Cherchi, "'*Quosdam historicos*' (*Rer. Mem. Lib., III 12*)," in *Studi Petrarcheschi* 18 (2005): 159–62. More than a philological note is the piece by Etienne Gilson, "Sur deux textes de Pétrarque: II. *In confinio duorum populorum*," in *Petrarca e Petrarchismo. Atti del terzo congresso dell'associazione internazionale per gli studi di lingua e letteratura italiana (Aix-en-Provence e Marsiglia, 31 marzo–5 aprile 1959)* (Bologna: Minerva, 1961), 43–50, which is quite insightful on the position of *Rerum memorandarum libri* between classical and humanistic terrain.

3.   For the reception of Valerius Maximus in the Middle Ages, see the fundamental studies by Dorothy D. Schullian, "A Preliminary List of Manuscripts of Valerius Maximus," in *Studies in Honor of B. L Ullman*, ed. Lillian B. Lawler et al. (Saint Louis: Saint Louis University Press, 1960), 81–95, and idem, "A Revised List of Manuscripts of Valerius Maximus," in *Miscellanea Augusto Campana* (Padua: Antenore, 1981), 695–728; and "Valerius Maximus," in *Catalogus Translationum et Commentariorum*, ed. F. Edward Cranz and O. P. Kristeller (Washington: Catholic University Press, 1984), 4:287–403. This last is the most important contribution for several aspects of Valerius Maximus's afterlife (manuscripts, commentaries, excerpts, editions). Some data, especially concerning his fortunes in the vernacular languages, are found in *Dionigi da Borgo di San Sepolcro fra Petrarca e Boccaccio*, ed. Franco Suitner (Città di Castello: Petruzzi, 2000), passim; but see more specifically the essay by Giuseppe Di Stefano, "Dionigi di Borgo di San Sepolcro e Valerio Massimo," 147–64. John Briscoe's recent edition, *Valeri Maximi facta et dicta memorabilia* (Stuttgart and Leipzig: B. G. Teubner, 1998), shows that text, selections, and translations of Valerius Maximus were transmitted in over eight hundred manuscripts, many from the later Middle Ages. See D. Wardles's review of this valuable contribution in the online *Bryn Mawr Classical Review* (1999.09.25).

4.   See Schullian, "Valerius Maximus," in *Catalogus*, 324–28; Di Stefano, "Dionigi di Borgo di San Sepolcro e Valerio Massimo," in Suitner, *Dionigi da Borgo di San Sepolcro*, 147–64. This volume is interesting for other data pertaining to the fortunes of Valerius in Italy during the fourteenth and fifteenth centuries.

5.   "Eque tristis et terrifica nec letioris exitus Cassii Parmensis quies. Post bellum actiacum, victo cui enixe faverat Antonio, Athenis, quo disperatis rebus se contulerat, per noctem dormiens quendam immensi corporis et ethiopici nigroris insueteque prorsum deformitatis hominem in cubiculum suum ingredientem cernere visus est et stupefactus aspectu ex eodem quisnam

foret exquirere; ille autem nescio quid horrisonum graeco murmure respondisse. Quo metu sompnum frangente trepidanter servos suos excivit, quis ea specie thalamum irrupisset interrogans. Quibus aperte negantibus quempiam introisse, curis eger rursum sompno succubuit; et eadem visione iterum experrectus ac territus, illato lumine servos suos lectum circumsistere precepit. Nocturno pavori diurnus successit dolor. Per eosdem enim dies ab Augusto Cesare, quem comuni insectatione non contentus nominatim gravibus maledictis irritaverat, capite multatus est." *Rerum memorandarum libri* (ed. Billanovich), 4.56.

6. "Vincit huiusce somnii dirum aspectum quod insequitur. Apud Actium M. Antonii fractis opibus, Cassius Parmensis, qui partes eius secutus fuerat, Athenas confugit. Ubi concubia nocte, cum sollicitudinibus et curis mente sopita in lectulo iaceret, existimauit ad se venire hominem ingentis magnitudinis, coloris nigri, squalidum barba et capillo immisso, interrogatumque quisnam esset respondisse κακον δαιμονα. Perterritus deinde taetro visu et nomine horrendo, servos inclamauit, sciscitatusque est ecquem talis habitus aut intrantem cubiculum aut exeuntem vidissent. Quibus adfirmantibus neminem illuc accessisse, iterum se quieti et somno dedit, atque eadem animo eius obversata species est. Itaque fugato somno lumen intro ferri iussit puerosque a se discedere vetuit. Inter hanc noctem et supplicium capitis quo eum Caesar adfecit parvulum admodum temporis intercessit." Valerius Maximus, *Memorable Doings and Sayings*, ed. and trans. D. R. Shackleton Bailey, Loeb Classical Library (Cambridge: Harvard University Press, 2000), bk. 1, chap. 7 (On Dreams), 88–89.

7. Op. cit., cxxii–cxxiii.

8. See Marco Ariani, *Petrarca* (Rome: Salerno Editrice, 1999), 104.

9. Paolo Cherchi, "Petrarch, Valerio Massimo, e le "concordanze delle storie," in *Rinascimento: Rivista dell'Istituto Nazionale di Studi sul Rinascimento*, 2nd ser., 42 (2002): 31–65.

10. Paolo Cherchi, *Polimatia di riuso—Mezzo secolo di plagio (1539–1589)* (Rome: Bulzoni, 1998).

Chapter Nine

The editors warmly thank Lisa Barca for her valuable professional assistance in translating and editing this essay.

1. The most recent edition is *Bucolicum carmen/Pétrarque,* Latin text with French trans. and comm. by Marcel François and Paul Bachmann with François Roudaut, preface by Jean Meyers (Paris: Champion, 2001). For the text with its earliest commentaries, see Antonio Avena, *Il Bucolicum carmen e i suoi*

commenti inediti (1906; Bologna: Forni, 1969). For an Italian prose translation
that accompanies the Latin, see Petrarch, *Bucolicum carmen,* ed. Tonino T.
Mattucci (Pisa: Giardini, 1970). For an English translation with succinct
commentary, see Thomas G. Bergin, ed., Petrarch's *Bucolicum Carmen* (New
Haven: Yale University Press, 1974). Bergin's translation faces Avena's text
(which follows the autograph MS Vat. Lat. 3358), and both are here cited.
See Domenico De Venuto, ed., *Il Bucolicum Carmen di Francesco Petrarca: Edizione diplomatica dell'autografo Vat. Lat. 3358* (Pisa: ETS, 1990); On questions of
dating, see Enrico Carrara, "I commenti antichi e la cronologia delle ecloghe
petrarchesche," *Giornale Storico della Letteratura Italiana* 28 (1897): 138–43;
Arnaldo Foresti, "La data della prima egloga" and "Quando il Petrarca fece
le grandi giunte al *Bucolicum?*" in *Aneddoti della vita di Francesco Petrarca* (1928;
Padua: Antenore, 1977), 204–8 and 471–84; Nicholas Mann, "The Making
of Petrarch's *Bucolicum Carmen:* A Contribution to the History of the Text,"
Italia Medioevale e Umanistica 20 (1977): 127–82; Nicholas Mann, "L'edizione
critica del *Bucolicum Carmen,*" *Annali della Scuola Normale Superiore di Pisa,*
3rd ser., 19 (1989): 231–38. The classic source on the early fourteenth-
century eclogue exchange between Dante and Giovanni del Virgilio is
Philip H. Wicksteed and Edmund G. Gardner, *Dante and Giovanni del Virgilio.
Including a Critical Edition of the Text of Dante's "Eclogae Latinae" and of the Poetic
Remains of Giovanni del Virgilio* (1902; Freeport: Books for Libraries Press,
1971). See also the more recent Dante Alighieri, *Le ecloghe,* text, trans. with
comm. by Giorgio Brugnoli and Riccardo Scarcia (Milan: Ricciardi, 1980).
For the Latin pastorals of Petrarch's great contemporary, see *Buccolicum
carmen,* ed. Giorgio Bernardi Perini, in Giovanni Boccaccio, *Tutte le opere,* ed.
Vittore Branca, vol. 4 (Milan: Mondadori, 1994), 689–1085; and Giovanni
Boccaccio, *Eclogues,* trans. and comm. by Janet Smarr (New York: Garland,
1987), both with an excellent apparatus that probes the complex relationship
between the "bucolics" of Boccaccio and Petrarch. See, for example, Smarr,
introduction to Bocaccio, *Eclogues,* xli–l. For the history of the genre more
broadly, Enrico Carrara's classic study is still important, *La poesia pastorale*
(Milan: Vallardi, 1909).

2.   King Robert of Anjou ("Robert the Wise," 1278–1343), ruler of Naples and
a papal ally, possessed great literary culture and had examined Petrarch on
the occasion of his poetic coronation in 1341. Petrarch befriended the brothers Giovanni and Giacomo of the powerful Roman Colonna family by 1330
and entered the latter's service that year as a chaplain. He resigned the position in 1347, troubled by Giovanni's opposition to the republican reformer
Cola di Rienzo (1313–54). Appointed in 1344 by Pope Clement VI notary of
the Roman treasury, Cola organized a popular uprising against the nobles

that had gained momentum by 1347, but he was defeated by the Colonna and Orsini families and denounced by the papacy as a heretic (an allegation of which he was later absolved). Petrarch was enthusiastic about Cola's dream, never realized, of making Rome the seat of political and moral regeneration, thus uniting and bringing peace to Italy. See Mario Emilio Cosenza, *Francesco Petrarca and the Revolution of Cola di Rienzo* (Chicago: University of Chicago Press, 1913).

3. For keys to the allegories generally, the most useful sources are Avena, *Il Bucolicum carmen e i suoi commenti inediti*, which publishes such early commentators as Benvenuto da Imola and Francesco Piendibeni; and Bergin, *Petrarch's Bucolicum Carmen*.

4. In *Familiares* 10.4, written to his brother, Petrarch summarizes and explains the content of this eclogue. "Monicus" is the epithet of the Cyclops, meaning *monoculus* or "one-eyed." Of the two eyes that nature gives each person, one for seeing whatever is earthly and the other for things divine, Gherardo only keeps open the latter, hence he is one-eyed. The name "Silvius," from the Latin for "woodland," is appropriate to Petrarch because this eclogue was composed in the woods, for which he has always felt an affinity. *Parthenias*, as Petrarch explains in the same letter, is Virgil, a guiding model. In the preface to his commentary on Virgil, Servius wrote that the Mantuan poet was called Parthenias ("virginal") from his reputation for upright morals and chastity. Smarr, introduction, in Boccaccio, *Eclogues*, xxvii, observes the natural suitability of the pastoral genre, which is about shepherds and their flocks, to a discussion of Christian themes.

5. As Petrarch explains in a letter of January 18, 1347, to Barbato da Sulmona, "by the shepherd full of eyes [Argus] is meant our most watchful lord king, who had been the far-sighted shepherd of his people; by 'Idaeus' I mean our 'Pythias' (for Jove was brought up on Ida of Crete); by Jupiter I mean our faithful Barbato from his signal renown for friendship; and since I may not assume this for myself, I have chosen to be not Damon but Silvius—both from my ingrained love of the woods, and because this form of poetry occurred to me . . . in my woodland solitude." See Bergin, *Petrarch's Bucolicum Carmen*, 220, who cites from *Variae* 49 (*Disperse* 7) as Englished by Edward Henry Ralph Tatham, *Francesco Petrarca, the First Modern Man of Letters, His Life and Correspondence* (London: Sheldon Press, 1925–26), 2:394. Ovid tells the story of Argus, shepherd with one hundred eyes, set by Juno to guard the heifer Io from Jupiter's advances; Jupiter dispatched Mercury to lull Argus to sleep and kill him, after which Juno put his eyes on the tail feathers of her bird, the peacock (*Metamorphoses* 622–746).

6. "Obstupuisti, credo, perstrinxitque oculos fulgor insolitus. Dicunt enim

stuporem amoris esse principium," Petrarch *Secretum* 3.152. See Michele Feo, "Per l'esegesi della III egloga del Petrarca," *Italia medioevale e umanistica* 10 (1967): 385–401. Petrarch uses the form "Dane" for Daphne.

7. Petrarch here follows the model of Virgil's seventh eclogue, which, according to the late Latin commentator Servius, showed a contest between Virgil and an inferior rival poet (Boccaccio, *Buccolicum carmen* [trans. Smarr], xlv).

8. Petrarch explains the political allegory in a letter from Vaucluse of late summer 1347, to Cola di Rienzo (*Variae* 42, *Disperse* 11), cited by Bergin, *Petrarch's Bucolicum carmen*, 225–26, as translated by Tatham, *Francesco Petrarca*, 2:407–8: "The two shepherds are two sorts of citizens living in the same city but differing widely as to its interests. One is 'Martius,' which is to say 'warlike' and restless . . . yet dutiful and compassionate towards his mother, who is Rome. The other brother is 'Apicius' (whom we know as a master of the culinary art . . . by whom you are to understand those given over to pleasure and indolence." Festinus is "the swift one," in other words, Fame, who travels fast to bear her tidings.

9. Clement VI (c. 1291–1352), was pope from 1342 to 1352, when the papacy had its seat at Avignon. In Rome, Clement initially supported Cola di Rienzo's movement but later excommunicated him.

10. See Ernest Hatch Wilkins, "Petrarch's Seventh Eclogue," in *Studies in the Life and Works of Petrarch* (Cambridge: Harvard University Press, 1955), 48–62. Epy is explained by Benvenuto da Imola, whom Bergin, *Petrarch's Bucolicum carmen*, 229, cites from Avena, *Il Bucolicum carmen e i suoi commenti inediti*, 219: "Mea Epicurea, id est, Ecclesia: sic Epicurus qui posuit felicitatem in gaudendo" [my Epicurea, that is, the Church, even as Epicurus, who put his happiness in pleasure].

11. See Minna Skafte Jenson, "Petrarch's Farewell to Avignon: *Bucolicum Carmen* VIII," in *Avignon and Naples: Italy in France, France in Italy in the Fourteenth Century*, ed. Marianne Pade, Hannemarie Ragn Jensen, and Lene Waage Petersen (Rome: L'Erma di Bretschneider, 1997), 69–82. For the allusions in the names, see Bergin, *Petrarch's Bucolicum carmen*, 232: "Ganymede, the mortal carried off to Olympus to join the gods" is Colonna, "exalted to the pomp and luxury of the College of Cardinals." The poor fisherman Amyclas (Lucan *De bello civile* 5.515–31; Dante *Paradiso* 11.68) is Petrarch.

12. See Giovanni Gasparotto, "Il Petrarca conosceva direttamente Lucrezio: Le fonti dell'egloga IX, 'Querulus' del *Bucolicum carmen*," in *Atti e Memorie della R. Accademia di Scienze, Lettere, e Arti in Padova* 80 (1967–68): 309–55.

13. Bergin, *Petrarch's Bucolicum Carmen*, 235, sees Philogeus and Theophilus as "allegories of emotional attitudes . . . both characters speak for Petrarch."

Evidence suggests that the eclogue was written when the plague was well underway, but before the poet learned of Laura's death.

14. Ludwig van Kempen is the dedicatee of Petrarch's *Epistolae familiares*.

15. See Giovanni Ponte, "Problemi petrarcheschi: La decima egloga e la composizione dei Trionfi," in *Rassegna della letteratura italiana* 69, no. 7.5 (1965): 517–29. See also sonnet 318 of the *Canzoniere* ("Al cader d'una pianta che si svelse"), which likewise employs the metaphor of the laurel, uprooted but immortal (Bergin, *Petrarch's Bucolicum Carmen*, 236).

16. The nymphs express different aspects of the poet's response to Laura's death. See Fredrik Amadeus Wulff, *En svensk Petrarca-bok till jubelfästen* (Stockholm: P. A. Norstedt & Söner, 1905), 86, accepted by Bergin, *Petrarch's Bucolicum carmen*, 248, which cites Piendibeni from Avena, *Il Bucolicum carmen e i suoi commenti inediti*, 285, on "Galatea" as a *senhal* for Laura, signifying "White Goddess." Niobe recalls Ovid's sorrowing mother, punished for boasting about her children by Apollo and Daphne, who killed her seven sons and seven daughters (*Metamorphoses* 6.165–312); Fusca in Latin means "dark"; Fulgida is "bright, refulgent"). Needless to say, eclogues 3, 10, and 11 express in a bucolic key a motif pervasive in the *Canzoniere*, Petrarch's cult of Laura as the laurel, studied, for example, by Robert M. Durling, "Petrarch's 'Giovene Donna Sotto un Verde Lauro,'" *MLN* 86, no. 1 (Jan. 1971): 1–20; John Freccero, "The Fig Tree and the Laurel," *Diacritics* 5 (1975): 34–40; Ugo Dotti, "Petrarca: Il mito dafneo," *Convivium* 37 (1969): 9–23; and Durling in his introduction to *Petrarch's Lyric Poems* (Cambridge: Harvard University Press, 1976), esp. 26–29.

17. Early commentators, cited by Avena, *Il Bucolicum carmen e i suoi commenti inediti*, understand Multivolus to be the vulgar mob. Volucer, literally a "winged creature" or "bird," suggests news that quickly travels, hence Bergin's translation "Swiftfoot" (250).

18. See especially sonnets 114, 117, 137, and 138 of the *Canzoniere*, in which the poet vituperates the Avignon papacy and compares the city to Babylon. So, too, in Petrarch *Sine nomine* 18, for example, with a scathing attack on the Church and final novella savagely satirizing its representative, a grotesque and goatish old lecher. For more on this collection of letters, see the essay by Ronald Martinez in the present volume.

19. "Es meritus post vincla crucem, post verbera ferrum./Supplicium breve! Quin potius sine fine dolores/Carceris eterni, vel si quid tristius usquam est,/Serve infide, fugax, dominoque ingrate benigno."

20. "Immortale homini nichil est; moriemur et ipsi./Ludere consilium, nec euntis temporis horam/Perdere segnitie, curasque repellere inanes;/Ni forsan tibi nunc aliud, dilecta, videtur."

21. On Petrarch's relationship to Virgil's eclogues, see Magrith Berghoff-Bührer, *Das Bucolicum Carmen des Petrarca: Ein Beitrag zur Wirkungsgeschichte von Vergils Eclogen* (Bern: Peter Lang, 1991).

22. Virgil, *Eclogues,* in *Eclogues, Georgics, Aeneid,* trans. H. Rushton Fairclough, Loeb Classical Library (Cambridge: Harvard University Press, 1974): "Tityre, tu patulae recubans sub tegmine fagi/silvestrem tenui musam meditaris avena:/nos patriae finis et dulcia linquimus arva."

23. "Monice, tranquillo solus tibi conditus antro,/Et gregis et ruris potuisti spernere curas;/Ast ego dumosos colles silvasque pererro."

24. ". . . [t]um fusca nitentem/Obduxit Phebum nubes, precepsque repente/Ante expectatum nox affuit; horruit ether/Grandine terribili; certatim ventus et imber/Sevire et fractis descendere fulmina nimbis./Altior, ethereo penitus convulsa fragore,/Corruit et colles concussit et arva cupressus."

25. ". . . Daphnis pastoribus olim,/Et tibi nunc ingens merito cantabitur Argus."

26. On the myth of Polyphemus and Galatea and its development from Virgil to Ovid and subsequent use in the Italian Renaissance, see F. Battera, "Sulla pístola di Polifemo e Galatea: Primi appunti," *Compar(a)ison: An International Journal of Comparative Literature* 2 (1993): 35–64.

27. "Dulcior his silvis et gramine dulcior arvi,/Gratior his antris, et gratior amne sonoro,/Huc modo, dum sum solus, ades, mea nobilis Epy."

28. "Candidior folio nivei Galatea ligustri,/floridior pratis, longa procerior alno,/splendidior vitro, tenero lascivior haedo,/levior adsiduo detritis aequore conchis,/solibus hibernis, aestiva gratior umbra,/nobilior pomis, platano conspectior alta,/lucidior glacie, matura dulcior uva,/mollior et cygni plumis et lacta coacto,/et si non fugias, riguo formosior horto." The translation is Ovid, *Metamorphoses,* trans. Frank Justus Miller, Loeb Classical Library (Cambridge: Harvard University Press, 1968), 13:789–97.

29. Petrarch *Bucolicum carmen* (trans. Bergin, modified). On the use of elements of Terence's comedies in the Renaissance pastoral genre, particularly in England, see Clark L. Chalifour, "Sir Philip Sidney's Old Arcadia as Terentian Comedy," in *SEL: Studies in English Literature* 16, no. 1 (Winter 1976): 51–63.

30. See Guido Martellotti, *Dalla tenzone al carme bucolico: Giovanni Del Virgilio, Dante, Petrarca,* in Guido Martellotti, *Dante e Boccaccio e altri scrittori dall'Umanesimo al Romanticismo,* foreword by Umberto Bosco (Florence: Olschki, 1983), 71–89. For a panorama on the *tenso,* as this form of poetic debate was called in Provencal, see *Il genere "Tenzone" nelle letterature romanze delle Origini,* ed. Matteo Pedroni and Antonio Stäuble (Ravenna: Longo, 1997).

31. Petrarch *Familiares* 10.4: "est quod nisi ex ipso qui condidit auditum, intelligi non possit." For Benvenuto's view, see Fausto Ghisalberti, *Le chiose virgiliane di Benvenuto da Imola,* in *Studi virgiliani pubblicati in occasione delle celebrazioni*

bimillenarie della Reale Accademia Virgiliana (Mantua: Reale Accademia Virgiliana, 1930), 117, n. 1: "est impossibile quod aliquis intelligat bucolica nisi habeat aliquid ab illo qui composuit."

32. Petrarch *Bucolicum carmen* 12.160: "I nunc, in rebus spem certam pone secundis."

33. See Petrarch, *Laurea occidens. Bucolicum carmen X*, trans. and ed. Guido Martellotti (Rome: Edizioni di Storia e Letteratura, 1968). This eclogue constitutes, in Bergin's view, the "most 'mediaeval' of the series" due to its extraordinarily lengthy and pedantic cataloging of ancient poets. Here, more than in any other eclogue of the *Bucolicum*, "The Virgilian element is completely overshadowed" (237). Bergin, *Petrarch's Bucolicum carmen*, also points out that this section displays a direct blending, rare in Petrarch's opus, of the poet as ardent lover, on the one hand, and the pedantically meticulous philologist, on the other.

34. "Laurea culta michi, nec me situs asper et horrens / Arcuit incepto; propriis nec viribus ausus, / Externos volui consultor adire colonos. / Nec longe tenuere vie, nec tempus iniquum / Ac durum tardavit opus. . . ."

35. On the merging of Laura and the Laurel in Petrarch's poetics, see Paolo Cherchi, "Dispositio e significato del sonetto LXVII," in *The Flight of Ulysses: Studies in Memory of Emmanuel Hatzantonis*, ed. Augustus A. Mastri (Chapel Hill: Annali d'Italianistica, 1997), 82–96, esp. 86–89.

36. "Sed letum fortuna oculo suspexit iniquo: / Forte aberam, silvasque ieram spectare vetustas; / Pestifer hinc eurus, hinc humidus irruit auster; / Ac, stratis late arboribus, mea gaudia laurum / Extirpant franguntque truces, terreque cavernis / Brachia ramorum, frondesque tulere comantes." According to Bergin, *Petrarch's Bucolicum carmen*, 247, "These lines refer to the plague of 1348. Eurus, the southeast wind, and Auster, the south wind, are perhaps meant to indicate the direction from which the plague struck Provence."

37. ". . . laurum non eurus et auster, / Sed superi rapuere sacram, et felicibus arvis / Inseruere Dei; pars corticis illa caduci / Oppetiit, pars radices vivacior egit / Elisiosque novo fecundat germine campos."

38. "Heu nimis arcta domus, tanto domus atra decori! / Hec sedes Galathea tibi est? Quam fulgere cernens, / Sol stupuit, fassusque parem, fassusque subinde / Maiorem, attonitus serum se se abdidit undis."

39. "Hei michi! Quo nunc fessus eam? Quibus anxius umbris / recreer, aut ubi iam senior nova carmina cantem?"

40. ". . . Huc genitor profugus me ruris aviti / Finibus infantem rapuit, ripaque palustri / Exposuit miserum, atque abiit."

41. "Meminit haud ignobilis Italie civitas, Aretium, quo pulsus patria pater magna cum bonorum acie confugerat. Inde mense septimo sublatus sum

totaque Tuscia circumlatus prevalidi cuiusdam adolescentis dextera; qui—
quoniam iuvat laborum discriminumque meorum tecum primitias
recordari—linteo obvolutum, nec aliter quam Metabus Camilam, nodo de
stipite pendentem, ne contactu tenerum corpus offenderet, gestabat. Is, in
transitu Arni fluminis, lapsu equi effusus, dum honus sibi creditum servare
nititur, violento gurgite prope ipse periit." For Petrarch's comparison of himself to Ulysses and further discussion of this important letter, see the essay
in this volume by Giuseppe Mazzotta as well as S. Carrai, "Il mito di Ulisse
nelle 'Familiari,'" in *Motivi e forme delle Familiari di Francesco Petrarca*, ed. Claudia Berra (Milan: Cisalpino, 2003), 167–73.

42. "Theocritus syragusanus poeta, ut ab antiquis accepimus, primus fuit qui
greco carmine buccolicum excogitavit stilum, verum nil sensit preter quod
cortex ipse verborum demonstrat. Post hunc latine scripsit Virgilius, sed
sub cortice nonnullos abscondit sensus. . . . Post hunc autem scripserunt et
alii, sed ignobiles, de quibus nil curandum est, excepto inclito preceptore
meo Francisco Petrarca, qui stilum preter solitum paululum sublimavit et
secundum eglogarum suarum materias continue collocutorum nomina aliquid significantia posuit." Giovanni Boccaccio, *Epistole*, ed. and trans. Ginetta
Auzzas, in Giovanni Boccaccio, *Tutte le opere*, ed. Vittore Branca, vol. 5, pt. 1
(Milan: Mondadori, 1992), 493–856, quotation on 712.

43. "Quis insuper adeo insanus erit, ut putet preclarissimum virum atque chris-
tianissimum Franciscum Petrarcam, . . . expendisse tot vigilias, tot sacras
meditationes, tot horas, dies et annos, quot iure possimus existimare inpen-
sos, si *Buccolici* sui carminis gravitatem, si ornatum, si verborum exquisitum
decus pensemus, ut Gallum fingeret Tyrheno calamos exposcentem, aut
iurgantes invicem Panphylum et Mitionem et alios delirantes eque pastores?"
Giovanni Boccaccio, *Genealogie deorum gentilium*, ed. Vittorio Zaccaria, in
Giovanni Boccaccio, *Tutte le opere*, ed. Vittore Branca, vols. 7–8 (Milan:
Mondadori, 1998), 8:1420–23.

44. See Boccaccio, *Eclogues* (ed. Smarr), xxviii–xxxi; Carrara, *La poesia pastorale;*
and Nicholas Mann, "Il 'Bucolicum Carmen' e la sua eredità," *Quaderni Petrarcheschi* 9–10 (1992–93): 513–35. On the posterity of Petrarch's pastorals
more generally in Europe, see William J. Kennedy, "The Virgilian Legacies
of Petrarch's *Bucolicum carmen* and Spenser's 'Shepheardes Calendar,'" in
The Early Renaissance: Virgil and the Classical Tradition, ed. Anthony Pellegrini,
Center for Medieval and Renaissance Studies (Binghamton: State University of New York Press, 1985), 79–106; Richard Cody, *The Landscape of the
Mind* (Oxford: Clarendon Press, 1969); Louise George Clubb, *Italian Drama
in Shakespeare's Time* (New Haven: Yale University Press, 1989); and Andrew
Ettin, *Literature and the Pastoral* (New Haven: Yale University Press, 1984).

45. For the text, see Angelo Poliziano, *Silvae,* ed. Francesco Bausi (Florence: Olschki, 1996). Poliziano's chief model for the *Nutricia* was Petrarch's tenth eclogue, on which see Martellotti's discussion in his edition of Petrarch's *Laura occidens.*

Chapter Ten

1. Petrarch, *De vita solitaria,* in *Opere latine,* ed. Antonietta Bufano, 2 vols. (Turin: Unione Tipografico-Editrice Torinese, 1975), bk. 1, 1:374, translation, Petrarch, *The Life of Solitude by Francis Petrarch,* trans. Jacob Zeitlin (Urbana: University of Illinois Press, 1924), bk. 1, 180–81.

2. Petrarch, *Petrarch's Lyric Poems: The Rime sparse and Other Lyrics,* trans. Robert M. Durling (Cambridge: Harvard University Press, 1976); cf. Italian text in Petrarch, *Canzoniere,* ed. Marco Santagata (Milan: Mondadori, 2001). On Petrarch's ecstatic vision in the *Canzoniere,* see Marjorie O' Rourke Boyle, *Petrarch's Genius: Pentimento and Prophecy* (Berkeley: University of California Press, 1991), 65–68.

3. Vinicio Pacca, *Petrarca* (Bari: Laterza, 1998), 95–96. Cf. Nicholas Mann, *Petrarch* (New York: Oxford University Press, 1984), 42; Kenelm Foster, *Petrarch* (Edinburgh: Edinburgh University Press, 1984), 8; and Arnaud Tripet, *Pétrarque ou la connaissance de soi* (Geneva: Droz, 1967), 50–52. In *Prolegomeni al "De vita solitaria" di Petrarca* (Parma: Scuola Tip. Benedettina, 1967), Francesco Serpagli connects *De vita solitaria* to Augustine's *De moribus ecclesiae catholicae,* 55–62. Unless otherwise noted, all translations are mine.

4. Peter von Moos, "Les solitudes de Pétrarque. Liberté intellectuelle et activisme urbain dans la crise du XIVe siècle," in *Rassegna europea di letteratura italiana* 7 (1996): 23–58, esp. 25.

5. Von Moos, "Les solitudes de Pétrarque," 26; Michael Jasenas; *Petrarch in America* (Washington and New York: The Folger Shakespeare Library and The Morgan Library, 1974), 35.

6. Charles Edward Trinkaus, *In Our Image and Likeness: Humanity and Divinity in Italian Humanist Thought* [electronic resource] (Notre Dame: Notre Dame University Press, 1995), part 1.1, 4. Cf. Antonietta Bufano, "Introduzione," in Petrarch, *Opere latine,* 1:27; and Jacob Zeitlin, introduction to Petrarch, *De vita solitaria,* 55–67; on the ideal nature of the book, 56.

7. Etienne Gilson, "Sur deux texts de Pétrarque," in *Studi Petrarcheschi* 7 (1959): 35–50, esp. 36.

8. On the crucial importance of friendship for Petrarch, see Claude Lafleur, *Pétrarque et l'amitié* (Paris: Librairie Philosophique J. Vrin, 2001), 33–50; and Pietro Paolo Gerosa, *Umanesimo cristiano del Petrarca* (Turin: Bottega d'Erasmo, 1966), 99–104.

9. Giorgio Ficara, "Introduzione," in Petrarch, *De vita solitaria*, ed. Marco Noce (Milan: Mondadori, 1992), xxvi.

10. Guido Martellotti, "Introduzione alle prose," in *Scritti petrarcheschi*, ed. Michele Feo and Silvia Rizzo (Padua: Antenore, 1983), 220–39, esp. 228, Petrarch, *TC* 1.17, in *Trionfi*, ed. Vinicio Pacca and Laura Paolino (Milan: Mondadori, 2000), translation, *Triumphs of Petrarch*, trans. Ernest H. Wilkins (Chicago: Chicago: University of Chicago Press, 1962).

11. See Marco Ariani, "Petrarca," in *Storia della letteratura italiana*, ed. Enrico Malato (Rome: Salerno, 1995), 2:601–726, esp. 2:640–51. On the thorny issues of its composition, see B. L. Ullman, "The Composition of Petrarch's 'De vita solitaria' and the History of the Vatican Manuscript," in *Miscellanea Giovanni Mercati* (Vatican City: Biblioteca Apostolica Vaticana, 1946), 4:117–31.

12. Ernest Hatch Wilkins, *Life of Petrarch* (Chicago: University of Chicago Press, 1963), 17–18.

13. Wilkins, *Life of Petrarch*, 231–32.

14. Gerosa, *Umanesimo cristiano del Petrarca*, 339. On Petrarch's borrowings from the Bible and Augustine's *Confessions* with special emphasis on the *Canzoniere*, see Giovanni Pozzi, "Petrarca, i Padri e soprattutto la Bibbia," in *Alternatim* (Milan: Adelphi, 1996), 143–89.

15. Cf. Petrarch, *Invective contra medicum*, in *Opere latine*, ed. Antonietta Bufano (rept., 1987), 2: 920–22; and *De suis ipsius et multorum ignorantia*, in *Opere latine*, 2: 1118. As Petrarch's epistles are concerned, see *Familiares* 2.9, 16.4, 17.1. In *De otio religioso*, the first quotation from *De vera religione* is in its opening pages. Cf. Petrarch, *De otio religioso*, in *Opere latine*, 1:581.

16. Augustine, *De vera religione*, ed. William Green (Vienna: Hoelder-Pichler-Tempsky, 1961), chap. 3, section 3, 5.

17. Augustine, *De vera religione*, chap. 42, section 79, 58.

18. Augustine, *De vera religione*, chap. 4, section 6, 8–9.

19. Augustine, *De vera religione*, chap. 3, section 5, 7.

20. Augustine, *De vera religione*, chap. 26, section 48, 34.

21. Petrarch *Secretum* bk. 2, in *Opere latine*, 1:94.

22. Petrarch *Secretum* bk. 2, in *Opere latine*, 1:140. Cf. Trinkaus, *In Our Image and Likeness*, part 1.1, 3–50.

23. Petrarch *De vita solitaria* in *Opere latine*, bk. 1, 328. In his article on the codex 2201 of the Bibliothèque nationale in Paris that contains Augustine's *De vera religione* with Petrarch's summaries and glosses, Francisco Rico points out that Petrarch transcribed the above sentence from Cicero's *Tusculanae disputationes* on top of Augustine's text, as if to state that Augustine's treatise originates from Cicero's text. As Rico explains, Petrarch first read Augustine's brief treatise circa 1335 and continued to reflect on it for the rest of his

life. See Francisco Rico, "Petrarca y el '"De vera religione,'" in *Italia mediev-ale e umanistica* 17 (1974): 313–64, 327–28.

24. Cicero, *Tusculan Disputations*, trans. J. E. King, Loeb Classical Library (Cambridge: Harvard University Press, 2001), book 3.1.2, 227.

25. Cicero, *Tusculan Disputations* bk. 3.1.3, 226–27.

26. Cicero, *Tusculan Disputations* bk. 1.16.37–38, 45.

27. "veder mi parve un mondo/ novo, in etate immobile ed eterna,/ e'l sole e tutto 'l ciel disfar a tondo/ con le sue stelle, anchor la terra e'l mare,/ e rifarne un più bello e più giocondo."

28. For a complete list of biblical references, see Petrarch, *Trionfi* (ed. Pacca and Paolino), 514–15.

29. Petrarch *TE* 31–32 (trans. Wilkins, 108).

30. Petrarch *Familiares* 3.5, translation, *Rerum familiarum libri I–VIII*, trans. Aldo S. Bernardo (Albany: State University of New York Press, 1975) 126.

31. Petrarch, *De vita solitaria*, dedicatory epistle, 262.

32. *De vita solitaria* (trans. Zeitlin), 97. Pozzi speaks of Petrarch's "parodic" use of biblical passages. By "parody" Pozzi means that Petrarch slightly modifies a text in order to use it in a different context. See Pozzi, "Petrarca, i padri e soprattutto la bibbia," 154.

33. *De vita solitaria* (trans. Zeitlin), 100. Cf. Petrarch, *De vita solitaria*, 268.

34. *De vita solitaria* (trans. Zeitlin), 98; Petrarch, *De vita solitaria*, 264.

35. *De vita solitaria* (trans. Zeitlin), 105. I have modified Zeitlin's translation slightly to highlight the reference to the non-place of solitude, which disap-pears in his English version. Petrarch, *De vita solitaria*, bk. 1, 272.

36. *De vita solitaria* (trans. Zeitlin), 220; Petrarch, *De vita solitaria*, bk. 2, 430.

37. Petrarch, *De vita solitaria*, bk.1, 276 and 278. Cf. Petrarch *Seniles* 2.1. On the opposition between the two ideal men, see von Moos, "Les solitudes de Pé-trarque," 37–38; Ilaria Tufano, "La notte, la paura, il peccato: Il ritratto dell' 'occupatus' nel "De vita solitaria,'" in *Rassegna europea di letteratura italiana* 22 (2003): 37–52. The emphasis of this essay is on the connection between the "occupatus," the worldly man, and "Franciscus," the protagonist of the *Secre-tum*. On the concept of *phantasma* in its relation to *De vera religione*, see 46. See also Sandra Isetta, "Il linguaggio ascetico di Francesco Petrarca nel *De vita solitaria*," in *Studi umanistici piceni* 23 (2003): 75–94, on the two opposite men, 85.

38. Augustine, *De vera religione*, chap. 26, section 48, 34.

39. Augustine, *De vera religione*, chap. 26, section 49, 35.

40. Petrarch, *De vita solitaria*, bk. 1, 274.

41. For the echoes of Pseudo-Basilius in *De vita solitaria*, see Petrarch, *De vita solitaria. Buch I*, ed. K. A. E. Enenkel (Leiden: Brill, 1990), 172–74.

42. Peter Damian, *Opusculum undecimum,* in *PL* 145 (Paris: Thibaud, 1867), chap. 19, col. 246.

43. Palladius Helenopolitanus (368–431) is the author of the *Historia lausiaca.* He became a monk of the Mount of Olives at the age of twenty. His *Historica lausiaca* is a history of the monks of Egypt and Palestine in the form of anecdotes and short biographies. Its name comes from the dedication to Lausos, a chamberlain of Theodosius II (408–50 C.E.). For the English text, see Palladius, *Lausiac History,* trans. Robert Meyer (Westminster: Newman Press, 1965).

44. Peter Damian, *Opusculum undecimum,* chap. 19, col. 246.

45. Petrarch, *De vita solitaria,* bk. 1, 324.

46. *De vita solitaria,* bk. 1, 328 and 324–26. Cf. Seneca, *Ad Lucilium,* 25.5–6. On the centrality of Christ in Petrarch, cf. Trinkaus, *In Our Image and Likeness,* pt. 1.1, 37–40.

47. Augustine, *De vera religione,* chap. 2, section 2, 3.

48. Petrarch, *RVF* 251.7. See also the canzone 73.37. Gerosa, *Umanesimo cristiano del Petrarca,* 341.

49. Ernst Cassirer, *The Individual and the Cosmos in Renaissance Philosophy,* trans. Mario Domandi (Mineola: Dover Publications, 1963), 143. Cf. Paolo Cherchi, "La simpatia della natura nel *Canzoniere* di Petrarca," in *Cultura Neolatina* 63, nos. 1–2 (2003): 83–113, esp. 89–90. On the personified presence of "natura" in the Middle Ages, see Barbara Newman, *God and the Goddesses: Vision, Poetry, and Belief in the Middle Ages* (Philadelphia: University of Pennsylvania Press, 2003), 51–137.

50. Nicholas Mann, "Preface," in Petrarch, *De vita solitaria,* ed. Christophe Carraud (Grenoble: Millon, 1999), 18.

51. Palladius Helenopolitanus, *Historia lausiaca,* in *PL* 73 (Paris: Garnier, 1879), col. 1091.

52. Petrarch, *De vita solitaria,* bk. 2, 382. Palladius Helenopolitanus, *Historia lausiaca, PL* 73, col. 1093.

53. Palladius Helenopolitanus, *Historia lausiaca,* chap. 8, *PL* 73, col. 1099.

54. *Historia lausiaca,* chap. 8, 1100.

55. Petrarch, *De vita solitaria* bk. 2, 382–84; Palladius Helenopolitanus, *Historia lausiaca,* chap. 12, *PL* 73, cols. 1103–4.

56. Petrarch, *De vita solitaria,* bk. 2, 390; Palladius Helenopolitanus, *Historia lausiaca,* chap. 4, *PL* 73, cols. 1094–95.

57. Petrarch *De vita solitaria* bk. 2, 394.

58. *De vita solitaria,* bk. 2, 394 and 404. Cf. Jeremiah 8:23–9:1.

59. *De vita solitaria,* bk. 2, 428.

60. *De vita solitaria,* bk. 2, 406–8.

61. *De vita solitaria,* bk. 2, 408; Ambrose, "Epistola 49," in *PL* 16 (Paris: Garnier, 1880), col. 1203.

62. Ambrose, "Epistola 49," 1204.

63. Virgil, *Georgics,* trans. H. R. Fairclough (Cambridge: Harvard University Press, 2001), 3.215–16.

64. Cf. Ficara, "Introduzione," in Petrarch *De vita solitaria* (ed. Noce), xiii–xiv. Ficara stresses the abstract connotation of Petrarch's concept of solitude. Ficara holds that, for Petrarch, no place on earth can ever be perfect for the solitary man. Cf. Giorgio Ficara, *Solitudini* (Milan: Garzanti, 1993), 71–98.

65. Theodore J. Cachey Jr., introduction to *Petrarch's Guide to the Holy Land* (South Bend: University of Notre Dame Press, 2002), 19. Cf. chapter 14 in this volume.

66. Petrarch, *De vita solitaria,* bk. 2, 416.

67. *De vita solitaria,* bk. 2, 424.

68. *De vita solitaria,* bk. 2, 440.

69. Cf. Petrarch, *Against a Detractor of Italy,* in Petrarch, *Invectives* (trans. Marsh), 375 and 385.

70. Petrarch, *De vita solitaria,* bk. 2, 456.

71. *De vita solitaria,* bk. 2, 460. Similar invective appears in *TF* 2.139–44.

72. *De vita solitaria,* bk. 2, 478.

73. *De vita solitaria,* bk. 2, 466.

74. *De vita solitaria,* bk. 2, 486.

75. *De vita solitaria,* bk. 2, 526.

76. Ronald G. Witt, introduction in Petrarch, *On Religious Leisure,* ed. and trans. Susan S. Schearer (New York: Italica Press, 2002), xiv.

77. Petrarch, *De vita solitaria,* bk. 2, 528. Cf. Cicero, *Dei doveri,* ed. Dario Arfelli (Milan: Mondadori, 1994), bk. 3.1, 206.

78. Ambrose, *De officis ministrorum,* 3.1, *PL* 16, cols. 145–47.

79. 1 Kings 18:17.

80. Petrarch, *De vita solitaria,* bk.2, 530.

81. *De vita solitaria,* bk. 2, 532.

82. *De vita solitaria,* bk. 2, 534.

83. Tore Janson, *Latin Prose Prefaces* (Stockholm: Almqvist and Wiksell, 1964), chap. 1, 64. See also the "conclusion," 158–61. Cf. *De vita solitaria. Buch 1* (ed. Enenkel), 133–41.

84. Petrarch, *De vita solitaria,* 270.

85. *De vita solitaria,* bk. 2, 536.

86. *De vita solitaria,* bk. 2, 538.

87. *De vita solitaria,* bk. 2, 550; Petrarch, *De vita solitaria* (trans. Zeitlin), 307.

88. "O felice colui che trova il guado/ Di questo alpestro e rapido torrente/ Ch'a nome vita ed a molti è sì a grado."

89. Petrarch, *TE,* 49.

90. Petrarch, *De otio religioso,* in *Opere latine,* bk. 1, 1:570. On this treatise, see Jean-Luc Marion, "Préface," in Petrarch, *De otio religioso: Le repos religieux,* ed. Christophe Carraud (Grenoble: Millon, 2000), 5–10. See also Carraud's introduction to his edition, 11–26. Carraud highlights the connections among the *Secretum, De vita solitaria,* and *De otio religioso.*

91. Petrarch, *De otio religioso,* bk. 2, 808.

92. Petrarch, *De vita solitaria,* bk. 2, 562.

93. *De vita solitaria,* bk. 2, 564.

94. *De vita solitaria* (trans. Zeitlin), 316.

95. On the possible date of this poem, see Petrarch, *Canzoniere* (ed. Santagata), 686–87.

96. Petrarch, *RVF,* sestina 142, stanza 2, v. 8, 685.

97. "A la dolce ombra de le belle frondi/ corsi fuggendo un dispietato lume/ che'n fin qua giù m'ardea dal terzo cielo."

Chapter Eleven

1. Petrarch mentions the episode in *De otio religioso,* 1. On Montrieux and Gherardo, see Henry Cochin, *Le frère de Pétrarque et le livre "Du repos des religieux"* (Paris: Boullion, 1930); and Arnaldo Foresti, "Quando Gherardo si fece monaco," in *Aneddoti della vita di Francesco Petrarca,* Studi sul Petrarca, 1 (Padua: Antenore, 1977), 108–14.

2. There is no critical edition of *De otio religioso.* The best available edition of the Latin text is by Giovanni Rotondi and Guido Martellotti, *Il "De otio religioso" di Francesco Petrarca* (Vatican City: Biblioteca Apostolica Vaticana, 1958). Translations based on Rotondi and Martellotti's edition are *Opere latine di Francesco Petrarca,* vol. 1, ed. Antonietta Bufano, with B. Aracri and C. K. Regiani (Turin: Unione Tipografico-Editrice Torinese, 1974); *Le repos religieux,* ed. Christophe Carraud (Paris: Millon, 2000); *On Religious Leisure,* ed. and trans. by Susan S. Schearer with an introduction by Ronald Witt (New York: Italica Press, 2002). See also Giuseppe Rotondi, "Note al *De otio religioso,"* *Studi Petrarcheschi* 2 (1949): 153–66; and "Le due redazioni del *De otio religioso,"* *Aevum* 9 (1935): 22–77. Petrarch's works are cited with their original Latin title. Unless otherwise stated, English translations and page references are from the Schearer edition.

3. See Ugo Dotti, *Vita di Petrarca* (Rome and Bari: Laterza, 1992), 136–75. See also Enrico Fenzi, "Petrarca a Milano: Tempi e modi di una scelta meditata,"

in *Petrarca e la Lombardia: Atti del Convegno di Studi, Milano, 22–23 maggio 2003*, ed. Giuseppe Frasso, Giuseppe Velli, and Maurizio Vitale (Padua: Antenore, 2005), 221–63.

4. See Berthold L. Ullman "The Composition of Petrarch's *De vita solitaria* and the History of the Vatican Manuscript," in *Miscellanea Giovanni Mercati* (Vatican City: Biblioteca Apostolica Vaticana, 1946), 124–25. See also Dotti, *Vita di Petrarca*, 151–54.

5. Of the codices examined by Rotondi, three (the Marciano Lat. 476, the Vat. Pal. 1730, and the Vat. Barb. Lat. 2110) contain a shorter text than the others do. Six codices have a longer version (the Vaticano Urbinate Lat. 333; the Estense a. R. 6.7; the fragmented codex Brera AD, XIV, 27; the very short fragment of Laurenziano Santa Croce pl. XXVI, sin. N. 9, copied by Fra' Tedaldo della Casa; the Paris. Lat. 6502, and the London Harl. 6348). Rotondi almost completely collated the last two codices, and based his edition on Vat. Urb. Lat. 333. The printed editions (Venice 1501, 1503; Basilea 1554, 1581; Berne 1604) reproduce the short text, probably written in 1347. The other is probably from the first half of the 1350s. On the Wolfenbüttel codex, perhaps made for Tito Vespasiano Strozzi (fig. 5), see Agostino Sottili, *I. codici del Petrarca nella Germania occidentale* (Padua: Antenore, 1978), 2:639–40.

6. See Martellotti's introduction in *Il "De otio religioso" di Francesco Petrarca*, 8–12. Based on a new manuscript, the Chicago, Newberry Library, f. 95, and on an attentive reading of Harl. 6348, Giulio Goletti proposes two additions to the text, "Due integrazioni testuali al *De otio religioso*," in *Petrarca nel tempo: Tradizione lettori e immagini delle opere; Catalogo della mostra. Arezzo, Sottochiesa di San Francesco, 22 novembre 2003–27 gennaio 2004*, ed. Michele Feo (Pontedera: Bandecchi e Vivaldi, 2003), 418–22. See also Giulio Goletti, "Restauri al *De otio religioso* del Petrarca," in *Studi Medievali e Umanistici* (2004): 295–307; and his new edition, *De otio religioso* (Florence: Le Lettere, 2007).

7. Rotondi, notes on *De otio religioso*, 155–56.

8. Jean Mombaer (Mauburnus, 1460–1501), recommended Saint-Thierry's *Golden Letter* and Petrarch's *De otio religioso* in his *Rosetum exercitiorum spiritualium et sacrarum meditationum. In quo etiam habetur materia predicabilis per totum anni circulum* (1494). Jean Mombaer, from Brussels, was abbot of Livry and an important figure in the movement of *devotio moderna* that developed in Belgium. The *Rosetum* introduced a series of subjects and a method for individual meditation or mental prayer. Prior to the *Rosetum*, there were no texts on methodical meditation. Monastic orders such as that of the Carthusians prescribed special times for mental prayer but no regulation in terms of subjects and method existed. From this point of view, Petrarch's *De otio religioso* was a path-breaking work.

9. See Rotondi and Martellotti, *Il "De otio religioso" di Francesco Petrarca*, 1. 4, n. 3.

10. Petrarch did not directly challenge religious life: "he was contributing to an eventual challenge to the notion that the professional religious were inherently more meritorious or more pious than lay Christians." Charles Trinkaus, *In Our Image and Likeness* (London: Constable, 1970), 662.

11. "Ita vero moderabor stilum, ut quasi ad presentes sermo michi sit ad absentes epystola." Petrarch, *De otio religioso*, 5. According to Giuseppe Mazzotta, "Petrarch's soliloquies are radically dialogic . . . the recognition of contradictory voices lodged in the reflexive center of the self." Giuseppe Mazzotta, *The Worlds of Petrarch* (Durham: Duke University Press, 1993), 148. For the characteristics of humanist dialogue, see David Marsh, *The Quattrocento Dialogue: Classical Tradition and Humanist Innovation* (Harvard: Harvard University Press, 1980).

12. Guillaume de Saint-Thierry, *Lettre aux frères du Mont-Dieu* (Paris: Vrin, 1946).

13. "We know this certainly: that this Being is unutterable, incomprehensible, and inaccessible to our minds." Petrarch, *De otio religioso*, 58.

14. For Petrarch's "poetic theology," see Charles Trinkaus, *In Our Image and Likeness*, 689–97; and Charles Trinkaus, *The Poet as Philosopher: Petrarch and the Formation of Renaissance Consciousness* (New Haven: Yale University Press, 1979), 90–113.

15. See also Giovanni Boccaccio, *Genealogie deorum gentilium*, 15.8.2, ed. Vittorio Zaccaria, vols. 7–8, in Giovanni Boccaccio, *Tutte le opere*, ed. Vittore Branca (Milan: Mondadori, 1998), 8:1544–47. Petrarch *Familiares* 10.4.1, addressed to Gherardo, restates that theology was nothing but poetry on God.

16. Cf. Witt, introduction to *Petrarch on Religious Life*, 14.

17. "Etsi enim non sit in virtute finis noster, ubi eum philosophi posuere, est tamen per virtutes iter rectum eo ubi finis est noster; per virtutes, inquam, non tantum cognitas, sed dilectas. Hi sunt ergo veri philosophi morales et virtutum utiles magistri, quorum prima et ultima intentio est bonum facere auditorem ac lectorem, quique non solum docent quid est virtus aut vitium preclarumque illud hoc fuscum nomen auribus instrepunt, sed rei optime amorem studiumque pessimeque rei odium fugamque pectoribus inserunt." Petrarch, *De sui ipsius et multorum ignorantia*, ed. Enrico Fenzi (Milan: Mursia, 1999), 4, 148.

18. For the genres of medieval religious literature, see Jean Leclercq, *L'amour des Lettres et le désir de Dieu* (Paris: Cerf, 1990), 87–107, 145–78. For the importance of *De vera religione*, see Francisco Rico, "Petrarca y el *De vera religione*," *Italia Medioevale e umanistica* 17 (1974): 313–64.

19. On Petrarch's knowledge of classical and patristic texts, see Pierre de Nolhac, *Pétrarque et 'l'humanisme* (Paris: Honoré Champion, 1907); Giuseppe

Billanovich, *Petrarca letterato: Lo scrittoio del Petrarca* (Rome: Edizioni di Storia e letteratura, 1947); and *Petrarca e il primo umanesimo* (Padua: Antenore, 1996). See also Giuseppe Velli, *Petrarca e Boccaccio: Tradizione, memoria, scrittura* (Padua: Antenore, 1979). On the complexity of Petrarch's relation to classical thought, see Trinkaus, *Poet As Philosopher*, 1–51, now published in F. Edward Cranz, *Reorientations of Western Thought from Antiquity to the Renaissance*, ed. N. Streuver (Aldershot, Ashgate, 2006).

20. Petrarch further developed the anti-Scholasticism visible in the *De otio religioso* in works such as *Invective contra medicum* and *De sui ipsius et multorum ignorantia*. The English translations of these works are from Petrarch, *Invectives* ed. and trans. David Marsh (Cambridge: Harvard University Press, 2003).

21. Petrarch, *De sui ipsius et multorum ignorantia*, 149: "Itaque longe errant qui in cognoscenda virtute, non in adipiscenda, et multo maxime qui in cognoscendo, non amando Deus tempus ponunt. Nam et cognosci ad plenum Deus in hac vita nullo potest modo, amari autem potest pie atque ardenter."

22. Cranz illustrates Petrarch's paradoxical use of ancient sources on the themes of conversion: of "seeing with the mind"; of *aegritudo* (sadness); and finally the theme of "meditation upon death." Edward F. Cranz, "Some Petrarchan Paradoxes," speech delivered at the New England Renaissance Conference, Wheaton College, 1984.

23. "Vacatio" means freedom from ordinary occupations so as to be able to dedicate oneself to something more elevated. In the Bible the term is rare and usually negative, but it is frequent in patristic literature. *Otium*, and its Greek equivalent *scholé*, were well-established notions in classical literature. For the meaning of *quies, otium*, and *vacatio* in monastic literature, see Jean Leclercq, *Otia monastica: Études sur le vocabulaire de la contemplation au moyen âge*, Studia Anselmiana, 51 (Rome: Herder, 1963), 13–49.

24. Theologians such as Augustine, Jerome, Benedict, and Bernard, among others, used this verset to exhort to contemplation. Augustine followed the *Vetus Itala*, a Latin version of the Bible in use before the Vulgate, which translated from the Greek Septuagint: "Agite otium, et agnoscetis quia ego sum Dominus." "Agite otium" corresponds to "scholasate," reflecting the classical ideal of study and contemplation (*scholé*). By adopting Augustine's translation to comment on the "vacatio," Petrarch maintained this meaning. This version is found in the Italian edition of Augustine's treatise *De vera religione* 35 (Milan: Mursia, 1987), but it is absent in his *Enarrationes in Psalmos* (*Psalm* 45) (Nuova Biblioteca Agostiniana, http://www.sant-agostino.it/nba.htm), *Biblia Sacra Vulgatae Editionis*, Sixti V Pontificis Maximi iussu recognita et Clementis VIII auctoritate edita (Milan: San Paolo, 1995). The English translation is from the Douay version of the Latin Vulgate, available at http://www.drbo.org/lvb.

25. *De otio et solitudine* is the title of book 1 of Petrarch's *Rerum memorandarum libri*, which initially Petrarch wanted to entitle *Rerum humanarum*. Unike *De vita solitaria*, this book does not include religious examples. See Petrarch, *Rerum memorandarum libri*, ed. Giuseppe Billanovich, Edizione nazionale delle opere di Francesco Petrarca, 5 (Florence: Sansoni, 1945), 1. The *otium* is also the theme of *De vita solitaria*, book 4 of the *Invective contra medicum*, and many *Familiares* (e.g., 9, 4; 11, 15; 7, 5) and *Seniles* (e.g., 10, 1; 15, 3; 16, 3).

26. For a brief *excursus* on the meaning of *otium* from antiquity to the Middle Ages, see Ronald Witt, introduction to *Petrarch on Religious Life*, 12–14. See also Leclercq, *Otia monastica*.

27. "Otio etenim est opus non resoluto et inerti atque enervante animos, sed strenuo et, quod maxime vestrum est, religioso et pio . . . Ubi enim ieronimiana translatio habet: 'Vacate,' vetustior habebat: 'Otium agite.'" *De otio religioso*, 64–65. I have slightly changed the Schearer translation of "agite otium" to show the closeness of the *Vetus Itala* verset and Petrarch's idea of *otium*.

28. "Our Lord's bees" [dominice apes]. Petrarch, *De otio religioso*, 4.

29. Petrarch, *De otio religioso*, 65; Virgil *Georgics* 4.150–280. In Christian iconography, honey symbolized both Christ and the virginity of Mary. A sign of religious eloquence, this image was recurrent in the writings of Ambrose and Bernard of Clairvaux. Ambrose associated honey with the Holy Spirit and the beehive with the Church. In his view, the Christian was the hardworking bee, whose virtue adds "honey" to the community. In Petrarch it also symbolizes the work of the *literatus*.

30. "Come and behold ye the works of the Lord: what wonders he hath done upon earth, Making wars to cease even to the end of the earth. He shall destroy the bow, and break the weapons: and the shield he shall burn in the fire. *Be still and see that I am God;* I will be exalted among the nations, and I will be exalted in the earth. The Lord of armies is with us: the God of Jacob is our protector," emphasis added [Venite et videte opera Domini, / quae posuit prodigia super terram. / Auferet bella usque ad finem terrae, / arcum conteret et confringet arma / et scuta comburet igne. / Vacate et videte quoniam ego sum Deus: / exaltabor in gentibus et exaltabor in terra]. Psalm 45 (46):9–11.

31. "Quid est enim aliud 'Vacate et videte'? Vacate, quies presens; videte, requies eterna. Vacate in terra, in cielo videbitis, et in terra etiam quantum purus et detersus, sed adhuc carneus, videre oculus potest." *De otio religioso*, 7. I have slightly changed Schearer's English translation. The term "quiet" instead of "rest" seems closer to the technical spiritual meaning the word "quies" had in the religious literature. I also preferred to translate literally "videte" with "to see" as it stresses the meaning of knowledge as vision on which Psalm 45

insists. It also suggests the relevance of the material act of seeing for the achievement of a superior spiritual vision.

32. "Virtus semita, Deus finis videndus in Syon." *De otio religioso*, 130.

33. See the same idea in *Remedies for Fortune Fair and Foul*, ed. Conrad H. Rawski (Bloomington: Indiana University Press, 1991), preface, 8.

34. "Neque vero vos tutus arbitremini quia in castris Cristi agitis; quamvis enim sub optimo duce militetis et castra munitissima ac fortissima sint, nullus tamen locus ad plenum tutus extimandus est quem insomnes et feri hostes obsident atque circumsonant . . . " *De otio religioso*, 22–23.

35. "Suspecta securitas et que non spiritales tantum profectus impediat, sed etiam temporales." *De otio religioso*, 28.

36. "Omni custodia servate cor vestrum et cavete iugi studio que damnosa cognoscistis. Quod facile erit expertis in seculo quid insidiosum, quid violentum, quid precipue moribus vestris formidabile fuerit. Que nocentiora sensistis cautius declinate: hunc ira torquebat, hunc libido, hunc superbia extollebat, hunc deprimebat accidia, hunc avaritia et hunc gula, hunc tristis coquebat invidia: quisque familiarem suum hostem in prelio recognoscat et inde maxime caveat, unde sibi noceri amplius solitum recordatur." *De otio religioso*, 22.

37. See Hugh of Saint-Victor, *Didascalicon. De studio legendi* (New York: Columbia University Press, 1991); and Elspeth Whitney, *Paradise Restored: The Mechanical Arts from Antiquity through the Thirteenth Century*, Transactions of the American Philosophical Society (Philadelphia: American Philosophical Society, 1990).

38. Petrarch argued that this life "if properly governed, could be the most happy and gratifying of all things" [si rite ageretur, felicissima prorsus ac iocundissima rerum erat]. Petrarch *De remediis utriusque fortune* 1.10.

39. "It is not suitable to Him to hate anything he created" [Dignus nichil odisse omnium que fecit]. Petrarch, *De otio religioso*, 15.

40. "O inenarrabile sacramentum! Nam quo altius humanitas attolli poterat, quam ut homo ex anima rationali et humana carne subsistens, homo mortalis casibus, periculis, necessitatibus nostris obnoxious et, ut paucis absolvam, verus ac perfectus homo, et a Verbo filio Dei Patrique consubstantiali et coeterno in Deum atque in unitate persone ineffabiliter assumptus, duas in se naturas mira rerum prorsus imparium aggregatione coniungeret."

41. Petrarch's attitude toward the clergy indicates "that the privileged and special position of sanctity and merit granted to the religious in medieval Catholicism was being diluted and that the difference between layman and regular clergy was becoming one of degree, or lesser degree." Trinkaus, *In our Image and Likeness*, 662.

42. The comparison of the additions to *De vita solitaria* and *De otio religioso* reveals that Petrarch revised them in parallel. See Martellotti, *Introduzione al De otio*, 13. Cf. Ullman, "The Composition of Petrarch's *De vita solitaria* and the History of the Vatican Manuscript," 123–25; Rico, "Petrarca y el *De vera religione*," 355.

43. Petrarch, *Rerum senilium libri*, trans. by Aldo S. Bernardo, Saul Levin, and Reta A. Bernardo (Baltimore: Johns Hopkins University Press, 1992), idem, *Seniles* 6.5, to Philippe of Cabassoles. This letter accompanied in 1366 the completed version of the *De vita solitaria*.

44. Petrarch revised the *De vita solitaria* until 1370. For a commentary on the first book, see K. A. E. Enenkel, *De Vita Solitaria. Buch I. Kritische Textausgabe Und Ideengeschichtlicher Kommentar* (Leiden: Brill, 1990).

45. See Trinkaus, *In Our Image and Likeness*, 654–62; and Mazzotta, *Worlds of Petrarch*, 147–66.

46. See Ugo Dotti, *Petrarca civile: Alle origini dell'intellettuale moderno* (Rome: Donzelli, 2001), 73–91; Enrico Fenzi, "Preveggenze umanistiche di Petrarca," *Saggi petrarcheschi* (Florence: Cadmo, 2003), 633–53; and, on Petrarch's poetic "profession," consult Douglas Biow, *Doctors, Ambassadors, Secretaries: Humanism and Professions in Renaissance Italy* (Chicago: University of Chicago Press, 2002), 27–44.

47. According to Jean-Luc Marion, *Familiares* 4.1 and the two treatises on solitude constitute a triptych. See his introduction to the French edition of *De otio religioso*.

48. Petrarch *Invective* bk. 4.170 (trans. Marsh, 145): "And you should see that solitude is not the enemy of the polity."

49. According to Billanovich, the letter was written in 1353, even if Petrarch sets the narration in 1336, presumably the date of the ascent. Giuseppe Billanovich, "Petrarca e il Ventoso," *Italia medioevale e Umanistica* 9 (1966): 389–401; and Bortolo Martinelli, *Petrarca e il Ventoso* (Milan: Minerva Italica, 1977), 147–215. See also Robert M. Durling, "Il Petrarca, Il Ventoso e la possibilità dell'allegoria," *Revue des Études Augustiniennes* 23, nos. 3–4 (1977): 304–23.

50. Petrarch sent the book and the letter in 1348–49. Monicus was a Cyclops whose name meant "one eye" or "monocular." It alluded to Gherardo's condition as a monk, having only one eye to look at the heaven. The name Silvius alludes to Petrarch's love for the woods and symbolizes his choice of "humanistic" solitude.

51. Monicus and Silvius correspond to Davidic poetry (a genre Petrarch explored in his *Penitential Psalms*) and to morally engaged secular poetry (epics inspiring virtue through exemplary figures), respectively.

52. Saint Basil the Great was the author of a famous letter to young people
in which he exhorted them to study the ancient poets because in teaching
virtue, these authors would prepare their souls to receive Christ's evangelical
message. The letter, translated in 1400 by Leonardo Bruni, had a wide circulation and became a milestone in the debate on the reform of the curriculum
of study.

Chapter Twelve

1. The standard edition is in Petrarch, *Prose,* ed. Guido Martellotti, Pier Gior-
gio Ricci, Enrico Carrara, Enrico Bianchi (Milan and Naples: Riccardo
Ricciardi Editore, 1955). Among the most important studies of the work are
Francisco Rico, *Vida u obra del Petrarca. I. Lectura del Secretum* (Padua: Anten-
ore, 1974); Hans Baron, *Petrarch's Secretum: Its Making and Its Meaning* (Cam-
bridge: Medieval Academy of America, 1985); and Carol Everhart Quillen,
Rereading the Renaissance: Petrarch, Augustine, and the Language of Humanism
(Ann Arbor: University of Michigan Press, 1998). Petrarch, *Secretum,* ed.
Enrico Fenzi (Milan: Mursia, 1992), offers an Italian translation and valu-
able notes.

2. Cf. the allegorical introduction of book 2 of Petrarch, *Rerum memorandarum
libri,* ed. Giuseppe Billanovich, Edizione nazionale delle opere di Francesco
Petrarca, 5 (Florence: Sansoni Editore, 1943), 43: "Ingredienti michi quidem
reverenter velut religiosssimi cuiuspiam templi fores primogenita sororum
occurrit in limine. Ea est Prudentia" [As I entered the portals of a sort of
most holy temple, the first-born of the sisters meets me at the threshold. She
is Prudence]. On book 1 of the work as a sort of "vestibule" to the following
books, cxxiv–cxxv.

3. See the manuscript illumination *Truth, Petrarch, and St. Augustine,* Bruges,
Grootseminarie, MS 113/78, fol. 1r (fig. 6, p. 210). On the opening scene, see
Marco Ariani, *Petrarca* (Rome: Salerno Editrice, 1999), 116: "The opening
bears some affinity to the introductory cantos of the *Comedy:* Virgil, sent by
three ladies, appears to Dante, who is lost in the forest of sin."

4. Petrarch, *Prose,* 28: "A. Quid agis, homuncio? . . . An non te mortalem esse
meministi?" [What are you doing, little man? . . . Don't you remember that
you are mortal?] The emphasis on memory and writing evokes Augustine's
Soliloquia. See Francesco Tateo, *Dialogo interiore e polemica ideologica nel "Secretum" del Petrarca* (Florence: Casa Editrice Le Monnier, 1965), 18–19. Petrarch
also calls himself *homuncio* in his *Posteritati:* see *Prose,* 2: "Vestro de grege
unus fui autem, mortalis homuncio" [I was one of your herd, a mortal little
man]. Augustinus's reproach seems to echo the opening of Anselm's *Proslo-
gion:* "Eia nunc, homuncio, fuge paululum occupationes [Come now, little

man, briefly leave your worries]: see Bortolo Martinelli, "'Abice ingentes historiarum sarcinas . . . dimitte Africam': Il finale del 'Secretum,'" *Revue des études italiennes* 29 (1983): 58–73, at 66.

5.   Cf. Petrarch *Seniles* 14.1 (later printed as *De republica optime administranda*), an epistle written in 1373 to Francesco da Carrara, in which Petrarch refers to the *Somnium Scipionis* as "fictum illud in celi arce colloquium" [that conversation imagined in the citadel of heaven]: see Petrarch, *Opera* (Basileae: Henrichus Petri, 1554; Ridgewood, N.J.: Gregg Press, 1965), 1:421. Petrarch also calls his tract *De sui ipsius et multorum ignorantia* a "conversation": Petrarch, *Invectives*, ed. and trans. David Marsh (Cambridge: Harvard University Press, 2003), 222–23: "Liber quidem dicitur, colloquium est" [I have called this work a book, but it is really a conversation]. In *Familiares* 4.3.7 (to Robert of Naples, 26 December 1338), Petrarch refers to Cicero's *De amicitia* as "in dyalogo Lelii, qui de vera amicitia est" [in the dialogue *Laelius*, which is about friendship].

6.   See Petrarch *Familiares* 24.5.2 (to Seneca, August 1, 1348 or 1350): "Iuvat vobiscum *colloqui*, viri illustres, qualium omnis etas penuriam passa est, nostra vero ignorantiam et extremum patitur defectum" [I like to converse with you, illustrious men, who are rare in every age, but unknown and utterly lacking in ours]. Cf. *Familiares* 4.12 (to Cardinal Giovanni Colonna, January 5, 1342), Petrarch writes "Recognosce mecum singula, pater optime, nec de germano *colloqui* pigeat cum illo qui in fratre tuo decus suum sibi prereptum luget . . . " [Recall each thing with me, holy father, and do not hesitate to converse with someone who mourns the loss of his glory in your brother]. Cf. *De vita solitaria* 1.6, in *Prose* (ed. Martellotti et al.), 356: "versari passim et colloqui cum omnibus, qui fuerunt gloriosi viri" [(We must) everywhere dwell and converse with all the glorious men of the past].

       Petrarch also uses the verb *alloquor:* see *Familiares* 10.3.3 (to his brother Gherardo, September 25, 1348): "Dum ergo te *alloquor*, ipse res meas ago . . ." [While I speak to you, I deal with my own affairs]; and *Familiares* 24.12.1 (to Homer, October 9, 1360): "Dudum te scripto *alloqui* mens fuerat" [Some time ago I resolved to speak to you in writing].

7.   The heading "dyalogus" was introduced in the Basel 1554 edition: see Petrarch, *Les remèdes aux deux fortunes, 1354–1366*, ed. and trans. Christophe Carraud (Grenoble: Éditions Jérôme Millon, 2002), 1:22, n. 1. Ariani, *Petrarch*, 357, refers to the humanist's "model of the man of letters who dialogues with the world solely by virtue of his culture."

8.   Petrarch *Familiares* 10.3.56: "Lege Gregorii dyalogum."

9.   Gregory, *Dialogi*, ed. Umberto Moricca (Rome: Tipografia del Senato, 1924), 13–16: "Quadam die, nimiis quorundam saecularium tumultibus depraessus,

quibus in suis negotiis plerumque cogimur solvere etiam quod nos certum est non debere, secretum locum petii amico merori, ubi omne quod de mea mihi occupatione displicebat se patenter ostenderit, et cuncta quae infligere dolore consueverant congesta ante oculos licenter venirent. Ibi itaque cum adflictus valde et diu tacitus sederem, dilectissimus filius meus Petrus diaconus adfuit, mihi . . . qui gravi excoqui cordis languore me intuens ait: numquidnam novi aliquid accedit quod plus te solito moeror tenet? . . . Si sola, Petre, referam quae de perfectis probatisque viris unus ego homuncio vel bonis ac fidelibus viris attestantibus agnovi, vel per memetipsum dedici, dies, ut opinor, antequam sermo cessabit."

10. See Petrarch, *De vita solitaria* 2.1–8 in *Prose*, 406–80, idem, *De vita solitaria*, ed. Marco Noce (Milan: Arnoldo Mondadori Editore, 1992), 142–226, and idem, *De vita solitaria: La vie solitaire, 1346–1366*, ed. and trans. Christophe Carraud (Grenoble: Éditions Jérôme Millon, 1999), 176–265. For *Invective contra medicum*, see Petrarch, *Invectives*, 110–11.

11. For some Petrarchan themes in Alberti, see David Marsh, "Petrarch and Alberti," in *Renaissance Essays in Honor of Craig Hugh Smyth*, ed. Sergio Bertelli and Gloria Ramakus (Florence: Giunti-Barbera, 1985), 1:363–75.

12. See *Familiares* 10.3–5, 16.2, and 17.1. *Familiares* 10.4 in fact explicates the allegory of this eclogue. On the affinities of *Parthenias* and the *Secretum*, see Martinelli, "Il finale del 'Secretum,'" 70–71.

13. See the recent edition with French translation: Petrarch, *L'Afrique, 1338–1374*, preface by Henri Lamarque, intro., trans., and notes by Rebecca Lenoir (Grenoble: Éditions Jérôme Millon, 2002), and esp. 27–28 of the introduction, on the poem as "counterpoint" to the *Secretum*.

14. Ovid *Remedia amoris* 581–87: "non tibi secretis (augent secreta furores) / est opus; auxilio turba futura tibi est . . . / nec fuge colloquium nec sit tibi ianua clausa . . ."

15. Petrarch, *Prose* (ed. Martellotti et al.), 336, citing Quintilian 10.3.27–30: "Est lucubratio, quotiens ad eam integri ac refecti venimus, optimum secreti genus. Sed silentium et secessus et undique liber animus, ut sunt maxime optanda, ita non semper possunt contingere . . . quare in turba, itinere, conviviis etiam cogitatio ipsa faciat sibi secretum." This passage may have influenced Lorenzo Valla's dialogue *De voluptate* (1431), in which Leonardo Bruni observes that seclusion and silence promote discussion: see Lorenzo Valla, *De vero falsoque bono*, ed. Maristella De Panizza Lorch (Bari: Adriatica Editrice, 1971), 143–44: "Secretum et silentium magis disputationibus convenit."

16. Petrarch, *Prose* (ed. Martellotti et al.), 32: "unum illud indignor, quod quenquam vel esse miserum suspicaris invitum." On this passage, see Rico, *Lectura*, 44–71.

17. On the voluntaristic thesis of book 1, see Petrarch, *Secretum* (ed. Fenzi), 293–95, nn. 9–18.

18. Petrarch, *Prose* (ed. Martellotti et al.), 130–32: "A. Duabus adhuc adamantinis dextra levaque premeris cathenis . ꞅ . / F. Quenam sunt quas memoras cathene? / A. Amor et gloria."

19. Augustine *Confessions* 8.5.10: "velle meum tenebat inimicus, et inde mihi catenam fecerat, et constrinxerat me. quippe ex voluntate perversa facta est libido, et dum servitur libidini, facta est consuetudo, et dum consuetudini non resistitur, facta est necessitas. quibus quasi ansulis sibimet innexis— unde catenam appellavi—tenebat obstrictum dura servitus. voluntas autem nova, quae mihi coeperat, ut te gratis colerem, fruique te vellem, deus, sola certa iucunditas, nondum erat idonea ad superandum priorem vetustate roboratam. ita duae voluntates meas, una vetus, alia nova, illa carnalis, illa spiritualis, confligebant inter se, atque discordando dissipabant animam meam " Cf. also *Confessions* 6.12. 21: "trahebam catenam meam solvi timens" [I dragged my chain, fearing to be released].

20. Rico, *Lectura*, 259: "el protagonista es ahora fundamentalmente el Francesco escritor" [the protagonist is now essentially Franciscus as writer].

21. For the text of Petrarch's coronation speech, see Carlo Godi, "La 'Collatio Laureationis' del Petrarca," *Italia medioevale e umanistica* 13 (1970): 1–27; for its ambitious program, see Stefano Gensini, "'Poeta et historicus': L'episodio della laurea nella carriera e nella prospettiva culturale di Francesco Petrarca," *La Cultura* 18 (1980): 166–94.

22. By the same token, in book 9 of the *Africa* Ennius is crowned with laurel, even though he has not yet written his epic of Roman history. Cf. Aldo S. Bernardo, *Petrarch, Scipio, and the "Africa": The Birth of Humanism's Dream* (Baltimore: Johns Hopkins University Press, 1962), 48: "the crowning of Ennius appears strange. He seems, indeed, to be rewarded from something he is yet to do, namely, a poem honoring Scipio." In *Bucolicum carmen* 3, the shepherd Stupeus (Petrarch) is likewise awarded a laurel wreath.

23. Cf. the observation of Augustinus in *Prose* 210: "Tu quoque nunc etate florida superbus alios calcas, mox ipse calcaberis" [Now in the prime of life, you haughtily tread on others, but soon you yourself will be trodden underfoot]; and the opening dialogue of *De remediis utriusque fortune* 1.1, "De etate florida et spe vite longioris" [On the prime of life and hope for long life], in Petrarch, *Prose* (ed. Martellotti et al.), 606–13, and in Petrarch, *De remediis utriusque fortune* (ed. Carraud), 1:22–27.

24. Petrarch's expressions "solis ardores" and "solis ardoribus" (*Prose*, 194, 200) recall a Sallustian phrase describing Africa—"loca exusta solis ardoribus"

[regions burned by the sun's hot rays], *Bellum Iurgurthinum* 19.6—which Jerome had echoed in his *Epistle* 22.7 (to Eustochium, on virginity) and which Petrarch cites in book 2 of his *De vita solitaria* (ed. Noce), 180, 375, n. 3; and Petrarch, *De vita solitaria* (ed. Carraud), 218, and 418, n. 486.

25. Petrarch, *Prose* (ed. Martellotti et al.), 194: "A. Quid tamen tam grande facturum esse te iudicas?/F. Preclarum nempe rarumque opus et egregium./A. . . . hoc ipsum preclarum neque late patet, neque in longum porrigitur, locorumque ac temporum angustiis coartatur." Petrarch also refers to space and time in his letter "To Posterity" (2): "dubium sit an exiguum et obscurum longe nomen seu locorum seu temporum perventurum sit" [it is doubtful whether my paltry and obscure name can travel far in space or time].

26. Ibid.: "Intelligo istam veterem et tritam iam inter philosophos fabellam: terram omnem puncti unius exigui instar esse, annum unum infinitis annorum milibus constare; famam vero hominum nec punctum implere nec annum. . . . Hec enim relatu magis speciosa quam efficacia sum expertus." All the same, Petrarch was not averse to using geographical descriptions in his Latin poetry: cf. *Africa* 6.839–84 (the Tuscan coast), and *Africa* 9.189–99 (Homer's vivid description of Greece).

27. For a detailed description of Petrarch's sources, see Rico, *Lectura*, 391 n. 486.

28. On Macrobius and Petrarch's *Africa*, see Simone Marchesi, "The *Africa*: Petrarch's Philological Epic," in this volume, esp. n. 24.

29. See Petrarch, *De remediis utriusque fortune*, 1:92, 1:96, and 2:68; Latin text with French translation in Petrarch, *De remediis utriusque fortune* (ed. Carraud), 396, 428, and 834; English translation in *Petrarch's Remedies for Fortune Fair and Foul*, trans. Conrad H. Rawski (Bloomington: University of Indiana Press, 1991), 1:245, 1: 264, and 3:157.

30. Augustine *City of God* 16.9 on the existence of the antipodes. On this passage, see Rico, *Lectura*, 401–3; and Petrarch, *Secretum* (ed. Fenzi), 404–6, n. 371.

31. Petrarch, *Prose* (ed. Martellotti et al.), 200: "Ea ne est fabula, queso, que geometricis demonstrationibus terre totius designat angustias?"

32. Cicero *De natura deorum* 2.204–14.

33. Petrarch *Africa* 2.361–63: "angustis arctatus finibus orbis / insula parva situ est, curvis quam flexibus ambit/Occeanus." Cf. also *Africa* 2.470–71: "annorum, nate, locorumque / estis in angusto positi." Both passages are quoted in Rico, *Lectura*, 392 n. 486.

34. Petrarch, *Prose* (ed. Martellotti et al.), 204: "A. Habes de gloria iudicium meum . . . nisi forte nunc etiam fabulosa tibi hec omnia videntur./F. Minime quidem, neque michi more fabularum affecerunt animum, quin imo veteris abiciendi novum desiderium iniecerunt."

35. See J. B. Harley and David Woodward, *Cartography in Prehistoric, Ancient, and Medieval Europe and the Mediterranean* (Chicago: University of Chicago Press, 1987), 144–46.

36. Cf. Petrarch, *Secretum* (ed. Fenzi), 289–90, nn. 17, 21.

37. Dante, *Paradiso* 22.133–35: "Col viso ritornai per tutte quante / le sette spere, e vidi questo globo/tal, ch'io sorrisi del suo vil sembiante." Cf. Chaucer *Troilus and Criseyde* 5.1814–22, in *The Works of Geoffrey Chaucer*, ed. F. N. Robinson, 2nd ed. (Boston: Houghton Mifflin, 1961), 479: "And down from thennes faste he gan avyse/This litel spot of erthe, that with the se/ Embraced is, and fully gan despise/This wrecched world and held al vanite/To respect of the pleyn felicite/That is in hevene above; and at the laste,/Ther he was slayn, his lokyng down he caste,/And in himself he lough right at the wo/Of them that wepten for his deth so faste."

38. See Dante *Convivio* 3.5 in *Le opere di Dante*, Testo critico della Società Dantesca Italiana, ed. M. Barbi et al., 2nd ed. (Florence: Nella Sede della Società, 1960), 203–6.

39. Dante, *Questio de aqua et terra*, 52–54 in *Le opere di Dante*, 438: "Nam, ut demonstratum est in theorematibus mathematicis, necesse est circumferentiam regularem spere a superficie plana sive sperica, qualem oportet esse superficiem aque, emergere semper cum orizonte circulari. Et quod terra emergens habeat figuram qualis est semilunii, patet et per naturales de ipsa tractantes, et per astrologos climata describentes, et per cosmographos regiones terre per omnes plagas ponentes. Nam, ut comuniter ab omnibus habetur, hec habitabilis extenditur per lineam longitudinis a Gadibus, que supra terminos ab Hercule positos ponitur, usque ad hostia fluminis Ganges, ut scribit Orosius."

40. Cf. *Collatio* 2.47–49, in Carlo Godi, La "Collatio Laureationis" del Petrarca," *Italia medioevale e umanistica* 13 (1970): 15: "Et ex hoc nimirum fonte procedunt illa ludibria usque ad extremum vite tempus inutiliter et inefficaciter in hac facultate laborantium, qualia non nulla legimus in libris de scolastica disciplina" [And indeed this is the source of those ludicrous trifles, written by men who toil vainly and ineffectually all their lives in such fields, that we sometimes find in reading books of Scholastic teaching].

41. Petrarch, *Prose* (ed. Martellotti et al.), 206: "F. Labores ne meos interruptos deseram?/A. Abice ingentes historiarum sarcinas . . . Dimitte Africam."

Chapter Thirteen

1. There were actually three versions of the Psalter translated, or at least adapted, by Jerome. The one used in the liturgy, called the Roman Psalter, was, like most biblical texts in medieval liturgies, an ancient translation from

the Septuagint (Greek Jewish) Bible, the Gallican Psalter was a slightly more elaborated translation of the Greek text, and the later Hebrew Psalter was a close translation of the Hebrew. Even though the Old Roman text was used liturgically, the Gallican was the preferred Psalter for study in most of Europe. Deluxe editions of the Psalms showed all three versions. All first references to the Psalms in this article will be according to the Septuagint-Vulgate numbers, with the Hebrew numbering found in most English translations given in parentheses where appropriate. The major shifts of numbering occurred in two places: Hebrew Psalms 9 and 10 are combined as Vulgate Psalm 9; and Vulgate Psalms 146 and 147 are combined as Psalm 147 in the Hebrew. This means that between Psalm 10 and 146 of the Hebrew numbering, the Vulgate psalm numbers are one less, but that all Latin versions and the Hebrew Psalter count 150 psalms.

2. Walter Drum, *The Catholic Encyclopedia*, vol. 12 (New York: Robert Appleton, 1911), s.v. "The Psalms." For general information on the Psalms in medieval Christianity, see *The Place of the Psalms in the Intellectual Culture in the Middle Ages*, ed. Nancy van Deusen (Albany: State University of New York, 1999).

3. Alcuin of York, *Enchiridion seu expositio pia ac brevis in Psalmos Poenitentiales, in Psalmum CXVIII et Graduales*, in *PL* 100:569–640 (570–84 for the Penitential Psalms).

4. The text is published as Gregory the Great, *In septem Psalmos Poenitentiales, Expositio* in *PL* 79:549–660, with a reference to it as "Auctor Incertus" (Gregory VII?), *Commentarius in VII Psalmos Poenitentiales* in *PL* 148. A. Mercati, working from a history of the manuscripts and printed editions, thought the text was written by Heribert, twelfth-century bishop of Reggio Emilia, "L'autore della *Expositio in Septem Psalmos poenitentiales* fra le opere di S. Gregorio Magno," *Revue Bénédictine* 31 (1914–19): 250–57. The text is no. 2649 in F. Stegmüller, *Repertorium Biblicum Medii Aevi* (Madrid, 1950).

5. Auctor incertus (Innocent III?), *Commentarium in Septem Psalmos Poenitentiales, PL* 217:967–1130 (from the Cologne edition of 1575); no. 4005 in Stegmüller, *Repertorium Biblicum Medii Aevi*.

6. Martin Luther, "The Seven Penitential Psalms," trans. by Arnold Guebert, *Luther's Works*, vol. 14 (Saint Louis: Concordia Publishing House, 1958), 137–205. For a general study of Luther on the Psalms, see Scott H. Hendrix, *Ecclesia in via: Ecclesiological Developments in the Medieval Psalms Exegesis and the Dictata Super Psalterium (1513–1515) of Martin Luther* (Leiden: Brill, 1974).

7. The *Sette salmi penitenziali* attributed to Dante were first published in Venice "Nel Beretin Convento della Ca' Grande," about 1475; the better-attested edition is Dante Alighieri, *I sette salmi penitenziali ed il Credo, trasportati alla volgar poesia, illustrate con annotazioni dall'abate Francesco Saverio Quadrio* (Bolo-

gna: Giovani Gottardi, 1753), reprinted in Milan by G. Silvestri in 1851, and published in the *Biblioteca scelta di opere italiane antiche e moderne*, vol. 562. For another edition, with the Latin Psalm texts on facing pages, cf. *I sette salmi penitenziali di Dante Alighieri e di Francesco Petrarca* (1821; Florence: Dalla Società Tipografica, 1827). These poems in terza rima may have been the first Italian versions of the Penitential Psalms; see Maria Palermo Concolato, "Il Viaggio del testo: *I Salmi penitenziali* dall'Aretino al Wyatt," in *Per una topografia dell'Altrove. Spazi altri nell'immaginario letterario e culturale di lingua inglese*, ed. Maria Teresa Chialant and Eleonora Rao (Naples: Liguori Editore, 1995), 399–412, reference to Dante on 401; and Salvatore Floro di Zenzo, *Studio critico sull'attribuzione a Dante Alighieri di un antico volgarizzamento dei Setti salmi penitenziali* (Naples: Laurenziana, 1984).

8. Laura Battiferra degli Ammannati, *I sette salmi penitenziali di David con alcuni sonetti spirituali*, ed. Enrico Maria Guidi (Urbino: Accademia Raffaello, 2005). For the most recent study of Aretino, Battiferra, and other versions and their influence on English poetic translations, see Hannibal Hamlin, *Psalm Culture and Early Modern English Literature* (Cambridge: Cambridge University Press, 2004), 111–44.

9. See Hamlin, *Psalm Culture*, 173, for the reference to George Chapman. Other studies include T. M. C. Lawler, "Some Parallels between Walter Hilton's *Scale of Perfection* and St. John Fisher's *Penitential Psalms*," *Moreana: Bulletin Thomas More* 9 (1966): 13–27; Kenneth Muir, "The Texts of Wyatt's *Penitential Psalms*," *Notes and Queries* 14 (1967): 442–44; Robert G. Twombly, "Thomas Wyatt's Paraphrase of the Penitential Psalms of David," *Texas Studies in Literature and Language: A Journal of the Humanities* 12 (1970): 345–80; and Danielle Clarke, " 'Lover's Songs Shall Turne to Holy Psalmes,' Mary Sidney and the Transformation of Petrarch," *Modern Language Review* 92 (1997): 282–84. In my study of the Penitential Psalms in English I have been helped by Clare Costley King'oo, "David's 'Fruytfull Saynges': The Penitential Psalms in Late-Medieval and Early-Modern England" (Ph.D. diss., University of Pennsylvania, 2005).

10. Donatella Coppini, "Don Giuseppe de Luca e l'incompiuta edizione dei *Salmi penitenziali* del Petrarca," *Quaderni Petrarcheschi* (1993): 413–35. I am grateful to Stefano Cracolici and Francesco Caruso for help with the elusive bibliography on Petrarca's *Salmi penitenziali*.

11. Coppini, "Don Giuseppe de Luca," 415, 430–35.

12. Petrarch, *Les psaumes pénitentiaux, publiés d'après le manuscript de la Bibliothéque de Lucerne*, ed. Henry Cochin (Paris: L. Rouart et Fils, 1929). Coppini identifies the manuscript as Zentralbibliothek BB S 20. 4o, "Don Giuseppe de

Luca," 424, n. 45, even though Cochin and de Luca never mention the shelf mark. For this manuscript, see O. Besomi, *Codici petrarcheschi nelle biblioteche svizzere* (Padua: Antenore, 1967), 49–51; and the description of Donatella Coppini in *Petrarca nel tempo: Tradizione lettori e immagini delle opere, Catalogo della mostra, Arezzo, Sottochiesa di San Francesco, 22 novembre 2003–27 gennaio 2004*, ed. Michele Feo (Pontedera: Edizioni Bandecchi & Vivaldi, 2003), 452–53. I am grateful to Peter Kamber of the Zentral- und Hochschulbibliothek Luzern for information about this manuscript in the form of a scroll.

13. Petrarch, *Psalmi penitentiales* (ed. Cochin), 83–89.

14. Petrarch, *Poesie Latine*, ed. Guido Martellotti and Enrico Bianchi (Turin: Einaudi, 1976), 214–23, and idem, *Salmi penitenziali*, ed. Roberto Gigliucci (Rome: Salerno Editrice, 1997), intro., 19.

15. The latest edition by Ida Garghella, *I sette salmi* (Naples: Edizioni scientifiche italiane; Perugia: Università degli studi di Perugia, 2002) contains only selections.

16. The review appeared in *Frontespizio*, June, 1931, 13; cf. Coppini, "Don Giuseppe de Luca," 423, n. 44.

17. Pierre de Nolhac, "Préface," in Petrarch, *Les psaumes pénitentiaux* (ed. Cochin), 1–7; on p. 6 he calls the work "un recueil d'amour" (a love miscellany).

18. Petrarch, *Psalmi penitentiales* (ed. Cochin), 9.

19. Petrarch, *Psalmi penitentiales* (ed. Cochin), 87.

20. Quoted by Coppini, "Don Giuseppe de Luca," 423, my translation.

21. For a history of the scholarship on dating of the *Psalmi*, see Vinicio Pacca, *Petrarca* (Bari: Laterza, 1998), 131, and 171–72, n. 42; and Marco Ariani, *Petrarca* (Rome: Salerno, 1999), 127, esp. n. 16.

22. Petrarch, *Seniles*. 10.1, quoted by Pacca, *Petrarca,* 131.

23. Petrarch, *Psalmi penitentiales* (ed. Gigliucci), 10; Pacca, *Petrarca,* 132.

24. Petrarch, *Bucolicum carmen* 1, *Parthenias*, 101–110.

25. For the first edition (Venice: Albert Stendal, 1473), see Ariani, *Petrarca,* 127, n. 16 and Petrarch, *Psalmi penitentiales* (ed. Cochin), 90; the edition at the University of Pennsylvania is *Ludolfi Carthusiensis qui et autor fuit vite Christi In Psalterium expositio: in qua subiecte reperiuntur materie: Psalmi penitentiales et co[n] fessionales elegantes et deuoti Domini Francisci Petrarche poete laureati: tabula cunctorum Dauiticorum Psalmorum: tabula versiculorum omnium . . . : tabula materia[rum] principaliu[m] in marginib[us] annotataru[m]: additur in margi[n]e ad solita[m] Hieronymi tra[n]slatione[m], Diui Augustini accuratissima de Hebreo in Latinu[m] tra[n]slatio* ([Paris]: Venundatur Parrhisijs in vico Diui Iacobi a Mag[ist]ro Bertholdo Rembolt [et] Ioha[n]ne Paruo, [10 Mar. 1514]).

26. Coppini, "Don Giuseppe de Luca," 448.

27. As it is usually translated into English: "Glory to the Father and to the Son and to the Holy Spirit / As it was in the beginning, is now, and ever shall be / World without end. / Amen."

28. Petrarca, Psalmus 1, *Salmi penitentiales* (ed. Gigliucci), 23.

29. Flavius Cassiodorus Senator, *Expositio Psalmorum*, ed. M. Adriaen, Corpus Christianorum Series Latina, 97–98 (Turnhout: Brepols, 1973); and *Explanation of the Psalms*, trans. by P. G. Walsh (New York: Paulist Press, 1990).

30. See an extensive list of sources in the notes to Petrarch, *Salmi penitenziali* (ed. Gigliucci).

31. This has been noted by many critics. The introduction to the 1827 edition explains: "Petrarca wrote the Penitential Psalms in Latin prose" (4); Pacca says: "Petrarca opts for a serial prose, made up of brief syntactical units, that seeks to reproduce the biblical style" (*Petrarca*, 132). See also Hamlin, *Psalm Culture*, 2.

32. Ariani, *Petrarca*, 218. Ariani's reference here is to a letter from Petrarch to Gherardo on the Vulgate Bible, *Familiares* 10.4.31, but *Parthenias* 103 also asks that the Psalms not be seen as "rough": "ne raucum dixeris, oro" (Don't call it rough, I beg of you).

33. Giovanni Pozzi, "Petrarca, i Padri e soprattutto la Bibbia," *Studi Petrarcheschi* 6 (1989): 125–69, reprinted in Giovanni Pozzi, *Alternatim* (Milan: Adelphi, 1996), 143–89.

Chapter Fourteen

1. Petrarch, *Le familiari*, ed. Vittorio Rossi and Umberto Bosco (Florence: Sansoni, 1933–42): "Statum meum vis audire; atque si a stando status dicitur, nullus hic homini status est, sed fluxus iugi ac lapsus atque ad ultimum ruina. Quid velis tamen intelligo: quam seu suaviter seu duriter res mee non stant, dico, sed volvuntur." For the English, see *Letters on Familiar Matters*, trans. Aldo S. Bernardo (1975; reprint, Baltimore: Johns Hopkins University Press, 1982–1985).

2. Petrarch, *Petrarch's Guide to the Holy Land. Itinerary to the Sepulcher of Our Lord Jesus Christ*, ed. Theodore J. Cachey, Jr. (Notre Dame: University of Notre Dame Press, 2002), pr. 5: "Longam mortem et peiorem morte nauseam, non de nichilio quidem sed expertus, metuo."

3. Petrarch *Itinerarium* Pr. 7: "Nichilominus te animo comitabor et, quoniam ita vis, his etiam comitabor scriptis, que tibi brevis itinerarii loco sint. Morem enim secutus amantium, cuius presentia cariturus es, imaginem flagistasti, qua utcumque tuam absentiam solareris, non hanc vultus imaginem, cuius in dies mutatio multa fit, sed stabiliorem effigiem, animi ingeniique mei que, quantulacumque est, profecto pars mei optima est."

4. Petrarch can be considered the founder of the early modern genre of cartographic writing. See Theodore J. Cachey, Jr., "Petrarchan Cartographic Writing," *Medieval and Renaissance Humanism: Rhetoric, Representation and Reform*, ed. Stephen Gersh and Bert Roest (Leiden: Brill, 2003), 73–91; and Tom Conley, *The Self-Made Map: Cartographic Writing in Early Modern France* (Minneapolis: University of Minnesota Press, 1996).

5. "de qua si tam parvo in spatio loqui velim, intolerande nimis audacie sim."

6. "Inde mons prealtus, cui carminibus potens Circe nomen imposuisse creditur."

7. "Hinc utinam tu secundis ventis et cursu tam facili proveharis ut ego ad Italie finem facili provehar stilo!"

8. Michele Feo, "Di alcuni rusticani cestelli di pomi," *Quaderni Petrarcheschi* 1 (1983): 23–24.

9. See Petrarch *Itinerarium* 20.1 for the anecdote. Thomas M. Greene, "Petrarch *Viator:* The Displacements of Heroism," *Yearbook of English Studies* 12 (1982): 46.

10. Petrarch *Itinerarium* 21.0: "Quod enim iter tu tribus forte vix mensibus, hoc ego triduo consummavi."

11. Mary W. Helms, *Ulysses' Sail: An Ethnographic Odyssey of Power, Knowledge, and Geographical Distance* (Princeton: Princeton University Press, 1988), 5.

12. Marco Ariani, "Petrarca," *Storia della letteratura italiana* (Rome: Salerno editrice, 1995–), 633.

13. Petrarch, *Canzoniere*, ed. Marco Santagata (Milan: Mondadori, 2004), 110. Translations are from *Petrarch's Lyric Poems: The Rime sparse and Other Lyrics*, trans. and ed. by Robert M. Durling (Cambridge: Harvard University Press, 1976).

14. Ernest Hatch Wilkins, *Life of Petrarch* (Chicago: University of Chicago Press, 1961), 159–60.

15. Petrarch, *Canzoniere* (ed. Santagata), 1392; but see also Marco Santagata, *Frammenti dell'anima: Storia e racconto nel Canzoniere di Petrarca* (Bologna: Il Mulino, 1992), 251–52.

16. "Siquidem post compressos adolescentie turbines et flammam illam benificio maturioris etatis extinctam—o quid poquor cum tot libidinosos passim ac deliros senes videm, turpe iuvenibus vel spectaculum vel exemplum—imo igitur post illud incendium celesti rore Cristique refrigerio consopitum, prope unus semper vite mec tenor fuit, et cum sepe interim loca mutaverim, ille mansit immobilis."

17. Santagata, *I frammenti*, 143–90; see also Guglielmo Gorni, "Metamorfosi e redenzione in Petrarca. Il senso della forma Correggio del *Canzoniere*,"*Lettere italiane* 30 (1978): 4–13. In speaking of a "Correggio" form for which no man-

uscript evidence survives, one should bear in mind the caveats of Teodolinda
Barolini, "The Making of a Lyric Sequence: Time and Narrative in Petrarch's 'Rerum vulgarium fragmenta,'" *MLN* 104 (1989): 18–19.

18. Wilkins, *Life,* 158. See also for the biographical information that follows,
Ugo Dotti, "Gli anni milanesi (1353–1361): L'attività letteraria," in *Vita di
Petrarca* (Rome and Bari: Laterza, 1992), 318–53.

19. Nicholas Mann, "The Making of Petrarch's *Bucolicum Carmen,*" *Italia Medioevale e Umanistica* (1977): 127–82.

20. Wilkins, *Life,* 19.

21. William Kennedy, *The Site of Petrarchism: Early Modern National Sentiment in
Italy, France and England* (Baltimore: Johns Hopkins University Press, 2004);
and see also Roland Greene, *Unrequited Conquest: Love and Empire in the Colonial
Americas* (Chicago: University of Chicago Press, 1999).

22. Theodor Adorno, *Minima moralia* (London: Verso, 2003), 87.

23. In the introduction to his edition of the *Trionfi,* Marco Ariani characterizes
the poem's incubation during this period in terms of an "integral expression
of [Petrarch's] experimentalism that at the beginning of the 1350s became
the lucid awareness of a poetic project." See Petrarch, *Trionfi,* ed. Marco
Ariani (Milan: Mursia, 1988), 6. Marco Santagata, in his introduction to the
poem, notes that "the surviving annotations document nearly uninterrupted
work on the entire poem from beginning to end between 8 September 1357
and 12 February 1374." See Marco Santagata, "Introduzione," in Petrarch,
Trionfi; Rime estravaganti; Codice degli abbozzi, ed. Vinicio Pacca (Milan: Mondadori, 1996), 50.

24. "Ego interim anhelo vigilo sudo esuo nitor in adversum, et ubi densior dif-
ficultatum sepes, eo alacrior gresum fero, ipsa rerum novitate seu asperitate
excitus atque impulsus. Certus labor, fructus incertus, malum michi comune
cum ceteris stadium hoc ingressis."

25. "Nolo ducem qui me vinciat sed precedat; sint cum duce oculi, sit iudicium
sit libertas; non prohibear ubi velim pedem ponere et preterire aliqua et
inaccessa tentare; et breviorem sive ita fert animus, planiorem callem sequi et
properare et subsistere et divertere liceat et reverti."

26. *Petrarch's Triumphs: Allegory and Spectacle,* ed. Konrad Eisenbichler and Amilcare A. Iannucci (Ottawa: Dovehouse Editions, 1990).

27. Petrarch, *Trionfi* (ed. Ariani), 18.

28. Marziano Guglielminetti, *Memoria e scrittura: L'autobiografia da Dante a Cellini*
(Turin: Einaudi, 1977), 130.

29. "Ipsa sed oculis erit Inarime que sese obviam dabit, insula poetarum nota
preconio, Isclam moderni vocitant, sub qua, Iovis edicto, obrutum Typheum

gigantem fama est; fecitque locum fabule vapor, velut hominis anhelantis, et Ethneo more estuare solitum incendium."

30. Petrarch, *Triumphus Pudicitie* (ed. Pacca and Paolino), 109–14; *The Triumphs of Petrarch*, trans. Ernest Hatch Wilkins (Chicago: University of Chicago Press, 1962), 43.

31. *Sine nomine* 18 (April–May, 1358), in Petrarch, *Epistole*, ed. Ugo Dotti (Turin: Unione Tipografico-Editrice Torinese, 1978), 606–607: "Taceo denique illa prodigia, que insensibilis vereque orbus terrarum orbis tamdiu quasi Etnam Enceladus aut Typheus Inarimen pati potest, quorum omnium mesta nimis et severa narratio est." For the English, see *Petrarch's Book without a Name: A Translation of the "Liber Sine nomine,"* trans. Norman P. Zacour (Toronto: Pontifical Institute of Medieval Studies, 1973), 113: "Finally I say nothing of those prodigies which a numb and truly destitute world can suffer only so long, like Enceladus buried under Mount Etna or Typheus under the island of Ischia. About all of this it is too sorrowful and gloomy to write."

32. Giuseppe Billanovich, "Tra Dante e Petrarca," *Italia medioevale e umanistica* (1965): 1–44, quotation on 39–40.

33. "Quid vero nunc cogitas? An nondum te desiderium nostri cepit, ut domum, ut patriam, ut amicos invisere animus sit? Credo id quidem, imo ne aliter fieri posse certus sum. Sed nullus est acrior stimulus quam virtutis. Ille nunc per omnes difficultates generosum animum impellit, nec consistere patitur, nec retro respicere cogitque non voluptatum modo, sed honestorum pignorum atque affectuum oblivisci, nichil aliud virtutis spetiem optare, nichil velle, nichil denique cogitare. Hic stimulus qui Ulixem Laertis et Penelopes et Thelemaci fecit immemorem, te nunc nobis vereor abstrahet quam vellemus."

34. See Enrico Fenzi, "Tra Dante e Petrarca: Il fantasma di Ulisse," in *Saggi petrarcheschi* (Florence: Cadmo, 2004), 493–517.

35. "[I]lle obstitit, et tum vehementius cepto incubuit, omnium negligens soliusque fame cupidus. In quo illum satis mirari et laudare vix valeam, quem non civium iniuria, non exilium, non paupertas, non simultatum aculei, non amor coniugis, non natorum pietas ab arrepto semel calle distraheret, cum multi quem magni tam delicati ingenii sint, ut ab intentione animi leve illos murmur avertat."

36. Theodore J. Cachey, Jr., "From Shipwreck to Port: *RVF* 189 and the Making of the *Canzoniere*," *MLN* 120, no. 1 (2005): 30–49.

37. For the literary relationship between Petrarch and Dante, see *Petrarch and Dante: Antidantism, Metaphysics and Tradition*, ed. Zygmunt G. Baranski and Theodore J. Cachey, Jr. (Notre Dame: University of Notre Dame, 2009).

Chapter Fifteen

I would like to thank Ronald Witt for his reading of this article in manuscript.

1. See the Latin-French edition by Christophe Carraud of Petrarch, *Les remèdes aux deux fortunes* (Grenoble: Millon, 2002); and the English edition and translation of Conrad Rawski, *Petrarch's Remedies for Fortune Fair and Foul* (Bloomington: Indiana University Press, 1991). On the dating of the work, see Klaus Heitmann, "La genesi del 'De remediis utriusque fortune' del Petrarca," *Convivium* 25 (1957): 9–30; and Ernest Hatch Wilkins, *Life of Petrarch* (Chicago: University of Chicago Press, 1961). See also the biography of Azzo da Correggio by Giorgio Montecchi in *Dizionario biografico degli italiani* (Rome: Istituto della Enciclopedia italiana, 1983), 29:425–30.

2. Fifteenth-century humanists were particularly exercised by the relation between virtue and fortune, as in Poggio Bracciolini's 1440 *De infelicitate principum* (*On the Unhappiness of Princes*). Leon Battista Alberti's vernacular dialogue *Theogenius* (c. 1440) directly adopts the thematic of Petrarch's treatise.

3. Klaus Heitmann, *Fortuna und Virtus: Eine Studie zu Petrarcas Lebensweisheit* (Cologne: Böhlau, 1958); see also Charles Trinkaus, *In Our Image and Likeness: Humanity and Divinity in Italian Humanist Thought* (Chicago: University of Chicago Press, 1970), 1:41–42, 179–80; Nicholas Mann, "The Manuscripts of Petrarch's *De remediis*: A Checklist," *Italia medioevale e umanistica* 14 (1971): 5–90; Randolph Starn, "Petrarch's Consolation on Exile: A Humanist Use of Adversity" in *Essays Presented to Myron P. Gilmore,* ed. Sergio Bertelli and Gloria Ramakus (Florence: La Nuova Italia Editrice, 1978), 1:241–54; and Heinrich C. Kuhn, "Petrarcas *De remediis*: Ethik ohne Richtschnur?" in *Ethik—Wissenschaft oder Lebenskunst? Modelle der Normenbegründung von der Antike bis zur Frühen Neuzeit,* ed. Sabrina Ebbersmeyer and Eckhard Kessler (Berlin: LIT Verlag, 2007), 127–41.

4. Petrarch, *Secretum,* ed. Enrico Carrara, in Petrarch, *Prose,* ed. Guido Martellotti, Pier Giorgio Ricci, Enrico Carrara, and Enrico Bianchi (Milan: Riccardo Ricciardi, 1955), 64.

5. Cicero *Tusculanae disputationes* 3.11.24–25 in Cicero, *Tusculan Disputations,* ed. and trans. J. E. King, Loeb Classical Library, 2nd ed. (Cambridge: Harvard University Press, 1945), 254–56. See also Cicero's reference to the twofold power of Fortune in *De officiis* 2.19 (*On Duties,* ed. and trans. by W. Miller, Loeb Classical Library [Cambridge: Harvard University Press, 1913], 186). On Petrarch's appreciation of Cicero, see Pierre de Nolhac, *Pétrarque e l'humanisme* (Paris: H. Champion, 1907), 1:213–68; B. L. Ullman, "Petrarch's Favorite Books," in his *Studies in the Italian Renaissance* (Rome:

Edizioni di Storia e Letteratura, 1955), 123–24. See also Petrarch *Familiares*
18.14.4, cited by Heitmann, *Fortuna*, 180, n. 163.

6. *De remediis fortuitorum liber*, in L. Annaeus Seneca, *Opera quae supersunt.
    Supplementum*, ed. F. Haase (Leipzig: B. G. Teubner, 1902), 44–55. An Eliza-
    bethan English translation of the work, entitled *The remedyes against all casual
    chaunces*, is reprinted in Ralph Graham Palmer, *Seneca's "De Remediis Fortuito-
    rum" and the Elizabethans* (Chicago: Institute of Elizabethan Studies, 1953),
    27–65. See Janet Levarie Smarr's recent *Joining the Conversation: Dialogues by
    Renaissance Women* (Ann Arbor: University of Michigan Press, 2005), 18–22,
    for examples of edifying dialogues in late-classical and medieval literature.

7. For example, the dialogues 64 and 65 of the first part, hereafter cited as *De
    remediis* 1.64–65; and 1.83–85, 1.95–96; *De remediis* 2.2–9, 2.19–22, 2.35–36,
    2.43–44, 2.52–53, 2.59–60, 2.62–63, 2.68–69, 2.71–73, 2.78–81, 2.91–92,
    2.117–125; see also Carraud's note to 1.57 (*De remediis*, ed. Carraud, 2:304).

8. Cicero *Tusculanae disputationes* 1.30.74 (trans. King, 86) citing *Phaedo* 67D,
    and in turn cited by Augustinus in the *Secretum* (*Prose*, ed. Carrara, 210);
    Seneca *Ep.* 70 and 82 in *Epistles*, ed. and trans. by R. M. Gummere, Loeb
    Classical Library (Cambridge: Harvard University Press, 1920), 57–72 and
    240–58.

9. *De remediis* 2.104–11.

10. Heitmann, *Fortuna*, 74–94, 139–49, 250, sees contradictions among these
    camps while admitting that Petrarch did not. One should bear in mind that
    the traditions of Stoicism itself, early, middle and late, incorporated Plato-
    nism in varying degrees, and that Cicero himself, whom Heitmann views as
    a Stoic (19, 35, 111, 119), was self-consciously eclectic in his approach. This
    eclecticism and inconsistency no doubt appealed to the variable moods of
    the poet-humanist: see *Familiares* 6.2.1, in *Le familiari*, ed. Vittorio Rossi and
    Umberto Bosco (Florence: Sansoni, 1934–42), 2:55; also *Familiares* 2.5.3 (ed.
    Rossi and Bosco, 1:81).

11. Trinkaus, *In Our Image and Likeness*, 1:179–80, 1:190–95.

12. One problem with the readings of Heitmann and Trinkaus is that they fail
    to address the relation among the dialogues and treat them as individual,
    separate units; another is that they interpret the statements of Ratio to be
    expressions of the author himself. As Petrarch showed with respect to the
    figure of Franciscus in the *Secretum*, one should be cautious about establish-
    ing these identifications.

13. I have used the capitalization "Fortune" and feminine gender when discuss-
    ing how Petrarch personifies this force congruent to the conventions of his
    time. I have left Ratio untranslated to convey its philosophical character,
    adopted by Petrarch from Cicero, Seneca, and the Fathers.

14. See *De remediis* 1, preface (ed. Carraud, 1:16, lines 132–34), and *Familiares* 23.12.13, cited by Heitmann, *Fortuna*, 61; and by Rawski in *De remediis*, 2:22. See Heitmann's overview, *Fortuna*, 35–37.

15. The form also demarcates the work's divergence from its more systematic predecessors on the subject of Fortune. While Chalcidius, Augustine, and Boethius all design a metaphysical or theological concatenation of causes that subordinate Fortune to Fate or Providence, Petrarch by contrast confronts the various moments of human joy or sadness. For an overview of these thinkers, see Vincenzo Cioffari, "Fate, Fortune, and Chance," in *Dictionary of the History of Ideas*, ed. Philip P. Wiener (New York: Scribner, 1973), 2:225–36.

16. *De remediis* (ed. Carraud, 1:294–96, lines 20–22 [Petrarch *De remediis* 1.63, *De piscinis*]; trans. Rawski, 1:184, revised): "immo si rationi, subditus atque obediens est, ad meliorem finem rectiori calle vos duceret prestaretque ut multa que cupitis sperneretis."

17. *De remediis* (ed. Carraud, 1:854, lines 1 and 24 ["Animi discordia"; "philosophi"], 1:856, lines 31–32 (trans. Rawski, 3:171, modified): "coge, vel consilio, vel vi, partes ignobiles parere nobilibus." Rawski (*De remediis*, 4:259–61) cites the Platonic teaching transmitted in Cicero *Tusculanae disputationes* 1.10.20; and Augustine *De civitate dei* 14.9.

18. *De remediis* 1.2, see also 2.3, 1.89, 2.64, 2.117.

19. *De remediis* 2.117 (trans. Rawski, 4:468) cites *Tusculanae disputationes* 1.31.7; Carraud (ed. Carraud, 2:638) cites *De remediis fortuitorum* 2.7.

20. *De remediis* (ed. Carraud, 1:16, lines 132–34). For antecedents, see *De remediis* (trans. Rawski, 2:20–22); and (ed. Carraud, 2:176).

21. *De remediis* 2.97, 2.102.

22. *De remediis* 1.63.

23. *De remediis* 1.100, 2.56.

24. *De remediis* 2.1.

25. *De remediis* 2.7, 2.8.

26. *De remediis* 2.114, adapting Cicero's *Tusculanae disputationes* 2, as I shall explain below.

27. *De remediis* 1.11, 1.45, and 1.92.

28. *De remediis* 2.28 (ed. Carraud, 1:694, line 61; trans. Rawski, 3:83): "Non est vera virtus cui conscientie premium non sufficit" [If yours is true virtue it is sufficiently rewarded by your good conscience]. See also *De remediis* 2.25, 77, 102, 122. On this point see Cicero *Tusculanae disputationes* 2.26.64 (trans. King, 218), which discusses conscience only after a long section on the motivations of glory and custom for virtue.

29. *De remediis* 1.90, 1.106.

30. *De remediis* 2.31 (ed. Carraud, 1:706, lines 27–28; trans. Rawski, 3:88): "Quamvis nempe politicum et sociale animal dicatur homo, si verum tamen inspicitur, nullum minus [Man is called . . . a political creature and one whose nature it is to live with others. However, if the truth is carefully examined, he turns out to be nothing less than that].

31. *De remediis* 1.14, 2.119.

32. *De remediis* 2.17 (ed. Carraud, 1:644, lines 8–11; trans. Rawski, 2:60): "Quod miri autem volvi humana? Homo ipse volvitur et non stat, sed ut scriptum est, 'quasi flos egreditur, et conteritur, et fugit velut umbra, et nunquam in eodem statu permanet.'"

33. *De remediis*, 1.115, 2.2, see also 1.117.

34. See Tuomas M. S. Lehtonen, *Fortuna, Money, and the Sublunar World: Twelfth-Century Ethical Poetics and the Satirical Poetry of the Carmina Burana* (Helsinki: Finnish Historical Society, 1995); Jerold C. Frakes, *The Fate of Fortune in the Early Middle Ages: The Boethian Tradition* (Leiden: Brill, 1988); G. W. Trompf, *The Idea of Historical Recurrence in Western Thought: From Antiquity to the Reformation* (Berkeley: University of California Press, 1979), 62–64, 161–66, 197–98; Cioffari, "Fate, Fortune, and Chance"; F. P. Pickering, *Literature and Art in the Middle Ages* (Coral Gables: University of Miami Press, 1970), 168–222; John W. Fleming, *The Roman de la Rose: A Study in Allegory and Iconography* (Princeton: Princeton University Press, 1969), 123–25; Pierre Courcelle, *La consolation de philosophie dans la tradition littéraire: Antécédents et postérité de Boèce* (Paris: Études Augustiniennes, 1967), 113–39; and Howard Patch, *The Goddess Fortuna in Mediaeval Literature* (Cambridge: Harvard University Press, 1927), 20–22.

35. *De remediis* 2, preface (trans. Rawski, 3:1; ed. Carraud, 1:530, line 3): "Omnia secundum litem fieri."

36. *De remediis* 2.83 (trans. Rawski, 3:190, amended; ed. Carraud, 1:890, lines 9–15): "*Dolor.* Velocissime senui. *Ratio.* Dicebam tibi tempus fugere: iam credere incipis. Dici nequit, non modo inter opiniones hominum diversorum, sed unius hominis opinionis quid intersit. Iuvenis ante oculos etatem habens, longissimam opinatur; hanc ipsam senior a tergo respiciens, videt esse brevissimam." See also Petrarch *Familiares* 1.1.27–44 (ed. Rossi and Bosco, 1:8–13) and 24.1.22–31 (ed. Rossi and Bosco, 4:219–21).

37. See Heitmann, *Fortuna*, 113–14, citing *Familiares* 12.3.10. Ratio cites Horace's *Ars poetica* 38–53 to underscore that statements of the philosophers need to be adorned with "order" (*ordinis*) and "setting" (*iuncture*) so that they reach the minds of their listeners (2.117 [*De remediis*, ed. Carraud, 1:1054, lines 68–69]).

38. *De remediis* 1.63 and 1.93.

39. *De remediis* 2.79, and 1.79 (trans. Rawski, 1:220; ed. Carraud, 1:358, line 19): "Fusca enim et ambigua merx est homo."

40. See *De remediis* 2.21, 2.31, 2.36, 2.37, and 2.74.

41. *De remediis* 1.27.

42. *De remediis* 2.64–65, 2.54.

43. *De remediis* 2.67.

44. *De remediis* 1.116 (trans. Rawski, 1:312; ed. Carraud, 1:510, lines 31–32): "stultissimum et mali sui semper avidissimum animal est homo."

45. *De remediis* 1.121 (trans. Rawski, 1:322; ed. Carraud, 1:524, lines 13–14): "Vix tantum deberent niti homines ut salvi essent, quantum nituntur ut pereant."

46. *De remediis* (trans. Rawski, 1:264, with slight modification; ed. Carraud, 1:428, lines 202–9): "Proinde expergiscimini aliquando mortales! Aperite oculos neve semper falsis caligate fulgoribus, vestra metimini atque extimate corpuscula, circumspicite quibus septi estis anguistiis, nolite geometras ac philosophos contemnere: terra omnis punctus est . . . cum ascendere creditis descenditis et cum stare videmini, tum maxime ruitis; nec ullum animal magis suarum virium obliviscitur ac sepius vermes semimortui regna et imperia somniatis" (see also *De remediis* 2.58, 2.119). There is a reference to Cicero's *Dream of Scipio*, a work integral to the teaching of Augustinus in the *Secretum* (*Prose*, ed. Carrara, 194). See the note by Rawski in *De remediis* (trans. Rawski), 2:335–39 to *De re publica* 6 (*Somnium*); and Carraud's reference (*De remediis*, 2:362) to Boethius's *Cons.* 2, pr.7.

47. *De remediis* 1.18, 1.19, 2.4, 2.52.

48. *De remediis* 2.122, 2.118.

49. *De remediis* 2.71, 1.89, 2.91.

50. *De remediis* 2.50 (trans. Rawski, 3:120, modified; ed. Carraud, 1:768, lines 53–67): "Nunc fabellam accipe ridiculam, sed materie non ineptam. Circa litus Occeani, quod Britanniam ab adverso conspicit, ante non multo annos, fama est fuisse mulierculam inopem, sed forma appetibili, et insigni lascivia, hec duodecim parvos filios, totidem ex viris genitos habebat, annuis etatum interstitiis inter se distantes. Instante ante mortis hora, vocari prope virum iubet et: "non est, inquit, amplius ludi tempus: nullus horum puerorum ad te spectat, preter maiorem solum. Primo enim anno nostri connubii casta fui." Sedebant tunc forte pueri omnes, humi, circa ignem, more gentis aliquid manducantes. Stupente igitur viro, atque illis rei novitate suspensis, illa singulorum patres ordine nominat; quod audiens omnium minimus, qui triennis erat, panem quem dextera, et rapam quam habebat in manu altera, in terram posuit, at tremens desiderio et ambabus manibus in altum erectis, adorantis in morem, 'Da,' inquit, 'queso, michi, genitrix, aliquem patrem bonum!' cunque illa in fine verborum patrem parvuli nominasset, et famosum

quendam divitemque hominem, reassumpto in mandibus cibo, 'bene habet,' inquit, 'bonus est pater.'" See also the previous story in *De remediis* 2.50 (ed. Carraud, 1:766, lines 26–39), and 2.13.

51. *De remediis* 1.41, 1.23; see also 1.28 on comedians; 1.21 on two types of *otium*.

52. *De remediis* 2.93; Carraud (in *De remediis*, 2:589) refers to Cicero's *De natura deorum* 2, which is adapted by Augustine in *De civitate dei* 22.24.

53. *De remediis* 1.108 (trans. Rawski, 1:293; ed. Carraud, 1:472, lines 19–20): "Nemo igitur felix, priusquam ex hac miseriarum valle migraverit" (see also *De remediis* 2.96 and 97).

54. Cicero *Tusculanae disputationes* 2.21.47 (trans. King, 200): lacking reason, "nihil esse homine deformius." Cicero did recognize elsewhere that ethical teaching needed to be tailored to a person's character: *De officiis* 1.30–34 (trans. Miller, 108–28).

55. Modifying *De remediis* (trans. Rawski, 3:268–69, 274; ed. Carraud, 1:1024, line 9): "philosophice fabelle"; 1:1028, line 71: "hec inania que philosophica dicitis"; 1:1034, lines 155–57: "Nunc languori meo propius adhibes manum, docens ubi illa reperiam, que in hoc statu, Stoicorum opinionibus inhumanis et saxeis potiora et michi opportuniora confido, quamvis et confidendo diffidam."

56. Cicero *Tusculanae disputationes* 2.12.29–13.31 (trans. King, 176–78).

57. Sorrow begins to change its view when Ratio cites Cicero's notions of patience and perseverance in the face of suffering; yet Ratio itself acknowledges its verbal relief is ephemeral: *De remediis* (ed. Carraud), 1:1044, lines 300–302. Humanists in the fifteenth century would explore in various ways the limitations of Stoic theory: cf. Poggio's *De vera nobilitate* (*On True Nobility*); Giannozzo Manetti's *Dialogus consolatorius* (*Dialogue of Consolation*); Lorenzo Valla's *De voluptate* (*On Pleasure*); and Alberti's *Profugiorum ab erumna libri* (*On Refuges from Hardship*).

58. *De remediis* 2.122, 2.126. The limits of logic can be found in Ratio's argument to Sorrow in *De remediis* 2.119 (ed. Carraud, 1:1074, lines 17–19; trans. Rawski, 3:299): "non morereris utique, nisi mortalis esse; sin id defles quod mortalis sis, non est flendi locos ubi esse desinis, quod invitus es" [You would not die if you were not mortal. And if you deplore being mortal, then you have no cause to weep when you cease to be what you do not want to be]. Of course the basic sorrow is over one's mortality, for which death by definition offers no consolation.

59. *De remediis* 2.117 (trans. Rawski, 3:290; ed. Carraud, 1:1060, lines 151–53): "atque nil damnosus in humanis malis, quam Dei, suique ipsius et mortis oblivio, que tria numero sic connexa sunt, ut vix valeant dissolvi."

60. *De remediis* 2.122.

61. *De remediis* (trans. Rawski, 3:323; ed. Carraud, 1:1116, lines 45–46): "Nullam tam magnum peccatum esse potest, quin multo maior misericordia Dei est."

Chapter Sixteen

1. For the current authoritative edition of the text, see Petrarch, *Invective contra medicum: Testo latino e volgarizzamento di ser Domenico Silvestri,* ed. Pier Giorgio Ricci with an appendix by Bortolo Martinelli (Rome: Edizioni di Storia e Letteratura, 1978). This edition, based on only nine of the over forty manuscripts that transmit the text, was supposed to offer an entirely new edition with respect to the one Ricci himself had prepared for the same publisher in 1950, an edition already incisively criticized by Ruggero Raimondi in a long and meticulous review that appeared in *Studi Petrarcheschi* 4 (1951): 225–62. Ricci died in 1976, leaving his revision unfinished. His posthumous 1978 edition is in fact the result of a careful consideration of his handwritten notes that Bortolo Martinelli was able to study and discuss, producing a text that certainly improved the one previously published but that cannot be considered definitive. Francesco Bausi, "Il *mechanicus* che scrive libri: Per un nuovo commento alle *Invective contra medicum* di Francesco Petrarca," *Rinascimento* 42 (2002): 67–68, announced his new edition, since published as Petrarch, *Invective contra medicum* (Florence: Le Lettere, 2005). See too idem, "La sconosciuta redazione originaria delle *Invective contra medicum* di Francesco Petrarca (Libro I) in un codice di Danzica," *Rinascimento* 45 (2005): 91–115. For cultural context of Petrarch's views on medicine, see now *Petrarca e la medicina,* eds. Monica Berté, Vincenzo Fera, and Tiziana Pesenti (Messina: Centro Interdipartimentale di Studi Umanistici, 2006). For both the Latin text and the English translation, I will quote from "Invective contra medicum: Invectives against a Physician," in Petrarch, *Invectives,* ed. and trans. David Marsh, I Tatti Renaissance Library (Cambridge: Harvard University Press, 2003), 2–179, which is based on the 1978 posthumous edition of Ricci's text.

2. The thematic spectrum outlined here roughly reflects the order in which Petrarch treats the matter in the four books of the *Invectives*. Book 1 rejects the alleged equivalence between rhetoric and medicine by reaffirming the medieval distinction between liberal arts (grammar, rhetoric, dialectics, mathematics, music, geometry, and astronomy), on the one hand, and mechanical arts (fabric making, armament, commerce, agriculture, hunting, medicine, and theatrics), on the other, following the classification provided by Hugh of Saint-Victor in his *Didascalicon* (bk. 2, chap. 1); see Hugh of Saint-Victor, *Didascalicon: A Medieval Guide to the Arts,* trans. Jerome Taylor (New York: Columbia University Press, 1961), 74; and Bausi, "Il *mechanicus* che scrive libri,"

89–94. Books 2 and 3 contest the epistemological validity of both medicine and Scholastic philosophy by attacking their purportedly sterile cult of dialectics and exalting poetry as a form of true philosophy, described in book 3 as a discipline superior to both alike. Book 4 praises the solitary life of the countryside, described as the ideal environment for the liberal activity of the humanist, against the frenetic life of the city, portrayed as the natural habitat for the lucrative activity of the doctors. For further readings in English, see Conrad H. Rawski, "Notes on the Rhetoric in Petrarch's *Invective contra medicum*," in *Francis Petrarch, Six Centuries Later: A Symposium*, ed. Aldo Scaglione (Chapel Hill: Department of Romance Languages, University of North Carolina, 1975), 249–77; Thomas G. Benedek, "An Interpretation of Petrarca's 'Invective against Physicians,'" in *Thirty-first International Congress on the History of Medicine*, ed. Raffaele A. Bernabeo (Bologna: Monduzzi, 1990), 691–96; Nancy Struever, "Petrarch's 'Invective contra medicum': An Early Confrontation of Rhetoric and Medicine," *MLN* 108 (1993): 659–79; George A. Trone, "'You lie like a doctor!': Petrarch's Attack on Medicine," *Yale Journal of Biology and Medicine* 70 (1997): 183–90; and Carol E. Quillen, *Rereading the Renaissance: Petrarch, Augustine, and the Language of Humanism* (Ann Arbor: University of Michigan Press, 1998), 73–74 and 148–81.

3. For the recurrence of these themes in Petrarch's works, see Vinicio Pacca, *Petrarca* (Rome and Bari: Laterza, 1998), 163–67; and Marco Ariani, *Petrarca* (Rome: Salerno, 1999), 159–64. For a philosophical and historical appraisal of the concept of "moral perfectionism," see Stanley Cavell, *Conditions Handsome and Unhandsome: The Constitution of Emersonian Perfectionism* (Chicago: Chicago University Press, 1990), 1–17, and his most recent *Cities of Words: Pedagogical Letters on a Register of the Moral Life* (Cambridge: Harvard University Press, 2004), 313–39, 352–72.

4. See Ernest Hatch Wilkins, *Life of Petrarch* (Chicago: University of Chicago Press, 1961), 123–24; Ugo Dotti, *Vita di Petrarca* (Bari: Laterza, 1987) 252–57, Pacca, *Petrarca*, 117–78; Ariani, *Petrarca*, 41–51. Clement's illness might well be connected with his alleged addiction to wine. Still today, the pope's name is enshrined on the label of a red burgundy known as *Châteauneuf du Pape Clément*; on Clement's drinking reputation, see John E. Wrigley, "A Papal Secret Known to Petrarch," *Speculum* 39 (1964): 618. In the *Invective*, Petrarch fails to make any explicit reference to the papal penchant for the grape. But in *Bucolicum carmen* 6, Pamphilus (Saint Peter) accuses Mitio (Clement VI) of neglecting his pastoral duties precisely because of wine, see Ernest Hatch Wilkins, *Studies in the Life and Works of Petrarch* (Cambridge: Medieval Academy of America, 1955), 48. In the sonnets 136.7 and 137.3–4, famously known for Petrarch's attack on the papal court of Avi-

gnon, the poet characterizes the Curia as the "slave of wine" ("de vin serva") and devotee of Venus and Bacchus, rather than of Jove and Pallas ("à fatti suoi dèi/non Giove et Pallas, ma Venere et Bacco"). See Petrarch, *Canzoniere*, ed. Marco Santagata (Milan: Mondadori, 1996), 666 and 670. Santagata's commentary refers to *Seniles* 12.1.41, *Epystole* 3.26.42, *Sine nomine* 18, and *Vita solitaria* 1 but omits any reference to Petrarch's sixth eclogue.

5.   Petrarch *Familiares* 5.19 in *Rerum familiarum libri: I–VIII*, translated by Aldo S. Bernardo (Albany: State University of New York, 1975), 279; for the Latin text, see *Le Familiari*, ed. Vittorio Rossi and Umberto Bosco (Florence: Sansoni, 1933–42), 2:44.

6.   The question about the real identity of this doctor has puzzled the readers of the *Invective* since the time of de Sade's uncle. See Jacques-François-Paul-Aldonce de Sade, *Mémoires pour la vie de François Pétrarque* (Amsterdam: Arskée and Merkus, 1764–67), 3:209–16; Gaetano Luigi Marini, *Degli archiatri pontifici* (Rome: Stamperia Pagliarini, 1784), 1:79; Eduard Niçaise, *La Grande Chirurgie de Guy de Chauliac* (Paris: Alcan, 1890), 84–86; Pierre Pansier, "Les médecins des papes d'Avignon (1308–1403)," *Janus* 14 (1909): 405–34; Nicola Latronico, "I medici e la medicina nelle *Invettive* del Petrarca," *Castalia* 1–6 (1955 but 1936): 35–42, 79–91, 133–39, 77–86, 231–39, 79–84, available also as a separate publication (Milan: Tipografia Giuseppe Bianchi, 1956); Adalberto Pazzini, *Storia della medicina* (Milan: Società editrice libraria, 1947), 514–15; Mario Tabanelli, *Un secolo d'oro della chirurgia francese: Guy de Chauliac* (Forlì: Valbonesi, 1970); Martinelli, "Il Petrarca e la medicina," in *Invective contra medicum*, 209–11. Martinelli justly rejects the traditional identification with Jean d'Alais and Guy de Chauliac (211).

7.   Petrarch *Invective contra medicum* 2.88 (trans. Marsh, 70–71): "Illam certe premeditari, contra illam armari, ad illius contemptum ac patientiam componi, illi si res exigat occurrere, et pro eterna vita, pro felicitate, pro gloria brevem hanc miseramque vitam alto animo pacisci, ea demum vera philosophia est, quam quidam nichil aliud nisi cogitationem mortis esse dixerunt." This passage is to be read in conjunction with Petrarch *Secretum* 1 (ed. Carrara, 8): "*Aug.* . . . cum sit profecto verissimum ad contemnendas vite huius illecebras componendumque inter tot mundi procellas animum nichil efficacius reperiri quam memoriam proprie miserie et meditationem mortis assiduam; modo non leviter, aut superficietenus serpat, sed in ossibus ipsis ac medullis insideat" [For there can be no doubt that to recollect one's misery and to practice frequent meditation on death is the surest aid in scorning the seductions of this world, and in ordering the soul amid its stoles and tempests, if only such meditation be not superficial, but sink into the bones and marrow of the heart]. See *Petrarch's Secret*, trans. William Henry Draper (London: Chatto

and Windus, 1911). On the concept of medicine as a contemplation of death, see Klaus Bergdolt, "Die *meditatio mortis* als Medizin: Betrachtungen zur Ethik der Todesangst im Spätmittelalter und Heute," *Würzburger medizinhistorische Mitteilungen* 9 (1991): 249–57.

8. See Bausi, "Il *mechanicus* che scrive libri," 67–68. Bausi's scrutiny of the entire handwritten tradition of the *Invective* indicates that Petrarch's revision of the texts spans a much longer period of time than the one previously assumed by Ricci.

9. See Umberto Bosco, *Petrarca* (Turin: Unione Tipografico-Editrice Torinese, 1946), 9–10. The revision of the *Invective* coincided with the revision or the composition of the *Sine nomine*, the *Posteritati*, the *Secretum*, *De viris illustribus*, the *Remediis utriusque fortune*, the *Invective* against Jean de Caraman, *De otio religioso*, *De vita solitaria*, the *Bucolicum carmen*, the Correggio draft of the *Canzoniere*, and the *Triumphi*. See Vinicio Pacca, "Cronologia della vita e delle opere," in Pacca, *Petrarca*, 261–65.

10. See Klaus Bergdolt, *Artz, Krankheit und Therapie bei Petrarca: Die Kritik an Medizin und Naturwissenschaft im italienischen Frühhumanismus* (Weinheim: Acta Humaniora, 1992), with particular reference to *De otio religioso*, *De vita solitaria*, the *Secretum*, *De remediis utriusque fortune*, see 50–54, 55–57, 77–82, 90–101, respectively; see also, by the same author, "Petrarca, la medicina e le scienze naturali," *Kos*, n.s., 89 (1993): 43–49, where the invectives are presented as a key text to explain the shift from the Middle Ages to the early Renaissance, 43; and idem, "Precursori ed epigoni nella polemica petrarchesca contro i medici," in Berté, *et al.*, *Petrarca e la medicina*, 3–18.

11. For Petrarch's rhetorical models, see the annotated edition of the text in Petrarch, "Invective contra medicum: Invettive contro un medico," trans. Clara Kraus Reggiani, in Petrarch, *Opere latine*, ed. Antonietta Bufano (Turin: Unione Tipografico-Editrice Torinese, 1975), 2:818–981; and the discussion provided by Bausi, "Il *mechanicus* che scrive libri," 79–106. The reader interested in this particular aspect of Petrarch's *Invective* may refer to Wilhelm Süss, *Ethos: Studien zur älteren griechischen Rhetorik* (1910; Leipzig and Berlin: Teubner, 1975), 247–55; and Felice Vismara, *L'invettiva: Arma preferita dagli umanisti nelle lotte private, nelle polemiche letterarie, politiche e religiose* (Milan: Umberto Allegretti, 1900) 1–8; see, more recently, Severin Koster, *Die Invektive in der griechischen und römischen Literatur* (Meisenheim am Glan: Hain, 1980), 210–81.

12. See Susan L. Feagin, *Reading with Feeling: The Aesthetics of Appreciation* (Ithaca: Cornell University Press, 1996); Terrance Brown, "Affective Dimensions of Meaning," in *The Nature and Ontogenesis of Meaning*, ed. Willis F. Overton and David Stuart Palermo (Hillsdale: Lawrence Erlbaum Associates, 1994),

168–90; Maria Chiara Levorato, *Le emozioni della lettura* (Bologna: Il Mulino, 2000); and John Gibson, "Between Truth and Triviality," *British Journal of Aesthetics* 43 (2003): 224–37. If it is true that a viable theory of literary humanism must do justice to the idea that literature offers cognitive rewards to the attentive reader, the main goal of this approach is to provide clues for both a cognitive understanding and an aesthetic appreciation of Petrarch's works within the context in which it was once produced and the context in which it may be received today. Knowledge but also acknowledgment, understanding but also appreciation, idea but also emotion, meaning but also feeling represent the tentative set of dialectical keywords that may guide a new reading of Petrarch's *Invective* and, more generally, of his humanistic engagement.

13. See Jole Agrimi and Chiara Crisciani, *Medicina del corpo e medicina dell'anima: Note sul sapere del medico fino all'inizio del secolo XIII* (Milan: Episteme, 1979). For a pertinent anthology of primary texts, see Luigi Firpo, *Medicina medievale: Testi dell'alto medioevo, miniature del codice di Kassel, regole salutari salernitane, incisioni del 'Fasciculo de medicina,' anatomia di Mondino de' Liuzzi* (Turin: Unione Tipografico-Editrice Torinese, 1972).

14. Petrarch *Familiares* 5.19.3–4 (trans. Bernardo, 278–79). The Latin text reads as follows: "Lectum tuum obsessum medicis scio; hinc prima michi timendi causa est. Discordant enim de industria, dum pudet novi nichil afferentem alterius hesisse vestigiis. 'Nec est dubium' ut eleganter ait Plinius, 'omnes istos famam novitate aliqua aucupantes animas statim nostras negotiari . . . et in hac sola artium *evenire*, ut cuicunque se medicum profitenti statim credatur, cum sit periculum in nullo mendacio maius; non tamen illud intuemur, adeo blanda est sperandi pro se cuique dulcedo. Nulla preterea lex que puniat inscitiam capitalem, nullum exemplum vindicte; discunt periculis nostris et experimenta per mortes agunt, medicoque tantum hominem occidisse impunitas summa est.' Horum turbam velut inimicorum aciem, Clementissime Pater, intuere." Cf. Pliny *Naturalis historia* 29.8.11: "nec dubium est omnes istos famam novitate aliqua aucupantes anima statim nostra negotiari," together with 17–18: "itaque, Hercules, in hac artium sola evenit, ut cuicumque medicum se professo statim credatur, cum sit periculum in nullo mendacio maius. non tamen illud intuemur, adeo blanda est sperandi pro se cuique dulcedo. nulla praeterea lex quae puniat inscitiam capitalem, nullum exemplum vindictae. discunt periculis nostris et experimenta per mortes agunt, medicoque tantum hominem occidisse inpunitas summa est."

15. Petrarch *Invective contra medicum* 1.23 (Marsh trans., 18–21): "Non detraho claris viris, ne fiam tui similis, qui obtrectandi studio me cum Plinio miscuisti, quem si intelligere posses, esses hortandus ut legeres, et te ipsum in eo

speculo intuens, vel deformitatem tuam corrigeres, vel desineres superbire"
[I will not disparge famous men, lest I resemble you, who are so eager to
malign me that you confuse me with Pliny. For if you viewed yourself in that
mirror, you would either correct your deformity or cease to be proud].

16. Petrarch *Invective contra medicum* 1.3 (Marsh trans., 4–5): "Ego quidem (nam
memini) non artificium sed artifices improbavi, eosque non omnes, sed pro-
caces atque discordes" [For my part, I remember clearly that I did not criticize the medical profession, but merely its professionals—and not all of them,
but only the insolent and factious ones]; 1.26 (Marsh trans., 20–21): "invenies
me nil omnino contra medicinam nilque contra veros medicos locutum, sed
contra discerptores atque adversarios Ypocratis" [You'll find that that I said
nothing against medicine or true physicians, but only against the detractors
and adversaries of Hippocrates]; and 1.40 (Marsh trans., 30–31): "Hec non
adversus medicinam—quod sepe testatus sum—neque adversus excellentes
medicos, qui irasci non debent si, semper rari, nostra sint etate rarissimi,
sed adversus te delirantesque similiter dicta sint" [As I have often said, my
remarks are not directed at medicine, nor at excellent physicians, who should
not be angered that they are so rare in this age, when they have always been
rare].

17. See Paul Oskar Kristeller, "Humanism and Scholasticism in the Italian
Renaissance," *Byzantion* 17 (1944–45): 346–74; Eugenio Garin, *Italian Humanism: Philosophy and Civic Life in the Renaissance,* trans. Peter Munz (New
York: Harper & Row, 1965), 1–36; and Cesare Vasoli, *La dialettica e la retorica
dell'umanesimo: Invenzione e metodo nella cultura del XV e XVI secolo* (Milan: Feltrinelli, 1968).

18. Petrarch *Familiares* 5.19 (ed. Rossi, 2:44; trans. Bernardo, 279): "atque illis morientibus ypocraticos nodos tulliano stamine per miscentes, sinistro
quamvis eventu superbiunt, nec rerum effectibus sed inani verborum elegan-
tia gloriantur."

19. Randall Collins, "On the Acrimoniousness of Intellectual Disputes," *Common Knowledge* 8 (2002): 47–70; the article is substantially drawn from his
The Sociology of Philosophies: A Global Theory of Intellectual Change (Cambridge:
Harvard University Press, 1998), where Collins provides a general theory of
intellectual life based on a general theory of interaction rituals and a sociology of thinking.

20. On the long-lasting quarrel against the doctors after Pliny, see Klaus Bergdolt, "Die Kritik am Arzt im Mittelalter: Beispiele und Tendenzen vom 6. bis
zum 12. Jahrhundert," *Gesnerus* 48 (1991): 43–64, and idem, "Zur antischolastischen Arztkritik des 13. Jahrhunderts," *Medizinhistorisches Journal* 26
(1991): 264–81.

21. For an account of the genre of the invective in Italian humanism, see Pier Giorgio Ricci, "La tradizione dell'invettiva tra Medioevo e Rinascimento," *Lettere italiane* 26 (1974): 405–14; Lucia Cesarini Martinelli, "Note sulla polemica Poggio-Valla e sulla fortuna delle 'Elegantiae,'" *Interpres* 3 (1980): 29–79; Claudio Griggio, "Note sulla tradizione dell'invettiva dal Petrarca al Poliziano," in *Bufere e molli aurette: Polemiche letterarie dallo Stilnovo alla 'Voce,'* ed. Maria Grazia Pensa (Milan: Guerini e Associati, 1996), 37–51, and idem, "Forme dell'invettiva in Petrarch," *Atti e memorie dell'Accademia patavina di scienze morali, lettere e arti. Memorie della classe di scienze morali, lettere e arti* 109 (1996–97): 375–92.

22. See Petrarch *Invective contra medicum* 3.162 (trans. Marsh, 134–35): "et cum nulla gens magis rethoricis floribus nuda sit, nulla minus illis indigeat, tamen rethorici, et oratores, et poete, et philosophi, et apostoli, ac suscitatores corporum dici vultis; et penitus nihil estis, nisi verba inania nugeque volatiles" [Although no group lacks rhetorical embellishments more, and need them less, you still insist on being called rhetoricians, orators, poets, philosophers, apostles, and raisers of the dead. Yet you are absolutely nothing but empty words and fleeting trifles]. As early as the first invective, Petrarch compares himself to Demosthenes, in order to justify the fact that his reply is longer than the letter of his detractor, as "the defense of Demosthenes is longer than the accusation of Aeschines" [Ideoque et maior defensio Demosthenis quam Eschinis accusatio est], see 1.40 (trans. Marsh, 31–32): For the concept of *gravitas nervosa,* see Leonardo Bruni Aretino, *Humanistisch-philosophische Schriften mit einer Chronologie seiner Werke und Briefe,* ed. Hans Baron (Leipzig: Teubner, 1928) 130; as discussed in Giovanni Ponte, "La 'gravitas nervosa' del Poliziano," in *Poliziano nel suo tempo: Atti del VI Convegno internazionale (Chianciano-Montepulciano 18–21 luglio 1994),* ed. Luisa Secchi Tarugi (Florence: Francesco Cesati Editore, 1996), 107–15; and more recently in Stefano Cracolici, "Alberti e la 'gravitas nervosa': Note su un contributo di Giovanni Ponte," in *Leon Battista Alberti (1404–72) tra scienze e lettere: Atti del Convegno (Genova, 19–20 novembre 2004),* ed. Alberto Beniscelli and Francesco Furlan (Genoa: Accademia Ligure di Scienze e Lettere, 2005), 287–308.

23. On this crucial event in Petrarch's life, see Renee Neu Watkins, "Petrarch and the Black Death: From Fear to Monuments," *Studies in the Renaissance* 19 (1972): 196–223; Klaus Bergdolt, "Petrarca und die Pest," *Sudhoffs Archiv* 76 (1992): 63–73; and Francesco Gianni, "Per una storia letteraria della peste," in *The Regulation of Evil: Social and Cultural Attitudes to Epidemics in the Late Middle Ages,* ed. Agostino Paravicini Bagliani and Francesco Santi (Florence: Sismel, 1998), 63–124.

24. These topics are to be found also in Petrarch's correspondence with vari-

ous contemporary physicians, notably Francesco Casini and Giovanni
Dondi dall'Orologio, who agreed to his position and partially also to his
polemic; see Antonio Zardo, *Petrarca e i Carraresi* (Milan: Hoepli, 1887),
105–24; Klaus Bergdolt, "Petrarca and die Pest," and "Petrarca, la medicina
e le scienze naturali"; Tiziana Pesenti, "Dondi dall'Orologio, Giovanni," in
Dizionario Biografico degli Italiani (Rome: Istituto dell'Enciclopedia Italiana,
1992), 41:96–104; Giuseppe Dell'Anna, "Il Petrarca e la medicina," in *Petrarca
e la cultura europea*, ed. Luisa Rotondi Secchi Tarugi (Milan: Nuovi Orizzonti, 1997), 203–322; Matilde Conde Salazar, "El médico en las epístolas de
Séneca y Petrarca," in *Séneca dos mil años después: Actas del congreso internacional
conmemorativo del bimilenario de su nacimiento (Córdoba, 24–27 de septiembre, 1996)*
(Córdoba: Publicaciones de la Universidad de Córdoba y Obra Social y Cultural CajaSur, 1997), 637–44.

25. Petrarch *Invective contra medicum* 1.9 (trans. Marsh, 8–10): "O si quod ominari
horreo, sed, licet immortalis Dei vicarius, est tamen ipse mortalis—si ergo
tunc nature debitum persolvisset, quanta fuisset inter vos et quam indecisa
discordia de pulsu, de humoribus, de die cretico, de farmacis! Celum ac terram dissonis clamoribus implessetis, causam ipsam egritudinis ignorantes.
Miseri qui sub auxilii vestri fidutia egrotant! Cristus autem, in cuius manu
salus hominum sita est, salvum illum, ignorantibus omnibus vobis, fecit—et
faciat precor quantum sibi, quantum Ecclesie cui presidet, est necesse!"

26. See Agrimi and Crisciani, *Medicina del corpo e medicina dell'anima*, 34–36, 90,
n. 174; Nancy G. Siraisi, *Medieval and Early Renaissance Medicine: An Introduction to Knowledge and Practice* (Chicago: University of Chicago Press, 1990),
chap. 3, idem, "Die medizinische Fakultät," in *Geschichte der Universität in Europa*, ed. Walter Rüegg (Munich: Beck, 1993), 1:321–342, and idem, *Medicine
and the Italian Universities, 1250–1600* (Leiden: Brill, 2001), 161–63; David D.
Lines, "Natural Philosophy in Renaissance Italy: The University of Bologna and the Beginning of Specialization," *Early Science and Medicine* 6 (2001):
267–323; and George W. McClure, *The Culture of Profession in Late Renaissance
Italy* (Toronto: University of Toronto Press, 2004), 6–12.

27. Petrarch describes his medical detractor as "declaiming, arguing, and
shouting" and quotes Virgil's characterization of medicine in the *Aeneid*
(12.396–97) as the "mute art." See Petrarch *Invective* 3.161 (trans. Marsh,
134–35): "Expediret tibi, sed multo magis egris tuis, ut mutus esses, non
orator . . . Certe non ad artis ignominiam, nec a casu, medicinam Virgilius
mutam vocat, sed quoniam muta debet esse, non loquax . . . Solebant medici
veteres taciti curare: vos perorantes, et altercantes, et conclamantes oc-
ciditis" [It would be better for you, and even better for your patients, if you
were mute and not an orator . . . It is clearly neither a slur on the profession

nor an accident when Virgil calls medicine mute: it should be mute and not verbose . . . Ancient physicians used to give care in silence. You kill while declaiming, arguing, and shouting]. The Virgilian characterization of medicine as a silent art, which also returns in his correspondence to Giovanni Dondi dall'Orologio and Francesco Casini (see *Seniles* 3.8), classicizes, in fact, a well-established recommendation of monastic medicine. See Agrimi and Crisciani, *Medicina del corpo e medicina dell'anima*, 9; and Firpo, *Medicina medievale*, 28, 38, 40. For the convergence here implicit between classical and Christian imitation practices, see Dina De Rentiis, *Die Zeit der Nachfolge: Zur Interdipendenz von 'imitatio Christi' und 'imitatio auctorum' in 12.-16. Jahrhundert* (Tübingen: Max Niemeyer, 1996).

28. Petrarch *Invective contra medicum* 1.11 (Marsh trans., 10–11): "at Romano Pontifici, gravi tunc egritudine laboranti, metu ac devotione dictantibus, epystolam scripsi brevem."

29. See, in particular, Brian Stock, "Reading, Writing, and the Self: Petrarch and His Forerunners," *New Literary History* 26 (1995): 717–30, which expands and applies to Petrarch an argument previously presented in "The Self and Literary Experience in Late Antiquity and the Middle Ages," *New Literary History* 25 (1994): 839–52. For the patristic and monastic influences on Petrarch's thought, see Giuseppe Billanovich, *Un nuovo esempio delle scoperte e delle letture del Petrarca: L'Eusebio-Girolamo-PseudoProspero* (Krefeld: Scherpe, 1954), as well as his fundamental "Nella biblioteca del Petrarca," *Italia medioevale e umanistica* 3 (1960): 1–58; Jean Leclercq, "Temi monastici nell'opera del Petrarca," *Lettere italiane* 43 (1991): 42–54, now in *Spiritualità e lettere nella cultura italiana e ungherese del basso Medioevo*, ed. Sante Graciotti and Cesare Vasoli (Florence: Olschki, 1995), 149–62; and George W. McClure, *Sorrow and Consolation in Italian Humanism* (Princeton: Princeton University Press, 1990), 18–72.

30. Petrarch *Invective contra medicum* 3.136 (Marsh trans., 112–13).

31. Judson Boyce Allen, *The Ethical Poetic of the Later Middle Ages: A Decorum of Convenient Distinction* (Toronto: University of Toronto Press, 1982), 12.

32. For the definition of *ethica docens* and *ethica utens*, see Egidio Colonna, *De regimine principum libri III: Recogniti et una cum vita auctoris in lucem editi per Hieronymum Samaritanium* (Aalen: Scientia Verlag, 1967), 3; see also Georg Wieland, *Ethica, scientia practica: Die Anfänge der philosophischen Ethik im 13. Jahrhundert* (Münster: Aschendorff, 1981), 103, as well as his "Ethica docens— Ethica utens," in *Sprache und Erkenntnis im Mittelalter,* ed. Jan P. Beckmann (Berlin: Walter de Gruyter, 1981), 593–601.

33. See Charles G. Osgood, *Boccaccio on Poetry* (Princeton: Princeton University Press, 1930) 122–23. For the Latin text, see Giovanni Boccaccio, *Genealogie*

deorum gentilium, 15.8.5, ed. Vittorio Zaccaria, in Giovanni Boccaccio, *Tutte le opere*, ed. Vittore Branca, vols. 7–8 (Milan: Mondadori, 1998), 2:1548, "Equo modo, si quis poetas dicat theologos, nulli facit iniuriam. Si sacros quis illos dicunt, quis ades demens est quin videat quoniam mentiretur? Esto non unquam, ut in precedentibus patet, circa honesta eorum theologia versetur, que sepissime potius physiologia aut ethologia quam theologia dicenda est, dum eorum fabule naturalia contegunt aut mores."

34. For a comparison between Petrarch's and Boccaccio's theories of poetry, with a thoughtful comment on the passage in question, see Vittorio Zaccaria, "La difesa della poesia: Dal Petrarca alle *Genealogie* del Boccaccio," *Lectura Petrarce* 19 (1999): 211–29.

35. On Petrarch's therapeutic eloquence, see Jerrold E. Seigel, *Rhetoric and Philosophy in Renaissance Humanism: The Union of Eloquence and Wisdom; Petrarch to Valla* (Princeton: Princeton University Press, 1968), 37–42; Charles Trinkhaus, *The Poet as Philosopher: Petrarch and the Formation of Renaissance Consciousness* (New Heaven: Yale University Press, 1979), 90–113 and 119–20; and George W. McClure, "Healing Eloquence: Petrarch, Salutati, and the Physicians," *Journal of Medieval and Renaissance Studies* 15 (1985): 317–46. For an account of the ancient relationship between poetry and medicine, see Pedro Laín Entralgo, *The Therapy of the Word in Classical Antiquity*, trans. L. J. Rather and John M. Sharp (New Haven: Yale University Press, 1970).

Chapter Seventeen

1. The circumstances of its composition are as follows: In September 1362 Petrarch moved from Milan and Padua to Venice with the intention of bequeathing to the Republic a permanent public library based on his books; in spring 1365 he initiated a friendship with four men who would malign him the following fall while he was visiting Padua. Upon his return to Venice in January 1366, another friend, Donato Albanzani, informed him of their slander, but he did not respond to the charges until May 1367, when he began writing *De ignorantia* during a trip to Pavia. In January 1368 he wrote to Donato (*Seniles* 13.5) about revising the project. The following March he left Venice permanently, taking up residence first in Padua and then two years later (after trips to Pavia and Milan) at his house in Arquà (on land given by Francesco da Carrara). There he completed *De ignorantia* and dated his personal copy on 25 June 1370.

2. Quotations throughout refer to Petrarch, *Invectives*, ed. and trans. David Marsh, I Tatti Renaissance Library (Cambridge: Harvard University Press, 2003), here cited from 284–85 and 224–25. I have profited also from the detailed annotations in *De sui ipsius et multorum ignorantia*, ed. Enrico Fenzi

(Milan: Mursia, 1999). An earlier translation by Hans Nachod appears in *The Renaissance Philosophy of Man,* ed. Ernst Cassirer, Paul Oskar Kristeller, and John Herman Randall (Chicago: University of Chicago Press, 1948), 47–133.

3.   Sigmund Freud, *The Standard Edition of the Complete Psychological Works of Sigmund Freud,* trans. James Strachey in collaboration with Anna Freud, 24 vols. (London: Hogarth Press, 1953–74), vol. 8, *Jokes and Their Relation to the Unconscious* (London: Hogarth Press, 1960), 42–45.

4.   Freud, *Jokes and Their Relation,* 102.

5.   During his periodic visits to Padua, Petrarch lived in a small house adjoining the cathedral and university precincts. Pietro da Moglio had moved to the university from Bologna in 1362, and returned to Bologna in 1368; see Arnaldo Foresti, "Pietro da Moglio a Padova e la sua amicizia col Petrarca e col Boccaccio," *L'Archiginnasio* 15 (1920): 163–73, and Ernest Hatch Wilkins, *Petrarch's Later Years* (Cambridge: Medieval Academy of America, 1959), 47–48 and 178. Lombardo della Seta (?–1390) was an independent scholar who introduced himself to Petrarch in 1368 and completed *De viris illustribus* after the poet's death; see Giuseppina Ferrante, "Lombardo della Seta, Umaninsta padovano," *Istituto veneziano di scienze, lettere, ed arti: Atti* 93 (1933–34): 445–87; and Wilkins, *Later Years,* 160–65, 292–302. Giovanni de' Dondi (1330–89) constructed a celebrated mechanical clock at Padua and later a planetarium at Pavia; see Vincenzo Bellemo, *Jacopo e Giovanni de' Dondi* (Chioggia: Duse, 1894); and Wilkins, *Later Years,* 166, 186–87, 194–97. Before Petrarch's time, the University of Padua was particularly noted for the study of law and rhetoric; its faculty included Rolandino da Padova after 1260, Lovato Lovati in the late thirteenth century, Giovanni d'Andrea in 1307–9, and Albertino Mussato in 1315. Its faculty of medicine and natural philosophy included Dino del Garbo in 1300 and Pietro d'Abano (a teacher of Marsilio of Padua) in 1307–15. See J. K. Hyde, *Padua in the Age of Dante* (Manchester: Manchester University Press, 1966); Nancy Siraisi, *Arts and Science at Padua: The Studium of Padua before 1350* (Toronto: Pontifical Institute of Medieval Studies, 1973); Paul Oskar Kristeller, "Umanesimo e scholasticismo a Padova fino al Petrarca," *Studies in Renaissance Thought and Letters IV* (Rome: Edizioni di storia e letteratura, 1996), 11–26; and Ronald G. Witt, *In the Footsteps of the Ancients: The Origins of Humanism from Lovato to Bruni* (Boston: Brill, 2000).

6.   Only one passage in *De ignorantia* refers to Averroes (twice in two paragraphs, 322–23, to be cited below). Another passage offers a mocking parody of certain philosophers whose mania for quantifying "how many hairs a lion has" (238–39), perhaps evokes the Oxford Calculators at Merton College, heirs of William of Ockham's terminist logic. The ensuing examples are con-

ventional, derived from such thirteenth-century encyclopedic texts as Vincent of Beauvais's *Speculum naturale,* Alexander Neckham's *De rerum naturis,* or Bartholomaeus Anglicus's *De proprietatibus rerum.* An allusion to those who fix their eyes on "some god . . . that desires iniquity" (242–43) might evoke William of Ockham's thought experiment about *odium dei.* Petrarch expresses contempt for the Scholastic argument of double truth (300–301) which might validate conflicting claims of philosophy and theology, an argument long since condemned by the bishop of Paris in 1277. Elsewhere the invective alludes briefly to the Pythagorean doctrine of metempsychosis (294–97), the Democritean and Epicurean doctrines of atomism (296–97), and the Aristotelian theory of the eternity of the material world (296–97, 304–11).

7. They are identified in two fifteenth-century glosses, one printed for the first time by Giovanni Degli Agostini in 1752, the other by Emmanuele Cicogna in 1830. See Paul Oskar Kristeller, "Petrarch's Averroists," *Studies in Renaissance Thought and Letters, II* (Rome: Edizioni di Storia e Letteratura, 1985), 209–16; and *De sui ipsius* (ed. Fenzi, 105–7).

8. For the impact of this endowment, see Bruno Nardi, "Letteratura e cultura veneziana del Quattrocento," in *La civiltà veneziana del Quattrocento* (Florence: Sansoni, 1957), 99–146.

9. Donato Albanzani taught grammar at Venice; among his pupils was Giovanni Malpaghini, who became Petrarch's copyist in summer 1364; after 1370, Albanzani volunteered a translation of *De viris illustribus* into Italian. See Wilkins, *Later Years,* 75, 92–93, 117–21, 173, 201; and Carmine Jannaro, "Donato Casentinese, volgarizzatore del Petrarca," *Studi Petrarcheschi* 1 (1948): 185–94.

10. All revisions are carefully noted in Marsh's edition, 480–89, with the translator's gracious acknowledgment of assistance by James Hankins in editing the Latin text.

11. For the economy of trecento Venice, see *Money and Banking in Medieval and Renaissance Venice,* vol. 1, Frederic C. Lane and Reinhold C. Mueller, *Coins and Moneys of Account* (Baltimore: Johns Hopkins University Press, 1985), and vol. 2, Reinhold C. Mueller, *The Venetian Money Market* (Baltimore: Johns Hopkins University Press, 1997), esp. 121–57, 288–358, and 453–87, with specific references to Petrarch's maligners Contarini and Talenti on 19–20, 152–53, 485–87, 576. For its commercial revolution in the fourteenth century, see Peter Spufford, *Power and Profit: The Merchant in Medieval Europe* (London: Thames and Hudson, 2002), 228–85. For its sociological composition, see Elisabeth Crouzet-Pavan, *Venice Triumphant: The Horizons of a Myth,* trans. Lydia G. Cochrane (Baltimore: Johns Hopkins University Press, 2002), 229–71.

12. See Kristeller, "Curriculum," 86. For a protohumanist emphasis on subjectivity in late-medieval Augustinian, Dominican, and Franciscan schools, see Richard Southern, *Scholastic Humanism and the Unification of Europe*, 3 vols. (Oxford: Blackwell, 1995–2001).

13. The fictive date of the discussion is 76 BCE. Its participants are C. Velleius the Epicurean, Q. Lucilius Balbus the Stoic, and C. Aurelius Cotta, the Neoplatonist Academic, who suspends judgment on both. See Cicero, *The Nature of the Gods*, trans. P. G. Walsh (Oxford: Clarendon, 1997).

14. For Petrarch's *theologica poetica* in *De ignorantia*, see Charles Trinkaus, *The Poet as Philosopher* (New Haven: Yale University Press, 1979), 91–113.

15. Petrarch, *Invective contra medicum* (trans. Marsh, 14–15), from Hugh of Saint-Victor's *Didascalion*, as cited in Marsh's notes (492).

16. See Alfred Ernout and Antoine Meillet, *Dictionnaire étymologique de la langue latine* (Paris: Klincksieck, 1932), 671–73.

17. Petrarch draws his account from Suetonius *Divus Augustus* 86.1–5, where Augustus criticizes Maecenas and Marc Antony for their convoluted styles, as noted by Marsh (*Invective contra medicum*, 510, n. 105).

18. He declines to say how much Greek he really knows, which is actually very little, perceptibly attested by his faulty transcription of ΜΕΤΕΜΨΙΚΟΣΙΣ (for the correct ΜΕΤΕΜΨΥΧΟΣΙΣ), 294–95.

19. Basing his example upon a misreading in medieval manuscripts of Seneca *Epistulae* 38.43, Petrarch identifies the author of this claim as the philosopher Pythagoras rather than the rhetorician Protagoras.

20. For Petrarch's sense of such colloquy, see Nancy Struever, *Theory as Practice: Ethical Inquiry in the Renaissance* (Chicago: University of Chicago Press, 1992), 7–56; and Carol Everhart Quillan, *Rereading the Renaissance: Petrarch, Augustine, and the Language of Humanism* (Ann Arbor: University of Michigan Press, 1998), 106–81.

21. Zeno used the word to amuse his Roman students who included Cotta, Cicero, and Atticus; see Philip B. Corbett, *The Scurra* (Edinburgh: Edinburgh University Press, 1986), 27ff.

22. For evolving communities of readership, see Erich Auerbach, *Literary Language and Its Public in Late Latin Antiquity and in the Middle Ages*, trans. Ralph Manheim (Princeton: Princeton University Press, 1965), 275–338.

Chapter Eighteen

1. The Latin text is taken from Enrico Bianchi's partial edition included in Petrarch, *Rime, Trionfi e poesie latine*, ed. F. Neri, G. Martellotti, E. Bianchi, N. Sapegno, La letteratura italiana: Storia e Testi, 6 (Milan and Naples: Riccardo Ricciardi Editore, 1951), 705–805. For the *Epystole* not present in this

edition, I used, with slight corrections in spelling and punctuation, *Poemata minora quae exstant omnia / Poesie minori del Petrarca,* ed. Domenico Rossetti, vols. 2–3 (Milan: Società Tipografica dei Classici Italiani, 1831–34). Unless otherwise noted, translations are mine.

2. For comprehensive and updated information on the manuscript tradition, title, and dating of the work's publication, see Michele Feo, "Francesco Petrarca," in *Storia della letteratura italiana,* ed. Enrico Malato, (Rome: Salerno, 2001), 10:294–96. For the dates and addressees of the single letters, Ernest H. Wilkins's "manual," *The "Epistolae metricae" of Petrarch* (Rome: Edizioni di Storia e Letteratura, 1956), remains valuable. A critical edition by Michele Feo is expected soon. See also Feo's attentive but somewhat labored presentation of the muddled picture of the various (mostly incorrect) proposals advanced for the title: "Fili petrarcheschi," *Rinascimento* 19 (1979): 3–26. The one commonly used in modern times, *Epistole metrice* is not, however, without a basis in Petrarch's writings, as Feo himself shows (12).

3. Petrarch, *Petrarch's Lyric Poems,* ed. and trans. by Robert M. Durling (Cambridge: Harvard University Press, 1976), 36, emphasis added.

4. Petrarch, *Poemata minora* (ed. Rossetti), 2:208. To translate is to interpret. In this case it is possible to err. Is the writer saying that he has *really* tamed his flesh? This is what Vinicio Pacca thinks (*Petrarca* [Rome and Bari: Editori Laterza, 1998], 148). He translates "domata finalmente la carne." *Vix* can hardly mean *finally,* but it could express temporality, an action immediately preceding another: "*as soon as, once* I have tamed my flesh." The early nineteenth-century translator, Giuseppe Adorni, is correct when he writes "Domata *a stento* la mia carne," in Petrarch, *Poemata minora* (ed. Rossetti), 2:204.

5. See Feo, *Fili petrarcheschi,* 45, for this farewell implying the author's ultimate responsibility for the organization of the work in its entirety. Enrico Carrara, quoting the very same verses (3.34.39–40) had in 1935 already acutely made this point (*Enciclopedia italiana,* 27:15).

6. Adequate attention has not been paid to the fact that Giovanni Boccaccio, in copying *Epystole* 1.14 in his notebook (Florence, Biblioteca Medicea Laurenziana, MS 29.8, fol. 72r–v), gives for its date 1340. Only this early date can explain the epistle's echoes in the famous description of the Black Death at the beginning of the *Decameron.* See Giuseppe Velli, "Il *De Vita et moribus domini Francisci Petracchi de Florentia* del Boccaccio e la biografia del Petrarca," *MLN* 102 (1987): 32–39, esp. 34.

7. Enrico Fenzi's assumption that the writer, in *Epystole* 2.18, is indulging in a metaphor implying the composition of *Africa* is hardly justified by the text. See Petrarch, *Il mio segreto,* ed. Enrico Fenzi (Milan: Mursia, 1992), 33–37.

The poem is the main subject up to v. 15, with the poet's expected conclusion that the glory coming from it is vain. Then, the *cura secunda* (the second commitment), *the house*, equally strong (*par*) takes over: "Cura secunda domus michi par. . . ." The distinction is clear. In her edition and translation of Petrarch, *L'Afrique* 1338–1374 (Grenoble: Éditions Jérôme Millon, 2002), 29–35). Rebecca Lenoir picks up what could be at most a hypothesis and makes an allegory out of Fenzi's metaphor, giving free play to unbridled considerations (see her "interpretation" of the *rimula* [small crack] in a wall). The translation of the entire epistle (29–31) is not faultless.

8. *Petrarch at Vaucluse: Letters in Verse and Prose,* trans. Ernest Hatch Wilkins (Chicago: University of Chicago Press, 1958), 8.

9. Ibid., 10.

10. *The Letters of Machiavelli,* trans. Allan Gilbert (New York: Capricorn Books, 1961), 142, emphasis added.

11. Christian Bec uses E. R. Curtius's topos in the chapter "Dal Petrarca al Machiavelli: Il dialogo tra lettore ed autore," first published in *Rinascimento* 16 (1976): 3–19, and then in his volume *Cultura e società a Firenze nell'età del Rinascimento* (Rome: Salerno, 1981), 228–44. His reference to Curtius has no relevant hermeneutic effectiveness. This is true not only for the afterlife of the Petrarchesque formulations of the theme but also for their sources, which may be different depending on their specific stylistic form. To recur to the anonymous and impersonal topos is of little use, but identifying the actual "readings" behind Petrarch's individual passages is important (Let me say that Seneca has a central position: *De brevitate vitae* 14–15; *Ad Lucillum* 62.67.104). That Machiavelli could not have known *Epystole* because "uscite a stampa più tardi" (they were printed later)—Bec relies on E. Scarpa—is a useless statement. Apart from the fact that Machiavelli might have had access to the manuscript tradition, *Epystole* are included in the Venetian editions of 1501 and 1503.

12. Petrarch, *Prose,* ed. G. Martellotti, P. G. Ricci, E. Carrara, and E. Bianchi (Milan and Naples: Ricciardi, 1955), 16.

13. Petrarch, *Rime, Trionfi e poesie latine,* 764. On his return to *Africa* and on the composition of the entire proem (1, vv. 1–70) which indeed took place in Selvapiana and Parma, see Giuseppe Velli, "Il proemio dell'*Africa*," in *Petrarca e Boccaccio: Tradizione—memoria—scrittura,* 2nd ed. (Padua: Antenore, 1995), 47–59.

14. *Petrarch's Lyric Poems* (trans. Durling), 504, reformatted and corrected.

15. Lucan *De bello civili (Pharsalia),* trans. J. D. Duff (1928; repr., Cambridge: Harvard University Press, 1969). Concerning the presence of Lucan in Petrarch's Latin works (not exclusively in *Africa*) and in his vernacular compo-

sitions, see the index of my *Petrarca e Boccaccio*. A mere hint at the constrictive strength of tradition: vv. 402–403 of Lucan "Hunc [lucum] non ruricolae Panes nemorumque potentes /Silvani Nymphaeque tenent" [No rural Pan dwelt there, no Silvanus, ruler of the woods, no Nymphs], are the opposite of Virgil, *Aeneid* 8.314 (*clausola*): "Haec nemora indigenae Fauni *Nymphaeque tenebant*" [In these woodlands native Fauns and Nymphs once dwelt]. *Aeneid*, *in Eclogues, Georgics, Aeneid, the Minor Poems*, trans. H. R. Fairclough (1916; repr., Cambridge: Harvard University Press, 1986).

16. Virgil *Catalepton* 14.1–4 in *Eclogues, Georgics, Aeneid, the Minor Poems*, 2:507–9.

17. Cf. the chapter "La memoria poetica del Petrarca" in my *Petrarca e Boccaccio*, 35–36.

18. Ovid, *Remedies for Love*, in *The Art of Love and Other Poems*, trans. J. H. Mozley (1929; repr., Cambridge: Harvard University Press, 2004), 191.

19. The rhetorician Claudian was much loved by Petrarch, who probably owned more than one manuscript of his works. One manuscript is extant (Paris, Bibliothèque nationale, MS Par. Lat. 8082), rich in *notabilia* and glosses of that exceptional reader. For the presence of Claudian in the works of Petrarch see Velli, *Petrarca e Boccaccio*, particularly 22–23n., 68, 68n.

20. Claudian, *In Rufinum*, in *Claudian*, trans. Maurice Platnauer (1922; repr., Cambridge: Harvard University Press, 1963), 41.

21. Note the different position of the verb; the anaphora *horridus hunc; rusticus hunc* (*Epystole* 2.16.41–42), but discontinued in 43 where the third subject *custos* is at the very end of the hexameter; the recurrence of the *r* for 'low' subject matter (*r*usticus—*r*ast*r*is.), doubled only once ("ho*rr*idus")—because Petrarch tends to avoid *rr* within a context, even a large one, where it is frequent. For his proposed correction in *Africa* 3.446, see Vincenzo Fera, *La revisione petrarchesca dell'Africa* (Messina: Centro di Studi umanistici, 1984), 105.

22. Torquato Tasso, *Gerusalemme liberata*, ed. Anna Maria Carini (Milan: Feltrinelli, 1961), 13.3.1–8; reprinted on-line at http://www.liberliber.it. Compare Tasso's "(né) guida *bifolco* mai, guida *pastore*" with Petrarch's "né *pastori* appressavan né *bifolci*"; and Tasso's "ma lunge passa e la *dimostra a dito*" with Petrarch's "*digito*que hunc *signat* . . . custos." The connections are indisputable. For the *Fortleben* of Tasso's passage, see, for example, Giambattista Marino, *La strage de gl'innocenti* 1.15, "correr *bifolci* poi correr *pastori*"; where the substantives (in the plural) come from Petrarch, but Tasso's subtler influence is felt at the "musical" level (doubling of the same verb; the rhythm of the hendecasyllable).

23. Torquato Tasso, *Jerusalem Delivered*, trans. by Joseph Tusiani (Rutherford: Fairleigh Dickinson University Press, 1970), 287.

Chapter Nineteen

1. The edition of record is Paul Piur, *Petrarcas 'Buch ohne Namen' und di päpstliche Kurie: Ein Beitrag zur Geistesgeschichte der Frührenaissance* (Halle and Saale: Max Niemeyer, 1925). Petrarch, *Sine nomine: Lettere polemiche e politiche*, ed. Ugo Dotti (Bari: Laterza, 1974), follows Piur's text. An English translation is Norman P. Zacour, *Petrarch's Book without a Name: A Translation of the "'Liber Sine nomine'"* (Toronto: Pontifical Institute of Medieval Studies, 1973). Nine letters are translated into English in Robert Coogan, *Babylon on the Rhone* (Potomac: Studia humanitatis, 1983). References to the *Familiar Letters* are to *Le familiari* (*Rerum familiarum libri* 24), ed. Vittorio Rossi, 4 vols., Florence: Sansoni, 1933–42 [Edizione nazionale, vols. 10–13]; references to the *Rerum vulgarium fragmenta* are to Petrarch, *Canzoniere*, ed. Marco Santagata, 2nd ed. (Milan: Mondadori, 1997); for the *Variae*, see Petrarch, *Lettere disperse, varie, e miscellanee*, ed. Alessandro Pancheri (Guanda: Parma, 1994).

2. For the writing and arrangement, see Petrarch *Sine nomine* (ed. Piur, 147–60); Ernest Hatch Wilkins, *Studies in the Life and Works of Petrarch* (Cambridge: Medieval Academy of America, 1955), 81–181, esp. 179–81; Ernest Hatch Wilkins, *Petrarch's Eight Years in Milan* (Cambridge: Medieval Academy of America, 1958), 48–49, 166–67, 179, 184, 202; and *Petrarch's Book without a Name* (trans. Zacour), 19–23. Translations are mine unless otherwise noted.

3. Marco Ariani, *Petrarca* (Naples: Sellerio, 2000), 188. Another recent account is Vinicio Pacca, *Petrarca* (Bari: Laterza, 1998), 140–43.

4. For the manuscripts, see Petrarch *Sine nomine* (ed. Piur, 241–90). The name of the collection is discussed by Michele Feo in "Fili petrarcheschi," *Rinascimento* 19 (1979): 3–89, esp. 22–23.

5. *Sine nomine, praefatio* (ed. Piur, 164).

6. See *Sine nomine* 11 (ed. Piur, 204). In terms of *ars dictaminis*, Petrarch's letters include intrinsic parts from exordium to conclusion but lack the extrinsic *allocutio* or address and the signature or seal, *communitio*. These are essential for several theorists (see Emil J. Polak, *A Textual Study of Jacques de Dinant's Summa dictaminis* [Geneva: Droz, 1975]: 67, 124–25), without them the letter does not transmit the writer's thoughts to a remote addressee, as its definition requires.

7. See *Familiares* 24.13.6 ("I have uprooted from the order of these [the *Familiares*] other similar writings that remain to me, which will make up another volume"); other references to the *Sine nomine* in the *Familiares* are at 15.12.2 and 20.6.2; they appear to establish the dating of the first (1353) and second (1359–60) versions of the *Sine nomine*. Petrarch assembled the first, twenty-book collection of the *Familiares* in 1359.

8. See *Sine nomine* 2 (ed. Piur, 167): "those very words, which might have soft-

ened hearts of marble, were torn up and scattered . . . Your courier was captured at the Durance, tortured, whipped, forbidden entrance to the city and sent off with threats, bruises, and blows, returning to your feet with bloodied head."

9. Petrarch *Sine nomine* (ed. Dotti, 2); see *Familiares* 21.1.2: "I long ago fashioned and composed many things . . . when I go from here, they will break out from their concealment and show me to have been a disciple of the truth, though hidden for fear of the Jews" (cf. John 16:19).

10. See Petrarch's *praefatio* (ed. Piur, 164): "if anyone judges that they should be erased or separated out, they can more easily uproot a part of the work without disfiguring the whole."

11. Vergerio included parts of six letters; see Coogan, *Babylon on the Rhone,* 14–15.

12. Piur's edition depends on over forty manuscripts of the collection, partial or complete, between the late trecento and the late quattrocento; all identify the work as Petrarch's (see *Sine nomine,* ed. Piur, 244–90).

13. Petrarch *Sine nomine praefatio* (ed. Piur, 164): "If, as the satirist pleases to say, it is safe for the living to talk about the dead, surely it is safer for the dead to talk about the living." For the citation, see Juvenal, *Satire,* ed. and trans. Luca Canali (Milan: Rizzoli, 1976), 1.162.

14. Petrarch *Sine nomine* 6 (ed. Piur, 190–91): "I shall write, truth will dictate, the whole human race will bear witness; Posterity, you be the judge, unless you are deaf to our ills because of your own!"

15. Petrarch *Sine nomine* 19 (ed. Piur, 237); for *Sine nomine* 11 (ed. Piur, 204): "you know who I am, and you recognize my voice." In *Sine nomine* 4 (ed. Piur, 181), Petrarch, made a Roman citizen at his coronation, writes, "I add this, that it is a Roman citizen who speaks."

16. For Petrarch's "grandiose" self, see Pierre Blanc, "Petrarca ou la poétique de l'ego: Éléments de psychopoétique pétrarquienne," *Revue des Études Italiennes* 29 (1983): 122–69, esp. 144.

17. For the dates of individual letters, some highly conjectural, see Petrarch *Sine nomine* (ed. Piur, 313–407), passim; Wilkins, *Studies in the Life of Petrarch,* idem, *Petrarch's Eight Years in Milan;* and Petrarch *Sine nomine* (ed. Dotti), passim.

18. For the chronology, see Wilkins, *Studies in the Life of Petrarch,* 179–81, but see esp. note 106. *Sine nomine* 5–13, written, except for letter 12, from late 1351 to spring of 1352, were ordered as follows (digits represent the letter's place in the likely chronological order): 7, 9, 8, 10, 11, 6, 5, 13. See Dotti in *Sine nomine* (ed. Dotti), xxx–xxxi.

19. Petrarch *Sine nomine* 7 (ed. Piur, 192); see also 5 (ed. Piur, 185): "I was happier in my Italian Helicon"; 6 (ed. Piur, 188, 190): "Give back Nero, I beg, give back Domitian"; "Do you think I lack subjects for a tragic poem?"

20. *Sine nomine* 5 (ed. Piur, 185): "Now I am held by the Gallic world, by western Babylon."

21. *Sine nomine* 10 (ed. Piur, 196–97), begins: "You will be amazed at the sub-scripts (*subscriptiones*) to my letters," referring to signing the previous letter "written, full of indignation, by the waters of Babylon."

22. Babylon appears in *Sine nomine* 14 (ed. Piur, 211): "who I ask you would not flee from Babylon?" Other references in *Sine nomine* 17 (ed. Piur, 220, 227); 18 (ed. Piur, 228); and seven other uses; 19 (ed. Piur, 235). The last three letters were all likely written to Francesco Nelli, though the latter two are fictional letters never sent. See E. H. Wilkins, *Studies* 192–212, and idem, "A Survey of the Correspondence between Petrarch and Francesco Nelli," *Italia Medioevale e Umanistica* 1 (1958): 351–58.

23. See *Sine nomine* 9 (ed. Piur, 196): "Under this burden of persecution enslaved Italy sighs in our time" [*serva . . . suspirat Italia*]. The end of *Sine nomine* 8 and beginning of *Sine nomine* 9 are closely linked verbally (ed. Piur, 195): "it is unseemly for a man to want (*velle*) what just now he spurned (*nolit*)"; and "There are two kinds of persecution: one we endure unwillingly [*nolentes*], the other willingly (*volentes*)."

24. *Sine nomine* 13 (ed. Piur, 208).

25. *Sine nomine* 14 (ed. Piur, 214): "See Rome, Milan, Venice . . . only do not look upon Babylon; do not descend living into the Inferno." *Sine nomine* 15 (ed. Piur, 216): "If not snatched away by God (*nisi Deus eripiat*), who could escape from here?" *Sine nomine* 16 (ed. Piur, 216): "reditus tuus, namque ire in patriam redire est" (translated in the text).

26. *Sine nomine* (ed. Piur, 234) notes that Dedalus is said to have "swum" as he flew (*enatavit*) in Virgil *Aeneid* 6.16; Deucalion, escaping the flood, swims (*enatavit*) in *Sine nomine* 11 (ed. Piur, 203).

27. "viventium infernus" (the hell of the living; *Sine nomine* 8 [ed. Piur, 195]) de-rives from Psalm 54.16; *evasimus* is also used anaphorically of Petrarch's and Gherardo's escapes from youthful error in Avignon, *Familiares* 10.3.39–40. *enatasti* and *evasisti* also echo the first of the *Sine nomine* (ed. Piur, 166): "see if there is any raft fit for swimming with (*enatandum tabula*), so that holding it we may escape to the dry land (*in siccum evadamus*)."

28. Virgil *Aeneid* 6.128: "sed revocare gradum superasque *evadere* ad auras"; also *Sine nomine* (ed. Piur, 365, 370–71): "*eripe* me his, invicte, malis . . ." (empha-ses added).

29. In numerous passages, Petrarch grafts Palinurus's plea to be snatched from Acheron into Hades with pleas to Christ for the soul's rescue from Hell ("a porta inferni erue me, domine," 2nd Nocturns of Matins in the Office of the Dead) and for the liberation of the just from Limbo, as narrated in the

Gospel of Nicodemus; see especially *Familiares* 23.12, quoted in Petrarch, *Secretum*, ed. Enrico Fenzi (Milan: Mursia, 1992), 308; see also *Canzoniere* 214 (ed. Santagata), vv. 28–29, and *Seniles* 16.8.

30. Petrarch *Sine nomine* 19 (ed. Piur, 237).

31. For Petrarch's use of invective, see Franco Suitner, "L'invettiva antiavignonese del Petrarca e la poesia infamante medievale," in *Studi Petrarcheschi,* n.s., 2 (1985): 201–10; see also Emilio Pasquini, "Il mito polemico di Avignone nei poeti italiani del Trecento," in *Aspetti culturali della società italiana nel periodo del papato avignonese* (Todi: Accademia Tudertina, 1981), 257–309, esp. 270–87. For the rhetoric of medieval invective and satire, see also Maurizio Perugi, "Il sordello di Dante e la tradizione mediolatina dell'invettiva," in *Studi Danteschi* 55 (1983): 23–135; and Hugo Kindermann, *Satyra: Die Theorie der Satire im Mittellateinischen Vorstudie zu einer Gattungsgeschichte* (Nurenberg: Hans Carl, 1978).

32. Horace *Sermones* 1.4.39–42; Kindermann, *Satyra,* 24, cites a twelfth-century *accessus* to Juvenal that prescribes verse for satire, prose for invective.

33. Martellotti's suggestion, reported in Feo, "Fili petrarcheschi," 23, that the *titulus Sine nomine* attests to a reluctance to pin down the collection with a title, offers some guidance.

34. See *Canzoniere* (ed. Santagata), 133–35, and Santagata's notes; on the *Epystole* to Nelli, see Wilkins, *Studies in the Life of Petrarch,* 193–204.

35. In Martianus Capella (*De nuptiis* 1.2, cited in Kindermann, *Satyra,* 26), Petrarch could have found the Roman comic formula used to applaud satire.

36. Petrarch *Sine nomine, praefatio* (ed. Piur, 164): "this idea led me . . . to write the *Bucolicum carmen,* an obscure kind of poem (*poematis genus ambigui*) which though understood by few might possibly please many."

37. *Sine nomine* 6 (ed. Piur, 190): "do you think I lack a subject for a tragic poem (*tragico carmine*)? . . . the Linen books will agree with the annals . . . You need no other work of tragedy or history."

38. *Sine nomine* 3 (ed. Piur, 172): " a formal debate was held on the question: would it not be best for the world if the city of Rome and Italy were united and at peace?"

39. See *Sine nomine* (ed. Dotti), 88, 126–32.

40. Petrarch *Sine nomine* 17 (ed. Piur, 221): "With all their strength they drag him again and again to Calvary–scoffed at, naked, helpless, scourged—and to blasphemous applause they affix him once again to the cross."

41. Isidore of Seville, cited in Kindermann, *Satyra:* "They are called satirists (*Satyrici*) . . . because their fullness and abundance means they speak at once of many things; or because of that platter (*lance*) that crammed with various fruits and produce was borne to pagan temples; or the name was taken from

the satyrs (*Satyris*), who hold pardonable what is said because of drunkenness" (31–37, quotation from 31).

42. Dotti in *Sine nomine* (ed. Dotti), xxxiv–xxxv; see also Ariani, *Petrarca*, 187.

43. John Wrigley, "A Rehabilitation of Clement VI," *Archivum historiae pontificiae* 3 (1965): 127–38, makes an elaborate case for the adulterous couple as Louis of Taranto and Joanna I of Spain, not Clement VI and the Vicountess of Turenne, as argued by the abbé de Sade.

44. Juvenal *Satura* 1.160: ". . . digito compesce labellum"; cf. *Sine nomine* 19 (ed. Piur, 238), citing Job 39:34–35.

45. Juvenal *Satura* 1.52–54: "Heracleas aut Diomedeas aut mugitum labyrinthi/et mare percussum puero fabrumque volantem" [the exploits of Hercules or Diomedes, or the bellowing of the labyrinth, or the sea struck by the boy, or the flying craftsman . . .].

46. Juvenal *Satura* 1.79–80: "Si natura negat, facit indignatio versum/qualemcumque potest" [If nature holds back, it is outrage itself that, as best it may, drives me to verses]. See Ariani, *Petrarca*, 187; Kindermann, *Satyra*, 76, 118.

47. Giuseppe Velli, "Il Dante di Francesco Petrarca," in *Studi Petrarcheschi*, n.s. 2 (1985): 185–99, esp. 190–92; see also Giuseppe Billanovich, *Petrarca letterato I. Lo scrittoio del Petrarca* (Rome, 1947), 165–66; Pasquini, "Il mito polemico di Avignone"; Perugi, "Il sordello di Dante," 87–97; Suitner, "L'invettiva antiavignonese del Petrarca."

48. See Perugi, "Il sordello di Dante," 81–108.

49. For this aspect of Lamentations commentary, see Ronald L. Martinez, "Mourning Beatrice: The Rhetoric of Threnody in the *Vita nuova*," *MLN* 113 (1998): 1–29 and idem, "Lament and Lamentation in *Purgatorio* and the Role of Dante's Statius," *Dante Studies* 117 (1997): 46–82.

50. See Petrarch *Sine nomine* (ed. Piur, 168); that this passage also echoes Dante, *Purgatorio* 6.76–78 is noted by Kenelm Foster, *Petrarch, Poet and Humanist* (Edinburgh: Edinburgh University Press, 1984), 11–12. See *Sine nomine* 2 (ed. Piur, 168): "Is this the way you honor your mistress (*dominam*) Rome? . . . Do you not know the origins of the name 'Provençe' (Provincie nomen)? . . . Is this the way your revere the mistress of the Provinces (*provinciarum dominam*)?"

51. See *Sine nomine* (ed. Piur, 196); there are some ten passages, including six from Dante's *Purgatorio* 6 and political epistles (5–7, 11); only four, all previously identified, are registered in Marco Baglio, "Presenze dantesche nel Petrarca latino," *Studi Petrarcheschi* 9 (1992): 77–137, esp. 134–36.

52. See *Sine nomine* 18 (ed. Piur, 230): "Now rejoice, Babylon, rejoice at least for being the opposite of the mistress of virtues . . ."

53. Ezio Raimondi, "Un esercizio satirico del Petrarca," in *Metafora e Storia* (Turin: Einaudi, 1970), 189–208. All the letters to Nelli include a narrative

anecdote of some kind, another distinguishing feature of the letters added in the late fifties.

54. Petrarch *Sine nomine* 18 (ed. Piur, 234): "And just like the Psyche of Lucius Apuleius, to be honored in happy marriage, she enters the chamber of a man unknown to her."

55. *Sine nomine* 18 (ed. Piur, 234–35).

56. Similar spousal (and adultery) metaphors are found in Petrarch's *Bucolicum carmen* 6.149–157, describing simoniacal "adultery" (cf. Dante *Inferno* 19.3), and the subsequent infidelities of the Avignon harlot.

57. For Guido da Pisa, Dante is not only a comic and lyric poet but "a satirist, too, on account of the reproaches he makes of vices and the recommendations to virtue; and a tragedian as well, because of the great deeds of high personages that he narrates" (my trans.); see Guido da Pisa, *Expositiones et glose super Comediam Dantis facte per Fratrem Guidonem Pisanum*, ed. Vincenzo Cioffari (Albany: State University of New York Press, 1974).

Chapter Twenty

1. Petrarch, *Lettere disperse, varie e miscellanee,* ed. Alessandro Pancheri (Parma: Guanda, 1994), 78–80 (*Lettere disperse* 9): "litteras tuas, que istinc ad nos ueniunt, non extimes apud eos, quibus destinantur, permanere, sed confestim ab omnibus tanta sedulitate transcribi tantoque studio per aulas Pontificum circumferri, quasi non ab homine nostri generis, sed a superis uel antipodibus misse sint." Translations are mine unless otherwise noted.

2. Barbato's letter is quoted and dated by Marco Vattasso, *Del Petrarca e di alcuni suoi amici* (Rome: Tipografia Vaticana, 1904), 13–14: "nedum prolixas epistolas, sed fragmenta tui eloquij undecumque possum querito. . . ." This responded to Petrarch's letter, "Aliquotiens, Barbate, queri soleo" (*Familiares* 22.4).

3. Petrarch *Lettere disperse* (ed. Pancheri), 268 (*Lettere disperse* 33): "eadem amicitie vis compellet, que te adeo solicitum ardentemque coacervandis opusculis meis fecit, que ut memoras, ab innumeris et mirum in modum patria, moribus ac professione distantibus mendicasti. . . . michi propter perseverantiam admiratio quotidie recens est, quod ita nichil affectui tuo detrahat cuncta consumens etas." On Barbato's passion for Petrarch's writing, see also *Lettere disperse* 5 and *Lettere disperse* 51.

4. In addition to the *Familiares* and *Seniles,* Petrarch grouped nineteen letters together in the *Liber sine nomine.* The letters were explicitly excluded from the *Familiares* because they were too controversial, so much so that Petrarch did not want them published until after his death. The letters in the three collections together number about five hundred.

5. Vittorio Rossi, "Un archetipo abbandonato di epistole di Petrarca," in *Studi sul Petrarca e sul Rinascimento*, ed. Vittorio Rossi (Florence: Sansoni, 1930), 176. See, for example, also Giorgio Pasquali, *Storia della tradizione e critica del testo* (Florence: Le Monnier, 1952), 458, 64; Aldo S. Bernardo, "Letter-Splitting in Petrarch's *Familiares*," *Speculum* 33, no. 2 (1958): 236–41; and below, n. 7.

6. For the 350 *Familiares*, for instance, Silvia Rizzo estimates that an original version exists for less than one-quarter (or about eighty-eight); ("Il latino del Petrarca nelle *Familiari*," in *The Uses of Greek and Latin*, ed. A. C. Dionisotti, Anthony Grafton, and Jill Kraye [London: Warburg Institute, 1988], 53). For an early list of precanonical versions of these letters, see Paul Piur, "Die Korrespondenz Petrarcas," in *Briefwechsel des Cola di Rienzo*, vol. 2, ed. Konrad Burdach and Paul Piur (Berlin: Weidmannsche Buchhandlung, 1928), 133–34.

7. Vittorio Rossi described Petrarch's general procedure in refining his letters: after drafting the letter and making additions, subtractions, and corrections, he had two copies of the letter made, the *transmissiva* to send to his addressee and the *transciptio in ordine* to keep for himself. Petrarch did not, however, unerringly follow this procedure. See Rossi, "Un archetipo," 175.

8. In the mid-nineteenth century, Giuseppe Fracassetti issued the first large compilation of letters extraneous to the structured prose letter collections. From manuscript and printed sources, Fracassetti published sixty-five of these extraneous letters as *Epistolae variae* and included eight more in an *Appendix litterarum:* Francisci Petarcae, *Epistolae de rebus familiaribus et variae*, ed. Giuseppe Fracassetti (Florence: Le Monnier, 1859–1863), 3:309–536. Of these seventy-three letters, twelve have since been excluded, but the sixty-one others form the most important nucleus of the *Lettere disperse*. In 1962, E. H. Wilkins and Giuseppe Billanovich collected and published other extraneous letters and letter fragments as *"Miscellaneous letters"* in "The Miscellaneous Letters of Petrarch," *Speculum* 37, no. 2 (1962): 226–43. With only two exceptions, the seventy-six letters in the modern edition of the *Lettere disperse*, edited by Alessandro Pancheri, were first collected as *variae* or *miscellaneae*. The exceptions are the letter that begins "Invitus ducur" (*Lettere disperse* 37), published in 1991 by Giovanna Rao in Michele Feo, ed., *Codici latini del Petrarca nelle biblioteche fiorentine* (Florence: Le Lettere, 1991), 474–79; and the "D'Orville letter" (*Lettere disperse* 61), published in 1974 by Nicholas Mann as "'O Deus, qualis epistola!' A New Petrarch Letter," in *Italia medioevale e umanistica* 17 (1974): 242–43. Pancheri's edition is now the key reference work for study of the *Disperse*, where the various provenances of the letters are discussed in the textual note, xxvii–xxxiv.

9. Mikhail Bakhtin writes, for instance, that "the letter, like a rejoinder in a di-

alogue, is addressed to a specific person, and it takes into account the other's possible reactions, the other's possible reply." *Problems of Dostoevsky's Poetics* (Ann Arbor: Ardis, 1973), 205.

10. Giles Constable, "Letters and Letter-Collections," *Typologie des sources du moyen âge occidental* 17 (1976): 11.

11. Although there are some exceptions (including the Viscontean letters, discussed below), Petrarch largely spurned the rigid rules of composition of the *ars dictaminis* and embraced the more open and personal style of expression of classical letter writing. See, for example, Ronald Witt, "Medieval 'Ars Dictaminis' and the Beginnings of Humanism: A New Construction of the Problem," *Renaissance Quarterly* 35, no. 1 (1982): 1–35, especially 28–35; and Ronald Witt, *In the Footsteps of the Ancients: The Origins of Humanism from Lovato to Bruni* (Leiden: Brill, 2000), 230–91.

12. Pancheri, introduction, xvii. As Pancheri explains, since Petrarch wrote many more letters than he could include in his planned collections, many of the *lettere disperse* (along with the hundreds or thousands of other letters that have not survived) were not deliberately rejected as much as they were not chosen. Petrarch several times commented on his nearly obsessive compulsion to write (see, for example, *Familiares* 13.7), and wrote that he burned at least a thousand of his poems and letters (*Familiares* 1.1). See also *Seniles* 16.3.

13. Venice, MS Marciano Lat. XIII 70 = 4309. See Giuseppe Billanovich, *Petrarca letterato. I. Lo scrittoio del Petrarca* (Rome: Edizioni di Storia e Letteratura, 1947), 23; Michele Feo, "Fili petrarcheschi," *Rinascimento*, 2nd ser., 19 (1979): 63.

14. The dating between late 1363 and 1365 is offered by Rossi, "Un archetipo," 184; see also Feo, "Fili," 64.

15. These letters are *Lettere disperse* 45–47 and *Lettere disperse* 55–58. Some of the letters from the codex M were also moved to the *Seniles*. On codex M, see for example Rossi, "Un archetipo"; Billanovich, *Petrarca letterato*, 23–24; Pancheri, introduction, xx–xxii.

16. Petrarch might have removed *Lettere disperse* 46 to Giovanni Boccaccio because it repeated the narration, also found in *Familiares* 21.10, of an injury Petrarch received from an unwieldy Ciceronian codex; the first part of the letter returned, in any case, in amplified form, in *Seniles* 10.2; he might have eliminated *Lettere disperse* 47 as repetitive of *Familiares* 22.4 (Pancheri, introduction, xx).

17. *Lettere disperse* 45 announced publication of a work, *De vita solitaria*, that was not yet ready when Petrarch was having the definitive version of the *Familiares* copied (see Feo, "Fili," 64). *Lettere disperse* 55–57 were eliminated from the final collection because they regarded the copyist of the codex M, who

was not the copyist of the final manuscript (see Rossi, "Un archetipo," 185). *Lettere disperse* 58 discussed Petrarch's plan to donate his codices to found a public library in Venice; although Petrarch still lived in Venice when the final books of the *Familiares* were being transcribed, his decision to exclude this letter seems to Pancheri a sign that he was already contemplating leaving the city (Pancheri, introduction, xxi.)

18. Michele Feo, "L'epistola come mezzo di propaganda politica in Francesco Petrarca," in *Le forme della propaganda politica nel due e nel trecento*, ed. Paolo Cammarosano (Rome: École Française de Rome, 1994), 224. Pancheri's edition names only Bernabò in association with the letter. Cf. *Lettere disperse* (ed. Pancheri), 289.

19. Petrarch *Lettere disperse* (ed. Pancheri), 290: "Tu quidem, quantum intelligi datur, credens forte tibi rem esse cum pueris, multipliciter visus es ut nos ventoso tonitru et verborum inanium fragoribus deterreres. Nos . . . insolentiae tuae minas ac dicta contemnimus, omnino muscularum murmur, ac vanus strepitus non horremus."

20. Feo gives a summary of who does and does not attribute authorship of this letter to Petrarch; by Feo's counts, eleven critics sustain that Petrarch wrote it; two allow that it is probably his; two doubt it; and four deny it. Based on the sources that Feo cites, no critic after Paul Piur in 1933 has denied authorship. See Michele Feo, "Francesco Petrarca e la contesa epistolare tra Markwart e i Visconti," in *Filologia umanistica per Gianvito Resta*, ed. Vincenzo Fera and Giacomo Ferraú (Padua: Antenore, 1997), 683–84. Feo here also provides a critical edition of Markwart and Petrarch's letters.

21. For the string of setbacks that brought Bussolari to extreme measures, see Luisa Vergani-Zamboni, "Per una nuova lettura delle epistole del Petrarca a Iacopo Bussolari," *Filologia e Letteratura* 15, no. 2 (1969): 131–32.

22. Petrarch *Lettere disperse* (ed. Pancheri), 312.

23. Bussolari, and Petrarch's condemnation of him, are matters of historical controversy. Scholars who criticize Petrarch's actions in this episode include Dotti, *Vita di Petrarca* (Rome: Laterza, 1987), 334; Michele Feo, "Nuove petrarchesche," *Belfagor* 46, no. 2 (1991): 151, and idem, "Propaganda," 220. Other historians, in implicit criticism, draw a parallel between Bussolari and Cola di Rienzo, whose struggle for Roman liberty Petrarch passionately supported. See, for instance, Francesco Cognasso, *I Visconti* (Milan: Dall'Oglio, 1966; rpt. 1987), 235. Vittorio Rossi argues, however, that Petrarch at least saw their struggles as fundamentally different and the condemnation of Bussolari as necessary: "Petrarca a Pavia," in *Studi sul Petrarca e sul Rinascimento*, ed. Vittorio Rossi (Florence: Sansoni, 1930), 9.

24. Other troublesome letters among those Petrarch wrote for the Visconti are

those denouncing the captain Pandolfo Malatesta (*Lettere disperse* 37 and 38), who was a friend and correspondent of the poet's; Feo doubts he could have written these letters without "some moral uneasiness" ("Nuove," 151).

25. For a discussion of his friends' reactions, and especially Boccaccio's, see, inter alia, Billanovich, *Petrarca letterato,* 180–86; and Ugo Dotti, *Petrarca a Milano: Documenti milanesi 1353–1354* (Milan: Ceschina, 1972), 51–75.

26. Petrarch *Lettere disperse* (ed. Pancheri), 130: "desueta iugo colla submisi." His freedom was limited enough that he had to obtain permission from the Visconti to leave the city. See the editor's note in Petrarch, *Lettere,* ed. Giuseppe Fracassetti (Florence: Le Monnier, 1863–1867), 3:467.

27. For dating, see Ernest Hatch Wilkins, *Petrarch's Eight Years in Milan* (Cambridge: Mediaeval Academy of America, 1958), 40, with whom Dotti concurs, *Petrarca a Milano,* 67–68.

28. On him, see Ludovico Frati, "Gano di Lapo da Colle e le sue rime," *Il Propugnatore,* n.s., 6, no. 2 (1893): 195–226. His sonnet to Petrarch, which also lauded Petrarch and evidently contrasted Florentine freedom to Milanese tyranny, has not survived.

29. Petrarch *Lettere disperse* (ed. Pancheri), 166: "quod discedat a tyrannide dominorum de Mediolano et accedat ad libertatis locum." The words are from an explanatory note in the manuscript Vat. Barb. Lat. 56, fol. 21r, that precedes Petrarch's letter of response (ibid., 167, n. 5).

30. Ibid., 166: "Sed error facti magna sepe fallit ingenia."

31. Wilkins, *Eight Years,* 69–71.

32. Petrarch *Lettere disperse* (ed. Pancheri), 190: "id enim agis non ut vulgare aliquid, sed ut suprema vitae gaudia, libertatem, solitudinem, otium, silentium, id agis ut laborum ferias, ut tranquillae mentis statum, ut te postremo, ut me mihi restituas." Also in the *dispersa* that follows this one, to Gui de Boulogne, Petrarch expresses hope (vain, as it turned out) that Cabassoles will win his freedom.

33. The dating is from Wilkins, *Eight Years,* 91.

34. Petrarch *Lettere disperse* (ed. Pancheri), 200: "At quotiens ad plebeias atque humiles curas, quas nec stilo dignas putem, aliqua rerum necessitas me attraxerit, plebeium quoque characterem non recuso, ne forte plus operae verbis impendam quam sententiis debeatur."

35. The dating is from Wilkins, *Eight Years.*

36. Petrarch *Lettere disperse* (ed. Pancheri), 318: "omnibus una mens est moram meam his in locis: nisi sat reliquae vitae meae consentaneam probare."

37. Critics differ on what this is: see Wilkins, *Eight Years,* 102; Arnaldo Foresti, *Aneddoti della vita di Francesco Petrarca* (Padua: Antenore, 1977), 523; Dotti, *Vita,* 310–11; *Lettere disperse* (ed. Pancheri), 318, n. 8.

38. Petrarch *Lettere disperse* (ed. Pancheri), 318: "ubi si res meas: non dicam ir-reprehensibiles aut laudabiles: sed tolerabiles excusabilesque: mira vero & illi amico & alijs miratoribus meis siue amantibus siue temptantibus siue ex professo carpentibus puto responsum erit."

39. In *Lettere disperse* 46, again to Boccaccio, Petrarch also pleads the necessity of his choice, since he has no other place to go (*Lettere disperse,* ed. Pancheri, 344).

40. This was the second of three consecutive letters to Nelli on the issue.

41. Dotti, *Petrarca a Milano,* 74–75.

42. Petrarch *Lettere disperse* (ed. Pancheri), 38: "Sed quibus iterum verbis utar in tam repentino tamque inopinato gaudio? Quibus votis exultantis animi motus explicem? Usitata sordescunt, inusitata non audeo."

43. Petrarch *Lettere disperse* (ed. Pancheri), 92 (*Lettere disperse* 10): "uindex libertatis unice." The two letters to Cola in the *Sine nomine,* a collection of letters that Petrarch himself explains were deliberately excluded from the *Familiares,* similarly discuss Cola's revolution at its apex and address Cola in exaltative terms.

44. The surviving letters to Cola thus number seven: the four *disperse;* two in the *Sine nomine;* and one in the *Familiares.* Since Petrarch said he wrote the tribune every day (*Lettere disperse* 9) and that writing to him soothed his worries (*Lettere disperse* 10), we must imagine that these letters represent only a fraction of those actually written.

45. Petrarch, *Le familiari,* ed. Vittorio Rossi (Florence: Sansoni, 1934), 2.110–11: "Mundus ergo te videbit de bonorum duce satellitem reproborum? . . . Immortale decus est, immortalis infamia," translated by Aldo Bernardo as *Letters on Famliar Matters I–VIII* (New York: Italica Press, 2005), 350–51.

46. Petrarch says as much in *Lettere disperse* 8, *Lettere disperse* (ed. Pancheri), 74–75, and *Lettere disperse* 9, *Lettere disperse* (ed. Pancheri), 82–85.

47. Demonstrations of its authenticity in Arnaldo Della Torre, "Aneddoti pe-trarcheschi," *Giornale Dantesco* 16 (1908): 82–88; and Billanovich, *Petrarca letterato,* 257, n. 1, followed by Ernest Hatch Wilkins, *Studies on Petrarch and Boccaccio* (Padua: Antenore, 1978), 126; but Feo expresses some reservation about whether the letter was originally in Italian ("Fili," 56).

48. Petrarch *Lettere disperse* (ed. Pancheri), 366–67: "o' pregato che cerchi alcuni libbri et se forse trovasse cosa alcuna . . . prego che vi piaccia pagare i denari infino a cento fiorini, et terrete i libbri" [I asked him to look for certain books, and if he happens to find any of them . . . I ask that you please pay up to 100 Florins and hold the books.]

49. Horace, *Sermones* 1.9; *Lettere disperse* (ed. Pancheri), 158, n. 6.

50. On Nelli and the correspondence between him and Petrarch, see Henry Co-

chin, *Un amico di Francesco Petrarca: Le lettere del Nelli al Petrarca* (Florence: Le Monnier, 1901).

51. Petrarch *Lettere disperse* (ed. Pancheri), 160: "coenatus . . . solis fabulis."

52. Ibid., 166: "ut ego testificor, lingua, incolumem pervenisse."

53. This same bothersome visitor is mentioned in several other letters among the *Familiares, Lettere disperse,* and *Seniles;* on him, see Foresti, *Aneddoti,* 305–18.

54. Plus two (*Lettere disperse* 10) to unknown correspondents. Only a slight majority of the addressees of the *disperse* were also addressees of the *Familiares, Seniles, Sine nomine,* or the *Epystole.* Compare tables in Petrarch *Lettere* (ed. Fracassetti), 1.153–61, "Indice dei nomi di tutti coloro cui il Petrarca scrisse lettere"; and Alessandro Pancheri, textual note to Petrarch, *Lettere disperse* (ed. Pancheri), xxxiv–xxxvi.

55. Petrarch also wrote Gui de Boulogne independent of his work for the Visconti in *Lettere disperse* 27.

56. The close friendship is also testified by letters to Azzo's natural and legitimate sons, *Lettere disperse* 14 and 33. In his ordered collections, however, Petrarch does not mention Azzo, *signore* of Parma who might himself have been accused of despotism.

57. Only one letter from an ordered collection is addressed to him.

58. Both Bruni and Barbato are frequent addressees also in the ordered collections.

59. See Feo, *Codici,* 348–52.

60. See p. 301 above. On a miscellany gathered by Barbato, see also Vattasso, *Petrarca;* and Ernest Hatch Wilkins, *Studies in the Life and Works of Petrarch* (Cambridge: Mediaeval Academy of America, 1955), 242–52. Paul Piur names Barbato and Moggio among the most dedicated collectors of Petrarch's letters ("Korrespondenz," 140, n. 3).

Chapter Twenty-one

1. I have used Petrarch, *Le Familiari,* ed. Vittorio Rossi (Florence: Sansoni, 1933). The Latin quotations from *Familiares* 1.1 are taken from Petrarch, *Le Familiari,* intro. and trans. Ugo Dotti (Rome: Archivio Guido Izzi, 1991), who bases his text on that of Rossi. The number in each quotation refers to the paragraph of the letter. The English translations are taken from Petrarch, *Rerum familiarum libri I–VIII,* trans. Aldo S. Bernardo (Albany: State University of New York Press, 1975). The other letters are to be found in *Letters on Familiar Matters. Rerum Familiarum Libri,* trans. Aldo S. Bernardo (Baltimore: Johns Hopkins University Press, 1982 and 1985).

2. Petrarch *Familiares* 1.1 (trans. Bernardo, 1:9; ed. Dotti, 56): "Prima quidem scribentis cura est, cui scribat attendere; una enim et quid et qualiter cet-

erasque circumstantias intelliget. Aliter virum fortem, aliter ignavum decet
alloqui; aliter iuvenem inexpertum, aliter vite muneribus functum senem;
aliter prosperitate tumidum, aliter adversitate contractum; aliter denique
studiosum literisque et ingenio clarum, aliter vero non intellecturum siquid
altius loquaris."

3. *Familiares* 24.13 (trans. Bernardo, 1:8; ed. Dotti, 52–53): "usque ad hoc
tempus vita pene omnis in peregrinatione transacta est. Ulixeos errores
erroribus meis confer: profecto, si nominis et rerum claritas una foret, nec
diutius erravit ille nec latius. Ille patrios fines iam senior excessit; . . . [ego]
periclitari cepi antequam nascerer et ad ipsum vite limen auspicio mortis
accessi. . . . pulsus patria pater magna cum bonorum acie confugerat. Inde
mense septimo sublatus sum totaque Tuscia . . . Finis tusci errores, Pise;
unde rursus etatis anno septimo divulsus ac maritimo itinere transvectus
in Gallias, hibernis aquilonibus haud procul Massilia naufragium passus,
parum abfui quin ab ipso rursus nove vite vestibulo revocarer. . . . quot inter
errandum periculorum timorum ve species pertulerim, preter me unum nemo
te melius novit. Que idcirco memorare nunc libuit, . . . si modo iam senui, et
non graviora michi in senio reservantur."

4. Giovanni Boccaccio, *Trattatello in Laude di Dante*, ed. Pier Giorgio Ricci, in
Tutte le opere di Giovanni Boccaccio, ed. Vittore Branca (Milan: Mondadori,
1974), 3:455–57, parags. 72, 82: "Uscito adunque in cotale maniera Dante
di quella città, della quale egli non solamente era cittadino, ma n'erano li
suoi maggiori stati reedificatori, e lasciatevi la sua donna, insieme con l'altra
famiglia, male per picciola età alla fuga disposta. . . . Non poterono gli amo-
rosi disiri, né le dolenti lagrime, né la sollecitudine casalinga, né la lusinghev-
ole gloria dei pubblici ofici, né il miserabile esilio, né la intollerabile povertà
giammai con le loro forze rimuovere il nostro Dante dal principale intento,
cioè da' sacri studii; perciò che, sì come si vederà dove appresso partitamente
dell'opere da lui fatte si farà menzione, egli, nel mezzo di qualunque fu più
fiera delle passioni sopra dette, si troverà componendo essersi esercitato";
Giovanni Boccaccio, *The Life of Dante (Trattatello in laude di Dante)*, trans. by
Vincenzo Zin Bollettino (New York: Garland Publishing, 1990), 20–23:
"And so Dante departed from that city where he had not only been a citizen,
but which his ancestors had rebuilt. He left behind his wife, together with
the rest of his family, whose youthful age poorly adapted them to share his
flight. . . . Neither Dante's ardent passion, nor painful tears, nor domestic
anxieties, nor the seductive glory of public office, nor the misery of his exile,
nor unendurable poverty could ever with all their force turn our poet away
from his main objective, which was his complete dedication to sacred studies.
For, as will be seen later, when mention shall be made of each of the works he

composed, in the middle of whatever was most threatening of the trials just named one will find that Dante always pursued his writing with great intensity." Cf. *Inferno* 26.94–96, which, after the attack against Florence, features Ulysses' speech: "Né dolcezza di figlio, né la pieta/del vecchio padre, né il debito amore,/lo qual dovea Penelopè far lieta" [neither fondness for my son, nor reverence for my aged father, nor the due love which would have made Penelope glad."] Text and translation are cited from Dante Alighieri, *The Divine Comedy*, trans. with comm. by Charles S. Singleton (Princeton: Princeton University Press: 1970–76), 1:276–77.

5. For a reading of Dante's rhetorical and philosophical ambiguities in the representation of Ulysses, see Giuseppe Mazzotta, *Dante Poet of the Desert: History and Allegory in the Divine Comedy* (Princeton: Princeton University Press, 1979), 66–106.

6. For the historical development of this practice, see Marcello Simonetta, *Il Rinascimento segreto: Il mondo del segretario da Petrarca a Machiavelli* (Milan: Franco-Angeli, 2004). The issue of Petrarch's ambiguities has recently been treated with historical precision by Riccardo Fubini, "Pubblicità e controllo del libro nella cultura del Rinascimento," in *Humanisme et église en Italie et en France méridionale (XV siècle–milieu du XVI siècle)*, ed. Patrick Gilli (Rome: École Française, 2004), 207–10.

7. Petrarch *Familiares* (ed. Dotti), 48: "hec igitur tibi, frater, diversi coloribus, ut sic dicam, liciis texta dicaverim; ceterum, si stabilis sedes . . . contigerit . . . nobiliorem et certe uniformem telam tuo nominee meditor ordiri."

8. "È dunque da sapere che 'autoritate' non è altro che 'atto d'autore.' Questo vocabulo, cioè 'autore,' senza quella terza lettera C, può discendere da due principi. . . . L'altro principio onde 'autore' discende, sì come testimonia Uguiccione nel principio de le sue Derivazioni, è uno vocabulo Greco che dice 'autentin,' che tanto vale in latino quanto 'degno di fede e obedienza.'" *Convivio*, in *Opere Minori*, vol. 1, pt. 2, ed. Cesare Vasoli and Domenico de Robertis (Milan : Ricciardi, 1988).

Chapter Twenty-two

1. See Petrarch, *Letters of Old Age: Rerum senilium libri*, 16.3, trans. Aldo S. Bernardo, Saul Levin, and Reta A. Bernardo (Baltimore: Johns Hopkins University Press, 1992), 609; Kenelm Foster, *Petrarch: Poet and Humanist* (Edinburgh: Edinburgh University Press, 1984), 19–21; and Marco Ariani, *Petrarca* (Rome: Salerno Editrice, 1999), 180–86.

2. See Ernest Hatch Wilkins, *Petrarch's Later Years* (Cambridge: Medieval Academy of America, 1959), 18; Petrarch, *Seniles* (trans. Bernardo et al.), xvii–xviii.

3. See Wilkins, *Later Years*, 146, 305–6. See further, "Petrarca, Boccaccio e

Zanobi da Strada," in Giuseppe Billanovich, *Petrarca e il primo umanesimo* (Padua: Editrice Antenore, 1996), 158–67.

4. See Wilkins, *Later Years*, 308–11.

5. See *Seniles* (trans. Bernardo et al.), ix–x; all translations from *Seniles* follow this edition. This volume translates from the *Librorum Francisci Petrarche annotatio impressorum* (Venice, 1501), with questionable readings checked against fifteenth-century manuscripts. Ironically, the very greatness of Petrarch's reputation as Latinist and philologist seems to have inhibited efforts to provide a workable edition of *Seniles:* there is now (since 1998) a book series entitled "Materiali per l'edizione Nazionale delle Opere di Francesco Petrarca," sponsored by the 'Commissione per l'edizione Nazionale delle Opere di Francesco Petrarca," building painstakingly toward the monumental edition. The "Commissione" was established by "legge dello Stato 365" on July 11, 1904, by way of marking the sixth hundredth anniversary of Petrarch's birth. The first volume of the series, Nicola Festa's edition of the *Africa*, was published in 1926; the four volumes of the *Familiares*, edited by Vittorio Rossi (and latterly Umberto Bosco) appeared between 1933 and 1942. To mark the seven hundredth anniversary, the CNP is launching a new, faster-track series (in book and CD-ROM formats) that will cover all Petrarch's works; authorial variants will be reported, but there will be no commentary. The *Seniles* volume will be edited by Silvia Rizzo and Monica Berté, with the participation of Michele Feo and Vincenzo Fera.

6. See now Petrarch, *Lettres de la vieillesse (Rerum Senilium)*, ed. Elvira Nota, trans. Frédérique Castelli, François Fabre, and Antoine de Rosny, annotated by Ugo Dotti (Paris: Les Belles Lettres, 2002–). As Pierre Laurens argues, "this is certainly the first time, since the editions of Venice (1501, 1503) and of Basle (1554, 1581) that we will have a complete text of the second of Petrarch's great epistolary works at our disposal; and, even better, a text established (for the first time) as a critical edition that will be regarded as authoritative" (1:x).

7. On the slaves at Venice, see *Seniles* 10.2 (370–71); for analysis of this passage in the context of European slaving and humanist practice, see David Wallace, *Premodern Places* (Oxford: Blackwell, 2004), 190–92.

8. Nicholas Mann, *Petrarch* (Oxford: Oxford University Press, 1984), 98.

9. For a fine edition of *Seniles* 5.2, first fruit of the series "Materiali per l'Edizione Nazionale delle Opere di Francesco Petraraca," see Petrarch, *Senile V, 2*, ed. Monica Berté (Florence: Casa Editrice Le Lettere, 1998).

10. On *amor hereos*, see Mary Frances Wack, *Lovesickness in the Middle Ages: The Viaticum and Its Commentaries* (Philadelphia: University of Pennsylvania Press, 1990).

11. See J. Burke Severs, *The Literary Relationships of Chaucer's Clerkes Tale* (New Haven: Yale University Press, 1942). See further Severs, "The Clerk's Tale," in *Sources and Analogues of Chaucer's Canterbury Tales*, ed. W. F. Bryan and Germaine Dempster (New York: Humanities Press, 1958), 288–331; all quotations from the Latin of Petrarch's Griselda story, *Seniles* 17.3, follow this text. The base text of Severs's edition is Biblioteca Apostolica Vaticana, Rome, MS Vat. Lat. 1666. For an edition based upon Peterhouse, Cambridge, MS 81 (collated with eight other manuscripts), see Thomas J. Farrell, "The Story of Griselda," in *Sources and Analogues of the Canterbury Tales*, vol. 1, ed. Robert M. Correale and Mary Hamel (Cambridge: D.S. Brewer, 2002), 108–29. There are some 150 uncollated versions of *Seniles* 17.3 (which circulated independently, as well as part of the collection): see Charlotte C. Morse, "Exemplary Griselde," *Studies in the Age of Chaucer* 7 (1985): 51–86, in particular 64.

12. Chaucer, "Clerk's Tale," *Canterbury Tales*, 4.32–3. All references follow *The Riverside Chaucer*, ed. Larry D. Benson (Oxford: Oxford University Press, 1987).

13. See Eve Kosofsky Sedgwick, *Between Men: English Literature and Male Homosocial Desire* (New York: Columbia University Press, 1985), 25–26.

14. See *Decameron*, ed. Vittore Branca (Milan: Mondadori, 1976), 10.8; Victoria Kirkham, "The Classic Bond of Friendship in Boccaccio's Tito and Gisippo (*Decameron* 10.8)," in *The Classics in the Middle Ages: Papers of the Twentieth Annual Conference of the Center for Medieval and Early Renaissance Studies*, ed. Aldo S. Bernardo and Saul Levin (Binghamton: Center for Medieval and Renaissance Texts and Studies, 1990), 223–35; David Wallace, *Giovanni Boccaccio: Decameron* (Cambridge: Cambridge University Press, 1991), 103–4; Louis Sorieri, *Boccaccio's Story of Tito e Gisippo in European Literature* (New York: Institute of French Studies, 1937).

15. It is fascinating to note that nameless and exemplary Griselda comes between Petrarch and Boccaccio in the opening, title-bearing rubric of Biblioteca Apostolica Vaticana, Rome, MS Vat. Lat. 1666, fol. 17r: "Francisci Petrarce, Poete Laureati, de Insigni Obedientia et Fide Uxoris, ad Johannem Bocacium de Certaldo" (fol. 17r.; Severs, "Clerk's Tale," 296). The embedded title, "On the Distinctive Obedience and Faithfulness of a Wife," has authority, although so too does the one adopted from MS Peterhouse, Cambridge, 81 by Farrell: "Historia Griseldis." Ambivalence about quite how to characterize or moralize the tale begins, it seems, with the author himself and with his scribes: "scribes produced" (in copying the final part of 17.3, Thomas J. Farrell observes) "many and widely divergent versions of Petrarch's statement about his purpose and moral" ("The Story of Griselda," 129).

16. Severs notes that of the seventy-two manuscripts and early prints he has examined, five have "stilo alto" ("Clerk's Tale," 330; see further, for further variations, Farrell, "The Story of Griselda," 129). Chaucer's Clerk speaks of Petrarch writing "in heigh stile" (4.41).

17. See Severs, "Clerk's Tale," 330; Petrarch *Seniles* (trans. Bernardo et al.), 668.

18. Petrarch *Seniles* 17.4 (trans. Bernardo et al.), 669. On this circle of humanist men friends, see Vittore Branca, *Boccaccio Medievale*, 5th ed. (Florence: Sansoni, 1981), 390.

19. On the *duplex causa efficiens* (twofold efficient cause) that sees God as the force that moves the human author to write, see *Medieval Literary Theory and Criticism, c. 1100–c. 1375: The Commentary Tradition*, ed. A. J. Minnis and A. B. Scott with the assistance of David Wallace (Oxford: Clarendon Press, 1988), esp. 198.

20. See David Wallace, *Chaucerian Polity* (Stanford: Stanford University Press, 1997), 225–26, 261–98.

21. Petrarch *Seniles* 17.2 is conveniently available in Petrarch, *Prose*, ed. Guido Martellotti et al. (Milan: Riccardo Ricciardi, 1955), 1135–59 (p. 1142).

22. "Opto ego vobis salvis mori, et post me relinquere quorum in memoria et in verbis vivam, quorum precibus adiuver, a quibus amer ac desider" (ed. Martellotti et al., 1154; ed. Bernardo et al., 652).

23. Alan Bray, *The Friend* (Chicago: University of Chicago Press, 2003). See especially chapter 4, "The Body of the Friend," which is largely dedicated to intimate behaviors such as eating, drinking, and sleeping together; emptying chamberpots; and exchanging gifts and letters.

24. "Me too, by night." See J. T. Muckle, "Abelard's Letter of Consolation to a Friend [*Historia Calamitatum*]," *Medieval Studies* 12 (1950): 163–213, quotation from 165. Petrarch is likely referring to his own fall from horseback on February 23, 1345.

25. This suggestion, concerning "un examen de conscience particulièrement réservé aux péchés de la chair," is made by Pierre de Nolhac, *Pétrarque et l'humanisme*, 2nd ed, 2 vols. (Paris: Champion, 1907), 2:290. The manuscript in question is Bibliothèque nationale de France, Paris, MS Lat. 2923.

26. "Saepe humanos affectus aut provocant aut mitigant amplius exempla quam verba" (*Abaelard's Historia calamitatum*, ed. and trans. (into German) by Dag Nikolaus Hasse (Berlin: Walter de Gruyter, 2002), 2; "there are times when example is better than precept for stirring or soothing human passions" (*The Letters of Heloise and Abelard*, trans. Betty Radice [Harmondsworth: Penguin, 1974], 57).

27. See Victoria Kirkham, "L'immagine del Boccaccio nella memoria tardogotica e rinascimentale," in *Boccaccio visualizzato: Narrare per parole e per im-*

magini fra medioevo e rinascimento, ed. Vittore Branca (Turin: Einaudi, 1999), 1:85–144, quotation from 105. In Giorgio Vasari's famous *Ritratto di sei poeti toscani* (1544), Boccaccio appears with "viso rotondo, mascella robusta, labbra piene e sensuali" (85).

28. "olim iuvenis edidisti," 290. Burke Severs includes the "Preface" to *Seniles* 17.3 *after* his edition of the French and Latin texts in *Literary Relationships.*

29. "Egit me tui amor et historie," ed. Severs in *Literary Relationships,* 291.

30. *Of Mountains, Woods, Fountains, Lakes, Rivers . . . Oceans:* see now the edition by Manlio Pastore Stocchi in Branca, *Tutte le opere di Giovanni Boccaccio,* vol. 8 (Milan: Mondadori, 1998). On Boccaccio as geographer, see Wallace, *Premodern Places,* 212–13. Chaucer's Clerk thinks Petrarch's display of geography "a thing impertinent" (4.54).

31. Chaucer works hard to associate his version of the Griselda story with *Lumbardye,* a place he consistently associates with *tyrannye:* his opening geographical account speaks of "West Lumbardye" and his Walter is, "to speke as of lynage, The gentilleste yborn of Lumbardye" (4.46, 71–2). See further, Wallace, *Chaucerian Polity,* 40–54, 267–77, 367.

32. "Quid iussu principum perdiderim . . . ," 1148.

33. *Decameron* 10.10.3 ("mad bestiality"; equivalent language recurs at 10.10.61, where Walter speaks of those who repute him "crudele e iniquo e bestiale").

34. "Quam quidem an mutata veste deformaverim an fortassis ornaverim," Petrarch declares to Boccaccio, "tu iudica" (ed. Severs in *Literary Relationships,* 291): "whether I have deformed it or, perhaps, beautified it by changing its garment, you judge" (656).

35. "Nomine ego cum principibus fui, re autem principes mecum fuerunt" (1146).

36. "Non sumus paris meriti" (1138).

37. See *Variae* 56, discussed in Wallace, *Chaucerian Polity,* 348.

38. See Wallace, *Chaucerian Polity,* 268.

39. "neque in hoc unquam fatigabor aut lentescam dum spiritus huius reliquie ulle supererunt," 324.

40. Latin text follows Petrarch, *Opera Latina omnia,* 3rd ed. (Venice: Simone Gabi, called Bevilacqua, 1503), not paginated.

41. *Opera Latina omnia* ("Francesco Petrarca to posterity, greetings").

42. See Louise O. Fradenburg, "The Manciple's Servant Tongue: Politics and Poetry in *The Canterbury Tales,*" *ELH* 52 (1985): 86, 103–8.

43. See Pier Giorgio Ricci, "Posteritati," in Petrarch, *Prose,* 1161; Petrarch, *Selected Letters,* ed. Craig Kallendorf (Bryn Mawr: Thomas Library, Bryn Mawr College, 1986), 136. Kallendorf supplies a Latin text of *Seniles* 18.1. On Petrarch's will (Padua, April 4, 1370), see *Petrarch's Testament,* ed. and

trans. Theodor E. Mommsen (Ithaca: Cornell University Press, 1957); and the last essay in this volume.

44. Petrarch, *Seniles* (trans. Bernardo et al.), 671, lightly modified; *Opera Latina omnia:* "Promiseram memini in quadam ordinis huius epistola me deinceps in epistolis brevius scriptuarum declivi iam temporis urgente penuria; promissum implere non valui; multoque facilius ut intelligi datur silentium cum amicis est quam breviloquium tantus est ubi semel incepimus ardor colloquendi ut facilius fuerit non coepisse quam frenare impetum cepti sermonis: sed promissum. Nonne sat promissum implet qui plus prestat? Eram credo dum promitterem oblitus Catonis illud apud Ciceronem late notum: quo natura ipsa loquencior est senectus. Valete amici. Valete epistolae. Inter colles euganeos. 6 idus Iunias."

Chapter Twenty-three

1. Petrarch, "Last Will," in *Petrarch's Testament,* ed. and trans. Theodor E. Mommsen (Ithaca: Cornell University Press, 1957), 93.

2. Theodor E. Mommsen, "The Last Will: A Personal Document of Petrarch's Old Age," in *Petrarch's Testament,* 10.

3. Jacques Chiffoleau, *La comptabilité de l'au-delà* (Rome: École Française de Rome, 1980), 39.

4. Mommsen, "The Transmission of the Text," in *Petrarch's Testament,* 51.

5. Petrarch *Seniles* 11.17. I quote from Ernest Hatch Wilkins, *The Life of Petrarch* (Chicago: University of Chicago Press, 1961), 224, on the *Testamentum,* see 223–25. For a complete translation of this letter, see Petrarch, *Letters of Old Age,* trans. Aldo S. Bernardo, Saul Levin, and Reta A. Bernardo (Baltimore: Johns Hopkins University Press, 1992), 2:433–37.

6. We make minimal changes to Mommsen's translation (*Petrarch's Testament,* 70).

7. Samuel K. Cohn, Jr., *Death and Property in Siena, 1205–1800* (Baltimore: Johns Hopkins University Press, 1988), 59.

8. *Il testamento di Giovanni Boccaccio secondo l'originale in pergamena* (Siena: Alessandri e Landi, 1853), 9. Compare the incomplete form in vernacular reproduced at the end of the "Proemio" of *Annotationi et discorsi sopra alcuni luoghi del Decameron di M. Giovanni Boccaccio* (Florence: Giunti, 1574), in particular, on the relationship between the final Latin version and the Italian draft, 3–5. A translation in modern Italian is also present in Cesare Marchi, *Boccaccio* (Milan: Rizzoli, 1975), 303–10. On Boccaccio's testament, see Vittore Branca, *Giovanni Boccaccio: Profilo biografico* (Florence: Sansoni, 1977), 187–89; Thomas Caldecot Chubb, *The Life of Giovanni Boccaccio* (1930; repr., Port Washington: Kennikat Press, 1969), 258–59.

9. Cicero *De senectute* 20.74; *Tusculanae disputationes* 1.48.115. I find the reference to *De senectute* in Mommsen's edition (69).

10. Petrarch, *Letters of Old Age*, trans. Aldo S. Bernardo, Saul Levin, and Reta A. Bernardo (Baltimore: Johns Hopkins University Press, 1992), 1:18 and 23. Instead of "literature," as we find in Bernardo's version, I translate "literis" as "letters." On the significance of this letter, see Vinicio Pacca, *Petrarca* (Bari: Laterza, 1998), 222–23.

11. Saint Francis of Assisi, *Testamentum*, in *Opuscula sancti patris Francisci assisiensis*, ed. Caietanus Esser O.F.M. (Rome: Collegii S. Bonaventurae, 1978), 12:307–17, quotation on 315.

12. On Francis's testament, see Giovanni Miccoli, *Francesco d'Assisi* (Turin: Einaudi, 1991), 41–56.

13. Saint Francis of Assisi, *Testamentum*, 308, 307.

14. Cf. Cohn, *Death and Property in Siena*, 59–60.

15. Chiffoleau, *La comptabilité de l'au-delà*, 77.

16. Chiffoleau, *La comptabilité de l'au-delà*, 77–78.

17. Chrodegangus Metensis, *Regula canonicorum secundum recensionem Dacherii*, in *PL* 89, ed. J. P. Migne (Paris: Migne, 1850), chapter 32, col. 1072: "Imprimis prosterne te humiliter in conspectu Dei in terra ad orationem, et roga beatam Mariam cum sanctis apostolis, et martyribus, et confessoribus, ut ipsi intercedant pro te ad Dominum, et Deus omnipotens dignetur tibi dare sapientiam perfectam, et scientiam, et intelligentiam veram, ad confitendum peccata tua." Johannes Caietanus, *Ordo Romanus XIV*, in Jean Mabillon, *Museum Italicum* (Luteciae Parisionum: Martin, 1689), 2:246–443, quotation on 329. On the evolution of this sacrament, see Cyrille Vogel, *Le pécheur et la pénitence au moyen âge* (Paris: Cerf, 1969), 15–47; Philippe Rouillard, *Histoire de la pénitence* (Paris: Cerf, 1996), 65–75. The basic information on the *Confiteor* comes from the entry "Confiteor" in *The Catholic Encyclopedia* (http://www.newadvent.org/cathen/04222a.htm). For a general overview of the concept of penance and confession, see the entry "pénitence" in *Dictionnaire de spiritualité*, 78–79 (Paris: Beauchesne, 1984), 943–1010. In particular, on the medieval view of penance, 970–80. On the issue of confession in Petrarch's *Secretum*, see Timothy Kircher, *The Poet's Wisdom* (Leiden: Brill, 2006), 145–84.

18. Mommsen, *Petrarch's Testament*, 70.

19. Petrarch, *Salmi penitenziali*, ed. Roberto Gigliucci (Rome: Salerno, 1997), psalm 3, 36, and 38.

20. Mommsen, "The Last Will: A Personal Document of Petrarch's Old Age," in *Petrarch's Testament*, 16. Cf. Wilkins, *Life of Petrarch*, 243–44.

21. Petrarch, *Canzoniere*, canzone 366, ed. Marco Santagata (Milan: Mondadori, 2001), 1397–1416, on the date of composition, 1401.

22. Petrarch, *Canzoniere*, canzone 366, vv. 135–37 (ed. Santagata, 1401).

23. Cohn, *Death and Property in Siena*, 60–61.

24. On Francesca and Francescuolo da Brossano, see Mommsen, *Petrarch's Testament*, 40–41; Wilkins, *Life of Petrarch*, 177–78.

25. Petrarch, *Lettres de la veillesse* (*Rerum senilium*), book 14, epistle 1, edited by Elvira Nota, (Paris: Les Belles Lettres, 2006), 4:228–307.

26. Petrarch *Seniles* (ed. Nota), 2: 551.

27. Petrarch *Seniles* (ed. Nota), 4: 307.

28. On this epistle and the broader issue of mourning women in medieval Italy, see Diane Owen Hughes, "Mourning Rites, Memory, and Civilization in Premodern Italy," in *Riti e rituali nelle società medievali*, ed. Jacques Chiffoleau, Lauro Martines, and Agostino Paravicini Bagliani (Spoleto: Centro Italiano di studi sull'Alto Medioevo, 1994), 23–38.

29. Mommsen, *Petrarch's Testament*, 72.

30. Nicholas Mann, *Petrarch* (New York: Oxford University Press, 1984), 6.

31. Cf. Mann, *Petrarch*, 4.

32. *Il testamento di Giovanni Boccaccio secondo l'originale in pergamena*, 10.

33. Giovanni Boccaccio, *Genealogie deorum gentilium*, ed. in *Tutte le opere*, ed. Vittore Branca (Milan: Mondadori, 1998), 8:1486. Giovanni Boccaccio, *Trattatello in laude di Dante*, ed. in *Tutte le opere*, edited by Vittore Branca (Milan: Mondadori, 1974), 3:463, paragraph 105.

34. Boccaccio, *Genealogie deorum*, 1484 and 1488.

35. Wilkins, *Life of Petrarch*, 82.

36. Wilkins, *Life of Petrarch*, 96.

37. Petrarch, *De vita solitaria*, in *Opere latine*, ed. Antonietta Bufano (Turin: Unione Tipografico-Editrice Torinese, 1975), book 2, 1:530.

38. Cf. Chiffoleau, *La comptabilité de l'au-delà*, 165–71.

39. See Samuel Cohn, "Burial in the Early Renaissance: Six Cities in Central Italy," in *Riti e rituali nelle società medievali*, ed. Jacques Chiffoleau, Lauro Martines, and Agostino Paravicini Bagliani (Spoleto: Centro Italiano di studi sull'Alto Medioevo, 1994), 39–57.

40. Mommsen, *Petrarch's Testament*, 70.

41. Mommsen, *Petrarch's Testament*, 74.

42. Mommsen, *Petrarch's Testament*, 77.

43. Cohn, *Death and Property in Siena*, 27.

44. Mommsen, *Petrarch's Testament*, 81; on Petrarch's admiration for Giotto, 22–23.

45. Mommsen, *Petrarch's Testament*, 80.

46. *Il testamento di Giovanni Boccaccio secondo l'originale in pergamena*, 12.

47. Mommsen, *Petrarch's Testament*, 81–83.

48. Mommsen, *Petrarch's Testament*, 90.

49. Mommsen, *Petrarch's Testament*, 83.

50. Mommsen, *Petrarch's Testament*, 87.

51. Mommsen, *Petrarch's Testament*, 86.

52. Mommsen, *Petrarch's Testament*, 93.

53. Timothy J. Reiss, *Mirages of the Selfe: Patterns of Personhood in Ancient and Early Modern Europe* (Stanford: Stanford University Press, 2003), chapter 11 ("Multum a me ipso differre compulsus sum"), 303.

54. Mommsen, "The Last Will: A Personal Document," in *Petrarch's Testament*, 7.

BIBLIOGRAPHY

PRIMARY LITERATURE

Abelard, Peter. *Abaelard's Historia Calamitatum*. Edited and translated by Dag Nikolaus Hasse. Berlin: Walter de Gruyter, 2002.

———. "Abelard's Letter of Consolation to a Friend [*Historia Calamitatum*]." Edited by J. T. Muckle. *Medieval Studies* 12 (1950): 163–213.

———. *The Letters of Heloise and Abelard*. Translated by Betty Radice. Harmondsworth: Penguin, 1974.

Alcuin of York. *Enchiridion seu expositio pia ac brevis in Psalmos Poenitentiales, in Psalmum CXVIII et Graduales*. In *PL* 100, col. 569–640. Paris: Garnier, 1851.

Ambrosius. "Epistola XLIX." In *PL* 16, col. 991–93. Paris: Garnier, 1880.

———. *De officiis ministrorum*. In *PL* 16, col. 1–142. Paris: Garnier, 1880.

Anonymous (Innocent III?). *Commentarium in Septem Psalmos Poenitentiales*. *PL* 217, col. 967–1130. Paris: Garnier, 1855.

Aristotle. *Physics*. In *The Basic Works of Aristotle*. Edited by Richard McKeon. Translated by R. P. Hardie and R. K. Gaye. New York: Random House, 1941.

Augustine. *City of God Against the Pagans*. Translated by George E. McCracken. 7 vols. Loeb Classical Library. Cambridge: Harvard University Press, 1966–72.

———. *Confessions*. Translated by R. S. Pine-Coffin. London: Penguin, 1961.

———. *Confessions*. Translated by William Watts. 2 vols. Loeb Classical Library. Cambridge: Harvard University Press; London: Heinemann, 1976.

———. *De vera religione*. Edited by William Green. Vienna: Hoelder-Pichler-Tempsky, 1961.

———. *De vera religione*. Milan: Mursia, 1987.

———. *Enarrationes in Psalmos*. Nuova Biblioteca Agostiniana, http://www.sant-agostino.it/nba.htm.

———. *The True Religion*. Translated by C. A. Hangartner and G. R. Sheahan. In *The Essential Augustine*. Edited by Vernon Bourke. Indianapolis: Hackett, 1953.

Battiferra degli Ammannati, Laura. *Laura Battiferra and Her Literary Circle: An Anthology*. Edited by Victoria Kirkham. Chicago: University of Chicago Press, 2006.

———. *I sette salmi penitenziali di David con alcuni sonetti spirituali*. Edited by Enrico Maria Guidi. Urbino: Accademia Raffaello, 2005.

Benzo da Alessandria. *Cronica*. In Joseph Berrigan, "Benzo da Alessandria and the Cities of Northern Italy." *Studies in Medieval and Renaissance History* 4 (1967): 125–92.

Biblia Sacra Vulgatae Editionis. Sixti V Pontificis Maximi iussu recognita et Clementis VIII auctoritate edita. Milan: San Paolo, 1995.

Boccaccio, Giovanni. *Annotationi et discorsi sopra alcuni luoghi del Decameron di M. Giovanni Boccaccio*. Florence: Giunti, 1574.

———. *Boccaccio on Poetry*. Translated by Charles G. Osgood. Princeton: Princeton University Press, 1930.

———. *Buccolicum Carmen*. Edited by Giorgio Bernardi Perini. In Giovanni Boccaccio, *Tutte le opera*, edited by Vittore Branca, 4:689–1085. Milan: Mondadori, 1994.

———. *Decameron*. Edited by Vittore Branca. In Giovanni Boccaccio, *Tutte le opere*, edited by Vittore Branca, vol. 4. Milan: Mondadori, 1976.

———. *De montibus, silvis, fontibus, lacubus, fluminibus, stagnis seu paludibus et de diversis nominibus maris*. Edited by Manlio Pastore Stocchi. In Giovanni Boccaccio, *Tutte le opere*, edited by Vittore Branca, 8:1815–2122. Milan: Mondadori, 1998.

———. *Eclogues*. Translated by Janet Levarie Smarr. New York and London: Garland, 1987.

———. *Epistole*. Edited by Ginetta Auzzas. In Giovanni Boccaccio, *Tutte le opere*, edited by Vittore Branca, vol. 5, part 1, 495–856. Milan: Mondadori, 1992.

———. *The Fates of Illustrious Men*. Translated and abridged by Louis Brewer Hall. New York: Frederick Ungar, 1965.

———. *Genealogie deorum gentilium*. Edited by Vittorio Zaccaria. In Giovanni Boccaccio, *Tutte le opera*, edited by Vittore Branca, vols. 7–8, 11–1813. Milan: Mondadori, 1998.

———. *Il testamento di Giovanni Boccaccio secondo l'originale in pergamena*. Siena: Alessandri e Landi, 1853.

———. *Trattatello in laude di Dante*. Edited by Pier Giorgio Ricci. In Giovanni Boccaccio, *Tutte le opere*, edited by Vittore Branca, vol. 3, 413–538. Milan: Mondadori, 1974.

———. *Vita e costume di messer Francesco di Petracco, di Firenze*. Edited by Renata Fabbri. In Giovanni Boccaccio, *Tutte le opere*, edited by Vittore Branca, vol. 5, pt. 1, 897–11. Milan: Mondadori, 1992.

Bruni, Leonardo. *Ad Petrum Paulum Histrum Dialogus*. In *Prosatori latini del Quattrocento*. Edited by Eugenio Garin, 39–99. Milan and Naples: Ricciardi, 1952.

———. *Humanistisch-philosophische Schriften mit einer Chronologie seiner Werke und Briefe*. Edited by Hans Baron. Leipzig: Teubner, 1928.

Caietanus. *Ordo Romanus XIV*. In Jean Mabillon, *Musei Italici*, vol. 2. Luteciae Parisionum: Martin, 1689.

Cassiodorus, Flavius. *Explanation of the Psalms*. Translated by P.G. Walsh. New York: Paulist Press, 1990.

———. *Expositio Psalmorum*. Edited by M. Adriaen. In *CCL* 97–98. Turnhout: Brepols, 1973.

Chaucer, Geoffrey. *The Riverside Chaucer*. Edited by Larry D. Benson. Oxford: Oxford University Press, 1987.

———. *The Works of Geoffrey Chaucer*. Edited by F. N. Robinson. 2nd ed. Boston: Houghton Mifflin, 1961.

Chrodegangus Metensis. *Regula canonicorum secundum recensionem Dacherii*. In *PL* 89. Paris: Migne, 1850.

Cicero. *De officiis. On Duties*. Translated by Walter Miller. Loeb Classical Library. Cambridge: Harvard University Press, 1913.

———. *Dei doveri*. Edited and translated by Dario Arfelli. Milan: Mondadori, 1994.

———. *The Nature of the Gods*. Translated by P.G. Walsh. Oxford: Clarendon Press, 1997.

———. *The Speech on Behalf of Archias the Poet*. In *Pro Archia, Post reditum ad quirites, Post reditum in senatu, De domo sua, De haruspicum responsis, Pro Plancio*. Translated by N. H. Watts. Loeb Classical Library. 1923. Reprint, Cambridge: Harvard University Press, 1979.

———. *Tusculanes disputationes. Tusculan Disputations*. Translated by J. E. King. Loeb Classical Library. 1927. Reprint, Cambridge: Harvard University Press, 2001.

Claudian. *The First Book against Rufinus*. In *Claudian*. Translated by Maurice Plautner. 2 vols. Loeb Classical Library. 1922. Reprint, Cambridge: Harvard University Press, 1963.

Colonna, Egidio (Aegidius Romanus). *De regimine principum libri III: Recogniti et una cum vita auctoris in lucem editi per Hieronymum Samaritanium*. Aalen: Scientia Verlag, 1967.

Dante Alighieri. *"La Commedia" secondo l'antica vulgata*. Edited by Giorgio Petrocchi. 4 vols. Milan: Mondadori: 1966–67.

———. *Convivio*. Edited by Cesare Vasoli. In *Opere minori*, vol. 5.1, part 2. Milan: Ricciardi, 1988.

———. *Dante and Giovanni del Virgilio. Including a Critical Edition of the Text of Dante's "Eclogae Latinae" and of the Poetic Remains of Giovanni del Virgilio*. 1902. Reprint, Freeport: Books for Libraries Press, 1971.

———. *De vulgari eloquentia*. Edited by Aristide Marigo. 3rd ed. Pier Giorgio Ricci. Florence: Le Monnier, 1968.

————. *The Divine Comedy.* Translated by Charles S. Singleton. 6 vols. Bollingen Series. Princeton: Princeton University Press, 1970–75.

————. *Le ecloghe.* Edited and translated by Giorgio Brugnoli and Riccardo Scarcia. Milan: Ricciardi, 1980.

————. *Le opere di Dante. Testo critico della Società Dantesca Italiana.* Edited by M. Barbi and others. 2nd ed. Florence: Nella Sede della Società, 1960.

————. *Tutte le opere di Dante.* Edited by Edward Moore. 3rd ed. Oxford: Oxford University Press, 1904.

[Dante Alighieri, spurious attribution]. *I sette salmi penitenziali di Dante Alighieri e di Francesco Petrarca.* Bergamo: Mazzoleni, 1821; reprint, Florence: Società Tipografica, 1827.

————. Spurious attribution. *I sette salmi penitenziali ed il Credo, trasportati alla volgar poesia, illustrate con annotazioni dall'abate Francesco Saverio Quadrio.* Bologna: Giovani Gottardi, 1753. Reprinted in Biblioteca scelta di opere italiane antiche e moderne, 562. Milan: G. Silvestri, 1851.

Ferreto dei Ferreti. *Historia rerum in Italia gestarum.* In *Le opere di Ferreto de' Ferreti vicentino.* Edited by Carlo Cipolla. Fonti per la Storia d'Italia, 42–43bis. Rome: Forzani, 1908–20.

Francis of Assisi. *Testamentum.* In *Opuscula sancti patris Francisci assisiensis.* Vol. 12. Edited by Caietanus Esser, O.F.M. Grottaferrata. Rome: Collegii S. Bonaventurae, 1978.

Freud, Sigmund. *The Standard Edition of the Complete Psychological Works of Sigmund Freud.* Translated by James Stnachey with Anna Freud. 24 vols. London: Hogarth Press, 1953–1974.

Giovanni da Cremenate. *Historia Johnannis de Cremenate, notarii mediolanensis.* Edited by L. A. Ferrai. Fonti per la Storia d'Italia, 2. Rome: Forzani, 1889.

Gregory the Great. *Dialogi.* Edited by Umberto Moricca. Rome: Tipografia del Senato, 1924.

————. (attr.; Pope Gregory VII? Heribert of Reggio Emilia?) *In septem Psalmos Poenitentiales Expositio.* In *PL* 79:549–660.

Guido da Pisa. *Expositiones et glose super Comediam Dantis facte per Fratrem Guidonem Pisanum.* Edited by Vincenzo Cioffari. Albany: State University of New York Press, 1974.

Hugh of Saint-Victor. *Didascalicon: A Medieval Guide to the Arts.* Translated by Jerome Taylor. New York: Columbia University Press, 1961.

————. *Didascalicon: De studio legendi.* Edited by Charles H. Buttimer. Washington, D.C.: Catholic University of America Press, 1939.

————. *Didascalicon. De studio legendi.* New York: Columbia University Press, 1991.

Isidore of Seville. *Etymologiarum sive originum libri XX.* Edited by W. M. Lindsay. Oxford: Clarendon Press, 1911.

Juvenal, *Satire.* Edited and translated by Luca Canali. Milan: Rizzolis, 1976.

Livy. *Ab urbe condita.* Translated by B. O. Foster. 14 vols. Loeb Classical Library. Cambridge: Harvard University Press, 1919–67.

Lucan. *The Civil War (Pharsalia) [Bellum civile].* Translated by J. D. Duff. Loeb Classical Library. 1928. Reprint, Cambridge: Harvard University Press, 1969.

Ludolph of Saxony (Ludolph the Carthusian). *Ludolfi Carthusiensis qui et autor fuit vite Christi In Psalterium expositio : in qua subiecte reperiuntur materie : Psalmi penitentiales et co[n]fessionales elegantes et deuoti Domini Francisci Petrarche poete laureati: tabula cunctorum Dauiticorum Psalmorum : tabula versiculorum omnium . . . : tabula materia[rum] principaliu[m] in marginib[us] annotataru[m] : additur in margi[n] e ad solita[m] Hieronymi tra[n]slatione[m], Diui Augustini accuratissima de Hebreo in Latinu[m] tra[n]slatio.* [Paris]: Venundatur Parrhisijs in vico Diui Iacobi a Mag[ist]ro Bertholdo Rembolt [et] Ioha[n]ne Paruo, [10 Mar. 1514].

Luther, Martin. "The Seven Penitential Psalms." Translated by Arnold Guebert. In *Luther's Works,* vol. 14, 137–205. Saint Louis: Concordia Publishing House, 1958.

Macrobius. *A Commentary on the Dream of Scipio.* Translated by William H. Stahl. New York: Columbia University Press, 1962.

Mussato, Albertino. *Historia augusta Henrici VII caesaris et alia quae extant opera.* Edited by Laurentii Pignorii vir. Clar. Spicilegio necnon Foelici Osia et Nicolae Villani etc. Venice: Ducali Pinelliana, 1636.

Nelli, Francesco. *Un ami de Pétrarque: Lettres de Francesco Nelli à Pétrarque.* Edited by Henry Cochin. Paris: Champion, 1892.

———. *Un amico di Francesco Petrarca. Le lettere del Nelli al Petrarca.* Edited by Henry Cochin. Florence: Le Monnier, 1901.

Novelle inedite intorno a Bernabò Visconti. Edited by Piero Ginori Conti. Florence: Fondazione Ginori Conti, 1940.

Ovid. *Metamorphoses.* Translated by Frank Justus Miller. 2 vols. Loeb Classical Library. Cambridge: Harvard University Press, 1968.

———. *Remedies for Love.* In *The Art of Love and Other Poems.* Loeb Classical Library. 1929. Reprint, Cambridge: Harvard University Press, 2004.

Palladius Helenopolitanus. *Historia Lausiaca.* In *PL* 73, col. 709–83. Paris: Garnier, 1879.

Pastrengo, Guglielmo. *De viris illustribus et de originibus.* Edited by G. Bottari. Studi sul Petrarca, 21. Padua: Antenore, 1991.

Petrarch. *Africa.* Edited by Nicola Festa. Edizione Nazionale delle Opere di Francesco Petrarca, 10. Florence: Sansoni, 1926. Reprint, Florence: Le Lettere, 1998.

———. *L'Afrique: 1338–1374*. Edited and translated by Rebecca Lenoir. Grenoble: Jérôme Millon, 2002.

———. *L'Afrique. Affrica*. Edited and translated with introduction and notes by Pierre Laurens. Paris: Belles Lettres, 2006.

———. *Arenga facta Mediolani*. In *Scritti inediti di Francesco Petrarca*. Edited by Attilio Hortis, 335–40. Trieste: Tipografia del Lloyd Austro-Ungarico, 1874.

———. *Arenga facta per dominum Franciscum Petrarcham poetam laureatum in Civitate Novarie*. In *Scritti inediti di Francesco Petrarca*, 341–58.

———. *Arenga facta per dominum Franciscum Petrarchum poetam laureatum in Civitate Novarie*. In *Francesco Petrarca a Novara e la sua aringa ai novaresi*. Translated by Carlo Negroni. Novara: Fratelli Miglio, 1876.

———. *Arenga facta Veneciis*. In *Scritti inediti di Francesco Petrarca*, 329–33.

———. *Bucolicum carmen*. Edited by Tonino T. Mattucci. Pisa: Giardini, 1970.

———. *Bucolicum carmen*. Translated by Thomas Goddard Bergin. New Haven: Yale University Press, 1974.

———. *Bucolicum carmen*. Edited and translated by M. François and P. Bachmann, with the collaboration of F. Roudaut. Paris: Champion, 2001.

———. *Il Bucolicum carmen di Francesco Petrarca: Edizione diplomatica dell'autographo Vat. Lat. 3358*. Edited by Domenico De Venuto. Pisa: ETS, 1990.

———. *Il Bucolicum carmen e i suoi sommenti inediti*. Edited by Antonio Avena. 1906. Reprint, Bologna: Forni, 1969.

———. *Canzoniere*. Edited by Gianfranco Contini. Turin: Einaudi, 1964.

———. *Canzoniere*. Edited by Marco Santagata. Milan: Mondadori, 2004.

———. *Il Canzoniere e i Trionfi*. Edited by Andrea Moschetti. Milan: Vallardi, 1908.

———. *Il codice Chigiano L.V.176, autografo di Giovanni Boccaccio*. Edited by Domenico De Robertis. Rome: Archivi Edizioni, 1974.

———. *Collatio brevis coram Iohanne Francorum rege*. Edited by Carlo Godi. In "L'orazione del Petrarca per Giovanni il Buono." *Italia Medioevale e Umanistica* 8 (1965): 45–83. Reprinted with Italian translation and notes in *Opere latine*, 2:1285–1309.

———. *Collatio in Capitolio*. Translated by Victor Develay. In "Pétrarque au Capitole." *Le Livre* 6, no. 2 (1885): 278–88.

———. *Collatio inter Scipionem, Alexandrum, Annibalem et Pyrhum*. Edited by Guido Martellotti. Philadelphia: University of Pennsylvania Libraries, 1974.

———. "La *Collatio inter Scipionem Alexandrum Hanibalem et Pyrhum*, un inedito del Petrarca nella Biblioteca della University of Pennsylvania." Edited by Guido Martellotti. In *Classical, Mediaeval, and Renaissance Studies in Honor of Berthold*

Louis Ullman, edited by Charles Henderson Jr., 2:145–68. Rome: Edizioni di Storia e Letteratura, 1964. Reprint in Guido Martellotti, *Studi petrarcheschi*, edited by Michele Feo and Silvia Rizzo, 321–46. Padua: Antenore, 1983.

———. *Collatio laureationis*. In Carlo Godi, "La 'Collatio laureationis' del Petrarca nelle due redazioni." *Studi Petrarcheschi* 5 (1988): 1–58.

———. *Contro un medico: Invettive*. Edited by Emilio Di Leo. Salerno: Giacomo, 1953.

———. *De gestis Cesaris*. In *Le vite degli uomini illustri di Francesco Petrarca volgarizzate da Donato degli Albenzani da Pratovecchio*. Edited by Luigi Razzolini. 2 vols. Collezione di opere inedite o rare dei primi tre secoli della lingua. Bologna: Gaetano Romagnoli, 1874–79.

———. *De otio religioso*. See *Le Repos religieux*.

———. *De otio religioso*. Edited by Giulio Goletti. Edizione Nazionale delle Opere di Francesco Petrarca. Florence: La Lettere, 2007.

———. *Il "De otio religioso" di Francesco Petrarca*. Edited by Giovanni Rotondi and Guido Martellotti. Vatican City: Biblioteca Apostolica Vaticana, 1958.

———. *De remediis utriusque fortune*. See *Les Remèdes aux deux fortunes*.

———. *De sui ipsius et multorum ignorantia*. Edited by Enrico Fenzi. Milan: Mursia, 1999.

———. *De viris illustribus*. Edited by Guido Martellotti. In Petrarch, *Prose*, edited by Guido Martellotti, Pier Gorgio Ricci, Enrico Carrara, and Enrico Bianchi, 217–67. Milan and Naples: Ricciardi, 1955.

———. *De viris illustribus*. Edited by Guido Martellotti. Edizione Nazionale delle Opere di Francesco Petrarca, no. 2, pt. 1. Florence: Sansoni, 1964.

———. *De viris illustribus libri nondum editi*, Pars I–IV. Edited by Carl Ernest Christian Schneider. Breslau: n.p., 1829–1834.

———. *De vita et rebus gestis C. Julii Caesari*. Edited by Carl Ernest Christian Schneider. Leipzig: Gerhard Fleischerum, 1827.

———. *De vita solitaria*. Edited by Marco Noce. Milan: Arnoldo Mondadori Editore, 1992.

———. *De vita solitaria. Buch I*. Edited by K. A. E. Enenkel. Leiden and New York: Brill, 1990.

———. *De vita solitaria. La vie solitaire: 1346–1366*. Edited and translated by Christophe Carraud. Grenoble: Jérôme Millon, 1999.

———. *Discorso ai Novaresi*. Translated by Dorino Tuniz. In *Petrarca a Novara*, 17–27.

———. *Epistolae de rebus familiaribus et variae*. 3 vols. Edited by Giuseppe Fracassetti. Florence: Le Monnier, 1859–63.

———. *Epistole*. Edited by Ugo Dotti. Turin: Unione Tipografico-Editrice Torinese, 1978.

————. *Le familiari.* Edited by Vittorio Rossi and Umberto Bosco. Edizione Nazionale delle Opere di Francesco Petrarca, 10–13. 4 vols. Florence: Sansoni, 1926–42.

————. *Le familiari.* Edited by Ugo Dotti. 3 vols. Rome: Archivio Guido Izzo, 1991.

————. *Francesco Petrarca a Novara, e la sua Aringa ai Novaresi.* Translated by Carlo Negroni. Novara: Fratelli Miglio, 1876.

————. *Invective contra medicum. Testo latino e volgarizzamento di ser Domenico Silvestri.* Edited by Pier Giorgio Ricci and Bortolo Martinelli. Rome: Edizioni di storia e letteratura, 1978.

————. *Invective contra medicum.* Edited by Francesco Bausi. Florence: Le Lettere, 2005.

————. *Invectives.* Edited and translated by David Marsh. I Tatti Renaissance Library. Cambridge: Harvard University Press, 2003.

————. *Laurea occidens. Bucolicum carmen X.* Edited and translated by Guido Martellotti. Rome: Edizioni di Storia e Letteratura, 1968.

————. *Lettera ai posteri.* Edited by Gianni Villani. Rome: Salerno, 1990.

————. *Lettere.* Translated by Giuseppe Fracassetti. 5 vols. Florence: Le Monnier, 1863–67.

————. *Lettere disperse, varie e miscellanee.* Edited by Alessandro Pancheri. Parma: Ugo Guanda, 1994.

————. *Letters of Old Age. Rerum senilium libri.* Translated by Aldo S. Bernardo, Saul Levin, and Reta A. Bernardo. 2 vols. Baltimore: Johns Hopkins University Press: 1992.

————. *Letters on Familiar Matters.* Translated by Aldo Bernardo. 1975–85. Reprint, New York: Italica Press, 2005.

————. *Letters on Familiar Matters. Rerum familiarum libri IX–XVI.* Translated by Aldo S. Bernardo. Baltimore: Johns Hopkins University Press, 1982.

————. *Letters on Familiar Matters XVII–XXIV.* Translated by Aldo S. Bernardo. Baltimore: Johns Hopkins University Press, 1985.

————. *Lettres de la veillesse. Rerum senilium.* Edited by Elvira Nota. 5 vols. Paris: Les Belles Lettres, 2002–. [vol. 5 forthcoming].

————. *Librorum Francisci Petrarche annotatio impressorum.* Venice, 1501.

————. *The Life of Solitude by Francis Petrarch.* Translated by Jacob Zeitlin. Urbana: University of Illinois Press, 1924.

————. *Il mio segreto.* Edited by Enrico Fenzi.

————. "The Miscellaneous Letters of Petrarch." See Wilkins and Billanovich.

————. *On Religious Leisure.* Edited and Translated by Susan S. Schearer. New York: Italica Press, 2002.

————. *Opera Latina Omnia.* 3rd ed. Venice: Simone Gabi [Bevilacqua], 1503.

———. *Opera quae extant omnia.* 4 vols. Basel: Henrichus Petri, 1554.

———. *Opera quae extant omnia.* 4 vols in 3. Basel: Henric Petri, 1554. Reprint, Ridgewood: Gregg Press, 1965.

———. *Opere latine di Francesco Petrarca.* 2 vols. Edited by Antonietta Bufano. Turin: Unione Tipografico-Editrice Torinese, 1975.

———. *Orationes contra tempestates.* In *Scritti inediti di Francesco Petrarca,* edited by Attilio Hortis. Trieste: Tipografia del Lloyd Austro-ungarico, 1874.

———. *Panegyricum in funere matris.* Edited by Carlo Muscetta. *Revue des Études Italiennes,* n.s., 29, nos. 1–3 (1983): 180–83.

———. *Petrarca a Novara. 13 giugno 1358.* Introduction by Francesco Cognasso. Novara: Interlinea, 2004.

———. *Il Petrarca nuovamente revisto e ricorretto.* Edited by Lodovico Dolce. Venice: Gabriel Giolito de' Ferrari, 1557.

———. *Petrarcas 'Buch ohne Namen' und di päpstliche Kurie: Ein Beitrag zur Geistesgeschichte der Frührenaissance.* Edited by Paul Piur. Halle and Salle: Max Neimeyer, 1925.

———. "Petrarcas *Privilegium laureationis.*" Edited by D. Mertens. In *Litterae Medii Aevi. Festschrift für Johanne Autenrieth zu ihrem 65. Geburtstag,* edited by Michael Borgolte and Herrad Spilling, 225–47. Sigmaringen: Jan Thorbecke Verlag, 1988.

———. *Petrarch at Vaucluse. Letters in Verse and Prose.* Translated by Ernest Hatch Wilkins. Chicago: University of Chicago Press, 1958.

———. *Petrarch's "Africa."* Translated and annotated by Thomas G. Bergin and Alice S. Wilson. New Haven: Yale University Press, 1997.

———. *Petrarch's Book without a Name. A Translation of the Liber sine monime.* Translated by Norman P. Zacour. Toronto: Pontifical Institute of Medieval Studies, 1973.

———. "Petrarch's *Coronation Oration,*" in Wilkis, *Studies in the Life and Works of Petrarch,* 300–13. Cambridge: Medieval Academy of America, 1955.

———. *Petrarch's Guide to the Holy Land. Itinerary to the Sepulcher of Our Lord Jesus Christ.* Edited and translated by Theodore J. Cachey Jr. Notre Dame: University of Notre Dame Press, 2002.

———. *Petrarch's Lyric Poems: The Rime sparse and Other Lyrics.* Edited and translated by Robert Durling. Cambridge: Harvard University Press, 1976.

———. *Petrarch's Remedies for Fortune Fair and Foul.* Translated by Conrad Rawski. 5 vols. Bloomington: Indiana University Press, 1991.

———. *Petrarch's Secret.* Translated by William Henry Draper. London: Chatto and Windus, 1911.

———. *Petrarch's Testament.* Edited and translated by Theodor E. Mommsen. Ithaca: Cornell University Press, 1957.

———. *Poesie latine.* Edited by Guido Martellotti and Enrico Bianchi. 1951. Reprint, Turin: Einaudi, 1976. 214–23.

———. *Poesie minori del Petrarca sul testo latino ora corretto volgarizzate da poeti viventi o da poco defunti.* Edited by Domenico Rossetti. 3 vols. Milan: Società Tipografica de' Classici Italiani, 1829–34.

———. *Posteritati.* See *Lettera ai posteri.*

———. *Les Psaumes Pénitentiaux, publiés d'après le manuscript de la Bibliothèque de Lucerne.* Edited by Henry Cochin. Paris: L. Rouart et Fils, 1929.

———. "Prefaces to the *De viris illustribus.*" Edited by Benjamin Kohl. *History and Theory* 14 (1974): 132–45.

———. *Prose.* Edited by G. Martellotti, Pier Giorgio Ricci, Enrico Carrara, Enrico Bianchi. Milan and Naples: Ricciardi Editore, 1955.

———. *Les remèdes aux deux fortunes. De remediis utriusque fortune: 1354–1366.* Edited and translated by Christophe Carraud. 2 vols. Grenoble: Éditions Jérôme Millon, 2002.

———. *Le repos religieux. De otio religioso: 1346–1357.* Edited by Jean-Luc Marion. Paris: Jérôme Millon, 2000.

———. *Rerum familiarum.* Edited by Ugo Dotti. Paris: Les Belles Lettres, 2002.

———. *Rerum familiarum libri I–VIII.* Translated by Aldo S. Bernardo. Albany: State University of New York Press, 1975.

———. *Rerum memorandarum libri.* Edited by Giuseppe Billanovich. Edizione Nazionale delle Opere di Francesco Petrarca, 14. Florence: Sansoni Editore, 1945.

———. *Rerum vulgarium fragmenta. Codice Vat. Lat. 3195.* 2 vols. *Edizione in fac-simile* (vol. 1 [2003]) and *Commentario* (vol. 2 [2004]). Edited by Gino Belloni, Furio Brugnolo, H. Wayne Storey, and Stefano Zamponi. Rome: Antenore: 2003–4.

———. *Le Rime.* Edited by Giosuè Carducci and Severino Ferrari. 1899. Reprint, Florence: Sansoni, 1957.

———. *Rime disperse di Francesco Petrarca o a lui attribuite.* Edited by Angelo Solerti. Florence: Sansoni, 1909. Reprint, Introduction by Paola Vecchi Galli. Florence: Le Lettere 1997.

———. *Rime, Trionfi e poesie latine.* Edited by Ferdinando Neri, Guido Martellotti, Enrico Bianchi, Natalino Sapegno. Milan and Naples: Ricciardi, 1951.

———. *Salmi penitenziali.* Edited by Roberto Gigliucci. Rome: Salerno Editrice, 1997.

———. *Scritti inediti di Francesco Petrarca.* Edited by Attilio Hortis. Trieste: Tipografia del Lloyd Austro-Ungarico, 1874.

———. "La seconda ambasceria di Francesco Petrarca a Venezia." Edited by Vittorio Lazzarini. In *Miscellanea di studi critici pubblicati in onore di Guido Mazzoni.*

2 vols. Edited by A. Della Torre and P. L. Rambaldi, 1:173–83. Florence: Tipografia Galileiana, 1907.

———. *The Secret*. Edited and translated by Carol E. Quillen. Boston and New York: Bedford/St. Martin's, 2003.

———. *Secretum*. Edited by Enrico Carrara. In Petrarch, *Prose*, edited by Guido Martellotti, Pier Giorgio Ricci, Enrico Carrara, and Enrico Bianchi, 21–215. Milan and Naples: Ricciardi, 1955. Reprint, Turin: Einaudi, 1977.

———. *Secretum. Il mio segreto*. Edited by Enrico Fenzi. Milan: Mursia, 1992.

———. *Selected Letters*. Edited by Craig Kallendorf. Bryn Mawr: Thomas Library, Bryn Mawr College, 1986.

———. *Senile V 2*. Edited by Monica Berté. Florence: Le Lettere, 1998.

———. *I sette salmi*. Edited by Ida Garghella. Naples: Edizioni Scientifiche Italiane. Perugia: Università degli studi di Perugia, 2002.

———. *I sette salmi penitenziali di Dante Alighieri e di Francesco Petrarca*. Bergamo: Mazzoleni, 1821. Reprint, Florence: Società Tipografica, 1827.

———. *Sine nomine: Lettere polemiche e politiche*. Edited by Ugo Dotti. Bari: Laterza, 1974.

———. *Trionfi, Rime estravaganti, Codice degli abbozzi*. Edited by Vinicio Pacca and Laura Paolino. Milan: Mondadori, 2000.

———. *Die Triumphe*. Edited by Carl Appel. Halle an der Saale: Niemeyer, 1901.

———. *Triumphi*. Edited by Marco Ariani. Milan: Mursia, 1988.

———. *The Triumphs of Petrarch*. Translated by Ernest Hatch Wilkins. Chicago: University of Chicago Press, 1962.

———. *La vita di Scipione l'Africano*. Edited by Guido Martellotti. Milan: Ricciardi, 1954.

———. *Le vite degli nomini illustri di Francesco Petrarca volgarizzate da Donato degli Albenzani*. Edited by Luigi Razzolini. 2 vols. Collezione di opera inedited orare dei primi tre secoli della lingua. Bologna: Romagnoli, 1874–79.

Petrus Damianus. *Opusculum undecimum*. In *PL* 145, col. 221–42. Paris: Thibaud, 1867.

Pliny, the Elder. *Natural History*. Translated by H. Rackham. 10 vols. Loeb Classical Library. Cambridge: Harvard University Press, 1949–62.

Poliziano, Angelo. *Silvae*. Edited by Francesco Bausi. Florence: Olschki, 1996.

Riccobaldi Ferrariensis. *Compendium romanae historiae*. Edited by A. Teresa Hankey. Fonti per la Storia d'Italia, 108. vol. 1. Rome: Istituto Storico Italiano per il Medioevo, 1984.

———. *Chronica parva Ferrariensis*. Edited by Gabriele Zanella. Ferrara: Deputazione Provinciale Ferrarese di storia Patria, 1983.

Saint-Thierry, Guillaume de. *Un traité de la vie solitaire. Lettre Aux Frères Du Mont-Dieu. Epistola ad fratres de Monte-Dei.* Paris: Vrin, 1946.

Seneca, L. Annaeus. *Epistles.* Translated by Richard M. Gummere. 3 vols. Loeb Classical Library. Cambridge: Harvard University Press, 1917–25.

———. *Opera quae supersunt. Supplementum.* Edited by Friederich Haase. Leipzig: B. G. Teubner, 1902.

Statius. *Silvae, Thebaid, Achilleid.* Translated by J. H. Mozley. 2 vols. Loeb Classical Library. 1928. Reprint, Cambridge: Harvard University Press, 1967.

Tasso, Torquato. *La Gerusalemme liberata.* Edited by Lanfranco Caretti. 1961. Reprint, Turin: Einaudi, 1993.

———. *Gerusalemme liberate.* Edited by Anna Maria Carini. Milan: Feltninelli, 1961.

———. *Jerusalem Delivered.* Translated by Joseph Tusiani. Rutherford: Fairleigh Dickinson University Press, 1970.

Valerius Maximus. *Facta et dicta memorabilia.* Edited by John Briscoe. 2 vols. Stuttgart and Leipzig: Teubner, 1998.

———. *Faits et dits mémorables.* Edited and translated by Robert Combès. Paris: Les Belles Lettres, 1995.

———. *Fatti e detti memorabili.* Translated by Luigi Rusca. 2 vols. Milan: Rizzoli, 1972.

———. *Memorable Doings and Sayings.* Translated by D. R. Shackleton Bailey. 2 vols. Loeb Classical Library. Cambridge: Harvard University Press, 2000.

Valla, Lorenzo, *De vero falsoque bono.* Edited by Maristella De Panizza Lorch. Bari: Adriatica Editrice, 1971.

Virgil. *The Aeneid.* Translated by Robert Fitzgerald. New York: Vintage Classics. 1990.

———. *Eclogues, Georgics, Aeneid, the Minor Poems.* Translated by H. Rushton Fairclough. 2 vols. Loeb Classical Library. 1916. Reprint, Cambridge: Harvard University Press, 2001.

———. *Publi Vergili Maronis Aeneidos. Liber quartus.* Edited by A. Pease. Cambridge: Harvard University Press, 1935.

SECONDARY LITERATURE

Adorno, Theodor. *Minima moralia.* London and New York: Verso, 2003.

Agrimi, Jole, and Chiara Crisciani. *Medicina del corpo e medicina dell'anima: Note sul sapere del medico fino all'inizio del secolo XIII.* Milan: Episteme, 1979.

Allen, Judson Boyce. *The Ethical Poetic of the Later Middle Ages: A Decorum of Convient Distinction.* Toronto: University of Toronto Press, 1982.

Ariani, Marco. *Petrarca.* Rome: Salerno Editore, 1999.

————. "Petrarca." In *Storia della letteratura italiana*. Directed by Enrico Malato. Vol. 2, 601–726. Rome: Salerno, 1995–2004.

Auerbach, Eric. *Literary Language and Its Public in Late Latin Antiquity and in the Middle Ages*. Translated by Ralph Mannheim. Princeton: Princeton University Press, 1965.

Avesani, Rino. "Il preumanesimo veronese." In *Storia della cultura veneta*, 2:111–41. Vicenza: Neri Pozza, 1976.

Baglio, Marco. "Presenze dantesche nel Petrarca latino." *Studi Petrarcheschi* 9 (1992): 77–137.

Bakhtin, Mikhail. *Problems of Dostoevsky's Poetics*. Ann Arbor: Ardis, 1973.

Balduino, Armando. *Boccaccio, Petrarca e altri poeti del Trecento*. Florence: Olschki, 1984.

Baranski, Zygmunt G., and Theodore J. Cachey, Jr., eds. *Petrarch and Dante: Antidantism, Metaphysics and Tradition*. Notre Dame: University of Notre Dame, 2009.

Barber, Joseph A. "Il sonetto CXIII e gli altri sonetti a Sennuccio." *Lectura Petrarce 2* (1982): 21–39.

Barchiesi, Alessandro. *Speaking Volumes: Narrative and Intertext in Ovid and Other Latin Poets*. London: Duckworth, 2001.

Barolini, Teodolinda. "The Making of a Lyric Sequence: Time and Narrative in Petrarch's *Rerum vulgarium fragmenta*." *MLN* 104 (1989): 1–38. Reprinted in *Dante and the Origins of Italian Literary Culture*, 193–223. New York: Fordham University Press, 2006.

————. "Notes toward a Gendered History of Italian Literature, with a Discussion of Dante's *Beatrix Loquax*." In *Dante and the Origins of Italian Literary Culture*, 360–78. New York: Fordham University Press, 2006.

————. "Petrarch at the Crossroads of Hermeneutics and Philology: Editorial Lapses, Narrative Impositions, and Wilkins' Doctrine of the Nine Forms of the *Rerum vulgarium fragmenta*." In *Petrarch and the Textual Origins of Interpretation*, edited by Teodolinda Barolini and H. Wayne Storey, 21–44. Columbia Series in the Classical Tradition. Leiden: Brill, 2007.

————. "Petrarch As the Metaphysical Poet Who Is Not Dante: Metaphysical Markers at the Beginning of the *Rerum vulgarium fragmenta*." In *Petrarch and Dante*, edited by Zygmunt Baranski and Theodore Cachey. Notre Dame: Notre Dame University Press, forthcoming.

————. *The Undivine Comedy: Detheologizing Dante*. Princeton: Princeton University Press, 1992.

Baron, Hans. *From Petrarch to Leonardo Bruni: Studies in Humanistic and Political Literature*. Chicago: University of Chicago Press, 1968.

————. *Petrarch's Secretum: Its Making and Its Meaning.* Cambridge: Medieval Academy of America, 1985.

————. "The State of Petrarch Studies." In *From Petrarch to Leonardo Bruni: Studies in Humanistic and Political Literature,* 7–50.

Bartuschat, Johannes. "Sofonisba e Massinissa: Dall'*Africa* e dal *De viris* ai *Trionfi.*" In *Petrarca e i suoi lettori,* edited by Vittorio Caratozzolo and Georges Güntert, 109–41. Ravenna: Longo, 2000.

Battaglia Ricci, Lucia. "Immaginario trionfale: Petrarca e la tradizione figurativa." In Berra, *I Triumphi,* 255–98.

Battera, Francesca. "Sulla pístola di Polifemo e Galatea: Primi appunti." *Compar(a)ison: An International Journal of Comparative Literature* 2 (1993): 35–64.

Bausi, Francesco. "Il *mechanicus* che scrive libri: Per un nuovo commento alle *Invective contra medicum* di Francesco Petrarca." *Rinascimento* 42 (2002): 67–111.

————. "La sconosciuta redazione originaria delle *Invective contra medicum* di Francesco Petrarca (Libro I) in un codice di Danzica." *Rinascimento* 45 (2005): 91–115.

Bec, Christian. "Dal Petrarca al Machiavelli: Il dialogo tra lettore ed autore." *Rinascimento* 16 (1976): 3–19. Reprinted in *Cultura e Società a Firenze nell'età del Rinascimento,* 228–44. Rome: Salerno, 1981.

Bellemo, Vincenzo. *Jacopo e Giovanni de' Dondi.* Chioggia: Duse, 1894.

Bellucci, Laura. "Palinodia amorosa in una 'dispersa' del Petrarca." *Studi e Problemi di Critica Testuale II* (1971): 103–28.

Benedek, Thomas G. "An Interpretation of Petrarch's 'Invective against Physicians.'" In *Thirty-first International Congress on the History of Medicine,* edited by Raffaele A. Bernabeo, 691–96. Bologna: Monduzzi, 1990.

Bergdolt, Klaus. *Artz, Krankheit und Therapie bei Petrarca: Die Kritik an Medizin und Naturwissenschaft im italienischen Frühhumanismus.* Weinheim: Acta Humaniora, 1992.

————."Die Kritik am Arzt im Mittelalter: Beispiele und Tendenzen vom 6. bis zum 12. Jahrhundert." *Gesnerus* 48 (1991): 43–64.

————. "Die *meditatio mortis* als Medizin: Betrachtungen zur Ethik der Todesangst im Spätmittelalter und Heute." *Würzburger medizinhistorische Mitteilungen* 9 (1991): 249–57.

————. "Petrarca, la medicina e le scienze naturali." *Kos,* n.s., 89 (1993): 43–49.

————. "Petrarca und die Pest." *Sudhoffs Archiv* 76 (1992): 63–73.

————. "Precursori ed epigone nella polemica petrarchesca contro i medici." In Berté, *et al., Petrarca e la Medicina,* 3–18.

————."Zur antischolastischen Arztkritik des 13. Jahrhunderts." *Medizinhistorisches Journal* 26 (1991): 264–81.

Berghoff-Bührer, Margrith. *Das Bucolicum Carmen des Petrarca: Ein Beitrag zur Wirkungsgeschichte von Vergils Eclogen.* Bern and New York: P. Lang, 1991.

Bernardo, Aldo S. Introduction to Petrarch, *Rerum familiarum libri I–VIII*, xvii–xxxii.

———. "Letter-Splitting in Petrarch's *Familiares.*" *Speculum* 33, no. 2 (1958): 236–41.

———. "Petrarch's Autobiography: Circularity Revisited." *Annali d'Italianistica* 4 (1986): 45–72.

———. *Petrarch, Scipio, and the "Africa": The Birth of Humanism's Dream.* Baltimore: Johns Hopkins University Press, 1962.

Bernardo, Aldo S., ed. *Francesco Petrarca Citizen of the World: Proceedings of the World Petrarch Congress Washington, D.C., April 6–13, 1974.* Padua: Antenore, 1980.

Berra, Claudia, ed. *I Triumphi di Francesco Petrarca (Gargnano del Garda, 1998).* Milan: Cisalpino, 1999.

———. "La varietà stilistica dei *Trionfi.*" In Berra, *I Triumphi*, 175–218.

Berté, Monica, Vincenzo Fera, and Tiziana Pesenti, eds. *Petrarca e la medecina.* Messina: Centro Interdipartimentale di Studi Umanistici, 2006.

Bertolani, Maria Cecilia. *Il corpo glorioso: Studi sui Trionfi del Petrarca.* Rome: Carocci, 2001.

Besomi, Ottavio. *Codici petrarcheschi nelle biblioteche svizzere*, 49–51. Padua: Antenore, 1967.

Bettarini, Rosanna. "Perché 'narrando' il duol si disacerba (Motivi esegetici dagli autografi petrarcheschi)." In *La critica del testo. Problemi di metodo ed esperienze di lavoro. Atti del Convegno di Lecce, 22–26 ottobre*, 305–20. Rome: Salerno, 1985.

Bianchi, Dante. "Intorno alle 'rime disperse' del Petrarca: Il Petrarca e i fratelli Beccari." *Studi Petrarcheschi* 2 (1949): 107–35.

Billanovich, Giuseppe. "L'altro stil nuovo: Da Dante teologo a Petrarca filologo." *Studi Petrarcheschi*, n.s., 11 (1994): 1–98.

———. "Dall' *Epystolarum mearum ad diversos liber* ai *Rerum familiarium libri XXIV.*" In *Petrarca letterato*, 1–55.

———. "Laura fantasma del *Canzoniere.*" *Studi Petrarcheschi*, n.s., 11 (1994): 149–58.

———. *Un nuovo esempio delle scoperte e delle letture del Petrarca: L'Eusebio-Girolamo-PseudoProspero.* Krefeld: Scherpe, 1954.

———. "Petrarca, Boccaccio e Zanobi da Strada." In *Petrarca e il primo umanesimo*, 158–67.

———. "Petrarca e Cicerone." In *Miscellanea Giovanni Mercati.* 4:88–106. Vatican City: Biblioteca Apostolica Vaticana, 1966.

———. *Petrarca e il primo umanesimo.* Padua: Editrice Antenore, 1996.

——. *Petrarca letterato I. Lo scrittoio del Petrarca*. Rome: Edizioni di Storia e Letteratura, 1947.

——. "Petrarch and the Textual Tradition of Livy." *Journal of the Warburg Institute* 14 (1951): 137–208.

——. *Restauri boccacceschi*. Rome: Edizioni di Storia e Letteratura. 1947.

——. "Uno Suetonio della Biblioteca del Petrarca (Berlinese Lat. Fol. 337)." *Studi Petrarcheschi* 6 (1956): 23–33.

——. "Petrarca e il Ventoso." *Italia Medioevale e Umanistica* 9 (1966): 389–401.

——. "Tito Livio, Petrarca, Boccaccio." *Archivio Storico Ticinese* 97 (1984): 3–10.

——. "Tra Dante e Petrarca." *Italia Medioevale e Umanistica* 8 (1965): 1–44.

——. *La tradizione del testo di Livio e le origini dell'Umanesimo: Tradizione e fortuna di Livio tra medioevo e umanesimo*. Vol. 1.1. Studi sul Petrarca, 9. Padua: Antenore, 1981.

Biow, Douglas. *Doctors, Ambassadors, Secretaries: Humanism and Professions in Renaissance Italy*. Chicago: University of Chicago Press, 2002.

Bishop, Morris, ed. *Catalogue of the Petrarch Collection in Cornell University Library*. Millwood: Kraus-Thomson Organization, 1974.

Blanc, Pierre. "Petrarca ou la poétique de l'ego: Éléments de psychopoétique pétrarquienne." *Revue des Études Italiennes*, n.s., 29 (1983): 124–69.

Borchardt, Frank L. "Petrarch: The German Connection." In *Francis Petrarch*, ed. Scaglione. 418–31.

Bosco, Umberto. *Francesco Petrarca*. Bari: Laterza, 1968.

——. "Particolari petrarcheschi. 1. Precisazioni sulle *Invective contra medicum*." *Studi Petrarcheschi* 1 (1948): 97–109.

——. "Il Petrarca e l'umanesimo filologico." *Giornale Storico della Letteratura Italiana* 120 (1942): 84–89.

Bowron, Edgar Peters. "Giorgio Vasari's 'Portrait of Six Tuscan Poets.'" *Minneapolis Institute of Arts Bulletin* 60 (1971–73): 43–54.

Boyle, Marjorie O'Rourke. *Petrarch's Genius. Pentimento and Prophecy*. Berkeley: University of California Press, 1991.

Branca, Vittore. *Boccaccio medievale*. 5th edition. Florence: Sansoni, 1981.

——. "Francesco Petrarca." *Dizionario critico della letteratura italiana*, 3:419–32. Turin: Unione Tipografico-Editrice Torinese, 1986.

——. *Giovanni Boccaccio. Profilo biografico*. Florence: Sansoni, 1977.

——. "Intertestualità fra Petrarca e Boccaccio." *Lectura Petrarce* 14 (1994): 359–80.

Bray, Alan. *The Friend*. Chicago: University of Chicago Press, 2003.

Brown, Terrance. "Affective Dimensions of Meaning." In *The Nature and Onto-*

genesis of Meaning, edited by Willis F. Overton and David Stuart Palermo, 168–90. Hillsdale: Lawrence Erlbaum Associates, 1994.

Bruère, Richard T. "Lucan and Petrarch's *Africa.*" *American Journal of Philology* 56 (1961): 83–99.

Cachey, Theodore J. Jr. "From Shipwreck to Port: *RVF* 189 and the Making of the *Canzoniere.*" *MLN* 120, no. 1 (2005): 30–49.

———. "Petrarchan Cartographic Writing." In *Medieval and Renaissance Humanism: Rhetoric, Representation and Reform,* edited by Stephen Gersh and Bert Roest, 73–91. Leiden and Boston: Brill, 2003.

Calcaterra, Carlo. "La concezione storica del Petrarca." *Annali della Cattedra Petrarchesca* 9 (1939–40): 3–25. Reprinted in *Nella selva del Petrarca,* 415–33.

———. *Nella selva del Petrarca.* Bologna: Cappelli, 1942.

Caratozzolo, Vittorio, and Georges Güntert, eds. *Petrarca e i suoi lettori.* Ravenna: Longo, 2000.

Carducci, Giosuè. "Ad Arquà, presso la tomba del Petrarca." In *Prose scelte.* Edited by Emilio Pasquini, 224–26. Milan: Biblioteca Universale Rizzoli, 2007.

———. *Ai parentali di Giovanni Boccacci in Certaldo.* Bologna: Zanichelli, 1876.

Carrai, Stefano. "Il mito di Ulisse nelle 'Familiari.'" In *Motivi e forme delle Familiari di Francesco Petrarca,* edited by Claudia Berra. Milan: Cisalpino, 2003.

Carrai, Stefano, ed. *La poesia pastorale nel Rinascimento.* Padua: Antenore, 1998.

Carrara, Enrico. "I commenti antichi e la cronologia delle Egloghe petrarchesche." *Giornale Storico della Letteratura Italiana* 28 (1895): 123–53.

———. "Petrarca, Francesco." In *Enciclopedia italiana,* 27 (1935).

———. *La poesia pastorale.* Milan: Vallardi, 1909.

Cassirer, Ernst. *The Individual and the Cosmos in Renaissance Philosophy.* Translated by Mario Domandi. Mineola: Dover Publications, 1963.

Cassirer, Ernst, Paul Oskar Kristeller, and John Herman Randall, eds. *The Renaissance Philosophy of Man.* Chicago: University of Chicago Press, 1948.

The Catholic Encyclopedia. http://www.newadvent.org/cathen/04222a.htm.

Cavedon, Annarosa. "Intorno alle 'Rime estravaganti' del Petrarca." *Revue des Études Italiennes,* n.s., 29 (1983): 86–108.

———. "La tradizione 'veneta' delle Rime estravaganti del Petrarca." *Studi Petrarcheschi* 8 (1976): 1–73.

Cavell, Stanley. *Cities of Words: Pedagogical Letters on a Register of the Moral Life.* Cambridge: Harvard University Press, 2004.

———. *Conditions Handsome and Unhandsome: The Constitution of Emersonian Perfectionism.* Chicago: Chicago University Press, 1990.

Cervigni, Dino, ed. "Petrarch and the European Lyric Tradition." Special issue, *Annali d'Italianistica* 22 (2004).

Cesarini Martinelli, Lucia. "Note sulla polemica Poggio-Valla e sulla fortuna delle *Elegantiae*." *Interpres* 3 (1980): 29–79.

Chalifour, Clark L. "Sir Philip Sidney's Old Arcadia as Terentian Comedy." *SEL: Studies in English Literature* 16, no. 1 (Winter 1976): 51–63.

Cherchi, Paolo. "Dispositio e significato del sonetto LXVII." In *The Flight of Ulysses: Studies in Memory of Emmanuel Hatzantonis*, edited by Augustus A. Mastri, 82–96. Chapel Hill: *Annali d'Italianistica*, 1997.

———. "Petrarca, Valerio Massimo, e le 'concordanze delle storie.'" *Rinascimento* 2nd ser., 42 (2002): 31–65.

———. *Polimatia di Riuso – Mezzo secolo di plagio*. Rome: Bulzoni, 1998.

———. "'Quosdam historicos' (Rer. Mem. Lib., III 12)." *Studi Petrarcheschi* 18 (2005): 159–62.

———. "La simpatia della natura nel *Canzoniere* di Petrarca." *Cultura Neolatina* 43, nos. 1–2 (2003): 83–113.

Chiappelli, Carolyn. "The Motif of Confession in Petrarch's 'Mt. Ventoux.'" *MLN* 93, no. 1 (Jan. 1978): 131–36.

Chiffoleau, Jacques. *La comptabilité de l'au-delà*. Rome: École Française de Rome, 1980.

Chiffoleau, Jacques, Lauro Martines, and Agostino Paravicini Bagliani, eds. *Riti e rituali nelle società medievali*. Spoleto: Centro Italiano di Studi sull'Alto Medioevo, 1994.

Chubb, Thomas Caldecot. *The Life of Giovanni Boccaccio*. 1930. Reprint, Port Washington: Kennikat Press, 1969.

Cioffari, Vincenzo. "Fate, Fortune, and Chance." In *Dictionary of the History of Ideas*, edited by Philip P. Wiener, 2:225–36. New York: Scribners, 1973.

Clarke, Danielle. "'Lover's Songs Shall Turne to Holy Psalmes': Mary Sidney and the Transformation of Petrarch." *Modern Language Review* 92 (1997): 282–94.

Clubb, Louise George. *Italian Drama in Shakespeare's Time*. New Haven: Yale University Press, 1989.

Cochin, Henry. *Le frère de Pétrarque et le livre "Du repos des religieux."* Paris: Boullion, 1930.

Cody, Richard. *The Landscape of the Mind: Pastoralism and Platonic Theory in Tasso's Aminta and Shakespeare's Early Comedies*. Oxford: Clarendon Press, 1969.

Cohn, Samuel K. Jr. "Burial in the Early Renaissance: Six Cities in Central Italy." In *Riti e rituali nelle società medievali*. Chiffoleau, *et al.*, 39–57.

———. *Death and Property in Siena, 1205–1800*. Baltimore: Johns Hopkins University Press, 1988.

Collins, Randall. "On the Acrimoniousness of Intellectual Disputes." *Common Knowledge* 8 (2002): 47–70.

———. *The Sociology of Philosophies: A Global Theory of Intellectual Change.* Cambridge: Harvard University Press, 1998.

Concolato, Maria Palermo. "Il Viaggio del testo: *I Salmi penitenziali* dall'Aretino al Wyatt." In *Per una topografia dell'Altrove. Spazi altri nell'immaginario letterario e culturale di lingua inglese,* edited by Maria Teresa Chialant and Eleonora Rao, 399–412. Naples: Liguori, 1995.

Conde Salazar, Matilde. "El médico en las epístolas de Séneca y Petrarca." In *Séneca dos mil años después: Actas del congreso internacional conmemorativo del bimilenario de su nacimiento (Córdoba, 24–27 de septiembre, 1996),* 637–44. Córdoba: Publicaciones de la Universidad de Córdoba y Obra Social y Cultural CajaSur, 1997.

Conley, Tom. *The Self-Made Map: Cartographic Writing in Early Modern France.* Minneapolis: University of Minnesota Press, 1996.

Constable, Giles. "Letters and Letter-Collections." *Typologie des sources du Moyen Âge Occidental* 17 (1976): 7–65.

———. "Petrarch and Monasticism." In Bernardo, *Francesco Petrarca Citizen of the World,* 53–99.

Conte, Gian Biagio. "Il proemio della *Farsalia.*" *Maia* 18 (1966): 42–53.

Coogan, Robert. *Babylon on the Rhone.* Potomac: Studia Humanitatis, 1983.

Coppini, Donatella. "Don Giuseppe de Luca e l'incompiuta edizione dei *Salmi penitenziali* del Petrarca." *Quaderni Petrarcheschi* (1993): 413–35.

Corbett, Philip B. *The Scurra.* Edinburgh: Edinburgh University Press, 1986.

Corsaro, Antonio. "Fortuna e imitazione nel cinquecento." In Berra, *I Triumphi,* 429–85.

Cosenza, Mario Emilio. *Francesco Petrarca and the Revolution of Cola di Rienzo.* Chicago: University of Chicago Press, 1913. 2nd ed., Ronald G. Musto. New York: Italica Press, 1986.

Costley, Clare. *The Penitential Psalms and Theologies of Penance.* Ph.D. diss., University of Pennsylvania, 2005.

Courcelle, Pierre. *La consolation de philosophie dans la tradition littéraire: Antécédents et postérité de Boèce.* Paris: Études Augustiniennes, 1967.

Cracolici, Stefano. "Alberti e la 'gravitas nervosa': Note su un contributo di Giovanni Ponte." In *Leon Battista Alberti (1404–72) tra scienze e lettere: Atti del Convegno (Genova, 19–20 novembre 2004),* edited by Alberto Beniscelli and Francesco Furlan, 287–308. Genova: Accademia Ligure di Scienze e Lettere, 2005.

Crouzet-Pavane, Elizabeth. *Venice Triumphant: The Horizons of a Myth,* trans. Lydia G. Cochrane. Baltimore: Johns Hopkins University Press, 2002.

Daniele, Antonio, ed. *Le lingue del Petrarca.* Udine: Forum (Società Editrice Universitaria Udinese), 2005.

Debenedetti, Santorre. "Per le 'disperse' di Francesco Petrarca." *Giornale Storico della Letteratura Italiana* 56 (1910): 98–106.

Dell'Anna, Giuseppe. "Il Petrarca e la medicina." In *Petrarca e la cultura europea*, edited by Luisa Rotondi Secchi Tarugi, 203–322. Milan: Nuovi Orizzonti, 1997.

Della Torre, Arnaldo. "Aneddoti petrarcheschi." *Giornale Dantesco* 16 (1908): 69–88.

Del Puppo, Dario, and H. Wayne Storey. "Wilkins nella formazione del canzoniere di Petrarca." *Italica* 80 (2003): 295–312.

De Luca, Giuseppe. Review of *Pétrarque, Les Psaumes Pénitentiaux, publiés* [under pseudonym "Odoscopos"] *d'après le manuscript de la Bibliothèque de Lucerne*. Edited by Henry Cochin. Paris: L. Rouart et Fils, 1929. In *Frontespizio* (June 1931): 13.

De Rentiis, Dina. *Die Zeit der Nachfolge: Zur Interdipendenz von 'imitatio Christi' und 'imitatio auctorum' in 12.-16. Jahrhundert*. Tübingen: Max Niemeyer, 1996.

De Robertis, Domenico. Introduction. *Il codice chigiano L. V. 176, autografo di Giovanni Boccaccio*. Rome: Archivi Edizioni, 1974.

De Sanctis, Francesco. *Storia della letteratura italiana*. Edited by Paolo Arcari. 1870–71. Reprint, Milan: Fratelli Treves, 1925.

Desmond, Marilynn. *Reading Dido: Gender, Textuality, and the Medieval "Aeneid."* Minneapolis: University of Minnesota Press, 1994.

Dewar, Michael. "Laying It on with a Trowel: The Proem to Lucan and Related Texts." *Classical Quarterly* 44 (1994): 199–211.

Di Stefano, Giuseppe. "Dionigi di Borgo San Sepolcro e Valerio Massimo." In Suitner, *Dionigi da Borgo San Sepolcro fra Petrarca e Boccaccio*, 147–64.

Di Zenzo, Salvatore Floro. *Studio critico sull'attribuzione a Dante Alighieri di un antico volgarizzamento dei Sette salmi penitenziali*. Naples: Laurenziana, 1984.

Dictionnaire de spiritualité. 17 vols. Paris: Beauchesne, 1932–.

Dotti, Ugo. *Petrarca a Milano: Documenti milanesi, 1353–1354*. Milan: Ceschina, 1972.

———. *Petrarca a Parma*. Reggio Emilia: Edizioni Diabasis, 2006.

———. *Petrarca civile. Alle origini dell'intellettuale moderno*. Rome: Donzelli, 2001.

———. "Petrarca: Il mito dafneo." *Convivium: Filosofia Psicologia Humanidades* 37 (1969): 9–23.

———. *Vita di Petrarca*. 1987. Reprint, Bari: Laterza, 1992.

Drum, Walter. "The Psalms." In *The Catholic Encyclopedia*. Vol. 12. New York: Robert Appleton, 1911.

Durling, Robert. "The Ascent of Mt. Ventoux and the Crisis of Allegory." *Italian Quarterly* 18, no. 69 (Summer 1974): 7–28.

———. "Petrarch's 'Giovene Donna Sotto un Verde Lauro.'" *MLN* 86, no. 1 (Jan. 1971): 1–20.

Dutschke, Dennis. "The Anniversary Poems in Petrarch's *Canzoniere.*" *Italica* 58 (1981): 83–101.

———. "Le figure bibliche « in ordine»." In Berra, *I Triumphi*, 135–52.

———. *Francesco Petrarca: Canzone XXIII from First to Final Version.* Ravenna: Longo, 1977.

Eisenbichler, Konrad, and Amilcare Iannucci, eds. *Petrarch's Triumphs: Allegory and Spectacle.* Toronto: Dovehouse, 1990.

Ernout, Alfred and Antoine Meillet. *Dictionnaire etymologique de la langue latine.* Paris: Klincksieck, 1932.

Ettin, Andrew V. *Literature and the Pastoral.* New Haven: Yale University Press, 1984.

Farrell, Thomas J. "The Story of Griselda." In *Sources and Analogues of the Canterbury Tales,* edited by Robert M. Correale and Mary Hamel, 1:108–29. Cambridge: D.S. Brewer, 2002.

Feagin, Susan L. *Reading with Feeling: The Aesthetics of Appreciation.* Ithaca: Cornell University Press, 1996.

Fentonia [pseudo.]. "I sette salmi." *Notes and Queries: A Medium of Inter-Communication for Literary Men, General Readers, Etc.* 3rd ser., 5 (Jan.–June 1864): 409.

Fenzi, Enrico. "Di alcuni palazzi, cupole e planetary nell'*Africa* di Petrarca." In *Saggi petrarcheschi,* 233–35.

———. "L'ermeneutica petrarchesca tra libertà e verità." *Lettere Italiane* 54 (2002): 170–209.

———. "Petrarca a Milano: Tempi e modi di una scelta meditata." In *Petrarca e la Lombardia: Atti del Convegno di Studi, Milano, 22–23 maggio 2003,* 221–63, edited by Giuseppe Frasso, Giuseppe Velli, and Maurizio Vitale. Padua: Antenore, 2005.

———. "Preveggenze umanistiche del Petrarca." In *Saggi petrarceschi,* 633–53.

———. *Saggi petrarceschi.* Fiesole: Cadmo, 2003.

———. "Tra Dante e Petrarca: Il fantasma di Ulisse." In *Saggi petrarcheschi,* 493–517.

Feo, Michele. "Di alcuni rusticani cestelli di pomi." *Quaderni Petrarcheschi* 1 (1983): 23–75.

———. "L'epistola come mezzo di propaganda politica in Francesco Petrarca." In *Le forme della propaganda politica nel due e nel trecento,* edited by Paolo Cammarosano, 203–26. Rome: École Française de Rome, 1994.

———. "Fili petrarcheschi." *Rinascimento* 19 (1979): 3–89.

———. "Francesco Petrarca." In *Storia della letteratura italiana,* edited by Enrico Malato, 10:294–96. Rome: Salerno, 2001.

———. "Francesco Petrarca e la contesa epistolare tra Markwart e i Visconti." In *Filologia umanistica per Gianvito Resta,* edited by Vincenzo Fera and Giacomo Ferraú, 621–92. Padua: Antenore, 1997.

————. "'In vetustissimis cedulis.' Il testo del postscriptum della senile XIII 11 γ e la 'forma Malatesta' dei *Rerum vulgarium fragmenta.*" *Quaderni Petrarcheschi* 11 (2001): 119–148.

————. "Note petrarchesche. I: Petarca e Enrico da Iernia. II: Le 'due redazioni' della *Collatio laureationis.*" *Quaderni Petrarcheschi* 7 (1990): 186–203.

————. "Nuove petrarchesche." *Belfagor* 46, no. 2 (1991): 129–52.

————. "Per l'esegesi della III ecloga del Petrarca." *Italia Medioevale e Umanistica* 10 (1967): 385–401.

Feo, Michele, ed. *Codici latini del Petrarca nelle biblioteche fiorentine.* Florence: Le Lettere, 1991.

————. *Petrarca nel tempo: Tradizione lettori e immagini delle opere.* Pontedera: Bandecchi and Vivaldi, 2003.

Fera, Vincenzo. *La revisione petrarchesca dell'Africa.* Messina: Centro di Studi Umanistici, 1984.

Ferrante, Giuseppina. "Lombardo della Seta, Umanista padovano." *Istituto Veneziano di Scienze, Lettere ed Arti: Atti* 93 (1933–34): 445–87.

Festa, Nicola. *Saggio sull'Africa.* Palermo: Sandron, 1926.

Ficara, Giorgio. *Solitudini.* Milan: Garzanti, 1993.

Finucci, Valeria, ed. *Petrarca: Canoni, Esemplarità.* Rome: Bulzoni, 2006.

Firpo, Luigi. *Medicina medievale: Testi dell'Alto Medioevo, miniature del codice di Kassel, regole salutari salernitane, incisioni del Fascicolo de medicina, anatomia di Mondino de' Liuzzi.* Turin: Unione Tipografico-Editrice Torinese, 1972.

Fisher, John. *Commentary on the Seven Penitential Psalms.* Edited by J. S. Phillimore. London: Manresa Press, 1914–15.

Fleming, John W. *The Roman de la Rose: A Study in Allegory and Iconography.* Princeton: Princeton University Press, 1969.

Folena, Gianfranco. "L'orologio del Petrarca." *Libri e Documenti* 5, no. 3 (1979): 1–12.

Foresti, Arnaldo. *Aneddoti della vita di Francesco Petrarca.* 1928. Reprint, Studi sul Petrarca, 1. Edited by Antonia Tissoni Benvenuti. Padua: Antenore, 1977.

————. "La data della prima ecloga." In *Aneddoti,* 204–8.

————. "Quando Gherardo si fece Monaco." In *Aneddoti,* 108–14.

————. "Quando il Petrarca fece le grandi giunte al *Bucolicum?*" In *Aneddoti,* 471–84.

Forster, Leonard. *The Icy Fire: Five Studies in European Petrarchism.* Cambridge: Cambridge University Press, 1969.

Forte, Stephen L. "John Colonna O.P., Life and Writings (ca. 1298–1340)." *Archivum Fratrum Praedicatorum* 20 (1950): 394–402.

Foster, Kenelm. *Petrarch: Poet and Humanist.* Edinburgh: Edinburgh University Press, 1984.

Fradenburg, Louise O. "The Manciple's Servant Tongue: Politics and Poetry in *The Canterbury Tales.*" *ELH* 52 (1985): 85–118.

Frakes, Jerold C. *The Fate of Fortune in the Early Middle Ages: The Boethian Tradition.* Leiden: Brill, 1988.

"Francesco Nelli." *Rai International Online.* http://www.italica.rai.it/rinascimento/parole_chiave/schede/136nelli.htm.

Frasso, Giuseppe. *Itinerari con Francesco Petrarca.* Padua: Antenore, 1974.

————. "Minime divagazioni petrarchesche." In *Il genere "tenzone" nelle letterature romanze delle Origini,* edited by Matteo Pedroni and Antonio Stäuble, 159–63. Ravenna: Longo, 1999.

Frati, Ludovico. "Gano di Lapo da Colle e le sue rime." *Il Propugnatore,* n.s., 6, no. 2 (1893): 195–226.

Freccero, John. "The Fig Tree and the Laurel: Petrarch's Poetics." *Diacritics* 5 (1975): 34–40.

Freund, Elizabeth. *The Return of the Reader: Reader-Response Criticism.* London and New York: Methuen, 1987.

Friedersdorff, Franz. "Die poetischen Vergleiche in Petrarcas *Africa.*" *Zeitschrift für Romanische Philologie* 20 (1896): 471–91; 21 (1897): 58–72; 22 (1898): 9–48.

Fubini, Riccardo. "Pubblicità e controllo del libro nella cultura del Rinascimento." In *Humanisme e église en Italie et en France méridionale (XV siècle-milieu du XVI siècle),* edited by Patrick Gilli, 207–10. Rome: École Française, 2004.

————. Review of *Doctors, Ambassadors, Secretaries: Humanism and Professions in Renaissance Italy,* by Douglas Biow. *Renaissance Quarterly* 56 (2003): 1152–53.

Fucilla, Joseph G. *Oltre un cinquentennio di scritti sul Petrarca (1916–1973).* Padua: Antenore, 1982.

Garfagnini, Gian Carlo. "Note sull'uso degli *Auctores* nelle *Seniles.*" *Quaderni Petrarcheschi* 9–10 (1992–1993): 669–83.

Garin, Eugenio. "Guarino Veronese e la cultura a Ferrara." In *Ritratti di umanisti,* 69–106. Florence: Sansoni, 1967.

————. *Italian Humanism: Philosophy and Civic Life in the Renaissance.* Translated by Peter Munz. New York: Harper & Row, 1965.

————. *Ritratti di umanisti.* Florence: Sansoni, 1967.

Gasparotto, Giovanni. "Il Petrarca conosceva direttamente Lucrezio. Le fonti dell'egloga IX, 'Querulus' del *Bucolicum carmen.*" *Atti e Memorie della R. Accademia di Scienze, Lettere, e Arti in Padova* 80 (1967–68): 309–55.

Gensini, Stefano. "'Poeta et historicus': L'episodio della laurea nella carriera e nella prospettiva culturale di Francesco Petrarca." *La Cultura* 18 (1980): 166–94.

Gerosa, Pietro Paolo. *Umanesimo cristiano del Petrarca.* Turin: Bottega d'Erasmo, 1966.

Getto, Giovanni. *"Triumphus Temporis:* Il sentimento del tempo nell'opera di Francesco Petrarca." In *Letterature comparate: problemi e metodo. Studi in onore di Ettore Paratore,* 3:1243–72. 4 vols. Bologna: Patron, 1981.

Ghisalberti, Fausto. "Le chiose virgiliane di Benvenuto da Imola." In *Studi virgiliani pubblicati in occasione delle celebrazioni bimillenarie della Reale Accademia Virgiliana.* Mantova: Reale Accademia Virgiliana, 1930.

Giannarelli, Elena. "Fra mondo classico e agiografia cristiana: Il *Breve panegyricum defuncti matri* di Petrarca." *Annali della Scuola Normale di Pisa* 9, no. 3 (1979): 1099–118.

Giannetto, Nella, ed. *Vittorino da Feltre e la sua scuola. Umanesimo, Pedagogia, Arti.* Florence: Olschki, 1981.

Gianni, Francesco. "Per una storia letteraria della peste." In *The Regulation of Evil: Social and Cultural Attitudes to Epidemics in the Late Middle Ages,* edited by Agostino Paravicini Bagliani and Francesco Santi, 63–124. Florence: Sismel, 1998.

Gianola, G. M. "La raccolta di biografie come problema storiografico nel *De viris* di Giovanni Colonna." *Bollettino dell'Istituto Storico Italiano per il Medio Evo e Archivio Muratoriano* 89 (1991): 509–40.

Gibson, John. "Between Truth and Triviality." *British Journal of Aesthetics* 43 (2003): 224–37.

Gilson, Etienne. "Sur deux texts de Pétrarque." *Studi Petrarcheschi* 7 (1959): 35–50.

———. "Sur deux texts de Pétrasque: II. *In confinio duorum populum.*" In *Petrarca e Petrarchismo. Atti del Terzo Congresso dell'Associazione Internatzionale per gli Studi di Lingua e Letteratura Italiana (Aix-en-Provence e Marsiglia, 31 marzo – 5 aprile 1959,* 43–50. Bologna: Minerva, 1961.

Ginori Conti, Piero. *Novelle inedite intorno a Bernabò Visconti.* Florence: Fondazione Ginori Conti, 1940.

Giunta, Claudio. "Memoria di Dante nei *Trionfi.*" *Rivista di Letteratura Italiana* 11 (1993): 411–52.

———. *Versi ad un destinatario. Saggio sulla poesia italiana del Medioevo.* Bologna: Il Mulino, 2002.

Godi, Carlo. "La 'Collatio laureationis' del Petrarca." *Italia Medioevale e Umanistica* 13 (1970): 13–27.

———. "La 'Collatio laureationis' del Petrarca nelle due redazioni." *Studi Petrarcheschi* 5 (1988): 1–58.

Goletti, Giulio. "Due integrazioni testuali al *De otio religioso.*" In Feo, *Petrarca nel tempo,* 418–22.

————. "Restauri al *De otio religioso* del Petrarca." *Studi Medievali e Umanistici* 2 (2004): 295–307.

Gorni, Guglielmo. "Metamorfosi e redenzione in Petrarca. Il senso della forma Correggio del *Canzoniere*." *Lettere Italiane* 30 (1978): 3–13.

Graf, Arturo. *Attraverso il Cinquecento*. Turin: Chiantore, 1926.

Greene, Roland. *Unrequited Conquest: Love and Empire in the Colonial Americas*. Chicago: University of Chicago Press, 1999.

Greene, Thomas. *The Light in Troy: Imitation and Discovery in Renaissance Poetry*. New Haven: Yale University Press, 1982.

————. "Petrarch *Viator:* The Displacements of Heroism." *Yearbook of English Studies* 12 (1982): 25–57.

Griggio, Claudio. "Forme dell'invettiva in Petrarca." *Atti e Memorie dell'Accademia Patavina di Scienze Morali, Lettere e Arti. Memorie della Classe di Scienze Morali, Lettere e Arti* 109 (1996–97): 375–92.

————. "Note sulla tradizione dell'invettiva dal Petrarca al Poliziano." In *Bufere e molli aurette: Polemiche letterarie dallo Stilnovo alla 'Voce,'* edited by Maria Grazia Pensa, 37–51. Milan: Guerini e Associati, 1996.

Grimes, Kristen Ina. "A proposito di *Rvf* 285: Petrarca tra Laura e Monica." *Atti e Memorie dell'Accademia Galileiana di Scienze, Lettere ed Arti già Ricovrati e Patavina* 117 (2004–5): 273–95.

Guglielminetti, Marziano. *Memoria e scrittura: L'autobiografia da Dante a Cellini*. Turin: Einaudi. 1977.

Hainsworth, P. R. J. "The Myth of Daphne in the *Rerum vulgarium fragmenta*." *Italian Studies* 34 (1979): 28–44.

————. *Petrarch the Poet: An Introduction to the "Rerum vulgarium fragmenta*." London: Routledge, 1988.

Hamlin, Hannibal. *Psalm Culture and Early Modern English Literature*. Cambridge: Cambridge University Press, 2004.

Hankey, A. Teresa. *Riccobaldo of Ferrara: His Life, Works and Influence*. Rome: Istituto Storico Italiano per il Medio Evo, 1996.

Harley, J. B., and David Woodward. *Cartography in Prehistoric, Ancient, and Medieval Europe and the Mediterranean*. Chicago: University of Chicago Press, 1987.

Heitmann, Klaus. *Fortuna und Virtus: Eine Studie zu Petrarcas Lebensweisheit*. Cologne: Böhlau, 1958.

————. "La genesi del 'De remediis utriusque fortune' del Petrarca." *Convivium* 25 (1957): 9–30.

Helms, Mary W. *Ulysses' Sail: An Ethnographic Odyssey of Power, Knowledge, and Geographical Distance*. Princeton: Princeton University Press, 1988.

Hendrix, Scott H. *Ecclesia in via: Ecclesiological Developments in the Medieval Psalms*

Exegesis and the Dictata Super Psalterium (1513–1515) of Martin Luther. Leiden: Brill, 1974.

Holmes, Olivia. *Assembling the Lyric Self: Authorship from Troubadour Song to Italian Poetry Book.* Minneapolis: University of Minnesota Press, 2000.

Hughes, Diane Owen. "Mourning Rites, Memory, and Civilization in Premodern Italy." In Chiffoleau, *et al.*, *Riti e ritual*, 23–38.

Holub, Robert C. *Reception Theory: A Critical Introduction.* London and New York: Routledge, 1984.

Hüttig, Albrecht. *Macrobius im Mittelalter: Ein Beitrag zur Rezeptionsgeschichte der "Commentarii in Somnium Scipionis."* Frankfurt am Main: Peter Lang, 1990.

Hyde, J. K. *Padua in the Age of Dante.* Manchester: Manchester University Press, 1966.

Iliescu, Nicolae. *Il "Canzoniere" petrarchesco e Sant'Agostino.* Rome: Società Accademica Romena, 1962.

Iser, Wolfgang. *The Act of Reading: A Theory of Aesthetic Response.* Baltimore: Johns Hopkins University Press, 1978.

Isetta, Sandra. "Il linguaggio ascetico di Francesco Petrarca nel *De vita solitaria*." *Studi Umanistici Piceni* (2003): 75–94.

Jannaro, Carmine. "Donato Casentinese, volgarizzatore del Petrarca." *Studi Petrarcheschi* 1 (1948): 185–94.

Janson, Tore. *Latin Prose Prefaces.* Stockholm: Almqvist and Wiksell, 1964.

Jasenas, Michael. *Petrarch in America: A Survey of Petrarchan Manuscripts.* Washington and New York: The Folger Shakespeare Library and The Pierpont Morgan Library, 1974.

Jenson, Minna Skafte. "Petrarch's Farewell to Avignon: *Bucolicum carmen* VIII." In *Avignon and Naples: Italy in France, France in Italy in the Fourteenth Century*, edited by Marianne Pade, Hannemarie Ragn Jensen, and Lene Waage Peterson, 69–82. Rome: "L'Erma" di Bretschneider, 1997.

Kablitz, Andreas. "Das Ende des Sacrum Imperium. Verwandlung der Repräsentation von Geschichte zwischen Dante und Petrarca." In *Mittelalter und Frühe Neuzeit.* Edited by W. Haug, 499–549. Tübingen: Niemeyer, 1999.

Kennedy, William J. *Authorizing Petrarch.* Ithaca: Cornell University Press, 1994.

———. *The Site of Petrarchism. Early Modern National Sentiment in Italy, France and England.* Baltimore: Johns Hopkins University Press, 2004.

———. "The Virgilian Legacies of Petrarch's *Bucolicum carmen* and Spenser's Shepheardes Calendar." In *The Early Renaissance: Virgil and the Classical Tradition*, edited by Anthony L. Pellegrini, 79–106. Binghamton: Medieval and Early Renaissance Studies, 1985.

Kessler, Eckhard. *Petrarca und die Geschichte. Geschichtsschreibung, Rhetorik, Philosophie im Übergang vom Mittelalter zur Neuzeit.* Munich: W. Fink, 1978.

Kindermann, Hugo. *Satyra: Die Theorie der Satire im Mittellateinischen: Vorstudie zu einer Gattungsgeschichte.* Nurenberg: Hans Carl, 1978.

Kircher, Timothy. *The Poet's Wisdom: The Humanists, the Church, and the Formation of Philosophy in the Early Renaissance.* Leiden: Brill, 2006.

Kirkham, Victoria. "A Canon of Women in Dante's *Commedia.*" *Annali d'Italianistica* 7 (1989): 16–41.

———. "The Classic Bond of Friendship in Boccaccio's Tito and Gisippo (*Decameron* X, 8)." In *The Classics in the Middle Ages. Papers of the Twentieth Annual Conference of the Center for Medieval and Early Renaissance Studies,* edited by Aldo S. Bernardo and Saul Levin, 223–35. Binghamton: Medieval and Renaissance Texts and Studies, 1990. Reprint in *The Sign of Reason,* 237–48.

———. "Dante's Polysynchrony: A Perfectly Timed Entry into Eden." *Filologia e Critica* 20 (1995): 329–52.

———. *Fabulous Vernacular: Boccaccio's 'Filocolo' and the Art of Medieval Fiction.* Ann Arbor: University of Michigan Press, 2001.

———. "Giovanni Boccaccio: Latin Works." In *Encyclopedia of Italian Literary Studies,* edited by Gaetana Marrone, 1:255–60. New York: Routledge Taylor and Francis, 2007.

———. "L'immagine del Boccaccio nella memoria tardo-gotica e rinascimentale." In *Boccaccio visualizzato. Narrare per parole e per immagini fra Medioevo e Rinascimento,* edited by Vittore Branca, 1:85–144. 3 vols. Turin: Einaudi, 1999.

———. "Painters at Play on the Judgment Day (*Decameron* VIII, 9)." *Studi sul Boccaccio* 14 (1983–84): 256–77. Reprint in, *The Sign of Reason,* 215–35.

———. "The Parallel Lives of Dante and Virgil." *Dante Studies* 110 (1992): 233–53.

———. *The Sign of Reason in Boccaccio's Fiction.* Florence: Olschki, 1993.

Kirkham, Victoria, ed. *Laura Battiferra and her Literary Circle: An Anthology.* The Other Voice in Early Modern Europe. Chicago: University of Chicago Press, 2006.

Kirkham, Victoria, and María Rosa Menocal. "Reflections on the 'Arabic' World: Boccaccio's Ninth Stories." *Stanford Italian Review* 7, nos. 1–2 (1987): 95–110.

Kirkham, Victoria, and Jennifer Tonkovich." How Petrarch Became Boccaccio: A Bronze Bust from the Morgan Library." *Studi sul Boccaccio* 33 (2005): 269–98.

Kleinhenz, Christopher, and Andrea Dini, eds. *Approaches to Teaching Petrarch and the Petrarchan Tradition.* New York: Modern Language Association, 2009.

Koster, Severin. *Die Invektive in der griechischen und römischen Literatur.* Meisenheim am Glan: Hain, 1980.

Kristeller, Paul Oskar. "Humanism and Scholasticism in the Italian Renaissance." *Byzantion* 17 (1944–45): 346–74.

———. "Petrarch's Averroists." *Studies in Renaissance Thought and Letters II,* 209–16. Rome: Edizioni di Storia e Letteratura, 1985.

———. "Umanesimo e scolastica a Padova fino al Petrarca." *Studies in Renaissance Thought and Letters IV,* 11–26. Rome: Edizioni di storia e letteratura, 1996.

Kuhn, Heinrich C. "Petrarcas *De remediis:* Ethik ohne Richtschnur?" In *Ethik – Wissenschaft oder Lebenskunst? Modelle der Normenbegrundung von der Antike bis zur Frühen Neuzeit,* edited by Sabrina Ebbersmeyer and Eckhard Kessler, 127–41. Berlin: LIT Verlag, 2007.

Lafleur, Claude. *Pétrarque et l'amitié.* Paris: Librairie Philosophique J. Vrin, 2001.

Laín Entralgo, Pedro. *The Therapy of the Word in Classical Antiquity.* Translated by John M. Sharp and L. J. Rather. New Haven: Yale University Press, 1970.

Lammers, Stephen E., and Allen Verhey, eds. *On Moral Medicine: Theological Perspectives in Medical Ethics.* Grand Rapids: Eerdmans, 1987.

Lane, Frederic C., and Reinhold C. Mueller. *Money and Banking in Medieval and Renaissance Venice.* 2 vols. Baltimore: Johns Hopkins University Press, 1985 and 1997.

Lanzillotta, Maria Accame. "Le *antiquitates romanae* di Petrarca." In *Preveggenze umanistiche di Petrarca. Atti delle giornate petrarchesche di Tor Vergata, Rome/ Cortona, 1–2 giugno 1992.* , 213–39. Pisa: ETS, 1994.

Latronico, Nicola. *I medici e la medicina nelle Invettive del Petrarca.* Milan: Quaderni di Castalia, 1956.

Lawler, Lillian, Dorothy M. Robathan, and William C. Korfmacher, eds. *Presented to Him on the Occasion of his Seventy-fifth Birthday.* St. Louis: Classical Bulletin, St. Louis University, 1960.

Lawler, T. M. C. "Some Parallels between Walter Hilton's *Scale of Perfection* and St. John Fisher's *Penitential Psalms.*" *Moreana: Bulletin Thomas More* 9 (1966): 13–27.

Lazzarini, Vittorio. "La seconda ambasceria di Francesco Petrarca a Venezia." In *Miscellanea di studi critici pubblicati in onore di Guido Mazzoni dai suoi discepoli,* 1:173–83, edited by Arnaldo Della Torre and P.L. Rambaldi. Florence: Successori B. Seeber, 1904.

Leclercq, Jean. *L'amour de lettres et le désir de Dieu.* Paris: Cerf, 1990.

———. *Otia monastica: Études sur le vocabulaire de la contemplation au Moyen Âge.* Studia Anselmiana, 51. Rome: Herder, 1963.

———. "Temi monastici nell'opera del Petrarca." *Lettere Italiane* 43 (1991): 42–54.

Reprinted in *Spiritualità e lettere nella cultura italiana e ungherese del basso Medioevo*, edited by Sante Graciotti and Cesare Vasoli, 149–62. Florence: Olschki, 1995.

Lehtonen, Tuomas M. S. *Fortuna, Money, and the Sublunar World: Twelfth-Century Ethical Poetics and the Satirical Poetry of the Carmina Burana*. Helsinki: Finnish Historical Society, 1995.

Lerer, Seth. "Medieval English Literature and the Idea of the Anthology." *PMLA* 118 (2003): 1251–67.

Levorato, Maria Chiara. *Le emozioni della lettura*. Bologna: Il Mulino, 2000.

Lines, David D. "Natural Philosophy in Renaissance Italy: The University of Bologna and the Beginning of Specialization." *Early Science and Medicine* 6 (2001): 267–323.

Macola, Novella. "I ritratti col Petrarca." In Daniele, *Le lingue del Petrarca*, 135–57.

Malato, Enrico, ed. *Storia della letteratura italiana*. 14 vols. Rome: Salerno, 1995–2004.

Mann, Nicholas. "Il 'Bucolicum carmen' e la sua eredità." *Quaderni Petrarcheschi* 9–10 (1992–93): 513–35.

———. "L'edizione critica del *Bucolicum carmen*." *Annali della Scuola Normale Superiore di Pisa: Classe di Lettere e Filosofia* 19, no. 1 (1989): 231–38.

———. "The Making of Petrarch's *Bucolicum Carmen*." *Italia Medioevale e Umanistica* (1977): 127–82.

———. "'O Deus, qualis epistola!' A New Petrarch Letter." *Italia Medioevale e umanistica* 17 (1974): 206–43.

———. *Petrarch*. Oxford: Oxford University Press, 1984.

Marchesi, Simone. *Stratigrafie decameroniane*. Florence: Olschki, 2004.

Marchi, Cesare. *Boccaccio*. Milan: Rizzoli, 1975.

Marini, Gaetano Luigi. *Degli archiatri pontifici*. Rome: Stamperia Pagliarini, 1784.

Marsh, David. "Petrarch and Alberti." In *Renaissance Essays in Honor of Craig Hugh Smyth*, edited by Sergio Bertelli and Gloria Ramakus, 1:363–75. 2 vols. Florence: Giunti-Barbera, 1985.

———. *The Quattrocento Dialogue: Classical Tradition and Humanist Innovation*. Harvard: Harvard University Press, 1980.

Martellotti, Guido. "*La Collatio inter Scipionem, Alexandrum, Hanibalem et Pyrhum*. Un inedito del Petrarca nella biblioteca della University of Pennsylvania." In *Classical Mediaeval and Renaissance Studies in Honor of B.L. Ullman*, edited by Charles Henderson, Jr., 145–68. 2 vols. Rome: Edizioni di Storia e Letteratura, 1964. Reprinted in *Scritti petrarcheschi*, 321–46.

———. "Dalla tenzone al carme bucolico: Giovanni del Virgilio, Dante, Petrarca." In *Dante, Boccaccio e altri scritori*, 71–89.

————. *Dante e Boccaccio e altri scrittori dall'Umanesimo al Romanticismo (con una premessa di Umberto Bosco)*. Florence: Olschki, 1983.

————. "Epitome e compendio." *Orientamenti Culturali* 2 (1946): 205–16. Reprinted in *Scritti petrarcheschi*, 50–66.

————. "Linee di sviluppo dell'umanesimo petrarchesco." *Studi Petrarcheschi* 2 (1949): 51–80. Reprinted in *Scritti petrarcheschi*, 110–40.

————. "Petrarca e Cesare." *Annali della Scuola Normale Superiore di Pisa*, ser. 2, 16 (1947): 149–58. Reprinted in *Scritti petrarcheschi*, 77–89.

————. "Petrarca e Silio Italico: Un confronto impossibile." In *Scritti petrarcheschi*, 563–78.

————. Review of Francisco Rico, *Vida u obra de Petrarca. 1.Lectura del Secretum*. Studi sul Petrarca, 4. Padua: Antenore, 1974. In *Annali della Scuola Normale Superiore di Pisa*, ser. 3, 6 (1976): 1394–1401. Reprinted, with the title "Sulla data del *Secretum*," in *Scritti petrarcheschi*, 487–96.

————. *Scritti petrarcheschi*. Edited by Michele Feo and Silvia Rizzo. Studi sul Petrarca, 16. Padua: Antenore, 1983.

————. "Storiografia del Petrarca." In *Convegno internazionale Francesco Petrarca (Roma-Arezzo-Padova-Arquà Petrarca, 24–27 aprile 1974*. Atti dei Convegni Lincei, 10, 179–87. Rome: Accademia dei Lincei, 1976. Reprint, *Scritti petrarcheschi*, 475–486.

————. "Sulla *Philologia*." In *Scritti petrarcheschi*, 360–61.

————. "*Il Triumphus Cupidinis in Ovidio e nel Petrarca*." In *Scritti Petrarcheschi*, 517–24.

————. *La vita di Scipione l'Africano*. Milan and Naples: Ricciardi, 1954.

Martinelli, Bortolo. "'Abice ingentes historiarum sarcinas . . . dimitte Africam': Il finale del 'Secretum.'" *Revue des Études Italiennes* 29 (1983): 58–73.

————. "Il Petrarca e la medicina." In *Invective contra medicum: Testo latino e volgarizzamento di ser Domenico Silvestri*. Edited by Pier Giorgio Ricci and Bortolo Martinelli, 205–49. Rome: Edizioni di Storia e Letteratura, 1978.

————. *Petrarca e il Ventoso*. Milan: Minerva Italica, 1977.

————. "Sulla data del *Secretum* del Petrarca. Nova et vetera." *Critica Letteraria* 13 (1985): 431–82, 643–93.

Martinez, Ronald L. "Lament and Lamentation in *Purgatorio* and the Role of Dante's Statius." *Dante Studies* 117 (1997): 46–82.

————. "Mourning Beatrice: The Rhetoric of Threnody in the *Vita nuova*." *MLN* 113 (1998): 1–29.

————. "Petrarch's Lame Leg and the Corpus of Cicero: An Early Crisis of Humanism?" In *The Body in Early Modern Italy*. Edited by Julia L. Hairston and Walter Stephens. Baltimore: Johns Hopkins University Press, forthcoming.

Mazzotta, Giuseppe. "The *Canzoniere* and the Language of the Self." *Studies in Philology* 75 (1978): 271–96.

————. *Dante, Poet of the Desert. History of Allegory in the Divine Comedy.* Princeton: Princeton University Press, 1979.

————. *The Worlds of Petrarch.* Durham: Duke University Press, 1993.

McClure, George W. *The Culture of Profession in Late Renaissance Italy.* Toronto, Buffalo, London: University of Toronto Press, 2004.

————. "Healing Eloquence: Petrarch, Salutati, and the Physicians." *Journal of Medieval and Renaissance Studies* 15 (1985): 317–46.

————. *Sorrow and Consolation in Italian Humanism.* Princeton: Princeton University Press, 1990.

Mercati, A. "L'autore della *Expositio in Septem Psalmos poenitentiales* fra le opere di S. Gregorio Magno." *Revue Bénédictine* 31 (1914–19): 250–57.

Miccoli, Giovanni. *Francesco d'Assisi.* Turin: Einaudi, 1991.

Miller, Patricia Cox. *Dreams in Late Antiquity: Studies in the Imagination of a Culture.* Princeton: Princeton University Press, 1994.

Minnis, A. J., and A. B. Scott, eds., with the assistance of David Wallace. *Medieval Literary Theory and Criticism, c. 1100–c. 1375: The Commentary Tradition.* Oxford: Clarendon Press, 1988.

Mommsen, Theodor. "The Last Will: A Personal Document of Petrarch's Old Age." In *Petrarch's Testament,* 3–50.

————. "Petrarch and the Decoration of the *Sala virorum illustrium* in Padua." *Art Bulletin* 34, no. 2 (June 1952): 95–116.

————. "Petrarch's Conception of the 'Dark Ages.'" *Speculum* 17 (April 1942): 226–42.

Montecchi, Giorgio. "Correggio, Azzo da." In *Dizionario biografico degli italiani,* 29: 425–30. Rome: Istituto della Enciclopedia italiana, 1983.

Moos, Peter von. "Les solitudes de Pétrarque. Liberté intellectuelle et activisme urbain dans la crise du XIVe siècle." *Rassegna Europea di Letteratura Italiana* (1996): 23–58.

Morse, Charlotte C. "Exemplary Griselde." *Studies in the Age of Chaucer* 7 (1985): 51–86.

Muckle, J. T. "Abelard's Letter of Consolation to a Friend [*Historia calamitatum*]." *Medieval Studies* 12 (1950): 163–213.

Mueller, Reinhold C. *The Venetian Money Market.* Baltimore: Johns Hopkins University Press, 1997.

Muir, Kenneth. "The Texts of Wyatt's *Penitential Psalms.*" *Notes and Queries* 14 (1967): 442–44.

Murphy, Stephen. *The Gift of Immortality: Myths of Power and Humanist Poetics.* Madison, Teaneck: Farleigh Dickinson Press / Associated University Presses, 1997.

Musto, Ronald G. *Apocalypse in Rome: Cola di Rienzo and the Politics of the New Age.* Berkeley: University of California Press, 2003.

Nardi, Bruno. "Letteratura e cultura Veneziana del Quattrocento." In *La civiltà veneziana del Quattrocento*, 99–146. Florence: Sansoni, 1957.

Newman, Barbara. *God and the Goddesses. Vision, Poetry, and Belief in the Middle Ages.* Philadelphia: University of Pennsylvania Press, 2003

Niçaise, Eduard. *La grande chirurgie de Guy de Chauliac.* Paris: Alcan, 1890.

Nolhac, Pierre de. "Le *De viris illustribus* de Pétrarque." *Notices et Extraits des Manuscrits de la Bibliothèque Nationale et Autres Bibliothèques* 34, no. 1 (1891): 61–148.

———. *Pétrarque et l'humanisme.* 2 vols. Paris: Champion, 1907.

Novati, Francesco. "Il Petrarca e i Visconti." In *Francesco Petrarca e la Lombardia*, 9–84. Milan: Hoepli, 1904.

Oxford Classical Dictionary. Edited by Simon Hornblower and Antony Spawforth. 3rd edition. Oxford: Oxford University Press, 1996.

Pacca, Vinicio. *Petrarca.* Rome and Bari: Laterza, 1998.

Paden, William. "Petrarch as a Poet of Provence." *Annali d'Italianistica* 22 (2004): 19–44.

Palmer, Ralph Graham. *Seneca's "De remediis fortuitorum" and the Elizabethans.* Chicago: Institute of Elizabethan Studies, 1953.

Pancheri, Alessandro. *"Con suon chioccio." Per una frottola 'dispersa' attribuibile a Francesco Petrarca.* Padua: Antenore, 1993.

———. "Pro Confortino." In Segre, *et al.*, 49–59.

———. "Introduction" and "Textual Note." In Francesco Petrarca. *Lettere disperse, varie e miscellanee.* Edited by Alessandro Pancheri, ix–xxxvi. Parma: Ugo Guanda, 1994.

Pansier, Pierre. "Les médecins des papes d'Avignon (1308–1403)." *Janus* 14 (1909): 405–34.

Paolino, Laura. "'Ad acerbam rei memoriam.' Le carte del lutto nel codice Vaticano latino 3196 di Francesco Petrarca." *Rivista di Letteratura Italiana* 11 (1993): 73–102.

Parker, Deborah. "Vasari's *Portrait of Six Tuscan Poets:* A Visible Literary History." In Deborah Parker, ed. "Visibile parlare: Images of Dante in the Renaissance." Special issue, *Lectura Dantis* 22–23 (Spring–Fall 1998): 45–62.

Pasquali, Giorgio. *Storia della tradizione e critica del testo.* Florence: Le Monnier, 1952.

Pasquini, Emilio. "'Minori' in bilico fra le 'due corone.'" In *Le botteghe della poesia: Studi sul Tre-Quattrocento italiano.* Bologna: Il Mulino, 1991.

———. "Il mito polemico di Avignone nei poeti italiani del Trecento." In *Aspetti culturali della società italiana nel periodo del papato avignonese*, 257–309. Todi: Accademia Tudertina, 1981.

———. "Il Testo: Fra l'autografo e i testimoni di collazione." In Berra, *I Triumphi*, 11–37.

Pastore Stocchi, Manlio. Introduction to Francesco Petrarca, In Bufano, *Opere latine.*

Patch, Howard. *The Goddess Fortuna in Mediaeval Literature,* Cambridge: Harvard University Press, 1927.

Pazzini, Adalberto. *Storia della medicina.* Milan: Società Editrice Libraria, 1947.

Pedroni, Matteo, and Antonio Stauble, eds. *Il genere "Tenzone" nelle letterature romanze delle origini.* Ravenna: Longo, 1997.

Peron, Gianfelice. "Lingua e cultura d'oïl in Petrarca." In Daniele, *Le lingue del Petrarca,* 11–32.

Perugi, Maurizio. "Il Sordello di Dante e la tradizione mediolatina dell'invettiva." *Studi Danteschi* 55 (1983): 23–135.

Pesenti, Tiziana. "Dondi dall'Orologio, Giovanni." In *Dizionario biografico degli Italiani,* vol. 41, 96–104. Rome: Istituto dell'Enciclopedia Italiana, 1992.

Petrini, Mario. *La Risurrezione della carne: Studi sul Canzoniere.* Milan: Mursia, 1993.

Phelps, Ruth Shepard. *The Earlier and Later Forms of Petrarch's "Canzoniere."* Chicago: University of Chicago Press, 1925.

Piccini, Daniele. *Un amico del Petrarca: Sennuccio del Bene e le sue rime.* Rome and Padua: Antenore, 2004.

Pickering, F. P. *Literature and Art in the Middle Ages.* Coral Gables: University of Miami Press, 1970.

Picone, Michelangelo. "Il tema dell'incoronazione poetica in Dante, Petrarca e Boccaccio." *L'Alighieri* 25 (2005): 5–26.

Piur, Paul. "Die Korrespondenz Petrarcas." In *Briefwechsel des Cola di Rienzo.* Edited by Konrad Burdach and Paul Piur, Vom Mittelalter zur Reformation. 2:110–238. 5 vols. Berlin: Weidmannsche Buchhandlung, 1928.

———. *Petrarcas 'Buch ohne Namen' und die päpstliche Kurie: Ein Beitrag zur Geistesgeschichte der Frührenaissance.* Halle and Saale: Max Niemeyer, 1925.

Polak, Emil J. *A Textual Study of Jacques de Dinant's Summa dictaminis.* Geneva: Droz, 1975.

Ponte, Giovanni. "La decima Egloga e la composizione dei *Trionfi.*" In *Studi sul Rinascimento. Petrarca, Leonardo, Ariosto,* 63–90. Naples: Morano, 1994.

———. "La 'gravitas nervosa' del Poliziano." In *Poliziano nel suo tempo: Atti del VI Convegno internazionale (Chianciano-Montepulciano 18–21 luglio 1994),* edited by Luisa Secchi Tarugi, 107–15. Florence: Francesco Cesati Editore, 1996.

———. "Nella selva del Petrarca." *Giornale Storico della Letteratura Italiana* 167 (1990): 1–63.

———. "Problemi petrarcheschi: La decima egloga e la composizione dei *Trionfi.*" *Rassegna della Letteratura Italiana* 69, no. 7.5 (1965): 517–29.

Pozzi, Giovanni. "Petrarca, i padri e soprattutto la bibbia." *Studi Petrarcheschi* 6

(1989): 125–69. Reprinted in Giovanni Pozzi, *Alternatim,* 143–89. Milan: Adelphi, 1996.

Pulsoni, Carlo. *La tecnica compositiva nei Rerum vulgarium fragmenta: Riuso metrico e lettura autoriale.* Rome: Bagatto Libri, 1998.

Quillen, Carol Everhart. *Rereading the Renaissance: Petrarch, Augustine, and the Language of Humanism.* Ann Arbor: University of Michigan Press, 1998.

Quondam, Amedeo. *Petrarchismo mediato: Per una critica della forma antologia.* Rome: Bulzoni, 1974.

Raimondi, Ezio. "Un esercizio satirico del Petrarca." In *Metafora e Storia,* 189–208. Turin: Einaudi, 1970.

Rawski, Conrad H. "Notes on the Rhetoric in Petrarch's *Invective contra medicum.*" In Scaglione, 249–77.

Reeve, Michael D. "Classical scholarship." In *The Cambridge Companion to Renaissance Humanism,* edited by Jill Kraye, 20–46. Cambridge: Cambridge University Press, 1996.

Reeve, Michael D., and R. H. Rouse. "[Cicero's] Speeches." In *Texts and Transmission: A Survey of the Latin Classics,* edited by L. D. Reynolds, 54–98. Oxford: Clarendon Press, 1983.

Reiss, Timothy J. *Mirages of the Selfe: Patterns of Personhood in Ancient and Early Modern Europe.* Stanford: Stanford University Press, 2003.

Ricci, Pier Giorgio. *Miscellanea petrarchesca.* Edited by Monica Berté. Rome: Edizioni di Storia e Letteratura, 1999.

———. "La tradizione dell'invettiva tra Medioevo e Rinascimento." *Lettere Italiane* 26 (1974): 405–14.

Rico, Francisco. "Petrarca y el *De vera religione.*" *Italia Medioevale e Umanistica* 17 (1974): 313–64.

———. *El sueño del humanismo. De Petrarca a Erasmo.* Madrid: Alianza Editorial, 1993.

———. "'Ubi puer, ibi senex': Hans Baron y el *Secretum* de 1353." In *Il Petrarca latino e le origini dell'Umanesimo. Atti del Convegno internazionale. Firenze 19–22 maggio 1991,* 65–237. *Quaderni Petrarcheschi,* 9 and 10. (1992–93). Reprint, Florence: Le lettere, 1996.

———. *Vida u obra del Petrarca. I. Lectura del Secretum.* Studi sul Petrarca, 4. Padua: Antenore, 1974.

Ricucci, Marina. "L'esordio dei *Triumphi:* Tra *Eneide* e *Commedia.*" *Rivista di Letteratura Italiana* 12 (1994): 313–49.

Rizzo, Silvia. "Il latino del Petrarca nelle *Familiari.*" In *The Uses of Greek and Latin,* edited by A. C. Dionisotti, Anthony Grafton, and Jill Kraye, 41–56. London: Warburg Institute, 1988.

Robinson, James Harvey, with Henry Winchester Rolfe. *Petrarch: The First Modern Scholar and Man of Letters.* New York: Putnam, 1898.

Roche, Thomas. "The Calendrical Structure of Petrarch's *Canzoniere.*" *Studies in Philology* 71 (1974): 152–72.

Romanò, Angelo. *Il codice degli abbozzi (Vat. Lat. 3196) di Francesco Petrarca.* Rome: Bardi, 1955.

Ross, Braxton, W. "Giovanni Colonna, Historian at Avignon." *Speculum* 45 (1970): 533–63.

Rossetti, Domenico. *Petrarca, Giulio Celso e Boccaccio, illustrazione bibliologica delle Vite degli uomini illustri del primo, di Cajo Giulio Cesare attribuita al secondo e del Petrarca scritta dal terzo.* Trieste: G. Marenigh, 1828.

Rossi, Vittorio. "Un archetipo abbandonato di epistole di Petrarca." In *Studi sul Petrarca e sul Rinascimento,* 175–93.

———. "Petrarca a Pavia." In *Studi sul Petrarca e sul Rinascimento,* 3–81.

———. *Studi sul Petrarca e sul Rinascimento.* Florence: Sansoni, 1930.

Rotondi, Giovanni. "Le due redazioni del *De otio* del Petrarca." *Aevum* 9 (1935): 27–77.

———. "Note al *De otio religioso.*" *Studi Petrarcheschi* 2 (1949): 153–66.

———. "Un volgarizzamento inedito quattrocentesco del *De otio religioso.*" *Studi Petrarcheschi* 3 (1950): 47–96.

Rouillard, Philippe. *Histoire de la pénitence.* Paris: Cerf, 1996.

Sabbadini, Remigio. *Le scoperte dei codici latini e greci ne' secoli XIV e XV.* 2 vols. Florence: Sansoni, 1905–14.

Sade, Jacques-François-Paul-Aldonce de. *Mémoires pour la vie de François Pétrarque.* 3 vols. Amsterdam: Arskée and Merkus, 1764–67.

Santagata, Marco. *Dal sonetto al Canzoniere: Ricerche sulla preistoria e la costituzione di un genere.* Padua: Liviana, 1979.

———. *I frammenti dell'anima. Storia e racconto nel Canzoniere di Petrarca.* Bologna: Il Mulino, 1992.

———. *Per moderne carte: La biblioteca volgare di Petrarca.* Bologna: Il Mulino 1990.

Santini, Carlo. "Nuovi accertamenti sull'ipotesi di raffronto tra Silio e Petrarca." In *Preveggenze umanistiche di Petrarca,* edited by Giorgio Brugnoli and Guido Paduano, 111–39. Pisa: ETS, 1993.

Scaglione, Aldo, ed. *Francis Petrarch Six Centuries Later: A Symposium.* Chapel Hill and Chicago: North Carolina University Press and Newberry Library, 1975.

Scaramella, Pierroberto. "Medici e confessori: Medicina del corpo, medicina dell'anima." *Studi Storici* 40 (1999): 613–27.

Schullian, Dorothy M. "A Preliminary List of Manuscripts of Valerius Maximus." In *Studies in Honor of B.L. Ullman,* edited by Lillian B. Lawler *et al.,* 81–95. Saint Louis: Saints Louis University Press, 1960.

———. "A Revised List of Manuscripts of Valerius Maximus." In *Miscellanea Augusto Campana,* 695–728. Padua: Antenore, 1981.

———. "Valerius Maximus." In *Catalogus Translationum et Commentariorum,* edited by F. Edward Cranz and O. P. Kristeller, 4:287–403. Washington: Catholic University Press, 1984.

Sedgwick, Eve Kosofsky. *Between Men: English Literature and Male Homosocial Desire.* New York: Columbia University Press, 1985.

Segre, Cesare, Giovanni Giudici, and Alessandro Pancheri. *Le varianti e la storia: Il Canzoniere di Francesco Petrarca.* Turin: Bollati Boringhieri, 1999.

Seigel, Jerrold E. *Rhetoric and Philosophy in Renaissance Humanism: The Union of Eloquence and Wisdom: Petrarch to Valla.* Princeton: Princeton University Press, 1968.

Serpagli, Francesco. *Prolegomeni al "De vita solitaria" di Petrarca.* Parma: Scuola Tip. Benedettina, 1967.

Severs, J. Burke. "*The Clerk's Tale.*" In *Sources and Analogues of Chaucer's Canterbury Tales,* edited by W. F. Bryan and Germaine Dempster, 288–331. New York: Humanities Press, 1958.

———. *The Literary Relationships of Chaucer's Clerkes Tale.* New Haven: Yale University Press, 1942.

Shapiro, Marianne. *Hieroglyph of Time: The Petrarchan Sestina.* Minneapolis: University of Minnesota Press, 1980.

Simonetta, Marcello. *Rinascimento segreto: Il mondo del Segretario da Petrarca a Machiavelli.* Milan: FrancoAngeli, 2004.

Siraisi, Nancy. *Arts and Science at Padua: The Studium of Padua before 1350.* Toronto: Pontifical Institute of Medieval Studies, 1973.

———. *Medicine and the Italian Universities, 1250–1600.* Leiden and Boston: Brill, 2001.

———. *Medieval and Early Renaissance Medicine: An Introduction to Knowledge and Practice.* Chicago: The University of Chicago Press, 1990.

———. "Die medizinische Fakultät." In *Geschichte der Universität in Europa,* edited by Walter Rüegg, 1:321–42. München: Beck, 1993.

Smarr, Janet Levarie. "Boccaccio and the Choice of Hercules." *MLN* 92, no. 1 (1977): 146–52.

———. *Joining the Conversation: Dialogues by Renaissance Women.* Ann Arbor: University of Michigan Press, 2005.

Sorieri, Louis. *Boccaccio's Story of Tito e Gisippo in European Literature.* New York: Institute of French Studies, 1937.

Sottili, Agostino. *I codici del Petrarca nella Germania Occidentale*. Vol. 2. Padua: Antenore, 1978.

Southern, Richard. *Scholastic Humanism and the Unification of Europe*. 3 vols. Oxford: Blackwell, 1995–2001.

Spufford, Peter. *Power and Profit: The Merchant in Medieval Europe*. London: Thames and Hudson, 2002.

Stahl, William Harris. *Macrobius, A Commentary on the Dream of Scipio*. New York: Columbia University Press, 1962.

Starn, Randolf. "Petrarch's Consolation on Exile: A Humanist Use of Adversity." In *Essays Presented to Myron P. Gilmore*, edited by Sergio Bertelli and Gloria Ramakus, 1:241–54. Florence: La Nuova Italia, 1978.

Stegmüller, Friedrich. *Repertorium Biblicum Medii Aevi*. Madrid: Matriti, 1950.

Stevenson, James and Mark Julian Edwards. "Lactantius." In *Oxford Classical Dictionary*. Edited by Simon Hornblower and Antony Spawforth. 3rd ed. Oxford: Oxford University Press, 1996.

Stock, Brian. "Reading, Writing, and the Self: Petrarch and His Forerunners." *New Literary History* 26 (1995): 717–30.

————. "The Self and Literary Experience in Late Antiquity and the Middle Ages." *New Literary History* 25 (1994): 839–52.

Storey, H. Wayne. "Doubting Petrarca's Last Words: Erasure in MS Vat. Lat. 3195." In *Petrarch and the Textual Origins of Interpretation*, edited by Teodolinda Barolini and H. Wayne Storey. Columbia Series in the Classical Tradition. Leiden: Brill, 2007.

Struever, Nancy. "Petrarch's 'Invective contra medicum:' An Early Confrontation of Rhetoric and Medicine." *Modern Language Notes* 108 (1993): 659–79.

————. *Theory as Practice: Ethical Inquiry in the Renaissance*. Chicago: University of Chicago Press, 1992.

Sturm-Maddox, Sara. *Petrarchan Metamorphoses: Text and Subtext in the Rime sparse*. Columbia: University of Missouri Press, 1985.

Suitner, Franco. "L'invettiva antiavignonese del Petrarca e la poesia infamante medievale." *Studi Petrarcheschi*, n.s., 2 (1985): 201–210.

Suitner, Franco, ed. *Dionigi da Borgo di San Sepolcro fra Petrarca e Boccaccio*. Petruzzi: Città di Castello, 2000.

Suleiman, Susan, and Inge Crosman, eds. *The Reader in the Text. Essays on Audience and Interpretation*. Princeton: Princeton University Press, 1980.

Süss, Wilhelm. *Ethos: Studien zur älteren Griechischen Rhetorik*. Leipzig and Berlin: Teubner, 1910. Reprint, Aalen: Scientia Verlag, 1975.

Tabanelli, Mario. *Un secolo d'oro della chirurgia francese: Guy de Chauliac*. Forlì: Valbonesi, 1970.

Taddeo, Edoardo. "Petrarca e il tempo." *Studi e Problemi di Critica Testuale* 27 (1983): 69–108.

———. *Petrarca e il tempo e altri studi di letteratura italiana.* Pisa: ETS, 2003.

———. "Petrarca e il tempo: Il tempo come tema nelle opere latine." *Studi e Problemi di Critica Testuale* 25 (1982): 53–76.

Tateo, Francesco. *Dialogo interiore e polemica ideological nel "Secretum" del Petrarca.* Florence: Le Monnier, 1965.

———. "Sulla ricezione umanistica dei *Trionfi*." In Berra, *I Triumphi*, 375–401.

Tatham, Edward H. R. *Francesco Petrarca: The First Modern Man of Letters: His Life and Correspondence. A Study of the Early Fourteenth Century.* 2 vols. London: Sheldon Press, 1925–26.

Thorndike, Lynn. *A History of Magic and Experimental Science.* New York: Macmillan, 1923–58.

Trapp, J. B. "The Iconography of Petrarch in the Age of Humanism." *Quaderni Petrarcheschi* 9–10 (1992–1993): 11–73.

———. "Petrarch's Laura. The Portraiture of an Imaginary Beloved." *Journal of the Warburg and Courtauld Institutes* 64 (2001): 55–192.

———. "The Poet Laureate: Rome, *Renovatio* and *Traslatio Imperii*." In *Rome in the Renaissance: The City and the Myth,* edited by P. A. Ramsey, 93–130. Binghamton: Medieval and Early Renaissance Studies, 1982.

Trinkaus, Charles. *In Our Image and Likeness: Humanity and Divinity in Italian Humanist Thought.* 2 vols. Chicago: University of Chicago Press, 1970.

———. *The Poet as Philosopher.* New Haven: Yale University Press, 1979.

Tripet, Arnaud. *Pétrarque ou la connaissance de soi.* Genève: Droz, 1967.

Trompf, G. W. *The Idea of Historical Recurrence in Western Thought: From Antiquity to the Reformation.* Berkeley: University of California Press, 1979.

Trone, George A. "'You Lie Like a Doctor!': Petrarch's Attack on Medicine." *Yale Journal of Biology and Medicine* 70 (1997): 183–90.

Tufano, Ilaria. "La notte, la paura, il peccato. Il ritratto dell' 'occupatus' nel 'De vita solitaria.'" *Rassegna Europea di Letteratura Italiana* 22 (2003): 37–52.

Twombly, Robert G. "Thomas Wyatt's Paraphrase of the Penitential Psalms of David." *Texas Studies in Literature and Language: A Journal of the Humanities* 12 (1970): 345–80.

Ullman, Berthold Luis. "The Composition of Petrarch's *De vita solitaria* and the History of the Vatican Manuscript." In *Miscellanea Giovanni Mercati,* 4:124–25. 6 vols. Vatican City: Biblioteca Apostolica Vaticana, 1946.

———. "Petrarch's Favorite Books." In *Studies in the Italian Renaissance,* 123–24.

———. *Studies in the Italian Renaissance.* Rome: Edizioni di Storia e Letteratura, 1955.

Van Deusen, Nancy, ed. *The Place of the Psalms in the Intellectual Culture in the Middle Ages*. Albany: State University of New York, 1999.

Vasoli, Cesare. *La dialettica e la retorica dell'Umanesimo: Invenzione e metodo nella cultura del XV e XVI secolo*. Milan: Feltrinelli, 1968.

Vattasso, Marco. *Del Petrarca e di alcuni suoi amici*. Rome: Tipografia Vaticana, 1904.

Vecce, Carlo. "La 'Lunga Pictura': Visione e rappresentazione nei *Trionfi*." In Berra, *I Triumphi*, 299–315.

Vecchi Galli, Paola. "Per una stilistica delle 'disperse.'" In Daniele, *Le lingue del Petrarca*, 109–27.

———. "Rime disperse." In *Petrarca nel tempo*, ed. Feo, 159–68.

———. "I *Triumphi*. Aspetti della tradizione quattrocentesca." In Berra, *I Triumphi*, 343–73.

Velli, Giuseppe. "Il Dante di Francesco Petrarca." *Studi Petrarcheschi*, n.s., 2 (1985): 185–99.

———. "Il *De Vita et moribus domini Francisci Petracchi de Florentia* del Boccaccio e la biografia del Petrarca." *MLN* 102 (1987): 32–39.

———. *Petrarca e Boccaccio. Tradizione—memoria—scrittura*. Padua: Antenore, 1995.

———. "La poesia volgare del Boccaccio e i 'Rerum vulgarium fragmenta'. Primi appunti." *Giornale Storico della Letteratura Italiana* 169 (1992): 183–99.

———. "Il proemio dell'*Africa*." *Italia Medioevale e Umanistica* 8 (1965): 323–32.

Vergani-Zamboni, Luisa. "Per una nuova lettura delle epistole del Petrarca a Iacopo Bussolari." *Filologia e Letteratura* 15, no. 2 (1969): 128–43.

Vickers, Nancy. "Diana Described: Scattered Woman and Scattered Rhyme." *Critical Inquiry* 8 (1981): 265–79.

Vismara, Felice. *L'invettiva: Arma preferita dagli Umanisti nelle lotte private, nelle polemiche letterarie, politiche e religiose*. Milan: Umberto Allegretti, 1900.

Visser, Tamara. *Antike und Christentum in Petrarcas "Africa."* Tübingen: Gunter Narr Verlag, 2005.

Vogel, Cyrille. *Le pécheur et la pénitence au Moyen Âge*. Paris: Cerf, 1969.

Wack, Mary Frances. *Lovesickness in the Middle Ages. The Viaticum and Its Commentaries*. Philadelphia: University of Pennsylvania Press, 1990.

Wallace, David. *Chaucerian Polity*. Stanford: Stanford University Press, 1997.

———. *Giovanni Boccaccio: Decameron*. Cambridge: Cambridge University Press, 1991.

———. *Premodern Places: Calais to Surinam, Chaucer to Aphra Behn*. Oxford: Blackwell, 2004.

Walton, Steven A. "An Introduction to the Mechanical Arts in the Middle Ages." Assocation Villard de Honnecourt for Interdisciplinary Study of Medieval

Technology, Science, Art, University of Toronto, 2003, available at http://
    members.shaw.ca/competitivenessofnations/2.%20Articles.htm.

Wardle, D. Review of Valerius Maximus *Facta et dicta memorabilia*. *Bryn Mawr
    Classical Review*. Online.

Warner, J. Christopher. *The Augustinian Epic: Petrarch to Milton*. Ann Arbor: Uni-
    versity of Michigan Press, 2005.

Watkins, Renee Neu. "Petrarch and the Black Death: From Fear to Monuments."
    Studies in the Renaissance 19 (1972): 196–223.

Whitney, Elspeth. *Paradise Restored. The Mechanical Arts from Antiquity through
    the Thirteenth Century*. Transactions of the American Philosophical Society.
    Philadelphia: American Philosophical Society, 1990.

Wieland, Georg. "Ethica docens—Ethica utens." In *Sprache und Erkenntnis im
    Mittelalter*, edited by Jan P. Beckmann, 593–601. Berlin: Walter de Gruyter,
    1981.

———. *Ethica, scientia practica: Die Anfänge der philosophischen Ethik im 13. Jahrhun-
    dert*. Münster: Aschendorff, 1981.

Wilkins, Ernest Hatch. "The Coronation of Petrarch." In *The Making of the "Can-
    zoniere,"* 9–69.

———. *The "Epistolae metricae" of Petrarch. A Manual*. Rome: Edizioni di Storia e
    Letteratura, 1956.

———. "An Introductory Dante Bibliography." *Modern Philology* 17, no.11 (March
    1920): 623–32.

———. *Life of Petrarch*. Chicago: University of Chicago Press, 1961.

———. *The Making of the "Canzoniere" and Other Petrarchan Studies*. Rome: Edizioni
    di Storia e Letteratura, 1951.

———. "Peregrinus ubique." In *The Making of the "Canzoniere,"* 1–8.

———. "Petrarch's Coronation Oration." *PMLA* 68 (1953): 1242–50. Reprint,
    Studies in the Life and Works of Petrarch, 300–13.

———. *Petrarch's Correspondence*. Padua: Antenore, 1960.

———. "Petrarch's Ecclesiastical Career," *Speculum* 28, no. 4 (1953): 754–75.

———. *Petrarch's Eight Years in Milan*. Cambridge: Medieval Academy of America,
    1958.

———. *Petrarch's Later Years*. Cambridge: Medieval Academy of America, 1959.

———. "Petrarch's Seventh Eclogue." In *Studies in the Life and Works of Petrarch*,
    48–62.

———. *Studies in the Life and Works of Petrarch*. Cambridge: Mediaeval Academy of
    America, 1955.

———. *Studies on Petrarch and Boccaccio*. Padua: Antenore, 1978.

———. "A Survey of the Correspondence between Petrarch and Francesco
    Nelli." *Italia Medioevale e Umanistica* 1 (1958): 351–58.

Wilkins, Ernest Hatch, and Giuseppe Billanovich. "The Miscellaneous Letters of Petrarch." *Speculum* 37, no. 2 (1962): 226–43.

Witt, Ronald. "The *De tyranno* and Coluccio Salutati's View of Politics and Roman History." *Nuova Rivista Storica* 53 (1969): 434–74. Republished in Ronald Witt, *Italian Humanism and Medieval Rhetoric*.

———. *"In the Footsteps of the Ancients": The Origins of Humanism from Lovato to Bruni.* Leiden and New York: Brill, 2000.

———. *The Two Latin Cultures and the Foundation of Renaissance Humanism in Medieval Italy.* Cambridge: Cambridge University Press, forthcoming.

———. *Italian Humanism and Medieval Rhetoric.* Aldershot and Burlington: Ashgate/Variorum, 2001.

———. "Medieval 'Ars Dictaminis' and the Beginnings of Humanism: A New Construction of the Problem." *Renaissance Quarterly* 35, no. 1 (1982): 1–35.

———. "Petrarch's Conception of History." In *Petrarca. Canoni e Esemplarità*, edited by Valeria Finucci, 211–18. Rome: Bulzoni, 2006.

Wrigley, John E. "A Papal Secret Known to Petrarch." *Speculum* 39 (1964): 613–34.

———. "A Rehabilitation of Clement VI." *Archivum Historiae Pontificiae* 3 (1965): 127–38.

Wulff, Fredrik Amadeus. *En svensk Petrarca-bok till jubelfästen.* Stockholm: P. A. Norstedt and Söner, 1905.

Zaccaria, Vittorio. "La difesa della poesia: Dal Petrarca alle *Genealogie* del Boccaccio." *Lectura Petrarce* 19 (1999): 211–29.

Zacour, Norman P. *Petrarch's Book without a Name: A Translation of the 'Liber Sine nomine.'* Toronto: Pontifical Institute of Medieval Studies, 1973.

Zardo, Antonio. *Petrarca e i Carraresi.* Milan: Hoepli, 1887.

Zatti, Sergio. *L'uniforme cristiano e il multiforme pagano: Saggio sulla "Gerusalemme liberata."* Milan: Il Saggiatore, 1983.

CONTRIBUTORS

Teodolinda Barolini is the Lorenzo Da Ponte Professor of Italian at Columbia University. She is the author of *Dante's Poets: Textuality and Truth in the Comedy* (1984; Italian trans. 1993), winner of the Marraro Prize of the Modern Language Association and the John Nicholas Brown Prize of the Medieval Academy; *The Undivine Comedy: Detheologizing Dante* (1992; Italian trans. 2003); and *Dante and the Origins of Italian Literary Culture* (2006), winner of the Premio Flaiano. She has edited *Medieval Constructions in Gender and Identity* (2005) and, with H. Wayne Storey, *Dante for the New Millennium* (2003) and *Petrarch and the Textual Origins of Interpretation* (2007). Volume 1 of her commentary to Dante's lyrics is forthcoming from Rizzoli.

Susanna Barsella is assistant professor of modern languages and literatures at Fordham University. Her main area of research is in Italian medieval literature and Renaissance humanism with a specific interest in the literature of early humanism. She has published on medieval, Renaissance, and modern Italian authors. She is currently working on a book on the concept of work in early humanistic texts, a monograph on Dante Alighieri's angelology in the *Divine Comedy*, and, together with Francesco Ciabattoni, coediting a festschrift in honor of Salvatore Camporeale.

Theodore J. Cachey Jr. is professor of Romance languages and literatures and director of the William and Katherine Devers Program in Dante Studies at the University of Notre Dame. His research focuses on Dante, Petrarch, the "Questione della lingua," and the literature and history of travel. He is the editor of *Petrarch's Guide to the Holy Land* (2002), which received the Scaglione Prize of the Modern Language Association for a Manuscript in Italian Studies.

Stefano Carrai is professor of Italian literature at the University of Siena. He is the author of books on Italian poetry of the Middle Age and of the Renaissance (*Le muse dei Pulci* [1985], *La lirica toscana del Duecento* [1997], *I precetti di Parnaso* [1999]). His edition of Della Casa's poems with commentary was published in 2003. His latest book is *Dante elegiaco* (2006).

Paolo Cherchi has been professor of Italian literature at the University of Ferrara since 2003. From 1965 to 2002, he was at the University of Chicago, where he also taught medieval Spanish literature and Romance philology. He has published on a wide range of topics dealing with Renaissance encyclopedism, medieval courtly love, history of science, Baroque poetry and philology, and Spanish and Provençal literature. Among his books are *Capitoli di critica Cervantina* (1977); *Enciclopedismo e politica della riscrittura: Tommaso Garzoni* (1981); *Andreas and the Ambiguity of Courtly Love* (1994); *La metamorfosi dell'Adone* (1996); *Polimatia di riuso—Mezzo secolo di plagio (1539–1589)* (1998); and *L'onestade e l'onesto raccontare del Decameron* (2004). He has edited Tomaso Garzoni's *Opere* (1994) and *Piazza universale* (1996). His latest book is *Le nozze di filologia e fortuna* (2005).

Stefano Cracolici is senior lecturer in Italian at Durham University (U.K.). He has interests in the history of emotions with a particular focus on Italian humanism and its ethical, aesthetic, and medical implications. He is currently revising his first book in English, *Anger in the Ideal City: Intellectual Acrimony and the Sources of Militant Criticism.*

Fabio Finotti is the Mariano Di Vito Professor of Italian Studies and director of the Center for Italian Studies at the University of Pennsylvania. He has published four books: *Sistema letterario e diffusione del decadentismo nell'Italia di fine Ottocento* (1988); *Critica stilistica e linguaggio religioso* (1989); *Una ferita non chiusa: Misticismo, filosofia, letteratura in Prezzolini e nel primo Novecento* (1992); and *Retorica della diffrazione: Bembo, Aretino, Giulio Romano e Tasso: letteratura e scena cortigiana* (2004). He has edited the writings of Carducci, Fogazzaro, and D'Annunzio, among others.

William J. Kennedy is professor of comparative literature at Cornell University. He is the author of four books on European Renaissance literature, including *Authorizing Petrarch* (1994) and *The Site of Petrarchism: Early Modern National Sentiment in Italy, France, and England* (2003). He is currently working on a study of figurations of economic transaction and exchange in European poetry from Petrarch to Shakespeare.

Timothy Kircher is professor of history at Guilford College. He has written on fourteenth- and fifteenth-century Italian humanism and is the author of *The Poet's Wisdom: The Humanists, the Church, and the Formation of Philosophy in the Early Renaissance* (2006). He is presently examining the writings of Leon Battista Alberti.

Victoria Kirkham is professor of Romance languages and a member of the Graduate Group in Comparative Literature and the Center for Italian Studies at the University of Pennsylvania. She is the author of articles on Dante, Renaissance culture, and Italian cinema, and three books, most recently of *Fabulous Vernacular: Boccaccio's Filocolo and the Art of Medieval Fiction* (2001), winner of the Scaglione Prize of the Modern Language Association for a Manuscript in Italian Studies, and the editor and translator of *Laura Batti-*

ferra and Her Literary Circle: An Anthology (2006), published in the Other Voice in Early Modern Europe series by the University of Chicago Press.

Dennis Looney is associate professor of Italian and classics at the University of Pittsburgh. His book on the poetics of Boiardo, Ariosto, and Tasso, *Compromising the Classics: Romance Epic Narrative in the Italian Renaissance* (1996), was recognized by the Modern Language Association's Marraro-Scaglione Prize for Italian Literary Studies (1996–1997). He is coeditor (with Deanna Shemek) of *Phaethon's Children: The Este Court and Its Culture in Early Modern Ferrara* (2005) and editor and cotranslator of Sergio Zatti, *The Quest for Epic: From Ariosto to Tasso* (2006).

Armando Maggi is professor of Romance languages and a member of the Committee on History of Culture at the University of Chicago. He is the editor of the critical edition of Guido Casoni's (1591) treatise *Della magia d'amore* (2003), and the author of several books, most recently of *Satan's Rhetoric: A Study of Renaissance Demonology* (2001) and *In the Company of Demons: Unnatural Beings, Love, and Identity in the Italian Renaissance* (2006), and *The Resurrection of the Body: Pier Paolo Pasolini: From Saint Paul to Sade* (2009), the latter three published by the University of Chicago Press.

Simone Marchesi is assistant professor of French and Italian at Princeton University. His special interest is in the influence of classical and late-antique Latin works on Italian medieval writers, in particular Dante, Petrarch, and Boccaccio. His published work includes *Stratigrafie decameroniane* (2004) along with numerous articles on Dante, Boccaccio, Petrarch, and Giovanni della Casa, as well as on the tradition of the twentieth-century novel and contemporary Italian cinema.

David Marsh studied classics and comparative literature at Yale and Harvard Universities and is now professor of Italian at Rutgers, The State University of New Jersey. He is the author of *The Quattrocento Dialogue: Classical Tradition and Humanist Innovation* (1980) and *Lucian and the Latins: Humor and Humanism in the Early Renaissance* (1998). He has translated Leon Battista Alberti's *Dinner Pieces* (1987), Giambattista Vico's *New Science* (1999), and Paolo Zellini's *Brief History of Infinity* (2004). More recently he has edited and translated Petrarch's *Invectives* (2003) and the anthology *Renaissance Fables: Aesopic Prose by Leon Battista Alberti, Bartolomeo Scala, Leonardo da Vinci, and Bernardino Baldi* (2004).

Ronald L. Martinez is professor of Italian studies at Brown University. He has published on Dante, Petrarch, Boccaccio, Ariosto, Machiavelli, and Renaissance Italian drama. In addition to Dante and trecento studies, he has teaching and research interests in Italian Renaissance cultural history. Currently he is finishing, in collaboration with Robert M. Durling, an edition with translation and commentary of Dante's *Divine Comedy* (*Inferno* [1996]; *Purgatorio* [2003]; *Paradiso* [forthcoming]) and preparing a book-length study on Dante's appropriation of medieval Catholic liturgy for narrative and linguistic aspects of the *Commedia*.

E. Ann Matter is associate dean for arts and letters and the William R. Kenan, Jr., Professor of Religious Studies at the University of Pennsylvania. Her field is medieval and early modern Christianity, especially the history of biblical interpretation, spirituality, and mysticism. She is the author of *The Voice of My Beloved: The Song of Songs in Western Medieval Christianity* (1990). With Armando Maggi and Maiju Lehmijoki-Gardner, she edited the "Seven Revelations" of Lucia Brocadelli da Narni, court prophet of Ercole I d'Este of Ferrara, for publication in *Archivum fratrum praedicatorum;* she also translated the "Seven Revelations" into English for the Classics of Western Spirituality series.

Giuseppe F. Mazzotta is the Sterling Professor in the Humanities for Italian at Yale University. His scholarly interests focus mainly on medieval, Renaissance, and Baroque literature and thought. He has written several books: *Dante Poet of the Desert: History and Allegory in the Divine Comedy* (1979); *The World at Play in Boccaccio's Decameron* (1986); *The Worlds of Petrarch* (1993; rpt. 2000); *Dante's Vision and the Circle of Knowledge* (1993); *The New Map of the World: The Poetic Philosophy of Giambattista Vico* (1999); and *Cosmopoiesis: A Renaissance Experiment* (2003). He has also edited several volumes.

Justin Steinberg is associate professor of Italian at the University of Chicago. His scholarship focuses on medieval Italian literature, especially Dante, Petrarch, and the early lyric. He is the author of *Accounting for Dante: Urban Readers and Writers in Late Medieval Italy* (2007), winner of the Scaglione Prize of the Modern Language Association for a Manuscript in Italian Studies.

Giuseppe Velli has taught at the University of California, Los Angeles, and at Smith College. He has held the chairs of Medieval and Renaissance Philology at the University of Venice and of Italian Literature at the University of Milan. He is on the board of the National Academy "Francesco Petrarca" and is coeditor of the journal *Studi Petrarcheschi.* He is on the Executive Committee of the National Council for the Celebrations of the Seventh Centennial of Petrarch's birth. A past honorary president of the American Association of Italian Studies, he is the author of *Petrarca e Boccaccio: Tradizione— memoria—scrittura; Tra Lettura e creazione: Sannazaro—Alfieri— Foscolo;* and the editor of Giovanni Boccaccio, *Carmina* (1992).

David Wallace is the Judith Rodin Professor of English and a member of the Center for Italian Studies at the University of Pennsylvania. Most recently, he is the author of *Premodern Places* (2004), coeditor of *The Cambridge Companion to Medieval Women's Writing* (2003), and editor of *The Cambridge History of Medieval English Literature* (1999, 2002). His work for BBC Radio 3 includes documentaries on Bede, Margery Kempe, Sir Thomas Malory, and John Leland. His 2007 Clarendon Lectures will appear as *Strong Women: Life, Text, and Territory, 1347–1645*.

Lynn Lara Westwater is assistant professor of Italian at the George Washington University. She is currently completing a book on polemics between male and female writers entitled *Gender Wars in Seventeenth-Century Venice*. She coedited a critical edition of the letters of Venetian nun Arcangela Tarabotti, published in Italy in 2005, and her coedition and translation of Tarabotti's letters is forthcoming.

Ronald G. Witt is William B. Hamilton Professor of History (emeritus) at Duke University. He is the author of four books, most recently *In the Footsteps of the Ancients: The Origins of Humanism from Lovato dei Lovati to Bruni* (2000), which received the Phyllis Gordon Prize of the Renaissance Society of America, the Helen and Howard R. Marraro Prize of the American Historical Society, and the Jacques Barzun Prize of the American Philosophical Society. His manuscript, *The Italian Difference: The Two Latin Cultures of Medieval Italy (800–1250)*, is nearing completion.

INDEX